Glossary of Comprehension and Critical Thinking Terms

Allusions Allusions are references making comparisons to people, events, or places that clarify and make vivid a writer's point, e.g., "The boxer was strong, but when it came to speed, he was no Muhammad Ali."

Arguments Writers present readers with an opinion or conclusion followed by reasons, statistics, studies, or other evidence designed to convince readers to share the writer's point of view.

Bias Bias in writing reveals the author's personal inclination to support or criticize a particular idea or event.

Cause and effect pattern Readings that rely on the organization pattern show how one event produced or led to another.

Chains of repetition and reference Chains of repetition and reference consist of nouns, pronouns, synonyms, and implied or associated words that help the writer identify the topic and main idea for the reader.

Circular reasoning Writers who employ circular reasoning use different words to say the same thing twice.

Classification pattern Readings relying on the classification pattern describe how some larger group can be broken down into subgroups, each with its own set of specific characteristics.

Comparison and contrast pattern Readings that rely on the comparison and contrast pattern of development highlight the similarities or differences between two topics. Sometimes authors who use this pattern do both; they point out the similarities and the differences between two topics.

Concept maps Used for note-taking, concept maps show the main point of a reading in the center of the page with supporting details recorded on spokes, or lines, attached to the main idea.

Conclusions Conclusions are inferences a reader draws based on the writer's actual statements. However, they are not necessarily intended by the writer.

Connotations The associations, positive or negative, that come with a word.

Context The context of a word is the sentence or passage in which the word appears.

Definition pattern This organizational pattern usually begins with the word being defined highlighted or emphasized through the use of quotation marks, colored ink, boldface, or italics. Then the definition follows right after the word's first appearance.

Denotation The dictionary meaning of a word.

Explicit and implicit When a fact or idea is *explicit*, it's stated in the text. When a fact or idea is *implicit* it's suggested but not put into words.

Facts Statements of fact describe without evaluating or interpreting. They are not influenced by an author's personal experience or background. They can be checked or verified for accuracy.

Figurative language Language that makes sense in the imagination rather than in reality.

General sentences General sentences sum up or draw conclusions about a number of different but in some way related people, places, or events.

Graphic organizers Drawings or diagrams that readers use to take notes on texts heavy with physical descriptions.

Hasty generalizations Broad generalizations based on too few examples are considered "hasty."

Implied main idea The implied main idea of a reading is suggested but not directly stated.

Inferences Inferences are the conclusions a reader draws about ideas that are implied in a text but not directly stated. *Inappropriate inferences* are conclusions based more on the reader's personal experience than on the author's words.

Informed opinions Opinions that are backed by relevant reasons, facts, studies, and examples are informed and are therefore worthy of serious consideration. *Uninformed opinions* are opinions that fail to offer a convincing argument.

Informative writing Informative writing describes events or ideas without including personal judgments by the author.

Continued on inside back cover

aplia™

STUDENTS: Accessing Your Aplia
Course Through CengageBrain

CENGAGEbrain.com

CREATING YOUR APLIA ACCOUNT ON CENGAGEBRAIN BY VISITING:
login.cengagebrain.com

What is login.cengagebrain.com? Imagine that you are using Aplia along with another online study tool from Cengage Learning. Rather than having separate logins and passwords for both applications, Cengage offers a single access point through login.cengagebrain.com.

When you visit login.cengagebrain.com, you will see the following:

CENGAGE
brain
.com

Technical Support

Log In

Username
Enter your email address

Password

Forgot your password?

Login

Create a New Account

Already have an account with Cengage Learning, Aplia or iChapters.com?

Simply log into your existing account to register a new access code or a new Aplia Course Key

You do not need to create a new account.

✔ Gain instant access to your online learning materials

✔ Register an access code or Aplia Course Key

✔ Receive account holder exclusive promotions and discounts

Create an Account

> A **Single Sign-On (SSO)** account provides for one login to access Cengage Learning digital resources.
>
> For the purpose of this document, we will focus on the right side of this screen or "**Create a New Account**".
>
> Note: If you *do* have an existing account, CengageBrain accepts all prior login credentials, including Aplia and iChapters.

Step 1 | Begin by Creating an Account

1. Click the "Create an Account" button
2. The following page will load. Enter in the Aplia Course Key

YOUR COURSE KEY IS PROVIDED BY YOUR INSTRUCTOR TO ACCESS APLIA.

> Instructors often provide the Aplia Course Key on their **syllabus**, or the course web site. If you need help locating the **Aplia Course Key**, ask your instructor.

« Back to Log In / Register / Enter Code or Course Key

Enter Your Code or Key ⟩ Account Information ⟩ Access Materials

Enter Access Code or Aplia Course Key

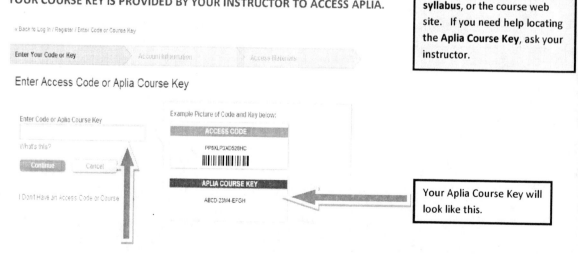

Enter Code or Aplia Course Key

What's this?

Continue   Cancel

I Don't Have an Access Code or Course

Example Picture of Code and Key below:

ACCESS CODE
PP5XLP3XD52SHC

APLIA COURSE KEY
ABCD-23M4-EFGH

> Your Aplia Course Key will look like this.

Step 2 | Confirm Your Course Information

The graphic below serves as an illustration for what you will see. Please confirm the displayed screen represents your enrolled course.

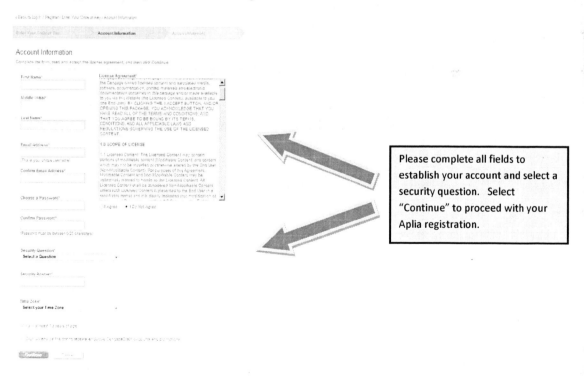

‹ Back to Log In / Register / Confirm Course

Enter Your Code or Key   Account Information   Access Materials

Confirm Course Information

Please confirm that this is the Aplia course for which you want to register

School:	Aplia University
Instructor:	Aplia Instructor
Course Name:	Dole Taggart's Activate
Start Date:	August 01, 2011
End Date:	December 18, 2011
Not the right course?	edit course key

Continue

> Confirm that the course information shown matches the course you are enrolled in. If yes, click the "**Continue**" button. If not, click on the "edit course key" link to re-enter the correct Course Key.

Step 3 | Complete Registration Form

As a new user, you must complete all fields in the registration form and click "Continue"

‹ Back to Log In / Register / Enter Your Code or Key / Account Information

Enter Your Product Key   Account Information   Access Materials

Account Information

Complete the form, read and accept the license agreement, and then click Continue

First Name*

Middle Initial

Last Name*

Email Address*

This is your chosen username

Confirm Email Address*

Choose a Password*

Confirm Password*

Password must be between 6-20 characters

Security Question*
Select a Question

Security Answer*

Time Zone
Select your Time Zone

License Agreement*

1.0 SCOPE OF LICENSE

> Please complete all fields to establish your account and select a security question. Select "Continue" to proceed with your Aplia registration.

Step 4 | My Home Dashboard Review

You have arrived at your **"My Home"** page. Here you can verify your e-Mail address with CengageBrain and pay for your course **(See Step 5).** Note that any prior (and future) Cengage Learning purchases will appear on this page. Additionally, the page provides support resources and a transaction history of your Cengage purchases – digital products, textbooks or rentals.

IMPORTANT: CengageBrain requires you to verify your e-mail address. Please go to your e-mail and check for a message from CengageBrain.com with the Subject **"Aplia Verification E-Mail".** If you don't see the message, check your SPAM folder.

Click the link to verify your e-mail. **Once verified, you will be prompted to log back in again with your e-mail and password from Step 3 above. Once you do, you will be brought back to your "My Home" Dashboard as shown below.**

Here is a complete view of the Dashboard showing all Cengage Learning resources instantly available in one spot. Also note transaction history and support options in the right hand field.

Step 5 | Completing Payment for Your Aplia Course

NOTE: YOUR APLIA ACCESS CODE IS CONTAINED IN THE PRINTED ACCESS CARD YOU HAVE ALREADY PURCHASED. THERE ARE <u>NO ADDITIONAL CHARGES TO ACCESS APLIA</u>. SIMPLY COMPLETE THE PAYMENT PROCESS BY CLICKING ON THE "SEE PAYMENT OPTIONS LINK" CIRCLED IN GREEN.

Activate: College Reading , 1st Edition
Ivan Dole, Leslie Taggart

Aplia: Dole Taggart's Activate   Open

Note: Payment for your Aplia course is due by the end of the day on August 21, 2011.

See Payment Options

Click on the "See Payment Options" link.

The below screen will appear

My Home   My Orders   My Account   My Rentals

Home / Aplia Payment

Pay for Your Aplia Course

Dole Taggart's Activate $60.00

The payment grace period will expire in 121 days. You will not be able to access your course when the grace period ends, but all your scores and course activity will be saved and accessible after you submit payment. Your payment is due by the end of the day on August 21, 2011.

How would you like to pay?

I've already paid by purchasing an Aplia Access Card.

If you've already purchased a standalone Aplia Access Card or a textbook bundle containing an Aplia Access Card, then you have a payment code that you must enter by selecting the option below.

○ Enter Payment Code inside my Aplia Access Card. What is a Payment Code?

Select "Enter Payment Code" (*also known as an "Access Code"*) and click on "Continue".

I'd like to pay Aplia directly.

○ Pay online with a credit or debit card.
○ Pay by mail with a check or money order in U.S. dollars.
○ Pay by mail with a check in Canadian dollars.

I'll pay later.

○ Go to my course.

Continue

Step 5 | Completing Payment for Your Aplia Course (cont.)

CENGAGE
brain

Find your Textbook or Materials

Enter ISBN, Book Title, Author

My Home   My Orders   My Account   My Rentals

Payment by Code What is this?

A Payment Code might be worth a portion of the cost or the full cost of your Aplia Course. Note: Payment Codes are single-use payments. Once you enter a Payment Code, it can not be used again. Refunds are not issued for Payment Codes.

Payment Information

Aplia ID:
Student Name:
Course Name: Dole Taggart's Activate
Instructor:
University: Aplia University
Start Date: August 01, 2011

Please enter your Payment Code and press Continue.

Payment Code: _____   What's this?

Your Payment Code should be similar to XXXXX-XXX-XXXXXXX-XX or PPXLP3XD529HC

If you need assistance, please go to Payment Support and send us a message.

Go Back   Continue

> Enter the *Access Code* that is **inside your Printed Access Card (PAC)**. Your Access Code should look similar to the one shown below:
>
> ACCESS CODE
> PPXLP3XD529HC
>
> **NOTE:** Your Access Code *is not* the same as your Course Key provided by your Instructor.

My Home   My Orders   My Account   My Rentals

Payment Confirmation

Please print this page for your records.

Your Payment Code has been accepted as payment for your Aplia course.

Order Summary

Student name:
Aplia ID:
Course: Dole Taggart's Activate
Instructor:
School: Aplia University
Course start date: 10/04/10
Course end date: 12/26/10
Grace period ends: 10/25/10
Payment code used: ZTRKF-FNB-JPGNP-PCB
Date and time of payment: 10/19/10, 08:21 AM

Please note that your Payment Code has now been used and will no longer work for any subsequent Aplia course.

Refund Policy

There are no refunds for Payment Codes. For more information, please read Aplia's Terms of...

If you have questions about your payment, please contact Aplia Support.

Continue

> This is a **Payment Confirmation** screen. Feel free to print the screen by clicking on the link that says "print" in blue at the top of the page.
> - - - - - - - - - - - - - - - - - -
> Click "Continue" to return to your My Home Dashboard and click on the **"OPEN"** button next to your Aplia course.

Step 6 | Accessing Your Course

Once click on the "Open" button, you will be directed to your Aplia course as shown below.

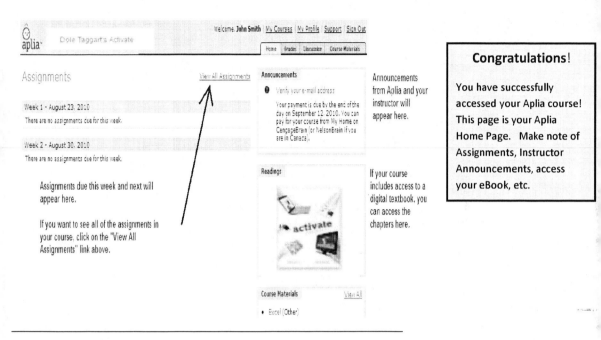

Congratulations!

You have successfully accessed your Aplia course! This page is your Aplia Home Page. Make note of Assignments, Instructor Announcements, access your eBook, etc.

Step 7 | Re-Entering Your Course After Logging Out

Now that you have created an account at login.cengagebrain.com, you can gain immediate access to your "My Home" page, simply by logging in at login.cengagebrain.com. Fill in your username and password to go directly to your "My Home" page and access your course!

Still Need Help?

Questions with your CengageBrain account?

- Check the FAQ's in the Support area of your CengageBrain home

  OR

- *E-Mail:* cengagebrain.support@cengage.com

  OR

- *Call:* 866-994-2427 Monday through Friday from 8:00AM to 6:00PM EST

Questions with your Aplia course?

- *Visit:* www.cengage.com/support

Reading for Results

Fox Valley Technical College

Special 11th Edition

Laraine Flemming

CENGAGE
Learning™

Australia • Brazil • Japan • Korea • Mexico • Singapore • Spain • United Kingdom • United States

CENGAGE
Learning™

Reading for Results; Fox Valley Technical College; Special 11th Edition

Reading For Results
Laraine Flemming
© 2011 Cengage Learning. All rights reserved.

Executive Editors:
Maureen Staudt
Michael Stranz

Senior Project Development Manager:
Linda deStefano

Marketing Specialist:
Courtney Sheldon

Senior Production/Manufacturing Manager:
Donna M. Brown

PreMedia Manager:
Joel Brennecke

Sr. Rights Acquisition Account Manager:
Todd Osborne

Cover Image:
Getty Images*

*Unless otherwise noted, all cover images used by Custom Solutions, a part of Cengage Learning, have been supplied courtesy of Getty Images with the exception of the Earthview cover image, which has been supplied by the National Aeronautics and Space Administration (NASA).

For product information and technology assistance, contact us at
Cengage Learning Customer & Sales Support, 1-800-354-9706

For permission to use material from this text or product,
submit all requests online at **cengage.com/permissions**
Further permissions questions can be emailed to
permissionrequest@cengage.com

This book contains select works from existing Cengage Learning resources and was produced by Cengage Learning Custom Solutions for collegiate use. As such those adopting and/or contributing to this work are responsible for editorial content accuracy, continuity and completeness.

Compilation © 2011. Cengage Learning.

ISBN-13: 978-1-133-34906-8

ISBN-10: 1-133-34906-4

Cengage Learning
5191 Natorp Boulevard
Mason, Ohio 45040
USA

Cengage Learning is a leading provider of customized learning solutions with office locations around the globe, including Singapore, the United Kingdom, Australia, Mexico, Brazil, and Japan. Locate your local office at:
international.cengage.com/region.
Cengage Learning products are represented in Canada by Nelson Education, Ltd.
For your lifelong learning solutions, visit **www.cengage.com/custom.**
Visit our corporate website at **www.cengage.com.**

Printed in the United States of America

Contents

7 Drawing Inferences from Visual Aids   381

8 Beyond the Paragraph: Reading Longer Selections   423

9   Recognizing Patterns of Organization in Paragraphs   492

Putting It All Together   689

Author Laraine Flemming combines research-based study strategies with stimulating readings to motivate student achievement

Focusing on
Supporting Details

5

IN THIS CHAPTER, YOU WILL LEARN

- more about the relationship between topic sentences and supporting details.
- how to distinguish between major and minor supporting details.
- how writers rely on readers to infer additional details.
- how to recognize the function of every sentence.

"God is in the details."
—Ludwig Mies van der Rohe, architect

"The devil is in the details."
—Anonymous

. . . [Reading for Results] has engaged my students and given them a sense of growth."
—Dr. Margaret E. Haynes, Delta College

New vocabulary exercises and more emphasis on vocabulary building

◆ Vocabulary Check Exercises

Each chapter ends with a new "Vocabulary Check" review of the words defined in the chapter.

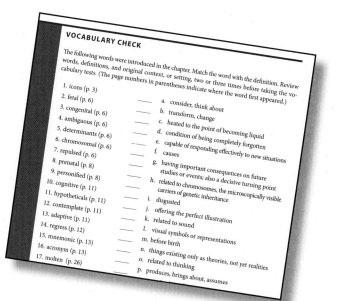

VOCABULARY CHECK

The following words were introduced in the chapter. Match the word with the definition. Review words, definitions, and original context, or setting, two or three times before taking the vocabulary tests. (The page numbers in parentheses indicate where the word first appeared.)

1. icons (p. 3)
2. fetal (p. 6)
3. congenital (p. 6)
4. ambiguous (p. 6)
5. determinants (p. 6)
6. chromosomal (p. 6)
7. repulsed (p. 6)
8. prenatal (p. 8)
9. personified (p. 8)
10. cognitive (p. 11)
11. hypotheticals (p. 11)
12. contemplate (p. 11)
13. adaptive (p. 11)
14. regress (p. 12)
15. mnemonic (p. 13)
16. acronym (p. 13)
17. molten (p. 26)

—— a. consider, think about
—— b. transform, change
—— c. heated to the point of becoming liquid
—— d. condition of being completely forgotten
—— e. capable of responding effectively to new situations
—— f. causes
—— g. having important consequences on future studies or events; also a decisive turning point
—— h. related to chromosomes, the microscopically visible carriers of genetic inheritance
—— i. disgusted
—— j. offering the perfect illustration
—— k. related to sound
—— l. visual symbols or representations
—— m. before birth
—— n. things existing only as theories, not yet realities
—— o. related to thinking
—— p. produces, brings about, assumes

◆ Increased Emphasis on Academic Vocabulary Building

More than two hundred new words, many drawn from academic texts, are introduced in context and then defined in footnotes. A series of end-of-chapter vocabulary tests follows the general review so that students get the repetition with variation they need to remember new words and meanings.

◆ A Comparison of Online and Print Dictionaries

Chapter 2, **Building Word Power**, describes what students can expect to find in online and print dictionaries, and explains the plusses and minuses of using an online dictionary. There's also a new section on figurative and literal meanings of words.

New features aid student comprehension and recall

◆ **"Review and Recall" Format for Learning Key Concepts**

Each chapter section concludes with a *Summing Up the Key Points* box that lists the section's key concepts, and a *Check Your Understanding* quiz that asks students to recall those same key points. Using this format of review and recall, both teachers and students can identify which concepts or skills might require additional discussion.

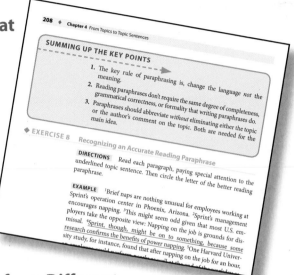

208 ◆ Chapter 4 From Topics to Topic Sentences

SUMMING UP THE KEY POINTS

1. The key rule of paraphrasing is, change the language *not* the meaning.
2. Reading paraphrases don't require the same degree of completeness, grammatical correctness, or formality that writing paraphrases do.
3. Paraphrases should abbreviate *without* eliminating either the topic or the author's comment on the topic. Both are needed for the main idea.

◆ **EXERCISE 8** Recognizing an Accurate Reading Paraphrase

DIRECTIONS Read each paragraph, paying special attention to the underlined topic sentence. Then circle the letter of the better reading paraphrase.

EXAMPLE [1]Brief naps are nothing unusual for employees working at Sprint's operation center in Phoenix, Arizona. [2]Sprint's management encourages napping. [3]This might seem odd given that most U.S. employers take the opposite view: Napping on the job is grounds for dismissal. [4]Sprint, though, might be on to something, because some research confirms the benefits of power napping. [5]One Harvard University study, for instance, found that after napping on the job for an hour,

◆ **Synthesizing Information from Different Sources**

A new feature called *Making Connections*, at the end of every chapter reading, encourages students to synthesize, or connect, new information with what's been previously learned.

◆ **More Coverage of Paraphrasing**

From Topics to Topic Sentences

4

Because paraphrasing is essential to comprehension, Chapter 4, **From Topics to Topic Sentences**, describes a new step-by-step system for paraphrasing. In addition, more exercises throughout the text ask for paraphrased answers and more examples illustrate the differences between accurate and inaccurate paraphrases.

New technique helps students learn to identify topics

◆ Method for Identifying Topics

Chapter 4 also introduces a new system for discovering paragraph topics. Students learn how to identify the *chains of repetition and reference*—pronouns, synonyms, and substitute words—a writer uses to keep the topic front and center in the paragraph.

More assistance for the visual learner, and help in understanding visual aids

◆ New chapter on understanding and interpreting visuals

Chapter 7, **Drawing Inferences from Visual Aids,** shows students how to interpret graphs, pie charts, drawings, and cartoons and relate them to the texts they illustrate. Connecting the text with the visual aid helps students see how essential inferences are to connecting verbal and visual material.

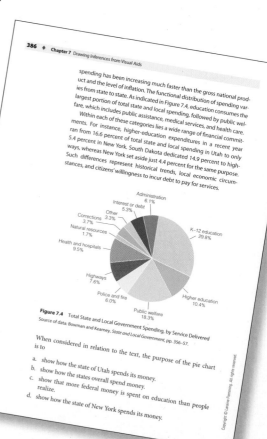

spending has been increasing much faster than the gross national product and the level of inflation. The functional distribution of spending varies from state to state. As indicated in Figure 7.4, education consumes the largest portion of total state and local spending, followed by public welfare, which includes public assistance, medical services, and health care. Within each of these categories lies a wide range of financial commitments. For instance, higher-education expenditures in a recent year ran from 16.6 percent of total state and local spending in Utah to only 5.4 percent in New York. South Dakota dedicated 14.9 percent to higher ways, whereas New York set aside just 4.4 percent for the same purpose. Such differences represent historical trends, local economic circumstances, and citizens' willingness to incur debt to pay for services.

Administration 6.1%
Interest or debt 5.3%
Other 3.3%
Corrections 3.7%
Natural resources 1.7%
Health and hospitals 9.5%
Highways 7.6%
Police and fire 6.0%
Public welfare 18.3%
Higher education 10.4%
K–12 education 29.8%

Figure 7.4 Total State and Local Government Spending, by Service Delivered
Source of data: Bowman and Kearney, *State and Local Government*, pp. 356–57.

When considered in relation to the text, the purpose of the pie chart is to

a. show how the state of Utah spends its money.
b. show how the states overall spend money.
c. show that more federal money is spent on education than people realize.
d. show how the state of New York spends its money.

Laraine Flemming's proven skills-and-strategies pedagogy

As in prior editions,

- Every chapter opens with an overview that outlines the chapter's objectives

- Every skill or concept introduced is accompanied by numerous models and exercises

- An entire chapter (Chapter 3) focuses on understanding the terms *general* and *specific*

- A complete chapter (Chapter 2) is dedicated to vocabulary building

- *Digging Deeper* multi-paragraph readings conclude each chapter

- End-of-chapter tests provide multiple chances for review

- The final section of the book, *Putting It All Together*, lets students apply everything they've learned from the previous chapters

Putting It All Together

The following readings give you a chance to practice everything you have learned about comprehension and critical reading. As you read, think about where you stand on the various events and experiences described. Ultimately reading is not just about understanding and remembering what other people say about the world. It's also about discovering your own point of view.

Additional Resources

◆ For Students

Aplia Developmental Reading, an online reading and learning solution, helps students become better readers by motivating them with compelling material, interactive assignments, and detailed explanations. In-text vocabulary features new and challenging words. Students receive immediate, detailed explanations for every answer, and grades are automatically recorded in the instructor's Aplia gradebook.

The Student Companion Website offers interactive practice quizzes, tips for reading and studying, advice for preparing for class and exams, live links to the websites mentioned in the textbook as well as to Online Writing Centers and Grammar Resources, and more.

New interactive vocabulary flashcards provide definitions to the vocabulary in the text and can be used to refresh students' knowledge of these key terms.

ReadSpace is a flexible and easy-to-use online reading tool that includes a wealth of interactive tools for virtually any reading student, at any level, all in one place. It is a comprehensive diagnostic and practice solution that can be used for online reading classes, in a reading lab, or in-class.

◆ For Instructors

The Instructor's Resource Manual and Test Bank offers suggestions for teaching each chapter and supplementary exercises for each skill introduced. These suggestions and exercises are great for the new instructor looking for support or the more experienced teacher looking for ideas. The Instructor's Resource Manual also provides a list of all the vocabulary words introduced in the book, along with a sample mid-term, final, and syllabus.

Examview® Test Bank, a text-specific test bank that features automatic grading, allows you to create, deliver, and customize tests and study guides (both print and online) in minutes. Instructors can see assessments onscreen exactly as they will print or display online, and build tests by entering an unlimited number of new questions or editing existing questions.

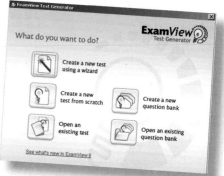

The Instructor Companion Website features a wide variety of teaching aids, including chapter-specific PowerPoint presentations, the Instructor's Manual and Test Bank, a semester final exam, and more.

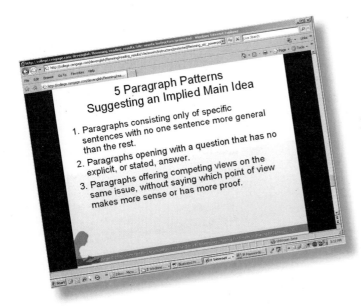

"Although I have tried other texts, I always return to Reading for Results."

—Carla Bell,
Henry Ford Community College

Acknowledgments

Many thanks to the following reviewers whose suggestions offered me a thoughtful and detailed blueprint for revision:

Carla Bell, *Henry Ford Community College*

Lynn Benaglio, *Erie Community College*

Etta Cantrell, *Big Sandy Community and Technical College*

Shannon Carter, *Phoenix College*

Karen Cowden, *Valencia Community College*

Sally S. Gabb, *Bristol Community College*

Felicia E. Grimes, *Tarrant County College*

Margaret E. Haynes, *Delta College*

Oscar Samuel Holton, *Swainsboro Technical College*

April Howell, *St. Pertersburg College*

JoAnne Lyons, *Bristol Community College*

Marta Mitten, *Chandler-Gilbert Community College*

Taralyn Pierce, *Lake-Sumter Community College*

Betty Raper, *Pulaski Technical College*

Adalia M. Reyna, *South Texas College*

Amanda Rogers, *Big Sandy Community & Technical College*

Anja-Leigh Russell, *Los Angeles Mission College*

In addition to the helpful comments of those who aided in the pre-revision review, I'd also like to thank the following instructors who have consistently been willing to offer their advice on any number of topics just about anytime I have asked for it. Their assistance has been invaluable and I am grateful to them for it: Geraldine LeVitre of Community College of Rhode Island, Jordan Fabish of Long Beach City College, Mary T. Nielsen of Dalton State College, Jenni Wessel of Black Hawk College, Denice Josten of Saint Louis Community College at Forest Park, and Dawn Sedik of Valencia Community College.

Strategies for Textbook Learning

IN THIS CHAPTER, YOU WILL LEARN

- how to use *SQ3R*, a reading method specifically created for learning from textbooks.

- what reading strategies are particularly appropriate for textbooks.

- what methods of reading and review might work best for you.

- how to match your reading rate to the material.

- how to use the World Wide Web to expand your background knowledge.

"Learning without thought is labor lost."
—Confucius

Because it was created more than half a century ago, *SQ3R*, the system for learning from textbooks introduced in this chapter, has sometimes been called obsolete, or out of date. But, in fact, Francis P. Robinson, the educational psychologist who created *SQ3R* in the 1940s, spent years teaching both college students and military personnel how to learn from textbooks. His system, if used consistently, can still produce big rewards. Although it needs some modifications, which you will learn about in the pages that follow, *SQ3R* (or one of the various study systems based on it[†]) will significantly boost your learning from textbooks as long as you use it on a consistent basis.

Chapter 1 also emphasizes the importance of writing while reading as a way of improving not just comprehension but remembering as well. In addition, you will learn how to vary your reading rate when completing your textbook assignments: You'll learn when to speed up and when to slow down. Finally, the chapter offers some suggestions for using the World Wide Web to expand your background knowledge and prepare for reading *before* starting your reading assignments.

Introducing *SQ3R*: Survey, Question, Read, Recall, Review

If you are reading a bestseller by a writer like Dan Brown[†] or Stephenie Meyer,[†] you more than likely let your mind drift along with the story, almost like you were dreaming it. However, this dreamy, unfocused approach, perfect for leisure reading, is not appropriate for textbooks. With textbooks, you need a systematic but flexible system that can take into account the difficulty of the material, the author's writing style, and the goals of your assignment. *SQ3R* is flexible enough to take all three elements into account.

S: Survey to Get a General Overview and Make Predictions

When you begin a textbook assignment, don't just open your textbook and start reading. Instead, **survey** or preview the material using the general

---

[†]PQRST is one popular alternative: Preview, Question, Read, Self-Recitation, Test.
[†]Brown is the author of *The Da Vinci Code.*
[†]Meyer is the author of *The Southern Vampire Series.*

sequence of steps described in the following box. Although the steps in a survey may increase or decrease according to text difficulty and your knowledge of the material, these seven steps are almost always essential. Take ten or twenty minutes to complete them before officially starting to read, and you will be well-rewarded in terms of both comprehension and remembering.

Seven Basic Steps in a Survey ◆	1. Read the title. Consider what it suggests about the chapter's content.
	2. Read all introductory material. That includes chapter outlines, lists of questions, goals, and objectives, all of which identify what the author expects readers to learn.
	3. Use the title and introduction to form a general question or two about what's covered in the chapter. Check your memory to see if you have any prior knowledge, or previous experience, with the topic discussed.†
	4. Read the headings and opening sentence of chapter sections. If the material is especially difficult or unfamiliar, expand this step: Read the last sentence of every chapter section or even the first and last sentence of every paragraph.
	5. Look at all visual aids. Visual aids include pictures, photos, maps, charts, boxes, icons,* and graphs. If captions, or explanations, accompany the visual aids, read them, too. Ask yourself what each visual aid suggests about the chapter's content. If specific icons are used consistently in the chapter, see if you can figure out what kinds of information they identify.
	6. Pay attention to words printed in boldface or in the margin of the page. With particularly important or difficult courses, expand this step to include jotting boldface or italicized terms in the margins. As you read, you can then add definitions to the terms noted in the margins.
	7. Read end-of-chapter summaries and questions. If there is no end-of-chapter summary, read the last page of the chapter.†

---

†More on developing prior knowledge using the World Wide Web on pages 40–51.
*icons: 1. visual symbols or representations, which, in textbooks, signal significance. 2. a person who is the object of much attention, as in "a pop *icon*."
†You'll be surveying a selection shorter than a chapter on pages 53–60. Note how the survey steps are adapted.

The Four Goals of a Survey

Whatever the length and depth of the survey, it should always give you the following: (1) a general overview of the material, (2) a feeling for the writer's style and organization, (3) a sense for what's important, and (4) an idea of the chapter's (or article's) natural breaks or divisions. This information can help you decide the number and length of your study sessions.

While most articles assigned for outside reading can be read and at least generally understood in a single study session, chapter assignments should be divided up and read in chunks of ten to fifteen pages.

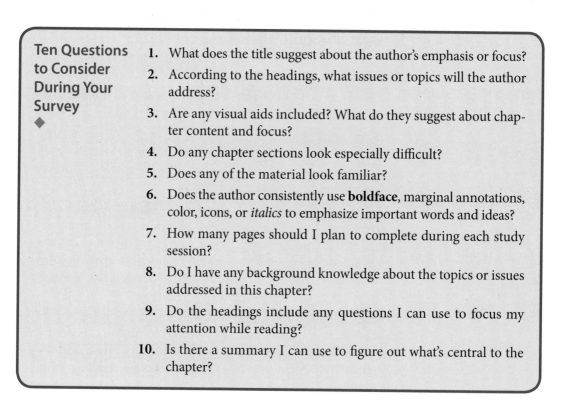

Ten Questions to Consider During Your Survey ◆	
1.	What does the title suggest about the author's emphasis or focus?
2.	According to the headings, what issues or topics will the author address?
3.	Are any visual aids included? What do they suggest about chapter content and focus?
4.	Do any chapter sections look especially difficult?
5.	Does any of the material look familiar?
6.	Does the author consistently use **boldface**, marginal annotations, color, icons, or *italics* to emphasize important words and ideas?
7.	How many pages should I plan to complete during each study session?
8.	Do I have any background knowledge about the topics or issues addressed in this chapter?
9.	Do the headings include any questions I can use to focus my attention while reading?
10.	Is there a summary I can use to figure out what's central to the chapter?

The Importance of Reading Flexibility

Before moving on to the next step in *SQ3R*, it's time to talk about the importance of **reading flexibility**, or the willingness to change reading strategies in accordance with the material. If, for example, flexible readers are studying a textbook chapter on marriage and the family and don't feel that the material is especially difficult, they might do an abbreviated survey: They would read just the introduction and the headings while ignoring the pictures and other visual aids.

But if those same readers were studying a biology chapter that was difficult, they would make their survey longer and more detailed. They would look at every clue to meaning in the chapter. They might even read the first sentence of every paragraph.

Flexible readers feel the same way about taking notes or reviewing. Difficult texts get a separate sheet of detailed notes and numerous reviews. Less difficult texts might be just as well-served by marginal notes and underlining, followed by one or two reviews.

READING TIP

Be a flexible reader who consciously adapts your reading strategies to the text in front of you. If, for instance, reading your history text at the same pace you were reading your health text leaves you feeling confused, be ready to adapt to the more difficult material by slowing down your reading rate.

SUMMING UP THE KEY POINTS

1. Surveying a chapter before you read it should fulfill four objectives: Your survey should (1) give you a general overview of the chapter, (2) give you a feel for the writer's style and method of organization, (3) help you figure out what's important in the chapter, and (4) identify chapter breaks that will help you decide how many pages you want to read in each study session.

2. Flexibility is crucial to surveying and every other aspect of reading. Each new reading assignment calls for a different set of reading strategies that reflect the kind of material you are reading, the author's style, and your own purpose in reading.

◆ **EXERCISE 1**   Surveying for Advance Knowledge

DIRECTIONS   Survey this selection by reading the headings and the first and last sentence of each paragraph, along with all visual aids. Based on the information drawn from your survey, answer the questions that follow.

Gender Identity: Our Sense of Maleness or Femaleness

Concept 1.1
Children early in life develop a firm gender identity, or psychological sense of being male or female.

1 By the age of three, most children have acquired a firm sense of their gender identity, of being either male or female. But what determines gender identity? The answer is not yet clear. Some research points to biological influences. Perhaps prenatal influences, such as fetal* sex hormones, sculpt the brain in ways that determine the later development of gender identity (Collaer & Hines, 1995). But research suggests that gender identity may not be fully stamped in at birth. In this research, children who were born with ambiguous* genitalia because of congenital* birth defects developed a gender identity that was consistent with the gender to which they were assigned and raised accordingly, even when the assigned gender conflicted with their chromosomal (XY or XX) sex (Slijper et al., 1998). All in all, most scientists believe that gender identity arises from a complex interaction of nature (biology) and nurture (rearing influences) (Diamond, 1996).

Concept 1.2 While researchers continue to explore the underpinnings of gender identity, both biological (hormonal) and environmental (rearing) influences may be involved.

2 Whatever the determinants* of gender identity may be, it is almost always consistent with one's chromosomal* sex. But for a few individuals gender identity and chromosomal sex are mismatched. These individuals have the gender identity of one gender but the chromosomal sex and sexual organs of the other.

Transsexualism: A Mismatch of Identity and Biology

Concept 1.3 Transsexuals have a gender identity that is at odds with their anatomic sex; they often undergo gender-reassignment surgery in order to correct what they perceive to be a mistake of nature.

3 People with transsexualism feel trapped in the body of the opposite gender by a mistake of nature. A transsexual man is anatomically a man but has the gender identity of a woman. A transsexual woman is anatomically a woman but possesses a male gender identity. Myths around transsexualism abound. Table 1.1 on page 7 exposes some of the more common myths.

4 Transsexual men and women may be repulsed* by the sight of their own genitals. Many undergo gender reassignment surgery to surgically

---

*fetal: related to unborn offspring still in the womb.
*ambiguous: uncertain, open to interpretation.
*congenital: present at birth.
*determinants: causes.
*chromosomal: related to chromosomes, the microscopically visible carriers of genetic inheritance.
*repulsed: disgusted.

Gender Reassignment Police officer Tom Ashton (left) underwent gender reassignment surgery and hormonal replacement, becoming Claire Ashton (right).

© David Burges/FSP/Gamma

alter their genitals to correct what they see as nature's mistake. Gender reassignment surgery transforms the genitalia to a workable likeness of those of the opposite gender. But since it cannot transplant the internal reproductive organs that produce the germ cells—the testes in the man

gender   The state of maleness or femaleness.

gender roles   The cultural expectations imposed on men and women to behave in ways deemed appropriate for their gender.

gender identity   The psychological sense of maleness or femaleness.

Table 1.1   Myths vs. Facts About Transsexualism

Myth	Fact
Only people who have sex-change operations are transsexuals.	Many transsexual men and women do not have gender reassignment surgery because they want to avoid postsurgical pain and complications or because the costs are prohibitive.
Men who wear women's clothes are transsexuals.	Some are. But others cross-dress to become sexually aroused, not because they are transsexual. Also, some gay males known as "drag queens" dress in women's clothing but are not transsexual.
Transsexualism is just a form of homosexuality.	Transsexualism should not be confused with homosexuality. People with a gay male or lesbian sexual orientation have an erotic attraction to, and preferences for, partners of the same gender. Yet their gender identity is consistent with their anatomic sex. A gay male, for instance, perceives himself to be a man who is sexually attracted to other men, not as a woman trapped in a man's body. Gay males or lesbians would no more want to rid themselves of their own genitals than would a heterosexual man or woman.

Concept 1.4 Each society defines masculinity and femininity by imposing a set of gender-based expectations about behavior and personality.

and the ovaries in the woman—reproduction is impossible. Thus, surgery does not change a man into a woman or a woman into a man, if what it means to be a man or a woman depends on having the internal reproductive organs of their respective sex. Nonetheless, gender reassignment surgery generally permits the individual to perform sexual intercourse. Hormonal replacement therapy is used to foster growth of the beard and body hair in female-to-male cases and of the breasts in male-to-female cases.

5   The underlying causes of transsexualism remain a topic of debate and scientific inquiry. Some scientists believe that a combination of sex hormones, genes, and environmental factors that influence the fetus during prenatal development may alter the architecture of the developing brain (Zhou et al., 1995). The result may be a mismatch of mind and body in which the brain becomes sexually differentiated in one direction during prenatal* development even as the genitals become sculpted in the other.

Concept 1.5 Though gender roles in our society have changed and are changing still, housekeeping and child-care roles still fall disproportionately on women.

Gender Roles and Stereotypes: How Society Defines Masculinity and Femininity

6   The cultural expectations imposed on men and women to behave in ways deemed appropriate for their gender are called *gender roles*. Fixed, conventional views of "masculine" and "feminine" behavior are called *gender-role stereotypes*. In our culture, the stereotypical female is perceived as nurturing, gentle, dependent, warm, emotional, kind, helpful, patient, and submissive. The stereotypical male, personified* by the ruggedly masculine characters in countless movies, is tough, self-reliant, and independent but also dominant and protective.

© Photo by Donald Miralle/Getty Images

Changing Gender Roles   Gender roles in our society have changed and are changing still.

7   Yet gender roles have changed and are changing still. Most women today work outside the home, and many are pursuing careers in traditionally male domains like law, medicine, and engineering. Some command naval vessels or pilot military helicopters. And in the legal profession, women now constitute 29 percent of lawyers as compared to only 15 percent in 1983 ("A Growing Gender Gap," 2000). Nevertheless, many traditional gender roles remain much as they were several generations ago. Women currently constitute 93 percent of registered

---

*prenatal: before birth.
*personified: offering the perfect illustration.

nurses (only a slight decrease from 96 percent in 1983) and 84 percent of flight attendants (an increase from 74 percent in 1983). Household and child-care responsibilities still fall more heavily on women, even on those who work in full-time jobs outside the home. (Nevid, *Psychology: Concepts and Applications*, pp. 332–34.)

1. The term *gender identity* refers to

   The psychological sense of maleness / femininess. pg. 7

2. Gender identity is a result of
   a. our genetic inheritance.
   b. our relationships to peers.
   c. our genetic inheritance and our social training.
   d. the genes we inherit and our training in elementary school.

3. Transsexuals feel they are

   trapped in the body of the opposite gender by a mistake of nature. pg-6

4. The term *gender roles* refers to → expectations

   Cultural roles deemed appropriate based on gender pg. 7

5. The author believes
   a. gender roles are changing.
   b. gender roles have not changed.
   c. gender roles should not change any more than they have.

CHECK YOUR UNDERSTANDING

1. What are the goals of a survey?

    _____

    _____

    _____

    _____

2. What does the term *reading flexibility* mean?

    _____

    _____

    _____

Q: Ask and Answer Questions While Reading

"A how-to-study program must be individualized to each student's needs."

—Francis P. Robinson

Many students complain that they lose concentration when they study. This isn't unusual. It happens to all of us when we try to absorb new and difficult material for any length of time. Still, the problem of failing concentration can be considerably reduced if you ask questions while reading. Raising and answering questions during a study session can help you remain mentally active throughout your reading. Using questions to maintain your concentration can also keep you alert to key points addressed in the chapter.

Use Introductory Lists of Questions

Many textbook chapters open with a list of questions or objectives the author (or authors) wants to address. When it comes to identifying what's essential to the chapter, such lists are extremely useful. Thus, it pays to jot some abbreviated version of them down before you begin reading. That way you can be alert to places in the text where questions get answered or objectives are fulfilled.

Turning Headings into Questions

Most textbook chapters are divided by major and minor headings. **Major headings** introduce the topics or issues addressed within the chapter. **Minor headings** further subdivide topics and issues introduced by the major headings. The following selection, for example, opens with the major heading "Personal, Social, and Cultural Influences on Identity Formation." Note how the minor headings further subdivide the selection.

Major Heading

Personal, Social, and Cultural Influences on Identity Formation

1 The adolescent's progress toward identity achievement is influenced by at least four factors: cognitive* growth, parenting, schooling, and the broader social-cultural context.

Minor Heading

2 **Cognitive Influences**   Cognitive development plays an important role in identity achievement. Adolescents who have achieved solid mastery of formal thought and who can reason logically about hypotheticals* are now better able to imagine and contemplate* future identities. Consequently, they are more likely to raise and resolve identity issues than are age-mates who are less intellectually mature (Berzonsky & Kuk, 2000; Boyes & Chandler, 1992).

Minor Heading

3 **Parenting Influences**   The relationships that adolescents have with their parents can also affect their progress at forging an identity (Grotevant & Cooper, 1998; Markstrom-Adams, 1992). Adolescents who move easily into identity achievement appear to have a solid base of affection at home combined with considerable freedom to be individuals in their own right (Grotevant & Cooper, 1998). In family discussions, for example, these adolescents experience a sense of closeness and mutual respect while feeling free to disagree with their parents and to be individuals in their own right. So the same loving and democratic style of parenting that helps children gain a strong sense of self-esteem is also associated with healthy and adaptive* identity outcomes in adolescence.

Minor Heading

4 **Scholastic Influences**   Does attending college help one to forge an identity? The answer is yes—and no. Attending college does seem to push people toward setting career goals and making stable occupational commitments (Waterman, 1982); but college students are often far behind

---

*cognitive: related to thinking.
*hypotheticals: things existing only as theories, not yet realities.
*contemplate: consider; think about.
*adaptive: capable of responding effectively to new situations.

their working peers in terms of establishing firm political and religious identities (Munro & Adams, 1977). In fact, some collegians regress* from identity achievement. But let's not be too critical of the college environment, for, like college students, many adults will later reopen the question of who they are if exposed to people or situations that challenge old viewpoints and offer new alternatives (Kroger, 2005).

Minor Heading   5   **Cultural-Historical Influences**   Finally, identity formation is strongly influenced by the broader social and historical context in which it occurs (Bosma & Kunnen, 2001)—a point that Erikson himself emphasized. In fact, the very idea that adolescents should choose a personal identity after carefully exploring many options may well be peculiar to industrialized societies of the twentieth century (Cote & Levine, 1988). As in past centuries, adolescents in many nonindustrialized societies today will simply adopt the adult roles they are expected to adopt, without any soul-searching or experimentation: Sons of farmers will become farmers, the children of fishermen will become (or perhaps marry) fishermen, and so on. For many of the world's adolescents, then, what [researchers] call *identity foreclosure* is probably the most adaptive route to adulthood. In addition, the specific life goals that adolescents pursue are necessarily constrained somewhat by whatever options are available and valued in their society at any given point in time (Bosma & Kunnen, 2001; Katsumoto, 2000). (Adapted from Shaffer, *Social and Personality Development*, pp. 192–93.)

All the headings shown in the previous selection are a source of questions that can guide your reading. Using words like *what*, *how*, and *why*, you can reframe those headings, turning them into questions such as "What are cognitive influences?" "How do cognitive influences affect identity formation?" "What role does parental influence play in identity formation?"

Form Questions Based on Key Terms

Authors frequently use boldface, italics, boxes, or notes in the margins to highlight key vocabulary. When you spot those highlighted terms during a survey, use them as the basis for questions; for example, the following two words appear as marginal notes in a chapter on memory. Both provide the basis for questions.

---

*regress: move backward.

Mnemonic* a device for improving memory

Acronym* a word composed of the first letter of a series of words

Questions: 1. What are some examples of mnemonics, and are they useful for all kinds of remembering?

2. What are some examples of acronyms, and how can they aid memory?

Use End-of-Chapter Summaries

Textbook authors frequently use a summary section to identify a chapter's core concepts. It follows then that readers should use these concluding sections as the basis for questions. Here's a brief excerpt from a summary of a chapter on early childhood development. Although the list states the key points to be learned from the chapter, the items in the list are fairly general. Questions can focus them more by asking for specific explanations or examples of what's been said.

Chapter Summary ◆

Early Social Relationships

1. A newborn infant has a natural tendency to actively participate in her social world.

   Question: How does the infant show this "natural tendency"?

2. *Infant-caregiver synchrony* refers to the closely orchestrated social and emotional interactions between an infant and his caregiver. It provides an important basis for the development of attachment relationships.

   Question: How does synchrony help form a basis for the development of attachments?

---

*mnemonic: memory aid; a famous and common mnemonic used for spelling is "*i* before *e* except after *c*."
*acronym: word created out of the first letter of several words or syllables; NATO (North Atlantic Treaty Organization) and SCUBA (Self-Contained Underwater Breathing Apparatus) are both acronyms.

3. The effects of nonmaternal care and maternal employment on infant and toddler development depend on the specific circumstances but in general do not appear to have negative effects.

   Question: How do the specific circumstances affect nonmaternal care and maternal employment?

4. When given the opportunity to do so, infants engage in active social interactions with their siblings and peers, and often prefer them to their parents as playmates.

   Questions: What are the social interactions infants engage in with siblings and peers? How do the infants show a preference?

Speaking of *Who, When,* and *Where*

The words *who, when,* and *where* can certainly be used to form questions. Just be aware that questions using these three words frequently produce brief answers that don't have much depth or detail; for example, When did Freud publish his landmark text, *The Interpretation of Dreams*? The answer is 1900, and that's all the information or insight you'll get from asking that question.

Question openers such as *what, why, how,* and *in what way* can help you dig more deeply into the text. The deeper, or more detailed, your understanding of the material, the easier it will be to remember what you've read.

SUMMING UP THE KEY POINTS

1. Readers who pose questions are less likely to lose their concentration while reading. They are also more likely to spot the most important passages in a chapter.

2. Questions used to guide your reading can be based on (1) introductory lists of questions and objectives, (2) major and minor headings, (3) key words highlighted in the text, and (4) summary sections of chapters.

◆ **EXERCISE 2**   **Using Questions to Focus Your Attention**

DIRECTIONS   Read the headings and the first sentence of every paragraph. Then make a list of questions you would use to guide your reading of this selection.

The Digestive System

All food which is eaten must be changed into a soluble, absorbable form within the body before it can be used by the cells. This means that certain physical and chemical changes must take place to change the insoluble complex food molecules into simpler soluble ones. These can then be transported by the blood to the cells and be absorbed through the cell membranes. The process of changing complex solid foods into simpler soluble forms which can be absorbed by the body cells is called **digestion**. It is accomplished by the action of various digestive juices containing enzymes. **Enzymes** are chemical substances that promote chemical reactions in living things, although they themselves are unaffected by the chemical reactions.

Digestion is performed by the digestive system, which includes the alimentary canal and accessory digestive organs. The **alimentary canal** is also known as the digestive tract or gastrointestinal (GI) tract. The alimentary canal consists of the mouth (oral cavity), pharynx (throat), esophagus (gullet), stomach, small intestine, large intestine (colon), and the anus. It is a continuous tube some 30 feet (9 meters) in length, from the mouth to anus.

The accessory organs of digestion are the tongue, teeth, salivary glands, pancreas, liver, and gallbladder.

Layers of the Digestive System

The walls of the alimentary canal are composed of four layers: (1) the innermost lining, called the mucosa, is made of epithelial cells; (2) the submucosa consists of connective tissue with fibers, blood vessels, and nerve endings; (3) the third layer, the muscularis consists of circular muscle; and (4) the fourth, the scrosa has longitudinal muscle. The mucosa secretes slimy mucus. In some areas, it also produces digestive juices. This slimy mucus lubricates the alimentary canal, aiding in the passage of food. It also insulates the digestive tract from the effects of powerful enzymes while protecting the delicate epithelial cells from abrasive substances within the food.

Lining of the Digestive System

The abdominal cavity is lined with a serous membrane called the peritoneum. This is a two-layered membrane with the outer side lining the abdominal cavity and the inner side, or visceral, lining covering the outside of each organ in the abdominal cavity. An inflammation of the lining of this cavity caused by disease-producing organisms is called **peritonitis**.

There are two specialized layers of peritoneum. The peritoneum that attaches to the posterior wall of the abdominal cavity is called the **mesentery**. The small intestines are attached to this layer. In the anterior portion of the abdominal cavity a double fold of peritoneum extends down from the greater curvature of the stomach. This hangs over the abdominal organs like a protective apron. This layer contains large amounts of fat and is called the **greater omentum**. The peritoneal structure between the liver and stomach is called the lesser omentum.

Functions of the Digestive System

The functions of the digestive system are to change food into forms that the body can use and to eliminate the waste products. These functions are accomplished in four major steps.

1. Break down food physically into smaller pieces
2. Change food chemically by digestive juices into the end products of fat, carbohydrates, and protein
3. To absorb the nutrients into the blood capillaries of the small intestines for use in the body
4. To eliminate the waste products of digestion (Scott and Fong, *Body Structures and Functions*, pp. 376–77.)

1) what are the four layers of the digestion system?

2) What are the functions of the Digestive System?

3) What does the lining of the digestive system do?

✔ CHECK YOUR UNDERSTANDING

1. Why is posing questions while reading beneficial?

_____

_____

2. What are some of the sources readers can use as the basis for questions?

_____

_____

R1: Read Difficult Material in Sections or Chunks

If you have an overall picture of a chapter or an article's contents and you know some of the questions you want to answer, it's time to start reading. Remember, though, that textbook study sessions shouldn't last more than one and a half to two hours. Your eyes could keep going a good deal longer than that, but your brain probably couldn't, and your concentration would be less focused. It's better to plan on a two-hour maximum study session so that you can stay focused the whole time.

Assign Yourself a Specific Number of Pages

Before you start reading, assign yourself a specific number of pages that you want to cover. The number should be determined by the length of the material and how much you already know about it. If you have no background knowledge about the subject under discussion, if the content is complex and the style difficult, consider reading only eight to ten pages per session. Just make sure you plan on at least three study sessions to get through the chapter. Think about reading a whole chapter in one sitting *only* if the material is familiar and the style easy to read.

Vary Your Assignments to Stay Sharp

If you wish, you can certainly take a half-hour break and then return to the chapter to finish it. But in terms of remembering what you read, you might be better off switching to a different assignment. Varying your assignments so that you aren't spending all your time on one subject helps concentration and remembering. Your brain feels refreshed and more alert simply because it's working on something new.

Be Prepared to Re-Read

For some odd reason, many people think that being a good reader means never having to re-read a single word. Yet, if anything, good readers have a knack for knowing when a passage requires a second or even a third reading. They also don't see re-reading as a sign of failure. They know that understanding almost any subject requires a willingness to read and re-read until the words start making sense.

Skilled readers also know that re-reading in the same way and at the same rate usually doesn't work. If they do a second reading, they slow down their reading rate and try a different reading strategy, say drawing a diagram or reading aloud.

> *"Students who use their notes to study tend to perform better on tests."*
>
> —Tim Urdan and Frank Pajares, *Adolescence and Education*
>
> *"Why mark a book? I may retort, why blaze a trail through a forest?"*
>
> —Peter.Slowreads.com

Write While You Read

If I could personally give every student who reads this book one piece of advice, it would be this: Keep a pen or pencil in hand while you read, and use it—a lot. With material that is somewhat familiar and written in an easy-to-absorb style, underline key words and jot brief notes in the margins of pages. With more complicated texts, especially those essential to your college career, do both—take brief marginal notes and make a more detailed set of notes in a separate notebook.

If you really want to make your way to the head of the class, then keep a highlighter close by. Use the highlighter for specific passages that seem especially significant—for example, ideas that might turn up on exams or prove useful for term papers. Because writing[†] while reading is critical to academic success, you'll hear more on this subject later on in the chapter.

SQ3R and Outlining

In his book *Effective Study*, Robinson told his readers to pose questions while reading and *write out* answers as a comprehension check. Robinson also believed that outlining while reading was a great study strategy. Given Robinson's endorsement of outlining, we can legitimately discuss it as part of *SQ3R* and later on talk about other writing strategies that Robinson did not explicitly mention.

Making an Informal Outline

Some students panic when they hear the word *outline* in the same sentence with the phrase "take notes." They panic because they think they have to create formal outlines, where every *a* is followed by a *b* and where strict rules dictate how the outline has to be completed. But that's not the case here. An informal outline used for note taking does not have to follow rigid rules. It just has to do the following:

1. Identify the main point or thought of each chapter section.

2. List some specifics used to explain that point or thought.

3. Indent to show relationships.

4. Leave plenty of space for the addition of more information later, during reviews.

[†]In this case, "writing" also includes marking, underlining, and drawing diagrams.

Here's an informal outline of the reading selection on pages 11–12.

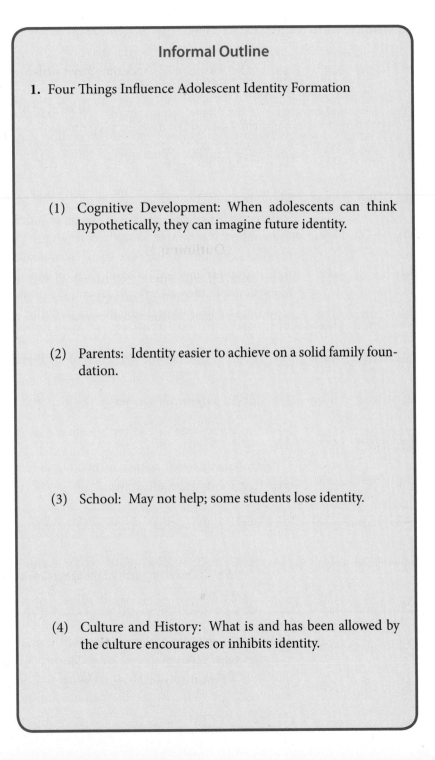

Informal Outline

1. Four Things Influence Adolescent Identity Formation

(1) Cognitive Development: When adolescents can think hypothetically, they can imagine future identity.

(2) Parents: Identity easier to achieve on a solid family foundation.

(3) School: May not help; some students lose identity.

(4) Culture and History: What is and has been allowed by the culture encourages or inhibits identity.

When you outline a chapter section by section while you read, you need to answer two questions: (1) What point does the author want to make in this section? and (2) What examples, definitions, reasons, facts, and so on, does the author use to explain or prove that point?

Unless you are very familiar with the material covered, your outline at this stage of your reading may not be especially detailed. That's the reason for all the space you see in the sample outline on page 19. The space is there to be filled in with details during later reviews.

Yes, sometimes when you start an outline, you won't even be sure you understand the writer's main point. Still that's important to know. If that's the case, you need to mark the passage for a second reading. That makes outlining an excellent way to monitor, or check, your comprehension.

Indenting Is Critical. How you line up or indent sentences or phrases in an outline is central to identifying relationships. If sentences, phrases, or words are aligned, they are equal in importance. If one sentence is indented under another, however, then the indented item is not equal in importance. Rather, it serves to explain the previous statement.

In the sample outline, these two thoughts are equally important:

> (1) Cognitive Development: When adolescents can think hypothetically, they can imagine future identity.
>
> (2) Parents: Identity easier to achieve on a solid family foundation.

The following two thoughts are not. On the contrary, indention indicates that one develops the other.

> 1. Four Things Influence Adolescent Identity Formation
>
> > (1) Cognitive Development: When adolescents can think hypothetically, they can imagine future identity.

Outlining chapter sections is certainly not appropriate for every reading assignment. However, for assignments that are detailed, dense with facts and figures, and short on **concreteness**, or words that can be easily visualized—for example, *rocks*, *houses*, and *mountains*—consider making an outline.

To be sure, you don't have to outline every chapter section. But do consider informal outlining for those parts of a chapter that seem difficult to process. Sorting the material to determine what goes into your outline and how the different pieces of information should be indented or aligned will help you understand the author's thinking.

SUMMING UP THE KEY POINTS

1. Reading at stretches of more than two hours can be self-defeating. Your eyes may still be moving across the page at the end of two hours, but more than likely your brain is not absorbing the meaning behind the words. Plan your study sessions accordingly.

2. Varying assignments so that you don't spend more than two hours learning material from one subject before switching to another is a good way to maintain concentration and promote remembering.

3. Writing while reading can help you really understand what you read. It's also an excellent way to encourage remembering.

4. Informal outlines do not follow a rigid format. The key goals of an informal outline are to (1) list the key points of a chapter section and (2) indicate their relationship to one another.

5. In an outline, indenting is how you show relationships between ideas. When items in an outline are equal in importance, they are aligned. When one statement explains another, it has to be indented under the statement it explains.

◆ **EXERCISE 3**   **Making an Informal Outline**

DIRECTIONS   Read and outline the selection that follows.

How to Read a Newspaper

1   Newspapers don't simply report the news; they report somebody's idea of what is news, written in language intended to persuade as well as inform. To read a newspaper intelligently, look for three things: what is covered, who are the sources, and how language is used.

Coverage

2   Every newspaper will cover a big story, such as a flood, fire, or presidential trip, but newspapers can pick and choose among lesser stories. One paper

will select stories about the environment, business fraud, and civil rights; another will prefer stories about crime, drug dealers, and "welfare cheats." What do these choices tell you about the beliefs of the editors and reporters working for these two papers? What do these people want you to believe are the important issues?

Sources

3 For some stories, the source is obvious: "The Supreme Court decided . . . ," "Congress voted . . . ," or "The president said. . . ." But for others the source is anonymous, and you should respond to them with questions. When you read phrases such as "a high official said today . . ." or "White House sources revealed that . . . ," always ask yourself this question: Why does the source want me to know this? The answer usually will be this: because if I believe what he or she said, it will advance his or her interests. This can happen in one of three ways. First, the source may support a policy or [an] appointment and want to test public reaction to it. This is called floating a **trial balloon**. Second, the source may oppose a policy or appointment and hope that by leaking word of it, the idea will be killed. Third, the source may want to take credit for something good that happened or shift blame onto somebody else for something bad that happened. When you read a story that is based on anonymous sources, ask yourself these questions: Judging from the tone of the story, is this leak designed to support or kill an idea? Is it designed to take credit or shift blame? In whose interest is it to accomplish these things? By asking these questions, you often can make a pretty good guess as to the identity of the anonymous source.

4   Some stories depend on the reader's believing a key fact, previously unknown. For example: "The world's climate is getting hotter because of pollution," "drug abuse is soaring," "the death penalty will prevent murder," "husbands are more likely to beat up on their wives on Super Bowl Sunday." Each of these "facts" is either wrong, grossly exaggerated, or stated with excessive confidence. But each comes from an advocate organization that wants you to believe it, because if you do, you will take that organization's solution more seriously. Be skeptical of key facts if they come from an advocacy source. Don't be misled by the tendency of many advocacy organizations to take neutral or scholarly names like "Center for the Public Interest" or "Institute for Policy Research." Some of these really are neutral or scholarly, but many aren't.

Language

5 Everybody uses words to persuade people of something without actually making a clear argument for it. This is called using **loaded language**. For example: if you like a politician, call him "Senator Smith"; if you don't like him, refer to him as "right-wing (or left-wing) senators such as Smith." If you like an idea proposed by a professor, call her "respected"; if you don't like the idea, call her "controversial." If you favor abortion, call somebody who agrees with you "pro-choice" ("choice" is valued by most people); if you oppose abortion, call those who agree with you "pro-life" ("life," like "choice," is a good thing). Recognizing loaded language in a newspaper article can give you important clues to the writer's own point of view. (Wilson and Dilulio, *American Government*, p. 304.)

Main Point How to read a Newspaper
Either to perform of pursuede

Specifics 1. Coverage
1) crime, fraud, government
civil rights

2. Sources
1) annonymous sources
2) obvious sources
3) trial balloon

3. Language
1) loaded language
2) writers point of view

CHECK YOUR UNDERSTANDING

1. Why should you avoid scheduling study sessions that are more than two hours long?

_____

_____

2. What is a good way to maintain your concentration even if you are studying for more than two hours?

_____

3. If you want to improve both comprehension and remembering, what should you do while reading?

_____

4. What should an informal chapter outline accomplish?

_____

_____

R2: See How Much You Can Recall Right After Reading†

When an author's words are right before our eyes, we usually think we understand them. Yet if we look away from the page and try to recall what we've read, we often discover that what we remember is muddled or incomplete. That's what makes the recall step of *SQ3R* so important. It's a way of monitoring your understanding before going on to the next section of a chapter or an article.

But there's another reason why recalling right after reading is critical: Most people are inclined to forget new information right after reading it. Fortunately, though, with the passage of time, the rate of forgetting slows down, and we forget less as time passes. That means anything we do to fix newly absorbed information into long-term memory *right after reading*—when the rate of forgetting is highest—

---

†Robinson used the word *recite*, but he included under that term "mentally reviewing the answer or writing it out," which is another way of saying "recall."

improves our chances of remembering what we have read, even weeks or months later.

As always with *SQ3R*, there are different ways to complete this step. The one you choose depends on the kind of material you are reading and the depth of understanding you want to achieve. Here again, flexibility is key.

Mental Recitation

With material that's not too difficult or too unfamiliar, you can try mentally reciting answers to the following questions: What topic, or subject, was discussed? What point did the author make about the topic? How did the author illustrate or argue the point? The last question of the three is usually the toughest to answer. If you can think of one illustration or reason after a first reading, you are doing just fine.

Try Writing Out the Answers

Robinson believed that readers were inclined to fool themselves if they only recited answers to their questions. In his opinion, it was too easy to accept a vague and confused answer. Posing questions about the material and writing out the answers was, in Robinson's opinion, a better comprehension check. By writing out the answers, readers could tell immediately what they did (and didn't) know.

Use Your Informal Outline

If you are making an informal outline of chapter sections, use it during the recall stage of your reading. Cover up everything except the opening thought or point of the outline and see how many details you can recall. Then, without even looking at the outline, see how well you can recall from memory the bare bones of the chapter section, i.e., the central thought and specific reasons, illustrations, etc.

Draw Rough Diagrams and Pictures

If you remember what you see even better than what you hear, consider translating words into pictures or diagrams during the recall step of your reading. Then check your drawing against the actual text to see what you've missed.

Here, for instance, is a passage about the layers of the earth, followed by a reader-made diagram. Note that the reader identified all four of the layers described in the passage. For a first reading, that's very good.

Four different layers make up the Earth: the inner core, outer core, mantle, and crust. The rocky and brittle crust is the outermost and

thinnest layer. In contrast, the thickest part of the Earth's mass is in the mantle, which is composed of iron (Fe), magnesium (Mg), aluminum (Al), silicon (Si), and oxygen (O) silicate compounds. Below the mantle lies the core, composed mostly of iron and so hot, it's molten.* The inner portion of the core, however, is under such intense pressure, it remains solid.

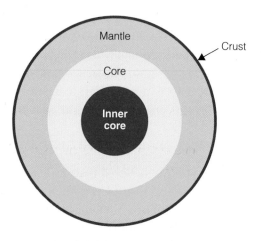

SUMMING UP THE KEY POINTS

1. Trying to recall what you've read right after reading is important for two reasons. First, it is a way of monitoring your understanding. It tells you how well you have or have not understood what you've read. Recalling right after reading also slows down the rate of forgetting and increases your chances of remembering what the author of the text actually said.

2. Flexibility is important in choosing the method of recall. In addition to mentally reciting after reading, you should also consider the following: (1) writing out answers to the questions you posed to guide your reading, (2) covering up parts of an informal outline and then trying to recall what remains on the page, and (3) making rough diagrams or drawing pictures. The method you choose depends on the kind of material you are reading.

*molten: heated to the point of becoming liquid.

◆ **EXERCISE 4**   **Recalling After Reading**

DIRECTIONS   Read the following excerpt. Then, from memory, fill in the boxes.

Steps in Delegation

1 The process of **delegation** essentially involves three steps. First, the manager assigns **responsibility**. That is, the manager defines the employee's duty to perform a task. For example, when a manager tells someone reporting to him to prepare a sales projection,* order additional raw materials, or hire a new assistant, he is assigning responsibility.

2   Second, the manager must also grant the **authority** necessary to carry out the task. Preparing a sales projection may call for the acquisition* of sensitive sales reports, ordering raw material may require negotiations on price and delivery dates, and hiring a new assistant may mean submitting a hiring notice to the human resource department. If these activities are not a formal part of the group member's job, the manager must give her the authority to do them anyway.

3   Finally, the manager needs to create **accountability**. This suggests that the group member incurs* an obligation to carry out the job. If the sales report is never prepared, if the raw materials are not ordered, or if the assistant is never hired, the group member is accountable to her boss for failing to perform the task. Indeed, if the manager is not careful, it is possible for some personnel to lose sight of their major task because they become focused on the wrong objectives. . . .

4   Of course, these steps are not carried out in rigid, one-two-three fashion. Indeed, in most cases they are implied by past work behavior. When the manager assigns a project to a group member, for instance, the group member probably knows without asking that he has the authority necessary to do the job and that he is accountable for seeing to it that it does, indeed, get done. (Adapted from Van Fleet and Peterson, *Contemporary Management*, pp. 252–53.)

Delegation Process

---

*projection: prediction of future sales.
*acquisition: the act of acquiring or obtaining something.
*incurs: produces, brings about, assumes.

CHECK YOUR UNDERSTANDING

1. What are two reasons why recalling right after reading is useful?

_____

_____

2. What are some of the methods readers can use to recall what they've read after finishing a chapter section?

_____

_____

_____

R3: Review Right After Completing the Assignment

Robinson's suggestion to review right after reading is a good one. But it needs some modification and clarification. Perhaps because he assumed students were also outlining chapters while they read, Robinson allotted only five minutes for review. Actually, you need at least fifteen to make this step productive.

Robinson also didn't always make it clear that the third *R* in his system represented only *the first* of several reviews. Trained as an educational psychologist, Robinson knew full well that *mastery of new material occurs with repeated reviews that extend over time.* He never assumed that the first review would be the reader's last.

The Goals of the First Review

At this stage of your reading, your first goal is to understand how the individual parts of the chapter fit together. For example, in a chapter titled "The Professional Sports Business," you would need to determine if the author was trying to give you a historical overview of how sports have become more about making money than a celebration of athletic prowess. Or perhaps the chapter focuses on the various elements that make up the business of sports, such as scouts, agents, contracts, owners, trainers, and endorsements. Once you have the larger chapter objective in mind, it becomes easier to see what each chapter section contributes.

The second goal of a first review is to confirm or revise your initial predictions about a chapter's contents. Did it, for example, describe critical management skills as you had thought? Or did the chapter actually veer away from your predicted topic to describe how technology has altered the role of management on a day-to-day basis? Rethinking your original prediction provides an important benefit: It anchors the chapter's actual contents firmly into your long-term memory.

Pick a Review Method That Suits You and Your Assignment

Robinson assumed that readers would be outlining while reading, thus he suggested that during the review stage of reading "the total outline should be looked over to get an overall, easily visualized picture." Although for some assignments and some readers outlining is an ideal learning strategy, and they therefore have an outline available for review, that's not always the case. Fortunately, there are other ways to complete a first review.

Look at All the Major Headings. Go through the chapter page by page. Look at each major heading and then look away to see how much you remember about the thoughts included under that heading. Give yourself just a few seconds to respond. If nothing comes to mind at the end of ten or fifteen seconds, mark the chapter or article section for another reading.

Draw Diagrams. If you remember pictures or images more readily than words, you might consider reviewing with diagrams. One popular diagram used for study purposes is called a **concept map**. With a concept map, you put the overall point of the chapter or article in the middle of the page and enclose it in a circle or box. Then you write down the headings of the individual chapter sections, attaching them by elongated arrows to the circled or boxed main thought, for example:

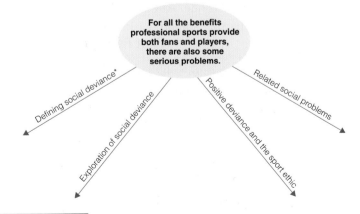

---

*deviance: the failure to follow established social rules.

To make your diagram, you don't have to call up everything in the chapter from memory. If you need to, leaf through the chapter and write down the headings. Then see how much you can recall about each one.

Here, for instance, is part of a diagram created for a chapter on disorders of the digestive system. Note how the reader has tried to fill in some of the details about the headings and left question marks under headings about which she recalled little or nothing.

Common Disorders of the Digestive System

stomatitis	hiatal hernia	pyloric stenosis	gastritis	enteritis	peptic ulcers	IBD[†]
inflammation of soft tissue in mouth	stomach protrudes above dia-phragm into esophagus opening	?	chronic inflammation of stomach lining	?	lesion in stomach lining, most bacterial caused	Crohn's disease and ?

While being able to recall the main point introduced under each heading is wonderful, recognizing that you can't recall much of anything is also useful. Your lack of recall tells you that the chapter section needs a second reading.

Work with a Classmate

Get someone in your class to review with you. Ask him or her to say the major headings aloud. Then respond by reciting what you remember about each one. Any time you draw a blank or remember very little, your partner should mark the passage for another reading.

Reviews and Recall Cues

The goals of reviews done right after reading and the long-term follow-up reviews you do for exam preparation are slightly different. Your first review, the last step in *SQ3R*, should give you a sense of the

---

[†]IBD: inflammatory bowel disease.

assignment as a whole. It should also help you determine what you do and don't know about the material you've just finished reading.

However, the reviews you do as follow-up preparation for exams should consistently focus on reducing the number of words, or **recall cues**, you need to call up the information you have learned. Although you may well start out reviewing with notes or diagrams based on complete sentences—"Gender identity refers to our sense of being male or female"; "Positive deviance refers to risky behavior that is made to seem acceptable in a specific setting"; "Delegation involves three basic steps"—you should end up with notes that include only a few key words and phrases, for example, "gender identity," "positive deviance," "steps in delegation." You can tell you are prepared for exams when just glancing at those key words and phrases triggers the explanations they represent.

SUMMING UP THE KEY POINTS

1. The third *R* in *SQ3R* refers to the review that takes place after a chapter is completed. However, Robinson knew that several reviews over an extended period of time were essential to mastery of new material. He never assumed that one review right after finishing a chapter would be enough.

2. The first goal of a review is to get a sense of how the parts of a chapter connect. Are they all effects of one cause, for instance, or do they describe a progression of events? Like the first step of *SQ3R*, the survey, use the review step to establish a sense of the chapter's general, or overall, goal.

3. Robinson suggested readers should review by looking over their informal outlines, but other methods can be used as well. You can look at all the major headings and then look away to see how much information you recall about each heading. You can make a concept map, which usually represents the chapter's central point along with the sub-topics or issues used to explain it. Or you can go over the chapter with a classmate who asks you what each major heading contributes to the overall point of the chapter.

Writing While Reading

Raising and answering questions while you read is one way to maintain your concentration and efficiently distribute your attention while you read. Combining writing with reading, however, will have the added bonus of helping you remember what you read long after you have put down the book or journal you are reading.

What follows are suggestions about how you can write and read at the same time. Over the course of several study sessions, try them all to see which ones you like best, and which ones are appropriate to specific kinds of texts. Underlining key words, for instance, probably works well with any kind of material from history to science. Diagramming, in contrast, is usually more effective with descriptions of physical events or processes.

Suggestions for Writing While Reading ◆

1. As you do a first reading, underline in pencil key words in selected sentences that you think are essential to the author's explanation.

2. When you do a second reading (or even a third one) for exam reviews, make final decisions about what's essential and what's not. This time, underline in pen.

3. Use boxes, circles, or stars to highlight key names, dates, and events.

4. If you have any personal knowledge about the subject matter, make personal comments in the margin.

Examples:

Uncle Bob went to Wild West show this summer.

Between 1872 and 1878, William "Buffalo Bill" Cody alternated between his career as a scout for the U.S. Cavalry and his starring roles in a series of melodramas popular in the East. By 1882, he had founded the enterprise that brought him even greater fame and shaped the country's view of itself, "Buffalo Bill's Wild West."

---

5. Use numbers to itemize individual parts of a definition, process, or procedure.

6. Paraphrase, or restate, the author's ideas in your own words.

Examples:

4 parts of emotions:
1. how you feel
2. how body responds
3. thoughts
4. purpose of

Emotions have several components: feelings, physiological responses, cognitions, and goals.

Number 8 is especially useful.

7. Use the margins to identify points of view that agree or disagree with the author's.

8. Use the top margin to summarize the contents of the page.

9. Use two different-colored pens, one to underline, another for marginal notes.

Examples:

Marshall Plan Provides Massive Aid

Comp. Howard Zinn on role of Marshall Plan.

The Marshall Plan was a four-year program proposed by U.S. Secretary of State George C. Marshall on June 5, 1947. Its goal was to provide foreign assistance to seventeen western and southern European nations as part of post–World War II reconstruction. Between 1948 and 1951, over $13 billion was dispensed through the Marshall Plan.

10. Whenever you find yourself struggling to understand an author's meaning for more than two or three sentences, mark the passage for a second and slower reading (e.g., *RR, x2, ??*).

11. Use arrows, labels, and abbreviations to make relationships between sentences clear.

12. Double underline, star, or otherwise highlight definitions.

Examples:

If you boil water on a stove, you can see a steamy mist above the kettle, and then higher still the mist seems to disappear into the air. Of course, the water molecules have not been lost.

Step ❶ → Step ❷

In the pan, water is in the liquid phase, and in the mist above the kettle, water exists as tiny droplets. These droplets then
Step ❸ →
Step ❹
evaporate, and the water vapor mixes with air and becomes invisible. Air generally contains some water vapor. **Humidity** is a measure of the amount of water vapor in air. (Turk and Turk, *Physical Science,* p. 410.)

13. Put quotation marks or rectangles around statements you think are particularly significant.

14. Mark a statement or passage you think might be a test question (e.g., *T.Q.*).

15. Use double lines in the margins to identify any statements you think could be the jumping-off point for a paper. Try to comment on the statement in a way that suggests how the paper might be developed.

Examples:

Effect of 1918 Influenza

How lethal was the 1918 influenza? It was twenty-five times more deadly than ordinary influenzas. This flu killed 2.5 percent of its victims. Normally just one-tenth of 1 percent of people who get the flu die. And since a fifth of the world's population got the flu that year, including 28 percent of Americans, the number of deaths was stunning. So many died, in fact, that the average lifespan in the United States fell by twelve years in 1918. If such a plague came today, killing a similar fraction of the U.S. population, 1.5 million Americans would die. (Adapted from Kolata, *Flu,* p. 216.)

T.Q.
Paper: There are signs bird flu could be worse than 1918.

Effect on mortality: average lifespan decreased.

Selectivity Is the Key

Whatever mix of notes, symbols, and underlining you come up with to make writing part of reading, remember this: Selectivity is the essence of marking a text. Your goal is not to emphasize every word on the page. Your goal is to make what's important stand out so that you can review key portions of the text at a later time without re-reading the entire chapter.

Recognizing Your Learning Style

Some people seem to have a natural bent, or inclination, for understanding diagrams. They look at a diagram and instantly know what it represents. Others have to study diagrams very carefully to pull out the meaning, even if the diagram illustrates a passage they understood. The point is this: Most of us have different learning strengths and weaknesses. To find out what yours might be, see the site listed under "Internet Resource."

Understanding your learning weaknesses is almost as important as knowing your strengths. If you realize, for instance, that you learn more easily from hearing information than from reading it, you might consider adding recitation to your study strategies.

INTERNET RESOURCE To learn more about your learning style, go to www.varklearn.com/english/index.asp. This link is available at the student companion website for this text: www.cengage.com/devenglish/flemming/rfr11e.

READING TIP Serious learners use trial and error to figure out what works for them and for the material they want to master. When one strategy doesn't work, they try another.

◆ **EXERCISE 5**   **Marking a Text**

> **DIRECTIONS**   Read each marked excerpt. Circle the letter of the one that better illustrates the advice given on pages 32–34. Then, in the blanks at the end, explain why you chose one over the other.

a. How Short-Term Memory Works

1 **Short-Term, or Working, Memory, the Mind's Blackboard.** Many sensory impressions don't just fade away into oblivion.* They are transferred into **short-term memory (STM)** for further processing. Short-term memory is a storage system that permits you to retain and process sensory information for a maximum of about thirty seconds. Short-term memory relies on both visual and acoustic* coding, but mostly on acoustic coding. For example, you attempt to keep a phone number in mind long enough to dial it by repeating it to yourself.

2   Most psychologists refer to short-term memory as *working memory*, since information held in short-term memory is actively "worked on," or processed, by the brain (Baddeley, 2001; Braver et al., 2001). Working memory is a kind of mental workspace or blackboard for holding information long enough to process it and act on it (Stoltzfus, Hasher, & Zacks, 1996). For example, we engage working memory when we form an image of a person's face and hold it in memory for the second or two it takes the brain to determine whether it is the face of someone we know. We also employ working memory whenever we perform arithmetical operations in our heads or engage in conversation. In a conversation, our working memory allows us to retain memory of sounds long enough to convert* them into recognizable words.

3   In the 1950s, psychologist (George Miller) performed a series of landmark* studies in which he sought to determine the storage capacity of short-term memory. Just how much Information can most people retain in short-term memory? The answer, Professor Miller determined, was about seven items, plus or minus two (Kareev, 2000). Miller referred to the limit of seven as the "Magic 7."

4   The magic number seven appears in many forms in human experience, including the "seven ages of man" in Shakespeare's *As You Like It*, the Seven Wonders of the World, the Seven Deadly Sins, and even the seven dwarfs of

---

*oblivion: condition of being completely forgotten.
*acoustic: related to sound.
*convert: transform, change.
*landmark: having important consequences on future studies or events; also a decisive turning point.

Disney fame (Logie, 1996). Investigators find that people can normally repeat a maximum of six or seven single-syllable words they have just heard (Hulme et al., 1999). Think about the "Magic 7" in the context of your daily experiences. Telephone numbers are seven-digit numbers, which means you can probably retain a telephone number in short-term memory just long enough to dial it. (Nevid, *Psychology: Concepts and Applications,* p. 221.)

b. How Short-Term Memory Works

1 **Short-Term, or Working, Memory, the Mind's Blackboard.** Many sensory impressions don't just fade away into oblivion.* They are transferred into **short-term memory (STM)** for further processing. Short-term memory is a storage system that permits you to retain and process sensory information for a maximum of about thirty seconds. Short-term memory relies on both visual and acoustic* coding, but mostly on acoustic coding. For example, you attempt to keep a phone number in mind long enough to dial it by repeating it to yourself.

Keeping phone number in mind

2 Most psychologists refer to short-term memory as *working memory*, since information held in short-term memory is actively "worked on," or processed, by the brain (Baddeley, 2001; Braver et al., 2001). Working memory is a kind of mental workspace or blackboard for holding information long enough to process it and act on it (Stoltzfus, Hasher, & Zacks, 1996). For example, we engage working memory when we form an image of a person's face and hold it in memory for the second or two it takes the brain to determine whether it is the face of someone we know. We also employ working memory whenever we perform arithmetical operations in our heads or engage in conversation. In a conversation, our working memory allows us to retain memory of sounds long enough to convert* them into recognizable words.

Form images, holding in memory to see if familiar

EX

T. Q.

3 In the 1950s, psychologist George Miller performed a series of landmark* studies in which he sought to determine the storage capacity of short-term memory. Just how much Information can most people retain in short-term memory? The answer, Professor Miller determined, was about seven items, plus or minus two (Kareev, 2000). Miller referred to the limit of seven as the "Magic 7."

Miller says we hold about 7 items in s.t. memory

4 The magic number seven appears in many forms in human experience, including the "seven ages of man" in Shakespeare's *As You Like It*, the Seven Wonders of the World, the Seven Deadly Sins, and even the seven dwarfs of Disney fame (Logie, 1996). Investigators find that people can normally

repeat a maximum of six or seven single-syllable words they have just heard (Hulme et al., 1999). Think about the "Magic 7" in the context of your daily experiences. Telephone numbers are seven-digit numbers, which means you can probably retain a telephone number in short-term memory just long enough to dial it. (Nevid, *Psychology: Concepts and Applications*, p. 221.)

_____

_____

_____

READING TIP   Using a variety of page-marking techniques will keep you focused and sharp. It will also help you remember what you read.

The Importance of Varying Your Reading Rate

> *"Readers make choices in the kinds of attention they give to texts—from scanning, skimming, and speed reading to deep reading and re-reading."*
>
> —Catherine L. Ross, professor, University of Western Ontario

Unless you are reading a very difficult text, where the complexity of the material forces you to maintain a low, phrase-by-phrase reading rate (see the following chart), the speed with which you read should vary. While re-reading the introduction you already surveyed, for instance, you can speed up to 500 or 600 words a minute. You need to slow down, though, when you start a chapter section, reducing your rate to around 250 or 300 words a minute.

With material that is familiar and not too difficult—introductions in textbooks, for instance, are often lists of single sentences rather than paragraphs—your reading rate can be on the boundary between skimming and study reading. If you are reading a chapter on childhood nutrition, for example, and already know much of the information from another course, then keep your reading rate fairly high, between 350 and 400 words a minute. If the text becomes difficult, don't be afraid to slow down and do an analytical, or close, reading, probably at 100 or 150 words a minute.

Reading Rates
◆

Good readers are flexible about reading rate. They vary it to suit the material and their reading purpose.

Reading Strategy	Purpose	Type of Assignment	Rate
Scanning	To locate a specific piece of information	You are searching for a specific fact, statistic, or study.	700 to 1,000 words a minute
Skimming	To get a general overview of an article or a chapter	You are preparing to read a chapter and previewing it to determine how much time and how many study sessions you will need to master the material.	400 to 800 words a minute
Study Reading	To understand an author's message or follow the plot of a novel or short story	You are reading a detailed but clearly written chapter in preparation for class.	250 to 400 words a minute
Close or Analytical Reading	To understand a hard-to-read passage or unfamiliar and complex material	You are trying to understand a chapter filled with new and ideas written in a hard-to-read style.	100 to 250 words a minute

INTERNET RESOURCE To learn more about both study skills and reading rate, go to www.studygs.net. You can find this link and all the others mentioned in the text at the student companion website for this text: www.cengage.com/devenglish/flemming/rfr11e.

Mining the Web for Background Knowledge

Around 1970, reading researchers began focusing on the relationship between background knowledge and comprehension. Almost unanimously they came to one conclusion: The more readers know about a subject *before* they begin reading, the more their comprehension improves.

In the 1970s, though, student readers couldn't really put this insight into practice. It would have required too much time searching for sources. Fortunately the arrival of the Internet and the World Wide Web has changed all that.

The World Wide Web Makes a Difference

Today, if you survey a textbook chapter and think, "Oh no, this reads as if it were written in a foreign language, that's how little I know about the subject," you can turn to the World Wide Web, a huge network of computerized documents linked together in cyberspace. The Web has information on just about any topic you can think of. With the Web, it is possible to develop background knowledge about whatever subject you are studying.

Why Bother with the Web?

Can you complete your reading assignments without turning to the Web for background knowledge? Absolutely. But if you use the Web to get a sense of what the chapter is about *before* you start reading, you will have a better understanding of your assignment. If, for instance, you are reading about personal finance and home ownership, you'll find the text makes sense more quickly if you know what terms like "fixed rate mortgages" and "adjustable rate mortgages" (or ARMs) mean *before* you begin reading.

Google and More

To get around on the Web, you need a **search engine**, or software that helps you move from website to website. Currently, Google is the most famous search engine, and it will certainly help you find the information you need. However, to get more varied results, you might consider using two search engines rather than one. For instance, in addition to Google.com, try search.yahoo.com or Microsoft's new search engine Bing.com. Studies indicate[†] that different search engines produce some results unique to the particular search engine. That means you might get better, more on-target results from one search engine than from another.

Search Terms Matter

Computers only give back what people put into them, and using a vague, general search term to guide your search engine won't get you what you want. More precisely, you won't get it in record speed. A carefully chosen search term, in contrast, can prepare you for your reading assignment in a matter of minutes.

Evaluating Websites

For an illustration, imagine that you are assigned a chapter on President Harry Truman's Cold War[†] policies following World War II. Let's imagine as well that you know absolutely nothing about this topic. All you know is that the Cold War was a period during which the Russians and the Americans were always threatening one another with military annihilation. To deepen your understanding of the era and of Truman, let's say you typed the single word "Truman" into a search engine. The kind of list you would get is shown on page 42.

With these results, most students would be likely to give up trying to get background knowledge for the assignment. Nothing on the list shown on page 42 promises an explanation of how Truman responded to the Cold War. However, the story changes dramatically if we use a phrase to make the search term narrower, or more specific. When we search with the phrase "Truman's Cold War Policies," the results shown on page 43 come up.

[†]Dogpile is a metasearch engine; i.e., it combines results from many different search engines. The owners of Dogpile, InfoSpace, have published two studies showing that results of different search engines do *not* reveal much overlap.
[†]Cold War: a competitive state of military tension and rivalry between nations that does not quite end up in a war. For the United States, the Cold War spanned the five decades following World War II.

Web Images Maps News Shopping Gmail more ▼   Sign in

Google | Truman | (Search) Advanced Search
                                                                Preferences

Web Books Images   Results 1 - 10 of about **17,100,000** for **Truman** [definition]. (**0.05** seconds)

Harry S. **Truman** - Wikipedia, the free encyclopedia
During World War I **Truman** served as an artillery officer. After the war he became part of the
political machine of Tom Pendergast and was elected a county ...
en.wikipedia.org/wiki/Harry_S._Truman - 417k -Cached - Similar pages

Truman State University
Research affiliation: Center for Research Libraries.
www.**truman**.edu/ - 8k - Cached - Similar pages

The H. **Truman** Scholarship Foundation | Home
Scholarships for college juniors who show leadership potential and have an interest in
government or public sector service.
www.**truman**.gov/ - 19k - Cached - Similar pages

Biography of Harry S. **Truman**
Biography of Harry S. **Truman**, the thirty-third President of the United States (1945-1953).
www.whitehouse.gov/history/presidents/ht33.html?PHPSESSID=
bfafb77cfd434ee5015680b531638c5a - 17k - Cached - Similar pages

Harry S. **Truman** Library and Museum
Jan. 21, 2009 ... **Truman** Presidential Library & Museum hosts documents, photographs, virtual
exhibits, audio files, oral histories, digital archives, ...
www.**truman**library.org/ - 36k - Cached - Similar pages

Truman - Google Books Result
by David McCullough - 2003 - Biography & Autobiography
Drawing on newly discovered archival material and extensive interviews with **Truman**'s own
family, friends, and Washington colleagues, McCullough tells the...
books.google.com/books?isbn=0743260295...

Truman College
Truman College is a community college on Chicago's north side offering two-year degrees,
career, ... **Truman** College is one of the City Colleges of Chicago.
www.**truman**college.cc/ - 46k - Cached - Similar pages

The **Truman** Show (1998)
Directed by Peter Weir. With Jim Carrey, Laura Linney, Noah Emmerich. An insurance
salesman/adjuster discovers his entire life is actually a TV show.
www.imdb.com/title/tt0120382/ - 59k - Cached - Similar pages

American Experience | **Truman**
Truman: The tragic story of America's first great songwriter.
www.pbs.org/wgbh/amex/**truman** - 19k - Cached - Similar pages

Amazon.com: **Truman**: David McCullough: Books
Truman and over 225,000 other books are available for Amazon Kindle .... This warm
biography of Harry **Truman** is both an historical evaluation of his ...
www.amazon.com/**Truman**-David-McCullough/dp/067189205 - 364k - Cached - Similar pages

Web Images Maps News Shopping Gmail more ▼

Sign in

Google | Truman's Cold War Policies | (Search)   Advanced Search
                                                          Preferences

---

Web   Results **1** - **10** of about **2,590,000** for **Truman's** Cold War Policies. (**0.25** seconds)

Cold War - Wikipedia, the free encyclopedia
These would become the main bureaucracies for US **policy** in the **Cold War**. .... of the **Cold War** that **Truman** and Eisenhower promoted politically, economically, ...
en.wikipedia.org/wiki/**Cold_War** - 330k - Cached - Similar pages

Cold War: The Balance of Terror
Feb 9, 2006 ... President **Truman's Cold War policy** became one of "containment" of the Soviets, which meant not challenging the Communists where they were ...
www.sagehistory.net/**coldwar**/topics/**coldwar**.html - 18k - Cached - Similar pages

The Truman Doctrine and NSC 68
Oct 28, 2002 ... Goals in the **Cold War**. **Cold War Policies**: 1945-1991 ... Daily Class Outline. 1. The **Truman** Doctrine and the Declaration of the **Cold War** ...
www. colorado.edu/AmStudies/lewis/2010/nsc68.htm - 48k - Cached - Similar pages

BBC - History - President Truman and the Origins of the Cold War
Jun 26, 2006 ... Undoubtedly, **Truman** profoundly shaped US foreign **policy** during 1945-53, ... wars that made America's **Cold War** 'victory' exceedingly costly. ...
www.bbc.co.uk/history/world**wars**/wwtwo/**truman**_01.shtml - 24k - Cached - Similar pages

79.02.01: The Foreign Policies of Harry S. Truman
First Lesson: **Truman** Takes Over the Presidency. Day 1: Foreign **Policies**: Ending the War in .... How the **Cold War** Was Played in Foreign Affairs, Vol. 51, No. ...
www. yale.edu/ynhti/curriculum/units/1979/2/79.02.01.x.html - 28k - Cached - Similar pages

This Day in History 1948: Henry Wallace criticizes Truman's Cold ...
Henry Wallace, former vice-president and current Progressive Party presidential candidate, lashes out at the **Cold War policies** of President Harry S. **Truman**. ...
www.history.com/this-day-in-history.do?action=Article&id=2622 - 57k - Cached - Similar pages

The National Archives Learning Curve | Cold War
The two events most associated with **Truman** and the **Cold War** are the **Truman** ... the arguments that Soviet **policy** in 1947 was largely defensive and reactive ... ...
www.learningcurve.gov.uk/**coldwar**/G3/cs3/default.htm - 12k - Cached - Similar pages

President Truman & Cold War Policy
An essay or paper on President **Truman** & **Cold War Policy**. President Harry S. **Truman**.
www.lotsofessays.com/viewpaper/1701223.html - Similar pages

The Cold War Begins
Stalin, by his **policy** in Poland and his broken promises, contributed to the ..... They too were blaming **Truman** for the **Cold War**, and they were upset and ...
www.fsmitha.com/h2/ch24cld.html - 57k - Cached - Similar pages

Free Seminars for Social Studies Teachers: Reassessing Harry ...
Sep 23, 2006 ... In this session, we will explore **Truman's** understanding and framing of the **Cold War** and examine the main foreign **policies** of the first years ...
www.teachingamericanhistory.org/seminars/2006/spalding_e.html - 27k - Cached - Similar pages

The sites on the list on page 43 are very different from those on the previous one. Because we included words in our search term that described more exactly what we were looking for—information related to "Truman's Cold War Policies" rather than just Truman—we got a list of sites that talk specifically about this topic instead of the Truman library or the Jim Carrey movie *The Truman Show*.

Even better, the list includes a page from Wikipedia, the Web-based encyclopedia. As long as the Wikipedia page is not undergoing revision[†] and the authors cite their sources, it's almost always a good place to get background knowledge about a topic. Certainly the entry that appears on page 45 seems perfect for our purposes.

If Wikipedia were not part of the list that came up in response to our search term, then the second site listed on page 43 also looks promising. The site description suggests the author will explain Truman's Cold War policies and, indeed, he does. As the web page on page 46 shows, the author gives readers a general overview of the Cold War, describes its origins, and evaluates Truman's policies.

Personal Websites

As good as the site on page 46 is, you'd still be better off checking out another site if this one was your first choice. Like many sites maintained by a person rather than an institution, there's a little too much opinion, or personal point of view, mixed in with the facts.

Look, for instance, at sentences like this one: "Harry Truman was ill-prepared to assume the duties of President upon FDR's death in April, 1945, and the blame for that must be laid at Roosevelt's feet." This is a perfectly legitimate opinion. Many people share it. But many others don't. In other words, the statement reveals a personal opinion or judgment.

When you are looking for background knowledge for a textbook assignment, all you really want is an overview of what events took place and who was involved in them. You don't want the website to spend much time evaluating either the events or the people associated with your topic. That's fine for later when you know the material, but it's best not to start off with a website that contains numerous personal opinions. Instead, try another website to find one with mostly factual information.

[†]Wikipedia's editors note when sources are not appropriate or the entry itself is not well-written. If you find an entry suggesting the need for revision, look elsewhere for information.

Cold War

From Wikipedia, the free encyclopedia

The Cold War was the state of conflict, tension and competition that existed between the United States and the Soviet Union and their respective allies from the mid-1940s to the early 1990s. Throughout this period, rivalry between the two superpowers was expressed through military coalitions, propaganda, espionage, weapons development, industrial advances, and competitive technological development, which included the space race. Both superpowers engaged in costly defense spending, a massive conventional and nuclear arms race, and numerous proxy wars.

Although the US and the Soviet Union were allied against the Axis powers during World War II, the two states disagreed sharply both during and after the conflict on many topics, particularly over the shape of the post-war world. The war had either exhausted or eliminated the pre-war "Great Powers" leaving the US and USSR as clear economic, technological and political superpowers. In this bipolar world, countries were prompted to align themselves with one or the other of the superpower blocs (a Non-Aligned Movement would emerge later, during the 1960s).

The US and the Soviet Union were the two superpowers during the Cold War, each leading its own sphere of influence. Here, the respective leaders Ronald Reagan (left) and Mikhail Gorbachev meet in 1985. Photo Courtesy Ronald Reagan Library.

The suppressed rivalry during the war quickly became aggravated first in Europe, then in every region in the world, as the US sought the "containment" and "rollback" of communism and forged myriad alliances to this end, particularly in Western Europe and the Middle East. Meanwhile, the Soviet Union fostered Communist revolutionary movements around the world, particularly in Eastern Europe, Latin America and Southeast Asia.

The Cold War saw periods of both heightened tension and relative calm. On the one hand, international crises such as the Berlin Blockade (1948–1949), the Korean War (1950–1953), the Berlin Crisis of 1961, the Vietnam War (1959–1975), the Soviet war in Afghanistan (1979–1989), and especially the 1962 Cuban Missile Crisis, raised fears of a Third World War. The last such crisis moment occurred during NATO exercises in November 1983, but there were also periods of reduced tension as both sides sought détente. Direct military attacks on adversaries were deterred by the potential for mutual assured destruction using deliverable nuclear weapons.

The Cold War drew to a close in the late 1980s and the early 1990s. With the coming to office of US President Ronald Reagan, the US increased diplomatic, military, and economic pressure on the Soviet Union, which was already suffering from severe economic stagnation. In the second half of the 1980s, newly appointed Soviet leader Mikhail Gorbachev introduced the *perestroika* and *glasnost* reforms. The Soviet Union collapsed in 1991, leaving the United States as the sole superpower in a unipolar world.

Part of a series on the
Cold War

Origins of the Cold War

Russian Revolution
World War II
Tehran Conference
Yalta Conference
Potsdam Conference
Iron Curtain

Cold War (1947-1953)
Cold War (1953-1962)
Cold War (1962-1979)
Cold War (1979-1985)
Cold War (1985-1991)

Contents

The Cold War: The Balance of Terror

Introduction

Copyright © 2005-6, Henry J. Sage

I believe that it must be the policy of the United States to support free peoples who are resisting attempted subjugation by armed minorities or by outside pressures. I believe that we must assist free peoples to work out their own destinies in their own way.

President Harry S. Truman—"The Truman Doctrine," 1947

The United States after World War II

Cold War Resources

General Overview: Now that the Cold War is over, it is relatively easy to view it objectively—to ask whether the United States played its cards correctly, to question whether we might have been able to lower tensions sooner and more sharply. Since the U.S. and its allies "won" the Cold War (and one can properly ask whether it is really over, or perhaps better, whether tensions at that level might indeed arise again) it is easy to say, well, of course we played it right—after all, we did win, didn't we? A more critical view might suggest that while Americans have indeed seen the fall of the Soviet Union and much of the apparatus of Communism, the U.S. might during those tension-filled years have pushed its luck so far that the only reason we did not get into a nuclear war was plain good fortune.

The Balance of Terror. In the aftermath of attacks on New York City and Washington on September 11, 2001, Americans certainly understand the fear that comes from threats of violence. Yet during the height of the Cold War in the 1950s and 1960s, the fear of nuclear war went beyond the fear of attacks on isolated cities or installations. For a time, the possibility of total nuclear war could not be ruled out, and questions were raised not only about the level of destruction that might result from a nuclear exchange, but also about what life might be like after a nuclear war. A dark joke went like this: "I don't know what they'll be using in World War Three, but in World War Four, they'll be using spears." In fact, movies like "On the Beach," based on the novel by Nevil Shute, raised the possibility of the extinction of all human life on Earth, and few saw that scenario as a far-fetched fantasy. The height of the terror came in October, 1962, when the Soviet Union began placing offense of nuclear weapons on the island of Cuba. There can be little doubt that the resulting "Cuban missile crisis" took the world to the brink; fortunately, cooler heads prevailed and disaster was averted. But nobody cheered when it was over—the shocking impact of what was possible had been too deep, and relief was a long time coming.

The Origins. The Cold War has no definite starting point—the struggle between Communist and non-Communist systems goes back to the Russian Revolution and even beyond. But the seeds of discord between the Soviet Union and the West were first sown in a tangible way, ironically, even as the need for winning World War II were bearing fruit. At the great wartime conferences among Churchill, Roosevelt and Stalin—with some participation by Chiang Kai-Shek and DeGaulle—the defeat of Germany (and Japan) grew closer, the tensions among those leaders became sharper. More than once, for example, Roosevelt became virtually a referee in the midst of the squabbles between Churchill and Stalin. From Casablanca to Tehran, Cairo and Yalta, the leaders tried to stake a claim for what they perceived as their national interests—and world interests—in the postwar era.

President Truman's Containment Policy. Harry Truman was ill-prepared to assume the duties of President upon FDR's death in April, 1945, and the blame for that must be laid at Roosevelt's feet. He did next to nothing to inform his hand-picked Vice President about the essential of his war policies, not even the atomic bomb research. Truman assumed the office while about 13 million Americans were still fighting in Europe and Asia and postwar problems were already beginning to emerge. President Truman's Cold War policy became one of "containment" of the Soviets, which meant not challenging the Communists where they were already established, but doing everything possible to see to it that their sphere did not enlarge itself at the expense of "free" nations.

See Harry S. Truman, Containment Speech, 1947. See also David McCullough's "Truman" and the fine HBO film of the same name with Gary Sinese. Truman wrote his own Memoirs as well.

A Note on Blogs

It's for precisely the reason mentioned in the previous section that blogs might not be the best place to start searching for background knowledge. Blogs,[†] by definition, represent a personal point of view that may or may not fit the general scholarly consensus, or informed group agreement, on a topic. When you are looking for background knowledge to supplement your reading, you need a general overview. The idiosyncratic, or individual, point of view found in blogs should come later when you are trying to develop a more complex and in-depth understanding of the subject.

Pointers on Choosing a Website for Background Knowledge ◆	1. **Read the website descriptions carefully, looking for references to words in your search term or people and events relevant to your chapter topics.** Search engines introduce each link with a title, description, and Web address. The most relevant links will include at least one or two words from your original search term. The least relevant ones either will not contain any words from your search term or will describe people and places that have little to do with the topic you're interested in.
	2. **If Wikipedia's Web description seems relevant to your topic, hit that link first.** If Wikipedia cites sources and the entry is not currently being revised, then it's an excellent site for a general overview and you probably don't need to look any further. Of course, if you'd like to deepen your understanding by reading at least two sources, that's always a good idea.
	3. **Eliminate those sites referring to documents, conference proceedings, addresses, interviews, and journal articles.** These will probably be too limited in scope to fulfill your pre-reading purpose: to enlarge your general background knowledge.

[†]Blog is the acronym for Web log, a Web page that, originally at least, was designed as a publicly accessible *personal* journal.

4. **Hold off clicking on websites referred to as outlines.** Because outlines and timelines pare information down to its most basic elements, they are usually too abbreviated to be valuable as pre-reading preparation. Websites set up as outlines or timelines are better for reviews.

5. **Avoid sites that end in *gov*.** If the Uniform Resource Locator (URL), which is a fancy phrase for website address, ends in *gov*, the U.S. government is the source of the Web page. Although resources from the government are fine for researching a term paper, they tend to be long, dry, and sometimes hard to read. For the purpose of gaining background knowledge, you want websites that provide information in a lively and easy-to-read manner. Thus you would be better off with URLs ending in or including *edu* (the source is an educational institution); *org* (nonprofit organization); and *com* (commercial organization).

   Note: htm and *html* do not tell you anything about the source of the information. These letters describe *how* the pages were created.

6. **Don't bother with sponsored sites.** Sponsored sites weren't just found by the Web crawler searching the Web. Someone paid a fee to make them come up in response to a particular set of search terms. You will very likely have to pay to use them. They are also likely to be **biased**, or inclined to show favoritism. With Google, sponsored sites generally appear on the right-hand side of the screen, but they can also make their way into the list of sites compiled randomly, or without plan, by the Web crawler. If a site seems to be selling products of any kind, cross it off your list of links.

7. **Avoid sites that emphasize a personal interpretation, or understanding, of the people and events.** Once you become familiar with a subject and know the traditional thinking on the topic, it's a good idea to read competing interpretations, such as "Harry Truman's handling of the Cold War was masterful" versus "Truman's manipulation of Cold War fears was a disaster" and decide what you think. But that's not how to start building background knowledge when you're first trying to understand a textbook topic.

SUMMING UP THE KEY POINTS

1. The more background knowledge you have about a textbook topic before you begin reading, the easier it will be for you to understand and remember the material.

2. The World Wide Web is an excellent source of background knowledge. Just make sure you use a search term specific enough to generate a list of websites related to your topic. Usually that means a phrase rather than a single word.

3. In selecting a site, make sure to choose one that does not express much personal bias. Your goal at this point is to understand what's traditionally thought or believed about the topic or topics included in your reading assignment. It's fine to learn about competing opinions or interpretations later, when you are thinking about writing term papers. Initially, though, your goal should be to understand the basic people, terms, and events related to the subject addressed in your text.

♦ **EXERCISE 6**   **Using the Web for Background Knowledge**

DIRECTIONS   Answer the questions by filling in the blanks or circling the correct response.

1. The letters *edu* indicate that a website is affiliated with, or connected to,

   _____.

2. During World War II, there was a resistance organization in Germany made up of teenagers who fought the Nazis until the entire group of young people was rounded up and executed. The group was called the "White Rose." Imagine that you are looking for more information about this organization. Would the search term "White Rose" be a good one? After circling your answer, please explain it.

   Yes or *No*. Please explain. _____

   _____

   _____

3. When a list of websites comes up in response to your search term, read the description to see if it contains _____

_____.

4. Imagine that you were looking for background information on President Franklin Delano Roosevelt and you landed on a website where you found the following description. Would this be a good site to use for background knowledge? Please circle your answer. Then explain your reasoning.

Franklin Delano Roosevelt held office during a time of financial crisis and economic instability: the Great Depression of the 1930s. Roosevelt, however, rose to the occasion. Gathering around him some of the finest minds in the country, known as "Roosevelt's brain trust," the president introduced a radical economic program called the "New Deal." At the heart of the New Deal was Roosevelt's willingness to intervene in the free market through government funding of programs that would create jobs and, at the same time, improve the goods and services available to U.S. citizens. The Works Progress Administration (WPA) was the largest federal agency in the government's program of economic relief. It provided close to 8 million jobs. The WPA affected almost every section of the country and was responsible for the building of much-needed bridges and roads still in use today. More than any president before or since, Roosevelt successfully used the government to enact essential social and political reforms.

Yes or *No*. _____

_____

_____

✔ **CHECK YOUR UNDERSTANDING**

1. What role can the World Wide Web play in helping you complete your reading assignments?

   _____

   _____

2. When using a search term, why is it better to use a phrase instead of a single word?

   _____

   _____

3. Why aren't blogs the best place to look when you are trying to gain background knowledge about topics in a textbook assignment?

   _____

   _____

   _____

   _____

VOCABULARY CHECK

The following words were introduced in the chapter. Match the word with the definition. Review words, definitions, and original context, or setting, two or three times before taking the vocabulary tests. (The page numbers in parentheses indicate where the word first appeared.)

1. icons (p. 3) _____
2. fetal (p. 6) _____
3. congenital (p. 6) _____
4. ambiguous (p. 6) _____
5. determinants (p. 6) _____
6. chromosomal (p. 6) _____
7. repulsed (p. 6) _____
8. prenatal (p. 8) _____
9. personified (p. 8) _____
10. cognitive (p. 11) _____
11. hypotheticals (p. 11) _____
12. contemplate (p. 11) _____
13. adaptive (p. 11) _____
14. regress (p. 12) _____
15. mnemonic (p. 13) _____
16. acronym (p. 13) _____
17. molten (p. 26) _____
18. projection (p. 27) _____
19. acquisition (p. 27) _____
20. incurs (p. 27) _____
21. deviance (p. 29) _____
22. oblivion (p. 36) _____
23. acoustic (p. 36) _____
24. convert (p. 36) _____
25. landmark (p. 36) _____

a. consider, think about
b. transform, change
c. heated to the point of becoming liquid
d. condition of being completely forgotten
e. capable of responding effectively to new situations
f. causes
g. having important consequences on future studies or events; also a decisive turning point
h. related to chromosomes, the microscopically visible carriers of genetic inheritance
i. disgusted
j. offering the perfect illustration
k. related to sound
l. visual symbols or representations
m. before birth
n. things existing only as theories, not yet realities
o. related to thinking
p. produces, brings about, assumes
q. move backward
r. prediction of future sales
s. not following accepted social standards
t. present at birth
u. the act of acquiring or obtaining something
v. related to unborn offspring still in the womb
w. memory aid
x. word created out of the first letter of several words or syllables
y. doubtful, open to interpretation

DIGGING DEEPER

Memories Are Made of This

Looking Ahead This reading, from a psychology text by Jeffrey Nevid, offers a detailed discussion of how new information gets stored in long-term memory.

> **To survey this reading, complete the following steps:**
>
> **1.** Read the title and all the topic headings.
>
> **2.** Read the definitions following all boldface terms.
>
> **3.** Look carefully at all the diagrams and marginal notes.
>
> **4.** Pose questions based on the title, headings, boldface terms, and visual aids.
>
> **5.** Read the opening and closing paragraphs along with the first sentence of every paragraph in between.
>
> **6.** Once you finish the survey, answer the questions on pages 60–61. Then go back and read the excerpt from beginning to end in order to answer the questions on pages 61–63.

1   **Memory storage** is the process of retaining information in memory. Some memories—your first kiss or your wedding, for example—may last a lifetime. But not all information becomes an enduring or long-term memory. As we shall see when we discuss the stages of memory, some information is retained for only a fraction of a second.

memory retrieval
The process of accessing and bringing into consciousness information stored in memory.

2   **Memory Retrieval: Accessing Stored Information**   Memory retrieval is the process of accessing stored information to make it available to consciousness. Retrieving long-held information is one of the marvels of the human brain. At one moment, we can summon to mind the names of the first three presidents of the United States, and at the next moment, recall our Uncle Roger's birthday. But memory retrieval is far from perfect ("Now, when is Uncle Roger's birthday anyway?"). Though some memories seem to be retrieved effortlessly, others depend on the availability of **retrieval cues**, cues associated with the original learning, to jog them into awareness.

retrieval cues   Cues associated with the original learning that facilitate the retrieval of memories.

Concept 1.1 The encoding specificity principle explains why victims of crime may be better able to recall details of the crime when they are brought back to the crime scene.

encoding specificity principle The belief that retrieval will be more successful when cues available during recall are similar to those present when the material was first committed to memory.

context-dependent memory effect The tendency for information to be better recalled in the same context in which it was originally learned.

state-dependent memory effect The tendency for information to be better recalled when the person is in the same psychological or physiological state as when the information was first learned.

3   Police detectives often take victims back to the scene of the crime to help jog their memories of the crime. You may perform better on an examination you take in the classroom where you originally learned the material. The question is, *why?* The most widely held explanation invokes the **encoding specificity principle** (Tulving, 1983). According to this principle, retrieval of particular memories will be more successful when cues available during recall are similar to those that were present when the information was originally encoded. The tendency for information to be better recalled in the context in which it was originally learned is called a **context-dependent memory effect**. Researchers believe that stimuli present in settings in which material is originally learned may be encoded along with the material itself. These stimuli may then serve as retrieval cues that help people access the learned material (Tulving & Thompson, 1973).

4   Consider a classic experiment that literally went underwater to demonstrate a context-dependent memory effect. Duncan Godden and Alan Baddeley (1975) had members of two university swim clubs learn a list of words. Members of one club learned the words on the beach; those in the other club learned them while submerged in water. The "beach group" showed better recall when they were tested on the beach than when immersed in water. The other group also showed a context-dependent effect; their retention was better when they were again submerged in water.

5   Bodily or psychological states may also serve as retrieval cues. A **state-dependent memory effect** occurs when people have better recall of information when they are in the same physiological or psychological state as when they first encoded or learned the information. Schramke and Bauer (1997) manipulated subjects' physiological states by having them either rest or exercise immediately before learning a list of twenty words. They found that recall after twenty minutes was better under the condition that prevailed in the original learning (rest or exercise). Similarly, people are generally better able to recall information when they are in the same mood (happy or sad) as when they learned the information (Bower, 1992). Bear in mind, however, that context- and state-dependent memory effects are not always observed, and when they are found, they often turn out to be rather weak (Eich, 1989).

Memory Stages

6   Some memories are fleeting; others are more enduring. The **three-stage model** of memory proposes three distinct stages of memory that vary with

Concept 1.2 The three-stage model of memory proposes three stages of memory organized around the length of time that information is held in memory: sensory memory, short-term memory, and long-term memory.

the length of time information is stored: *sensory memory*, *short-term memory*, and *long-term memory* (Atkinson & Shiffrin, 1971).

7 **Sensory Memory: Getting to Know What's Out There** **Sensory memory** is a storage system that holds sensory information in memory for a very short time. Visual, auditory, and other sensory stimuli constantly strike your sensory receptors, forming impressions you briefly hold in sensory memory in a kind of temporary storage device called a **sensory register**. This information lasts in memory for perhaps a fraction of a second to as long as three or four seconds. The sensory impression then disappears and is replaced by the next one.

8 **Short-Term, or Working, Memory: The Mind's Blackboard** Many sensory impressions don't just fade away into oblivion. They are transferred into **short-term memory (STM)** for further processing. Short-term memory is a storage system that permits you to retain and process sensory information for a maximum of about thirty seconds. Short-term memory relies on both visual and acoustic coding, but mostly on acoustic coding. For example, you attempt to keep a phone number in mind long enough to dial it by repeating it to yourself.

short-term memory (STM) The memory subsystem that allows for retention and processing of newly acquired information for a maximum of about thirty seconds (also called *working memory*).

Concept 1.3 People can normally retain a maximum of about seven items in short-term memory at any one time.

9 Most psychologists refer to short-term memory as *working memory*, since information held in short-term memory is actively "worked on," or processed, by the brain (Baddeley, 2001; Braver et al., 2001). Working memory is a kind of mental workspace or blackboard for holding information long enough to process it and act on it (Stoltzfus, Hasher, & Zacks, 1996). For example, we engage working memory when we form an image of a person's face and hold it in memory for the second or two it takes the brain to determine whether it is the face of someone we know. We also employ working memory whenever we perform arithmetical operations in our heads or engage in conversation. In a conversation, our working memory allows us to retain memory of sounds long enough to convert them into recognizable words.

10 In the 1950s, psychologist George Miller performed a series of landmark studies in which he sought to determine the storage capacity of short-term memory. Just how much information can most people retain in short-term memory? The answer, Professor Miller determined, was about seven items, plus or minus two (Kareev, 2000). Miller referred to the limit of seven as the "Magic 7."

11 The magic number seven appears in many forms in human experience, including the "seven ages of man" in Shakespeare's *As You Like It*, the Seven Wonders of the World, the Seven Deadly Sins, and even the seven dwarfs of Disney fame (Logie, 1996). Investigators find that people can normally repeat a maximum of six or seven single-syllable words they have just heard (Hulme et al., 1999). Think about the "Magic 7" in the context of your daily

experiences. Telephone numbers are seven-digit numbers, which means you can probably retain a telephone number in short-term memory just long enough to dial it. Before proceeding further, you can test your short-term memory by taking the challenge posed in the Try This Out feature below.

12   If you answered the challenge in the Try This Out feature, you probably found it easier to remember the numbers in Row 7 than those in Rows 5 and 6. Why? The answer is **chunking**, the process of breaking a large amount of information into smaller chunks to make it easier to recall. The sixteen-digit number in Row 7 consists of four chunks of consecutive years (1992, 1993, 1994, 1995). Instead of remembering sixteen separate bits of information, we need only remember four, which falls within the short-term memory capacity of most people. Similarly, children learn the alphabet by chunking series of letters. That's why they often say the letters *lmnop* as if they were one word (Rupp, 1998).

Try This Out

Breaking Through the "Magic 7" Barrier

At right are seven rows containing series of numbers. Read aloud the series in the first row. Then look away and repeat the numbers out loud in the order in which they appeared. Check whether your answer was correct or incorrect, and record it in the appropriate "yes" or "no" column. Repeat this procedure for each of the remaining rows.

How well did you do? Chances are you had little trouble with the first four series consisting of four to seven numbers. But you probably stumbled as you bumped up against the "Magic 7" barrier in the next two series, which have eight and ten digits. You may have had more success with the last series, which consists of sixteen digits. But why should you perform better with sixteen digits than with eight or ten? The text above offers an explanation.

Get It Right?

Row 1:	6293	___Yes	___No
Row 2:	73932	___Yes	___No
Row 3:	835405	___Yes	___No
Row 4:	3820961	___Yes	___No
Row 5:	18294624	___Yes	___No
Row 6:	9284619384	___Yes	___No
Row 7:	1992199319941995	___Yes	___No

---

maintenance rehearsal The process of extending retention of information held in short-term memory by consciously repeating the information.

13   Most information that passes through short-term memory fades away after a few seconds or is transferred to long-term memory. You can extend short-term memory beyond thirty seconds by engaging in **maintenance rehearsal**, the conscious rehearsal of information by repeating it over and over again in your mind. You practice maintenance rehearsal whenever you try to remember a person's name by rehearsing it again and again in your mind. But when your rehearsal is interrupted, even for just a few seconds, the contents of short-term memory quickly fade away. This is why it is

Concept 1.4 The major contemporary model of working memory holds that it consists of three components, or subsystems: the phonological loop, the visuospatial sketchpad, and the central executive.

14

difficult to keep a particular thought in mind and at the same time follow what someone is saying in conversation.

Memory theorists have developed a number of models to explain how working memory functions. The leading model, called the *three-component model*, was formulated by Alan Baddeley and Graham Hitch (1974; Baddeley, 1996). They proposed that working memory consists of three components (sometimes called *subsystems*): the *phonological loop*, the *visuospatial sketchpad*, and the *central executive* (see Figure 1.1).

1. The **phonological loop** is the speech-based, or verbal, part of working memory. It is a storage device that holds numbers and words we mull over in our minds at any given moment, such as telephone numbers, people's names, or plans for dinner. The phonological loop is engaged when you rehearse auditory material, such as by silently repeating a phone number to keep it from fading out of memory (Logie, 1996; Willingham, 2001).

phonological loop The speech-based part of working memory that allows for the verbal rehearsal of sounds or words.

2. The **visuospatial sketchpad** is a kind of drawing pad in the brain (Logie, 1996). You engage your visuospatial sketchpad whenever you picture in your mind an object, pattern, or image—the face of your beloved, the map of your home state, or the arrangement of the furniture in your living room.

visuospatial sketchpad The storage buffer for visual-spatial material held in short-term memory.

3. The **central executive** is the control unit of working memory. It doesn't store information. Rather, it receives input from the other two components and coordinates the working memory system (Baddeley, 1996; Engle, 1996). It also receives and processes information from long-term

central executive The component of working memory responsible for coordinating the other subsystems, receiving and processing stored information, and filtering out distracting thoughts.

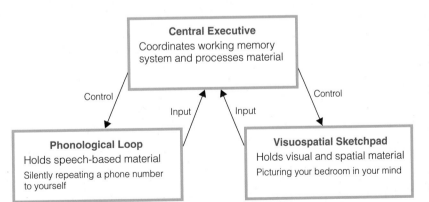

Figure 1.1   Three-Component Model of Working Memory
According to the three-component model, working memory consists of three subsystems: (1) a phonological loop for storing speech-based, or verbal, material; (2) a visuospatial sketchpad for storing visual and spatial material; and (3) a central executive that coordinates the other two subsystems, receiving and processing information retrieved from long-term memory, and filtering out distracting thoughts.

memory and filters out distracting thoughts so we can focus our attention on information we hold in mind at any given moment. The other components—the phonological loop and the visuospatial sketchpad—are called "slaves" because they do the bidding of the central executive (Willingham, 2001).

15 Since the two "slaves" work independently, they can operate at the same time without interfering with one another. When you drive an automobile, visual images of the road are temporarily stored in the visuospatial sketchpad. At the same time, your phonological loop allows you to carry on a conversation with a passenger or sing along with a song on the radio. Conflicts can arise when two or more simultaneous demands are placed on either component. It is difficult, as well as dangerous, to drive and read a roadmap at the same time. It is also difficult to hold two conversations at the same time or to listen to the TV news while attending to what someone else is saying.

long-term memory (LTM) The memory subsystem responsible for long-term storage of information.

16 **Long-Term Memory: Preserving the Past**   **Long-term memory (LTM)** is a storage system that allows you to retain information for periods of time beyond the capacity of short-term memory. Though some information may remain in long-term memory for only days or weeks, other information may remain for a lifetime. Whereas the storage capacity of short-term memory is limited, long-term memory is virtually limitless in what it can hold. We may never reach a point at which we can't squeeze yet one more experience or fact into long-term memory.

consolidation The process of converting short-term memories into long-term memories.

17 **Consolidation** is the process by which the brain converts unstable, short-term memories into lasting, stable memories. The first twenty-four hours after information is acquired is critical for consolidation to occur. The dreams that occur during REM[†] sleep may play an important role in consolidating daily experiences into long-term memories (C. Smith, 1995). This means that if you are studying for a test you have the next day and want to increase your chances of retaining the information you've just learned, make sure you get a good night's sleep.

elaborative rehearsal The process of transferring information from short-term to long-term memory by consciously focusing on the meaning of the information.

18 Although short-term memory relies largely on acoustic coding, long-term memory depends more on semantic coding, or coding by meaning. One way of transferring information from short-term to long-term memory is maintenance rehearsal, which, as we've noted, is the repeated rehearsal of words or sounds. But a better way is **elaborative rehearsal**, a method of rehearsal in which you focus on the *meaning* of the material. A friend of mine has a

---

[†]REM: Rapid Eye Movement sleep, a very deep stage of sleep during which time the brain is extremely active.

Concept 1.5
According to the semantic network model, when you think of a particular concept, it causes a ripple effect to occur within the network of interlinking concepts, triggering memory of related concepts.

19

semantic network model A representation of the organizational structure of long-term memory in terms of a network of associated concepts.

20

21

22

telephone number that ends with the digits 1991, a year I remember well because it was the year my son Michael was born. I have no trouble remembering my friend's number because I associate it with something meaningful (my son's birth year). But I need to look up other friends' numbers that end in digits that have no personal significance for me.

How do we manage to organize our long-term memory banks so we can retrieve what we want to know when we want to know it? Imagine being in a museum where bones, artifacts, and other holdings were strewn about without any organization. It would be difficult, perhaps impossible, to find the exhibit you were looking for. Now imagine how difficult it would be to retrieve specific memories if they were all scattered about in long-term memory without any rhyme or reason. Fortunately, long-term memory is organized in ways that provide relatively quick access to specific memories.

A leading conceptual model of how long-term memory is organized is called the **semantic network model** (A. M. Collins & Quillian, 1969; A. M. Collins & Loftus, 1975). This model proposes that information is held in networks of interlinking concepts. We understand the meaning of something by linking it to related things. For example, the concept of "animal" might be linked to concepts of "fish" and "bird," which in turn might be linked to associated concepts, such as "salmon" and "robin," respectively. The act of thinking of a particular concept causes a ripple effect throughout the semantic network. This rippling effect, called *spreading activation*, triggers recall of related concepts. In other words, you think of "fish" and suddenly related concepts begin springing to mind, such as "salmon" or "cod," which in turn trigger other associations such as "is pink," "tastes fishy," and so on.

Now think where else you may have encountered this notion of jumping between interlinking concepts. It is the basic principle underlying the hyperlinked structure of the World Wide Web. The inventor of the World Wide Web, English physicist Tim Berners-Lee, modeled it on how the human brain creates meaning (Berners-Lee, 1999). Berners-Lee said, "I like the idea that a piece of information is really defined only by what it's related to, and how it's related. . . . There really is little else to meaning. The structure is everything" (cited in Hafner, 1999, p. 20). Thus, when you go surfing in cyberspace by clicking on one link after another, you are modeling what your brain does naturally when it creates meaning by linking related concepts to each other.

We began our discussion of how memory works by recognizing that memory depends on underlying processes (encoding, storage, retrieval) that proceed through a series of stages (sensory memory, short-term memory, long-term memory). Figure 1.2 shows the three stages in schematic form.

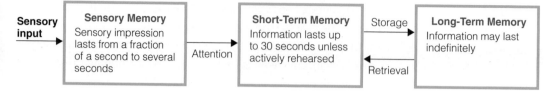

Figure 1.2 Three-Stage Model of Memory
Although human memory is more complex than the three-stage model would suggest, it does provide a useful framework for understanding relationships among the three memory storage systems. *Sensory input* (visual images, sounds, etc.) creates impressions that are held briefly in temporary storage buffers called sensory registers. If we attend to this information, it may enter *short-term memory*. We can use active rehearsal strategies (maintenance rehearsal and elaborative rehearsal) to transfer information from short-term memory into *long-term memory*. Once information is stored in long-term memory, it must be retrieved and enter short-term memory again before it can be used.

Through these steps, we come to form long-term memories that we can recall at will or with some help (retrieval cues). Next we focus on the contents of long-term memory—the kinds of memories that enrich our lives. (Adapted from Nevid, *Psychology: Concepts and Applications*, pp. 219–25.)

Questions Based on Your Survey

DIRECTIONS   Answer the questions by circling the letter of the correct response or the answer itself.

1. *True* or *False. Memory retrieval* is the process of accessing stored information that has been stored in long-term memory.

2. *True* or *False. Sensory memory* stores new impressions for a lifetime.

3. *True* or *False. Working memory* is another way of referring to short-term memory.

4. *Context-dependent memory effect* refers to
    a. the way in which we remember new information depending on the mood we are in at the time: If we are in a good mood, we remember it; in a bad mood, we don't remember as much.
    b. how new information is stored depending on how much we already knew about it previously.
    c. how we are likely to recall information more easily if we are in a situation similar to the one in which the information was originally learned.

5. Based on what you have read so far, it makes sense to predict that human memory can hold at one time how many chunks of information?
   a. five
   b. seven
   c. ten
   d. twelve

6. *True* or *False*. Information that enters short-term memory always fades away after only a few seconds.

7. *Maintenance rehearsal* refers to
   a. memorizing long lists of unrelated words.
   b. learning how to recite aloud from memory.
   c. repeating new information in order to remember it.
   d. connecting new information to what's been previously learned.

8. *True* or *False*. *Consolidation* refers to our ability to ignore information not related to our current task.

9. *True* or *False*. Remembering proceeds through a series of three stages; it does not usually happen in one single step or moment.

10. *True* or *False*. In working memory, the *central executive* is the control unit.

Questions Based on Your Reading

DIRECTIONS   Answer the questions by filling in the blanks or circling the letter of the correct response.

1. Overall, this selection describes
   a. the causes of forgetting.
   b. how memories are stored.
   c. the role of language in remembering.
   d. the changes in memory produced by aging.

2. Which of the following descriptions illustrates context-dependent memory?

   a. Even after his friend Marlene had showed him how to do it, David couldn't remember how to increase the size of the text on his phone screen. But when he went into the kitchen, where Marlene had first showed him how to make the text bigger, he suddenly remembered that all he had to do was tap the screen twice.

   b. Ellen couldn't seem to remember that John Adams had been the second president of the United States and Thomas Jefferson the third. So she imagined the two men drinking tea together and wearing football jerseys. Adams had a *2* on his jersey and Jefferson a *3*. When she wanted to remember the order of the two presidents, she called up that image.

3. The fact that bodily states can serve as retrieval clues that aid remembering is called

   a. sensory memory state.

   b. state-dependent memory effect.

   c. short-term memory principle.

4. Sensory memory holds onto information

   a. for a very long time.

   b. for a very short time.

   c. for a lifetime.

5. The author refers to short-term memory as the mind's

   _____.

6. What did George Miller discover through his experiments?

   _____

   _____

   _____

7. What is "chunking" and how can it affect a person's ability to remember a large amount of information?

   _____

   _____

8. *True* or *False.* The central executive is the storehouse of working memory.

9. According to the "Three-Component Model" of working memory, if you repeat an address to yourself in order to remember it, what part of working memory are you using?

   _____

10. According to the reading, the hyperlinked structure of the World Wide Web was modeled on _____.

Making Connections Based on what you know about *SQ3R*, do you think Francis Robinson knew that rehearsing new information was essential to remembering it?

Yes or *No.* Please explain.

_____

_____

_____

Drawing Your Own Conclusions Based on the information in the reading, which piece of advice for learning from textbooks would be more useful?

a. To remember the information in a textbook passage, identify the key sentences and repeat them at least three times before going on to the next chapter section.

b. To remember the information in a textbook passage, identify the key sentences and paraphrase them by substituting your words for the author's.

Please explain what in the reading led you to select this answer.

_____

_____

_____

_____

◆ **TEST 1**   **Vocabulary Review**

DIRECTIONS   Fill in the blanks with one of the words listed below.

cognitive	hypothetically	determinants	adaptive	personified
repulsed	prenatal	chromosomes	icons	contemplating

1. The skydiver's close call had frightened her more than she realized. Just _____ the idea of another jump gave her an anxiety attack.

2. Roaches have been around for millions of years because they are very _____ creatures; no matter what situation they find themselves in, they can find something to eat, from plaster to paint to sugar cubes, glue, and other roaches.

3. At first, it seemed as if the man was describing being kidnapped by aliens, but when reporters skeptically questioned his story, the man claimed he had been speaking _____.

4. The great baseball player Roberto Clemente, who died tragically young in an air crash, _____ everything an athlete and role model should be.

5. She had never taken care of her own health, but once she found out that she was pregnant, she made sure she got the best of _____ care for both herself and her baby.

6. A high-fat diet and lack of exercise seem to be two _____ in the onset of diabetes.

7. The mathematician had first-rate _____ skills, but emotionally he could barely function.

8. His wife tried not to show it, but she was _____ by the changes the disease had produced in his face.

9. The _____ on the screen were meant to resemble the functions they stood for; the one representing the print function, for instance, looked like a tiny printer.

10. At one time, people believed criminality was carried in the _____.

▶ **TEST 2** **Vocabulary Review**

DIRECTIONS   For each italicized word, write a definition in the blank.

1. The metal was heated until it was *molten* and could be poured into the molds, which were shaped like birds.

   Molten means _____.

2. As soon as he started to play, the guitarist realized the hall had serious *acoustic* problems and every chord produced an unpleasant echo.

   Acoustic means _____.

3. The 1966 case *Miranda v. Arizona* produced a *landmark* decision that profoundly affected those who had been accused of a crime: According to the *Miranda* decision, every person suspected of a crime had to be notified of the right to a lawyer.

   Landmark means _____.

4. The *acquisition* of several new companies by Cisco Systems is proof that the company is in good financial shape.

   Acquisition means _____.

5. Even after they have served their time, criminals jailed for sexual *deviance* are not welcomed back into society.

   Deviance means _____.

6. Having *incurred* a huge amount of debt, the banks found themselves in deep financial trouble.

   Incurred means _____.

7. After mentally *converting* euros to dollars, she realized how expensive the book really was.

   Converting means _____.

8. Chimpanzees do not make good pets; at a moment's notice, they can *regress* to being wild animals rather than household pets.

   Regress means _____.

9. The manager's sales *projections* for the next five years suggested that even more employees might be laid off.

   Projections means _____.

10. After years of being mobbed when he appeared in public, the wrestler descended into *oblivion* as newer and younger performers caught the public's fancy.

   Oblivion means _____.

Building Word Power

IN THIS CHAPTER, YOU WILL LEARN

- how a word's context, or setting, can help you develop a definition.
- how a knowledge of word parts can help you define an unfamiliar word.
- how to recognize specialized vocabulary words in textbooks.
- how context can change word meaning.
- how a dictionary can help you match meaning and context.
- how reading and writing vocabularies differ.
- when to use a print or an online dictionary.

> *"If you look after them, you can build bridges across incomprehension and chaos. They deserve respect."*
>
> —Playwright Tom Stoppard, on the power and importance of words

Enlarge your vocabulary while sharpening your comprehension skills and you'll be amazed at your increased ability to understand and remember what you read. As Wilfred Funk, one of the great dictionary makers of all time, aptly expressed it, "The more words you know, the more clearly and powerfully you will think . . . the more ideas you will invite into your mind."

Using Context Clues

What do you do when you come across an unfamiliar word? Do you just skip over it? Or do you pick up your dictionary and look for the definition? You probably already know that the first method is not recommended. Yet actually, the second one—turning to the dictionary every time—also has drawbacks. Looking up too many words can hurt your concentration. If you look up too many words, you can lose track of where you were on the page.

Fortunately, there are other alternatives to ignoring new words or looking them up. One alternative is to search the *context*, or setting, of the word to see if it contains a clue or clues to word meaning. Frequently, the sentence or passage in which the word appears can help you determine an **approximate definition** that allows you to keep reading without interruption. An approximate definition may not perfectly match a dictionary's definition. Still, it is close enough so that you can continue reading without interruption.

> When Russia was under the control of Josef Stalin, *dissidents* were routinely shot or imprisoned in hospitals for the mentally ill. Stalin did not allow anyone to express disagreement or discontent with his policies.

If you didn't know what the word *dissidents* in the first sentence meant, you could probably **infer**, or figure out, a definition from the sentence that follows. That sentence offers an example of what dissidents do: They disagree with their government.

Although there are several different kinds of context clues, most fall into one of four categories: example, contrast, restatement, and general knowledge.

Example Clues

As you already know from the previous illustration, the context of an unfamiliar word sometimes provides you with an example of the behavior or thinking associated with the word. Here's another sentence in which an example can lead you to a definition, this time of the word *ambivalent*.

His feelings for his cousin were *ambivalent*: Sometimes he delighted in her company; at other times, he couldn't stand the sight of her.

What's an example of ambivalent feelings? They are in conflict with one another. Because this is an example of what it feels like to be ambivalent, we can infer the following approximate definition: To be ambivalent is to experience conflicting emotions.

Contrast Clues

Context clues can also tell you what a word does not mean. Fortunately, knowing what a word doesn't mean can often lead you to a good approximate definition. Here's an example of a passage that provides a contrast clue:

As a child, she liked to be alone and was fearful of people; but as an adult, she was remarkably *gregarious*.

This sentence suggests that someone who is *gregarious* does not exactly flee the company of others. In fact, the sentence implies just the opposite: People who are gregarious like to be in the company of others. Thus, "liking the company of others" would be a good approximate definition.

Words That Signal Contrast Clues

In addition to knowing what a contrast clue is, you should also know that words such as *but, yet, nevertheless*, and *however* frequently introduce reversal or contrast clues. These words are all **transitions**—verbal bridges that help readers connect ideas. The transitions mentioned here tell readers to be on the lookout for a shift or change in thought. Note how the word *however* in the following sentence changes the author's train of thought and paves the way for a contrast clue that helps define the word *frivolous*.

After having had a really bad day, she wanted to read something *frivolous*. Normally, however, she preferred serious novels.

So what does the word *frivolous* mean? "Silly," "light," or "not serious" are all good approximate definitions.

Restatement Clues

To avoid tedious word repetition, authors often use a word and then follow it with a **synonym**, a word or phrase similar in meaning:

> The journalist had the *audacity* to criticize the president to his face. Oddly enough, her boldness seemed to amuse rather than irritate him.

In this case, the author doesn't want to overuse the word *audacity*, so she follows it with a synonym, *boldness*. For readers not sure what *audacity* means, the synonym *boldness* restates the word in language they can understand and provides them with a definition.

Restatement Clues in Textbooks

Intent on supplying readers with the **specialized vocabulary** essential to mastering an academic subject, textbook authors often introduce a word and then carefully define it. For example, the authors of the following passage want to be sure that their readers have exact definitions for the terms *brand recognition* and *ad recognition*. To make sure their readers have no doubt what these two terms mean, the authors define them in parentheses:

> Two important types of recognition in marketing are *brand recognition* (we remember having seen the brand before) and *ad recognition* (we remember having seen the ad before). (Hoyer and MacInnis, *Consumer Behavior*, p. 17.)

In addition to parentheses, authors use other devices to tell readers, "Here is the definition for the word I just introduced." Dashes, for instance, are also common.

> Reconversion—the transition from wartime production to the manufacture of consumer goods—ushered in a quarter century of ever-expanding prosperity. (Boyer et al., *The Enduring Vision*, p. 790.)

In this case, the authors realize their readers might not know what *reconversion*, particularly in this context, means. To avoid confusion, they enclose the definition in dashes right after the word first appears.

In addition to dashes or parentheses, textbook authors like to signal a restatement clue by first introducing the word being defined, in either boldface or italics. Then they follow the word with a comma and a definition. Here's an example:

> A major buzzword in leadership and management is *vision*, the ability to imagine different and better conditions and the ways to achieve them. (Dubrin, *Leadership*, p. 62.)

Here, the author is well aware that readers might think they know the meaning of the word *vision*—the ability to see. Yet within this particular context, the author has a specialized definition in mind, and he is careful to provide it right after he introduces the word.

Textbook authors go to great lengths to make sure you have the right definitions for the words essential to their academic field. In turn, your job as a reader is twofold: (1) Pay attention to the devices that signal the presence of restatement or definition clues; and (2) When those definitions appear, read them carefully. Consider as well jotting both words and definitions in a notebook for later review. The chances are good that the definitions will not reappear in later chapters, though the words themselves will.

General Knowledge Clues

Example, contrast, and restatement context clues are important. However, some context clues are not so obvious. Often your knowledge of the situation or events described will be your only real clue to word meaning. The following passage illustrates this point:

> For months he had dreamed of being able to *redeem* his medals. He had been unable to think of anything else. Now, with the vision of the medals shimmering before him, he hurried to the pawnshop.

None of the context clues previously discussed appears in the passage. However, your general knowledge should tell you that the word *redeem*, in this context at least, means "reclaim" or "recover." Most people go to a pawnshop to buy or to sell, and the man described as hurrying to the pawnshop probably wouldn't be in such a rush to sell something he had dreamed of for months. He is going to buy back what he has already sold.

1. **Example Clue**	"The discussion was becoming increasingly *belligerent*; no matter what was said, someone in the group would challenge it in an angry voice."
2. **Contrast Clue**	"At first the smell was almost flower-like, but in a matter of minutes it became harsh and *acrid*."
3. **Restatement Clue**	"*Cognition*—thinking or knowing— has been the subject of numerous studies."
4. **General Knowledge Clue**	"Football and basketball coaches are frequently known for their *volatile* tempers."

SUMMING UP THE KEY POINTS

1. Often, the sentence or passage in which an unfamiliar word appears can tell you what the word means. The words or sentences that supply the meaning are called *context clues*.

2. Context clues don't necessarily give you an exact dictionary definition, but they can supply an "approximate definition" that allows you to keep reading without interruption.

3. Of the many different kinds of context clues, four are particularly common: example, contrast, restatement, and general knowledge.

4. An example clue includes the behavior, attitude, event, or experience associated with a word.

5. A contrast clue provides the reader with a word that is opposite in meaning.

6. A restatement clue follows the unfamiliar word with a synonym substitute. In textbooks, authors explicitly define the word, often within dashes or parentheses.

7. General knowledge clues are descriptions of events or experiences that are likely to be familiar to readers.

◆ EXERCISE 1 Using Context Clues

DIRECTIONS Use context clues to develop an approximate meaning for each italicized word.

EXAMPLE To the old dog lying under the table, the smell of frying bacon was almost unbearably tantalizing, and he stared at the pan with obvious longing.

Tantalizing means <u>appealing, exciting; desirable but out of reach</u>.

EXPLANATION In this case, the sentence offers a general knowledge clue. Even readers who don't have pets would undoubtedly know that to a dog, the smell of frying bacon is extremely appealing or exciting.

1. According to the myth, the hero Achilles was *vulnerable* in just one area of his body. He could be killed only if he was wounded in the heel.

   Vulnerable means <u>exposed to harm</u>.

2. The candidate had expected to win, but instead she was *trounced* by her opponent, who won by a landslide.

   Trounced means <u>~~beat by~~ beaten bad by</u>.

3. Forced to sell their lands and homes at whatever prices they could obtain, Japanese Americans were herded into detention camps in the most desolate areas of the West. Sadly, few Americans protested the *incarceration* of their Japanese-American countrymen. (Boyer et al., *The Enduring Vision*, p. 778.)

   Incarceration means <u>punishment / being jailed</u>.

4. Before allowing someone to deliver a personal opinion on the air, most television news programs issue a disclaimer denying all responsibility for the views expressed.

   Disclaimer means <u>paper / waiver / authorized statement</u>.

5. Killed by an obsessed fan in 1995, the Latina entertainer Selena was deeply mourned because she was so much more than an entertainer: Selena was the *embodiment* of Mexican-American culture—representing devotion to the family, hard work, and a sense of community.

(Adapted from Hoyer and MacInnis, *Consumer Behavior*, p. 295.)

Embodiment means _leader / icon , symbol_.

6. Unjustly accused of spying, Captain Alfred Dreyfus[†] (1859–1935) was convicted and sentenced to life in prison on the ill-famed Devil's Island; pardoned in 1899, Dreyfus was fully *exonerated* of all charges in 1906.

Exonerated means _clear / free of guilt_.

7. The Chinese novelist Ha Jin is an amazingly *perceptive* writer: He understands human behavior in a way that few novelists do.

Perceptive means _insightful_.

8. Confusion and *delusions* (false and distorted beliefs) are typical signs of sleep deprivation. (Coon, *Essentials of Psychology*, p. 34.)

Delusions means _false and distorted beliefs_.

9. Queen Marie Antoinette's *hedonistic* lifestyle was one of the things that made her hated by the people of France; close to starvation themselves, they could not love a queen who seemed to care about nothing but pleasure.

Hedonistic means _rich / pleasure seeking / only care about fun._

10. In his 1939 novel *The Grapes of Wrath*, novelist John Steinbeck movingly describes the *plight* of migrant farm workers in California forced to work under brutal and dehumanizing conditions.

Plight means _life / working conditions / distressed. Sad situation_

◆ **EXERCISE 2**   **Using Context Clues**

DIRECTIONS   Use context clues to write an approximate meaning for each italicized word.

1. The reporters were sent out to cover the fighting that had broken out in the streets, but under no condition were they to get involved in the *upheaval*.

Upheaval means _____.

[†]What came to be known as the "Dreyfus Affair" polarized the French people. Many rightly suspected that Dreyfus was being persecuted because he was Jewish, and that fact appalled some and pleased others.

2. The millionaire did not expect the judge to hand down such a *punitive* sentence.

   Punitive means _____.

3. All over the country, people were starving and desperately *scavenging* for food.

   Scavenging means _____.

4. Looking filthy and *disreputable* after being lost for a month in the woods, the children were finally discovered by a team of hunting dogs.

   Disreputable means _____.

5. Her boss didn't need to make an effort to be nasty; he was *inherently* so and thought nothing of publicly humiliating his employees.

   Inherently means _____.

6. Because I can't spell very well, I was happy to learn there is no apparent *correlation* between the ability to spell and a high IQ.

   Correlation means _____.

7. The jockey hoped that *submersing* himself in the hot tub would soothe his aching body.

   Submersing means _____.

8. Inventors don't necessarily care if their inventions are *lucrative*; often they just have an idea they are desperate to make a reality, and money doesn't matter.

   Lucrative means _____.

9. Research on people who have lived to be more than eighty years old has consistently revealed a connection between low body weight and *longevity*.

   Longevity means _____.

10. How is it that so many doctors who *advocate* diet and exercise are overweight couch potatoes?

    Advocate means _____.

◆ **EXERCISE 3**   **Using Context Clues**

DIRECTIONS   Use context clues to write an approximate definition for each italicized word.[†]

EXAMPLE   People driven by *intrinsic* motivation don't need external rewards such as praise from others; instead, they find satisfaction in simply completing a task.

Intrinsic means <u>internal; inside or within oneself</u>.

EXPLANATION   In this case, the sentence offers a contrast clue. If people do not need external rewards, they must be motivated by rewards that are internal, or inside themselves. These are all good approximate definitions of the word *intrinsic*.

1. African-American novelist Richard Baldwin was an outspoken advocate of civil rights, who did not believe that racism would disappear on its own. Friends enjoyed relaying *anecdotes* about Baldwin's fiery and often funny responses to anyone claiming it would.

   Anecdotes means ⎯⎯⎯⎯⎯⎯⎯⎯⎯⎯⎯⎯⎯⎯⎯⎯⎯.

2. Emperor Justinian gathered together all of Rome's disorganized laws and made them into a *coherent* legal system.

   Coherent means ⎯⎯⎯⎯⎯⎯⎯⎯⎯⎯⎯⎯⎯⎯⎯⎯⎯.

3. Corporate raiders spend their days figuring out how to acquire new companies while offering the previous owners as little *compensation* as possible.

   Compensation means ⎯⎯⎯⎯⎯⎯⎯⎯⎯⎯⎯⎯⎯⎯.

4. By embracing drug use, rock music, "free love," and non-Western religions, the rebellious hippies of the 1960s and 1970s rejected *conventional* rules.

   Conventional means ⎯⎯⎯⎯⎯⎯⎯⎯⎯⎯⎯⎯⎯⎯.

[†]The italicized words in Exercises 3 and 4 are all from the Academic Word List developed by the School of Linguistics and Applied Language Studies at Victoria University of Wellington in New Zealand.

5. If *preliminary* testing of a new drug indicates potential benefits, the drug is then tested again for a longer period of time and on a larger sample population.

   Preliminary means _____.

6. Electricity is *generated* from a variety of energy sources, including coal, oil, wood, nuclear reactors, wind, sunlight, and water.

   Generated means _____.

7. *Proponents* of the bill were disheartened when the vote was put off until spring; the bill's critics, however, were jubilant.

   Proponents means _____.

8. Milton Hershey certainly didn't invent chocolate, but his *innovations* to the recipe and manufacture of it turned a luxury for the wealthy into an affordable treat for all.

   Innovations means _____.

9. The lawyer's *cogent* argument convinced the court, and she was allowed to submit the fibers as evidence.

   Cogent means _____.

10. After the Twenty-second Amendment to the U.S. Constitution took effect in 1951, all *ensuing* presidents were limited to two terms each.

    Ensuing means _____.

◆ **EXERCISE 4   Using Context Clues**

DIRECTIONS   Use context clues to write an approximate definition for each italicized word.

1. Although global warming has been *attributed* to the burning of fossil fuels, a few scientists argue that it's actually caused by natural climate cycles.

   Attributed means ___exposed/Connected to___.

2. U.S. military officials believed that dropping atomic bombs on Japan was the only way to save millions of American lives and end World War II; however, others have argued that there was no *justification* for killing more than 140,000 Japanese citizens and injuring another 100,000.

   Justification means ___reason, explination___.

3. Based on research and observation, scientists propose theories, or explanations, of events; then they conduct experiments that either prove a theory's *validity* or else reveal its inaccuracy.

   Validity means ___accuracy___.

4. In the U.S. Army, a general is the highest rank of officer, whereas the most *subordinate* officer rank is second lieutenant.

   Subordinate means ___begining or lowest rank___.

5. The final event of the American Civil War occurred on April 9, 1865; Confederate General Robert E. Lee officially *terminated* the conflict by surrendering to Union commander Ulysses S. Grant at the Appomattox, Virginia, courthouse.

   Terminated means ___ended / fred___.

6. Medical research rules require that human subjects know they are participating in an experiment; therefore, scientists must obtain each subject's *consent*, or permission, before giving him or her any treatment.

   Consent means ___permission___.

7. When scientists attempt to create a clone, they *extract* the DNA from the cell of one organism and then insert it into the egg cell of another organism of the same species.

   Extract means ___take / used remove___.

8. The kilometer is the unit of length used in Europe, Canada, and other countries; it is *equivalent*, or equal, to 0.62 miles.

   Equivalent means ___equal to___.

9. Because they can explode when mixed together, *incompatible* chemicals spelled with the same first letter, like cadmium chlorate and cupric sulfide, must be kept apart; they should never be stored alphabetically in a laboratory.

   Incompatible means <u>non cooperative</u>.

10. A paperback dictionary includes only some of our language's most commonly used words; the *Oxford English Dictionary*, however, aims to present all words from the earliest records to the present day. Its over 400,000 entries make it our language's most *comprehensive* dictionary.

    Comprehensive means <u>versatal / complete / All-inclusive</u>.

Context and Meaning

There are few situations in life where context isn't important. Certainly, words are no exception. Change a word's context and you are likely to change its meaning. For instance, if you are buying a new air conditioner, you might ask the salesperson how big a room the unit can *cool*. Here the word means "lower the temperature." But if someone asks your opinion of the Black Eyed Peas' new CD, you might say, "It's cool," and you wouldn't be talking about the group's temperature.

CHECK YOUR UNDERSTANDING

1. When readers get definitions from context, should the definition be almost the same as the one that appears in a dictionary? Please explain your answer.

2. What are the most common kinds of context clues?

3. The following sentence gives what kind of context clue for the italicized word?

   "Stress is the negative emotional and physiological process that occurs as individuals try to adjust to or deal with *stressors*, which are environmental circumstances that disrupt, or threaten to disrupt, individuals' daily functioning." (Bernstein et al., *Psychology*, p. 509.)

   Type of context clue: *Restatement Clue*

4. The following sentence gives what kind of context clue for the italicized word?

   "They offered the older teachers *incentives* for taking early retirement: They could have one full year of health benefits and a three-hundred-dollar bonus."

   Type of context clue: *Example Clue*

5. The following sentence gives what kind of context clue for the italicized word?

   "In the 1960s, members of opposing political parties worked together to pass important legislation, but today members of Congress are much more *polarized*, which makes it difficult to get anything done unless one party has a majority."

   Type of context clue: *Contrast Clue*

6. The following sentence gives what kind of context clue for the italicized word?

   "After all the cars leaving the game streamed onto the highway, there was complete *gridlock* going north and away from the stadium."

   Type of context clue: *General Knowledge Clue.*

Defining Words from Their Parts

In addition to using context clues to determine approximate meanings for unfamiliar words, check to see if you know any of the word's parts. For example, imagine you read this sentence and were initially puzzled by the word *dermatitis*: "The deadly disease began with a seemingly minor symptom—a light *dermatitis* on the arms and legs." Even if you had never heard or used the word *dermatitis*, you could come up with a definition simply by knowing that *derma* means skin and *itis* means inflammation, or outbreak. Given the context and your knowledge of the word's parts, you would be correct to say that *dermatitis* means "inflammation of the skin," or "rash."

Learning Roots, Prefixes, and Suffixes

To determine meaning from word parts, you need to know some of the most commonly used roots and prefixes, along with a few suffixes. The exercises in this chapter will introduce you to a good many, and it's worth your while to learn a few new word parts every day, averaging about twenty a week. If you review them regularly, you will be amazed at how quickly your vocabulary expands.

1. **Roots** give words their fixed meaning. Prefixes and suffixes can then be attached to the roots to form new words. For example, the following words are all based on the root *spec*, which means "look" or "see": re*spec*t, in*spec*tion, *spec*tacles, *spec*ulation.

2. **Prefixes** are word parts that appear at the *beginning* of words and modify the root meaning, as in *in*clude and *ex*clude or *in*voke and *re*voke.

3. **Suffixes** are word parts that appear at the *end* of many words. Although suffixes do occasionally affect word meaning, they are more likely to reveal what part of speech a word is, as in quick*ness* and quick*ly*. Words ending in *ness* are usually nouns. Those ending in *ly* are usually adverbs.

STUDY TIP

When you make a list of word parts, put the definitions on the far right. Each time you review, cover one side of the list and *recall from memory* either the word part or the definition.

INTERNET RESOURCE To learn more about prefixes, roots, and suffixes, go to www.virtualsalt.com/roots.htm. You can find this link at the student companion website for this text: www.cengage.com/devenglish/flemming/rfr11e.

◆ **EXERCISE 5**   **Learning Word Parts**

DIRECTIONS   Read each sentence and note what meaning the missing or partial word should convey. Then fill in the blanks with one—or, in some cases, two—of the word parts listed below.

Prefixes	Roots
bi = two	*chron* = time
im = not	*gam* = marriage
per = through	*lat* = side
poly = many	*mob* = move
	pel = force
	popul = people
	rect = straight, straighten

EXAMPLE   When we talk about events being ordered according to time, we are talking about events that are described in ___chron___ ological order.

EXPLANATION   The partially completed word needs to say something about "time." Thus, we need a word part that brings that meaning to the blank. The obvious choice would be the root *chron*, meaning "time."

1. When a situation can't be fixed or straightened out, we say that it cannot be ~~rdent~~ rec ified.

2. If a city is filled with people, it can be described as _popul_ ous.

3. When a disease goes away and repeatedly comes back over time, it is called _chron_ ic.

4. Human skin is called _per_ meable because substances, both good and bad, can pass through it.

5. An interesting book that almost forces you to keep reading is often described as com _pel_ ling.

6. An agreement that has to be signed by two sides is called ___*bi*___ _____ eral.

7. Being married to two people at the same time is called ___*big*___ ___*om*___ y.

8. Being married to several people at the same time is called ___*poli*___ ___*gam*___ y.

9. If someone or something can move, we say that he, she, or it is ___*mob*___ ile.

10. In contrast, someone or something that cannot move would be described as ___*en*___ ___*mob*___ ile.

STUDY TIP

Because the word parts introduced in Exercise 5 appear in many different words, you should start learning them right now. Repeated reviews done over an extended period of time are the key to mastery.

Combine Forces: Use Context Clues *and* Word Parts

Although recognizing word parts and using context clues are, by themselves, effective methods of determining meaning, they are even more powerful when combined. Take, for example, the following sentences: "I can't imagine a more *credulous* person. He actually believed I saw a flying saucer on the way home." To a degree, knowing that the root *cred* means "belief" and the suffix *ous* means "full of" are helpful clues to meaning. We can start off, then, by saying that to be *credulous* is to be "full of belief." Yet what exactly does that mean? You can imagine a bottle full of juice or wine, but how can a person be "full of belief"?

This is where context comes in. Look at the example clue the author offers: "He actually believed I saw a flying saucer on the way home." Apparently, a credulous person is likely to believe a story that most people might laugh at or question. After a closer look at the context, we can come up with a more precise definition of *credulous*: "gullible" or "easily fooled."

A knowledge of word parts can also help you sharpen or improve an approximate definition derived from context. Suppose you are not sure how to define the word *ambiguous* in a sentence like this one: "The finest poems are usually the most *ambiguous*, suggesting that life's big questions defy easy answers." Relying solely on context, you might decide that *ambiguous* means *puzzling* or *difficult*. Those definitions are certainly acceptable. But once you know that the prefix "ambi" means "both," you could make your definition more precise by defining *ambiguous* as "open to more than one interpretation," which would, in fact, be a better definition.

SUMMING UP THE KEY POINTS

1. Recognizing the meaning of prefixes or roots within a word can unlock a word's meaning, especially if you can combine that knowledge with context clues.

2. Roots give words their central, or core, meaning. Attaching new beginnings (prefixes) or endings (suffixes) to the word will change the meaning of the whole word, but the essential meaning of the root won't change. Just think, for instance, of how the meaning of *invent* stays the same in the following sequence, *re*invent, invent*or*, invent*ion*, even though the words as a whole assume different (but related) meanings.

3. Prefixes modify root meanings, and they can do so rather dramatically. Consider, for example, the difference between the words "do" and "*un*do."

4. Suffixes can tell you something about word meaning. Suffixes like *er* and *or* at the end of a word indicate that the word refers to a person who can perform or do something mentioned in the root—for example, farm*er*, creat*or*, invent*or*. On the whole, though, suffixes reveal more about a word's grammatical function—noun, verb, adjective, and so on—than they do about the definition.

5. By themselves, context clues or word parts are great clues to meaning. But if you can combine the two, you double your chances of getting the exact definition for the word that is puzzling you. Thus, it pays to learn as many common word parts as you possibly can, giving special attention to those drawn from Greek and Latin. The words appropriate to academic subject matter rely heavily on these two languages.

◆ EXERCISE 6 Using Word Parts and Context Clues

DIRECTIONS Use context clues and word parts to come up with an approximate definition for each italicized word. *Note*: Some of the words in the following sentences use prefixes or roots from the previous exercise.

Prefixes	Roots	Suffixes
mono = one	*for* = to bore into	*ism* = state, condition, or quality
pseudo = false	*the* = god	
mal = bad	*vit* = life	*ize* = to cause to be, to treat or affect
re = again, back		
syn, sym = together		*onym* = name, word

1. The Egyptian pharaoh Akhenaton rejected *polytheism*, advocating *monotheism* instead, but his decision to worship one god over many led to his downfall.

   Monotheism means _____.

   Polytheism means _____.

2. The International Olympic Committee took a long time to acknowledge how difficult it is for *synchronized* swimmers to execute the same movement at the same time while submersed in water.

   Synchronized means _____.

3. The kidnapper's actions were so *repellent* that it was hard to have any sympathy for her. Most agreed with the prosecution and hoped to see her incarcerated for a very long time.

   Repellent means _____.

4. During the operation, the surgeon's knife almost *perforated* the patient's lung.

   Perforated means _____.

5. The injection had completely *immobilized* the bear, allowing the ranger to approach it without fear.

   Immobilized means ⎯⎯⎯⎯⎯⎯⎯⎯⎯⎯⎯⎯⎯⎯⎯⎯⎯⎯⎯.

6. Amazingly, the drug had *revitalized* him after everyone thought he would not last the night.

   Revitalized means ⎯⎯⎯⎯⎯⎯⎯⎯⎯⎯⎯⎯⎯⎯⎯⎯⎯⎯.

7. In the nineteenth century, many women writers used *pseudonyms* because they were afraid of being labeled "unladylike" and didn't want their real names to be known.

   Pseudonyms means ⎯⎯⎯⎯⎯⎯⎯⎯⎯⎯⎯⎯⎯⎯⎯⎯⎯.

8. It can be brief, but management wants to see your *vita* before any contract gets signed.

   Vita means ⎯⎯⎯⎯⎯⎯⎯⎯⎯⎯⎯⎯⎯⎯⎯⎯⎯⎯⎯⎯⎯.

9. In an effort to win elections, politicians spend too much time *maligning* one another.

   Maligning means ⎯⎯⎯⎯⎯⎯⎯⎯⎯⎯⎯⎯⎯⎯⎯⎯⎯⎯.

10. Even at an advanced age, the legendary salsa singer Celia Cruz had the *vitality* of a much younger performer.

    Vitality means ⎯⎯⎯⎯⎯⎯⎯⎯⎯⎯⎯⎯⎯⎯⎯⎯⎯⎯.

✔ CHECK YOUR UNDERSTANDING

1. Why should you learn as many Greek and Latin prefixes and roots as you possibly can?

⎯⎯⎯⎯⎯⎯⎯⎯⎯⎯⎯⎯⎯⎯⎯⎯⎯⎯⎯⎯⎯⎯⎯⎯⎯⎯⎯⎯⎯⎯⎯⎯⎯⎯⎯⎯⎯⎯

⎯⎯⎯⎯⎯⎯⎯⎯⎯⎯⎯⎯⎯⎯⎯⎯⎯⎯⎯⎯⎯⎯⎯⎯⎯⎯⎯⎯⎯⎯⎯⎯⎯⎯⎯⎯⎯⎯

⎯⎯⎯⎯⎯⎯⎯⎯⎯⎯⎯⎯⎯⎯⎯⎯⎯⎯⎯⎯⎯⎯⎯⎯⎯⎯⎯⎯⎯⎯⎯⎯⎯⎯⎯⎯⎯⎯

2. How is a prefix different from a root?

_____

_____

_____

3. What do suffixes reveal about a word?

_____

4. Why is it a good idea to use both kinds of clues to meaning, context and word parts?

_____

_____

More Pointers About Specialized Vocabulary

Pages 71–72 introduced some common methods textbook authors use to highlight and define specialized vocabulary. But, in fact, textbook authors use several other important devices to highlight the words and terms essential to their discipline, or subject.

Recognizing Key Terms

Each time you open a textbook, you should immediately determine how an author signals to readers that a particular word or term is significant. Some authors consistently boldface key words or terms and then follow with a definition. Others introduce specialized vocabulary in boldface or italics, follow it with a definition, and then repeat both word and definition in the margin. Look, for example, at the following passage:

Goal-Setting Theory A theory of motivation suggesting that employees are motivated to achieve goals they and their managers establish together.

> **Goal-setting theory** suggests that employees are motivated to achieve goals they and their managers establish together. The goal should be very specific, moderately difficult, and one the employee

will be committed to achieve. Rewards should be directly tied to goal achievement. (Pride, Hughes, and Kapoor, *Business*, p. 232.)

Here the authors use three different devices to highlight the term *goal-setting theory*: They introduce it in boldface, provide a definition, and repeat that definition in a marginal annotation, or note. Whenever a word or phrase gets so much attention, it's important, and you should add both the word and the definition to your notes.

Paragraphs Devoted to Definitions

Although many textbook authors use multiple devices to make specialized vocabulary stand out, not all of them do. Sometimes, the only real clue to key terms is how much space the author has devoted to defining them. Any word or phrase that gets a whole paragraph to itself is bound to be essential to the subject you are studying. Look, for example, at the following paragraph, in which the author not only defines *stereotyping* but also gives you a brief history of its meaning.

> **Stereotyping** occurs when members of one group attribute characteristics to members of another group. Typically, these characteristics carry a positive or negative evaluation. In the United States, race and gender groups are often stereotyped. The meaning of the word *stereotype*, however, has changed considerably since its introduction in 1824 by James Morier, when it was used to describe a printing process. A century later Walter Lippmann defined stereotypes as "pictures in our heads" and argued that stereotypes are not merely descriptions of others, but include an emotional component that is driven by one's self-respect and value orientations. In more recent times, the word *stereotype* has taken on negative connotations, or associations. (Adapted from Neulip, *Intercultural Communication*, p. 150.)

Typically for the definition paragraph, this one opens with the word that is being defined; the definition follows right on its heels. The opening focus on word and definition is the key characteristic of a definition paragraph. What follows after that can vary, ranging from examples of the word in action to a brief history of its meanings. The main thing to remember is any word that earns a paragraph deserves your close attention. (For more on definition paragraphs, see pages 493–95.)

Checking the Glossary

If you feel unsure about any definitions of specialized vocabulary, check to see if your textbook has a glossary in the back. Most do. **Glossaries** list all the specialized terms in a textbook. If a definition is vague or unclear in the text, referring to the glossary will usually help clear up any confusion.

> **STUDY TIP**
>
> Make separate lists of specialized vocabulary for each of your courses. Review one list per day by covering the definitions and looking only at the words. Try to recall the definitions from memory. Look at them only to check that your definition is correct or to double check a definition you can't seem to recall.

◆ Connotations and Denotations of Words

The more words you add to your reading vocabulary, the more inclined you will be to try them out in your own writing. That's wonderful. However, to use words effectively, you need to know more than their **denotation**, or dictionary definitions. You also need to know whether a word carries with it any connotations. **Connotations** are the associations or implications some words develop over time.

For example, the words *pruning* and *slashing* both refer to the act of cutting. Their connotations, however, are very different, as you can see from the following brief passage. "My wife asked me why I was *slashing* her rose bushes. I told her I was just *pruning* them." By using the word *pruning*, the husband suggests he is shaping the bushes, whereas the wife's use of the word *slashing* implies he is destroying them.[†] Yet if you look up the two words in the dictionary and find their definitions—also known as their denotations—you will see that the definitions are not all that different. What gives *pruning* and *slashing* different meanings in the above sentences are the connotations the words carry with them. Pruning is associated with gardening, whereas slashing has a long history of being linked to violent acts (there's a genre of movies, after all, known as "slasher" films).

In the following pairs of sentences, you have two words to choose from in parentheses. In the first pair, underline the word that would

---

[†]This example comes from Joseph Trimmer, *Writing with a Purpose*.

encourage readers to have a positive response to the person or group under discussion.

a. Over the years, the lawyer Gloria Allred has taken on some truly (off-the-wall *or* unconventional) cases.

b. The students managed to (spend *or* waste) a few hours at the library.

Now underline the words that would encourage readers to react negatively.

c. (Gobbling *or* Eating) lunch at her desk, the receptionist was clearly not pleased to see so many new arrivals.

d. Henry Wallace, Franklin Delano Roosevelt's third-term vice president, was famous in Washington for his (weird *or* unusual) interests and hobbies.

Connotation, Denotation, and Context

Not all words have positive or negative connotations. Words like *table*, *chair*, and *molecule*, for instance, usually carry with them only their denotation. Then, too, some words have strong connotations in one context and no connotations in another. Take, for example, the word *pill* in the following sentence: "Can you give me some water so that I can take a *pill*?" Here, the word *pill* has no positive or negative associations. Yet in the next sentence, the word has a distinctly negative connotation: "My boss is a real *pill*; every time I sit down, she finds something else for me to do."

When learning new words, pay attention to and record examples of how they are used so that you begin to develop a sense for the appropriate context. Yes, a *domicile* is a house, but it is a rather formal word for house, more likely to be used in insurance or tax forms than in everyday conversation. So you might see a sentence like the following: "The company's *domicile* should not affect its tax advantage." But it would be rare for you to see a sentence like this one: "The dog hated to sleep in his *domicile*; he preferred his owner's bed." The word *domicile* is at home in the first sentence, out of place in the second.[†]

> *"The meaning of a word is not a set, cut-off thing like the move of a knight or pawn on a chessboard. It comes up with roots, with associations."*
>
> —Ezra Pound, poet

[†]Thanks to one of the finest teachers I have ever met, my friend and colleague Joan Hellman of Catonsville Community College, for this example.

SUMMING UP THE KEY POINTS

- - - - - - - - - - - - - - - - - - ➤

1. In textbooks, authors are usually consistent about how they identify the specialized vocabulary of their subject. They might, for instance, boldface the term in the text and annotate it in the margins. Or else they might rely on printing key terms in blue or red and following with a definition. Whatever the method or methods authors use, you need to identify them early on so that you can quickly spot those words essential to the subject you are studying.

2. When authors use an entire paragraph to define a word or phrase, you should take notice. Make sure you understand the meaning, noting it perhaps in the margins of your textbook or on an index card.

3. Glossaries, lists of words essential to the subject matter you are studying, are a part of most textbooks. If you are struggling with a definition in the text, check the glossary to see if the language there is clearer.

4. The more you want to use the words you learn, the more attentive you need to be to their context. The dictionary will give you a word's *denotation*, or formal meaning. But the *connotations*, or associations, the word carries only become clear after you have seen it used in multiple contexts.

5. Context can dramatically shift a word's meaning along with its connotations. Teachers telling "stories" to children are just doing their job. But an employee who tells "stories" about coworkers probably doesn't have many friends. Context makes all the difference.

♦ **EXERCISE 7**   **Understanding Connotation**

DIRECTIONS   Underline the word with more positive connotations.

1. (Crude, Direct) in the way he expressed himself, he often offended people even when he meant no harm.

2. She (giggled, guffawed) her amusement at her husband's quick-witted response.

3. Today's fashion models are almost always tall and (slender, skinny).

4. He didn't expect to pay such a high price for a (preowned, used) vehicle.

5. Clothes for (overweight, husky) boys are located on the second floor.

◆ **EXERCISE 8** **Understanding Connotation**

DIRECTIONS Underline the word with more negative connotations.

1. The student (called, blurted) out the answer before the teacher had finished reading the question.

2. The couple spent days (deliberating, disputing) how to spend their tax refund.

3. She was (stubborn, determined) and refused to change her mind.

4. His (carelessness, recklessness) caused the accident.

5. He (tossed, hurled) her suitcase out the window.

CHECK YOUR UNDERSTANDING

1. Why is it important for readers to note words that are defined in the margins, printed in bold, or explained in a paragraph?

_____

_____

2. When you don't completely understand the meaning of a word that seems essential to the subject matter discussed in your textbook, where should you look first?

_____

3. What's the difference between a word's *connotation* and its *denotation*?

_____

_____

4. Once you learn a new word, can you assume that it means the same thing in every context? Please explain your answer.

_____

_____

Turning to the Dictionary

The specialized vocabulary words necessary to understanding a particular subject are often defined in the margins of textbooks. If they aren't, you can always turn to the glossary. Context clues can also provide you with approximate definitions for both specialized and non-specialized vocabulary.

However, despite help from marginal annotations, the glossary, and context, there still will be times when you have to turn to the dictionary to learn the meaning of a word. What that means, of course, is that you need to have good dictionary skills. To make sure that you do, here's a quick review of what you can expect from a dictionary.

Getting Down the Basics: Syllable Count, Pronunciation Guide, and Parts of Speech

Whether you are looking up a word at Dictionary.com[†] or in the *American Heritage Dictionary*, you can expect the **entry word**, or word being defined, to appear in boldface. The entry word will itself be divided into syllables by dots (jus·ti·fi·ca·tion) or it will be followed by a hyphenated version of the word, indicating where the syllable breaks appear (jus-ti-fi-ca-tion).

Whether electronic or paper, most dictionary entries provide a sequence of symbols in parentheses (ĭn·strŭkt′). The letters and symbols tell you what sounds to give the vowels and consonants that make up the word, and an accent mark (′) or **boldface** tells you what syllable gets the most emphasis. Following the guide to pronunciation in brackets or parentheses, comes the part of speech either spelled out (*noun, adjective*) or abbreviated (*n, adj, adv*).

For illustrations of how these elements appear in an entry, look at these two entries for the word *didactic*, which generally means "intended to instruct." The first one comes from Dictionary.com, the second from the *American Heritage Dictionary*.

1. **di·dac·tic** ◀)) [dahy-**dak**-tic] – adjective
2. **di·dac·tic** (dī-dăk′tĭk) also **di·dac·ti·cal** *adj.*

[†]I know there are many other online dictionaries, but I find this site one of the least cluttered and most reliable.

Both entry words offer similar kinds of information, but they do it in slightly different ways. The electronic entry uses boldface to tell you that the second syllable of *didactic* gets the emphasis, whereas the print version uses an accent mark. *The American Heritage Dictionary* uses symbols like long (–) and short (˘) vowel sounds[†] to tell you how a word is pronounced. Dictionary.com provides sound-alike syllables. It also offers an audio link where you can hear the word spoken.

While the *American Heritage Dictionary* uses abbreviations for parts of speech, Dictionary.com spells out the word's grammatical function: It's an adjective. Despite minor differences, though, both dictionaries have the same objectives when they introduce entry words. They want readers to know how to pronounce the word, break it into syllables, and use it correctly in a sentence.

READING TIP If you are a student of English as a second language (ESL), pronunciation of new words is especially important to you. Anytime you can access an online dictionary, you should use it. Hit the audio link (◀ᴾ), which will allow you to hear the words pronounced, over and over again if need be.

◆ **EXERCISE 9** **Using the Dictionary**

DIRECTIONS Use a dictionary to answer the following questions. It can be an electronic or a print dictionary. However, if you use a dictionary online, please use Dictionary.com.

1. The word *heinous*, meaning "horribly wicked," is often mispronounced. Should the first syllable rhyme with *hey* or *hi*? _____

2. What part of speech is the word *heinous*? _____

3. How many syllables are there in the word *prevaricate*, meaning to mislead or lie? _____

[†]Long vowel sounds: pāy, mē, bīte, gō, cūte. Short vowel sounds: păt, mĕt, bĭt, gŏt, cŭt.

4. *Hyssop* is a woody plant with small blue flowers. How many syllables does the word have, and which one gets the strongest accent? _____ Is the *y* in *hyssop* pronounced like the *i* in *hi* or the *i* in *him*? _____

5. During World War II, a kamikaze was a pilot trained to make a suicidal attack, usually on ships. How many syllables does the word have? _____ Which one gets the strongest accent? _____ Is the *e* at the end of the word silent or spoken? _____ Are the *a*'s in the word pronounced like the *a* in *father* or the *a* in *pat*? _____ The word is a noun, but it can also play what other part of speech? _____

Sorting Through Multiple Meanings

As you already know, one single word can have multiple meanings. Those different meanings, however, can seem confusing when they appear together in a dictionary entry.

To avoid feeling overwhelmed when faced with a lengthy entry, just keep in mind that your goal is to determine what an unfamiliar word means *within a specific context*. That specific context will help you sort through any number of definitions and find the right one. Say, for instance, that the word *scald* in the following sentence sent you to the dictionary. "The dental instruments need to be *scalded* before being reused." Here's what you'd find:

> **scald'** (skôld) *v.* **scald·ed, scald·ing, scalds** —*tr.* **1.** To burn with or as if with hot liquid or steam. **2.** To subject to or treat with boiling water, *scalded the hide to remove the hair, scalded and peeled the tomatoes.* **3.** To heat (a liquid, such as milk) almost to the boiling point. **4.** To criticize harshly; excoriate.[†] —*intr.* To become scalded. ❖ *n.* **1.** A body injury caused by scalding. **2.** *Botany* **a.** A superficial discoloration on fruit, vegetables, leaves, or tree trunks caused by sudden exposure to intense sunlight or the action of gases. **b.** A disease of

---

[†]excoriate: another way of saying "to criticize harshly."

some cereal grasses caused by a fungus of the genus *Rhynchosporium*. [Middle English *scalden*, from Old North French *escalder*, from Late Latin *excaldāre*, to wash in hot water : Latin *ex-*, ex- + Latin *calidus*, *caldus*, warm, hot.]

With a lengthy entry like this, it's easy to feel unsure about which meaning to pick. Yet, actually, you can find the meaning through the simple process of elimination. For example, you can immediately eliminate the definitions following the word "Botany," which is a **special context label**. The label tells you that the word *scald* only has this particular meaning when used in a discussion related to botany. Because our sample sentence has nothing to do with botany, we can ignore this definition.

Next you can eliminate the end-of-entry material in brackets. This is how dictionary entries provide the **etymology**, or history, of words. They bracket them at the end. Etymologies are extremely interesting in their own right, but you can browse them some other time, when you are not in pursuit of a word's meaning.

Once you eliminate these two items in the entry, you have five meanings left, but the fifth one is a noun and *scald* in our sentence is used as a verb. You can tell that from the "ed" on the end. That means you can eliminate the fifth meaning from the list.

Of the four meanings, the second one is probably the best choice because the sentence that sent you to the dictionary in the first place used *scald* in a way that suggests some kind of special treatment or handling. Note, however, that even if you picked meaning number 1, "to burn with or as if with hot liquid or steam," it, too, would give you a solid sense of the original sentence's meaning. In fact, even if you picked meaning 3, you'd still be able to get the meaning of the sentence.

The only meaning that would be dead wrong if you plugged it into the sentence would be meaning number 4, "to criticize harshly." That meaning simply does not fit the original sentence. It represents a **figurative meaning**, or sense, of the word *scald*.

Figurative Versus Literal Meanings

Words used in a figurative sense imply a resemblance between two things that seem totally different. For instance, we can use the word *frozen* to describe ice cream. That would be using the word literally, or realistically. We would be using it to physically describe the state or consistency of ice cream.

However, we can also say that someone's opinions have "frozen with time." That phrase uses the figurative meaning for *frozen*. It suggests that a person's opinions haven't changed in any way, much like frozen ice cream hasn't changed from its original state to a more liquid one.

Similarly, if we use *scald* figuratively, we aren't talking about literally burning someone with heat or steam. We are talking about a person saying something so harsh that it feels *as if* the words could burn.

READING TIP Next time you turn to a dictionary to look up an unfamiliar word and find several definitions, quickly eliminate any meanings that have no bearing on the word's context. Then look for the meaning that makes the most sense within the original sentence or passage.

SUMMING UP THE KEY POINTS

1. In addition to providing definitions, dictionary entries tell you how a word is pronounced, broken into syllables, and used in a sentence.

2. Special context labels tell you that certain meanings apply only with a particular setting such as botany, architecture, or law.

3. Etymology is the history of a word. Most dictionaries present word history at the end of the entry, usually enclosed in brackets.

4. If you are looking up an unfamiliar word from your reading, there is no need to panic if the entry contains several definitions. Just sort through them using the original context of the word as a guide to your selection. Then, too, different definitions are often somewhat related in meaning, so even if you don't pick the exactly right one, you may still be able to get an approximate definition. That approximate definition will allow you to continue your reading.

5. Figurative meanings of words imply a resemblance between two things that, on the surface, seem totally different.

◆ EXERCISE 10   Using the Dictionary

DIRECTIONS   Read each sentence and look carefully at the italicized word. Then look at the dictionary entry and pick the meaning that best fits the context. *Note*: All dictionary entries are excerpted from the *American Heritage Dictionary*.

1. *Sentence*: Many of those who had *collaborated* with the enemy during the war somehow managed to escape punishment when the war was over.

   Entry: **col•lab•o•rate** (k-lăb′ə-rāt) *intr.v.* **–rat•ed, –rat•ing, –rates**
   1. To work together, especially in a joint intellectual effort. **2.** To cooperate treasonably, as with an enemy occupation force in one's country. [Late Latin *collabōrāre, collbōrāt-* : Latin *com-* + Latin *labōrāre,* to work (from *labor,* toil).] **–col•lab′o•ra′tion** *n.*
   –col•lab′o•ra′tive *adj.* **–col•lab′o•ra′tor** *n.*

   What is the best meaning for the word *collaborated* in the above

   sentence? ＿＿

2. *Sentence*: After giving the same presentation for four *consecutive* days, the accountant had a difficult time concealing his boredom.

   Entry: **con•sec•u•tive** (kən-sĕk′yə-tĭv) *adj.* **1.** Following one after another without interruption; successive, *was absent on three consecutive days; won five consecutive games on the road.* 2. Marked by logical sequence. 3. *Grammar* Expressing consequence or result: *a consecutive clause.* [French *consecutive,* from Old French, from Medieval Latin *cōnsecūtīvus,* from *cōnsecūtus,* past participle of Latin *cōnsequī,* to follow closely. See CONSEQUENT.]
   –con•sec′u•tive•ly *adv.* **–con•sec′u•tive•ness** *n.*

   What is the best meaning for the word *consecutive* in the above

   sentence? ＿＿

3. *Sentence*: The young reporter volunteered to act as a *conduit* between the rebels and the government.

   Entry: **con•duit** (kŏn′doo-ĭt) *n.* **1.** A pipe or channel for conveying fluids, such as water. **2.** A tube or duct for enclosing electric wires or cable. **3.** A means by which something is transmitted: *an arms dealer who served as a conduit for intelligence data.* **4.** Archaic † A fountain [Middle English, from Old French, from Medieval Latin *conductus,* from Latin past participle of *condūcere,* to lead together. See CONDUCE.]

   What is the best meaning for the word *conduit* in the above sentence?

   ＿＿

---

†Archaic: used to describe an early meaning no longer in use.

4. *Sentence*:   Keeping in mind the needs of the reader is an *integral* part of effective writing.

Entry: **in•te•gral** (ĭn′tĭ-grəl, ĭn-tăg′rəl) *adj.* **1.** Essential or necessary for completeness; constituent: *The kitchen is an integral part of any house.* **2.** Possessing everything essential; entire. **3.** (ĭn′tĭ-grəl) *Mathematics* **a.** Expressed or expressible as or in terms of integers. **b.** Expressed as or involving integrals. ❖ *n.* **1.** A complete unit; a whole. **2.** (ĭn′tĭ-grəl) *Mathematics* **a.** A number computed by a limiting process in which the domain of a function, often an interval or planar region, is divided into arbitrarily small units, the value of the function at a point in each unit is multiplied by the linear or areal measurement of that unit, and all such products are summed. **b.** A definite integral. **c.** An indefinite integral. [Middle English, from Old French, from Medieval Latin *integrālis*, making up a whole, from Latin *integer*, complete. See INTEGER.] **–in′te•gral′i•ty** (-grăl′ĭ-tē) *n.* **–in′te•gral•ly** *adv.*

What is the best meaning for the word *integral* in the above sentence? _____

✔ CHECK YOUR UNDERSTANDING

1. The opening of a dictionary entry usually introduces three elements. What are the three?

_____

2. If an entry contains several different definitions, what should guide your choice of meaning?

_____

3. What does etymology refer to?

_____

4. Look over the pairs of sentences that follow and circle the letters of the sentences that use the italicized words figuratively.

   a. The coach had to call a "time out," when two parents of the players got into a *heated* argument.

   b. The little boy *heated* the soup on the stove and then carried the pot to the table.

a. The cookies were on a very *high* shelf where the dog could not reach them.

b. The Tejano singer was *high* on nothing more than the enthusiasm of the crowd.

5. Look over the pairs of sentences that follow. Circle the letters of the sentences that use the italicized words literally.

a. The young girl had learned how to *weave* from her Cherokee grandmother.

b. Unlike writers in the nineteenth century, modern ones are not inclined to *weave* morals, or lessons, into their short stories.

a. The surgeon *cut* a hole on the top of the man's head in order to relieve the pressure on his brain.

b. The police captain told his lieutenant to *cut* the chatter and get to the point.

The Difference Between Reading and Writing Vocabularies

Mastering new vocabulary, whether for reading or writing, involves the regular collecting and reviewing of new words. However, with your reading vocabulary, the goal is to develop *automatic* word recognition: You see the word; you know its meaning, without having to consciously think about it. Learning researchers call this *automaticity*. That's a fancy way of saying your grasp of word and meaning are so firmly embedded in your memory that you don't have to mentally search for a definition. Understanding words at this automatic level is like driving a car for a long time. After a certain point, you have practiced your driving skills to such a degree, they feel like a natural instinct rather than a learned activity.

Mastering new vocabulary for writing is a little different. Your writing vocabulary should *not* involve automatic word choices. When you are looking for words to express your thoughts, you may need to think a bit about the most appropriate ones. The ones that come automatically to mind may be those you have heard so often, they are considered *clichés*—overused expressions which suggest the writer has given up on original thought and shifted into automatic pilot. This is never the impression you want to create as a writer. Whatever *tone*, or attitude, you convey with words, you want those words to seem fresh and carefully chosen. Thus, adding words to your writing vocabulary requires more than collection and review.

STUDY TIP

Use *mnemonic devices*, or memory tricks, to learn new words. Associate new words with images or examples; connect them to sample sentences or to people, e.g., "The word *anecdote* reminds me of how my dad gives advice. He always starts with an anecdote."

A Personal Note on Web-Based Dictionaries

So many dictionaries are available on the Web now, I can't claim to have studied all of them. But having looked at quite a few and compared them to print dictionaries, let me offer a moderately informed opinion: For reading purposes,[†] I believe a Web-based dictionary will serve you as well as a print dictionary, largely because the context of the word you are looking up is going to ensure that you don't choose a completely inappropriate meaning.

That being said, however, not all the dictionaries on the Web are equally complete or equally easy to use. In some cases, the layout of the webpage is so cluttered, it's hard to find the entry word among all the ads for other products and services. Other Web dictionaries bring together a number of different entries from several sources and, for some reason, they don't always put the best or most complete entries at the top of the list. That means you have to scroll through a number of entries before finding one that seems both clear and comprehensive.

Some dictionaries seem to have been created just for the Web, and they occasionally have meanings that don't seem to appear anywhere except on that website. Yet when you look up a word in a dictionary, you want to know that you are getting the generally accepted definitions for

---

[†]Where writing is concerned, I'd be inclined to stick with a print dictionary. The online dictionaries are occasionally a bit too creative with things like syllabication.

that word, not one lexicographer's, or dictionary maker's, opinion of what the word means.

When it comes to clearly organized and comprehensive entries, I have long favored Dictionary.com, with yourdictionary.com coming in a close second. However, I have to admit a growing affection for Wordnik.com, which has a perfectly splendid array of sample sentences accompanying each entry-word. In fact, this is precisely the point of the site: "to show you as many example sentences as we can find for each word."

Whichever Web dictionary you choose, make sure it fulfills these criteria:

1. The webpage should be easy to read. If you have to study the page to separate the entry from the ads and promotional sidebars, keep looking. Busy webpages can often prove a distraction and you may end up browsing phone applications rather than defining an unfamiliar word.

2. The various elements in the entry—for example, pronunciation guide, audio link, and word history—should be clearly laid out. Whenever you have to look at the page for a long time to determine where, say, the meanings leave off and the history begins, this is not the dictionary you want to be using.

3. The definitions of words should be clearly written. If you have to puzzle over how a definition is worded because it doesn't quite make sense, it's probably the definition and not you.

4. The definitions should come from several different sources so that you can compare the meanings from various sources.

5. If the online dictionary uses only one source for its definitions, the meanings listed in the entry should be fairly similar to the meanings listed in other dictionary entries for the same word. (Yes, this means you have to do some cross-referencing.) If you find a definition for a word that doesn't appear anywhere else, you should probably not use this dictionary.

6. In addition to definitions, the most useful dictionaries have examples of the words in context and audio links that let you hear the words pronounced.

DIGGING DEEPER — Word Lovers and Word Histories

Looking Ahead The discussion of dictionary skills on pages 94–98 mentioned that etymologies, or word histories, are interesting in their own right. The following excerpt from a poem called "Retirement" by the eighteenth-century writer William Cowper (1731–1800) suggests that, in his time at least, learning the history of a word could be a passionate pursuit. *Note*: In Cowper's time, the word *philologist* was used to describe a person who loved word history. Now the word has a narrower meaning and refers to someone interested in the study of literature.

> Learn'd philologists who chase
>
> A panting syllable through time and space,
>
> Start it at home, and hunt it in the dark,
>
> To Gaul,[†] to Greece, and into Noah's Ark.
>
> —William Cowper

Sharpening Your Skills

DIRECTIONS Answer the following questions by filling in the blanks or circling the letter of the correct response.

1. In the third line, what does the first *it* refer to?

   _____

   What does the second *it* refer to?

   _____

2. In the poem, Cowper describes a situation that is
   a. literal.
   b. figurative.

[†]Gaul: The name the Romans used to refer to the region where France and Belgium are now located.

3. What did Cowper mean when he talked about philologists tracing "a panting syllable through time and space"?

_____

_____

4. What word parts can you identify in the word *philologist*?

_____

5. The poem implies that philologists
   a. were not people of action.
   b. were interested only in certain words.
   c. are committed to uncovering the history of words.

   To help you understand why some people think learning etymologies is fun, not a chore, here are five words with a colorful past.

Ostracize	When the ancient Greeks wanted to vote on whether someone should be banished from their community, they would write their vote on a piece of pottery, called an *ostracon*. From that practice came the word *ostracize*, which means to banish or exclude.
Chauvinist	Nicolas Chauvin was a nineteenth-century French soldier famous mainly for being completely devoted to France's ruler Napoleon Bonaparte. From Chauvin's name comes the word *chauvinist*, meaning someone unthinkingly prejudiced in favor of one's country or group.
Martinet	Jean Martinet was a seventeenth-century French general, who passionately believed in strict discipline for his soldiers. Disagreement with his rules was neither encouraged nor allowed. From the general, then, comes the word *martinet*, meaning someone who follows rules to the letter and expects others to do the same.

Titan	According to Greek mythology, the Titans were members of a gigantic family of gods who inhabited the earth before people did. The Titans were huge and powerful. Today when we describe something as "titanic," we mean that it is huge or enormous. When we say that someone is a "titan," we mean that he or she has a great deal of power or is outstanding in some field.
Herculean	Hercules was a Greek hero who possessed extraordinary strength. It was said that he could perform fantastic feats. Today when we use the word *herculean*, we are talking about something that demands a great deal of effort or someone in possession of enormous strength.

Now see if you can correctly match those words to the blanks in the following sentences.

6. At one time, the creators of Google were ready to take on the _____ task of putting whole libraries online.

7. The new soldiers were depressed at learning the drill sergeant was a _____.

8. In the rock world of the 1970s and 1980s, Freddie Mercury, lead singer of the group Queen, was a _____, but fame did not save him from AIDS, and he died in 1991.

9. As a traveler, he was a _____; any deviation from what he was used to in his own country just had to be bad.

10. After a pair of male penguins stole eggs from some of the other birds, replacing them with stones, the two birds were _____ by the rest of the flock.

Making Connections Use the Web to answer this question: What is it that links these three men together: Samuel Johnson, James A. H. Murray, and Noah Webster?

Drawing Your Own Conclusions If Jean Martinet were transplanted to the twenty-first century and made the supervisor of a software programming department, what do you think he would say if his employees said they wanted to change the dress code on Fridays and come in wearing whatever they felt like wearing, as opposed to their normal professional attire? Please explain.

▶ TEST 1   Using Context Clues

DIRECTIONS   Use context clues to select an approximate definition for each italicized word.

1. In the face of real danger, he didn't even try to display his usual *bravado*: When the bull charged, he ran like a scared rabbit.
   a. extreme shyness
   b. love of animals
   c. false bravery
   d. quick wit

2. With age, the financial wizard and penny pincher Hazel Green grew increasingly eccentric: She wore *bizarrely* unfashionable clothes, trusted no one, went on strange diets, and generally seemed to be out of step with the world.
   a. stingily
   b. weirdly
   c. colorful
   d. cleverly

3. In *The Country of the Pointed Firs*, the nineteenth-century writer Sarah Orne Jewett created the remarkable and compelling Mrs. Todd, a country woman who uses her vast store of herbal *lore* to cure the ailing and aging.
   a. knowledge
   b. mystery
   c. myths
   d. poisons

4. After her face was *disfigured* by an automobile accident, the super-model realized that there really were people in the world who could love her for who she was rather than what she looked like.
   a. enriched
   b. abandoned
   c. rebuilt
   d. ruined

5. In order to justify his claim to visitation rights, Adam was willing to undergo a *paternity* test that would prove David was indeed his son.

   a. relative

   b. brotherhood

   c. fatherhood

   d. chemical

6. In the nineteenth century, girls and boys were rigidly *socialized*: Girls were encouraged to be subordinate to boys, and boys were told they could conquer the world.

   a. restricted by class

   b. punished for misbehavior

   c. taught to obey

   d. taught appropriate social roles

7. Although the curse of Tutankhamen's tomb has never been scientifically proven, the *irrational* belief persists that those who discovered the tomb met an early death.

   a. dishonest

   b. sensational

   c. fast-spreading

   d. unreasonable

8. In the fairy tale, the wolf tried to disguise his *predatory* nature by dressing up as Little Red Riding Hood's elderly grandmother.

   a. insensitive

   b. youthful

   c. dangerous

   d. wild

9. He wanted to work on their relationship by regularly seeing a therapist; she opted for a more *radical* solution and filed for divorce.

   a. insignificant

   b. drastic

c. quiet

d. expensive

10. The lawyer *systematically* worked his way through the document and eliminated all references to the coauthor.

a. casually

b. slowly

c. quickly

d. carefully

▶ TEST 2   Using Context Clues

DIRECTIONS   Use context clues to develop an approximate definition for each italicized word.

1. The artist, who is clearly a Democrat, uses his *satirical* cartoons to expose the follies of Republican politicians.

   Satirical means _____.

2. They decided against buying the house because of its *proximity* to the airport.

   Proximity means _____.

3. Having a child outside of marriage no longer carries the punitive *stigma* it did twenty-five years ago.

   Stigma means _____.

4. On the highway running through the city, a vehicle accident can cause *gridlock* that stretches for miles.

   Gridlock means _____.

5. To provide her children with intellectual *stimulation*, the young mother often took them to museums, bookstores, and concerts.

   Stimulation means _____.

6. When Martha asked her husband if she was getting fat, he said "yes" without thinking and quickly regretted his *candor*.

   Candor means _____.

7. George Washington was the first and last U.S. president to govern from Philadelphia; all *subsequent* presidents have resided in the White House in Washington, D.C.

   Subsequent means _____.

8. When the *Apollo 11* astronauts landed on the moon, they found a rocky, *barren* landscape.

   Barren means _____.

9. The diplomat had a *supercilious* expression on his face and seemed to be looking down his nose at the other guests.

   Supercilious means _____.

10. The Rev. Martin Luther King Jr.'s *charismatic* leadership inspired millions of people to demand civil rights for black Americans.

   Charismatic means _____.

▶ **TEST 3**   **Using Context Clues**

DIRECTIONS   Use context clues to develop an approximate definition for each italicized word.†

1. The 1938 Fair Labor Standards Act signed by Franklin D. Roosevelt prevents the *exploitation* of children; it prohibits anyone under the age of thirteen from working in most jobs.

   Exploitation means _____.

2. The Louisiana Purchase, President Thomas Jefferson's *acquisition* of 5.3 million acres of French territory in 1803, doubled the size of the United States.

   Acquisition means _____.

3. Wilbur and Orville Wright succeeded in building the first "flying machine" because they systematically *modified* their design, making changes and improvements following each test flight.

   Modified means _____.

4. By the end of the twentieth century, America's economy had begun to shift from one based *predominantly* on manufacturing to one based mostly on employees' knowledge and skills.

   Predominantly means _____.

5. The Common Era, also known as the Christian Era, began with the year Jesus was believed to have been born; the years *preceding* this date are followed by B.C., an abbreviation for "Before Christ."

   Preceding means _____.

---

†The italicized words are all from the Academic Word List developed by the School of Linguistics and Applied Language Studies at Victoria University of Wellington in New Zealand.

6. The American Civil War *commenced* on April 12, 1861, when the South fired the first shots at Union troops in Charleston, South Carolina, and ended on April 9, 1865.

   Commenced means _____.

7. According to one *hypothesis*, the impact of an asteroid 65 million years ago led to the extinction of the dinosaurs, but this explanation is not a proven fact.

   Hypothesis means _____.

8. The legal document known as a "living will" provides *explicit* instructions about what caregivers should and should not do in the event that a person becomes comatose or requires long-term life support.

   Explicit means _____.

9. According to many scientists, global warming could have dangerous *implications* for the future, including a destructive rise in sea levels, damage to ecosystems and agriculture, and an increase in extreme weather events like hurricanes.

   Implications means _____.

10. In economics, *fluctuations* in the prices of goods are caused by similar increases and decreases in the availability of and demand for those goods.

    Fluctuations means _____.

♦ **TEST 4**   **Word Analysis and Context Clues**

DIRECTIONS   Use context clues and word parts to develop an approximate definition for each italicized word.

Prefixes	Roots
anti = against	*cred* = belief
extra = over, outside, beyond	*dict* = say or speak
dis = apart from, not, without	*sect* = cut, divide
ad = to, toward	*here* = stick

1. The doctors were fearful the boy would die because they had no *antidote* for the snakebite.

   Antidote means _____.

2. The girl refused to *dissect* the frog because she couldn't bear the thought of wasting a frog's life just so some student could cut up the body.

   Dissect means _____.

3. Because the Shaker religion forbade sex even in marriage, it had a hard time keeping *adherents*.

   Adherents means _____.

4. The report included too much *extraneous* information: The committee wanted only the essential facts of the situation, not silly gossip about dress and personal behavior.

   Extraneous means _____.

5. If she wants to run in the next campaign, she needs to *disassociate* herself from well-known gamblers and gangsters.

   Disassociate means _____.

6. Dr. Sorenson thinks of himself as an expert on ocean environment, but he lacks the proper *credentials*: He's a dentist, not a marine biologist.

   Credentials means _____.

7. My mother always told me to follow the *dictum* "neither a borrower nor a lender be," but I am always borrowing money from my friends.

   Dictum means _____.

8. The bank official desperately tried to *extricate* himself from the financial crisis he had helped to create, but all his influence couldn't get him out of trouble this time.

   Extricate means _____.

9. Once the suspect gave a *credible* account of his actions the night before, the police decided to let him go.

   Credible means _____.

10. Even with the glue in place, the pictures simply would not *adhere* to the shiny wallpaper.

    Adhere means _____.

▶ **TEST 5**   **Word Analysis and Context Clues**

DIRECTIONS   Use context clues and word parts to develop an approximate definition for each italicized word.

Prefixes	Roots
in, im = in, into, not	*clin* = lean
multi = many	*plac* = calm, please
omni = all	*ven* = come
circum = around	*sci* = know
	vor = eat

1. As my uncle got older, he became less *implacable*; more mellow with age, he was much easier to please.

    Implacable means _____.

2. The entertainer Lena Horne was determined to *circumvent* the racism that once ruled Las Vegas. When hotel owners told her they didn't allow African-Americans to rent rooms, Horne told them no room, no performance. As usual, Lena got her way.

    Circumvent means _____.

3. President Lyndon B. Johnson's first *inclination* in a difficult situation was to sweet-talk whomever he needed on his side; if that didn't work, he could quickly turn into a bully.

    Inclination means _____.

4. In George Orwell's famous novel *1984*, "Big Brother" is an *omniscient* political leader, so all-knowing that privacy simply doesn't exist in the world he controls.

    Omniscient means _____.

5. The United States had a *multiplicity* of reasons for not entering World War II, but after Japan bombed Pearl Harbor, every one of those reasons disappeared like smoke.

Multiplicity means _____.

6. When millions died during the civil war in Rwanda, both Europe and the United States were harshly criticized for not *intervening* early on, when lives might have been saved.

Intervening means _____.

7. Roaches have survived for centuries because they are *omnivorous*; they eat anything and everything—from paste to nail filings.

Omnivorous means _____.

8. While the angry *multitudes* shouted outside the gates of the palace, the frightened king and queen tried to leave in secret, knowing full well that there was no way to calm their starving subjects.

Multitudes means _____.

9. The mother *placated* the child with a chocolate chip cookie; in a matter of seconds, he went from tears to giggles.

Placated means _____.

10. Not anxious to return to work, the boy took the most *circuitous* route he could think of, and a fifteen-minute trip took him three-quarters of an hour.

Circuitous means _____.

▶ **TEST 6**   **Word Analysis and Context Clues**

DIRECTIONS   Use context clues and word parts to develop an approximate definition for each italicized word.

> **Prefixes**
> *pre* = before or preceding, prior to
> *super* = over, beyond, above
> *sub* = under, from below, put under
>
> **Roots**
> *locut, loqu* = speech
> *voc* = voice, call
> *fic, fact, fect* = to make, to do
> *gen* = to give birth to, to produce, to cause

1. She has an amazing mind; in a single class session, she can *generate* one original idea after another, and most of them are quite good.

   Generate means _____.

2. After having their reports censored by military officials, the reporters were *vocal* in their complaints; they told anyone who would listen that their right to free speech had been ignored by the high command.

   Vocal means _____.

3. As a *prelude* to his speech, the scientist told a silly joke; as he had hoped, the comic introduction warmed up the audience and made them more attentive.

   Prelude means _____.

4. Patricia Henley's novel *Hummingbird House* wonderfully *evokes* the lush and beautiful landscape of Guatemala; she is particularly good at describing the country's colorful birds and gorgeous flowers.

   Evokes means _____.

5. What exactly is the *genesis* of the word *bedlam*? I've heard two different stories about its origin, and I am not sure which one is accurate.

   Genesis means _____.

6. Although the two men work together very well, they couldn't be more different: Bob is relaxed and *loquacious*, whereas Will is tense and silent most of the time.

   Loquacious means _____.

7. To avoid being followed by reporters, the famous couple used *fictitious* names when they checked into the hotel, but they used their real names after they had crossed over the border into Mexico.

   Fictitious means _____.

8. In an effort to trim her speech down to no more than fifteen minutes, the union organizer carefully crossed out any *superfluous* details that weren't directly related to her message.

   Superfluous means _____.

9. The previous group leader encouraged independent thought; unfortunately, the current leader tries to *subdue* all signs of it.

   Subdue means _____.

10. Sometimes truth is stranger than *fiction,* and the real world can be odder than the one you find in books.

    Fiction means _____.

Prefixes, Roots, and Suffixes Introduced in Chapter 2
◆

Prefixes

ad = to, toward
anti = against
bene = well, good
bi = two
circum = around
dis = apart from, not, without
extra = over, outside, beyond
im = not
in, *im* = in, into, not
mal = bad
mono = one
multi = many
omni = all
per = through
poly = many
pre = before, preceding, prior to
phil = love
pseudo = false
re = again, back
syn, *sym* = together
sub = under, from below, put under
super = over, beyond, above

Roots

bellum = war
chron = time
clin = lean
cred = belief
derma = skin
dict = say or speak
fic, *fact*, *fect* = to make or to do
for = to bore into
gam = marriage
gen = to give birth to, to produce, to cause
here = stick
lat = side
locut, *loqu* = speech
mob = move
pel = force
plac = calm, please
popul = people
rec, *rect* = straight, straighten
sci = know
sect = cut, divide
the = god
ven = come
vi, *vit*, *viv* = life
voc = voice, call
vor = eat

Suffixes

ism = state, condition, or quality
itis = inflammation
ize = to cause to be, to treat or affect
onym = name, word
ous = full of

Connecting the General
to the Specific in Reading
and Writing

Holger Mette/Shutterstock

IN THIS CHAPTER, YOU WILL LEARN

- how general and specific words differ.
- how general and specific sentences work together to create the author's meaning.
- how writers must generalize to make a point and include specific details to explain it.
- how readers respond by searching out general statements along with the specific details used to develop them.

"To generalize means to think."
—Friedrich Hegel, philosopher

"The truth, if it exists, is in the details."
—Anonymous

Throughout this book you'll see numerous references to the words *general*[†] and *specific*. To make sure you have a clear understanding of these terms, this chapter explains the meaning of both in some detail.

General and Specific Words

You'll soon be working with general and specific sentences, but let's begin with general and specific words. Once you learn to distinguish, or see the difference, between general and specific words, it's easy to identify general and specific sentences.

Here are two lists of words, one labeled *general*, the other *specific*. As you read each list, think about these two questions: How do the words in each list differ? What makes one word general and another one specific?

General	Specific
creatures	dogs
silver	nickels
expression	smile
object	statue
liquid	ink
flower	daisy
machine	computer

Did you notice that the words on the left can be interpreted, or understood, in a variety of ways? The word *creatures*, for example, is broad enough to include everything from cows to children. The word *dogs*, however, quickly eliminates both the cows *and* the children. We are now talking about a specific type of creature—one that barks, has four legs, and wags its tail.

Similarly, the word *silver* can refer to table settings or to money. The word *nickels*, however, quickly eliminates all other possibilities. It refers to coins rather than forks.

With these illustrations in mind, we can sum up the differences between general and specific words.

General words are broad in scope. They refer to or include a wide variety of different things and thus can be understood in several ways.

[†]The word *generalize* describes the thinking process that creates general categories from ideas, individual examples, events, or thoughts.

Specific words, in contrast, are much narrower in focus. Because they cover less territory, they can't be understood in so many different ways. General words expand meaning; specific words narrow or focus it. To make ourselves understood, we need both kinds of words. We need general words to sum up our experiences and specific words to explain or clarify them.

Let's look at two more pairs of words. This time, it's up to you to label them. Write a *G* next to the general word. Write an *S* next to the more specific one.

sound __G__   scream __S__

dance __S__   movement __G__

Did you put a *G* next to *sound* and an *S* next to *scream*? If you did, you're on the right track. The word *sound* covers everything from a meow to a giggle. Thus it's the more general of the two.

If you put an *S* next to the word *dance* and a *G* next to the word *movement*, you again labeled the words correctly. The word *movement* refers to many activities, from playing baseball to doing a tango. The word *dance*, however, eliminates playing baseball along with a host of other possibilities, such as kicking a football or waving good-bye.

♦ **EXERCISE 1**   **Coming Up with Specifics**

DIRECTIONS   After each general word, list at least three more specific words that could be included under that heading.

EXAMPLE

communication

speech

signs

television

EXPLANATION   Because all three words refer to a specific type of communication, we can include all three under the more general heading.

1. feelings

___happiness___

___sadness___

___joy___

2. music

<u>Country</u>

<u>Hip Hop</u>

<u>Rap</u>

Putting the Terms *General* and *Specific* into Context

To be meaningful, the terms *general* and *specific* need a context. Sure, *dog* seems like a general word, but if you place it next to the word *animals*, it's the more specific of the two. Similarly, if you put the word *dog* next to the name of a specific dog, say, a labrador retriever named *Tonka*, the word *dog* becomes the more general of the two.

For an illustration of how a word can become more general or specific with context, see the following diagram:

animals | The word *animals* refers to all kinds of living beings. Members of the group called *animals* are very different from one another; they are more dissimilar than similar.

quadrupeds | The term *quadrupeds* refers only to those animals having four legs; all other animals are excluded. Members of the group are more dissimilar than similar.

dogs | The word *dogs* refers to one particular group of quadrupeds. Members of the group called *dogs* are more similar to one another than are members of the group called four-legged animals.

pedigrees | The word *pedigrees* now includes only dogs whose parentage is clear; all mixed breeds have been excluded.

labs | The word *labs* refers to one particular pedigree, the labrador retriever. The members of this group look alike. At this level, all other breeds are excluded.

Tonka | The word *Tonka* refers only to labs bearing the name "Tonka." All other labrador retrievers are excluded from this level.

SUMMING UP THE KEY POINTS
- ➤

1. General words sum up people, objects, experiences, and events that are in some way related. The more general a word is, the greater number of things it refers to or includes and the more different from each other those things can be.

2. As words become increasingly general, the things they refer to can be quite dissimilar. Imagine, for example, all of the things that a general word like "communication" can refer to. That's why specific words need to accompany general ones. The specific words focus more on individual events, people, and experiences. When combined with general words, they nail down the broader meanings.

3. To be evaluated correctly, general and specific words need a context. On its own, the word "books" seems quite general. After all, there are all kinds of books, ranging from novels to encyclopedias. But if you compare the word "books" to the phrase "printed matter," then the word "books" is more specific than the phrase.

◆ **EXERCISE 2**   **Seeing the Difference Between General and Specific Words**

DIRECTIONS   Underline the more specific word in each pair.

EXAMPLE

a. entertainment, <u>movies</u>

b. <u>*Newsweek*</u>, magazines

EXPLANATION   The word *movies* is more specific than the word *entertainment*. It refers to a fewer number of things, and the things to which it refers are more alike than unalike. The word *Newsweek* is more specific than the word *magazines*. It refers to one particular magazine rather than to a variety of publications.

1. architecture, churches

2. crimes, robbery

3. Usher , rapper

4. Congress, government

5. documents, Constitution

◆ **EXERCISE 3**   **Seeing the Difference Between General and Specific Words**

DIRECTIONS   Underline the more general word in each pair.

1. creature, person

2. Earth, planet

3. pollution, smog

4. phobia, claustrophobia

5. flag, symbol

◆ **EXERCISE 4**   **Finding a General Category**

DIRECTIONS   Find one word or term *general enough* to include all the other words listed.

EXAMPLE   academic subjects

> American history
> English composition
> sociology
> algebra

EXPLANATION   In this case, all four items can be included under the heading "academic subjects." Now it's your turn.

1. ___Movies / Books___

> *The Da Vinci Code*
> *Harry Potter and the Deathly Hallows*
> *Breaking Dawn*
> *The Kite Runner*

2. *Female Singers*

Shakira
Beyoncé
Kelly Clarkson
Alicia Keys

3. *female Super heros*

Superwoman
Buffy the Vampire Slayer
Xena
Cat Woman

4. *Cartoons / Male*

Homer Simpson
Calvin and Hobbes
Dilbert
SpongeBob SquarePants

5. *Scarry movies*

The Ring
Night of the Living Dead
The Texas Chainsaw Massacre
Saw IV

◆ **EXERCISE 5**   **General and Specific in Context**

DIRECTIONS   Fill in the accompanying diagrams with the appropriate letters. The letter of the most general word goes on top. The letter of the most specific word goes on the bottom.

EXAMPLE

a. musician   b   (*most general*)
b. artist   a   (*more specific*)
c. violinist   c   (*most specific*)

EXPLANATION   The word *artist* can refer to many different kinds of people, for example, painters, sculptors, or writers. As the most general word, it goes on the top level. *Musician* is somewhat more specific than *artist*. It excludes all people who are not concerned with music. Therefore, it goes on the middle rung. *Violinist* is the most specific word; it refers only to people who play the violin.

1. a. flu
   b. disease
   c. bird flu

2. a. water
   b. Indian Ocean
   c. ocean

3. a. detergent
   b. product
   c. Tide

4. a. continent
   b. land mass
   c. South America

✔ CHECK YOUR UNDERSTANDING

1. What is the function of general words?

_____

_____

2. What happens when words become more general?

_____

_____

3. Why is it important for specific words to accompany general ones?

_____

_____

4. Why is a context important to evaluating general and specific words?

_____

_____

_____

Understanding the Difference Between General and Specific Sentences

To test your understanding of the terms *general* and *specific* when they are applied to sentences, read the following two examples. See if you can explain what makes the first sentence more general than the second.

General Sentence **1.** Anger can take many different forms.

Specific Sentence **2.** Some people grow quiet when they get angry, while others scream and shout.

Did you notice that the more general sentence, like more general words, could be interpreted, or understood, in several ways? Based on sentence 1, we could assume that anger might be expressed in tears, shouts, silence, or laughter. It all depends on how readers choose to interpret the key phrase "many different forms." The more specific sentence brings the general one into focus. It narrows, or limits, expressions of anger to just two responses: being quiet or noisy.

Here's another pair of sentences. Put a *G* in the blank next to the general sentence and an *S* next to the more specific one.

1. When they are in a classroom, many people are afraid to ask questions or disagree. ___S___

2. Our behavior is often affected by the presence of others. ___G___

If you labeled sentence 1 specific and sentence 2 general, you are correct. Sentence 2 says that our behavior is affected by the presence of others, but it doesn't zero in on any one situation. Instead, it sums up and includes any and all situations where people are present.

Sentence 1, in contrast, focuses on one particular setting—the classroom. It also identifies two particular kinds of behavior—asking questions or disagreeing. Sentence 1 clarifies and helps us understand sentence 2, making sentence 1 the more specific sentence.

> **READING TIP**
>
> As soon as you spot a general sentence, check to see how the sentences that follow clarify or explain it.[†]

General and Specific Sentences in Textbooks

Below is another example of general and specific sentences working together. This pair of sentences is drawn from a criminology textbook. Note how the first sentence makes a general point about police using the Internet. In answer to the question readers might raise about the general sentence—"How have police expanded their search for fugitives to the World Wide Web?"—the specific sentence offers an illustration.

> [1]Some police agencies have expanded their search for fugitives to the World Wide Web. [2]The Internet was credited for helping capture Rogge, the Seattle bank robber discovered in Guatemala, after a 14-year-old neighbor spotted the fugitive's photograph on the FBI's "10 Most Wanted" website. (Schmalleger, *Criminal Justice*, p. 184.)

After reading the first sentence, readers might imagine a number of ways that police have expanded their search for fugitives to the Web. But in this instance, at least, the specific sentence limits those possibilities to one: The FBI displayed the picture of the bank robber on their "10 Most Wanted" website and that led to his arrest.

Throughout your college career, numerous reading assignments will require you to make connections between general and specific sentences. Like the example shown here, your textbooks will introduce generalizations that sum up a number of different events, people, or experiences. The specific sentences that follow will then identify some of the events, people, or experiences on which the general statement was based.

[†]This advice will become crucial in Chapter 4, when you look for the main idea or message of a paragraph.

SUMMING UP THE KEY POINTS

- - - - - - - - - - - - - - - - - - - ➡

1. General sentences, like general words, are broad in meaning and can be understood in different ways. While they are essential to summing up events and experiences, they usually need specific sentences for clarification.

2. Specific sentences don't sum up as many events or experiences as general ones do. They focus on individual events or experiences and are less open to different interpretations. That's why they are so helpful for clarifying general statements.

◆ **EXERCISE 6**   **Recognizing General and Specific Sentences**

DIRECTIONS   Read each pair of sentences. Then label the general sentence *G* and the specific one *S*.

EXAMPLE

a. The focus in elementary schools has switched from girls to boys, and researchers now have a whole new set of educational concerns. __G__

b. In the 1990s, educational research focused on how to help girls excel in science and math, but now the emphasis is on helping boys become better readers and writers. __S__

EXPLANATION   Sentence *a* is more general because we don't have specific meanings for the words *focus* and *concerns*. Note how sentence *b*, the more specific sentence, defines both terms and puts limits on how they can be understood.

1. a. Early in U.S. history, newspapers didn't pretend to be without political bias. __G__

   b. In the eighteenth century, American politicians often funded and controlled newspapers. __S__

2. a. In the past twenty years, health care around the world has markedly improved, especially for infants. __G__

   b. Thanks to improved health care, the number of babies who die in the first year of life has decreased markedly over the last twenty years. _S_

3. a. In Japan, readily revealing one's emotions to others is not encouraged, but in America the opposite is true. _S_

   b. Culture affects behavior in a number of ways, particularly within the context of personal relations. _G_

4. a. Like many of his victims, Jesse James was shot in the back. _S_

   b. The outlaw Jesse James met what some have called a fitting end. _G_

5. a. By 2050, the U.S. Census Bureau predicts that the number of Hispanic individuals living in the United States will increase from 45.5 million to 132.8 million. _S_

   b. People of Hispanic origin make up about 15 percent of the total population in the United States, but the U.S. Census Bureau expects a dramatic increase in that number over the course of time. _G_

◆ **EXERCISE 7**   **Connecting General and Specific in Textbooks**

   DIRECTIONS   Each item in this exercise introduces one general sentence taken from a textbook paragraph. Three additional sentences follow, but only one is a more specific sentence that further explains the first. Circle the letter of that sentence. *Note*: The sentence you choose has to (1) be more specific than the opening sentence and (2) further illustrate or explain the opening sentence.

   EXAMPLE

General Sentence In the early twentieth century, behavioral psychologists like John Watson maintained that human nature is a product of learning and experience.[1]

Specific Sentences a. Psychologists have long argued over the role genetic inheritance plays in human development.

   _____
   [1]Adapted from Nevid, *Psychology: Concepts and Applications*, p. 344.

(b.) Watson even boasted that he could take healthy infants and, through control of the environment, turn them into doctors, lawyers, or even beggars and thieves.

c. John Broadus Watson was an American psychologist.

EXPLANATION Sentence *b* is the only one of the three that could be correct. Sentence *b* illustrates how deeply Watson believed that "human nature is a product of learning and experience." Answer *a* won't work because it's more general than the first sentence. It discusses the broader category of psychologists rather than the more specific "behavioral psychologists." Except for the use of Watson's name, sentence *c* doesn't pick up on anything said in the first sentence.

General Sentence 1. Pressure injury is caused when placing pressure against tissue leads to a decrease in blood flow to the area.[2]

Specific Sentences   a. Electrical injury is the result of contacting unprotected or inadequately insulated electrical wiring.

    b. Calluses are not painful; in fact, they provide protection for the hands.

    (c.) Corns and calluses are two common kinds of pressure injury.

General Sentence 2. In the context of the law, the exclusionary rule means that evidence illegally seized by the police cannot be used in a trial.[3]

Specific Sentences   a. One of the first Supreme Court cases directly affecting the collection of evidence was *Weeks v. United States* in 1914.

    b. All evidence recovered by illegal means is called "fruit of the poisonous tree" and is grounds for a mistrial.

    (c.) The exclusionary rule applies mainly to those instances where officers have failed to obtain a warrant authorizing them to conduct a search.

General Sentence 3. There are many theories regarding the reason behind the Chinese practice of footbinding.[4]

Specific Sentences   a. In ancient Chinese culture, only the poorest of women were allowed freedom of movement.

---

[2]Neighbors and Tannehill-Jones, *Human Diseases*, p. 358.
[3]Schmalleger, *Criminal Justice Today*, p. 249.
[4]Flemming, *Reading for Success*, p. 40.

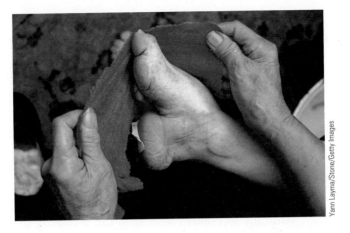

The perfectly bound foot was only 3″ long. Women who got their feet bound could not walk, run, or dance.

Yann Layma/Stone/Getty Images

b. According to one theory, the binding of women's feet when they were children made them physically dependent and therefore easily controlled.

c. The Chinese practice of footbinding is difficult for most people to understand because it was such a cruel thing to do.

General Sentence 4. Caffeine is an addictive stimulant found in coffee, chocolate, tea, cola drinks, and some over-the-counter medications.[5]

Specific Sentences

a. Many substances that seem a natural part of everyday life are actually addictive.

b. Those who are addicted to caffeine, for instance, often suffer uncomfortable withdrawal symptoms such as headache and fatigue if they are deprived of substances containing it.

c. Tobacco is also addictive and is also a stimulant; it narrows the blood vessels and raises heart rate and blood pressure.

✔ CHECK YOUR UNDERSTANDING

What's the role of general sentences in communication, and why is it a good idea to follow them with more specific sentences?

_____

_____

_____

---

[5]Adapted from Neighbors and Tannehill-Jones, *Human Diseases*, p. 413.

The Reader's Role

Readers need to follow the writer's train of thought through all of its twists and turns. On the most basic level, this means being on the lookout for general statements that sum up a variety of people, events, or ideas. Having spotted those statements, readers need to connect them to the more specific sentences used as clarification or proof. It's only by connecting the two kinds of sentences that the reader can determine the author's meaning.

Fulfilling the reader's role and making the right connections come naturally to readers who keep the following three questions in mind while reading:

1. Where are the most general statements in the reading?

2. What questions do they raise?

3. Where are the specific sentences that answer those questions?

"The existence of literature depends as much on readers reading as it does on authors writing."

—Stephen Mailloux, professor and writer

If they cannot answer one of these three questions, *experienced readers are quick to retool their approach* and ask different questions. For instance, if they can't find any general statements, they start asking what general idea or point is suggested, or implied, by the specific sentences in the passage (more about implied main ideas in Chapter 6). Should the specific sentences in the reading seem unrelated to the general sentence that initially appeared to be the focal point of the passage, experienced readers start looking for another general sentence (more on this in Chapter 4).

◆ **EXERCISE 8**   **Relating the Specific to the General**

DIRECTIONS   Read the three specific sentences. Then look at the general sentences that follow. Put a check in the blank next to the one general statement that the specific sentences could best support.

EXAMPLE

Specific Sentences

a. Before 1980, most doctors worked alone, but today more than half are salaried employees who work for medical companies.

b. Twenty-five years ago, doctors could count on the respect of their patients, but recent polls show a decline in patients' respect for physicians.

c. Increasingly, doctors must seek permission from government agencies or insurance companies to give special treatments to patients.

General Sentences

_____ **1.** The number of women and minorities applying to medical school has increased greatly.

__✓__ **2.** The professional life of physicians has changed dramatically in the past twenty-five years.

_____ **3.** Most people who enter medical school do so because they have been influenced by family doctors.

EXPLANATION General sentences 1 and 3 are not good choices because the specific sentences do not mention medical schools or why people apply to them.

Specific Sentences 1.

a. The tradition of using candles at funerals began with the Romans, who used them to frighten away evil spirits.

b. Tombstones originated as a way of keeping the dead in the underworld.

c. The original purpose of coffins was to keep the dead safely underground.

General Sentences

_____ **1.** Anthropologists have found evidence that funeral traditions existed during the Neanderthal age (100,000–40,000 BCE).

_____ **2.** Different cultures have different ways of mourning their dead.

_____ **3.** Many of the modern customs associated with mourning came from a fear of the dead and what they might do to the living.

Specific Sentences 2.

a. The citizens of Sparta, a city-state of ancient Greece, were not allowed to become farmers; they were made to train as warriors instead.

b. Family life in Sparta was severely limited because both boys and girls spent long hours in physical training.

c. From age seven to age thirty, the boys received instruction in the art of waging war.

General Sentences

_____ **1.** The Spartans were obedient to the laws of their land.

_____ **2.** The Spartan life was hard and devoted to war.

_____ **3.** Spartan men and women were known for their heroism in war.

Specific Sentences **3.** a. During World War II, German invaders destroyed Russia's richest agricultural regions.

b. According to official reports, more than seven million Russians were killed while defending their country against German attacks.

c. Many Russians lost their lives in concentration camps.

General Sentences

_____ **1.** The Russians suffered heavy losses in World War II.

_____ **2.** Russia suffered more losses than any of the other great powers.

_____ **3.** Russia has never recovered from the tragedy of World War II.

Specific Sentences **4.** a. During World War II, the War Department finally approved the training of African-American pilots.

b. In 1941 Benjamin O. Davis Jr. became the first African-American to lead a squadron of pilots.

c. President Franklin D. Roosevelt's Executive Order 8802 required employers in defense industries to make jobs available "without discrimination* because of race, creed* or color."

General Sentences

_____ **1.** For many African-Americans, World War II offered a chance to break down racial barriers.

_____ **2.** During World War II, racial violence broke out on several military bases.

_____ **3.** World War II brought out the best in Americans.

*discrimination: the act of showing prejudice in favor of or against a particular group.
*creed: belief, religion.

Initially barred from flight training because of his race, Benjamin O. Davis Jr. went on to become the first African-American to achieve the rank of general in the Air Force.

© Corbis

Specific Sentences 5. a. Between 1933 and 1939, about 150,000 square miles of U.S. farmland lost its topsoil.

b. Huge dust storms turned day into night all over the Great Plains.

c. During the same period, more than 500 million tons of rich earth dried out and turned to powder.

General Sentences

_____ 1. American land has been overplowed and overplanted for decades.

_____ 2. In the 1930s, a large part of the United States turned into what came to be called the "Great Dust Bowl."

_____ 3. Poor farming techniques cause hardships for many countries.

Specific Sentences 6. a. The creators of the search engine Google are not particularly happy that "to google" has become a verb referring to Web searches performed with search engines other than Google.

b. Xerox Corporation produced the first plain paper photocopier in 1959, which became so famous, "xeroxing" became a synonym for "photocopying."

c. The company Kimberly-Clark came up with the brand name Kleenex sometime in the 1920s; however, many people now refer to facial tissues as "kleenex," even if they are not talking about the ones produced by Kimberly-Clark.

General
Sentences

_____ **1.** In the twentieth century, American companies earned a reputation for creativity and originality by creating products and services that revolutionized daily life.

_____ **2.** Over time, some brand-name products became so popular, people began using the brand name to describe the thing being sold or used.

_____ **3.** Google is not the only company unhappy about having its trademark used as a general descriptive term.

Specific Sentences **7.** a. When actor Robert Coates liked the lines in one of Shakespeare's death scenes, he would repeat the scene over and over until angry theatergoers pelted him with oranges.

b. Coates forgot his lines every night, so he made up his own for well-known plays such as *Hamlet* and *King Lear*.

c. England's theater critics laughingly called the actor "Romeo" Coates because he would stop the show to wave to friends and chat with people in the audience.

General
Sentences

_____ **1.** Robert Coates, a nineteenth-century stage performer, may have been the most incompetent Shakespearean actor who ever lived.

_____ **2.** Actor Robert Coates played many of Shakespeare's most famous characters during the early 1800s.

_____ **3.** Handsome costumes mattered very much to British actor Robert Coates.

Specific Sentences **8.** a. A blue fireball exploded above central Siberia when an asteroid* hit near the Tunguska River on June 30, 1908.

---
*asteroid: small or minor planet.

b. A mushroom cloud bloomed in the air, and trees were uprooted and scorched for dozens of miles.

c. An entire herd of reindeer died because of the heat the asteroid produced, while its impact shattered windows as far away as 600 miles.

General Sentences

_____ **1.** Scientists believe that asteroids are ancient chunks of matter that never clumped together to become planets.

_____ **2.** Most asteroids are grouped into belts that hang in space.

_____ **3.** When an asteroid crashed to earth in 1908, it caused great damage.

Specific Sentences **9.**

a. In sign language, we use hands and other body parts to make gestures that stand for letters, words, and concepts.

b. Morse code requires a wire telegraph machine to produce sounds—dots and dashes—that are translated into letters, numbers, and punctuation.

c. Often seen at airports, the semaphore, or flag signaling system, works this way: A person stands holding a flag in each hand, then moves his or her arms to positions that indicate letters and numbers.

General Sentences

_____ **1.** Mass communication means that messages are sent to large audiences.

_____ **2.** Some communication methods do not rely on written language.

_____ **3.** Simple writing systems date back to the Sumerians of 3000 B.C.

Specific Sentences **10.**

a. Using the milk from 6,000 cows, a 13,440-pound cheese was produced for an exhibit at the 1937 New York State Fair.

b. In 1801, a Massachusetts preacher, John Leland, presented President Andrew Jackson with a 1,200-pound Cheshire cheese made in Leland's hometown.

c. The Wisconsin Cheese Foundation collected 183 tons of milk for its display in the 1964 World's Fair: a cheese wedge that weighed more than 34,500 pounds and stood six feet high.

General Sentences	_____ 1.	Ancient Romans who created huge cheeses were considered quite eccentric.
	_____ 2.	Canadians proudly show their skill at cheese making during the annual Toronto Fair.
	_____ 3.	Over the years, cheese-loving Americans have produced some pretty big cheeses.

♦ **EXERCISE 9**   **Clarifying General Sentences**

DIRECTIONS   Read each general sentence or generalization. Then circle the letters of the specific sentences that help explain it.

EXAMPLE

General Sentence   After interviewing eighty-five couples who had been married at least fifteen years, author Francine Klagsbrun identified several characteristics that make a happy marriage.

Specific Sentences   (a.) The ability to change and to tolerate change was high on the list of characteristics that make a happy marriage.

b. Married men tend to live longer than single ones do.

c. Women usually marry men who are a few years older than themselves.

(d.) According to Klagsbrun, a belief that marriage is a long-term commitment* appears to be essential to a happy marriage.

(e.) Many married couples insisted that "trust" and fidelity* are key characteristics of a happy marriage.

f. Compared with Europeans, Americans are more likely to get married.

EXPLANATION   The general sentence leaves readers wondering what characteristics make a happy marriage. Specific sentences *a*, *d*, and *e* answer that question, whereas sentences *b*, *c*, and *f* do not.

General Sentence   1. The German psychologist Hermann Ebbinghaus was the first person to systematically study the process of forgetting.

Specific Sentences   a. One theory of forgetting suggests that we forget when new information interferes with old.

b. Ebbinghaus spent thousands of hours memorizing nonsense syllables.

---

*commitment: the state of being bonded emotionally or intellectually to another person.
*fidelity: faithfulness, loyalty.

    c. After learning the nonsense syllables, Ebbinghaus measured the time it took to forget them.

    d. Another theory of forgetting stresses that we forget whenever we don't intend to remember.

    e. As a result of his research, Ebbinghaus discovered that the greatest memory loss occurs right after learning.

    f. Another memory researcher, A. P. Bumstead, discovered that several learning sessions stretched out over time actually decreased forgetting.

General Sentence 2. It's easy to understand why the threat of rabies inspires great fear.

Specific Sentences

    a. In its final stages, rabies produces hallucinations.

    b. Few people recover from rabies once symptoms appear.

    c. Rabies has been around a long time; there are references to it as early as 700 BCE.

    d. Once the disease takes hold, the victim can neither stand nor lie down comfortably.

    e. Recently, scientists have improved the treatment for rabies; the new treatment is much less painful than the old.

    f. In the early stages of rabies, a dog is likely to appear tired and nervous; it will try to hide, even from its master.

General Sentence 3. Many people believe that mystery stories are a product of modern times, but the mystery story actually has a long history.

Specific Sentences

    a. Historians of the detective story claim to have found elements of the mystery story in the pages of the Bible.

    b. Dorothy Sayers was for some years an enormously popular mystery writer.

    c. Poe's "The Murders in the Rue Morgue," published in 1841, presented the classic mystery problem of a dead body found in a sealed room.

    d. Mystery historians are continually arguing about which books may or may not be classified as true mystery stories.

    e. In the nineteenth century, Charles Dickens created a highly amusing character, Inspector Bucket, who in many ways resembles modern-day detectives.

    f. Some mystery writers do not use their real names.

General Sentence 3. Muhammad, the spiritual leader of the Muslims,[†] had an enormous influence on world history.

Specific Sentences
    a. Muhammad was born somewhere around the year 570 CE.

    b. Muhammad founded a religion, Islam, which was to become a major world religion.

    c. Until his fortieth year, Muhammad lived the ordinary life of a well-to-do merchant.

    d. Muhammad's teachings were the source of the Koran, the sacred text of the Muslims, which is still accepted by Muslims as the final authority on all spiritual matters.

    e. Muhammad founded an empire that included lands in Syria, northern Africa, and Spain.

    f. Muhammad was born in Mecca.

Connecting General and Specific Sentences in Paragraphs

Writers always have to make choices about how to approach their readers. Scholarly writers, for instance, often begin by reviewing what other authors have said about the topic or subject. Reviewing past research is the writer's way of giving readers a context so that they can better judge his or her contribution to the discussion.

Writers of newspaper editorials, in contrast, might well open with a colorful anecdote to attract readers and make them keep reading until they get to the point of the article. Textbook writers, however, know they have to pass on numerous new ideas to their readers. Thus they are inclined to open paragraphs with the general point they want to communicate. Here's an example:

General Sentence
[1]Anthropologists who study line-forming behavior have concluded that the way people wait in line reveals a good deal about cultural values.

Specific Sentences
[2]In some Arab countries, where women do not have equal rights, men routinely cut in front of women waiting in line. [3]They see no reason why a man should wait in back of a woman. [4]In Britain and the U.S., where men and women are at least officially considered equal, few men would dare cut ahead of a woman who was standing ahead of them in line. [5]In countries like Italy and Spain, where individuality is

[†]Muslims: believers in Islam, a religion based on the teachings of Muhammad. Muslims believe in one God (Allah). They also believe in paradise and hell.

highly prized above social conformity,* lines are little more than an annoyance to be ignored at will. [6]Men and women routinely jostle for the best position in line, and the poor soul who stands and waits his or her turn is considered to be lacking in spirit.

In this example, the first sentence is a general sentence that announces the paragraph's **main idea** or central point. The remaining more specific sentences then define phrases like "line-forming behavior" and "cultural values." The writer uses the general opening sentence to announce the point of the paragraph and the remaining more specific sentences for clarification and support.

General Sentences in Last Position

Writers of essays sometimes reverse the previous approach. They open with a series of specific sentences leading up to a larger generalization. It's the writer's way of stimulating audience interest. Here's an illustration:

Specific Sentences

[1]Speed dating is currently popular among single men and women in pursuit of a mate. [2]On a "speed date," the women sit at tables while the men circulate, spending anywhere from two to five minutes with any number of females. [3]When the prescribed time is up, the men move on with the temporary couple having decided either to meet again or forget the brief encounter. [4]In another widely reported-on trend, high school students don't talk about "dating," "going steady," or "courting," all of which are considered old-fashioned and uncool. [5]Instead, more and more teenagers agree to be "friends with benefits." [6]This means there will be a certain amount of physical contact, maybe even intercourse, but the two friends are not, or claim not to be, emotionally involved. [7]The physical part of the relationship is the "benefit," and that benefit can end as soon as one friend or the other decides they are no longer interested. [8]There are also anecdotal* reports among women that men no longer bring flowers on a first date while the men complain that young women are more interested in a male's financial success than they are in romantic behavior or courting techniques.

General Sentence

[9]To those of us who remember an earlier time, it's sad but seemingly true that romance is disappearing from the lives of the young and single.

Here the sentences start out specific and build up to a general statement that explains their meaning.

---

*conformity: obedience; willingness to follow rules.
*anecdotal: not scientific; based on personal stories.

READING TIP If the second sentence in a paragraph explains the first, the chances are good that the opening general sentence expresses the main idea.

♦ **EXERCISE 10** Locating the Main Idea

DIRECTIONS Read each paragraph. Then underline the general sentence expressing the main idea. *Note*: That sentence can be the first sentence in the paragraph or the last.

EXAMPLE [1]Senator Joseph McCarthy, the man who did untold harm to the country in the 1950s, pretended to be a dedicated patriot, but all he truly cared about was his own personal ambition. [2]In the early 1940s and 1950s, Americans were anxious about the spread of Communism within their country. [3]At the same time, McCarthy was looking for an attention-getting campaign platform. [4]Taking advantage of the country's fearful mood, the senator decided to launch a modern-day witch hunt. [5]Claiming to possess a list of Communists who were secretly working inside the U.S. government, McCarthy falsely accused not only civil servants[†] but also people in the military, academia, and even Hollywood's film industry. [6]Ultimately, the senator's relentless investigation failed to produce even one Communist. [7]But McCarthy had gotten the publicity he so desperately wanted and, more importantly for his ambitious ego, he had become a powerful man in Washington.

EXPLANATION In this passage, the first sentence is general enough to sum up and include all the others. The more specific supporting sentences explain how McCarthy "pretended to be a dedicated patriot" when he was really dedicated to "his own personal ambition."

1. [1]The eye is made up of many different parts, each one playing a significant role in an individual's ability to see. [2]The eyeball is surrounded by three layers of protective tissue. [3]The outer layer, called the *sclera*, is made from firm, tough, connective tissue and is white in color. [4]The middle layer, called the *choroids coat*, is a delicate network of connective tissue that contains many blood vessels. [5]The inner layer, which is called the *retina*, contains the nerve receptors for vision and approximately ten different layers of nerve cells. [6]Two

[†]civil servants: people working for state and local government.

kinds of nerve cells are contained within the retina: *cones*, which are used mainly for light vision, and *rods*, which are used when it is dark or dim. (Clover, *Sports Medicine Essentials*, p. 385.)

2. [1]Many of the world's most famous artists were either undervalued or ignored during their lifetime. [2]Nineteenth-century impressionist[†] painter Vincent van Gogh, whose paintings now sell for millions of dollars, sold only one painting in his lifetime and died penniless. [3]One of van Gogh's contemporaries, the now-famous painter Paul Gauguin, also died in poverty. [4]The seventeenth-century Dutch painter Rembrandt van Rijn had to file for bankruptcy at age fifty because the art critics of his time dismissed his work as unfashionable. [5]While he was alive, another celebrated Dutch painter, Jan Vermeer, found few buyers for his paintings. [6]Vermeer fell into complete obscurity* after his death in 1675. [7]His work was not rediscovered until the nineteenth century. [8]Of the more than 1,000 works of musical genius Johann Sebastian Bach (1685–1750), only eight were published during his lifetime. [9]Considered a good organ player, Bach was viewed as a mediocre composer. [10]The nineteenth-century poet Emily Dickinson wrote 1,775 poems, but only ten of these were published during her lifetime. [11]Dickinson's slightly older contemporary, *Moby-Dick* author Herman Melville was forced to abandon the idea of earning a living from writing when the public showed little enthusiasm for his work. [12]The sage* of Concord, Henry David Thoreau, sold only 1,700 copies of *Walden* in 1855, the year after it was published. [13]Fewer than 300 copies sold over the next five years, so the publisher did not reprint it. (Source of information: Lucius Furius, "Genius Ignored," www.serve.com/Lucius/GI.index.html.)

3. [1]In addition to the $1, $2, $5, $10, $20, $50, and $100 bills that circulate today, the U.S. Federal Reserve Board once issued and circulated bills in the amount of $500, $1,000, $5,000, and $10,000. [2]On July 14, 1969, however, the Treasury Department announced that these four bills would no longer be printed because they were rarely used. [3]As a result, the $100 bill is the highest denomination* in

---

[†]impressionist: an artist who creates a personal impression or sense of the world rather than a realistic picture.
*obscurity: the state of being unknown.
*sage: wise person; also, wise.
*denomination: a group of units having specific values.

circulation today. [4]Over the years, the Federal Reserve Board has also stopped producing several coin denominations. [5]The denominations include the half-cent, two-cent, three-cent, and twenty-cent copper coins, as well as a small silver coin that was called a half-dime (replaced by the nickel). [6]Although half-dollar and dollar coins are still in circulation, they are no longer either gold or silver as they were in the past. [7]As these examples illustrate, the Federal Reserve Board can and does discontinue or alter both coin and paper currency.

4. [1]In 1968, Billie Jean King joined with several other female tennis players to negotiate professional contracts that would increase their income. [2]Angered that male players received more prize money than females, King was the guiding force in making the women's Virginia Slims Tour a reality in 1970. [3]The next year, she became the first female athlete to win more than $100,000. [4]And no one will forget her 1973 victory over Bobby Riggs in the match that came to be known as the "Battle of the Sexes." [5]King beat Riggs in three sets and forever laid to rest the notion that women choked under pressure. [6]Not surprisingly, Billie Jean King is considered one of the most influential women in the history of tennis.

5. [1]In Poland, soup lovers can now choose from eight different varieties of Campbell's *zupa*, including *flaki*—tripe soup spiced with lots of pepper. [2]In Australia, Campbell's bestseller is pumpkin. [3]To please Mexican palates, Campbell came up with hot and spicy *crema de chile poblano* and *flor de calabaza* (squash soup). [4]Working in its Hong Kong test kitchen, Campbell concocted some recipes it hoped would appeal to the more than two billion consumers in Malaysia, Indonesia, Thailand, the Philippines, Vietnam, and Japan. [5]What did Campbell chefs come up with? [6]Successes include watercress and duck gizzard soup, radish-carrot soup, fig soup, and date soup. [7]The soup maker also developed several flavors of corn soup specifically for markets in Taiwan, Hong Kong, and Singapore. [8]What Campbell discovered is that Asian consumers are willing to buy lots of canned soup if the right soup is in the can. [9]Encouraged by the successful efforts of its chefs in Hong Kong, Campbell decided to launch seventeen varieties of soup in the Chinese province of Guangdong. [10]Clearly, the Campbell Soup Company is trying hard to please an international market. (Adapted from Pride, Hughes, and Kapoor, *Business*, p. 319.)

VOCABULARY CHECK

The following words were introduced in the chapter. Match the word with the definition. Review words, definitions, and original context two or three times before taking the vocabulary test. (The page numbers in parentheses indicate where the word first appeared.)

1. discrimination (p. 138) _____	a. small or minor planet
2. creed (p. 138) _____	b. faithfulness, loyalty
3. asteroid (p. 140) _____	c. wise person; also, wise
4. commitment (p. 142) _____	d. the act of showing prejudice in favor of or against a particular group
5. fidelity (p. 142) _____	e. not scientific; based on personal stories
6. conformity (p. 145) _____	f. belief, religion
7. anecdotal (p. 145) _____	g. obedience; willingness to follow rules
8. obscurity (p. 147) _____	h. a group of units having specific values
9. sage (p. 147) _____	i. the state of being unknown
10. denomination (p. 147) _____	j. the state of being bonded emotionally or intellectually to another person

DIGGING DEEPER Going Global

Looking Ahead   Here's another selection describing how American businesses are wooing an international market. As you read it, look carefully at the sentences to see which ones are more general and which ones are more specific.

1   Ken Krusensterna, owner of a Dallas trucking company, had driven across the border into Mexico for business reasons every week for five years without mishap. The trip was simply part of his routine—until the day he was kidnapped, beaten, and held for ransom. Although he was rescued after two weeks, Krusensterna sold his company rather than return to Mexico on business again.

2   Kidnapping and robbery are relatively remote but real dangers for multinational firms' employees and managers who work in or travel to other countries. Kidnappers in parts of Mexico, Brazil, Argentina, Colombia, and other developing nations sometimes target foreign business people whose employers seem able to pay ransoms totaling thousands or millions of dollars. Thieves also may assault and rob foreign business people. Now companies doing business in other countries are taking a number of precautions to keep their personnel safe from both kidnappers and robbers.

3   Many firms educate their employees about the risks of working and traveling abroad through seminars and frequent updates. Nova Chemicals, based in Canada, sends out regular e-mail warnings about problem areas so that employees know what to expect when they travel. Employees of Nortel Networks know to check the company's intranet for comprehensive safety information before and during an international business trip. Nortel also gives its employees a toll-free phone number to call from any country, at any hour, if they run into trouble and need emergency assistance.

4   Other multinationals go even further. For example, Japanese companies with operations near Tijuana often require transferred executives to live in southern California and travel to their factories on buses protected by armed guards. Some companies hire security specialists to teach their business travelers how to survive if they are attacked or kidnapped, even conducting mock kidnappings to reinforce the skills. At a minimum, experts say that employees who work or travel in other nations should not call attention to themselves. They also should avoid flashing cash in public and keep corporate symbols hidden. Finally, varying the daily routine will make it more difficult for criminals to plan a kidnapping or robbery. (Adapted from Pride, Hughes, and Kapoor, *Business*, p. 317.)

Sharpening Your Skills

DIRECTIONS Answer the questions by circling the letters of the correct response.

1. Which one of the following general statements sums up the entire reading?
   a. Although he was rescued after two weeks, Krusensterna sold his company rather than return to Mexico on business again.
   b. Thieves may assault and rob foreign businesspeople.
   c. Companies doing business in other countries are now taking a number of precautions to keep their personnel safe.
   d. Many firms educate their employees about the risks of working and traveling abroad through seminars and frequent updates.

2. Which of the following statements about paragraph 1 is correct?
   a. The first sentence is the most general.
   b. The last sentence is the most general.
   c. The first and last sentences are equally specific.

3. Which description fits paragraph 2?
   a. The first sentence is the most general sentence in the paragraph; it sums up the more specific details that follow.
   b. The last sentence is the most general sentence with the previous, more specific sentences illustrating it.

4. In paragraph 3, the more specific sentences answer which question?
   a. What are the risks of traveling abroad?
   b. How often do companies provide frequent updates?
   c. How do firms educate employees about risks?

Making Connections What general statement can you come up with that could include both the information from the selection you just read and the information from the paragraph on page 148?

_____

_____

_____

_____

_____

Drawing Your Own Conclusions   Based on the reading, do you think all the companies doing business overseas view the threat of robbery and kidnapping with the same degree of seriousness?

_____

_____

_____

▶ TEST 1   Vocabulary Review

DIRECTIONS   Fill in the blanks with one of the words listed below.

creed	discrimination	asteroid	sage	denominations
conformity	fidelity	obscurity	anecdotal	commitment

1. In October 2008, scientists celebrated the first successful prediction of when a(n) _____ would fly into Earth's atmosphere.

2. King Arthur loved both his queen Guinevere and his young knight Lancelot, never doubting for a moment their _____ to him, and for that, Arthur paid dearly.

3. Once the accident had mutilated his face, the actor wanted nothing more than to lead his life in complete _____, so no one would ever recognize him.

4. There is no scientific proof that mind reading is possible; all of the so-called proof is purely _____.

5. When she cashed her check, she asked for bills in various _____.

6. For the young nun, the Catholic _____ was nothing to joke about, and she blushed deeply at her companion's remarks.

7. When people get older, they are supposed to become wiser, but my uncle is no more a(n) _____ now than he was when he was twenty.

8. In the late nineteenth century, the Chinese immigrants who worked on the railroad were victims of _____: Although their labor was much prized, they were treated badly by both employers and coworkers.

9. Like many ambitious people, he could not decide whether his _____ should be to his family or to his job; in the end, he chose his job and lost his family.

10. _____ plays a big role in the lives of many teenagers; they are uncomfortable if they don't share the interests and behavior of their peers.

▶ TEST 2   Distinguishing Between General and Specific Sentences

DIRECTIONS   Read each pair of sentences. Then mark the general sentence with a *G* and the more specific one with an *S*.

1. a. In wintertime, the body temperature of a woodchuck undergoes a steep drop of many degrees. _____

    b. In wintertime, the body temperature of a woodchuck drops from 90°F to around 40°F. _____

2. a. The fats found in fish, nuts, and vegetables may actually help protect you from heart disease. _____

    b. Not all fats are bad; in fact, some may be good for you. _____

3. a. The temperature of Antarctica is changing; it is not as cold as it used to be. _____

    b. Current Antarctic temperatures are nine degrees higher than they were fifty years ago. _____

4. a. According to a sixteen-year-long class action suit, the oil company Texaco (now owned by Chevron) dumped billions of gallons of toxic waste water into the rainforest of Ecuador between 1964 and 1990. _____

    b. For years, the country of Ecuador and the oil company Chevron have been locked in a lawsuit; the suit involves claims that the oil giant is responsible for massive pollution of the country's Amazon rainforest. _____

5. a. Many records claim that baseball was first played in 1846, but some evidence suggests the game is older than that. _____

    b. In her 1818 novel *Northanger Abbey*, author Jane Austen refers to a game called baseball, suggesting that the game was played before 1846. _____

▶ **TEST 3**   **Distinguishing Between General and Specific Sentences**

DIRECTIONS   Read each pair of sentences. Then mark the general sentence with a G and the more specific one with an S.

1. a. We tend to take birds for granted, but birds, like most living creatures, can surprise us with their unusual abilities. _____

   b. The ruby-throated hummingbird has the rare ability to fly backward and upside-down. _____

2. a. In the early fifties, Puerto Rico's form of government underwent a major change. _____

   b. In June 1950, Puerto Ricans voted to make the island a commonwealth.† _____

3. a. Around the Caribbean island of Bequia, ten-man teams hunt forty-ton humpback whales in wooden sailboats, armed only with harpoons the fishermen throw by hand. _____

   b. In the Caribbean, a small group of fishermen pursue their prey much like their ancestors once did, using old-fashioned methods and tools. _____

4. a. In the 1970s, the first U.S. space shuttle got its name from a popular science fiction television series. _____

   b. In 1977, urged by fans of the TV series *Star Trek*, President Gerald Ford asked NASA to name the first U.S. space shuttle *Enterprise*. _____

---

†commonwealth: self-governing political unit voluntarily associated with the United States.

▶ **TEST 4**   ### Recognizing the Most General Sentence

DIRECTIONS   In each group of sentences, one is more general than the others. Circle the letter of the most general statement.

1. a. When a Hmong† person dies, a string must be knotted around his or her finger and tied to a slaughtered cow or pig.

    b. Hmong mourners burn small boats folded from gold or silver paper, and do so very close to the dead person's body.

    c. One Hmong death ritual is to play a mouth organ with long reed pipes, pound on a drum, and strike a metal gong.

    d. When the Hmong, a mountain people from Southeast Asia, settled in the United States, they brought with them their funeral customs.

    e. At a Hmong funeral two relatives dress in the dead person's clothes and pretend to be him or her, greeting guests who come to view the body.

    f. Hmong mourning starts with a twenty-four-hour vigil attended by hundreds of people who chant, wail, and cry as loudly as possible.

2. a. In ancient Britain, gathering and hanging mistletoe were winter traditions.

    b. During feasts, the ancient Romans draped their homes with mistletoe.

    c. The custom of kissing or embracing under a branch of mistletoe has been around for centuries and is part of many cultures.

    d. The early Scandinavians considered mistletoe a symbol of love.

    e. In ancient Britain, if enemies met under the mistletoe, they would have to lay down their weapons and embrace.

    f. In the fourth century, the Christian Church outlawed the hanging of mistletoe because it was associated with pagan traditions, but many people ignored the church's law.

3. a. In Mexican-American families, young children are rarely separated from their mothers.

    b. Unless forced to by financial need, Mexican-American mothers generally stay home with their children.

---

†Hmong: a group of people who made their home in Laos and who supported the United States during the Vietnam war (1961–1975).

c. In Mexican-American families, the children usually come first.

d. Although the children are mainly the mother's responsibility, fathers are deeply involved in decisions about the children's upbringing and future.

e. Fathers often work two or more jobs so that mothers can stay home with the children.

f. When a baby is born to a Mexican-American couple, both parents frequently rearrange their lives to care for the child.

4. a. In AD 1466, Pope Gelasius ordered a celebration in honor of the martyred Saint Valentine.

b. The earliest known valentine was written in 1415.

c. Saint Valentine's Day has been celebrated for centuries.

d. By the sixteenth century, it had become a tradition for lovers to exchange gifts on Saint Valentine's Day.

e. It was in the sixteenth century that the image of Cupid became associated with Saint Valentine's Day.

f. In 1797, a British publisher put together *The Young Man's Valentine Writer*, a collection of verses for young men who needed help writing their own valentines.

5. a. People who use amphetamines tend to perceive situations unrealistically and as a result don't handle them well.

b. People who use large doses of amphetamines have trouble sleeping.

c. People who use amphetamines often find that they are unable to stop talking.

d. Under the influence of amphetamines, people usually feel they are working more efficiently; unfortunately, this impression is seldom accurate.

e. Amphetamines, also known as *speed*, are dangerous drugs with serious side effects.

f. Loss of appetite is a common side effect of amphetamines.

▶ **TEST 5**   ## Recognizing the Most General Sentence

DIRECTIONS   In each group of sentences, one is more general than the others. Circle the letter of the most general statement.

1. a. In the African country of Dahomey, music historians were carefully trained to preserve important records.

    b. There was a time when the music of Africa was also the history of the African people.

    c. In the African country of Burundi, singers followed soldiers to war and recorded great actions in song.

    d. Many African countries trained men and women to be living books who could record important events in song.

    e. If the songs contained important information, some African musicians had to learn them in secret.

    f. In the Sudan, singers recited the history of the nation at public gatherings and sang the deeds of great heroes.

2. a. Tornadoes are clouds shaped like funnels: they reach all the way to the ground, doing enormous damage.

    b. Although all storms have fearful aspects, tornadoes are the most frightening.

    c. Winds within the funnel of the tornado can reach speeds of more than several hundred miles per hour.

    d. Tornadoes strike without warning: they seem to come out of nowhere.

    e. Sometimes buildings actually blow up as the tornado passes over them.

    f. The heavy rain and hail that accompany a tornado also do much damage.

3. a. Because of the way he looked, John Merrick (1862–1890) could not go into the street without being mobbed by curious strangers who stared at and ridiculed him.

    b. Before he came under a doctor's care, John Merrick was exhibited in the circus, like an animal.

c. The victim of a terrible and deforming disease, John Merrick could not sleep like other people; he had to sit up with his heavy head resting on his knees.

d. The head of the Elephant Man was enormous and misshapen.

e. John Merrick, also known as the Elephant Man, had a brief and all too painful life.

f. John Merrick never forgot the brutal beatings and terrible humiliation of his life in the circus.

4. a. It took a while for L. Frank Baum, author of *The Wonderful Wizard of Oz*, to find just the right title for his masterpiece.

b. While the book was in production, Baum changed the title to *From Kansas to Fairyland*.

c. An author sometimes has great difficulty choosing the title of a book.

d. When Baum first submitted his manuscript in 1899, it was called *The Emerald City*.

e. Just before the book appeared in print, Baum changed the title again, this time to *The City of the Great Oz*.

f. In the end, the book was published in 1900 as *The Wonderful Wizard of Oz*.

5. a. Supervisors at the Levi Strauss company patrol hallways, making sure no one wears tank tops or flip-flops.

b. When major corporations relax their dress codes, they still use a variety of methods to let employees know what's acceptable.

c. The S. C. Johnson Wax firm prints a pamphlet with "What's Hot and What's Not" clothes guidelines, then distributes it with paychecks.

d. Two Sears mannequins are dressed in casual clothing, then placed in the cafeteria of the company's headquarters.

e. Morgan Stanley, an investment firm, issues formal memos that outline changes in policy—for example, allowing women executives to shed their pantyhose in warm weather.

f. The Society of Human Resources Management holds an "outfits" fair for employees, offering information booths, trivia games, and prizes.

▶ **TEST 6**   Identifying General Sentences in Paragraphs

DIRECTIONS   Read each paragraph and underline the general sentence that opens or closes the paragraph.

1. [1]One of the ancient world's seven wonders, the Great Pyramid of Giza, was the tallest structure in the world for forty-three centuries. [2]Consisting of about two million blocks of stone, each weighing two tons, the Great Pyramid was pushed or pulled into place with human muscle alone. [3]The other tomb on the list of seven wonders, the 140-foot-tall Mausoleum at Halicarnassus, was not only gigantic but also adorned with beautiful statues and carvings. [4]Another wonder, the Hanging Gardens of Babylon, consisted of tiers of terraces that were supported with stone columns. [5]Each terrace was watered with a complex irrigation system so that lush plant life would thrive above ground level and over visitors' heads. [6]The Lighthouse at Alexandria, which was as tall as a 40-story building, was covered with white marble and contained a mirror that could reflect light for miles. [7]Among the seven wonders were two statues considered wondrous for both size and artistry. [8]Made of ivory and gold, the statue of Zeus stood as tall as a 4-story building. [9]The statue of the sun god Apollo, called the Colossus of Rhodes, was a 110-foot-high bronze structure that took twelve years to build. [10]The seventh wonder, the Temple of Artemis at Ephesus, was widely considered to be the most beautiful structure in the world. [11]Built to honor the Greek goddess of hunting and nature, this marble building included 127 columns, each 60 feet high, and housed paintings and statues created by the greatest artists of the time. [12]The Seven Wonders of the Ancient World were all massive marvels of engineering genius. (Source of information: Alaa Ashmawy, "The Seven Wonders of the Ancient World," http://ce.eng.usf.edu/pharos/wonders/.)

2. [1]Federalist[†] architecture was designed to reflect democratic ideals. [2]The government buildings erected in the Federalist style from 1790 to 1820 were inspired by the temples of Greece and Rome because America's founders admired these two ancient civilizations. [3]Like the

---

[†]Federalist: related to the belief that individual states should recognize the authority of a central government.

structures they were modeled after, Federalist buildings were constructed of materials such as stone, brick, and marble to symbolize the enduring nature of democracy. [4]The huge buildings' columns and domes suggested the grand and dignified proceedings that were to take place within them. [5]Their Roman porticos, or porches, were designed to draw citizens to the great meeting places where they could participate in government. [6]And the buildings' shapes and symmetry reflected the equality, order, and stability of republican values. [7]The rectangular floor plans and the balanced, parallel features of the structures' exteriors signified the democratic nature of the government functions they housed. [8]The round shapes of the rotundas and circular windows stood for the eternal nature of democratic principles.

3. [1]Odd as it may seem, several journalists who plagiarized or in some cases simply invented their stories ultimately profited from their wrongdoing. [2]In 2003, reporter Jayson Blair was fired by the *New York Times* when it was found that he had plagiarized news stories and made up dozens of others. [3]Just months after the scandal broke, however, Blair was in discussion with television producers about selling his story. [4]He had also begun writing a book expected to bring him handsome profits. [5]Another fraud, writer-editor Stephen Glass, made up stories and printed them as fact. As a result, he was fired in 1998 by his employer, *New Republic* magazine. [6]Five years later Glass had six-figure movie and book deals based on his life story. [7]Then there was *Boston Globe* columnist Mike Barnicle, who was forced to resign in 1998 when his plagiarism became public knowledge. [8]Today, Barnicle is a columnist for the *Boston Herald* and he regularly appears on television as a critic and commentator. [9]Barnicle's fellow *Boston Globe* columnist Patricia Smith was fired for inventing quotes in her stories, yet she now writes for several publications. [10]Elizabeth Wurtzel was fired by the *Dallas Morning News* for plagiarism, too, but she went on to write for *New York* magazine as well as *The New Yorker*, and she has authored a number of best-selling books. (Source of information: Maria Puente, "Disgrace, Dishonor, Infamy: They're Not So Bad Anymore," *USA Today*, May 22, 2003, p. 1D, www.usatoday.com/usaonline/20030522/5180112x.htm.)

4. [1]Textbooks have long taught that the seventeenth-century English settlement at Jamestown, Virginia, struggled and almost perished

because the colonists didn't like hard work. [2]Historians believed that the colonists were more interested in finding gold than in getting their hands dirty. [3]However, when scientists analyzed the rings of Jamestown cypress trees during a 1998 climate study, they found that the trees' growth was significantly stunted between 1606 and 1612. [4]Based on this information, the study's authors argued that when Jamestown was founded in 1607, a lack of rain caused fresh water supplies to dry up and parched corn to turn brown on the stalk. [5]The subsequent food shortage would have aggravated relations between the colonists and the Powhatan Indians, who were also forced to compete for scarce resources. [6]In 1608, Captain John Smith noted in his journal that the Indians would not trade corn for colonists' goods because that year's crop had been poor, and the Indians did not have enough for themselves. [7]Based on current research, it now seems possible that a drought, rather than laziness or greed, was to blame for Jamestown's troubles. (Source of information: Jeffery L. Sheler, "Rethinking Jamestown," *Smithsonian*, January 2005, pp. 48–56.)

From Topics to Topic Sentences

IN THIS CHAPTER, YOU WILL LEARN

- how to determine the *topic* of a paragraph.

- how to get from the topic to the *main idea* of the paragraph.

- how to recognize *topic sentences* expressing the main idea.

- the most common locations for textbook topic sentences.

- how to paraphrase topic sentences for reading notes.

*"Understanding depends on mutual empathy,
on reader and writer appreciating each other's task."*
—Larry Wright, professor and philosopher

Sometimes when you read a paragraph, the meaning will seem to jump out at you. This is especially true if you are familiar with the subject matter and have acquired the appropriate background knowledge. At other times, however, the text you are reading will take some effort to understand. To help you with those more difficult texts, this chapter offers a step-by-step strategy for getting to the author's meaning.

Determining the Topic

To make sense of paragraphs, particularly difficult ones, you first need to determine the **topic**, or the subject under discussion. The topic is the person, place, idea, object, or event the author wants to explore with readers. Because paragraphs usually mention several people, places, and events, you need a strategy for figuring out which one of those is actually the paragraph's topic.

The strategy recommended here is as follows: Look for the word or phrase most frequently repeated or referred to *throughout* the paragraph. Once you identify the word or words receiving the most *repetition and reference* throughout, you'll also know the paragraph topic. Take this example:

> [1]In the nineteenth century, baseball emerged as the most popular new urban sport. [2]The game first appeared in its modern form in the 1840s when a group of wealthy New Yorkers organized the Knickerbocker Club. [3]Then in 1862, in Brooklyn, William H. Cammeyer built the first enclosed baseball field in the country. [4]However, it was not until 1869 that teams began to charge admission and pay players. [5]In 1876, eight teams—New York, Philadelphia, Hartford, Boston, Chicago, Louisville, Cincinnati, and St. Louis—came together to form the National League of Professional Baseball Clubs. [6]By the late 1880s, annual attendance at National League games had reached eight million, while men and boys in vacant lots and empty streets were emulating professional players. (Adapted from Gillon and Matson, *The American Experiment*, p. 747.)

The topic of this paragraph has to be "baseball" because that's the word most frequently repeated or referred to in the paragraph. Let's look again at the paragraph. This time all references to baseball are in italics.

[1]In the nineteenth century, *baseball* emerged as the *most popular new urban sport.* [2]*The game* first appeared in *its modern form* in the 1840s when a group of wealthy New Yorkers organized the Knickerbocker Club. [3]Then in 1862, in Brooklyn, William H. Cammeyer built the first enclosed *baseball* field in the country. [4]However, it was not until 1869 that *teams* began to charge admission and pay *players.* [5]In 1876, eight *teams—New York, Philadelphia, Hartford, Boston, Chicago, Louisville, Cincinnati, and St. Louis—*came together to form the National League of Professional *Baseball* Clubs. [6]By the late 1880s, annual attendance at *National League games* had reached eight million, while men and boys in vacant lots and empty streets were emulating *professional players.*

The sample paragraph makes an important point about paragraph topics: Writers don't just repeat a word or phrase to keep the topic threading its way through a passage. Often they rely on substitutes. Take the second sentence of the baseball paragraph. Here the writers develop the topic—and avoid tedious repetition—by using a general category word, "game," to represent baseball. Because context eliminates any questions about which game the writer has in mind, the word *game* acts as a substitute or stand-in for "baseball." Writers use general-category substitutes like this to create **chains of repetition and reference** that keep the topic before readers' eyes without repeating the same words or phrases over and over again.

Notice, too, that in sentence 4 of the baseball paragraph, the authors mention the word *teams.* In the context of this paragraph, the word *teams* is clearly associated with the word *baseball* and, therefore, **implies**, or suggests, the topic.

This implied, or suggested, presence of a word or phrase is another common device writers use to refer to the topic: A word or phrase associated with the topic implies its presence and keeps the subject of the paragraph front and center in readers' minds.

Reference Through Examples

Another way writers imply, or suggest, the topic in addition to explicitly naming it is illustrated in the next paragraph. Here the author keeps the topic in front of readers mainly through examples, which illustrate the topic, "Charles Lindbergh's independent character":

Charles Lindbergh's strong and independent character shaped every event in his altogether spectacular life. In 1927, when he decided to fly nonstop over the Atlantic, everyone said it was impossible. But Lindbergh didn't listen. He flew anyway, becoming an international hero. In 1933, when the public demanded that he return a medal given to him by the Nazis, Lindbergh refused. No matter how unpopular his decision, he was not about to bend to the opinion of others. True to character, Lindbergh also planned his own funeral. Typically, he refused to leave such an important event in anyone else's hands. Charles Lindbergh wanted to die just as he had lived—on his own terms.

In this case, four examples of Lindbergh's behavior evoke, or call up, the topic of the paragraph—Lindbergh's independent character or spirit.

Reference Through Pronouns

In the paragraph that follows, the authors use pronouns that repeatedly refer to George Washington, the topic of the paragraph. The pronouns have been italicized to make them stand out.

[1]By February 4, 1789, the election of senators and Congress members was just about complete. [2]Now it was time for electors* in each state to meet and choose the nation's first president. [3]To no one's surprise, their choice was George Washington, a former general in the revolutionary army. [4]Although Washington had not sought the position, *he* knew the nation expected *him* to serve, and *he* was willing and ready to do so. [5]The general was among the very few in the revolutionary generation to have a national reputation. [6]*He* was hailed as the hero of the Revolution. [7]*He* also looked and acted the part of the dignified, virtuous patriot. [8]Thus, it's no surprise that Washington became president by a unanimous vote of the Electoral College.[†] [9]For regional balance—Washington was from Virginia—New Englander John Adams was chosen as *his* vice president. (Adapted from Berkin et al., *Making America*, p. 198.)

---

*electors: people chosen to cast their vote for president.
†Electoral College: The Electoral College refers to a process in which each state holds a specific number of votes. In the presidential election, whoever wins the state wins those electoral votes.

Using pronouns like *he* and *him*, the authors avoid excessive repetition while maintaining a chain of repetition and reference that spotlights their topic.

Here's the point of these examples: The topic of a paragraph can be mentioned or referred to in a variety of ways. Your job as a reader is to track the chain of repetition and references woven throughout the paragraph. It's that chain of repetition and reference that determines the topic under discussion.

READING TIP If a text is particularly difficult to read, pronouns are often the source of the confusion. If you are struggling with a passage, re-read it to nail down the *antecedent*, or reference, for every pronoun.

♦ **EXERCISE 1** **Determining the Topic**

DIRECTIONS Read each paragraph and circle the appropriate letter to identify the topic.

EXAMPLE In the nineteenth century, American and British fishermen nearly wiped out the seals of Antarctica. The Antarctic seals, however, after almost becoming extinct, have made an astonishing comeback, and the population is now rapidly increasing. Although scientists admit that other factors may be responsible for the seal's return, they are convinced that the severe decrease in the baleen whale population is a major cause. The baleen whale and the Antarctic seal once competed for the same food source—a tiny shellfish called krill. With the baleen whale practically extinct now, the seals have inherited an almost unlimited food supply. That increase in the seals' food supply is considered a major reason for the seals' comeback.

Who or what is most frequently mentioned or referred to in the paragraph?
a. the decline of the Antarctic seal
b. the disappearance of the baleen whale
c. the comeback of Antarctic seals

EXPLANATION Just about every sentence in the paragraph mentions or refers to the seals of Antarctica or their comeback from near extinction. Thus *c* is the correct answer. Neither the decline of the Antarctic seals nor the disappearance of the baleen whale is mentioned as frequently.

a brilliant military strategist. However, none of these activities interfered with the composer's love of music. Boulogne wrote and performed music throughout his lifetime, stopping only when he was imprisoned for a brief period after the Revolution.

a. French composers

b. Joseph Boulogne's all-black regiment

c. the exciting life of Joseph Boulogne

d. French Revolution

The Granger Collection, New York

Mary Love, who arrived in Montana in 1884, was six feet tall, packed a pair of six-guns, and threatened to break the nose of any man who dared to insult her.

2. When Americans think of the Wild West, they don't usually imagine it inhabited by African-Americans. Yet this image of the West—without the presence of black people—is completely inaccurate. In truth, thousands of African-Americans helped settle the West, even though few Hollywood films have acknowledged their existence. In 1951, for example, Hollywood released a movie called *Tomahawk*. The white actor Jack Oakie played a character named Sol Beckworth. Yet in reality, Beckworth was a black cowboy who struck it rich during the California gold rush. Similarly, Oklahoma, the location for many Westerns, was the site of several African-American communities, although none of them has ever appeared on film. It's time for Hollywood to acknowledge its historical error and make films showing African-Americans taking part in the westward movement.

a. African-Americans in Westerns

b. Jack Oakie

c. Oklahoma portrayed in Westerns

d. African-Americans in early films

3. If you could choose whether your baby would be male or female, would you do it? What about selecting your baby's eye and hair color, or deciding whether the child would be a talented athlete or an accomplished musician? If the polls are to be believed, many people would like the chance to make these decisions. Unfortunately, in a relatively short time, reproductive technology may well be available so that parents can, in fact, create the designer babies of their dreams. However, having the ability to create designer babies does not mean that we should allow parents to treat children as if they were cars. Although it's perfectly acceptable to go to the car dealer and select the options we want our cars to have, this same principle should

never be applied to human beings. It is morally wrong to create a child according to preference. In effect, this attitude toward human life amounts to playing God because God is the only one who should decide such matters, and we should not try to pick and choose our children's qualities or characteristics.

a. babies and cars
b. designer babies
c. polls about raising children
d. reproductive technology

4. When a new president is sworn in, Americans eagerly await the inaugural address, which has long seemed an essential part of the new president's arrival in office. What many don't realize, though, is that American presidents did not always think it so important to address their fellow citizens; like presidential powers, the inaugural address has evolved over the years. When George Washington was sworn in as the country's first president, he made a speech, to be sure. His audience, however, was limited to Congress, and making the speech had been Washington's personal choice. As the first president to be inaugurated in Washington, Thomas Jefferson did give a speech. But he gave it in the partially built Capitol building, and his audience was limited to members of Congress plus a few visiting dignitaries.* In 1817, James Monroe was the first to deliver his inaugural address in the open air, but he did not do so because he wanted to get closer to his fellow Americans. He did it because the Capitol was being renovated.* The president who finally made the inaugural address an institution was Andrew Jackson. Jackson addressed his speech to the American public, who turned out in droves to hear him.

a. the changes in the presidency
b. development of the inaugural address
c. Thomas Jefferson's inaugural address
d. Andrew Jackson's presidency

---

*dignitaries: people in high positions.
*renovated: repaired.

Phrasing the Topic

As you undoubtedly noticed when completing Exercises 1 and 2, the topic can't always be expressed in a single word. That raises the question, how do you know when a phrase rather than a single word is necessary? Here's the answer: If the topic needs to be expressed in a phrase, the paragraph will contain more than one chain of repetition and reference. Take, for example, the following:

> [1]Human beings, like all living creatures, are driven by certain innate instincts, drives, or needs. [2]All living organisms feel an impulse to maintain life, which causes them to seek nourishment. [3]They have a compulsion to reproduce, which finds its expression in sex. [4]Although much of the behavior of lower animals appears to be regulated by instincts, this is not true of human behavior. [5]Human beings have tamed their instincts and subordinated them to their attitudes toward the environment. [6]At times, human beings deny or disobey their natural instincts because of their social roles or relationships. [7]A prisoner of war may die rather than betray his or her country. [8]A child may refuse food if he believes that such a tactic gives him an advantage in a power struggle with his parents. (Adapted from Engler, *Personality Theories*, p. 99.)

In this passage, both human behavior and the role of instinct are repeatedly mentioned or referred to. When two different chains of repetition and reference make their way through a paragraph, as they do here, it indicates that the topic should be expressed in a phrase rather than a single word. Thus, the topic here would be "human beings and instinctive behavior," or "the role of instinct in human behavior," or even "human beings and instincts." And, yes, the phrase expressing the topic can take several forms as it does here. What's important is that the phrase incorporate the key words from both chains of repetition and reference.

Before turning to the next set of exercises, see if you can determine the topic of the following paragraph. When you think you know what person, place, event, or idea is most frequently repeated or referred to in the paragraph, write that topic into the blank at the end of the paragraph.

> [1]In 1804, as Lewis and Clark ascended the Missouri, they spent their first winter camped near the Mandan and Hidasa villages in modern North Dakota. [2]Like other nineteenth-century Europeans or Americans who visited these communities, the explorers were impressed by the

Mandans' large earth lodges. [3]Indeed, these lodges were among the largest and most substantial Native American residences north of Mexico, and they provided admirable shelter for people facing the central and northern Great Plains. [4]The artists Karl Bodmer and George Catlin later visited these villages, and their sketches and paintings provide a rich visual portrayal of the Mandans' lodge houses. (Adapted from Edmunds et al., *The People*, p. 199.)

If you figured out that the answer was not "Lewis and Clark" or "Bodmer and Catlin" but the "Mandans' earth lodges," then you have thoroughly understood this chapter section. Throughout the paragraph, the Mandans and the earth lodges are consistently referred to or repeated within the paragraph, making the phrase "Mandans' earth lodges" the logical topic.

SUMMING UP THE KEY POINTS

1. The topic is the person, place, event, idea, or thing being discussed or commented on in a paragraph.
2. The topic is repeatedly mentioned or referred to throughout a paragraph.
3. Readers can determine the topic by tracking the chain (or chains) of repetition and reference that identify the paragraph's topic.
4. Writers keep the topic before the reader's eyes by repeating the same word or referring to it through pronouns, examples, noun substitutes, and associated words.
5. If there is more than one chain of repetition and reference in a paragraph, the topic needs to be expressed in a phrase rather than a single word.

◆ **EXERCISE 3**   Phrasing the Topic

DIRECTIONS   Read each paragraph. In the blank at the end, write a phrase that identifies the topic.

EXAMPLE   The period 1950–1957 (these dates are rough approximations) is often called the first generation of computing. This era saw the appearance of UNIVAC I, the first computer built for sale, and the IBM 701, the first computer built by the company that would soon become a leader in this new field. These early systems were bulky, expensive, slow, and unreliable. They used vacuum tubes for processing and storage, and they were extremely difficult to maintain. The act of turning the machine on could alone blow out a dozen tubes! For this reason, first-generation machines were used only by trained personnel and only in specialized locations, such as in large corporations, in government and university labs, and on military installations, which could provide this expensive support environment.

On April 29, 1952, IBM President Thomas J. Watson Jr. announced to stockholders that he was building the "most flexible high-speed computer in the world."

Photo by Al Fenn/Time Life Pictures/Getty Images

Topic first-generation computers or computing; early computer systems, first computer

EXPLANATION The phrase expressing the topic of this paragraph has to combine two threads that run through the paragraph. It's certainly about computers. However, the topic is not just computers and how they work or what they can do. It's specifically about "first-generation computers" or the "first computers ever used."

1. Earlier lab tests had suggested that the herbal supplement ginkgo biloba could ward off Alzheimer's disease in the elderly. However, an

eight-year study of ginkgo biloba's use among the aging suggests that previous hopes for the herb's effect were unfounded. Starting in 2000, Steven DeKosky and his colleagues at the University of Virginia School of Medicine in Charlottesville studied a group of 3,000 subjects with an average age of 79. All participants in the study were free of Alzheimer's disease at the time the study started. All were given either two gingko pills per day or two placebos.* By 2006, just about equal numbers of the study participants—those taking the supplement and those not—had developed some degree of dementia,* a symptom that usually marks the onset of Alzheimer's disease. The trend continued into 2008, when the study ended. Thus the study results suggest that the supplement does nothing to delay the development of Alzheimer's.

Topic _____

2. Why do we dream? The short answer is that no one really knows. Some evidence suggests that dreaming may help us consolidate* old memories with the new learning that occurred during the day. Yet research support for these claims remains inconsistent. Dreams may have other functions as well. Ernest Hartmann, a leading dream investigator, believes dreams help us sort through possible solutions to everyday problems and concerns. Another prominent theory holds that dreams represent an attempt by the brain to make sense of the random* discharges of electrical activity that occur during REM sleep. The electrical activity arises from the brainstem, the part of the brain responsible for such basic functions as breathing and heart rate. According to this hypothesis, the brain creates a story line to explain those random signals. (Adapted from Nevid, *Psychology: Concepts and Applications*, p. 148.)

Topic *Reasons that we dream*

3. Although the debate continues to this day about how successful the Homestead Act of 1862 truly was—estimates range from a partial

_____

*placebos: substances that have no healing effect on the body but are believed by the people taking them to have medical value.
*dementia: loss of the normal ability to think, concentrate, and remember.
*consolidate: combine.
*random: not occurring according to a set pattern; inconsistent.

success to a total failure—one thing is clear: Many of those who expected great things from the Homestead Act were disappointed, and it did not prove the great blessing many had hoped for. Although the act gave five acres of publicly owned land to every person willing and able to farm it, estimates vary as to how many homesteaders were actually able to carry the land to "patent," i.e., finalize their claims of ownership. There is every indication that only about half of those claiming public lands were able or willing to hold on to them. Many of those homesteaders who went West determined to make a better life for themselves had no idea what they were getting into, and they were shocked by the level of hardship they were expected to endure. In response to the harsh weather and dry earth, many of the early homesteaders gave up and went home. Plagued by mistakes, mismanagement, and fraud, the Homestead Act of 1862 generally benefited land speculators* and big corporations as much as or a good deal more than the settlers it was designed to help.

Topic   <u>Homestead Act   The dissapointment
of the H. A.</u>

4. For decades, minor-to-moderate concussions caused by blows to the head were considered nasty consequences of playing amateur or professional football. Except for the most severe, though, concussions were thought to be disorienting* and painful, but not a huge threat to players' health and well-being. A growing body of evidence, however, suggests that concussions are serious head injuries, and parents of young children might want to think again about letting their kids play football "for fun." When, for instance, researchers studied the medical records of 548 World War II veterans, they discovered a consistent pattern: Veterans who had suffered multiple concussions during the war had a higher likelihood of developing Alzheimer's as they aged. In 2003, editors of the *Journal of Neurology, Neurosurgery & Psychiatry* were worried enough to suggest that those who faced risk of suffering multiple head injuries—for instance, football players or boxers—should be advised of their increased risk for developing Alzheimer's disease. In 2005, scientists at the "National Center for Catastrophic Sports Injury" provided what would seem to be conclusive*

---

*speculators: people who buy something with the expectation of a quick sale and a quick profit.
*disorienting: causing mental confusion.
*conclusive: final; putting an end to doubt.

proof: In testing more than 2,000 retired professional football play-ers, they found that former players who had suffered three or more concussions proved to have more brain disorders than players who had suffered two concussions or fewer. For children and teens who don't play sports in elementary or high school, the seeming connec-tion between concussions and disorders of the brain is not alarming because their chances of getting repeated concussions are small. Children and young adults who play football, however, are at a much higher risk. In any one football or soccer season, 10 percent of all college and 20 percent of all high school players sustain traumatic* brain injuries. In other words, they suffer a concussion, and that's in a single season. (Source of statistics: Robert Burton, "Should Johnny Play Linebacker?" Salon.com, January 13, 2009.)

Topic   *Concussions caused by playing football.*

✔ CHECK YOUR UNDERSTANDING

1. What is the topic of a paragraph?

_____

_____

2. How do you recognize the topic?

_____

3. Can readers locate the topic simply by circling the word that appears most often in the paragraph? Please explain.

_____

_____

4. What does it mean when two or more words are repeated or referred to in a paragraph?

_____

―――――――――

*traumatic: causing serious injury.

From Topic to Main Idea

Imagine that you overheard two friends in conversation and your name came up repeatedly. Curious, you asked them what they were talking about, and they replied in unison, "you." It's doubtful you would be satisfied with this answer. After all, you wouldn't know what your friends were saying *about* you. Their response supplies the topic of the conversation but leaves out the point. Were they saying what a generous, good-hearted person you are or complaining that you are mean-spirited and rude? More than likely, in this situation, you would ask—maybe even demand—to know the conversation's point.

Much the same thing happens with paragraphs. Once you know the subject under discussion, it's all but impossible not to ask, What does the author say about that topic? That's why, as soon as you have a word or phrase expressing the topic, you have to take the next step and identify the main idea. The **main idea** is the central message or point of the paragraph. It's the author's comment on or statement about the topic.

After all, if someone were to ask you what a paragraph was about and you answered with just a word or phrase, say, "the current view of concussions," the person posing the question would probably respond by asking, "Well, what does the author say *about* the current view of concussions?" He or she wouldn't be satisfied with just the topic, and neither should you.

Using the Topic as a Stepping Stone

To illustrate how to get from the topic to the main idea, let's look at the paragraph that follows and start by determining the topic. That means we have to answer the question, What subject does the author repeatedly mention or refer to throughout the paragraph?

[1]For a period of about seventy-five years (1765–1840), the Gothic novel, an early relative of the modern horror story, was popular throughout Europe. [2]Many of the most popular Go written by Horace Walpole, Ann Radcliffe, and M the thousands. [3]They were quickly translated, and giarized. [4]Gothic novels were popular largely beca a mysterious world where ghostly figures flitted thr sageways of ruined buildings, usually in the dead

Gothic novels were read and enjoyed by men and women of all classes, publishers, ever alert to a ready market, made sure that the books were available at bargain prices. [6]Even the poorest members of the working class could afford to pay a penny to enter the Gothic world of terror, and they paid their pennies in astonishing numbers.

In this paragraph, the Gothic novel is the subject to which the author repeatedly returns in every sentence, so we have the topic. Now we have to take the next step and ask another question: What idea is mentioned in general terms and further developed in specific detail? Once we know the answer to that question, we'll also know the main idea.

In this case, the paragraph opens with a general sentence telling us that the Gothic novel was extremely popular in Europe between 1765 and 1840. Notice that sentences 2 through 6 all pick up this thread and more specifically describe the source and extent of that popularity. We learn which authors were especially popular. We also learn that just about everyone enjoyed Gothic novels. Based on the relationship between the opening general sentence and the specific sentences that follow it, we can determine the main idea: "In the eighteenth and nineteenth centuries, Gothic novels were extremely popular throughout Europe."

◆ **EXERCISE 4**   **Identifying the Topic and Main Idea**

DIRECTIONS   Read each paragraph. In the blank at the end, write a phrase that identifies the topic. Then circle the appropriate letter to identify the main idea.

EXAMPLE   In 2009, Burger King created the "Whopper Sacrifice" campaign, offering a free "Big Whopper" to anyone who eliminated ten friends from their Facebook page. Creators of the campaign claimed that by the time it was over, 234,000 friendships had been eliminated from the website, and Burger King had garnered some new customers along with some useful publicity. However, Burger King's "unfriending" campaign also caused some hard feelings when it notified those people who had been dropped in exchange for a Whopper. Not surprisingly, some of those who had been cast off for the sake of a sandwich were miffed. As for those who had deleted their "friends," they didn't necessarily improve the situation with their explanations. Steven Schiff, for instance, wrote this on his personal blog: "Let's be honest here, questionable Facebook friend, we've been keeping you around all this time because we'd just feel bad if you ever found out that you got the ax. It's just, well, up until now nobody offered us a Whopper in exchange for your feelings." Facebook itself, however, was less accepting of Burger King's decision to notify those who had been abandoned for a Whopper. Burger King's access to the site was suspended. (Source of quotation: Douglas Quenqua, "Friends, Until I Delete You," *New York Times* Archives, January 29, 2009.)

Topic ____Facebook and the Whopper Sacrifice campaign; results of the Whopper____

____Sacrifice campaign____

Main Idea   a. Burger King proved that social-networking sites like Facebook and MySpace make a mockery of the word *friendship*.

      b. Burger King made a terrible mistake with its "Whopper Sacrifice" campaign, and the company insulted many of the people it hoped to win over.

      (c.) Burger King's "Whopper Sacrifice" campaign upset many of the people who were eliminated from Facebook in exchange for a Whopper.

> **EXPLANATION**   The correct answer is *c* because the paragraph tells readers about the "hard feelings" created by the campaign. The author might well believe that Facebook makes a mockery of friendship, but there is no attempt to argue that point in the paragraph. In particular, no attempt is made to criticize social-networking sites in general. The paragraph sticks to Facebook and recounts what happened as a result of Burger King's notifying the people who were dropped. Nothing in the paragraph suggests that Burger King made a horrible mistake; in fact, the author says the company got both customers and publicity as a result.

    1. The causes of depression in adolescents are complex and not completely understood by psychologists, but researchers have noticed that depressed children often have depressed parents. Studies of family relationships suggest that there is a genetic component to depression, but they also suggest that certain family climates are typical among depressed children. Children who witness or are victims of domestic violence seem to be particularly at risk for depression. Perhaps abusive parents, whose poor parenting skills may be a result of their own depression, weaken their children's ability to regulate their emotional highs and lows. It might also be true that abusive parents encourage their children to develop negative ideas about social relationships and a depressed outlook on life. (Adapted from Bukatko and Daehler, *Child Development*, p. 396.)

Topic _____

Main Idea
   a. The causes of depression in adolescents are unclear, but researchers believe that genetic inheritance plays a critical role.

   b. Children who suffer from depression have often witnessed domestic violence.

   c. Depression in adolescents can frequently be traced to their family situation.

2. Why does the moon rise at a different time each day? The moon travels in a complete circle about the earth about once a month. So let us say that today the moon rises at 6:00 p.m. Twenty-four hours later, the earth will have rotated once, but in the meantime the moon will have moved a short distance across the sky so that the earth must rotate a little bit extra in order to "catch up" with it. Thus the timing of the moon's rise depends on the moon's position above a point on the earth, and the position of the moon changes according to a cyclical pattern. (Turk and Turk, *Physical Science*, p. 516.)

Topic _____

Main Idea
   a. When the moon rises depends on its position in relation to the earth, which changes as the earth rotates.

   b. When the moon rises depends on how often the moon rotates in 24 hours.

   c. The moon makes a complete circle around the earth every other month.

Topic Sentences and Main Ideas

Topic sentences are general sentences that broadly state the point of the paragraph. Were someone to ask you what a paragraph was about, you could answer by quoting the author's topic sentence. Particularly in textbooks, the first sentence is often the topic sentence, as it is in the following paragraph:

[1]Inhalant abuse, an addictive habit with long-term, sometimes deadly consequences, is the intentional breathing of common household products in order to get high. [2]This intentional breathing is commonly called "huffing," "snuffing," or "bagging." [3]Bagging is the most dangerous

as it entails placing a plastic bag over the head to get a longer effect. [4]Using inhalants over a period of time may result in permanent brain, heart, kidney, and liver damage. [5]Some products like paint and gasoline contain lead and may cause death from lead poisoning. [6]Inhalant abuse is the third most common kind of substance abuse by individuals aged 12 to 14 years, surpassed only by alcohol and tobacco. [7]Symptoms of inhalant abuse include spots or sores around the mouth, a glassy-eyed look, fumes on the breath or clothing, anxiety, and loss of appetite. (Adapted from Neighbors and Tannehill-Jones, *Human Diseases*, p. 414.)

Using almost all the devices mentioned previously, the authors keep the topic "inhalant abuse" running through the paragraph. The associated words "huffing," "snuffing," and "bagging" maintain the topic in sentences 2 and 3, and an example in sentence 4 continues the chain of repetition and reference. However, the main idea related to the topic enters the paragraph via the first sentence, where we learn that inhalant abuse can have long-term consequences. The rest of the paragraph details those consequences.

More on Topic Sentences

Look now at the next paragraph, also from a textbook. Would you say that this paragraph introduces the main idea in the first sentence?

[1]In the 1920s, millions of Americans crowded into halls to watch boxers slug it out in the ring. [2]However, no boxer received more adulation than the boxer Jack Dempsey, who embodied the nation's frontier past. [3]Raised in Manassas, Colorado, he learned to fight in local bars against miners, cowboys, and anyone foolish enough to challenge him. [4]"Jack Dempsey hit like a sledgehammer and absorbed punishment like a sponge," wrote historian Michael Parrish. [5]"He was not a boxer but an earthquake that left blood, flesh, and bone scattered in its wake." [6]During the twenties, his two grueling championship bouts with Gene Tunney proved enormously popular. [7]In 1926, Tunney defeated Dempsey in their first fight before a rain-soaked crowd in Philadelphia. [8]While as many as 150,000 people paid to see their rematch the following year in Chicago, some 50 million listened to it on radio. [9]The referee's famous "long count" may have cost Dempsey the second fight when he knocked Tunney to the canvas but failed to go immediately to a neutral corner. (Gillon and Matson, *The American Experiment*, p. 936.)

In this example, the topic is "the boxer Jack Dempsey." Count how many times his name is repeated or referred to in the paragraph. Dempsey, however, is not even mentioned in the opening sentence. There's a reason for that. The first sentence is not a topic sentence. It's an introductory sentence. It provides context for the second sentence, which is, in fact, the topic sentence.

Introductory sentences provide background about the topic sentence but are not further developed in the paragraph. Once the topic sentence identifies the real focus of the paragraph, the idea in the introductory sentence all but disappears because its work has been done: It has prepared the reader for the topic sentence to follow. As you would expect, the introductory sentences cannot effectively sum up the paragraph.

READING TIP

To test whether a sentence is a topic sentence, turn it into a question. If the remaining sentences answer the question, you've found the topic sentence.

SUMMING UP THE KEY POINTS

1. The *main idea* is the general comment or point the author wants to make about the topic. It's the overall message readers are expected to take from a reading.

2. Like the topic, the author refers to the main idea in almost every sentence. Thus the main idea is developed in both general and specific terms.

3. The *topic sentence* is the sentence the author uses to sum up the main idea. Other people can use their own words to summarize the main idea, but their summary would not be a topic sentence. Only the author can supply that part of a paragraph.

4. Introductory sentences provide background about the topic sentence, but they are not developed after the topic sentence is introduced.

◆ **EXERCISE 5**   **Identifying the Topic Sentence**

DIRECTIONS   Circle the appropriate letter to indicate if the topic sentence is the first sentence or the second sentence in the paragraph.

1. [1]Robust expectations are important because the human body has a tendency to move along the path of the mind's expectations. [2]I learned recently of a study made of about one hundred patients awaiting similar surgery. [3]The patients were divided into two groups. [4]One group dreaded the surgery, regarded it as mutilation,* and tried to do everything possible to avoid going into the operating room. [5]Members of the second group viewed the surgery as an opportunity to liberate* their bodies from a dangerous intruder. [6]Careful observation of all patients following surgery revealed that those who had high expectations had a much more rapid recovery than those who feared the worst. (Adapted from Norman Cousins, "Taking Charge of Your Health," *Science Magazine*, July/August 1984, p. 20.)

    a. Sentence 1

    b. Sentence 2

2. [1]For centuries, earthquakes were considered warnings from the gods. [2]It is only in the twentieth century that a comprehensive* theory, called *plate tectonics*, seemed to adequately explain the cause of earthquakes. [3]According to this theory, the earth's surface consists of about a dozen giant rock plates, each seventy miles thick. [4]Propelled by unknown forces, the plates are continuously in motion. [5]Sometimes they collide and temporarily lock together. [6]The locking of the plates builds up stress on the plate edges, causing the rock to fracture. [7]The fracture causes the plates to resume their motion, but the sudden release of energy can also produce an earthquake. [8]The brainchild of Alfred Wegener, plate tectonics was initially derided when Wegener first proposed it in 1905. [9]Wegener died in 1930 without ever knowing that his theory would one day gain the respect of the scientific world.

    a. Sentence 1

    b. Sentence 2

---

*mutilation: the crippling or deforming of a body part.
*liberate: set free.
*comprehensive: wide-ranging or complete in coverage.

✔ **CHECK YOUR UNDERSTANDING**

1. What's the difference between the topic and the main idea?

_____

_____

2. Where can you expect to find references to the main idea?

_____

3. What's the difference between topic sentences and introductory sentences?

_____

_____

On the Alert for Reversal Transitions

As you learned in Chapter 2, *yet* is a reversal transition—that is, it tells readers the author is getting ready to challenge, revise, or modify what was previously said. When a reversal transition appears at the beginning of the second sentence in a paragraph, it's highly likely that the second sentence is the topic sentence. Here's an example:

Introduction

Reversal transition

Topic sentence

Specific details

[1]For the past twenty years, it's repeatedly been claimed that low self-esteem causes numerous social and psychological ills. [2]*Yet,* as it turns out, exaggerated self-esteem seems to be more prevalent and problematic than a sense of low self-esteem. [3]In a wide range of studies focused on self-esteem, participants consistently gave themselves higher ratings than they gave others. [4]They also overestimated their personal contribution to team efforts; exaggerated their ability to control life's events; and made unrealistic predictions about their future. [5]Participants in the studies also tended to get angry when things did not turn out as expected. [6]Similar research on self-image also shows that many people overestimate their intellectual and social skills. [7]What was particularly interesting about this tendency was that those who had the poorest intellectual and social skills were the most likely to overrate their performance in both areas. [8]For instance, researchers

Justin Kruger and David Dunning (1999) found that college students with the lowest scores on tests of logic and grammar generally assumed that their scores would be among the highest. [9]Interestingly enough, when these same students received training in grammar and logic, their self-assessments became less confident and more realistic. (Adapted from Brehm, Kassin, and Fein, *Social Psychology*, p. 138.)

As you can see in the second sentence of this example, the transition *yet* turns the paragraph away from the author's introductory point: Low self-esteem has long been considered the source of numerous problems. What the author really wants to communicate comes in sentence 2, where we learn that exaggerated self-esteem is more common and more troublesome.

Following the Author's Train of Thought

Whenever the second sentence of a paragraph fails to further explain the first, there's a high probability that the second sentence is the topic sentence. If, in addition, the second sentence opens with a reversal transition, you can be almost positive that the second sentence is the topic sentence. But if the third sentence continues the idea introduced in the second, you can be absolutely certain that the second sentence is the topic sentence.

You already know some reversal transitions from Chapter 2. Here is a more extensive list:

Contrast and Reversal Transitions ◆		
	Be that as it may	On the other hand
	But	Regardless
	Conversely	Still
	Despite that fact	That fact notwithstanding
	Even so	Tragically
	However	Unfortunately
	In contrast	When in fact
	In spite of	While that might be true, it's also true that
	Nevertheless	
	Nonetheless	Yet
	On the contrary	Yet as it turns out

INTERNET RESOURCE To learn more about introductory sentences, go to laflemm.com and look at "Introductory Sentences" under Key Concepts. You can find this link at the student companion website for this text: www.cengage.com/devenglish/flemming/rfr11e.

READING TIP When taking notes, think of the main idea as the headline you would write if the paragraph were a newspaper article—for example, "Citizens Blow Off Jury Duty" or "Excessive Self-Esteem More Common Than Low."

SUMMING UP THE KEY POINTS

1. Reversal transitions signal that the author is going to challenge, modify, or reverse the idea previously expressed.

2. When a reversal transition opens the second sentence of a paragraph, there's a good chance that the second sentence is the topic sentence.

3. If the second sentence opens with a reversal transition and the third sentence picks up on the point of the second, the second sentence is definitely the topic sentence.

◆ EXERCISE 6   Identifying Topics and Topic Sentences

DIRECTIONS Read each paragraph. Then circle the appropriate letter to identify the topic. Write *1* or *2* in the blank at the end to identify the topic sentence. If the topic sentence opens with a reversal transition, circle the transition.

EXAMPLE ¹When we read or hear about the suffering of wild animals illegally caught, shipped, and sold, we are likely to sigh deeply for about fifteen seconds, then forget the animals and their suffering. ²(However), we should be concerned about the wild animal trade, particularly right now, with the threat of bird flu hovering in the air. ³Imported animals don't come into the country alone. ⁴They carry with them parasites, germs, and diseases. ⁵In 2005, for instance, British inspectors identified a parrot carrying the bird flu virus. ⁶Because the parrot was being imported legally, it was under quarantine.* [7]But many parrots sold in Britain come into the country illegally and are never checked for disease. [8]One of those birds could also be infected with bird flu and spread the virus to its human owner.

The fear is that bird flu might one day turn into a pandemic rivaling the flu that killed millions in 1918, when emergency hospitals had to be constructed to treat the sick.

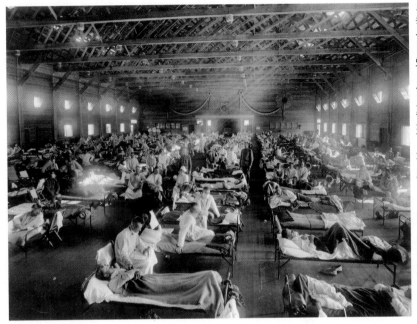

Courtesy of the National Museum of Health and Medicine, Armed Forces Institute of Pathology, Washington, D.C.

Topic   a. exotic animals
        b. illegal wild animal trade
        c. the suffering of animals
        d. the dangers of importing parrots

Topic Sentence ___2___

EXPLANATION   In this paragraph, the introductory sentence encourages the readers to think, "Yes, I have done that." Once potential readers feel personally drawn into the situation, they might just keep reading. The real point or main idea of the paragraph, however, comes in the second sentence. The topic sentence introduced by the reversal transition, *however*, announces the real point of the paragraph: Ignoring the illegal trafficking in wild animals can have serious consequences.

*quarantine: period of isolation to prevent the spread of disease.

1. ¹Communal movements[†] are almost as old as America itself. ²As early as the mid-1800s, writer and philosopher Ralph Waldo Emerson remarked that every other person seemed to carry in his pocket a plan for the "perfect society." ³Indeed Emerson and his friends eagerly experimented with group living at the much-written-about Brook Farm.[†] ⁴Doing their part for the communal movement, city newspapers ran ads for those interested in forming or joining communal associations. ⁵Historically, communal movements in America have been most prominent during times of social unrest. ⁶Thus, it follows that the movement saw a swell of enthusiasm in the 1840s and 1850s just prior to the outbreak of the Civil War. ⁷Following the war, the interest in communal movements persisted, and there were more than one hundred group-living communities. ⁸Most of them, however, survived only a few years. ⁹With the coming of the 1970s and the rise of social unrest and political activism, communal movements once again became popular in parts of the United States. (Adapted from McNeil, *The Psychology of Being Human*, p. 604.)

Topic

   a. Ralph Waldo Emerson

   b. American responses to social and political unrest

   c. the history of American communal movements

   d. alternative social arrangements

Topic Sentence   _____

2. ¹Men and women show that they're listening in different ways. ²A woman is more apt to give lots of support by murmuring a "Yeah" or "Uh-oh," nodding in agreement, and smiling. ³When listening, women also make more eye contact than do men, whose eyes are likely to wander away from the speaker (Brownell, 2002). ⁴In contrast to a woman, a man is more likely to listen quietly, without giving lots of listening cues as feedback. ⁵An analysis of calls to a crisis center in Finland revealed that calls taken by a female counselor were significantly longer for both male and female callers (Salminen & Glad, 1992). ⁶It's likely that the greater number of listening cues given

---

[†]communal movements: social experiments where people lived together without having blood ties.

[†]Brook Farm: a commune in West Roxbury, Massachusetts, that included several of America's greatest writers (1841–1847).

by the women encouraged the callers to keep talking. (Adapted from DeVito, *The Interpersonal Communication Book*, pp. 128–30.)

Topic   a. differences in how men and women listen
b. listening behaviors in men
c. conversational styles
d. making eye contact while listening

Topic Sentence   1

3. [1]Most Americans are accustomed to thinking that lie detectors, because they are machines, can, without error, separate the guilty from the innocent. [2]But, in fact, lie detectors can and do make mistakes. [3]For one thing, those who administer the tests are not necessarily qualified experts. [4]Many states don't employ licensed examiners trained to read and interpret lie detector printouts. [5]In addition, many subjects react to taking a lie detector test by becoming anxious. [6]As a result, their bodies behave as if the subjects were lying even when they are telling the truth. [7]Unfortunately, some people are smart enough to use relaxation techniques or tranquilizers to remain calm when they are telling a string of lies.

Topic   a. lie detector examiners
b. errors made by lie detectors
c. lie detector printouts
d. lie detector subjects who lie

Topic Sentence   2

Cards in the Rorschach Test are numbered 1 through 10, and the cards are always shown in numerical order.

Kheng Guan Toh/Shutterstock

4. [1]Researchers use interviews, rating scales, and questionnaires to identify observable psychological traits. [2]However, when seeking to uncover hidden or unconscious wishes, psychologists are likely to turn to *projective tests*. [3]In some projective tests, the subject is asked to tell a story about a picture or an image. [4]With others, subjects are told to respond to a word by calling up other words they associate with it. [5]Perhaps the most famous projective test is the Rorschach Technique. [6]Developed by Swiss psychologist Hermann Rorschach, the test consists of ten inkblots. [7]Subjects look at the inkblots and then describe what they see in them. [8]Yet another famous example of a projective test is the Thematic Apperception Test (TAT). [9]During the

TAT, subjects are shown pictures and asked to make up stories about the people depicted. [10]Although projective tests like the Rorschach and the TAT have been popular for decades, many psychologists now question their reliability as diagnostic tools.

Topic

   a. psychological testing

   b. unconscious wishes

   c. projective tests

   d. the Thematic Apperception Test

Topic Sentence   _2_

CHECK YOUR UNDERSTANDING

1. What do reversal and contrast transitions signal to the reader?

_____

2. What does a reversal and contrast transition at the beginning of the second sentence signal to readers?

_____

Locating Topic Sentences

Particularly in textbooks, topic sentences are most likely to be the first or the second sentence of the paragraph. However, topic sentences appear in other locations as well. As the following examples show, topic sentences can appear just about anywhere. In this next paragraph, for instance, two introductory sentences lead up to the topic sentence, which is the third sentence in the paragraph:

Introduction

Topic sentence

Specific details

[1]In the third century BCE, the Chinese were the first to sight Halley's comet. [2]In the fourteenth, the Florentine painter Giotto put the whirling ball of light into one of his paintings; in the sixteenth, William Shakespeare mentioned it in two of his plays. [3]**But it took the eighteenth-century astronomer Edmund Halley (1656–1742) to recognize that the comet seen by the Chinese, the Italians,**

and the British was the same comet returning on a fixed schedule. [4]While studying what seemed to be the appearance of many different comets, Halley realized that there might be only one comet that regularly appeared every seventy-six years. [5]As a result of his studies, he predicted that the comet would return in 1758. [6]His prediction was proven correct when the comet showed up on schedule. [7]From that moment on, the comet bore his name. [8]Unfortunately, Halley died without knowing that his prediction had come true.

In this case, the first two sentences provide background knowledge, and it isn't until the third sentence that the writer introduces a topic sentence summarizing the main idea.

Transitional Sentences

In addition to transitional words and phrases, be prepared as well for **transitional sentences**. These are complete sentences that connect sentences and paragraphs. For an example, see the underlined sentence in the following paragraph.

Introduction

Transitional sentence

Topic sentence

Specific details

[1]Jury duty is an essential part of living in a democratic society. [2]But you'd never know it from the way some American citizens behave. [3]**For many, jury duty is a burdensome inconvenience they try to avoid.** [4]At the least complicated level, there are those who simply throw away the summons to jury duty. [5]They know that if the state authorities come after them, it's easy enough to claim the notice never arrived. [6]Should the authorities pursue the issue—and they often don't—it's up to the state to prove that the notice actually got into the potential juror's hands, and that's not easy to do. [7]For those who lack the nerve to just chuck the notice into the wastebasket, there's a second choice. [8]During the interview stage of jury selection, jury dodgers can display their acting skills. [9]An agitated tone, much eyeball rolling, and excessive hand-wringing will signal that the potential juror is overly biased or else mentally unbalanced. [10]Both states of mind are reason for dismissal.

Here again, note that the paragraph opens with a general sentence. But that sentence is not developed in the remaining sentences. Instead, the transition—in this case a complete sentence—signals a shift in point of view, and paves the way for the topic sentence.

> **READING TIP** If the second sentence of a paragraph functions as a transition, then the third sentence is likely to be the topic sentence.

Topic Sentence at Mid-Point

As the paragraph about Halley's comet on pages 192–93 suggests, topic sentences can appear smack in the middle of a paragraph, as the following passage illustrates:

Specific details

Topic sentence

Specific details

[1]Most people know the gruesome story of Baron Frankenstein, the mad doctor who created a living creature from the bodies of corpses. [2]The story has been told and retold. [3]It has also been the subject of numerous films, and most people are familiar with the tale. [4]**What many people don't know, however, is that the chilling story of Dr. Frankenstein and his creature was written by a nineteen-year-old woman named Mary Shelley.** [5]As a young bride, Shelley liked to take part in storytelling competitions with her husband, poet Percy Bysshe Shelley, and his friend and fellow poet George Gordon Byron. [6]On one particularly long evening, Byron suggested that everyone write and read a ghost story. [7]Mary Shelley responded with the story of Frankenstein, and the rest, as they say, is history.

Topic sentences in the middle of a paragraph are not nearly as common as topic sentences at the beginning. But if a paragraph starts out specific, becomes general in the middle, and then returns to being specific, that general sentence in the middle is very likely the topic sentence.

Topic Sentence in Last Position

If no topic sentence turns up by the time you reach the middle of the paragraph, you have two choices to consider. Either the main idea is implied, or suggested, rather than stated (more about that in Chapter 6), or you are dealing with a paragraph where the topic sentence appears at the very end. Here's an example of a paragraph in which the topic sentence arrives last.

Specific details

Topic sentence

[1]Some people express their personal philosophies by tattooing themselves with phrases like "Live Hard" or "Love Thy Neighbor." [2]Others consider tattoos a way of displaying their taste in art. [3]They might tattoo a William Blake[†] etching[*] or a Georgia O'Keeffe[†] flower on some part of their bodies. [4]But in different cultures and eras, tattoos have also served religious purposes. [5]Mexico's Mayan people expressed their religious beliefs by tattooing themselves with images of jaguars, snakes, turtles, and toads. [6]From the 1700s until the present, many Muslims tattooed themselves to show their devotion to Allah. [7]Some Native American tribes used tattooing for medicinal purposes, believing that tattoos would ward off illness. [8]The Cree, for instance, would tattoo a cross on each cheek to protect against toothaches, and members of the Ojibwa tribe tattooed small circles on their temples to prevent headaches. [9]Throughout history tattooing has been widely used as a means of identification. [10]Before 787 CE, early Christians used tattoos to identify members of their faith. [11]Similarly, members of the military or fraternities may have themselves tattooed to publicly show their commitment. [12]Some cultures have tattooed prisoners, the most sinister example being the Nazis, who tattooed numbers on the arms of concentration camp victims during World War II. [13]**Tattoos, it's clear, have served many different purposes.**

Sentences 1 through 12 are too specific to summarize the paragraph. Only the very last sentence fits all the criteria of a topic sentence.

READING TIP If a paragraph maintains a consistent level of specific detail and suddenly branches out into a general statement at the end, that last sentence is probably the topic sentence.

[†]William Blake (1757–1827): British artist whose drawings and paintings have a fantastic otherworldly quality.
[*]etching: art made by imprinting an image on a metal plate.
[†]Georgia O'Keeffe (1887–1986): American artist known for her focus on flowers.

Doubling Up on Topic Sentences

To make sure that they get their point across, writers sometimes double up on topic sentences, stating the main idea at the beginning and at the end of a paragraph. Here's an example:

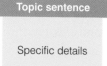

Topic sentence

Specific details

Topic sentence

¹**The career of George Smith Patton Jr., the much decorated four-star army general, stalled because he didn't know how to control his temper.** ²During World War II, in August 1943, Patton visited ailing and wounded soldiers in two separate army hospitals. ³On each visit, he publicly slapped a soldier who complained of losing the nerve to fight. ⁴Patton considered the men despicable and insisted that "real" soldiers should not have to look at gutless cowards afraid of battle. ⁵Although Patton thought his behavior perfectly appropriate, his commanding officer, Dwight D. Eisenhower, did not. ⁶Eisenhower forced Patton to apologize publicly to the hospital staff and to the men themselves. ⁷He also saw to it that Patton rose no higher in the chain of military command. ⁸**Thanks to his uncontrollable temper, General George Patton never climbed any higher on the military ladder.**

> **READING TIP**
>
> If a paragraph opens with a general statement, becomes more specific, and then turns more general again at the end, check to see if the opening and closing sentences say much the same thing. If they do, you are reading a paragraph with a double topic sentence.

Question and Answer

Writers, particularly textbook writers, are fond of opening paragraphs with questions. The opening question is there to direct readers' attention to the point of the paragraph. The opening question, however, is not the topic sentence. The answer, which usually follows quickly on the heels of the opening question, is the paragraph's topic sentence. Here's an example:

Opening question

Topic sentence answer

Specific details

¹What determines our long-term satisfaction, and why are some of us happier than others? ²**Seeking the roots of happiness, Ed Diener and his colleagues (1999) reviewed years of research and found that there are three key predictors of happiness.** ³The first is social

relationships: people with an active social life, close friends, and a happy marriage are more satisfied than those who lack these intimate connections. ⁴The second is employment status. ⁵Regardless of income, employed people are happier than those who are out of work. ⁶Finally, people who are physically healthy are happier than those who are not. (Adapted from Brehm, Kassin, and Fein, *Social Psychology*, p. 536.)

As is typical for this kind of paragraph, the sentence that answers the opening question is also the topic sentence of the paragraph.

◆ **EXERCISE 7**   **Locating Topic Sentences**

DIRECTIONS   Read each paragraph. Then write the number of the topic sentence in the blank at the end. *Note*: In these paragraphs, the topic sentence can be anywhere in the paragraph.

EXAMPLE   ¹During World War I and again during World War II, the U.S. Congress required Americans to observe daylight saving time (DST) to save energy for the production of war supplies. ²After U.S. Department of Transportation studies indicated that DST reduced the need for artificial light and decreased Americans' electricity usage, DST became permanent in most states. ³In addition to the energy savings, DST extended the daylight hours during warmer months when people were more inclined to be outdoors. ⁴DST is also said to prevent traffic accidents by allowing more people to return home from work or school in daylight. ⁵There is evidence, too, that DST reduces crime by decreasing the amount of time when people can move about in darkness. ⁶Clearly, there are some good reasons for observing daylight saving time.

Topic Sentence   6

EXPLANATION   The only sentence in the paragraph general enough to sum up all the benefits identified in sentences 1–5 is sentence 6, making that sentence the topic sentence expressing the main idea.

1. ¹Whether military or civilian, most professional training programs stress the value of self-confidence. ²Believe in yourself and you will succeed. ³Yet, in some cases, just the opposite is true. ⁴There are

people whose success stems not from self-confidence but from feelings of failure. [5]Feeling inadequate, these people push themselves hard, forcing themselves to achieve. [6]Viewed in this way, fear of failure becomes, paradoxically,* a source of success. [7]At least this was the view of the famed writer and critic Edmund Wilson. [8]As examples of his theory, Wilson cited the philosopher Karl Marx and the poet Edna St. Vincent Millay, two people driven to succeed by their feelings of inadequacy and failure.

Topic Sentence _____

2. [1]Early efforts at developing artificial intelligence (AI) focused on the computer's capabilities for formal reasoning, symbol manipulation, and problem solving. [2]Valuable as it is, this logic-based approach to AI has limitations. [3]For one thing, expert systems are successful only in narrowly defined fields. [4]And even here computers show limited ability. [5]That's because there is no way of putting into computer code all aspects of expert human reasoning. [6]Sometimes, even experts can say little more than, "I know it when I see it, but I can't put it into words." [7]Second, the vital ability to draw analogies* and make other connections is still beyond the grasp of current computer systems. [8]Finally, logic-based AI systems depend on "if-then" rules, and it is often difficult to tell a computer how to recognize an "if," or an under-what-circumstances condition, in the real world. (Adapted from Bernstein, *Psychology*, p. 299.)

Topic Sentence _____2_____

3. [1]When it was a republic of the Soviet Union,† Ukraine was sometimes called "Little Russia" or "The Breadbasket of the Soviet Union." [2]To the Ukrainians, the nickname must have seemed a cruel joke, given their sufferings under Russian rule. [3]No wonder the current

---

*paradoxically: ideas or events seemingly in contradiction, but actually making sense or fitting together, e.g., "Some day you will be old enough to start reading fairy tales again" (C. S. Lewis).

*analogies: comparisons between two unlike things that share a similar function or process, suggesting that two things alike in some respect are alike in others, e.g., "The heart is like a pump. The heart pumps blood from one part of the body to another like a pump pumps water from a reservoir that is fed by a stream" (from www.altoonafp.org/how_to_use_analogies.htm).

†Soviet Union: Before the fall of communism in Eastern Europe, this was the common name for Russia and the countries directly under the control of the Russian government.

president of Ukraine, Viktor Yushchenko, is determined to bring attention to the Soviet-created famine that killed millions of Ukrainians between 1931 and 1933, when the Russian dictator Josef Stalin ordered the confiscation of grain. [4]Although the Russians' own agricultural system was in chaos and underproductive, Stalin had another reason for his demand: He wanted to break the rebellious spirit of Ukrainian farmers, who were refusing to participate in his plan for collective, or group, farming. [5]Under Stalin's systematic confiscation of Ukrainian grain and livestock, millions of Ukrainians starved to death. [6]Some even resorted to cannibalism to survive. [7]In a speech given in November 2005, Yushchenko pressed his case for the United Nations to declare the famine genocide—a conscious plan to destroy the Ukrainian population.

Topic Sentence _____

4. [1]In his book *Influence*, writer and researcher Robert Cialdini opens with a confession: "I can admit it freely now. [2]All my life I've been timid about asserting myself." [3]Cialdini is not alone. [4]Many people find it difficult to be assertive in interpersonal situations and could use some help learning to say no. [5]Faced with an unreasonable request from a friend, spouse, or stranger, many of us become anxious at the mere thought of putting our foot down and refusing to comply. [6]Rather than saying no, we end up agreeing because a refusal makes us too uncomfortable. [7]Indeed, there are times when it is difficult for anyone to say no, and we probably all need a little assertiveness training. (Adapted from Brehm, Kassin, and Fein, *Social Psychology*, p. 248.)

2 topic sentences

Topic Sentence _4, 7_

5. [1]Few changes accompanying puberty are as explosive for families as the adolescent's increased interest in sex. [2]Still, anthropological* evidence indicates that the majority of cultures tend to permit or at least tolerate some sexual activity during the teenage years. [3]Western societies, however, have generally been more restrictive about sexual expression among teenagers and therefore are slow to recognize its reality. [4]For instance, research suggests that many mothers

*anthropological: related to the study of human cultures.

in the United States underestimate the sexual activity of their children. [5]The children, in turn, tend to underestimate the degree to which their parents disapprove of such activity (Jaccard, Dittus, and Gordon, 1998). [6]Whatever the misunderstandings on either side, it is simply true that large numbers of teenagers are sexually active at an early age. [7]One study reports that 30 percent of the students entering sixth grade in a large urban city had already engaged in sexual intercourse (Kinsman et al., 1998). [8]Levels of sexual activity similar to those found in the United States are also reported in other Western nations. (Adapted from Bukatko and Daehler, *Child Development*, p. 183.)

Topic Sentence _____

6. [1]A contusion is a bruise received from a sudden traumatic blow to the body, causing bleeding in the tissue, which later leads to discoloration at the injury site. [2]The severity of the contusion is directly related to the amount of soft tissue crushed and the amount of force applied to the tissue. [3]Contusions, or injuries that break the skin, are quite common with sports-related activities; therefore, it is recommended that athletes wear protective gear to decrease the possibility of injury. [4]Contusions commonly affect the quadriceps of basketball players and football running backs; however, it is important to note that contusions may occur to any part of the body. [5]A person with a mild contusion will experience tenderness and local pain at the injury site. [6]Limbs with mild contusions retain normal range of motion. [7]A severe contusion, however, will feature marked tenderness and a severe decrease in range of motion. (Adapted from Clover, *Sports Medicine Essentials*, p. 322.)

Topic Sentence _____

7. [1]For modern viewers, the critical admiration for D. W. Griffith's 1915 film *Birth of a Nation* is somewhat puzzling. [2]How is it possible that a film so crudely racist could be considered a cinematic triumph? [3]That's a good question, because the content is pretty awful. [4]What makes *Birth of a Nation* so memorable is not the nasty narrative, but Griffith's strikingly innovative* use of both the camera and the actors.

---

*innovative: original, inventive.

[5]When it comes to camera work, Griffith invented the *cross cut*, a technique that lets filmgoers watch a little of one scene, then some of another before returning to the first. [6]Through the use of the cross cut, Griffith was able to tell more complex stories than had previously been shown on screen. [7]Griffith also invented the camera *close-up*, which made it possible for audiences to feel they knew the stars on the screen. [8]But perhaps Griffith's greatest gift was his ability to make his actors abandon the overacting that had marred silent films for years. [9]Although to modern eyes Griffith's "stars" might still seem to be over-emoting, for the time, they showed a subtlety and realism seldom seen on the screen prior to Griffith's entry into films.

Topic Sentence _____

8. [1]Throughout the nineteenth century, many explorers failed to reach the North Pole. [2]Then in 1909, Dr. Frederick Cook claimed he had reached the Pole on April 21, spending two days there until drifting ice forced him to move westward. [3]The world press was quick to celebrate Cook's achievement until cables began arriving from naval lieutenant Robert Peary. [4]Peary insisted that he and three Eskimo companions had planted the flag of the United States at the North Pole on April 6, 1909. [5]Although a 1922 Congressional hearing decided that Cook's proof of his arrival at the Pole was falsified and that Peary was indeed the first man to arrive, the controversy continued with supporters of each man passionately taking sides. [6]At the same time, some of those not committed to either Peary or Cook insisted just as fervidly that the honor of being the first at the Pole belonged to Rear Admiral Richard Byrd, who, in 1926, claimed to be the first man to fly over the North Pole. [7]However, in 1996, the publication of Byrd's diary showed that although he had almost made it to the Pole, he had, just short of arrival, given up. [8]With Byrd out of the running, though, there was still another contender: the Russian scientist Otto Schmidt, who founded an ice station at the North Pole in 1938. [9]If Peary and Cook were *both* faking it, as some claimed, then Schmidt was indeed the first. [10]Given the amount of heated controversy surrounding who first arrived at the North Pole, we may never know for sure exactly who got there first.

last half

Topic Sentence _____ 10

9. ¹Perhaps there are those who are able to perceive the whole cosmetics scene as the massive PR campaign it is and remain unaffected by the industry's massive put-down of women's real bodies and faces, which it literally does. ²But in a society where women are generally overvalued for their personal appearance and undervalued for their contributions and competence, most women are to a certain extent vulnerable to the message of the cosmetic industry. ³What teenage girl does not harbor a secret desire to be the subject of a "makeover," believing that the answer to looking better is out there somewhere. ⁴The media, of course, tells us where that answer lies: in a tube, a bottle, a box. ⁵Not surprisingly, few women are immune. ⁶Even feminist author Susan Brownmiller, who admittedly has an anti-makeup bias, acknowledges that she dyes her own prematurely gray hair, although she considers it a "shameful concession to the wrong values." ⁷A job has been done on us all it seems. (Adapted from Sloane, *Biology of Women*, p. 523.)

Topic Sentence _____

10. ¹In the course of a day, there are many times when you need to keep some piece of information in your head for just a few seconds. ²Maybe it is a number that you are "carrying over" to do a subtraction, or a persuasive argument that you are going to make as soon as the other person finishes talking. ³Either way, you are using your short-term memory. ⁴This ability to hold on to a piece of information temporarily in order to complete a task is specifically human; it causes certain regions of the brain to become very active, in particular the *prefrontal lobe*. ⁵This region, at the very front of the brain, is highly developed in humans. ⁶It is the reason that we have such high, upright foreheads, compared with the receding foreheads of our cousins the apes.

Topic Sentence _____

VOCABULARY CHECK

The following words were introduced in pages 167–200. Match the word with the definition. Review words, definitions, and original context two or three times before taking the vocabulary tests. (The page numbers in parentheses indicate where the word first appeared.)

1. electors (p. 167) _____
2. dignitaries (p. 172) _____
3. renovated (p. 172) _____
4. placebos (p. 176) _____
5. dementia (p. 176) _____
6. consolidate (p. 176) _____
7. random (p. 176) _____
8. speculators (p. 177) _____
9. disorienting (p. 177) _____
10. conclusive (p. 177) _____
11. traumatic (p. 178) _____
12. mutilation (p. 185) _____
13. liberate (p. 185) _____
14. comprehensive (p. 185) _____
15. quarantine (p. 189) _____
16. etching (p. 195) _____
17. paradoxically (p. 198) _____
18. analogies (p. 198) _____
19. anthropological (p. 199) _____
20. innovative (p. 200) _____

a. comparisons between two unlike things that share a similar function or process, suggesting that two things alike in some respects are alike in others

b. ideas or events seemingly in contradiction, but actually making sense or fitting together

c. causing mental confusion

d. loss of the normal ability to think, concentrate, and remember

e. final; putting an end to doubt

f. combine

g. people who buy something with the expectation of a quick sale and a quick profit

h. people chosen to cast their vote for president

i. related to the study of human cultures

j. substances that have no healing effect on the body but are believed by the people taking them to be of medical value

k. period of isolation to prevent the spread of disease

l. art made by imprinting an image on a metal plate

m. people in high positions

n. original, inventive

o. causing serious injury

p. not occurring according to a set pattern; inconsistent

q. set free

r. the crippling or deforming of a body part

s. wide-ranging or complete in coverage

t. repaired

Paraphrasing to Test Comprehension

Recognizing the topic sentence and understanding the main idea of a paragraph are critical to understanding what you read. A word of caution here, though. It's easy to believe you have understood the main idea when the paragraph—and along with it, the topic sentence—are right before your eyes. In this situation, even the most experienced and skillful readers can fool themselves into thinking their understanding is better than it is. The truth—that our understanding of the main idea is somewhat fuzzy—only dawns on us when we try to recall the author's point in a class discussion or on a test. To avoid such unpleasant surprises, get into the habit of paraphrasing topic sentences whenever you are dealing with unfamiliar or hard-to-read material.

Reading Versus Writing Paraphrases

Any time you **paraphrase**, you use your own words to restate the author's ideas, changing the language but not the meaning. **Reading paraphrases**, however, don't require you to be as complete and grammatically correct the way paraphrasing for a term paper does. For reading paraphrases, all you have to do is to re-create, in your own words, a bare-bones version of the topic sentence. For an illustration, here are some of the topic sentences you have encountered so far, along with paraphrases appropriate to reading and writing.

Original	In the nineteenth century, baseball emerged as the most popular new urban sport.
Reading Paraphrase	19th century baseball big in cities.
Writing Paraphrase	Baseball became a favorite urban sport in the nineteenth century.
Original	The Antarctic seals, however, after almost becoming extinct, have made an astonishing comeback, and the population is now rapidly increasing.
Reading Paraphrase	After almost dying out, Antarctic seals make big comeback.

Writing Paraphrase	Once almost extinct, Antarctic seals are rebounding and their numbers are increasing.
Original	Although much of the behavior of lower animals appears to be regulated by instincts, this is not true of human behavior.
Reading Paraphrase	Instinct doesn't control our behavior like in animals.
Writing Paraphrase	Instinct regulates almost all behavior among lower animals, but it does not have the same control over human actions.
Original	For a period of about seventy-five years (1765–1840), the Gothic novel, an early relative of the modern horror story, was popular throughout Europe.
Reading Paraphrase	1765–1840, Gothic horror novels big sellers.
Writing Paraphrase	Between 1765 and 1840, the ancestor of the modern-day horror story, the Gothic novel, was widely read throughout Europe.

Pointers on Paraphrasing While Reading

As you can tell from the previous examples, paraphrases for reading are less formal than paraphrases created for term papers, where completeness and grammatical correctness are essential. However, that does not mean that there are no guidelines for the kind of reading paraphrases you should jot into the margins of your textbooks. There are some things you need to know and do in order to make paraphrasing topic sentences an effective comprehension strategy.

1. **Stick with the topic.** If you are paraphrasing a topic sentence, you already know the subject of the sentence. It's the same topic you identified based on the chain (or chains) of repetition and reference in the paragraph.

2. **Use your own words to comment on or describe the topic.** Finding your own words to express the author's original idea about the topic is what makes paraphrasing work. If you can't find different words to make the same point, that's an indication that you haven't understood the author's point. Yet even when you can find the right words to paraphrase the topic sentence, the time spent searching for those words gives your long-term memory a chance to store the idea away for later recall. This double benefit is what makes paraphrasing such an effective learning tool.

3. **Use the question about the main idea to get started.** When paraphrasing a topic sentence, use the same question that took you from the topic of the paragraph to the main idea: "What's the author saying about the topic?" Asking that question to paraphrase the topic sentence leads to any number of answers, for instance: "Antarctic seals survive near extinction," "Antarctic seals bounce back." Both paraphrases are correct because they both follow the central rule of paraphrasing: Change the language, not the meaning.

4. **Don't get bogged down trying to paraphrase word by word.** Instead, use the general question about the main idea to generate an answer. Then check to see how closely the answer, in terms of content and language, matches the original topic sentence. If your answer has almost the same wording as the topic sentence, see where you can substitute your own words for the author's.

5. **Recognize that some words and phrases can't be paraphrased.** Some words and terms in your textbooks are part of a highly specialized vocabulary specific to the subject matter. These specialized vocabulary words and terms might have few, if any, synonyms. Remember, for example, the paragraph on the "Mandan earth lodges." It would be hard to find a substitute for that particular phrase. For this reason, just about any paraphrase would keep the original wording of the topic, e.g., "19th-century Americans and Europeans bowled over by Mandan earth lodges."

6. **Don't stand on formality.** Note the use of the idiom[†] "bowled over" in the above paraphrase. Such informal language would be unacceptable

---

[†]Idioms are phrases peculiar to a particular language, and their meaning has been acquired through long usage in a specific context. Thus, idioms can't be understood through word-for-word translations, e.g., "Nobody buys a pig in a poke" has nothing to do with real pigs. It means you never buy anything sight unseen. "Sight unseen," by the way, is another idiom.

if you were paraphrasing for a research or term paper. But it's perfectly acceptable for a reading paraphrase because it's likely that you are the only one who will see the paraphrase during exam reviews.

7. **Abbreviate without losing the message.** Reading paraphrases, which go into the margins of your textbooks or the pages of your notebook, should be as brief as possible. Just don't make them too short. You'll need to re-read your notes later on to add details or to review for exams. At that time, you should be able to grasp the original meaning from the words jotted in your text or notebook. The examples in the following chart show the difference between effective and ineffective abbreviations.

Original	Western societies, however, have generally been more restrictive about sexual expression among teenagers and therefore are slow to recognize its reality.
Good Abbreviation	Western societies more likely to inhibit teenage sexual expression, therefore find it hard to acknowledge.
Poor Abbreviation	Western societies inhibit sexual expression.
Original	Although much of the behavior of lower animals appears to be regulated by instincts, this is not true of human behavior.
Good Abbreviation	Unlike lower animals, humans not controlled by instinct.
Poor Abbreviation	Humans not like lower animals.

WWW

INTERNET RESOURCE To learn more about paraphrasing, go to laflemm.com and look at "Paraphrasing" under Key Concepts. You can also find this link at the student companion website for this text: www.cengage.com/develenglish/flemming/rfr11e.

SUMMING UP THE KEY POINTS

1. The key rule of paraphrasing is, change the language *not* the meaning.

2. Reading paraphrases don't require the same degree of completeness, grammatical correctness, or formality that writing paraphrases do.

3. Paraphrases should abbreviate *without* eliminating either the topic or the author's comment on the topic. Both are needed for the main idea.

◆ **EXERCISE 8** **Recognizing an Accurate Reading Paraphrase**

DIRECTIONS Read each paragraph, paying special attention to the underlined topic sentence. Then circle the letter of the better reading paraphrase.

EXAMPLE [1]Brief naps are nothing unusual for employees working at Sprint's operation center in Phoenix, Arizona. [2]Sprint's management encourages napping. [3]This might seem odd given that most U.S. employers take the opposite view: Napping on the job is grounds for dismissal. [4]<u>Sprint, though, might be on to something, because some research confirms the benefits of power napping.</u> [5]One Harvard University study, for instance, found that after napping on the job for an hour, an employee could perform nearly as well at the end of the workday as at the beginning. [6]An earlier Japanese study reported that a twenty-minute nap improves employee performance. [7]Moreover, the National Sleep Foundation cautions that lack of sleep can take a high toll, leading to errors and accidents on the job as well as absenteeism. [8]This warning suggests that naps on the job might be a good thing.

Paraphrase a. Studies have shown that sleeping on the job is good for business.

(b.) Some studies suggest napping at work has advantages.

EXPLANATION Sentence *a* won't do because the word *sleeping* is too general as a paraphrase of *napping*. Naps are brief. The word *sleeping* could mean anything from a nap to an eight-hour snooze. Some studies have shown that short naps—not sleeping on the job—are good for business. Although both paraphrases change the wording, answer *b* is more accurate than answer *a*.

1. [1]Until the start of the twentieth century, it was assumed the U.S. Supreme Court would never get involved in state criminal trials. [2]However, in 1907 the Supreme Court set a new precedent* when it intervened in the case of Ed Johnson, a black man who had been unfairly convicted of rape and sentenced to death in Chattanooga, Tennessee. [3]Even though several witnesses placed Johnson miles away from the scene of the crime, an all-white jury found him guilty. [4]After hearing about Johnson's unjust conviction, a black lawyer named Noah Parden decided to take the case before the Supreme Court. [5]To everyone's surprise, the court ordered a stay of execution and a new trial. [6]In defiance of the court, the sheriff of Chattanooga, Joseph Shipp, a Ku Klux Klan member, helped Johnson get lynched by an angry mob. [7]Shipp incorrectly assumed that the Supreme Court would not punish him for flouting* its orders. [8]But when the court learned about Shipp's role in the lynching, the justices had the sheriff tried for contempt. [9]Although Joseph Shipp got off with a light sentence, from 1907 on, it was clear that the Supreme Court of the United States could and would intervene in state criminal trials.

Paraphrase

   a. Noah Parden's courageous decision to take Ed Johnson's case before Supreme Court was huge civil rights victory.

   b. With 1907 Ed Johnson case, Supreme Court showed readiness to intervene in state trials.

2. [1]Despite being hunted every fall, deer are not on the endangered list. [2]Actually, for a number of reasons, the wild deer population in the United States is skyrocketing. [3]Hunting regulations, including hunting bans and strict limits on the number of deer killed, have allowed the animals to thrive. [4]The rate of deer reproduction, too, has contributed to the growing population. [5]One doe usually gives birth to twins every year. [6]Furthermore, reduced numbers of natural predators* such as wolves, along with a series of mild winters, have resulted in a lower mortality, or death, rate. [7]Deer have also successfully adapted to the destruction of their habitats* by humans. [8]Even when forests are cut down, deer manage to find enough food and

---

*precedent: an example that becomes a pattern for future actions.
*flouting: showing contempt for or disregarding; commonly confused with *flaunting*, or showing off.
*predators: animals that kill to survive.
*habitats: living spaces for specific species.

shelter in the remaining vegetation. [9]They also boldly venture into suburbs to snack on tasty garden vegetables and flowers.

Paraphrase

a. Wild deer population on the rise mainly due to restrictions on hunters.

b. Several factors contributing to growing number of wild deer.

◆ **EXERCISE 9** **Recognizing the Best Reading Paraphrase**

DIRECTIONS Read each paragraph, paying special attention to the underlined topic sentence. Then circle the letter of the most accurate paraphrase.

1. [1]Western visitors to India are often astonished to see stray cows wandering in public places. [2]In some parts of the country, cows wander in and out of markets or browse in carefully cultivated* gardens, a seeming nuisance for the local populace. [3]<u>But for devotees* of Hinduism, cows are never an annoyance: They are considered sacred, and their presence is encouraged.</u> [4]In Hindu-populated regions of the country, cows are free to gather at the edges of highways, even if they occasionally cause traffic snarls. [5]Cows are also permitted to wander into the middle of busy intersections, along railroad tracks, and munch on park grass (grass is a staple* of their diet). [6]Hindus decorate young cows with garlands of flowers and bring the animals offerings of food. [7]Older cows are well taken care of. [8]They are boarded in homes especially designed for geriatric* bovines.

   a. In parts of India, Hindus treat cows as holy animals and won't chase animals from public places.

   b. Everywhere in India, cows worshipped like gods.

   c. In India, cows gather on highways and cause traffic jams.

2. [1]Microbats, the small, insect-eating bats found in North America, have tiny eyes that don't look like they'd be useful to predators navigating in the dark and spotting prey. [2]<u>Instead, the nocturnal* habits of bats are aided by their powers of *echolocation*, a special ability that makes feeding and flying at night easier than one might think.</u>

---

*cultivated: cared for.
*devotees: followers, believers.
*staple: a basic or essential part of something (especially in reference to diet).
*geriatric: related to the elderly.
*nocturnal: nighttime.

[3]To navigate in the dark, a microbat flies with its mouth wide open, emitting high-pitched squeaks humans cannot hear. [4]Some of these squeaks echo off flying insects as well as tree branches and other obstacles that lie ahead. [5]The bat hears the echo and gets an immediate mental picture of the object in front of it. [6]From the use of echolocation, or sonar, as it is also called, a microbat can tell a great deal about a mosquito or any other potential meal. [7]With pinpoint exactness, echolocation gives microbats the ability to perceive distance, speed, movement, and shape. [8]Thanks to echolocation, bats can also detect and avoid obstacles no thicker than a human hair. (Adapted from Pringle, *Batman: Exploring the World of Bats*, pp. 11–12.)

a. Due to echolocation, bats have superior vision.

b. Echolocation reason why bats can fly and feed at night.

c. Tiny eyes of microbats very powerful, can see better than almost all other nocturnal animals.

◆ **EXERCISE 10 Recognizing the Best Paraphrase**

DIRECTIONS   Read each paragraph. In the blank at the end, write the number of the topic sentence. Then circle the letter of the most accurate paraphrase. *Note*: In this case, the paraphrases are more complete, more like those you might use for a term paper.

EXAMPLE   [1]Between 1924 and 1933, research on worker productivity* was conducted at Hawthorne Works, Western Electric's plant in Cicero, Illinois. [2]The results of the research suggested that productivity would increase anytime workers were the subject of a study. [3]Thus, it didn't much matter which specific workplace conditions were altered. [4]This notion—that workers responded more to getting attention than to changes in the workplace—came to be known as the "Hawthorne Effect," and in the years since the research was conducted, countless psychology and sociology texts have cited the Hawthorne Effect as if it were a scientifically proven fact. [5]The Hawthorne Effect, however, despite its popularity, lacks a solid scientific foundation. [6]In 1998, science writer Gina Kolata outlined flaws in the study in a *New York Times* article titled "Scientific Myths That Are Too Good to Die." [7]As it turns out, only five workers participated in the original study. [8]As if that weren't bad enough, two of those five workers were replaced before the study was completed. [9]In other

*productivity: ability to produce goods.

words, the entire research sample consisted of three people. [10]Even more revealing, though, is the fact that numerous other workplace studies have contradicted or failed to confirm the existence of the Hawthorne Effect.

Topic Sentence ___5___

Paraphrase a. According to the "Hawthorne Effect," employee productivity increases when employees are under observation.

(b.) The Hawthorne Effect is based on inadequate scientific evidence and may not exist.

c. The Hawthorne Effect is the result of a scientific hoax.

d. Being the subject of a study has no effect on employees' productivity.

EXPLANATION Sentence 5 is further explained by the more specific sentences that follow. It's also developed until the end of the paragraph, while the introductory sentences about the results of the study are disproved or ignored. Both of these things make sentence 5 the topic sentence. The most accurate paraphrase of sentence 5 is sentence *b*, which stresses the lack of evidence for the existence of the Hawthorne Effect.

1. [1]Scientists have long known that some animals use tools. [2]Chimpanzees, for example, use sticks to catch insects. [3]Otters pry open shells with rocks. [4]Recently, though, researchers discovered that some bottlenose dolphins in western Australia also use tools to search for food. [5]Before the dolphins root around the ocean floor to find prey hiding in the sand, they stick sea sponges on their snouts. [6]Wearing the sponges allows the dolphins to locate prey they wouldn't otherwise be able to find without risking injury. [7]The sponges are like nose gloves. [8]They protect the dolphins' sensitive skin from hidden dangers, like poisonous stonefish and stingrays. [9]This dolphin behavior, scientists believe, is not based on instinct. [10]It appears that the dolphins learned how to use the sponges after they got their noses injured, and then passed their knowledge on to their offspring.

Topic Sentence _____

Paraphrase a. Dolphins are more intelligent than chimpanzees.

b. Australian bottlenose dolphins use tools when hunting for food.

c. Chimpanzees use sticks to get food, whereas dolphins use sponges.

d. Dolphins spend a long time teaching their young how to find food.

2. [1]Although the Clean Water Act has been justly credited for improving the condition of the waters in the United States, many lakes, streams, and rivers in the United States still suffer from high levels of toxic* pollutants.* [2]Among the serious threats posed by water pollutants are respiratory irritation, cancer, kidney and liver damage, anemia, and heart failure. [3]Toxic pollutants also damage fish and other forms of wildlife. [4]In fish they cause tumors or reproductive* problems; shellfish and wildlife living in or drinking from toxin-infested waters also develop genetic* defects. (Adapted from Pride, Hughes, and Kapoor, *Business*, p. 57.)

Topic Sentence   _____

Paraphrase

a. Birth defects among fish indicate the presence of polluted water.

b. Thanks to the Clean Water Act, the drinking supply is no longer in danger.

c. Despite the Clean Water Act, water sources in the U.S. are still polluted.

d. Polluted water is the main cause of cancerous tumors and birth defects.

3. [1]While making the 1996 hit movie *Evita*, the pop diva Madonna claimed to feel a special kinship for the movie's heroine, Eva Perón, once one of the most powerful women in Latin America. [2]But Madonna might want to think twice before paying homage* to the wife of Argentinean dictator Juan Perón. [3]Glamorous as Maria Eva Duarte (1919–1952) was, she was hardly a role model. [4]Nicknamed "Evita" by the people who loved her, Evita Perón said all the right things about helping the poor, but her devotion rarely went beyond grand gestures, designed to polish her image as a modern-day saint. [5]As the wife of the president, Evita traveled the country handing out small sums of money to anyone who reached out a hand. [6]Warmed by such seeming generosity, the poor of Argentina did not begrudge Evita the much larger sums of money she spent on clothes, jewelry, and travel. [7]Fond of starting spectacular housing and health projects that were dedicated to

---

*toxic: poisonous.
*pollutants: substances that are harmful.
*reproductive: related to birth.
*genetic: having to do with biological inheritance.
*homage: a show of respect.

helping the needy, Evita usually lost interest in the projects before completion. [8]Nevertheless, her personal charisma* seemed to protect her from the anger of those she disappointed. [9]For that matter, it still seems to enchant. [10]Even today many people insist, despite all evidence to the contrary, that she was an early feminist and generous philanthropist.

Topic Sentence _____

Paraphrase

a. Madonna adopts causes she doesn't understand.

b. Evita Perón used beauty and charm to claw her way to the heights of political power.

c. Evita Perón is still beloved by people all over the world.

d. Evita Perón, despite her glamour and power, was not someone to be admired.

4. [1]Video game players made *Grand Theft Auto* the top-selling game of 2001. [2]Since then, subsequent* versions of the game have won awards and critical acclaim. [3]However, because of its violent, sexual content, *Grand Theft Auto* has also generated heated controversy. [4]Assuming the role of criminal in a big city, a *Grand Theft Auto* player robs banks, sells drugs, commits arson, and assassinates city officials and civilians.[1] [5]Characters commit these crimes with only minor, temporary consequences and are rewarded with cash. [6]In *Grand Theft Auto III*, one mission requires the player to steal a car, have sex with a prostitute, and take her money after murdering her. [7]That same version created more uproar when it was discovered that players could also get access to secret and graphic* sex scenes. [8]This kind of content, insist the game's critics, encourages young people to engage in real-life sociopathic* behavior; consequently, some states have enacted laws prohibiting anyone under eighteen from buying it, while Australia banned the game altogether in 2005. [9]Several car thieves and murderers arrested in the United States have even claimed that the game instigated* their crimes, leading to lawsuits against the game's publisher.

---

*charisma: personal magnetism or charm.
*subsequent: following in time.
[1]Lou Kesten, in a review of *Grand Theft Auto IV* for the *Dallas Morning News*, wrote: "Eight hours into *Grand Theft Auto IV*, I've stolen 17 cars, run over 20 people, and killed another 15. . . ."
*graphic: obvious and vivid, often associated with sex and violence.
*sociopathic: lacking all moral or ethical sense.
*instigated: caused, motivated.

Topic Sentence _____

    Paraphrase

a. Despite popularity of the video game *Grand Theft Auto*, critics detest the game's violence.

b. Critically successful, *Grand Theft Auto* has also been a financial success and aroused envy among its competitors.

c. *Grand Theft Auto* encourages crime; for that reason alone, it should be banned.

d. *Grand Theft Auto* may well be the most popular video game ever created.

5. [1]In many ways, Latin American telenovelas resemble American soap operas, but there are noticeable differences between the two. [2]Both are highly dramatic, televised fictional serials focusing on personal relationships. [3]However, the American soap opera was designed to continue indefinitely, with some soap operas, such as *As the World Turns* and *Guiding Light*,[†] enduring for decades. [4]A telenovela, in contrast, usually lasts only six months to a year, and the show's creators know the entire story from the beginning. [5]Telenovela and soap opera story lines differ not only in length but in focus. [6]While soap operas explored the problems of families and included a number of different and ever-changing plots, telenovelas usually focus on one romantic relationship. [7]The most popular telenovela plot centers on a handsome hero who breaks up with his wealthy, but usually evil, girlfriend to be with a poor, beautiful, and kind-hearted heroine. [8]The nasty girlfriend and the hero's relatives work hard to separate the two lovers, but a climactic ending usually sees the villains punished in painful, even gory ways, while the hero and the heroine get married. [9]Soap operas, typically broadcast in the afternoons, were originally designed to appeal mostly to women; telenovelas, however, air during prime time and have always attracted a broader and more varied audience.

Topic Sentence _____

    Paraphrase

a. There are some similarities between soap operas and telenovelas, but the two also differ a good deal.

b. Telenovelas have a much wider audience than soap operas do.

c. Soap operas are a staple of afternoon television, whereas telenovelas belong to prime time.

d. Telenovelas are Latin American versions of American soap operas.

[†]*Guiding Light* went into its final season in the fall of 2009. It got its start on radio in 1937.

VOCABULARY CHECK

The following words were introduced in pages 209–14. Match the word to the definition. Review words, definitions, and original context two or three times before taking the vocabulary tests. (The page numbers in parentheses indicate where the word first appeared.)

1. precedent (p. 209)   _____
2. flouting (p. 209)   _____
3. predators (p. 209)   _____
4. habitats (p. 209)   _____
5. cultivated (p. 210)   _____
6. devotees (p. 210)   _____
7. staple (p. 210)   _____
8. geriatric (p. 210)   _____
9. nocturnal (p. 210)   _____
10. productivity (p. 211)   _____
11. toxic (p. 213)   _____
12. pollutants (p. 213)   _____
13. reproductive (p. 213)   _____
14. genetic (p. 213)   _____
15. homage (p. 213)   _____
16. charisma (p. 214)   _____
17. subsequent (p. 214)   _____
18. graphic (p. 214)   _____
19. sociopathic (p. 214)   _____
20. instigated (p. 214)   _____

a. living spaces for specific species
b. nighttime
c. ability to produce goods
d. caused, motivated
e. obvious and vivid, often associated with sex and violence
f. a show of respect
g. a basic or essential element of something
h. related to the elderly
i. followers, believers
j. an example that becomes a pattern for future actions
k. showing contempt for or disregarding
l. following in time
m. animals that kill to survive
n. lacking all moral or ethical sense
o. poisonous
p. having to do with biological inheritance
q. cared for
r. personal magnetism or charm
s. related to birth
t. substances that are harmful

DIGGING DEEPER — Jury Dodgers Beware!

Looking Ahead As the paragraph on page 193 explained, some citizens take jury duty very seriously, while others throw away their notices to report. As the following reading suggests, those who shirk jury duty might want to rethink their attitude.

1 Recently, in Passaic County, New Jersey, fourteen citizens were collected by the sheriff's department and brought before a judge at the county courthouse. Their offense? Refusing to respond to multiple notices to report for service as jurors. Their punishment? Fines up to $500 and assignment to jury duty.

2 The keystone of the U.S. justice system is the right to a trial by a jury of one's peers. Recently, however, many courts have experienced serious problems in getting people to perform their civic duty. Only one out of four adults have served as jurors, and jury avoidance is at an all-time high level. It is not uncommon for trials to be delayed because too few jurors are available.

3 Most juries continue to number twelve individuals, although six are sometimes used. Most jury decisions must be unanimous—anything short of that leads to a hung jury and either retrial or dismissal. Potential jurors are summoned by the court for assignment to a jury pool. Jurors usually must be U.S. citizens eighteen years of age or older. Questioning by the judge, prosecuting attorney, and defense attorney—known as *voir dire*—disqualifies individuals with potential conflicts of interest, bias, or other factors germane to the case. Once selected, the juror may be required to give a day or two to service, or months for the occasional long, complex trial. Remuneration is minimal, ranging from $5 a day in California and New Jersey to $40 in South Dakota and New York.

4 Why has jury-dodging become a problem? First, some individuals suffer a loss of income from not being able to work. Employers may be required to keep employee-jurors on their payroll and are prohibited from firing them for serving jury duty, but abuses occur. For the self-employed, jury duty can be a serious hardship, as it can be for potential jurors with small children and no day care arrangement. Other burdens of jury duty include time spent away from one's job, family, or leisure activities. Jurors in tough criminal cases can suffer psychological disturbances. A relatively minor—but annoying—problem is the uninviting, uncomfortable surroundings of many jury waiting rooms.

5   All states have provisions for excusing or postponing service for people selected for duty (such as old age, disability, undue hardship, extreme inconvenience, military duty). For those who ignore their summons, judges may respond with a stick, like the Passaic County judge. In Grant County, Washington, two randomly picked jury scofflaws are regularly brought to answer before the judge. In North Dakota, New Jersey, and other states, they are reported in the local newspaper. A judge in Baltimore once placed nonreporting jurors in jail for several hours. A kinder approach is to improve the quality of jury duty by, for instance, installing computer work stations, libraries, and other amenities in the jury lounges. Arizona's 2003 jury reform bill imposed a filing fee on civil cases that significantly hiked juror pay and promised jurors they would only serve one day every two years unless picked for a trial.

6   Gradually, courts are incorporating information technology to create a cyberjuror. Basic touch-tone telephone systems inform members of the jury pool whether they are going to be needed the next day. Online, twenty-four-hour interactive systems that qualify potential jurors by administering an electronic *voir dire* make specific assignments and process excuse and postponement requests. Postage savings alone can be substantial, and the new cyberjurors appreciate the convenience. (Adapted from Bowman and Kearney, *State and Local Government*, p. 247.)

Sharpening Your Skills

DIRECTIONS   Answer the questions by filling in the blanks or circling the letters of the correct response.

1. The topic of this reading is
   a. the right to trial by jury.
   b. excuses for jury dodging.
   c. the problem of jury dodgers.
   d. cyberjuries.

2. The overall main idea of the reading is that
   a. jury duty is the responsibility of all good citizens.
   b. penalties for jury dodgers are becoming harsher because so many people have failed to do their duty.

c. brief jail terms are becoming a common punishment for jury dodgers who don't seem to understand the seriousness of their crime.

d. the punishments and penalties for jury dodgers need to be increased.

3. Using your own words, paraphrase the definition for the term *voir dire.*

_____

4. Paragraph 2 has which shape?

a.

| Topic sentence |
| Specific details |
| Topic sentence |

b.

| Introductory sentence |
| Topic sentence |
| Specific details |

c.

| Introductory sentence |
| *Reversal transition* |
| Topic sentence |
| Specific details |

5. Based on the context, how would you define the words *germane* and *remuneration* in paragraph 3?

a. *Germane* means _____.

b. *Remuneration* means _____.

Making Connections Re-read the paragraph on page 193. In discussing people who try to avoid jury duty, what do the authors of the selection on pages 217–18 include that the author of the previous paragraph leaves out?

_____

_____

The paragraph on page 193 suggests that many people believe they can ignore a summons to jury duty and get away with it. They assume that the state won't bother coming after them. Does the selection you just read support or contradict that assumption? Please explain your answer.

_____

_____

_____

Drawing Your Own Conclusions In paragraph 4, the authors say, "Jurors in tough criminal cases can suffer psychological disturbances." However, they don't say anything more specific than that. How do you think "jurors in tough criminal cases" might suffer psychologically?

_____

_____

How do you think those who ignore a summons to jury duty should be handled?

_____

_____

INTERNET RESOURCE To learn more about main ideas and topic sentences, go to laflemm.com and look under Key Concepts. You can also find this link at the student companion website for this text: www. cengage.com/devenglish/flemming/rfr11e.

▶ **TEST 1**   **Vocabulary Review**

DIRECTIONS   Fill in the blanks with one of the words listed below.

conclusive	speculators	analogies	traumatic	innovative
placebos	quarantine	paradoxes	dementia	consolidating

1. As it turned out, the _____, which doctors had said was a result of old age, was actually caused by the medication. Once he stopped taking it, the patient was no longer confused and forgetful.

2. In the most current study, one-half of the subjects were given the new drug; the other half received _____.

3. More and more researchers believe that the brain is active during sleep. Sleep appears to be the time when the brain works at _____ new information with what's already been learned previously.

4. Unfortunately, the Homestead Act of 1862, which was supposed to benefit those struggling to earn a living in the cities, ended up enriching _____, who went West to buy land cheap and then sell it high.

5. Although police were convinced that the two men had been slain by members of a rival gang, they had no _____ evidence that would convict the suspects. As a result, they had to let them go.

6. The birds should have been placed in _____ upon their arrival at Heathrow airport, but somehow the sick birds slipped through customs. Three weeks later, the first case of parrot fever was reported in the human population.

7. The speaker was a fan of _____, and she compared the organization to a bee hive, where the employees were like the drones—the bees who do all the work in the hive—while the top executives played the role of queen bees.

8. After what appeared to be a(n) _____ blow to the head, the boxer crumpled to the floor.

9. The poet liked to use _____ like "blind me so that I may really see" and "capture my soul so that I may finally be free of sin."

10. Aware that traditional methods weren't working, the science teacher wanted to use more _____ techniques to teach her students about the laws of gravity, but her department head discouraged creativity on principle, making the teacher afraid of doing anything different or original.

▶ TEST 2   **Vocabulary Review**

DIRECTIONS   Fill in the blanks with one of the words listed below.

anthropological	flouting	dignitaries	homage	geriatric
disoriented	electors	habitats	etching	toxic

1. The visiting _____ weren't used to being greeted so informally; they expected to be treated as important officials. In other words, they required constant attention to their every whim.

2. The skater thought she was fine after falling headfirst on the ice, but once she got up and started wobbling the wrong way to the dressing room, she realized how dizzy and _____ she truly was.

3. The _____ hanging on the wall suggested an artist who had real drawing talent.

4. When the ancient tomb began to surface beneath a fine layer of dirt, the scientists knew they had discovered something of enormous _____ significance.

5. After the _____ gathered together for a vote, they began quarreling over which one should cast the first ballot.

6. The exhausted parents sent their son off to private school, where he continued _____ every rule on the books; the only ones he didn't disobey were the ones he didn't know.

7. At eight years, a dog starts to be old and is considered a(n) _____ case.

8. Given that so much of our water is polluted by _____ chemicals, it's no wonder that frogs with birth defects are turning up in huge numbers. Frogs spend much of their lives in water.

9. Because panda bears eat up to 84 pounds of bamboo shoots per day, they require very specialized _____ in which bamboo is extremely plentiful.

10. When he made the winning touchdown in the 2009 Superbowl, Pittsburgh Steeler Santonio Holmes paid _____ to basketball great LeBron James by mimicking his famous Nike chalk commercial. Like James, Holmes showed he could just "do it."

◆ **TEST 3**   **Vocabulary Review**

DIRECTIONS   Fill in the blanks with one of the words listed below.

productivity	graphic	precedent	genetic	staple
instigated	devotees	sociopathic	nocturnal	charisma

1. In Alaska, fish has long been a diet _____.

2. According to the legends, vampires are _____ creatures, who cannot survive the light of day.

3. _____ of Hinduism believe in reincarnation.

4. President Barack Obama's personal _____ was
   reflected in the huge crowds that turned out to see him during his
   run for the presidency.

5. The movie got an *R* rating because of the _____ violence.

6. The con man had a(n) _____ personality; swindling
   people out of their hard-earned money did not disturb him in the
   slightest.

7. When Supreme Court Justice Oliver Wendell Holmes decided to
   support freedom of speech, except in cases of clear and present danger, he set a(n) _____ for numerous other Supreme
   Court decisions that followed.

8. During the Civil War, the news that those who could afford to pay
   $300 would escape the draft _____ major riots
   among the poor.

9. When management decided to eliminate the annual bonuses, _____ declined dramatically.

10. Testing for _____ disorders that are passed on through generations is still controversial because some people do not want to know if they might get a terrible disease sometime in the future.

▶ TEST 4   **Vocabulary Review**

DIRECTIONS   Fill in the blanks with one of the words listed below.

random	renovations	comprehensive	predators	mutilation
pollutants	liberator	reproductive	subsequent	cultivated

1. Thanks to the money from the stimulus package, schools in the state were receiving much needed _____.

2. Simón Bolívar, the general who liberated much of South America from Spanish rule, is known as "The _____"; he is also sometimes called the George Washington of South America.

3. Increasingly, the land is being _____ by farmers, leaving Niger's giraffes with nowhere to graze.

4. The insurance agent was very knowledgeable; she was able to find the couple a(n) _____ health care package that would cover all their needs.

5. The police were desperately trying to find a pattern in the attacks, but so far the attacks seemed frighteningly _____.

6. During the party, the teenagers had thought it would be fun to carve their initials into the old cabinet, but to the party-giver's great-grandmother, the initials on what had once been her hope chest seemed like _____.

7. In an odd twist on the _____ cycle, it is the male seahorse who gives birth.

8. Initially, the mortgage broker's explanation made perfect sense, but then his _____ statements contradicted everything he had said the first time around.

9. Not surprisingly, porcupines have almost no _____; hunting these prickly creatures is simply more trouble than it's worth.

10. The water's dark blue color was a strong indication that it was filled with _____ that had run off from the factory farm nearby.

▶ **TEST 5**   Recognizing Topics and Topic Sentences

DIRECTIONS   Read each paragraph. Circle the appropriate letter to identify the correct topic. Then write the number of the topic sentence in the blank.

1. ¹In the early nineteenth century, many runaway slaves found refuge among Florida's Seminole Indians. ²Outraged, the U.S. government ordered the Seminoles to leave Florida. ³But Florida was their home, and they refused. ⁴When Osceola, the Seminoles' fierce leader, received the government's order in 1832, he speared it with a dagger, announcing, "This is the only treaty I will make with the whites!" ⁵These were not empty words. ⁶In 1835, Osceola launched a full-scale rebellion against federal rule that lasted for seven years. ⁷Although Osceola outwitted pursuers, he was captured in 1837. ⁸Placed in prison, he died the following year. ⁹The war, however, raged on. Convinced that Osceola had been murdered, the Seminoles were determined to avenge him. ¹⁰Still, by 1842, even the memory of Osceola was not enough to fuel what had become a bloody and hopeless battle. ¹¹Defeated, the Seminoles were force-marched to Oklahoma.

Topic   a. runaway slaves

             b. the U.S. government's treatment of the Seminoles

             c. Osceola's leadership of the Seminole rebellion

             d. the Seminole Indians' aid to runaway slaves

Topic Sentence   _____

2. ¹*Bulimia* is the Greek word for "hunger"; it's also the name of a serious, potentially life-threatening eating disorder that afflicts thousands of people. ²The disease has numerous triggers, ranging from family conflict to depression, but no one is quite sure of its causes. ³Victims of the disease are usually young women who engage in binge eating, consuming large quantities of food way past the point when their hunger is satisfied. ⁴To avoid gaining weight, they then purge themselves of the food they've consumed. ⁵Ninety percent of bulimics purge by vomiting. ⁶Others use laxatives or enemas or refuse to eat for long periods of time. ⁷Because these behaviors usually occur in secret, bulimic individuals—especially those who

maintain an average weight—can be difficult to recognize. [8]Others, though, become alarmingly thin, shrinking to little more than skin stretched over bones even as they continue to think they are too heavy. [9]Too often, their distorted self-image is fatal. [10]Even bulimics who manage to maintain a normal-looking appearance face severe health problems, including fluid loss, stomach disorders, ulcers, kidney collapse, heart failure, and even death.

Topic   a. eating disorders

         b. bulimia

         c. causes of bulimia

         d. health problems

Topic Sentence   _____

3. [1]Today's firefighters battle wildfires with a mixture of science, technology, and old-fashioned physical labor. [2]Some are accompanied by scientists who assist firefighters by tracking climatic changes that will affect the fire's spread. [3]Firefighters are also aided by specialists who study vegetation types and land features to predict the speed and direction of a fire's progress. [4]Technological advancements also help in the fight. [5]Global Positioning Systems can pinpoint the exact location and size of a fire while sophisticated aircraft track the fire, dropping fire-retardant chemicals and water from the sky. [6]Human muscle, though, is a third essential firefighting ingredient. [7]Crews armed with axes, saws, shovels, and hoses still work hard to deter and stop a fire by clearing brush and creating firebreaks by digging bushes and cutting down trees. [8]Modern firefighters use all of the weapons at their disposal—both the new advances and centuries-old techniques—to battle fire's destructive force.

Topic   a. modern firefighting methods

         b. wildfires

         c. Global Positioning Systems

         d. new technology for battling fires

Topic Sentence   _____

4. [1]Daredevil skydivers leap from airplanes at great heights, trusting that training, good equipment, and favorable weather will carry them safely to the ground. [2]Still, skydiving successfully from, say,

9,000 feet involves more than courage and luck; it requires real skill. ³When a skydiver takes the plunge, he or she begins to free fall, traveling through the air with the parachute tightly packed and no way to control the speed. ⁴A good skydiver, however, knows how to time the parachute's opening, allowing its dome-shaped cloth cover to blossom into the air. ⁵The canopy creates surface resistance and slows the diver's descent. ⁶Then it's up to the diver to steer the rig to a landing by pulling on lines attached to the parachute. ⁷A truly skillful skydiver also knows how to touch down on his or her feet. ⁸Still, millions of landings have been made on the knees or other, more delicate, body parts.

Topic   a. good and bad landings

          b. daredevils

          c. daredevil sports

          d. skillful skydiving

Topic Sentence   _____

5. ¹The white-tailed deer was one of the first animals to be protected by federal legislation. ²But as it turns out, unlike the passenger pigeon, white-tailed deer were not in much need of protection. ³They have proven to be highly adaptable creatures, and their population has not diminished despite the loss of wooded areas. ⁴Like squirrels and robins, white-tailed deer have adapted quite nicely to life on the edge of suburbia. ⁵In fact, they are happy to supplement their regular diets with fruits and vegetables from gardens. ⁶In addition, many homeowners are fond of these gentle creatures and put out blocks of deer food that help the animals make it through harsh winters.

Topic   a. the diet of white-tailed deer

          b. life on the edge of suburbia

          c. the survival of white-tailed deer

          d. wildlife in the suburbs

Topic Sentence   _____

▶ TEST 6   Recognizing Topics, Topic Sentences, and Transitions

DIRECTIONS   Read each paragraph. Circle the appropriate letter to identify the correct topic. Then write the number of the topic sentence in the blank. If the topic sentence is introduced by a reversal transition, circle the transitional word or phrase. Underline any transitional sentences.

1.   ¹Many parents and educators consider the Internet a powerful tool for learning. ²Others, though, are not so sure; these teachers and parents are concerned about the more than two hundred websites currently selling research papers to students, and they are determined to do something to correct the problem of Internet plagiarism. ³Websites like CheatHouse, PerfectTermPapers, and Researchpapers-on-time† sell papers on a variety of subjects, ranging from biology to poetry. ⁴Although most of these sites include disclaimer statements, insisting that the papers are simply "models," along with warnings against plagiarism, it's hard to believe that anyone takes either disclaimer or warning seriously. ⁵On the assumption that many students will be tempted to pay for a paper, two instructors at Coastal Carolina University, Margaret Fain and Peggy Bates, have created a list called "Cheating 101: Detecting Plagiarized Papers" (www.coastal.edu/library/presentations/plagiarz.html). ⁶Websites like Plagiarism.org have also sprung up to tell teachers how they can spot a stolen term paper. ⁷Similarly, companies like Turnitin.com will, for a fee, search every line of a student's paper and compare it, line by line, to their huge database of online papers and websites. ⁸If anything suspicious turns up in a student paper, Turnitin flags the passage and notifies the instructor.

Topic   a. CheatHouse

            b. plagiarism

            c. the problem of Internet plagiarism

            d. the effects of the Internet on education

Topic Sentence   _____

2.   ¹In 2005, a team of French surgeons performed successful face transplant surgery on a thirty-eight-year-old woman, whose face had

---

†In what has to be the height of hypocrisy, these sites tout the fact that the papers they sell aren't plagiarized but are written by staff writers.

been savagely ripped apart by a dog. [2]Monstrously disfigured, unable to eat or speak, the woman's only hope was a face transplant to supply her with a new nose, lips, and chin. [3]During a fifteen-hour operation, a team of eight surgeons stitched donated facial tissue on to what was left of their patient's ravaged face. [4]When the operation ended, the doctors pronounced the results to be even better than they'd imagined. [5]With her new face that is a combination of her own and the donor's, the patient does not look as she had before the injury. [6]Nevertheless, the operation is a promising breakthrough for those disfigured by disease or injury.

Topic

a. transplants

b. the first successful face transplant

c. transplant surgeons

d. people who have been disfigured in accidents

Topic Sentence _____

3. [1]In the past, South Koreans of marriageable age relied on their parents to find them a suitable spouse. [2]The current generation, however, has more options. [3]South Koreans in search of a mate are likely to use professional matchmakers or online dating services. [4]However, whichever method they choose, South Koreans, unlike Americans, are less focused on falling madly in love and more interested in finding husbands and wives who share their social goals and work ethic. [5]Men are looking for wives who can juggle their working lives with caring for the home. [6]Women are looking for men who are ambitious and hardworking; good looks or sex appeal are not considered an acceptable substitute for professional success. [7]Important, too, is the zodiac sign linked to the year a person was born. [8]Tradition claims, for example, that a man born in the year of the monkey would not be happy with a woman born in the year of the tiger. [9]Thus, many people in search of a mate are intent on knowing the birth sign of the person identified as a possible match.

Topic

a. searching for a mate in South Korea

b. romance in South Korea

c. the decline of matchmaking in South Korea

d. Korean dating services versus matchmakers

Topic Sentence _____

4. [1]In the 1930s and 1940s, the "zoot suit," with its tight-waisted, big-lapel jacket and baggy pants, wasn't just an item of clothing, it was a political statement. [2]Worn first in the jazz clubs of Harlem, the zoot suit, sometimes called "drapes," was popular with young African-American men intent on showing the rest of the world that they were hip, cool, and unimpressed by racist claims that they were second-class citizens. [3]That same refusal to be ignored or slighted motivated the embrace of the zoot suit by Hispanics in California, and in Los Angeles in particular. [4]Young Mexican-Americans in Los Angeles were fully aware that their flashy attire scared some of the city's less open-minded residents. [5]That's precisely what they liked about it. [6]For them, the zoot suit was a symbol of rebellion and a refusal to be ashamed of who they were. [7]Unfortunately, when riots broke out in Los Angeles in 1943, pitting soldiers on leave with the city's Mexican-American inhabitants, the zoot suit marked young men for attack, and wearing it was like displaying a target. [8]As a result, young men in zoot suits bore the brunt of both the attacks and the arrests (sailors rounded up were turned over to their commanding officers). [9]For that reason, the violence that flared up in Los Angeles in the summer of 1943 is remembered in history books as the "Zoot Suit Riots."

Topic

   a. African-American men wearing zoot suits

   b. riots in Los Angeles

   c. zoot suits

   d. racism in the 1930s and 1940s

Topic Sentence   _____

▶ TEST 7   Recognizing Topic Sentences

DIRECTIONS   Read each paragraph. Then write the number of the topic sentence in the blank at the end. *Note*: If there is a topic sentence at the beginning and the end of the paragraph, put both sentence numbers into the blank.

1. [1]On September 1, 1914, a twenty-nine-year-old passenger pigeon named Martha died in the Cincinnati Zoo. [2]Martha was the last known passenger pigeon in existence. [3]Yet in the nineteenth century, there were so many passenger pigeons in America that no laws were made to protect them, and that lack of legal protection proved their undoing. [4]Throughout the nineteenth century, large-scale pigeon shoots were a popular sport. [5]The killing often went on for days, mainly for the thrill of the kill, since the hunters' need for food had long been satisfied. [6]As the country grew more populated, passenger pigeons also found it increasingly difficult to locate the wide and uninhabited areas of land they needed for raising their young. [7]By the beginning of the twentieth century, Martha the passenger pigeon was all that was left from the huge flocks that had once ranged over the United States. [8]With the death of Martha, passenger pigeons disappeared forever.

Topic Sentence   _____

2. [1]By the time Elizabeth I became queen of England in 1558, her half-sister, Mary Tudor, had driven the country into chaos. [2]Mary, a Catholic, opposed the way her six-times-married father, Henry VIII, had abandoned the Catholic faith, so she started a new English church and attempted to force Catholicism on England. [3]She put non-Catholics on trial for challenging Church law and had some of them burned at the stake. [4]Protestants were forced to flee the country, and the queen became known as "Bloody Mary." [5]It was only after Mary died that peace again returned to England. (Armento et al., *Across the Centuries*, p. 459.)

Topic Sentence   _____

3. [1]Because of their great strength and high pain tolerance, pit bulls are greatly prized and often badly mistreated by those who make money from the so-called sport of dog fighting. [2]Their human owners breed and encourage the dogs to be aggressive, punishing and mistreating them if they are not. [3]Timid pit bulls—and such dogs do exist— purchased to make an owner rich are unlikely to have a very long life.

⁴They will be destroyed if they don't learn to be aggressive. ⁵Although pit bulls have been bred to fight, it's mainly greedy and abusive owners who have turned the breed into a real and imagined threat.

Topic Sentence _____

4. ¹In ancient times, Roman warriors used loud noise to frighten their enemies. ²Beating their swords against their shields, they'd yell taunts and insults, blow horns, and pound drums. ³During the Civil War, Union soldiers reportedly got chills when they heard their Confederate opponents' blood-curdling "rebel yell." ⁴Throughout history, it seems, loud noise has been employed as a weapon. ⁵Today, for instance, the U.S. Army uses noise to unsettle enemies and drive them out of hiding. ⁶Soldiers also play heavy metal or hard rock music to intimidate the enemy. ⁷In 1989, U.S. troops blasted high-volume rock music at the Vatican Embassy in Panama, where General Manuel Noriega, the Panamanian military leader wanted on drug charges, had taken refuge. ⁸During the Gulf and Iraq wars, right before an attack, American soldiers played grunge rock from mounted loudspeakers. ⁹Soldiers also sometimes use a "noise gun," the Long Range Acoustic Device (LRAD), which blasts a focused stream of harsh sounds so loud they can trigger nausea and fainting. (Source of examples: Anjula Razdan, "The Father of Acoustic Ecology," *Utne*, July–August 2005, p. 57.)

Topic Sentence _____

5. ¹Munchausen syndrome is a psychiatric disorder in which people fake illness in order to get attention and treatment. ²People affected with Munchausen syndrome will, for instance, scratch and cut themselves or add blood to their urine specimens. ³They may also inject a variety of substances into their blood or veins in order to cause illness. ⁴Those afflicted with Munchausen syndrome usually have the medical knowledge to make themselves appear convincingly sick. ⁵They will present themselves at emergency rooms, reporting a variety of symptoms, and willingly undergo any number of tests. ⁶If the test results do not match their symptoms, these individuals will often respond by reporting an entirely different set of symptoms. ⁷If confronted, victims of Munchausen syndrome are inclined to get hostile and demand treatment at another facility. (Adapted from Neighbors and Tannehill-Jones, *Human Diseases*, p. 420.)

Topic Sentence _____

▶ TEST 8   Recognizing the Most Accurate Paraphrase

DIRECTIONS   Read each paragraph. Write the number of the topic sentence in the blank. Then circle the letter of the most accurate paraphrase. *Note*: These paraphrases are the kind that would be appropriate for term papers.

1. [1]Cocaine became an outlawed substance in 1914. [2]But, for centuries before that, the drug was used for a variety of purposes. [3]Before the Spanish conquest of Peru, the coca plant was reserved for Inca[†] royalty, who used it in rituals and celebrations. [4]By the sixteenth century, when Spanish explorers first began arriving in South America, the native inhabitants had a 5,000-year history of chewing coca leaves to fight fatigue and hunger and increase endurance. [5]Then the Spanish explorers introduced coca leaves to Europe, where the leaves were smoked or consumed only occasionally until the nineteenth century. [6]In 1860, however, Germany's Albert Niemann isolated the coca plant's active ingredient and processed it into powder and liquid forms. [7]Thanks to Niemann, doctors were able to dispense cocaine for a variety of ailments, from toothaches to hay fever. [8]They also used it as an anesthetic during surgery. [9]It didn't take long before cocaine was available over the counter and as an ingredient in cigarettes, chocolate, and wine. [10]In 1886, Atlanta surgeon and chemist John Pemberton introduced Coca-Cola, a drink that contained about 60 mg of cocaine and was advertised as a cure for nervous ailments, "offering the virtues of coca without the vices of alcohol." [11]Not until the early 1900s did the medical community begin to understand cocaine's addictive nature, which led to its being banned. (Source of information: "In Search of the Big Bang," www.cocaine.org.)

Topic Sentence   _____

Paraphrase   a. Cocaine is destructive and highly addictive; it should remain illegal.

b. Cocaine offers medical benefits, but the dangers outweigh any positive effects.

c. Cocaine should never have been made illegal.

d. For hundreds of years, using cocaine was legal.

[†]Inca: Peruvian people who established an empire from Ecuador to central Chile.

2. [1]We humans spend millions of dollars every year trying to rid ourselves of insects, but some of those annoying bugs are actually essential to our survival. [2]Some insects, for instance, perform the vital function of fertilizing flowering plants. [3]Without the bugs' help, crops could not reproduce. [4]Insects are also essential to maintaining the balance of nature and preventing the uncontrolled spread of vegetation. [5]Diseases spread by insects also keep wild-animal populations from getting out of control. [6]In addition, insects dispose of animal remains and waste. [7]Dung beetles, for instance, have prevented Australia's grazing lands from being ruined by cattle droppings. [8]For some cultures, insects serve as food, with grubs, grasshoppers, and other bugs providing essential protein. [9]Insects also provide humans with many valuable products, such as silk, beeswax, and honey. [10]Insects may be pests, but they also provide us with countless benefits.

Topic Sentence   _____

Paraphrase

   a. Insects are essential to a garden: without them, there would be no flowers.

   b. In some cultures, insects are on the menu.

   c. Insects may be a nuisance, but some are beneficial.

   d. Insects provide many of life's luxuries.

3. [1]Many of the young heroes and heroines in children's literature—including popular characters like J. K. Rowling's Harry Potter, Roald Dahl's James Henry Trotter of *James and the Giant Peach*, and Lucy Maud Montgomery's Anne of *Anne of Green Gables*—are orphans. [2]Although the presence of so many orphans in young adult fiction may seem to suggest an unnecessarily pessimistic, or sad, worldview, literature experts say that orphaned characters actually serve a positive purpose. [3]According to English professor and children's literature specialist Philip Nel, an orphaned literary character expresses the powerlessness many young readers feel. [4]Still, says Nel, "many literary orphans are resilient characters who, despite their lack of power, find the emotional resources to beat the odds and make their way in the world." [5]Thus, orphaned characters make young readers believe it's possible to have some control over a world dominated by adults. [6]Nel also believes that literary orphans encourage children to think about growing up. [7]He says that a hero or heroine who has been prematurely separated from his or her parents encourages young readers to explore the idea of leaving and seeking independence.

[8]By imagining a world free of their parents, young readers prepare for the transition from child to adult. (Source of quotation: Deirdre Donahue, "Orphans in Literature Empower Children," *USA Today*, July 3, 2003, p. 7D.)

Topic Sentence ____

Paraphrase

a. The large number of orphans in children's fiction suggests kids don't want adults in their lives.

b. Some experts think orphaned literary characters help young readers feel more in control of their world.

c. The pessimism in children's literature is cause for concern.

d. Youthful readers need to express resentment toward parents; that's why there are so many orphans in children's literature.

4. [1]Men outrank women in all but one (Alzheimer's disease) of the fifteen causes of death, and women live an average of five years longer than men do. [2]Although many people believe that the reason for women's longevity is genetic, at least one study published in the *American Journal of Public Health* indicates that American men may be more likely than women to engage in risky, health-damaging behaviors. [3]For example, 26 percent of men smoke, compared to 22 percent of women; men are also far more likely to abuse drugs, drive without a seat belt, and ride motorcycles without helmets. [4]Thanks to an attitude that drives men to tackle danger head-on, they are twice as likely to get hit by lightning or to drown in floods. [5]Men also take less care of their bodies than do women, who are twice as likely as men to get an annual physical. [6]In addition, men are less likely to seek medical help when they experience health problems. [7]Then, too, men work in more dangerous professions than women, so males account for 90 percent of all on-the-job fatalities. [8]Clearly, this particular study suggests that men's behavior may actually be the reason they don't live as long as women do. (Source of statistics: Sanjay Gupta, "Why Men Die Young," *Time*, May 12, 2003, www.time.com/time/magazine/printout/0,8816,449501,00.html.)

Topic Sentence ____

Paraphrase

a. Men are more likely than women to develop Alzheimer's disease, and scientists are beginning to understand why.

b. Women live longer than men, and researchers are trying to find out why.

    c. Women's social involvement with others makes them live longer than men do.

    d. One study suggests that men's risky behavior results in a shorter life span for men than for women.

5. [1]In the past, snowmobile, motocross, and all-terrain vehicle (ATV) riders were criticized for damaging the fragile wilderness areas where they practice their sport. [2]Today, another group is being blamed for adversely impacting the landscape. [3]According to environmentalists, the rock-climbing enthusiasts who enjoy scrambling up rock faces and boulders are degrading many wilderness areas. [4]Although some climbers are attempting to follow a "leave no trace" policy, many others unthinkingly crush vegetation and interfere with wildlife like nesting birds. [5]In addition to harming wildlife, climbers are also leaving behind trash, climbing gear, and human waste. [6]The chalk they use on their hands to grip rocks, for instance, leaves smudges that don't wash away in the rain. [7]Climbers also damage cliffs by drilling bolts for safety ropes. [8]Some young climbers paint graffiti on the rocks they scale. [9]In Texas, unruly climbers scrawled graffiti on top of ancient rock art, forcing the state's park officials to place restrictions on rock climbing.

Topic Sentence   _____

Paraphrase   a. Some environmentalists believe that rock climbers are damaging wilderness areas.

    b. Too many rock climbers are painting graffiti on top of ancient landmarks.

    c. Rock climbing is popular, but its popularity shouldn't mask its danger.

    d. Rock climbers are worse than snowmobilers when it comes to damaging the environment.

Focusing on
Supporting Details

IN THIS CHAPTER, YOU WILL LEARN

- more about the relationship between topic sentences and supporting details.
- how to distinguish between major and minor supporting details.
- how writers rely on readers to infer additional details.
- how to recognize the function of every sentence.

"God is in the details."
—Ludwig Mies van der Rohe, architect

"The devil is in the deta
—Anonymo

Tischenko I

Chapter 4 described topic sentences and briefly mentioned the supporting details that explain them. Chapter 5 now looks more closely at supporting details and the topic sentences they develop. It also describes how readers add their own supporting details to flesh out the author's. Finally, we'll look at concluding sentences, which may not directly support the main idea but can still be significant.

Supporting Details Develop Topic Sentences

Paul: I thought June's behavior at that meeting was extraordinary.

Marisa: I thought the same thing. I couldn't believe how rude she was. She's too outspoken for my taste.

Paul: That's not what I meant at all. I thought she was great. When she believes in something, she's not afraid to speak her mind.

When the conversation between Paul and Marisa stays on a general level, both speakers are inclined to agree. It's only when Marisa moves to a more specific level that the speakers realize they actually disagree. This is a good example of how supporting details create good communication. As you might suspect, the kind of confusion that happens between Marisa and Paul isn't restricted to speech. It can also occur between

aragraphs

derstood if they don't supply enough support-
tails are more specific sentences that explain
e by providing reasons, examples, studies,
upporting details can take many different
the same: They help clarify, prove, or sug-

and supporting details work together,

eate serious psychological problems
ribute to continued joblessness.

By itself, the sentence tells us that long-term unemployment can do psychological damage. But what does the author mean by the general phrase "prolonged unemployment"? Is she talking about six months or six years? Exactly what kind of psychological problems does she have in mind? After all, that general phrase covers a good deal of ground. Also, how do psychological problems contribute to continued joblessness?

On its own, the sentence raises several questions. However, when it's followed by specific supporting details, those questions are answered:

> [1]Prolonged unemployment can create serious psychological problems that, in the long run, actually contribute to continued joblessness. [2]In a society that stresses the relationship between productive work and personal value, it is easy enough to equate long-term unemployment with personal worthlessness. [3]That is, in fact, precisely what many unemployed men and women begin to do. [4]Out of a job for a year or more, they begin to see themselves as worthless human beings without any value to society. [5]In what amounts to a vicious cycle, their sense of personal worthlessness further diminishes their chances of gaining employment. [6]Sometimes they stop looking for work altogether, sure in their despair that no one will hire them. [7]Or else they go on interviews, but they present themselves in such a defeated and hopeless way that the interviewer cannot help but be unimpressed and reject their application.

Do you see how the specific sentences in the paragraph help readers understand the topic sentence? Sentences 2 and 3 limit the ways in which readers can interpret the phrase "serious psychological problems." Sentence 4 defines "prolonged unemployment."

Sentence 5 explains the second half of the topic sentence by telling us how a sense of personal worthlessness can "contribute to continued joblessness." Sentences 6 and 7 provide two specific illustrations of how this happens.

Topic Sentences Can't Do It All

The supporting details in the paragraph define key phrases like "prolonged unemployment" and "serious psychological damage." They also illustrate the author's main idea and thereby answer a question readers might raise about the topic sentence, "How does prolonged unemployment contribute to continued joblessness?"

When reading a paragraph, you should always search for the author's topic sentence. However, by itself, that topic sentence is bound to raise some questions that only the supporting details can answer.

Actually, if you don't understand the supporting details the author uses to develop the topic sentence, you haven't truly understood the paragraph. Imagine, for example, that you were asked this question on an exam: "Explain how prolonged unemployment can contribute to continued joblessness." Without a thorough understanding of the paragraph's supporting details, you wouldn't be able to answer the question.

You can usually determine what supporting details contribute to your understanding of the topic sentence by asking two questions: (1) What type of supporting details—examples, reasons, studies, definitions, statistics—does the author supply? (2) What questions about the topic sentence do the supporting details answer?

READING TIP Once you think you have identified the topic sentence, ask yourself which of the remaining sentences provide clarification or evidence for that sentence. If the remaining sentences don't do either, you need to rethink your choice of topic sentence.

◆ **EXERCISE 1**   **Recognizing Supporting Details**

DIRECTIONS   The first sentence in each group of sentences is the topic sentence. That topic sentence is followed by five supporting details. Circle the letters of the three sentences that make the topic sentence clear and convincing.

EXAMPLE

Topic Sentence In April 1986, a tragic accident occurred at a nuclear power plant known as Chernobyl.

Supporting Details (a.) An explosion ripped through one of Chernobyl's four reactors, and radiation entered the atmosphere.

(b.) The plant burned for two weeks because technicians were unable to plug the leak caused by the explosion.

c. America had had its own nuclear scare when a meltdown occurred at Pennsylvania's Three Mile Island.

(d.) Immediately following the explosion at Chernobyl, thirty-one people died; several weeks later, 135,000 people were evacuated from the area.

e. Western Europe relies on nuclear power for much of its electricity.

EXPLANATION   The three supporting details that are circled tell us more about the tragic accident mentioned in the topic sentence. These are the three sentences that help make the topic sentence clear and convincing. The other two do not help explain the topic sentence.

Topic Sentence 1. The life of the Masai, a group of people who make their home in East Africa, is tightly linked to the raising of cattle.

Supporting Details a.) The diet of the Masai consists mainly of the blood and milk of cattle.

b.) Because they consider cattle sacred, the Masai do not slaughter or sell them.

c. Through a series of treaties, the British evicted the Masai from most of their homeland.

d.) The Masai follow their cattle from grazing site to grazing site.

e. The Masai are known to be fierce and proud warriors.

Topic Sentence 2. After close to forty years on NASA's[†] drawing boards, the Hubble space telescope went into orbit in 1990; but the telescope was plagued with problems throughout its voyage.

Supporting Details a. Edwin Hubble, for whom the telescope was named, was the son of a Missouri lawyer.

b.) The Hubble's ninety-four-inch mirror was off, and it sent blurred images back to earth.

c.) By 1993, some of the telescope's navigational equipment had begun to fail.

d. The current generation of land-based telescopes can do anything the Hubble can.

e.) During its early voyages in space, the Hubble telescope responded poorly to temperature change.

[†]NASA: a word formed from combining the initial letters in the words National Aeronautics and Space Administration. Another example of an acronym.

Topic Sentence 3. During World War I, new technology made war deadlier than it had ever been before.

Supporting Details

    a. During World War I, the czar of Russia took the Russians under his personal command.

    b. When World War I began, the U.S. Army consisted of only 92,710 men.

    c. In World War I, new technology allowed both sides to launch airplanes filled with explosives.

    d. After the Germans used poison gas in 1915, France, England, and the United States also began using it.

    e. New gasses were invented that could maim* and kill faster than ever before.

Topic Sentence 4. Before the introduction of a vaccine in 1954, the spread of polio terrorized the nation.

Supporting Details

    a. In 1916, a polio epidemic hit New York City; twenty-seven thousand people were paralyzed and six thousand died.

    b. The virus that causes polio was identified in 1908.

    c. In the early 1900s, physicians believed that polio was associated with the teething of infants, despite the fact that plenty of infants cut new teeth with no signs of fever or paralysis.

    d. Twenty-five thousand cases of polio were reported in 1946; most of them were children who were left paralyzed.

    e. Between 1952 and 1953, close to one hundred thousand people contracted polio.

◆ EXERCISE 2   Distinguishing Between Supporting Details and Topic Sentences

DIRECTIONS   Read each jumbled-up paragraph. In the blank at the end, write the number of the topic sentence. *Note*: Remember that topic sentences must be able to generally summarize the paragraph while the supporting details are necessarily more specific in nature.

EXAMPLE   [1]In April 1993, the nation watched as members of the Alcohol, Tobacco, and Firearms department were shot while attempting

—————————

*maim: injure severely, usually with scarring or loss of limbs.

to enter the cult compound* of David Koresh and the Branch Davidians. [2]The standoff between the two groups lasted until the compound burned to the ground with seventy-five members inside. [3]Cults, groups that demand complete obedience from their members, can sometimes have destructive and deadly effects on both their members and their critics. [4]One of the first and most notorious* cults to come to the attention of the public was Jim Jones's Peoples Temple in 1957. [5]Twenty years later in Guyana,[†] Jones erected "Jonestown," a town controlled by armed guards. [6]Tragically, in 1978, Jones ordered the "White Night," in which every member, a total of 909 adults and children, drank Kool-Aid laced with rat poison on command and died as a result. __3__

EXPLANATION   Only sentence 3 generally summarizes the specific examples provided by the supporting details. It's also the only sentence that's more general than all the others. The rest of the sentences are supporting details.

1. [1]Big dogs like German shepherds and Labrador retrievers, carefully bred for strength and appearance, frequently have hip problems that shorten their lives. [2]Pointers have become likely candidates for cancerous lymphomas, and Dobermans are inclined to suffer bleeding disorders. [3]Irish setters are frequently victims of eyesight problems. [4]Some people don't want to get dogs from the pound because they are afraid they might be inheriting someone else's problem pet, but pedigreed pooches are often the victim of overbreeding and more likely to have a host of health and temperament problems. [5]Bred for their sweet temperament, Golden retrievers also have become prey to skin and stomach disorders. [6]The much maligned pit bulls, in contrast, have been bred for aggression, and while they are loyal to their owners, they are not always safe around strangers. _____

2. [1]Delusions are false ideas that remain unchanged in the face of all logical arguments. [2]Victims of schizophrenia may, for instance, believe that they have the power to shape world events. [3]They may

---

*compound: building or buildings used as housing and surrounded by walls.
*notorious: famous for bad reasons.
[†]Guyana: officially the "Co-operative Republic of Guyana," located on the northern coast of South America.

see themselves as some powerful figure from the past like Napoleon or Jesus Christ. [4]Schizophrenia is characterized by delusions and hallucinations. [5]Hallucinations are perceptions of the world that occur in the absence of any external, or outside, stimuli. [6]They have no basis in reality. [7]Hallucinations include hearing nonexistent voices, seeing things that aren't there, having the sensation of being touched, or smelling and tasting things that are not, in fact, present either in the air or in food. [8]Schizophrenic delusions come in several forms. [9]Victims may feel that they are being persecuted by those who intend to do them harm. _____

3. [1]Wild animals can develop a real affection for their owners, but that does not mean they won't follow their instincts and attack if they feel threatened. [2]For a number of reasons, keeping wild animals as pets is not a good idea. [3]Baby chimpanzees, tigers, and lions are truly adorable, but they grow up, at which point adult animal behavior replaces the cuddly, dependent behavior of juveniles, and the animals may scratch, bite, or claw their owners. [4]Wild animals also carry diseases that are dangerous to people. [5]Thousands of people every year get salmonella infections from contact with reptiles and amphibians.* [6]The more people buy exotic animals as pets, the longer the exotic pet trade will continue and animals will be hunted and taken from their natural habitat to be sold as pets. _____

4. [1]Even a small amount of alcohol can bring about skeletal relaxation. [2]A larger amount can impair the respiratory* and cardiovascular* systems. [3]The consumption of alcohol has numerous mental and physical effects. [4]Consuming alcohol also alters our thinking so that sound judgment and concern for safety are reduced. [5]With heavy alcohol consumption, many people start to stagger and have difficulty walking. [6]Difficulty walking can become so intense that an individual falls to the ground. [7]Eventually, the person might find himself or herself in a complete stupor and unaware of what is happening in the external world. _____

---

*amphibians: animals that can live in water and on land.
*respiratory: related to breathing.
*cardiovascular: related to the heart and blood vessels.

◆ **EXERCISE 3**   **Identifying Irrelevant Details**

DIRECTIONS   Read each paragraph. Write the number of the topic sentence in the first blank. Each paragraph includes a supporting detail that has no relationship to the topic sentence. Write the number of that sentence in the second blank.

EXAMPLE   [1]Orthorexia nervosa is a new eating disorder that occurs when health-conscious individuals become obsessed with the quality of the food they eat. [2]People who suffer from this disorder base their self-esteem on their ability to maintain a diet of only healthy foods. [3]They decide, for example, that beans and rice are healthy and restrict themselves to eating only those two foods. [4]If they deviate from their restricted diet, they feel intensely guilty and depressed. [5]Bulimics overeat and then feel guilty until they are able to purge.* [6]Victims of orthorexia nervosa don't seem to realize that excessive reliance on a few select foods can deprive their bodies of critical nutrients.

Topic Sentence ___1___

Irrelevant Detail ___5___

EXPLANATION   With the exception of sentence 5, the supporting details in the sample paragraph all describe the eating disorder orthorexia nervosa. Sentence 5, however, talks about the eating disorder bulimia and never relates it to orthorexia, making the detail in sentence 5 irrelevant to the rest of the paragraph.

1. [1]In 1894, Japan waged war with China for the control of Korea; the Chinese, however, were no match for their opponents. [2]Within one year, the war was over, and the Japanese had almost completely destroyed the Chinese naval forces. [3]As a result of the war, China had to pay large sums of money to Japan and recognize the full independence of Korea; it also had to give up the resource-rich island of Taiwan. [4]Although the war was brief, it proved without a doubt that Japan was a military power to be reckoned with. [5]During World War II, Japan invaded China.

---

*purge: remove waste from the bowels or stomach; also, to eliminate or get rid of.

Topic Sentence   1

Irrelevant Detail   5

2. ¹Child abuse can take several forms. ²Sometimes the child is injured physically and may suffer from an odd or a disturbing combination of cuts, burns, bruises, or broken bones. ³Usually the parents or guardians claim that the child "had an accident," even though no normal accident could cause such injuries. ⁴Abused children have a greater chance of becoming abusive parents. ⁵But child abuse may also take the form of emotional neglect; the parents will simply ignore the child and refuse to respond to bids for attention. ⁶Children suffering from this kind of abuse often show symptoms of the *failure to thrive* syndrome*, in which physical growth is delayed. ⁷In still other cases of maltreatment, the child may be emotionally abused. ⁸One or both parents may ridicule or belittle the child. ⁹In this case, physical problems may be absent, but the child's self-esteem will be seriously undermined.

Topic Sentence   1

Irrelevant Detail   4

3. ¹Do you need to memorize a list of items in a particular order? ²If you do, you should take the *serial position effect* into account. ³The serial position effect refers to the tendency of many people to make the most errors when trying to remember the middle of a list or series. ⁴If, for example, you are introduced to a long line of people, you are most likely to forget the names of those in the middle of the line. ⁵People who deal with the public a lot can't afford to be forgetful. ⁶Anytime you need to learn a long poem or speech, be sure that you take the serial position effect into account. ⁷Give the middle of the speech or poem extra attention and practice.

Topic Sentence   3

Irrelevant Detail   5

4. ¹Most people run or scream in terror when they see a snake. ²Yet if snakes are examined without prejudice, they prove to be fascinating

*thrive: grow.

and relatively harmless members of the reptile family. ³Like other reptiles, they are cold-blooded, and their temperatures change with the environment. ⁴Although most people think that snakes are slimy and wet, the opposite is true. ⁵Their skins are cool and dry, even pleasant to the touch. ⁶The Hopi Indians perform ritual dances with live rattlesnakes in their mouths. ⁷Despite their reputation, most snakes do more good than harm by helping to control the rodent population.

Topic Sentence ___2___

Irrelevant Detail ___6___

Understanding the Difference Between Major and Minor Details

The two kinds of supporting details are *major* and *minor*. To understand the difference between the two, read the following paragraph. The major supporting details appear in **boldface**, the minor in *italics*.

> Psychologists have identified three basic styles of parenting. **Controlling parents think their children have few rights and many responsibilities.** *They tend to demand strict obedience to rigid standards of behavior and expect their children to obey their commands unquestioningly.* **Permissive parents, in contrast, require little responsible behavior from their children.** *Rules are not enforced, and the child usually gets his or her own way.* **Effective parents find a balance between their rights and their children's rights.** *They control their children's behavior without being harsh or rigid.*

In this paragraph, the topic sentence announces that psychologists have identified three different parenting styles. The natural response of most readers would be a question: "What are the three styles of parenting?" Notice how all the major details (printed in boldface) speak directly to that question.

Based on this illustration, we can say then that **major details** define key terms and clarify general words or phrases in the topic sentence. They further explain or develop those parts of the topic sentence that might otherwise confuse or even mystify readers. More specifically, major details answer questions raised by the topic sentence. Essential to understanding the main idea, major details should be paraphrased and included in your notes.

The Role of Minor Details

Look now at the minor details in the sample paragraph. Notice how they further explain the major details. Based on the example given, we can say that **minor details** help make major ones more specific. They can also repeat a key point for emphasis or add a colorful fact to hold the reader's interest. What minor details don't do is directly clarify or explain the topic sentence.

> **READING TIP**
> If you eliminate a minor detail from a paragraph, the main idea expressed by the topic sentence should remain clear and convincing. If it doesn't, the detail you eliminated is probably more major than minor.

Evaluating Minor Details

Unlike major details, minor details may or may not be essential to your understanding of the paragraph. If you need a minor detail in order to fully understand a major one, then, yes, include it in your reading notes. However, if the minor detail simply repeats or slightly expands a point clearly stated in a major detail, then you can safely leave it out.

To test your ability to recognize major and minor details, read the next sample paragraph. It contains only one minor detail. When you finish the paragraph, write the number of that sentence in the blank that follows.

[1]In the last forty-odd years, Native Americans have made numerous attempts to gain more political power. [2]In late 1969, a group of Native Americans publicized their grievances by occupying Alcatraz, the abandoned prison in San Francisco Bay, for nineteen months. [3]In 1963, tribes in the Northwest waged a campaign to have their fishing rights recognized in parts of Washington. [4]These were eventually granted by the Supreme Court in 1968. [5]In 1972, a group of Native Americans marched on Washington, D.C., to dramatize what they called a "trail of

broken treaties" and present the government with a series of demands. [6]In 1973, members of AIM, the American Indian Movement, took over Wounded Knee, South Dakota, for seventy-two days to protest the government's treatment of Native Americans. [7]Since the early 1980s, several tribes have filed lawsuits to win back lands taken from their ancestors. _____ (Adapted from Thio, *Sociology*, p. 255.)

In this paragraph, the topic sentence (sentence 1) tells us that in the last few decades, Native Americans have begun to demand more political power. Sentences 2, 3, 5, 6, and 7 are all major details that answer the obvious question raised by the topic sentence: How have Native Americans gone about demanding more political power?

The exception is sentence 4. This sentence provides an interesting detail: In at least one case, Native Americans triumphed in the Supreme Court. However, if that sentence were eliminated from the paragraph, we would still be able to answer the question "How have Native Americans gone about demanding more political power?" Thus, sentence 4 is clearly a minor detail. In this case, it gives us relatively little information about the author's main idea. Instead, it adds an interesting fact to an idea already introduced in sentence 3.

Diagrammed to show the relationship between major and minor details, the sample paragraph would look like this:

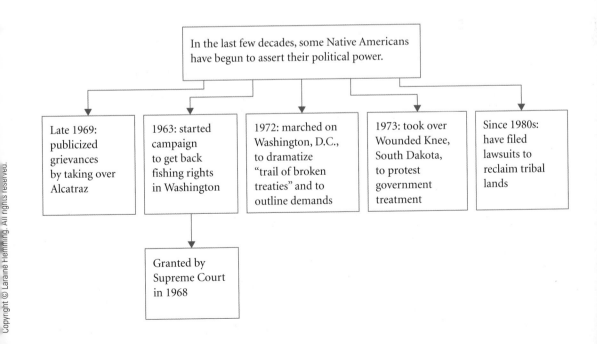

SUMMING UP THE KEY POINTS

Major Details

- are less general than topic or introductory sentences.
- provide the examples, reasons, statistics, and studies that help make the topic sentence clear and convincing.
- answer readers' questions about the topic sentence.
- must be included in reading notes.

Minor Details

- are the most specific sentences in the paragraph.
- further explain major details.
- repeat key points and add colorful details.
- may or may not be important enough to include in reading notes.

STUDY TIP

When taking notes, always evaluate the minor details, deciding which ones you need to include and which ones you can leave out.

◆ **EXERCISE 4**   Diagramming Major and Minor Details

DIRECTIONS   Read each paragraph. Then fill in the boxes. Be sure to paraphrase and abbreviate the sentences.

EXAMPLE   It seems impossible that large prehistoric creatures are alive today. Yet huge creatures from the dinosaur age may still exist beneath the sea. After all, as fossil remains show, dinosaurs had relatives who lived in the sea. They were huge and had long necks and snakelike heads. People who maintain that dinosaurs still live point to recent accounts of strange sea creatures that fit the description of ancient sea monsters. According to reports, the modern-day sea creatures also have long necks and snakelike heads.

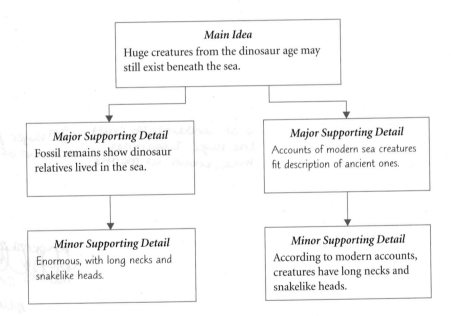

| **Main Idea** |
| Huge creatures from the dinosaur age may still exist beneath the sea. |

| **Major Supporting Detail** | **Major Supporting Detail** |
| Fossil remains show dinosaur relatives lived in the sea. | Accounts of modern sea creatures fit description of ancient ones. |

| **Minor Supporting Detail** | **Minor Supporting Detail** |
| Enormous, with long necks and snakelike heads. | According to modern accounts, creatures have long necks and snakelike heads. |

EXPLANATION   The topic sentence claims that huge creatures from the dinosaur age might still exist beneath the sea. Two major supporting details help make that statement more convincing. Each major detail is followed by a minor one that adds more information.

1. To the ordinary observer, the earth appears to be a solid mass. Scientists, however, know that the earth is composed of several distinct layers. Called the *outer crust*, the layer closest to the surface consists of lightweight rock that extends for about twenty miles beneath the earth's surface. Just underneath the crust is a second layer, about two thousand miles thick, known as the *mantle*. Portions of the mantle are extremely hot. The third layer, or the *core* of the earth, is made up of nickel and cobalt, and it too reaches extremely high temperatures. The temperatures are hot enough to melt both metals, but the sixty pounds of pressure borne by each square inch keeps them solid.

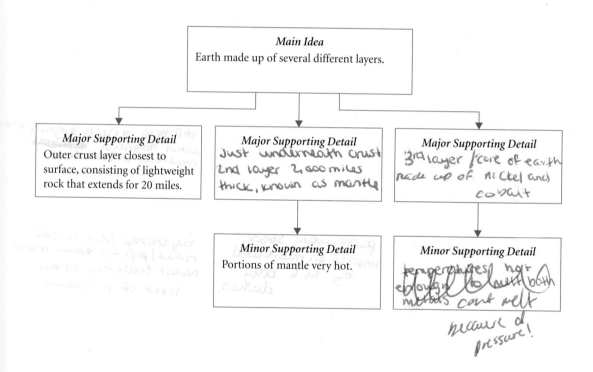

Main Idea
Earth made up of several different layers.

Major Supporting Detail
Outer crust layer closest to surface, consisting of lightweight rock that extends for 20 miles.

Major Supporting Detail
Just underneath crust 2nd layer 2,000 miles thick, known as mantle

Major Supporting Detail
3rd layer /core of earth made up of nickel and cobalt

Minor Supporting Detail
Portions of mantle very hot.

Minor Supporting Detail
temperatures hot enough to melt both metals cant melt

because of pressure!

2. Latin American music has had a powerful influence on popular music around the world. Since the 1930s, for example, Latin rhythms have been popular among West, Central, and East African musicians. Latin rhythms have also turned up in some Middle Eastern countries. In fact, they have had a particularly strong impact on the music used by Middle Eastern belly dancers. American hip hop reflects significant Latin American musical influences. The use of Latin American rhythms is a big change from earlier times, when popular music relied almost exclusively on the beat of the blues.

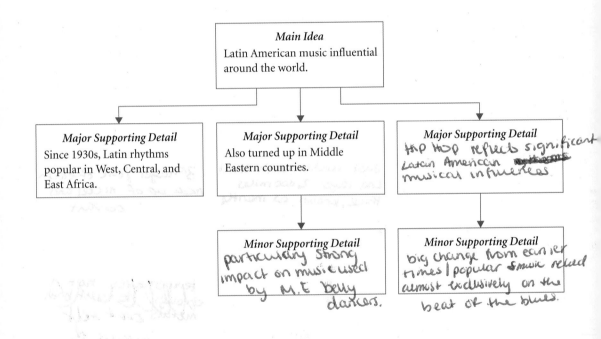

Main Idea
Latin American music influential around the world.

Major Supporting Detail
Since 1930s, Latin rhythms popular in West, Central, and East Africa.

Major Supporting Detail
Also turned up in Middle Eastern countries.

Major Supporting Detail
hip hop reflects significant Latin American musical influences

Minor Supporting Detail
particularly strong impact on music used by M.E belly dancers.

Minor Supporting Detail
big change from earlier times / popular music relied almost exclusively on the beat of the blues.

◆ **EXERCISE 5**   **Diagramming Major and Minor Details**

DIRECTIONS   Read each paragraph and fill in the boxes by paraphrasing and abbreviating the sentences.

1. Scientists who study identical twins have generally come to a similar conclusion. Even when identical twins are reared in different homes, they share many similarities. Observers are often struck by twins' identical facial expressions and personal habits. If, for example, one twin is a nail biter, the other is likely to be one too. Identical twins who have been separated are also likely to have similar IQ scores. They are even likely to share similar talents. If one excels in art, music, dance, or drama, the other is also likely to perform well in the same artistic fields.

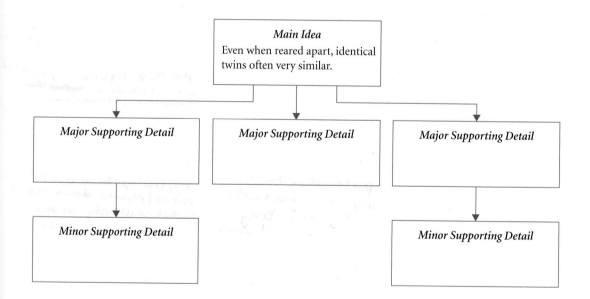

2. A little over a decade ago, the government of India started a program designed to clean up the Ganges River. The program failed because the Indian states did not have the money to keep it afloat. However, there is new hope on the horizon: Impressed with the scavenging behavior of carnivorous turtles, Indian officials in some states are using them to clean up river waste. According to officials, the turtles happily eat both animal and human carcasses. This is significant because among some religious groups, disposing of bodies in rivers is a common practice. In addition to their willingness to consume flesh, turtles also loosen the earth along the riverbanks, making it easier for plants to survive at the water's edge. The plants, in turn, help fight erosion at the banks, and some plants actually contribute to the water's purification. If the turtle experiment succeeds in a few states, it will be implemented throughout India, and even the Ganges may once again flow without pollutants.

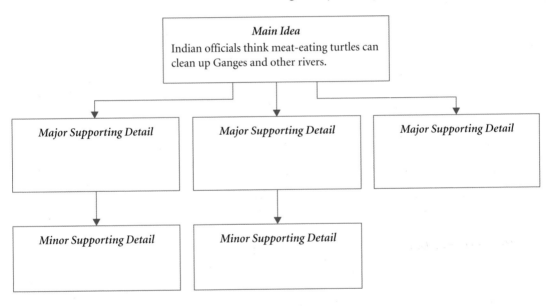

CHECK YOUR UNDERSTANDING

Explain the difference between major and minor details.

_____

_____

_____

IG TIP Evaluate minor details very carefully. If the minor details are essential to explaining a major detail, they belong in your notes.

Topic Sentences Help Identify Major Details

It pays to be alert to words and phrases in topic sentences that help readers identify major details. Note, for example, the underlined phrases in the following three topic sentences:

1. Child abuse can take <u>several different forms</u>.

2. Psychologists have identified <u>three styles of parenting</u>.

3. Even when identical twins are reared in different homes, they show <u>many similarities</u>.

All of the underlined phrases—several different forms, three styles of parenting, and many similarities—refer to some larger group that can be broken down into smaller subgroups. Such words and phrases are important because they tell you what kind of major supporting details you need to look for. In other words, each time you locate a different *form*, another *style*, or an additional *similarity*, you have also found a major detail.

For an illustration, read the next paragraph. Circle the word or phrase in the topic sentence that tells you what type of major detail you need to locate. Then label each of the supporting details as a major (*M*) or a minor (*m*) detail.

Topic Sentence
[1]<u>Feminists scored two impressive legal victories in the 1970s</u>. [2]In 1974, Congress passed the Equal Credit Opportunity Act, which enabled women to get bank loans and obtain credit cards on the same terms as men. _____ [3]Many states also revised their laws on rape, prohibiting defense lawyers from trying to discredit rape victims by revealing their previous sexual experience. _____ [4]Prior to this time, a woman's sexual history could be used to challenge her accusation of rape. _____ (Adapted from Norton et al., *A People and a Nation*, p. 1045.)

If you circled the phrase "two impressive legal victories," you're right; that is the key phrase. What about the supporting sentences? Did you label sentences 2 and 3 as major details and sentence 4 as a minor one? Correct again. Sentences 2 and 3 are major details because they introduce the two legal victories referred to in the topic sentence. Sentence 4 is a minor detail because it further explains the victory described in sentence 3.

Whenever you locate a topic sentence, look for words or phrases identifying some larger group that can be broken down into smaller sub-groups. By identifying the individual members of the larger group mentioned, you will also identify all the major details.

Although there are many such words and phrases, the following chart lists some of the most common. Watch for them as you read.

Topic Sentence Clues to Major Details ◆	Among the causes, results	Numerous cases, people, studies
	A number of ways	
	Categories	Precautions
	Causes	Problems
	Characteristics	Reasons
	Classes	Several advantages, cases, studies, goals
	Components	
	Consequences	Similarities
	Differences	Skills
	Effects	Stages
	Elements	Steps
	Examples	Strategies
	Factors	Studies
	Groups	Symptoms
	Kinds	Tactics
	Methods	Traits
	Motives	Traditions

◆ Transitions and Major Details

In addition to topic sentences that tell readers what type or kind of major detail they need to look for, there are other clues that can help you decide if a detail is major or minor. Transitions like *furthermore*, *moreover*, and *also* are the author's way of saying to readers, "Here's another major reason, illustration, advantage, or consequence to consider." Look, for example, at the following passage and pay close attention to the italicized transitions.

¹There are a number of reasons why parents should not allow young, impressionable children to watch televised wrestling. ²Wrestling suggests to children that physical violence causes no real harm. ³*After all*, in a wrestling match, no one seems to get hurt because most of the wrestlers come back the following week. ⁴*Furthermore*, wrestling suggests that people are valued according to the damage they can do since the superstars of wrestling are those men and women who most effectively hurt and humiliate their opponents. ⁵This is not an especially good message to be giving children. ⁶*In addition*, wrestling celebrates incredibly loutish behavior. ⁷Watching a wrestling match on television, viewers must find it difficult to say whose behavior is more disreputable,* the wrestlers shouting at the top of their lungs that they are going to demolish their opponent, or the scantily clad women who parade around exhibiting score cards and occasionally jump in the ring to join the fray.*

In this paragraph, the author opens with a topic sentence that sends a clear message: There are several reasons why young, impressionable children should not be allowed to watch televised wrestling. Then the transition *after all* announces that the author is following up on that claim.

To be sure that the remaining reasons stand out, the author signals their presence with the transitional words *furthermore* in sentence 4 and *in addition* in sentence 6. The transitions are her way of telling readers, "I'm continuing with the same train of thought, and here are additional reasons why you should share my point of view."

Transitions That Signal Addition or Continuation ◆			
After all	For one thing	Second, Third, Fourth
Also	For this reason	
And	Furthermore	Similarly
As a matter of fact	In addition	Then
Finally	Last	Therefore
First	Last of all	Thus
First and foremost	Lastly	Too
First of all	Moreover	
For example	Next	
For instance	One point, example, kind, etc.	

---

*disreputable: lacking in respectability.
*fray: battle, contest, test.

As you might suspect, transitions like the ones above don't always introduce major details. However, they introduce them often enough for you to be aware of the relationship between the two.

SUMMING UP THE KEY POINTS

1. When they appear in the topic sentence, words that refer to a larger group which can be subdivided—words such as *reasons, forms, styles, similarities,* and so on—are an important clue to major details. Much of the time, each individual reason, form, style, or similarity is a major detail.

2. Transitions that signal addition, such as *furthermore, also,* and *moreover,* are also likely to introduce major supporting details.

VOCABULARY CHECK

The following words were introduced in pages 246–62. Match the word to the definition. Review words, definitions, and original context two or three times before taking the vocabulary tests. (The page numbers in parentheses indicate where the word first appeared.)

1. maim (p. 246) _____

2. compound (p. 247) _____

3. notorious (p. 247) _____

4. amphibians (p. 248) _____

5. respiratory (p. 248) _____

6. cardiovascular (p. 248) _____

7. purge (p. 249) _____

8. thrive (p. 250) _____

9. disreputable (p. 262) _____

10. fray (p. 262) _____

a. related to breathing

b. related to the heart and blood vessels

c. grow

d. battle, contest, test

e. famous for bad reasons

f. lacking in respectability

g. injure severely, usually with scarring and loss of limbs

h. animals that can live in water and on land

i. remove waste from the bowels or stomach; also, to eliminate or get rid of

j. building or buildings used as housing and surrounded by walls

◆ **EXERCISE 6** **Using Topic Sentences and Transitions to Identify Major Details**

DIRECTIONS Read each paragraph. Circle any phrases in the topic sentence that offer a clue to the major details, and circle as well the transitions that signal continuation or addition. Then fill in the boxes by paraphrasing and abbreviating the sentences. *Note:* Not all topic sentences will include a phrase identifying the major details.

1. According to the sociologist Emile Durkheim, deviance (the violation of social rules) can serve a number of functions for society. First, it helps enhance conformity as a whole. Deviant behavior allows us to see the boundaries between right and wrong more clearly. Once aware of these boundaries, we are more likely to conform to standards of correct social behavior. Second, deviance strengthens solidarity among law-abiding members of society. Collective outrage against deviant behavior can unite people with different points of view. Third, deviance provides a safety valve for discontented people. Through relatively minor forms of deviance, those unhappy with society's rules can strike out at or insult the social order without doing major harm. Fourth, deviance can induce social change. As the civil rights movement has shown, people sometimes have to engage in deviant behavior in order to make society aware of its errors. (Adapted from Thio, *Society: Myths and Realities,* pp. 172–73.)

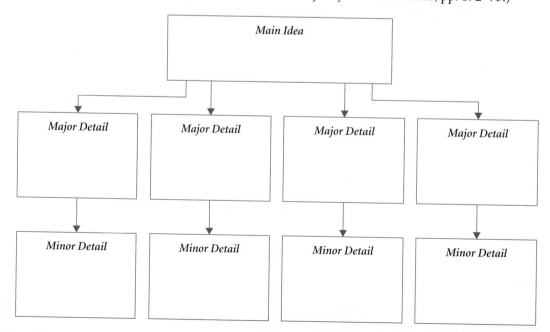

2. There are several benefits to having music education as part of the school curriculum. One benefit of musical training is that it seems to improve thinking skills. Students who have had music lessons score an average of 59 points higher on the verbal portion of the SAT and 44 points higher on the math portion than students who have not had music lessons, and studies show that youthful musicians tend to get good grades. Another important benefit of musical training is enhanced self-esteem. Researchers have also found that children who have had music education have more confidence in their own potential than do those who have not had music education and therefore are more likely to graduate from high school and less likely to use drugs. In addition music education helps children develop a host of other important skills. Learning to play an instrument requires self-discipline, concentration, and time management, while learning to make music with others helps young people learn how to cooperate and, above all, how to listen.

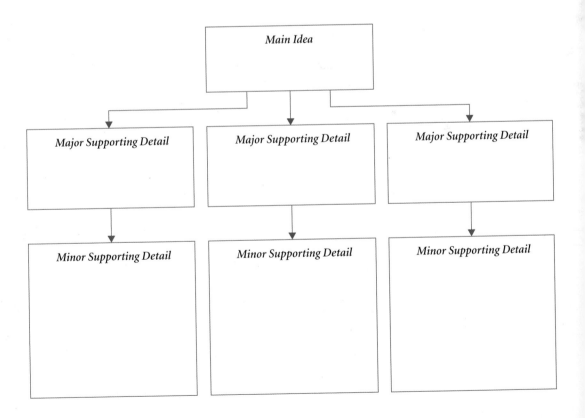

3. A 2003 poll sponsored by the American Automobile Association and other highway safety organizations revealed that most Americans are bad drivers who don't want to get better. Most drivers do little or nothing to improve their driving knowledge or skills. As a matter of fact, because the majority of states do not require motorists to periodically refresh their skills, adult drivers have generally not taken a test on road rules, road signs, or driving skills since they first got their driver's license as teenagers. In addition, motorists in our fast-paced society, pressed for time and in a hurry, drive recklessly. The poll reveals, for example, that more than 70 percent of drivers admit to speeding, and one-third say they have run yellow or even red lights. Finally, many drivers engage in distracting behaviors while behind the wheel. Sixty percent of drivers eat while they drive, 37 percent talk on cell phones while driving, and 14 percent say they even read while driving. (Source of information: Deborah Sharp, "A Poll Highlights Road Recklessness," *USA Today*, May 27, 2003, p. 3A.)

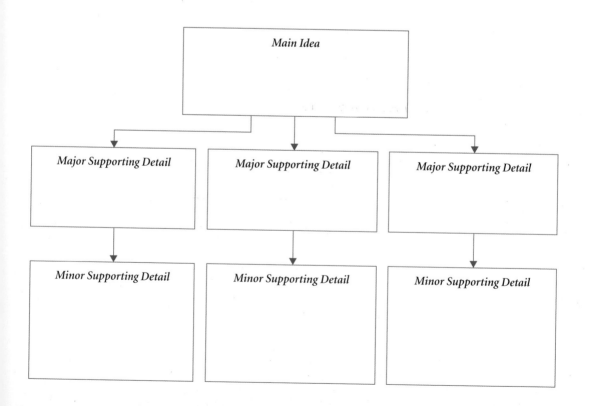

◆ EXERCISE 7   Identifying Topic Sentences and Major Details

DIRECTIONS   Read each paragraph and answer the questions about the topic sentence. Then paraphrase and list all the major details. Circle any transitions that signal continuation or addition.

EXAMPLE   ¹Although the famed magician Harry Houdini could have benefited from his audience's belief in the world of spirits, he tried in a number of ways to expose the fakery behind supposed supernatural* happenings. ²Throughout his career, Houdini carefully investigated and proved false hundreds of claims by people who said they could communicate with the spirit world. ³(Moreover,) he kept a file of fake mediums* and he instructed that, after his death, the file be made public. ⁴To ensure that his wishes were carried out, Houdini entrusted a key to the file to his friend and fellow magician Joseph Dunninger. ⁵Houdini (also) liked to dispel the "magic" behind his tricks and explain how they were performed. ⁶This was his way of proving to people that miracles could actually be faked.

a. Sentence __1__ is the topic sentence.

b. What word or phrase in the topic sentence provides a clue to the major details?

     a number of ways
     _____

c. Number and paraphrase all the major details according to the order in which they appear.

     1. Houdini investigated and disproved hundreds of fake claims
          about people in touch with spirits.

     2. Houdini kept file on people claiming to be in touch with the
          spirits, left instructions that file be published on his death.

     3. Houdini explained how his tricks were performed.

EXPLANATION   The topic sentence is the first sentence in the paragraph. It's the only sentence general enough to sum up the rest of the paragraph. The phrase "a number of ways" is a clue to the major details. It tells you that each way, or method, of exposing trickery is a major

---

*supernatural: relating to things not happening in the ordinary world; miraculous.
*mediums: people who claim they can communicate with the dead.

detail. Sentences 2, 3, and 5 all describe different techniques Houdini used to uncover fakes. These three sentences are major details and are paraphrased in the blank lines.

1. [1]The honeybee is a social insect that can survive only when it is part of a community. [2]Within that community, all of the honeybees have a number of special functions that help ensure survival. [3]The queen, for example, is the only sexually productive female; she gives birth to all of the drones, workers, and future queens. [4]Her capacity for laying eggs is enormous, and her daily output often exceeds 1,500 eggs. [5]Although lacking the ability to mate or reproduce, worker bees secrete wax, build the honeycomb, gather food, turn nectar into honey, guard the hive when necessary, and regulate its temperature. [6]When, for instance, the hive becomes too hot, worker bees cool the air by fanning their wings. [7]In contrast to the worker bees, drones have only one function—to mate with the queen. [8]After mating, which takes place in flight, a drone immediately dies; he has served his sole function and is no longer necessary to the community.

a. Sentence _2_ is the topic sentence.

b. What word or phrase in the topic sentence provides a clue to the major details?

   Number of special functions

c. Number and paraphrase all the major details according to the order in which they appear.

   1) Queen Bee: gives birth to drowns, worker
   2) worker Bee: wax, honeycomb, food, nectur
   3) Drone - mate w/ queen

2. [1]The religion of the Hopi Indians includes several different ceremonies intended to influence or pay respect to nature. [2]In the Bear Dance, for example, as many as two hundred masked and painted dancers represent the Kachinas, spirits associated with growing and

distributing food.[†] ³The purpose of the Bear Dance is to ensure that spring will bring a lush harvest. ⁴The Snake Dance, which takes place every second August, is a plea for rain. ⁵During the ceremony, the dancers twine live rattlesnakes around their shoulders. ⁶Once open to visitors, the Snake Dance is now closed to all outsiders. ⁷Visitors, however, may still be present for the Corn Dance, which is supposed to encourage a rich crop.

a. Sentence _____ is the topic sentence.

b. What word or phrase in the topic sentence provides a clue to the major details?

_____

c. Number and paraphrase all the major details according to the order in which they appear.

_____

_____

_____

_____

3. ¹One of the most common problems in old age is mental confusion, a condition extremely detrimental to the quality of life in later years. ²When it's the subject of study, mental confusion in the elderly is divided into three main categories. ³One kind of confusion is purely a result of illness, medication, or emotional and environmental stress. ⁴This category of confusion is usually reversible if caught early enough. ⁵The second type of confusion results from damage to the brain due to aging. ⁶This type is commonly referred to as "dementia." ⁷The third kind of confusion is produced by severe mental disorders such as psychosis.* (Adapted from Waughfield, *Mental Health Concepts*, p. 283.)

3 transitions
3 details

a. Sentence _2_ is the topic sentence.

b. What word or phrase in the topic sentence provides a clue to the major details?

Divided into 3 main categories

_____

[†]The word *Kachinas* can also refer to the spirits of ancestors and the forces of nature.
*psychosis: a mental disturbance that causes severe reality distortion.

c. Number and paraphrase all the major details according to the order in which they appear.

1) illness – medication / emotional stress
2) aging – dementia – brain damage.
3) mental disorders - psychosis

4. [1]Flow charts are excellent graphical devices for planning, scheduling, and controlling complex operations. [2]Frequently used by programmers who want to identify the individual components in tasks and quality-management teams who want to simplify tasks by eliminating wasted steps, flow charts have two main advantages. [3]Thanks to flow charts, managers at all levels and in all specialized areas can identify and sequence the key events and decisions involved in a process. [4]Flow charts are useful, too, because they force people to consider all relevant points or steps in a particular endeavor. [5]This is an advantage because conscious consideration of the individual points or steps encourages analytical thinking. (Adapted from Kreitner, *Management*, p. 171.)

a. Sentence _____ is the topic sentence.

b. What word or phrase in the topic sentence provides a clue to the major details?

c. Number and paraphrase all the major details according to the order in which they appear.

◆ **EXERCISE 8**   **Identifying Topic Sentences and Minor Details**

DIRECTIONS   Read each paragraph. Identify the topic sentence by writing the correct number or numbers in the blank at the end. Then go back and fill in each blank within the paragraph with the letter of the appropriate minor detail.

EXAMPLE   ¹The human ear is a complicated structure that can be divided into three main parts. ²The first part is the outer ear. ³It collects sound waves and directs them to the auditory canal. ⁴__c__ ⁵The middle ear contains three small bones. ⁶__a__ ⁷The middle ear is connected to the throat by a small tubelike structure known as the Eustachian tube. ⁸The inner ear contains the actual hearing apparatus, a small, shell-like organ filled with fluid and nerve endings. ⁹It is called the cochlea. ¹⁰__b__

Topic Sentence   __1__

Minor Details   a. These are called the hammer, anvil, and stirrup.

b. When the nerve endings receive vibrations from the fluid in the cochlea, they transmit them directly to the hearing portion of the brain.

c. At the very end of that canal is a membrane called the eardrum, or tympanum.

EXPLANATION   In this case, sentence 1 is the only sentence that could effectively sum up the paragraph. Choosing the correct minor supporting detail is easy if you use the right clues. Sentence 3, for example, mentions the auditory canal. Therefore, we put sentence *c*, which refers to the canal, into the first blank. Sentence 5 mentions three small bones. Therefore, the next sentence logically should be answer *a*, which identifies those bones. Sentence 9 introduces the cochlea. Therefore, answer *b*, which mentions the cochlea, is the appropriate choice to follow sentence 9 as a minor supporting detail. (Note, too, the importance of the minor details.)

1.   ¹In October 1957, the Russians leaped into the space age with the launching of a satellite* that became world famous as *Sputnik.* ²Awed by this breakthrough, America intensified its efforts to improve its satellite technology. ³Since that time, the United States has rivaled Russia by launching its own share of satellites. ⁴Hundreds of American satellites have been successfully propelled into the air. ⁵As our technology improves, scientists expect that many more satellites will be used. ⁶_____ ⁷The military, which already makes extensive use of satellites, will also continue to do so in the future. ⁸_____ ⁹Although they possess no satellites of their own, less industrialized countries have already laid claim to precious air space. ¹⁰_____

Topic Sentence   _____

---

*satellite: an object propelled into space to circle Earth or other planets.

Minor Details

   a. If they gain the technology to launch satellites in the future, these countries do not want to discover that all usable orbits* have been taken.

   b. Certainly the use of satellites in global communication will continue to increase.

   c. Military satellites are essential to intelligence gathering.

2. ¹The Galapagos are volcanic islands located about six hundred miles from South America's Pacific coast. ²With their barren* landscape, the islands do not seem the ideal spot for a summer vacation. ³Nevertheless, the Galapagos have begun to attract growing numbers of tourists, and that increase in tourism has caused a variety of problems. ⁴Some tourists, planning a long stay, have brought their pets with them. ⁵_____ ⁶In addition, many tourists have decided that the tortoises inhabiting the island make splendid souvenirs. ⁷_____ ⁸Even the tourists who bring no pets and steal no tortoises have managed to injure the island's fragile environment. ⁹They do not realize, for example, that killing a stray spider can actually harm the balance of nature. ¹⁰_____

Topic Sentence   _____

Minor Details

   a. Hundreds of tortoises have been captured and taken off the island.

   b. Unfortunately, those pets have often destroyed vegetation needed to support the wildlife population.

   c. Spiders are needed in great numbers to keep numerous island pests under control.

3. ¹Progeria is a genetic disorder that strikes children. ²Victims of the disease experience rapid aging. ³_____ ⁴First mentioned in the late nineteenth century, progeria is extremely rare. ⁵_____ ⁶Usually the disease goes undetected until just past infancy, when children suddenly stop growing. ⁷_____ ⁸Death usually occurs in the teens, often from a disease associated with aging, such as hardening of the arteries.

Topic Sentence   _____

---

*orbits: paths of movement.
*barren: unable to reproduce; dry; lacking in vegetation.

Minor Details

    a. It occurs about once in eight million births.

    b. Children with progeria seldom reach a weight of more than fifty pounds.

    c. For every one year, their bodies age ten.

4. [1]In 1954, the Supreme Court ruled in *Brown v. Board of Education* that "separate educational facilities are inherently* unequal." [2]The Supreme Court's *Brown* decision encouraged African-Americans to integrate all public facilities. [3]As a result, the civil rights movement officially began in Montgomery, Alabama, in December 1955 when Rosa Parks refused to give up her seat on a city bus to a white man. [4]_____ [5]Led by the Reverend Martin Luther King Jr., African-Americans reacted to her arrest by organizing a boycott. [6]_____ [7]The protests continued, with civil rights workers fanning out all over the South. [8]However, the civil rights bill designed to end segregation in all public facilities remained stalled in Congress. [9]_____

Topic Sentence   _____

Minor Details

    a. The bill finally passed in 1964.

    b. Consequently, Parks was arrested and taken to jail.

    c. The boycott lasted a year and ended when the federal court ruled that Alabama's bus segregation laws were unconstitutional.

5. [1]For centuries, the shroud of Turin has been an object of fascination to Christians and non-Christians alike, and so far, the many tests performed on the shroud have served only to increase its mystery. [2]A fourteen-foot piece of linen fabric, the shroud is believed to have been the cloth in which Jesus of Nazareth was wrapped after his death on the cross. [3]Normally it lies hidden behind the iron grille on a Turin altar. [4]But in 1978, an exhibition was held to celebrate the four hundredth anniversary of the shroud's discovery. [5]_____ [6]Markings on the shroud revealed the faded image of a naked man laid out for burial. [7]_____ [8]For a while, experts were puzzled when special photographs revealed

---

*inherently: at the core; by nature.

bulges around the eyes. [9]_____ [10]The shroud of Turin was also exhibited in 1998, when Pope John Paul II knelt before it in silent prayer. [11]Two years later, it was on exhibit again, from August 12 to October 22, 2000. [12]The next exhibit of the shroud is set for 2025.

Topic Sentence _____

Minor Details

a. But that mystery was solved when someone pointed out that the Romans placed coins over the eyes of the dead.

b. Strongly built and with regular features, his face is partially covered by a beard.

c. During the anniversary celebration, scientists were allowed to examine the cloth.

READING TIP To decide what major or minor details are essential to the main idea, ask yourself, How would I explain the content of this paragraph to someone who has never read it? The answer to that question will also identify essential details.

✔ CHECK YOUR UNDERSTANDING

1. What kinds of words in topic sentences are clues to major details?

_____

2. What are some examples of these words?

_____

3. What kinds of transitions are clues to major details?

_____

4. What are some examples of these transitions?

_____

Reader-Supplied Supporting Details

To thoroughly understand a paragraph, experienced readers know they have to draw inferences about supporting details that are implied rather than explicitly stated. For an illustration of how inferences contribute to a paragraph, read the following example. As you do, consider what information you have to add to the passage to fully understand it.

Topic Sentence

¹According to social exchange theory, the development and continuation of intimate relationships are associated with the rewards and costs involved. ²Research has shown that dating couples who experience increases in rewards as their relationship progresses are likely to stay together. ³In contrast, dating couples who experience fewer reward increases are less likely to stay together. ⁴Rewards and costs, however, do not arise on their own and in isolation. ⁵People bring to their relationships certain expectations. ⁶John Thibaut and Harold Kelley coined the term "comparison level" (CL) to refer to the expected outcome in relationships. ⁷A person with a high CL expects his or her relationships to be rewarding. ⁸Someone with a low CL does not. ⁹Even a bad relationship can look pretty good to someone who has a low CL. (Adapted from Brehm, Kassin, and Fein, *Social Psychology*, p. 208.)

In this paragraph, the main idea is spelled out in the first sentence. However, for the supporting details to fully clarify that topic sentence, readers have to draw inferences and add details.

Readers Working with the Author

Note that the writers of the paragraph on social exchange theory do not specifically define the meanings of the two key words, *rewards* and *costs*, even though both words need to be understood in a particular way: as emotional rather than financial rewards and costs. If those two words aren't defined in this way, the social exchange theory wouldn't make much sense when applied to intimate relationships. Yet the writers don't supply those specific meanings. They just supply the context for the two words. Then it's up to readers to draw the right inferences.

The need for reader-supplied supporting details, however, does not end with the definitions of these two words. Sentences 2 and 3 can only develop the topic sentence if readers infer a cause-and-effect relationship in which one event produces another. Dating couples who get an increased number of rewards stay together *because* they like the rewards. Similarly, couples who experience fewer rewards are less likely to stay together *because* there aren't enough rewards in the relationship. Even sentence 4, which looks so simple, requires readers to infer two implied phrases shown here in brackets: "Rewards and costs [*within couple relationships*] do not arise on their own or in isolation [*from all other influences*]."

In sentence 6, for the notion of a "comparison level" to make sense, the reader needs to infer that high or low expectations are based on *what people have previously experienced*. That's where the comparison comes in. In other words, if you come from a relationship with lots of rewards, you will expect those same rewards to be present in your new relationship. But, if your last relationship had more costs than benefits, there is a good chance you won't have high expectations for your next one. Significant as that piece of information is to understanding the theory, it is still implied rather than stated.

READING TIP　Never assume the writers provide you with every single word or phrase you need to construct their intended meaning. Be ready to fill in the gaps with the right inferences.

◆ **EXERCISE 9**　Drawing Inferences About Supporting Details

DIRECTIONS　Read the paragraph and underline the topic sentence. Then circle the appropriate letter to identify the inference readers need to add to the supporting details.

EXAMPLE　[1]Knowledge about emotions is learned, at least in part, from parents. [2]Children who display knowledge about emotions—who can label emotional expressions on faces, describe the feelings of another person in an emotional situation, and talk about the causes of emotions—typically have mothers willing to discuss and explain the power of emotions. [3]In the context of learning about emotions, these mothers are good "coaches." [4]However, when parents react negatively to children expressing emotion (e.g., "You're overreacting!"), children's understanding of emotions is poorer and, as a result, the children are less socially competent. [5]Parents who engage in such negative behaviors are missing opportunities to explain to their children the key elements of emotional responses. [6]The extreme case is represented by children who are physically abused or neglected by their parents. [7]These children lack the ability to call up the emotional expressions appropriate to particular situations, such as going to the zoo and getting a balloon or losing a pet to disease. (Adapted from Bukatko and Daehler, *Child Development*, p. 393.)

1. Which inference does the reader need to add to the supporting details?

    a. Mothers who criticize their children for not expressing how they feel create adults who are emotionally cold.

    b. Mothers open to talking about emotions are passing on their own knowledge of the role emotions play in life.

    c. Some mothers who are open to discussing emotions are likely to do so only when their children express negative emotions.

2. Which inference does the reader need to add to the supporting details?

    a. Parents who discourage their children from showing emotion do so because they themselves don't know how to express their feelings.

    b. When parents discourage their children from showing emotion, they do so because they equate showing emotion with weakness.

    c. Abused children whose emotional responses don't fit the social situation probably do not have parents who coach them on how to express emotions and respond to emotional situations.

EXPLANATION The authors use the word "coaches" to imply that some mothers teach their children about emotions in the same way coaches teach kids about sports. However, it's up to readers to draw that inference, which is answer *b*. Although the authors don't say it explicitly, it's very unlikely that abusive or neglectful parents would spend much time coaching their children in how to go about handling their emotions. Thus, answer *c* is correct.

1. [1]Violence on television and its effect on children has long been hotly debated. [2]Yet violence of a graphic nature has continued to play a big role in television programming. [3]In 2001, testifying before a U.S. Senate committee, the social psychologist and author of the report, "Television and the Aggressive Child," Leonard Eron warned that by the end of elementary school, a typical American child would see 8,000 murders and more than 100,000 additional acts of violence on television. [4]Eron, who died in 2007, was an especially vocal critic of televised violence because, along with Monroe M. Lefkowitz and Leopold Walder, he had authored a study that observed children's viewing habits and behavior over the course of forty years. [5]Still, the statistics on violence in television programming seem only to rise. [6]According to Parentstv.org, a website representing the Parents Television Council (PTC), the television season that began in the fall of 2005 was one of the most violent in recent history—averaging 4.41 instances of violence per hour of prime time. [7]This was a 75 percent increase since the 1998 television season.

1. Which of these inferences is the reader expected to add to the supporting details?

   a. Violence toward children is a growing threat in American society.

   b. In his testimony before the Senate, Leonard Eron argued that the amount of televised violence children were viewing would negatively affect them.

   c. In general, parents do not take seriously the warnings of people like Leonard Eron; they do not think that letting children watch televised violence is harmful in any way.

2. Which of these inferences is the reader expected to add to the supporting details?

   a. The major networks are seriously worried about the continual criticism of television's violent content.

b. The major networks have not been especially influenced or affected by the long-standing criticism of television's violent content.

c. Violence on America's six major networks is no greater than it is on European networks.

2. [1]When criminal acts are emphasized by television programming, viewers are encouraged to see themselves as victims. [2]Mass communications researchers have studied the degree to which watching television encourages a particular view of crime in viewers. [3]We know, for instance, that viewers who watch a lot of television consider themselves to be likely victims of crime or wrongdoing to a greater extent than is actually probable in the real world. [4]Heavy television viewers often seem to feel that they live in the TV world of violent crime. [5]This is not to say that crime is not a problem in American society. [6]But not everyone will be a victim of it. [7]Yet how can the public place the various aspects of life in any sort of realistic context when television news, in particular, suggests that the most important news is crime related? (Adapted from Leslie, *Mass Communication Ethics*, p. 170.)

1. Which of these inferences is the reader expected to add to the supporting details?

   a. People who watch a lot of television are more likely to engage in violent crimes because they believe that everyone else is doing the same thing.

   b. People who watch a lot of TV tend to have violent fantasies.

   c. People who watch a lot of television are inclined to think that what they see on television mirrors what's happening in the real world.

2. Which of these inferences is the reader expected to add to the supporting details?

   a. The author believes that lawsuits are turning an even greater number of people into victims.

   b. The author believes that people who watch a lot of television are quick to see themselves as victims of violent crime.

   c. The majority of the lawsuits being filed in the United States today are trivial and not worth the court's time.

3. [1]What would become one of the most dramatic symbols of the civil rights movement occurred in Mississippi in 1955. [2]In September, Emmett Till, a fourteen-year-old black youth from Chicago, visited relatives near Greenwood, Mississippi. [3]After buying some candy at a rural store, Till supposedly said "Bye, baby" to the white female clerk. [4]Three days later, after midnight, the girl's husband and brother dragged Till from his relatives' home, shot him through the head, cut off his testicles, and dumped his body in the Tallahatchie River. [5]After her son's death, Till's mother insisted on an open casket at the funeral so that, in her words, "All the world can see what they did to my boy." [6]The image of Till's mutilated body, captured on television, seared itself into the consciousness of a generation of black leaders. [7]Yet despite overwhelming evidence of guilt, an all-white, all-male jury found the two white suspects innocent of kidnapping. (Adapted from Gillon and Matson, *The American Experiment*, p. 1123.)

1. Which of these inferences is the reader expected to add to the supporting details?

   a. The family of the woman in the candy shop was outraged that a black man would speak in such a familiar way to a white woman.

   b. Till was dragged from his relatives' home by people who were ready to make trouble with the first person who crossed their path.

   c. The people who kidnapped Till were trying to avenge a similar crime that had been committed against another teenage boy who was white.

2. Which of these inferences is the reader expected to add to the supporting details?

   a. Till's mother never really cared about her son.

   b. Till's mother wanted the world to feel her horror and outrage.

   c. Till's mother was so distraught from grief, she could not think straight.

4. [1]The turning point of the 1960 presidential campaign came in a series of four televised debates between September 26 and October 24. [2]Facing off against Richard M. Nixon, John F. Kennedy used the debates—the first-ever televised debates between presidential

contenders—to demolish the Republican charge that he was inexperienced and poorly informed. [3]And he succeeded far better than his opponent in communicating the qualities of boldness, imagination, and poise. [4]Kennedy appeared alert, aggressive, and cool. [5]Nixon, who perspired profusely, looked nervous and uncomfortable. [6]Not surprisingly, radio listeners divided evenly on who won the debate. [7]However, television viewers, the overwhelming majority, gave Kennedy a decisive edge. [8]The performance energized Kennedy's campaign, and the debates institutionalized television's role as a major force in American politics. (Adapted from Gillon and Matson, *The American Experiment*, p. 1130.)

1. Which of these inferences is the reader expected to add to the supporting details?

   a. Kennedy was also perspiring.
   b. Kennedy was as uncomfortable as Nixon was on television, but he didn't show it.
   c. Because Kennedy didn't perspire, he seemed more relaxed and in control than Nixon.

2. Which of these inferences is the reader expected to add to the supporting details?

   a. Because the reception was not good, people who listened to the debate on radio couldn't hear what the candidates said with the same clarity as those watching it on television.
   b. Kennedy had spent a good deal of time being coached on how to debate, whereas Nixon had not.
   c. People who saw the debate on television were heavily influenced by the appearance and manner of the two men.

Concluding Sentences and Supporting Details

At this point, you are familiar with every kind of sentence that can appear in a paragraph except for one—the concluding sentence. As the name implies, **concluding sentences** come at the very end of paragraphs containing topic sentences. Unlike the supporting sentences that precede them, concluding sentences don't directly develop the topic sentence or even a major detail. Instead, they describe how some problem, event, or situation mentioned in the paragraph changed or should change over time. Although not all paragraphs end with concluding sentences, many do. More important, they usually contain significant information, even if they do not directly support the main idea expressed in the topic sentence.

The following paragraph illustrates how a concluding sentence differs from a supporting detail.

> From 1692 through 1693, Salem, Massachusetts, was the scene of a series of witchcraft trials. The trials began when two young girls, who appeared to be suffering fits, accused several men and women in the town of dealings with the devil. The girls' accusations were believed and, before the townspeople came to their senses, nineteen men and women had been hanged and many others were cruelly tortured and imprisoned. Following the events in Salem, witchcraft trials practically disappeared from the colonies.

The topic of the paragraph is witchcraft trials in Salem; the topic sentence of the paragraph tells readers that from 1692 through 1693 Salem was the scene of witchcraft trials. All the remaining sentences in the paragraph, except the last one, tell us more about the Salem trials. The last sentence tells us what happened in the colonies *after* the Salem experience. The last sentence is a good example of a concluding sentence.

If you are reading a paragraph and you encounter a concluding sentence, don't assume it's unimportant because it doesn't directly develop the main idea. Concluding sentences can include significant information about the topic under discussion. They deserve your attention. At the very least, you need to decide whether or not they are essential to your understanding of the paragraph.

SUMMING UP THE KEY POINTS

1. Experienced readers know that writers expect them to infer supporting details that are implied but not stated.

2. Concluding sentences don't directly develop the topic sentence or even a major detail. Instead, appearing at the very end of a paragraph, they describe how some situation or event mentioned in the paragraph changed or should change over time.

◆ **EXERCISE 10** **Recognizing Concluding Sentences**

DIRECTIONS The topic sentence in each paragraph has been under-lined. After reading the paragraph, circle the letter of the answer that best describes the final sentence of the paragraph.

EXAMPLE In 1856, Henry Bessemer invented a new method for man-ufacturing steel, one that consisted of three basic steps. First, a blast of cold air was forced through the mass of hot melting iron. The enormous heat created then burned out the impurities in the iron and left it ready for the final step—the addition of carbon, manganese, and other sub-stances that produced good-quality steel. The introduction of the Bessemer process revolutionized the steel industry, making steel an im-portant commodity* for American export.

a. The last sentence in the paragraph provides a supporting detail.

ⓑ The last sentence in the paragraph is a concluding sentence.

EXPLANATION The last sentence does not further explain the topic sentence. It does not describe one of the three basic steps in the Bessemer process. That eliminates answer *a*, making answer *b* the correct choice.

1. In 1886, French chemist Louis Pasteur believed that he had found a vaccine to combat the dreaded disease called rabies. Pasteur, how-ever, was fearful of using the rabies vaccine on human beings until the decision to do so was forced on him. On July 6, 1886, a young boy named Joseph Meister was brought to Pasteur for treatment. The boy had been bitten on the arms and legs by a rabid dog. Pasteur consulted with several physicians who assured him that the boy was going to die. It was only then that Pasteur decided to use his rabies vaccine. Meister lived to become gatekeeper of the Pasteur Institute and committed suicide fifty-five years later.

    a. The last sentence in the paragraph provides a supporting detail.

    b. The last sentence in the paragraph is a concluding sentence.

2. Although human beings like to think of themselves as the only ani-mals who possess total control over all their actions, this belief is not based on fact. A strong emotion such as fear can cause reactions that

---

*commodity: something that is bought or sold in the market.

are totally beyond human control. For example, it is well known that human beings often tremble when frightened. The trembling is involuntary and ceases only when the danger is past. Similarly, children and adults have been known to urinate when placed in fear-producing situations.

a. The last sentence in the paragraph provides a supporting detail.

b. The last sentence in the paragraph is a concluding sentence.

3. Until the sixteenth century, people believed that the earth was the center of the universe. <u>However, in 1543, Nicolaus Copernicus, a Polish astronomer, challenged the traditional worldview.</u> In his book *Concerning the Revolutions of the Heavenly Bodies*, Copernicus insisted that the earth revolved around the sun and that the sun was the real center of the universe. He further argued that the apparent revolution of the sun around the earth was caused by the earth's daily rotation on its own axis. Although Copernicus's theory was essentially correct, it was not accepted until well into the seventeenth century.

a. The last sentence in the paragraph provides a supporting detail.

b. The last sentence in the paragraph is a concluding sentence.

4. Whether a war should have been fought can always be debated. The prowar forces can always come up with a reason why a war should be waged; the antiwar forces are perfectly able to prove the opposite: <u>However, there was one war that everybody agreed had to be fought; that was World War II.</u> In the face of Hitler's murder of millions of human beings, few people were willing to question the need to stop him. And anybody who thought he could be persuaded by peaceful means just had to look at the promises he had broken when dealing with England and Russia.

a. The last sentence in the paragraph provides a supporting detail.

b. The last sentence in the paragraph is a concluding sentence.

5. Because viruses are difficult to classify, several different systems have been put forward. <u>Probably the most commonly used system classifies viruses according to their host cells; according to the system, there are three groups of viruses: animal, plant, and bacterial.</u> On the whole, animal viruses are much more complex than plant viruses and have, therefore, been given distinct names like *poxvirus* and

parvovirus. In contrast, plant viruses are named according to the host they invade, for example, the tobacco virus. Bacterial viruses, also called *bacteriophages*, or *phages*, are usually identified by a system of letters and numbers, like the T-2 bacteriophage.

 a. The last sentence in the paragraph provides a supporting detail.

 b. The last sentence in the paragraph is a concluding sentence.

◆ EXERCISE 11   Recognizing the Function of Every Sentence

DIRECTIONS   Read each paragraph. Then use the letters on the list that follows to identify the function of each sentence.

EXAMPLE   ¹One approach to minimizing the limitations of both computers and humans is to have them work together in ways that create a better outcome than either could achieve alone. __b__ ²In medical diagnosis, for example, the human's role is to establish the presence and nature of a patient's symptoms. __c__ ³The computer then combines this information in a completely unbiased way to identify the most likely diagnosis. __d__ ⁴Similarly, laboratory technologists who examine blood samples for the causes of disease are assisted by computer programs that serve to reduce errors and memory lapses by (1) keeping track of findings from previous tests, (2) listing possible tests that remain to be tried, and (3) indicating either that certain tests have been left undone or that a new sequence of tests should be done. __c__ ⁵This kind of human-machine teamwork can also help with the assessment of psychological problems. __c__ (Bernstein et al., *Psychology*, p. 300.)

 a. This is an introductory sentence that paves the way for the topic sentence.

 b. This is the topic sentence, summing up the general point of the paragraph.

 c. This is a major supporting detail that directly explains or argues the main idea.

 d. This is a minor supporting detail that further develops a major one.

 e. This is a transitional sentence that helps guide the reader from one sentence to the next.

 f. This is a concluding supporting sentence that describes the consequence of, solution for, or response to some problem or situation described in the paragraph.

EXPLANATION   This paragraph has no introductory sentence. Instead, the author opens with the topic sentence. The remaining blanks are all filled with the letters *c* or *d* because these sentences all introduce major or minor details.

1. [1]China was the first country to attempt to control drug abuse. _B_ [2]In the nineteenth century, opium was brought into the country by British traders. _C_ [3]As a result, the drug became so widespread in China that the government banned it with an imperial* edict.* [4]However, so much of the drug was smuggled in, despite the edict, that the banning attempt was unsuccessful. _C_ [5]Confiscation of large quantities of opium by the Chinese government led to the Opium War of 1839, in which the Chinese battled the British for control of the opium trade. _C_ [6]The Chinese lost the war and, as a result, the British were able to force the Chinese government to legalize the opium trade. _B_ [7]China eventually became the main source of opium and supplied the drug to the rest of the world. _E_ (Adapted from Waughfield, *Mental Health Concepts*, p. 354.)

   a. This is an introductory sentence that paves the way for the topic sentence.

   b. This is the topic sentence, summing up the general point of the paragraph.

   c. This is a major supporting detail that directly explains or argues the main idea.

   d. This is a minor supporting detail that further develops a major one.

   e. This is a transitional sentence that helps guide the reader from one sentence to the next.

   f. This is a concluding supporting sentence that describes the consequence of, solution for, or response to some problem or situation described in the paragraph.

2. [1]The process of settling criminal cases out of court at the discretion of the prosecutor and the judge is called "plea bargaining." _____ [2]With the exception of the victim and the general citizenry, everyone

---

*imperial: royal.
*edict: ruling, law.

benefits from plea bargaining, a fact that helps account for its extensive use. _____ ³The accused gets off with lighter punishment than she would face if the case went to trial and she lost. _____ ⁴The defense attorney frees up time to take on additional legal work. _____ ⁵The prosecuting attorney increases his conviction rate, which looks good if he has political ambitions. _____ ⁶The judge helps cut back the number of cases awaiting trial. _____ ⁷Even police officers benefit by not having to spend time testifying (and waiting to testify) and by raising the departments' clearance rate (the number of cases solved and disposed of). _____ (Bowman and Kearney, *State and Local Government*, p. 244.)

    a. This is an introductory sentence that paves the way for the topic sentence.

    b. This is the topic sentence, summing up the general point of the paragraph.

    c. This is a major supporting detail that directly explains or argues the main idea.

    d. This is a minor supporting detail that further develops a major one.

    e. This is a transitional sentence that helps guide the reader from one sentence to the next.

    f. This is a concluding supporting sentence that describes the consequence of, solution for, or response to some problem or situation described in the paragraph.

3. ¹As many vice presidents have pointed out, being vice president is not a particularly taxing job. _____ ²John Adams, for instance, described it as "the most insignificant office that ever the invention of man contrived." _____ ³Daniel Webster, for his part, rejected a vice-presidential nomination in 1848 with the statement, "I do not choose to be buried until I am really dead." _____ ⁴The only official task of the vice president is to preside over the Senate and to vote in case of a tie. _____ ⁵The two vice presidents who fulfilled this function the greatest number of times were John Adams, who broke a Senate tie on twenty-nine occasions, and John C. Calhoun, who cast the deciding vote twenty-eight times. _____ ⁶Since 1789, 244 Senate tie-breaking votes have been cast by a vice president. _____ ⁷Seven of those votes have been cast by George W. Bush's vice president, Dick Cheney. _____ ⁸Cheney is perhaps the only vice president who

escaped the inactivity of the vice president's office, and he played a crucial role in George W. Bush's presidency, including formulating foreign policy. _____

a. This is an introductory sentence that paves the way for the topic sentence.

b. This is the topic sentence, summing up the general point of the paragraph.

c. This is a major supporting detail that directly explains or argues the main idea.

d. This is a minor supporting detail that further develops a major one.

e. This is a transitional sentence that helps guide the reader from one sentence to the next.

f. This is a concluding supporting sentence that describes the consequence of, solution for, or response to some problem or situation described in the paragraph.

4. [1]Although there are those who insist privately owned prisons are the answer to the problem of prison overcrowding, members of Citizens Against Private Prisons (CAPP) do not agree. _____ [2]CAPP's members insist that private prisons ultimately do more harm than good, and they have some hard evidence to back up their claim. _____ [3]A 2005 report from the Irish Penal Reform Trust (IPRT), a group dedicated to prison reform, indicates that throughout the world private prisons have failed in their mission to decrease costs and improve performance. _____ [4]The IPRT report says that in the United States private prisons experience 50 percent more prisoner-on-staff assaults. _____ [5]CAPP also points out that Australia, in 2000, had to take control of the privatized Metropolitan Women's Correctional Centre. _____ [6]The government takeover was necessary because the private women's prison had been plagued by persistent problems and complaints that could not be resolved. _____ [7]In addition, CAPP members point to the United Kingdom, where private prisons have been touted as the answer to prison assaults and overcrowding; yet several private prison contractors have defaulted on their agreements with the governments and been heavily fined as a result. _____ [8]Because the movement toward private prisons seems to be gaining steam in the United States, CAPP needs to do more to publicize its efforts and its evidence before any more money is wasted on

contracts with private prison companies. _____ (Source of information: www.capp.50megs.com/recentnews296.html.)

    a. This is an introductory sentence that paves the way for the topic sentence.

    b. This is the topic sentence, summing up the general point of the paragraph.

    c. This is a major supporting detail that directly explains or argues the main idea.

    d. This is a minor supporting detail that further develops a major one.

    e. This is a transitional sentence that helps guide the reader from one sentence to the next.

    f. This is a concluding supporting sentence that describes the consequence of, solution for, or response to some problem or situation described in the paragraph.

✔ CHECK YOUR UNDERSTANDING

1. When it comes to supporting details, can you expect writers to include every detail you need to understand the main idea? Please explain your answer.

_____

_____

2. What makes concluding sentences different from supporting details?

_____

_____

_____

VOCABULARY CHECK

The following words were introduced in pages 267–86. Match the word to the definition. Review words, definitions, and original context two or three times before taking the vocabulary tests. (The page numbers in parentheses indicate where the word first appeared.)

1. supernatural (p. 267) _____
2. mediums (p. 267) _____
3. psychosis (p. 269) _____
4. satellite (p. 271) _____
5. orbits (p. 272) _____
6. barren (p. 272) _____
7. inherently (p. 273) _____
8. commodity (p. 283) _____
9. imperial (p. 286) _____
10. edict (p. 286) _____

a. at the core; by nature

b. ruling, law

c. people who claim they can communicate with the dead

d. royal

e. something that is bought or sold in the market

f. a mental disturbance that causes severe reality distortion

g. relating to things not happening in the ordinary world; miraculous

h. an object propelled into space to circle Earth or other planets

i. unable to reproduce; dry; lacking in vegetation

j. paths of movement

DIGGING Debating Private Prisons
DEEPER

Looking Ahead   As the paragraph on pages 288–89 already indicated, the privatization of prisons is a controversial issue. The authors of the following article outline some of the pros and cons.

1   Despite the rapid growth of private prisons throughout the 1980s and 1990s, prison privatization is a controversial idea. Those who support it claim that prisons built and operated by the private sector will save the taxpayers money. Because of less red tape, facilities can be constructed and operated more economically. Most importantly, advocates claim that private prisons reduce overcrowding.

2   Opponents of privatization, however, question whether firms can build and operate correctional facilities significantly less expensively than state or local governments can. They believe that the profit motive is misplaced in a prison setting, where firms may skimp on nutritious food, health care, or skilled personnel to cut operating costs. A company whose business benefits from filling up cell space as soon as it is built might foster a lock-'em-up-and-throw-away-the-key approach. Such a firm might also lobby for and contribute campaign dollars to legislators for stricter sentencing requirements and additional prisons.

3   Evidence on the economics of prison privatization is mixed. Most of the experimentation has involved juveniles, illegal aliens, and minimum- and medium-security offenders. The majority of studies indicate that operating-cost savings have been marginal or nonexistent. Corrections Corporation of America and other private prison firms have reported significant financial losses in recent years. And although overcrowded conditions may be relieved more promptly through privatization, the burden on the taxpayers appears to be about the same.

4   One of the basic questions to be addressed is whether the delegation of the corrections function to a private firm is constitutionally permissible. The U.S. Supreme Court and state courts will have to determine not only whether incarceration, punishment, deterrence, and rehabilitation can properly be delegated, but also who is legally responsible for a private facility. The Supreme Court spoke on one such issue by declaring that private prison guards who violate inmates' rights are not entitled to qualified immunity—unlike public-sector guards.

5   Another set of legal considerations concerns practical accountability for the day-to-day operation of jails and prisons. Consider, for example, this

case. In Texas, two men escaped from a private prison near Houston. They nearly made it to Dallas before they were caught. But Texas authorities couldn't prosecute them for their escape because by breaking out of a private facility, the men had not committed an offense under Texas law. The men, who had been sent to the Houston facility from Oregon, could not be prosecuted in Oregon because the escape happened in Texas.

6   Economic and legal issues aside, perhaps the most important question is, who should operate our jails and prisons? Legal scholar Ira Robbins suggests that we should remember the words of the novelist Fyodor Dostoevsky: "The degree of civilization in a society can be measured by entering its prisons." (Adapted from Bowman and Kearney, *State and Local Government*, p. 453.)

Sharpening Your Skills

DIRECTIONS   Answer the following questions by filling in the blanks or circling the letters of the correct response.

1. Which statement best expresses the main idea?

    a. Private prisons have not been as successful as supporters claim.
    b. Currently, the jury is still out on the effectiveness of privatizing prisons.
    c. Private prisons have been a complete failure.
    d. Privatizing prisons can solve the twin problems of overcrowding and prison violence against both guards and inmates.

2. In paragraph 3, Corrections Corporation of America is mentioned in a minor detail that clarifies a major detail. What is the point of the major detail?

    _____

3. "Evidence on the economics of prison privatization is mixed" is the topic sentence of paragraph 3. What word or words in this topic sentence need to be clarified in the supporting details?

    _____

4. What question do the supporting details in paragraph 4 need to answer?

_____

_____

5. In paragraph 5, the supporting details recount the escape of two men from a privately owned Texas prison. That example suggests that "practical accountability for the day-to-day operation of jails and prisons" is

   a. the responsibility of the state where the prison is located.
   b. the responsibility of the company running the prison.
   c. unclear.

6. Based on the context, what is a good approximate definition for the word *facilities* in paragraph 1?

_____

7. Based on the context, what is a good approximate definition for *marginal* in paragraph 3?

_____

8. Based on the context, what is a good approximate definition for *incarceration* in paragraph 4?

_____

9. According to *The American Heritage* dictionary, a deterrence can refer to measures taken by states to prevent hostile actions. But in paragraph 4 of the reading, the most likely definition for *deterrence* is

   a. to prevent someone from committing a crime.
   b. to prevent prison escapes.
   c. to prevent prison riots.

10. *The American Heritage* dictionary lists these definitions for *rehabilitate*: (1) To restore to good health or useful life, as through therapy and education; (2) To reinstate the good name of; (3) To restore the former rank, privileges, or rights of.

    Which of those definitions would best fit the use of *rehabilitation* in paragraph 4? _____

Making Connections Re-read the paragraph about private prisons on pages 288–89. Do you think the writer of that paragraph and the authors of the reading on pages 291–92 share the same attitude toward private prisons? Please explain your answer.

_____

_____

_____

Drawing Your Own Conclusions Where do you stand on the subject of private prisons? Is putting prisons under the control of private companies a good or a bad idea? Whatever your answer, please explain your reasoning.

_____

_____

_____

_____

▶ TEST 1   Vocabulary Review

DIRECTIONS   In the blank, write a definition for each italicized word.

1. The accident in the factory had left him *maimed* for life.

   Maimed means _____.

2. Many species of *amphibians*, like toads and frogs, are mysteriously disappearing.

   Amphibians means _____.

3. His clothing may have been elegant, but his manner was *disreputable*.

   Disreputable means _____.

4. His mother had expected her son to experience severe homesickness at camp, but his letters suggested that he was *thriving*.

   Thriving means _____.

5. Initially the events that occurred seemed to be *supernatural* in origin, but in the end they turned out to be the result of perfectly ordinary causes.

   Supernatural means _____.

6. When Senator Edward M. Kennedy died, well-wishers stood outside the Kennedy *compound* in Hyannisport holding candles.

   Compound means _____.

7. When a fight broke out on the field, several of the parents jumped into the *fray*.

   Fray means _____.

8. The woman was *inherently* good natured and people tended to take advantage of her open-hearted generosity.

   Inherently means _____.

9. Kanye West is *notorious* for being temperamental, but it's impossible to deny his talent.

   Notorious means _____.

10. The ability to climb stairs without heavy breathing is a sign of *cardiovascular* health.

    Cardiovascular means _____.

▶ **TEST 2**   **Vocabulary Review**

DIRECTIONS   Fill in the blanks with one of the words listed below.

commodity	imperial	psychosis	satellite	orbit
purged	edict	medium	respiratory	barren

1. The _____ circling the Earth was showing signs of malfunctioning, and no one on Earth or in the satellite itself was sure what was happening.

2. After the Russian dictator Josef Stalin came to power, he _____ the Communist Party of anyone who raised an objection or posed a question.

3. Normally the flu is an unpleasant _____ ailment that is deadly only for those with weakened immune systems; however, the mysterious flu of 1918 killed millions of young and healthy people.

4. We don't think of water as a(n) _____ that can be bought and sold by the highest bidder, but if it keeps getting scarce, that could happen.

5. When mapped, the planet's _____ looked like a sphere that circled the Earth.

6. After the crops were sprayed for insects, not only did the bugs die, but the lettuce and tomatoes went black as well; by the end of the month, the planting fields were completely _____.

7. The arrival of the dignitaries at the _____ palace was a cause of great excitement.

8. The _____ pretended to be possessed by the spirit of the famous magician, Cagliostro.

9. No one quite understands how cults function to subdue personal independence, but members often seem to share some kind of group _____.

10. After issuing the _____, the king left the balcony as the crowd roared its approval.

▶ **TEST 3**   **Recognizing Supporting Details**

DIRECTIONS   The first sentence in each group of sentences is the topic sentence. That topic sentence is followed by five supporting details. Circle the letters of the three sentences that help make the topic sentence clear and convincing.

Topic Sentence 1. Over the years, salamanders—small, lizardlike creatures that walk on four legs—have been the focus of numerous legends.

Supporting Details

a. In England, a salamander is also the name of a portable stove.

b. The philosopher Aristotle claimed that salamanders could put out fires simply by walking through them.

c. The word *salamander* comes from the Greek word *salamandra*.

d. It was once believed that twining a salamander around a tree would kill the tree and poison its fruit.

e. According to legend, four thousand soldiers died when they drank from a stream into which a salamander had fallen.

Topic Sentence 2. The Walt Disney film *Pinocchio* is based on a novel by nineteenth-century Italian writer Carlo Collodi, but the novel was far more violent than the film.

Supporting Details

a. In both the novel and the film, Pinocchio is transformed into a donkey.

b. Disney's *Pinocchio* did not achieve the popularity of the fabulously successful *Snow White*.

c. In Collodi's novel, when Pinocchio is attacked by a cat, he bites off the cat's paw.

d. In the Italian version, Pinocchio kills a talking cricket when the insect tries to keep him from getting into trouble.

e. In the novel, when Pinocchio falls asleep by the fire, he wakes up with his wooden feet burned off.

Topic Sentence 3. Until a cure was discovered in the nineteenth century, scurvy, a disease caused by a lack of vitamin C, plagued sailors on long sea voyages.

Supporting Details

a. In the late 1490s, the explorer Vasco da Gama lost more than half of his crew to scurvy.

b. In his autobiography, *Two Years Before the Mast*, nineteenth-century writer Richard Henry Dana described the sufferings of a fellow sailor who had contracted scurvy: "His legs swelled . . . his flesh lost its elasticity . . . and his gums swelled until he could not open his mouth."

c. Scurvy no longer plagues sailors who spend long periods of time at sea.

d. During the Napoleonic wars (1803–1814), French soldiers, who did not have daily doses of vitamin C, suffered from scurvy, but British soldiers, who drank daily doses of lime juice, escaped the disease.

e. British sailors became so associated with the drinking of lime juice that they were nicknamed "limeys"; the name stuck with them.

Topic Sentence 4. For centuries, dogs have held a very special place in the hearts of humans.

Supporting Details

a. In the fifteenth and sixteenth centuries, no high-born lady was complete without her lap dog, and many women took their pets to church.

b. Unlike most dogs, border collies would rather work than play.

c. The eighteenth-century poet and scholar Samuel Johnson was quick to put humans in their place, but he doted on his pet dog.

d. Even the French Emperor Napoleon (1769–1821) claimed that his beloved Josephine preferred her dog Fortune to him.

e. Some people do not understand the bond that can develop between human beings and their pets.

◗ **TEST 4**   **Identifying Topic Sentences and Supporting Details**

DIRECTIONS   Circle the appropriate letter to identify the one sentence in each group that could function as the topic sentence.

1. a. The digestive system performs several important functions from which the body benefits.

   b. During digestion, food is broken down into smaller pieces.

   c. The digestive juices turn the food we eat into fat, carbohydrates, and protein, all of which are needed by the body.

   d. During the digestive process, nutrients are absorbed into the bloodstream.

   e. At the end of digestion, waste products are eliminated from the body.

2. a. The California Department of Fish and Game uses GIS to track and monitor endangered species of plants and animals.

   b. The fire department in Greenville, South Carolina, uses GIS to map the best routes to a fire.

   c. Chicago uses GIS for parking violations and meter repair.

   d. Police in Denver use GIS to track crime trends throughout the city.

   e. The technology known as geographic information systems (GIS) is transforming the policies and operations of state and local governments. (Adapted from Bowman and Kearney, *State and Local Government*, p. 238.)

3. a. According to Gordon Allport, mature adults are interested in others and consider the welfare of others as important as their own.

   b. Gordon Allport believed that mature adults are problem solvers, who have developed the necessary skills to complete current and future tasks.

   c. The psychologist Gordon Allport developed several criteria for what he considered to be the "mature" personality.

   d. The ability to relate emotionally to other people was yet another of Gordon Allport's criteria.

   e. Self-insight was another character trait Gordon Allport associated with maturity.

4. a. People suffering from test anxiety worry they will perform poorly and be considered stupid as a result.

   b. Test anxiety is a very common problem with profound consequences.

   c. Test-takers who suffer from test anxiety often know the right answers, but they go blank due to high anxiety.

   d. Some children who suffer from test anxiety refuse to go to school.

   e. Boys and girls seem to suffer equally from test anxiety.

5. a. With the passage of the North American Free Trade Agreement (NAFTA) in 1994, it became easier for U.S. companies to move their plants to locations where labor was much cheaper than in the United States.

   b. Rulings by the World Trade Organization also made it easier for foreign products to be imported into the United States.

   c. American workers are no longer competing with one another; they are competing with workers around the world.

   d. In India and Russia, wages for computer programmers average less than 10 percent of the wages for programmers in the United States.

   e. During the recession of 2001–2003, more than 15 percent of the American jobs lost were outsourced to workers from other countries, where the labor was cheap.

▶ **TEST 5**　　　**Distinguishing Between Major and Minor Details**

DIRECTIONS　　Read each paragraph. Then fill in the boxes using either the numbers of the sentences or paraphrased versions of the topic sentence and major and minor details.

1.　[1]Parents worry about the violence in video games that require kids to shoot enemies, but some research shows that these games benefit children by improving their visual attention skills. [2]After as few as ten hours of play, kids show a 30 to 50 percent improvement in identifying objects in their peripheral, or side angle, vision. [3]These games also help children develop the brain's ability to shift attention rapidly from one thing to another. [4]In addition such shooting games improve players' ability to track many different items at one time. [5]This skill, in particular, is helpful in tasks such as driving. (Source of statistics: Sandra Blakeslee, "Video-Game Killing Builds Visual Skills, Researchers Report," *New York Times*, May 29, 2003, p. A1.)

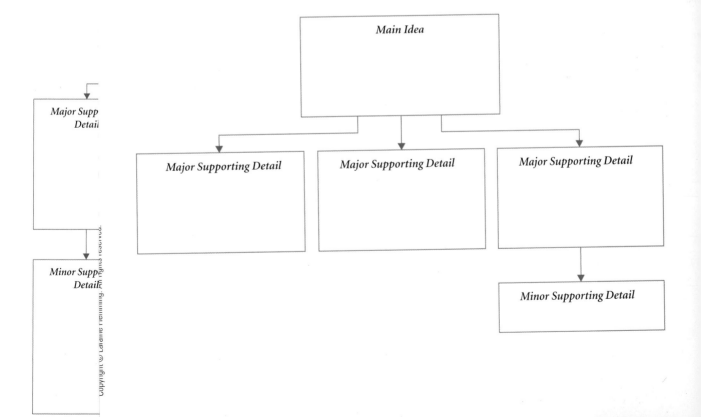

Main Idea

Major Supporting Detail

Major Supporting Detail

Major Supporting Detail

Major Supporting Detail

Minor Supporting Detail

Minor Supporting Detail

▶ **TEST 7**   **Recognizing Supporting Details and Concluding Sentences**

DIRECTIONS   Read each paragraph. The topic sentence in each paragraph is underlined. Label each of the following sentences as a major (*M*) or minor (*m*) detail. If you think the paragraph ends with a concluding sentence, write a *c* in the final blank.

1. ¹<u>Although we associate penguins with the Antarctic, only two of approximately twenty species live on the continent of Antarctica.</u> ²These are the two largest, the emperor and the king penguins. _____ ³Both of them stand about four feet high. _____ ⁴Most other species are found on the islands in the Antarctic region, but a few breed as far north as Australia, New Zealand, South Africa, and South America. _____

2. ¹<u>Leadership and management are in some ways similar forms of influence, but in one very crucial way they are quite different.</u> ²Managers can direct the efforts of others because of their status or power within an organization. _____ ³Simply put, employees follow the directions of a manager largely because they know that not to do so would endanger their jobs. _____ ⁴Leaders, in contrast, don't have to rely on their position or rank; often it is the power of their personality that makes them an influence to be reckoned with. _____ ⁵At the Marriott Corporation, for example, employees often go beyond their normal duties largely because they respect and admire Bill Marriott. _____

3. ¹Surprising as it may seem to those of us who grew up with him, Santa Claus was not always pictured as a roly-poly figure with chubby cheeks, a big belly, and a long white beard. ²<u>The Santa Claus we know today was created in the mid-nineteenth century by the cartoonist Thomas Nast.</u> ³The European ancestor of our Santa Claus, Saint Nicholas, was always pictured as a tall, lean, and bearded bishop who bore no trace of extra fat. _____ ⁴However, during the years 1863 to 1885, Nast was commissioned by *Harper's Weekly* to do a series of Christmas drawings; during that twenty-two-year period, he created the pudgy figure so beloved by children today. _____ ⁵It was Nast who decided that Santa should wear a fur-trimmed red suit and hat. _____ ⁶Nast's cartoons also showed the world how Santa spent his entire year—making toys, checking on children's behavior,

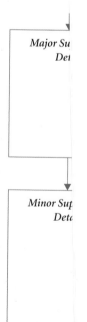

*Major Su
    Det*

*Minor Sup
    Det*

and reading their letters. _____ [7]Ultimately, however, Nast's fame rests not on his Santa Claus drawings but on his cartoons attacking political corruption.† _____

4. [1]The first American comic strip appeared in 1894. [2]<u>Comic books, however, arrived after the turn of the century, and it wasn't until the 1930s that comic books successfully became part of American culture.</u> [3]The first comic book, published by Dell Publishing Company, was a huge failure, but the second one, also published by Dell, succeeded. _____ [4]Called "Famous Funnies," the comic book cost ten cents, and all thirty-five thousand copies quickly sold out. _____ [5]Not surprisingly, many more comic books followed, most of them featuring cartoon characters, such as Popeye and Flash Gordon, that had originally appeared in newspapers. _____ [6]The biggest comic book breakthrough, however, came in 1938 with the introduction of a red-caped, blue-suited figure called Superman. _____ [7]Appearing in the first issue of *Action Comics*, Superman was an immediate sensation. _____ [8]Today, that first issue of *Action Comics* can fetch its owner around one hundred thousand dollars. _____

---

†corruption: dishonesty, wrongdoing.

◆ **TEST 8**   **Topics, Topic Sentences, and Inferring Supporting Details**

DIRECTIONS   Write a phrase that identifies the topic. Then underline the topic sentence, and circle the appropriate letters to identify the two inferences supplied by readers.

1. ¹More than half a century has passed since John Steinbeck wrote the novel *The Grapes of Wrath*. ²In it, he depicted the sorrows and trials of the Joads, a poverty-stricken family of migrants, seasonally employed people, who traveled from place to place looking for work. ³When Steinbeck wrote the book, there were no laws protecting migrant workers, and they were almost uniformly mistreated by their employers. ⁴After *The Grapes of Wrath* was published and widely read, the public's outcry for change was clear and strong, and reforms were undertaken; but most of the reforms never took effect, and even today many migrant workers still live under the worst possible conditions. ⁵Every year, the Department of Labor receives numerous complaints about improper recruitment procedures and failure to pay proper wages. ⁶But the charges are hard to prove, and workers often give up on getting justice. ⁷In addition, housing provided for migrant workers is frequently substandard. ⁸Migrant workers often live in barn-like dormitories or shacks, and overcrowding is the norm. ⁹Meals are equally inadequate, and poor nutrition causes widespread disease. ¹⁰Owners of farms employing migrant workers are often absent, leaving them in the hands of crew leaders. ¹¹Unfortunately, crew leaders, paid according to the amount they harvest, sometimes abuse their authority.

Topic   _____

Inferences   Which two of these inferences is the reader expected to add to the supporting details?

a. Steinbeck's book was not emotionally powerful enough to keep the desire for reform alive.

b. Steinbeck's book was so emotionally powerful, it made the public care about the unhappy lives forced upon migrant workers.

c. After the initial outpouring of sympathy for migrant workers, public outrage died down, and those who could improve the living conditions for migrant workers no longer felt the need to make an effort.

d. Farm owners would like to maintain better conditions, but the crew leaders they hire don't share their compassion.

e. The working conditions for migrant workers have actually gotten much worse since Steinbeck's book caused such an uproar.

2. [1]By 1939, gospel singer Marian Anderson had sung before most of Europe's royalty, but when she tried to rent Constitution Hall in Washington, D.C., for a concert, her request was denied because of racism. [2]The building was owned by the all-white Daughters of the American Revolution (DAR), and Anderson was the descendant of slaves. [3]Appalled by the thought of Anderson singing in their hall, the board of the DAR refused. [4]Fortunately, the DAR's refusal aroused considerable protest. [5]Eleanor Roosevelt, wife of President Franklin D. Roosevelt and a longtime champion of civil rights, promptly gave up her membership in the DAR. [6]In addition to Mrs. Roosevelt's very public protest, Interior Secretary Harold Ickes arranged an outdoor performance for Anderson on the steps of the Lincoln Memorial. [7]The concert was a smashing success, winning Anderson rave reviews. [8]In the end, it was Marian Anderson who had the last laugh.

Topic

Inferences

Which two of these inferences is the reader expected to add to the supporting details?

a. In 1939, everyone in the DAR had the same racist attitude as the board that refused Anderson's request.

b. Marian Anderson sang on the steps of the Lincoln Memorial.

c. Eleanor Roosevelt was known to champion the cause of the underdog.

d. Interior Secretary Harold Ickes did not like what the DAR had done.

3. [1]Early in their career, Wilbur and Orville Wright, the inventors of the airplane, weren't exactly an impressive pair. [2]Seeing them on the beach staring at birds in flight and flapping their arms in imitation, passersby made fun of the brothers. [3]As John T. Daniels, an early observer, put it, "We couldn't help thinkin' they were just a pair of poor nuts." [4]But Wilbur and Orville Wright were anything but nuts—and on December 17, 1903, they proved every one of their detractors wrong.

[5]On that day, their 745-pound invention, the *Flyer*, climbed ten feet into the air. [6]True, the flight came to a sudden halt when the plane nose-dived to the ground after only twelve seconds. [7]Still, the Wright brothers had proved that men could fly like those birds they had watched on the beach. [8]By 1908, the Wright brothers were ready to sign contracts to produce their flying machine with both the U.S. Army and a French industrial firm. [9]Wilbur, however, did not live long enough to really enjoy his triumph. [10]By 1912, he was dead of typhoid fever. [11]Luckier than his brother, Orville lived to continue his research; he died in 1948 at the age of seventy-seven.

Topic _____

Inferences Which two of these inferences is the reader expected to add to the supporting details?

   a. Wilbur and Orville Wright were remarkably unattractive men.
   b. Orville Wright survived the typhoid fever that killed his brother.
   c. By 1908, people were no longer dismissing the brothers as nuts.
   d. Passersby who made fun of the brothers because they thought the two looked silly flapping their arms didn't understand what the brothers were really doing.

4. [1]The Cuban hero José Martí devoted his life to making Cuba a free country. [2]Born in 1853, he was exiled to Spain at the age of seventeen for protesting Spanish domination of Cuba. [3]While in exile, he published a pamphlet describing the pain and humiliation of the political imprisonment he had suffered for demanding Cuban independence. [4]In 1878, Martí was allowed to return to Cuba under a general amnesty[†] for political prisoners. [5]But he was soon banished once again for plotting against the Spanish authorities. [6]After fleeing to the United States, where he stayed for a year in New York City, Martí left for Venezuela. [7]But his political work for Cuban independence made him unwelcome there, and he returned to New York City, where he lived from 1881 to 1895. [8]In 1895, he returned to Cuba to join the war for Cuban liberation and died in one of the early battles.

Topic _____

_____
[†]amnesty: release from a crime.

Inferences   Which two of these inferences is the reader expected to add to the supporting details?

a. Martí was banished the second time for again conspiring to free Cuba of Spanish rule.

b. Martí was not alone in his determination to make Cuba independent of Spain.

c. While Martí lived in New York, his every move was watched by the government.

d. If he could have, Martí would have become an American citizen.

More About Inferences

FROM THIS CHAPTER, YOU WILL LEARN

- how common inferences are in daily life.
- how to fill in the gaps in topic sentences.
- how to infer implied main ideas.

*"An inference is a statement about the unknown
made on the basis of the known."*
—S. I. Hayakawa, *Language in Thought and Action*

Step by step, Chapter 6 shows you how to draw infere̶ are looking at cartoons or reading textbooks. After a ᴜ̶ to everyday inferences, you'll learn how to infer main ideas tṟo̶ graphs, in which the message is strongly implied but left partially o̶ completely unstated.

Inferences in Everyday Life

In daily life, we draw inferences all the time. We draw conclusions, that is, about the unknown based on the known. If, for instance, neighbors come home with a new baby and shortly afterward start looking tired and worn, we might well infer that the baby was a light sleeper, who kept the parents awake, even if they themselves never complained. Similarly, if a room-mate goes on a blind date and comes home smiling and whistling, we'd probably assume, before hearing a word, that the date was successful.

Cartoons

Consider, too, how often we draw inferences when reading the comics section of a newspaper. Take, as an example, this Calvin and Hobbes comic strip. What's the boy thinking in the second frame? And what does he mean when he says, "I love loopholes"? In both cases, the car-toon's creator expects you to infer the boy's thoughts.

CALVIN AND HOBBES © 1995 Watterson. Dist. By UNIVERSAL PRESS SYNDICATE. Reprinted with permission. All rights reserved.

In the second frame, readers need to infer that Calvin has suddenly gotten an idea. To make this inference, they have to draw on the message of the first frame, where the boy's expression and the fact that he's reading a test say he's worried because he doesn't know how to answer one of the questions. Readers also need to know that exclamation points often signal excitement; in this case, the exclamation point suggests Calvin's excitement at finding a solution to his current problem.

To understand the final frame, readers have to infer a connection between Calvin's saying he loves "loopholes" and the gobbledygook he wrote in the previous frame. The inference they need to draw goes something like this: Calvin has interpreted the teacher's instructions to suit his own purposes. The teacher meant that students should paraphrase Newton's Law of Motion. Calvin, however, decides to supply his own meaning and interpret the instructions as "Explain the law in language of your own creation."

If you are thinking at this point that this is a lot of explanation for one simple cartoon, you are absolutely right. But in fact, a lot of explanation is required to describe the number of actual inferences you make when reading a simple cartoon. You just don't know you are doing it. Making inferences to read cartoons is so ingrained, or automatic, we don't realize how often we make them.

Quips* and Quotes

Quotes and quips also rely on you to figure out what was meant but left unsaid. For example, what did American author Mark Twain mean when he said, "Man is the only animal that blushes, or needs to"? And if you know anything at all about a hungry cat, you probably won't have problems understanding this quip: "There is no snooze button on a cat who wants breakfast."† My point is that you are no stranger to drawing inferences. You do it all the time. All you have to do at this point is think more consciously about how you draw inferences when you read.

◆ **EXERCISE 1**   **Understanding Inferences**

DIRECTIONS   Read each quotation. Infer the message it is meant to communicate and write your inference in the blank.

---

*quips: quick one-liners.
†www.re-quest.net/animals/domestic/cats/cat-quotes/index.htm.

1. "Nothing so needs reforming as other people's habits." (Mark Twain)

   Other people need to improve but we don't look @ improving ourselves

2. "If you want to make God laugh, tell him your future plans." (Woody Allen)

   We cn't predict future only he does

3. "The funniest line in English is 'Get it?' When you say that, everyone chortles.*" (Garrison Keillor)

   told joke / pretend to get it and laugh

4. "Why is it no one sent me yet
   One perfect limousine, do you suppose?
   Ah, no, it's always just my luck to get
   One perfect rose." (Dorothy Parker)

   roses are typical so get more creative

Idioms

Idioms are expressions that native speakers know from long usage but that non-native speakers stumble over because the expressions cannot be translated word for word and make sense. Idioms have evolved through usage and aren't related to the normal meanings of the words, so they often don't seem to fit the context for someone unfamiliar with the language. Tell a non-native speaker, for instance, that she shouldn't "rock the boat," and she'll wonder why you are talking about boating when you are in the library.

Idioms, like cartoons, quotes, and quips, rely on inferences to convey their meaning. For instance, if a friend is depressed and complaining about hard times, we might well say, "You've got to keep your chin up in times like these." Given the context of his complaints, we expect our friend to infer our idiomatic meaning, which has nothing to do with the direction of his chin. We expect him to infer, based on the context and his knowledge of the language, the meaning of the idiom we used: "Try to stay in a positive frame of mind."

---

*chortles: laughs, chuckles.

◆ EXERCISE 2 Understanding Idioms

DIRECTIONS Read each sentence. Note the italicized idiom. Then circle the letter of the inference the writer wants readers to draw from that idiom. *Note*: To complete this exercise, you will need access to a computer or a dictionary of idioms, available in all school libraries.

1. Harry Truman was famous for *shooting from the hip,* and his bluntness delighted his supporters and infuriated his critics.

   Based on the idiom used to describe Harry Truman, readers are supposed to infer that he

   a. was known for his eloquent speeches.

   b. was inclined to be impulsive.

   c. was famous for his skills with a rifle.

2. Because he was considered an *egghead,* Adlai Stevenson, the Democratic presidential candidate in 1952 and 1956, did not win over huge crowds in the way his opponent, Republican Dwight D. Eisenhower, did.

   Based on the idiom used to describe Adlai Stevenson, readers are supposed to infer that he

   a. pretended to be an ordinary working man and the pretense got on people's nerves.

   b. seemed to be an intellectual and that made him suspicious in the eyes of many.

   c. was overly critical of his opponent and people did not like him as a result.

3. In 1844, despite his being a *dark horse* candidate, James K. Polk managed to win the Democratic primary and eventually the presidency.

   Based on the idiom used to describe James K. Polk, readers are supposed to infer that he

   a. was popular enough to win the presidency despite the more moneyed and experienced competition.

   b. was a well-known gambler and voters found his weakness endearing.

   c. was a complete unknown when he became president.

4. The White House press secretary's job is to *carry water* for the president; the press secretary is not there to offer insight into current events.

   Based on the idiom used to describe the press secretary's job, readers are supposed to infer that the president's press secretary

   a. says what he or she is told to say by the president.
   b. is not expected to know anything about current events.
   c. is an excellent source of objective information about national and international events.

5. Franklin Delano Roosevelt's administration was highly successful in its first hundred days, and one reason for that success was Roosevelt's *brain trust*, which played a key role in shaping public policy.

   Based on the presence of the idiom "brain trust," readers are supposed to infer that

   a. Roosevelt had faith in his own judgment.
   b. Roosevelt liked people who were smarter than he was.
   c. Roosevelt liked to have the advice of experts when it came to crafting public policy.

Drawing Inferences to Construct Topic Sentences

As you already know from Chapter 5, inferences can play an important role in reading paragraphs. When necessary, they fulfill the function of supporting details.

As it turns out, inferences are even more important in paragraphs in which the author suggests but does not state the main idea in a single topic sentence. Sometimes, for example, writers do not express the main idea in one sentence. Instead, they put parts of the main idea into separate sentences and leave it to readers to weave the sentences together into a statement of the implied main idea; for example:

Topic Sentence   [1]At one time, the right side of the brain was regarded as the minor hemisphere, or half. [2]We now know, however, that it has its own special set of talents and isn't "minor" at all. [3]The right hemisphere is superior at recognizing patterns, faces, and melodies. [4]It's also involved in detecting and expressing emotions. [5]The right brain is actually better than the left at visualization skills, such as arranging blocks to match a pattern, putting together a puzzle, or drawing pictures.

The first sentence introduces the precise topic of the paragraph—the right side of the brain. However, the first sentence is not the topic sentence. The paragraph does not deal with the earlier notion that the right brain was the minor hemisphere. As the reversal transition "however" suggests, the author is going to revise the opening thought.

The real main idea of the paragraph turns up in the second sentence: We now know that the right brain is not inferior to the left; in fact, it has its own unique talents. But if you look at the topic sentence communicating that main idea in the example paragraph, you would notice it has some gaps: "We now know, however, that *it* has *its* own special set of talents and isn't 'minor' at all." Read that sentence a few weeks from now and you might not be so clear about the meanings of those pronouns, *it* and *its*. Then, too, if you want to paraphrase the sentence to take notes, you would first need to draw the correct inference and replace at least one of those pronouns with the right noun. Then you'd have a complete topic sentence: "We now know that the right side of the brain has its own special set of talents and isn't 'minor' at all."

Here's another example of a topic sentence that requires readers to fill in the gaps:

Topic Sentence

[1]In 1911, the English explorer Robert Scott set out to explore the South Pole. [2]Unfortunately, he made a fatal error, and his expedition to the South Pole resulted in tragedy. [3]When Scott left for the Pole, he carried with him not a team of sled dogs but nineteen small ponies. [4]Unlike the more widely used sled dogs, the ponies had a hard time navigating the harsh terrain* and could not withstand the freezing cold. [5]Ultimately, the ponies, along with Scott and his entire team, died in their attempt to reach the South Pole. [6]Roald Amundsen, the explorer who beat Scott to the Pole, later attributed his own success to his team's use of sled dogs rather than ponies.

Because the paragraph focuses on the specific effects of Scott's "fatal error," sentence 2 comes very close to being a complete topic sentence. But imagine that you underlined that sentence and re-read it to review for an exam, say, six weeks after your first reading. Could it stand on its

*terrain: an area of ground or land.

own as a summary sentence? Well, maybe it could if you were an expert in Antarctic exploration; however, most readers would need to know more. They would need, that is, a completed topic sentence like the following: "Unfortunately, the English explorer Robert Scott made a fatal error, and his 1911 expedition to the South Pole resulted in tragedy."

◆ **EXERCISE 3** **Constructing Topic Sentences**

DIRECTIONS Underline the partially completed topic sentence in each paragraph. Using information supplied by another sentence, write a completed version in the blank.

EXAMPLE [1]Who was Will Rogers? [2]He was the cowboy-philosopher who won America's heart in the 1920s. [3]Born in Oklahoma, Rogers began his career on stage playing a rope-twirling cowboy-comedian and in 1915 joined the Ziegfeld Follies.† [4]Soon his widely quoted wisecracks about the American political scene made him famous nationwide. [5]The public loved the way he ridiculed politicians. [6]"I am not a member of any organized party—I am a Democrat." [7]By the time he died in a plane crash in 1935, Rogers had made more than twenty films, and quotes from his newspaper column had appeared on the front page of the *New York Times*.

Will Rogers was the cowboy-philosopher who won America's heart in the

1920s.

EXPLANATION Sentence 2 is a partially completed topic sentence. To make it fully convey the author's meaning, readers need to combine sentences 1 and 2.

1. [1]As a relatively young man, Bela Lugosi became rich and famous. [2]Taken by his performance in 1931 as the blood-drinking Count Dracula, audiences willingly paid to see Lugosi's particular brand of elegance and evil. [3]But all that changed as Bela Lugosi grew older. [4]When he died, he had nothing left of the fame and fortune playing Dracula had brought him. [5]Because Lugosi had become so closely identified with the figure of the count, producers were hesitant to

---

†Ziegfeld Follies: a famous variety show created by Florenz Ziegfeld.

cast him in other roles. [6]In addition, his thick Hungarian accent, so effective in *Dracula*, was a handicap for other parts. [7]As a result, Lugosi was reduced to making ridiculous, low-grade thrillers like *Bela Lugosi Meets a Brooklyn Gorilla* and *Mother Riley Meets the Vampire*. [8]By the mid-1950s, Lugosi was all but forgotten by Hollywood and his fans. [9]By 1956, he was dead, a victim of drugs and alcohol.

Bela Lugosi died he had nothing left of the fame and fortune playing Dracula brought him.

2. [1]Throughout the 1800s, explorers had dreamed of reaching the North Pole. [2]But it wasn't until 1909 that anyone claimed to have done it. [3]Who got there first, though, is still the subject of argument. [4]Dr. Frederick Cook claimed that he had reached the Pole on April 21, 1908, spending two days there until drifting ice forced him to move westward. [5]The world press celebrated Cook's achievement until cables began arriving from Robert Peary, who insisted that he had been the first man to reach the Pole. [6]The controversy continued even after the two men had died. [7]In fact, some historians insist that both claims lacked the appropriate proof and therefore cannot be honored. [8]They propose instead that Richard Byrd was the first man to really arrive at the North Pole, flying over it in 1926. [9]Russian historians, for their part, dispute any such claims. [10]They insist that in 1937 the Russian scientist Otto Schmidt was the first person to ever set foot at the North Pole.

Who got to the North pole first is still the subject of arguement.

3. [1]Because of research indicating that drinking coffee contributes to diseases ranging from cancer to heart attacks, coffee has long been a guilty pleasure for many. [2]New research, however, suggests that it may actually offer significant health benefits. [3]For instance, researchers at the National Institute of Diabetes and Digestive Diseases found that coffee significantly reduces the risk of chronic liver disease. [4]Turning old research on its head, two new studies of American nurses have also shown that the biggest coffee drinkers actually have a lower risk for developing high blood pressure. [5]Drinking too much sometimes

causes the heart to race, but these palpitations* are apparently harmless. [6]Similarly, coffee's connections to breast cancer, osteoporosis, and dehydration have been exposed as weak and unproven. [7]What coffee does do is improve athletic ability by triggering a release of adrenaline that strengthens muscle contractions while improving speed and endurance. [8]And coffee's benefits aren't just physical. [9]Caffeine, functioning as a mild antidepressant, also helps to chase away the blues. [10]In one Harvard study of 80,000 American women, coffee drinkers were one-third less likely to commit suicide than non-coffee drinkers. (Source of study results: Kathleen McAuliffe, "Enjoy!" *U.S. News and World Report,* December 19, 2005, www.usnews.com.)

New research suggests that coffee may offer significant health benefits.

4. [1]In 2008, the tanker *Sirius Star* was hijacked by pirates; carrying two million barrels of oil, it was the largest tanker ever taken at sea. [2]Boarded in waters off the coast of Somalia, where the majority of pirate attacks occur, the seizure of the *Sirius Star* raised, yet again, the question haunting shipping companies, sailors, and maritime security organizations: How can ships at sea be kept safe from pirate attacks? [3]Vahan Simidian, the chief executive officer of HPV Technologies, believes his company's magnetic acoustic device (MAD), which functions as both alarm and weapon, provides the answer. [4]If the ship's captain is concerned about an approaching vessel, he can use MAD to produce a siren-like sound that tells pirates they have been sighted. [5]If the pirates keep coming, MAD can be notched up to another level of piercing sound. [6]At this point, the sound the device produces is so loud it's painful to the ears and can disorient those who hear it. [7]As Mr. Simidian says, when asked if MAD can do serious harm, "Absolutely." (Source of information: Daniel Emery, "Technology Sets Sights on Piracy," BBC News.)

---

*palpitations: unusually fast heartbeat.

Inferring Main Ideas

Sometimes writers don't give readers even parts of topic sentences. Instead, they supply a series of specific statements designed to lead readers to the implied main idea of the paragraph. For an illustration, read the following paragraph:

> [1]As a young man, the British soldier and writer T. E. Lawrence took part in an archaeological expedition in the Middle East. [2]The work fascinated him, as did the land, and he became possessed by a dream: The Arabs would overthrow Turkish rule and take control of their own country. [3]Lawrence sought to make his dream become reality during World War I when the British showed an interest in helping the Arabs revolt. [4]Seeing a chance for Arab independence, Lawrence arranged a meeting between British and Arab leaders. [5]Supplied with British arms and aided by Lawrence's military strategy, the Arabs rose up and captured several major Turkish[†] strongholds. [6]By 1919, the war was over, and the Turks had been defeated. [7]Thrilled by the Arab victory, Lawrence was now sure that his dream of Arab self-rule was about to become reality. [8]But when he was called to the Paris Peace Conference, he was stunned to discover that the British had no intention of giving up their control of the Middle East.

The author hasn't included a topic sentence in this paragraph. Instead, she leaves a trail of clues and expects readers to infer the implied main idea: "T. E. Lawrence was deeply disappointed at learning that the British were not going to give the Arabs their independence." The basis for that inference are the statements that follow:

1. Lawrence was, to use the writer's word, "possessed" by the dream of Arab independence. The word suggests Lawrence was passionately committed to it.

2. According to the author, Lawrence tried to turn "his dream" into a reality during World War I. The use of "his" suggests Lawrence's attachment to the idea.

3. The author says that Lawrence was "thrilled" to learn about the Arab victory and "sure that his dream of Arab self-rule was to become

---

[†]In World War I, Britain and Turkey were enemies.

reality." The use of the word *thrilled* emphasizes Lawrence's happiness at Arab self-rule.

4. The author uses the contrasting word *stunned* to describe the unpleasant surprise Lawrence felt about learning that the British were not giving up control of the Middle East.

Given the clues shown here, it would be hard not to infer that Lawrence was deeply disappointed at the British refusal to give the Arabs self-rule.

Anytime you read a passage and can't find a general sentence that even partially sums up the main idea, look at all the specific statements supplied by the author and ask yourself what these statements combine to suggest about the topic. Look, for instance, at the following paragraph. Study all the specifics given, then at the end write the implied main idea in the blank line that follows.

> [1]Ms. B, a twenty-three-year-old woman, complained of a phobia, or fear, of spiders that she had had for as long as she could remember. [2]She had no history of any other psychiatric symptoms. [3]In treatment, when first approached with a closed glass jar containing spiders, she breathed heavily, wept, and rated her distress as extremely high. [4]Suddenly she began scratching the back of her hand, stating she felt as though spiders were crawling under her skin, although she knew this was not really the case. [5]The sensation lasted only a few seconds and did not recur. [6]Her total treatment consisted of four one-hour sessions distributed over the span of a month. [7]At completion, she had lost all fear of spiders and was able to let them crawl freely about her arms, legs, and face, as well as inside her clothing, with no distress. [8]She remained free of fear at a one-year follow-up exam and expressed disbelief that she had allowed such a "silly fear" to dominate her life for so long (Curtis, 1981, p. 1095). (Adapted from Sue et al., *Understanding Abnormal Behavior*, p. 136.)

If your implied main idea goes something like, "Ms. B's treatment helped her overcome her fear of spiders," you drew a logical inference. It's logical because it's solidly based on the following details and how they add up:

1. Ms. B arrives for treatment unable to even look at spiders without having a violent reaction.

2. She then had four one-hour treatments.

3. After the treatments, she did not have a violent reaction and was actually able to let spiders crawl on her body.

Now, of course, you could claim that Ms. B's new response was a miracle. But that wouldn't be a **logical inference**. In other words, it wouldn't be based on the information in the paragraph. To be logical, reading inferences have to stem from what's actually said in the paragraph. You must, that is, be able to say: This is the implied main idea because of these words and statements. If you cannot point to anything in the paragraph that supports your version of the implied main idea, you and the author are no longer thinking along the same lines.

READING TIP Inferring implied main ideas is a two-step process. First, you need to understand what each sentence contributes to your knowledge of the topic. Next, you need to ask yourself what all the sentences combine to imply as a group. The answer to that question is the implied main idea of the paragraph.

SUMMING UP THE KEY POINTS

1. Inferences are essential to our understanding of cartoons, quotations, quips, and idioms.

2. Sometimes writers put parts of the main idea into separate sentences. To state the main idea, readers need to combine them.

3. If writers do not include a general sentence stating the main idea, readers need to look at all the specific statements in the paragraphs and consider what idea they suggest when taken together.

◆ **EXERCISE 4**   **Recognizing the Implied Main Idea**

DIRECTIONS   Each item in this exercise contains four sentences that combine to imply a main idea. Circle the letter of that implied main idea.

EXAMPLE

a. During the nineteenth century, factory owners hired young orphans, whom they could force to work fifteen hours a day.

b. Many factory owners preferred hiring women, who could move quickly among the machinery and were easily frightened by threats of dismissal.

c. Whenever possible, the employers increased their profits by reducing the workers' wages.

d. Workers who complained about the hours or poor working conditions were promptly fired; whenever possible, employers saw to it that rebellious workers were thrown into jail.

> Implied Main Idea
>
> (a.) Nineteenth-century factory owners cruelly exploited the men, women, and children who worked for them.
>
> b. In the nineteenth century, factory owners were quick to hire women because they were too timid to make any demands.
>
> c. In the nineteenth century, children were expected to work rather than play.

EXPLANATION   The first four sentences give examples of the way nineteenth-century employers abused *all* their employees, not just women and children. Thus, *a* is the only implied main idea that follows from all the specific statements given. It's certainly the only sentence that could summarize the opening four.

1. a. Workplace monitoring of employees is becoming more common thanks to new technology: Employers and supervisors can, if they wish, monitor employees' Web activity; screen their e-mail; and get screen shots of websites that employees visit.

   b. All sorts of records—from tax returns to sales receipts—have been digitized for storage in computerized databases, making it easier for people to locate personal information about others.

   c. Hackers have hacked into the computerized records of the Veterans Administration and Amazon.com among others.

   d. As part of the program for fighting terrorists, the government has asked for and, in many cases, gotten information about the sites computer users visit with the aid of search engines.

> Implied Main Idea
>
> a. Advances in computer technology have made it difficult to keep personal information private.
> b. Computers are eliminating the need for paper files, a trend that will undoubtedly continue.
> c. Workplace monitoring amounts to a serious, if not illegal, invasion of privacy.

2. a. On October 15, 1917, the famed Dutch dancer Mata Hari was taken before a French firing squad and executed as a spy.

   b. Although Mata Hari had agreed to spy for the Germans, there is no evidence that she ever gave them any information.

   c. Information about a new British tank, said to have been given to the Germans by Mata Hari, was actually provided by a British prisoner of war.

   d. The case against Mata Hari was based largely on telegrams supplied by the head of France's espionage agency, who had tampered with them before the trial.

> Implied Main Idea
>
> a. Mata Hari was executed not because she was a spy but because she was hated by the head of France's espionage bureau.
> b. Mata Hari may not have been guilty of the crimes that earned her a death sentence.
> c. There is no evidence Mata Hari agreed to spy for the Germans.

3. a. Thanks to Henry Ford's invention of a cheap automobile—called the first "people's car"—farmers from small rural towns were able to sell their products to larger markets located some distance away.

   b. Ford's Model T was introduced in 1908 and priced at $850; by 1923 it cost only $290, and people from all walks of life had the chance to own a car.

   c. Ford's Model T was so famous, popular songs and jokes alluded to it.

   d. In the early part of the twentieth century, almost half the American population lived in the country, but Ford's Model T made access to city life much easier, and the rural population began to diminish.

Implied Main Idea

(a.) The invention of the Model T had a profound effect on American life.

b. Henry Ford was determined to make a car that even working people could afford.

c. Henry Ford was a genius when it came to making money.

✓ 4. a. The month of January got its name from Janus, the Roman god of beginnings.

b. Saturday was named after Saturn, the Roman god of agriculture.

c. The sporting goods company Nike took its name from the Greek goddess of victory.

d. The planet Neptune was named after the Roman god of the sea.

Implied Main Idea

a. The gods and goddesses of Greek and Roman mythology had exotic and colorful names.

(b.) The names of the ancient gods and goddesses live on in our language.

c. Our calendar is a constant reminder of Greek mythology's long-lasting influence.

READING TIP The main idea you infer from the specific details should sum up the paragraph in the same way a topic sentence does.

◆ **EXERCISE 5**  Matching Details and Inferences

DIRECTIONS Read each paragraph. The implied main idea is written in the blank above the partially completed passage. One detail supporting that implied main idea is missing, however. Circle the letter of the detail that would make sense in relation to the implied main idea.

EXAMPLE

Implied Main Idea   The figure of the wolf is a common one in American idioms.

Perhaps because wolves over the years have menaced farmers' livestock, we are likely to call a smiling enemy "a wolf in sheep's clothing." The implication of the idiom is that the person pretending to be our friend is actually a threat and not to be trusted. We also use the idiom "wolfing down" food as a way of indicating that the person doing the eating is gobbling food like a hungry animal. Then there's the idiom to "cry wolf," meaning that a person's calls for help are no longer thought trustworthy. The person sounding the alarm is untrustworthy because he or she has too often called out for help when no real danger was present.

a.   And let's not forget the big bad wolf in "Little Red Riding Hood"; he's a fairy-tale figure that has been around for centuries.

b.   Then, too, we frequently call a person who likes to be alone a good deal, "a lone wolf."

c.   And finally, we have to consider how wolves have been hunted almost to extinction.

EXPLANATION   The correct answer is *b*. It's the only sentence that directly relates to the implied main idea. Answer *a* discusses the wolf in a fairy tale. Fairy tales aren't idioms, so answer *a* won't do. Answer *c* does pick up on the image in the first sentence of the wolf being part of the landscape. However, the paragraph as a whole is not concerned with real wolves in nature. It focuses on idioms that use the figure of the wolf.

Implied Main Idea   1.   Warren G. Harding wasn't exactly presidential material.

Those who claim that U.S. presidents must have a certain gravitas* to be elected president might want to consider the career of our twenty-ninth president, Warren G. Harding (1921–1923). Harding was considered none too bright by most of the people he worked with. An incurious man, he mainly liked to play poker, golf, drink, and chase women. Considered by most historians to be one of the worst presidents in history, Harding never really wanted the job, but his wife did, and Harding let his wife, Florence, stage manage most of his political career. Prodded by Florence, Harding rose from one office to another, but he never distinguished himself. Elected to the U.S. Senate in 1914,

---

*gravitas: dignity, seriousness.

he managed to be absent for two of the most important political debates—on women's suffrage* and Prohibition.[†] What Harding had going for him were his magnificent looks. As his admirers as well as his critics liked to point out, Harding *looked* distinguished and presidential. He also had a magnificent speaking voice, even if he had little to say.

   a. Harding gave few speeches during his campaign for the presidency, which was conducted mainly from his front porch, but his reluctance to campaign across the nation did not keep him from winning the office he sought.

   b. Still, Warren G. Harding defeated his opponent by a landslide and was remarkably popular throughout his presidency, which lasted only two years because Harding died unexpectedly of a stroke.

   c. According to a former Secretary of the Treasury, William McAdoo, Harding liked to make flowery speeches that consisted of "pompous phrases moving over the landscape in search of an idea."

Implied Main Idea 2. The consumption of alcohol and worries about its use have been with us for a very long time.

It's generally believed that during the Stone Age, humans chewed berries or grapes in order to make themselves giddy and lightheaded, similar to the way we now feel after consuming a couple of glasses of wine or beer. By 3000 B.C., the Egyptians had perfected the art of manufacturing beer and wine. By the first century A.D., the process of distillation* had been invented and was being used to make more potent alcoholic beverages. In the Middle Ages, even monks in monasteries were perfecting the manufacture of fine wines. Although some of those wines were used in religious ceremonies, many of the finer wines were sold to wealthy wine lovers. In America at least, the nineteenth century witnessed increasing anxiety over liquor consumption. The Temperance movement[†] emerged with women, in particular, insisting on the need for moderation in the consumption of alcohol.

   a. By 1919, worries about alcohol consumption had grown, and the Constitution was amended to prohibit the sale of alcohol throughout the United States.

---

*suffrage: the right to vote.
[†]Prohibition: the constitutional amendment forbidding the sale of alcohol.
*distillation: the process of heating a liquid until it boils and then collecting what's left after boiling; also, reducing something to its essence, or most basic elements.
[†]Temperance movement: movement with the goal of banning alcohol consumption.

b. The Eighteenth Amendment to the Constitution, prohibiting the sale of alcohol, is the only amendment ever to have been repealed, or revoked.

c. In a unique historical moment, the Twenty-First Amendment to the Constitution was introduced with the sole purpose of repealing the Eighteenth Amendment.

Implied Main Idea **3.** <u>The famed journalist H. L. Mencken did not have much respect for</u>

<u>either politicians or the reporters who covered them.</u>

According to Mencken, the American politician was "a man[†] who has lied and dissembled,[*] and a man who has crawled. . . . He has taken orders from his superiors . . . and he has wooed and flattered his inferiors in sense." True, Mencken voted for Franklin D. Roosevelt in the 1932 presidential election, but that didn't stop him from talking about the "imbecility of the New Deal.[†]" And even his praise for Roosevelt's presidency tended to be more about the man than about his policies. Mencken wrote of Roosevelt that people recognized in him "what is called, for lack of a better word, a gentleman." But if he damned Roosevelt with faint praise, Mencken was less kind to members of Congress, insisting in a 1934 speech before the Gridiron Club[†] that "Everyday in this country is April Fool's Day. . . . Where on earth will you find a match for Congress, now that John Ringling[†] has retired?"

a. In 1950, America's reigning literary critic, Edmund Wilson, called H. L. Mencken, "without question, since Poe, our greatest literary journalist."

b. And for the most part, Mencken was no kinder to his own colleagues, saving his most venomous barbs for Washington journalists, whom he considered "guilty of intolerable incompetence and quackery."

c. Friendly to Roosevelt initially, Mencken was stung when the president, after promising to go easy, attacked Mencken at the 1934 Gridiron Club dinner and made him a lifelong enemy.

[†]Presumably Mencken would have used the same tone of scorn to speak of the female politicians of today; there just weren't any during his time.
[*]dissembled: pretended.
[†]New Deal: the name given to Roosevelt's plan for stimulating the economy.
[†]Gridiron Club: founded in 1885, the Gridiron Club is the oldest journalistic organization in Washington, D.C.
[†]John Ringling: an allusion, or reference, to the man who founded the nation's biggest circus.

Questions for Evaluating Inferences

◆

1. **Is the inference solidly based on statements in the paragraph?** If asked to defend your inference, you should be able to point to specific words and sentences that support it.

2. **Are you relying more on the author's words than on your own personal point of view?** Even if the author has chosen a topic you think you know quite well, don't draw an inference based mainly on what you think or feel about the subject. When drawing inferences, it's the writer's mind you have to read, not your own.

3. **Are you sure that none of the author's statements contradict your inference?** If any of the sentences in a passage contradict the idea you've inferred, you probably haven't hit upon the main idea the author intended.

4. **Do the sentences in the paragraph connect to your implied main idea?** If you jot the implied main idea in the margins, you should immediately see how the supporting details help develop it.

WWW

INTERNET RESOURCE For a very comprehensive and detailed discussion of inferences, go to www.criticalreading.com/inferencetoc .htm. You can find this link at the student companion website for this text: www.cengage.com/devenglish/flemming/rfr11e.

◆ **EXERCISE 6**   **Recognizing the Implied Main Idea**

DIRECTIONS   Read each paragraph. Then circle the letter of the implied main idea.

1. In the past, many men and women decided to become flight attendants because they were attracted to the glamorous, fun, jet-setting lifestyle that came with the job. Now, however, flight attendants are spending most of their workdays dealing with rude, disgruntled passengers who are frustrated by delays, crowded flights, and the disappearance of perks like free food. These surly travelers often leave their manners in the airport terminal and bombard flight attendants with complaints. Then, too, flight attendants

must worry about the possibility of terrorism. Since the terrorist hijackings of four airliners on September 11, 2001, flight attendants have to scrutinize passengers' behavior, check suspicious baggage, and take many additional security measures. What's more, the crew must endure the stress and anxiety of working in an environment that is a terrorist target. Working in an industry that is struggling financially, flight attendants also now worry constantly about layoffs and wage or benefit cuts. As their employers slash jobs, those flight attendants still working are putting in longer hours as part of understaffed crews. (Source of information: Francine Parnes, "For Flight Attendants, Stress Comes with the Job," *New York Times*, August 12, 2003, www.nytimes.com/2003/08/12/business/12ATTE.html.)

Implied Main Idea

a. The airline industry is in a shambles.

b. The job of flight attendant has lost much of its glamour.

c. The September 11, 2001, terrorist attacks have significantly affected the airline industry.

d. Flight attendants have the most stressful job in America.

2. Many school officials favor installing Internet-wired video cameras in schools. With video cameras installed throughout the building, administrators would be able to review a videotape to see exactly what happened when a crime—say, a theft—occurred. The cameras could also generate an exact record of all classroom proceedings that could be used to monitor instructor performance as well as interactions between students and teachers. Some teachers want video cameras in their classrooms so that parents can see firsthand how their children behave. Parents think the cameras are a good idea for the opposite reason: They want to see and judge the teachers. Students, for their part, like the idea of being able to view what's going on in their classrooms should they miss a day or two because of illness. (Source of information: Greg Toppo, "Who's Watching the Class?" *USA Today*, August 11, 2003, p. 1D, www.usatoday.com/usatonline/20030811/5396054s.htm.)

Implied Main Idea

a. Video cameras are an excellent tool for improving security in our nation's schools.

b. Technology is improving today's schools in many different ways.

c. Administrators, teachers, and students all have different reasons for wanting to use video cameras in the schools.

d. Internet-wired video cameras in schools make parents more aware of what goes on in the classroom.

3. As far back as 1967, a study done at Harvard Medical School showed that during meditation, people use 17 percent less oxygen, lower their heart rates by three beats per minute, and increase the type of brain waves that occur during the state of relaxation preceding sleep. More recent studies of the brain have confirmed that meditation shifts activity from the right hemisphere of the prefrontal cortex to the left hemisphere. As a result, the brain switches to a calmer, more content state. For this reason, meditation can eliminate the need for medication to treat anxiety, tension, and even pain. As a matter of fact, many individuals are managing the pain of chronic diseases or injuries not with painkillers but with meditation, which helps people learn to accept their discomfort rather than struggle against it. Other patients suffering from diseases like cancer are meditating to actually boost their immune systems. Studies show that people who meditate have higher levels of disease-fighting antibodies in their blood.

Implied Main Idea

a. Meditation offers some significant health benefits.

b. Meditation is growing in popularity.

c. Meditation can sharpen one's ability to think.

d. Meditation has been shown to boost the immune system.

4. Was the 5,300-year-old, mummified body discovered in 1991 and now known as the "Iceman" killed, or did he freeze to death after being caught in a storm? One of the hikers who discovered the body in the Italian Alps said that before the Iceman was freed from a melting glacier, he had been clutching a knife in one hand. In 2001, an Italian radiologist discovered an arrowhead embedded in the shoulder of the Iceman; its position indicated that he had been hit from behind. Medical examiners have found a deep gash in one of the corpse's hands, in addition to a cut on his other hand and bruises on his body. Furthermore, DNA specialists have analyzed blood found on the arrows the Iceman was carrying. They have also found blood on the back of his cloak and his knife. They say

that this blood came from four different people. The blood of two people was found on the same arrow in the Iceman's quiver, suggesting that this arrow had struck two different individuals and then been pulled free.

Implied Main Idea

a. Scientists cannot decide if the Iceman froze to death or was murdered.

b. Evidence suggests that the Iceman was probably killed in a fight.

c. DNA testing has finally proven that the Iceman died after being shot in the back.

d. The Iceman discovered in 1991 has proven to be an intriguing and largely unsolvable mystery.

5. Is a diet high in sugar and carbohydrates responsible for American teenagers' acne problems? Although adolescents have long been warned to avoid chocolate and other kinds of junk food, studies in the 1970s and 1980s failed to prove the link between diet and pimples. However, research done in 2002 at Colorado State University revealed that refined foods like bread and cake cause an insulin surge in the body. This insulin stimulates the production of hormones that encourage the skin to secrete large quantities of a greasy substance known as sebum. Sebum promotes bacterial growth that causes the skin to break out. In addition, other studies have shown that for teenagers living in parts of the world where refined foods are uncommon, acne is virtually unknown. Anthropologists have noted that in remote places like Paraguay, Papua New Guinea, and the Amazon, where people eat low-carbohydrate diets, teenagers do not get acne at all, while 95 percent of American eighteen-year-olds do. Scientists also point to Inuit adolescents in Alaska, who began to suffer from acne only when they began eating a Western diet.

Implied Main Idea

a. Researchers have failed to prove that eating junk food causes adolescents' acne.

b. Research suggests that American teenagers' high-carbohydrate diet is causing their acne.

c. Recent studies have revealed that high levels of insulin are responsible for teenagers' problem with acne.

d. Research has shown that a sugar-free diet can eliminate acne.

> ## ✔ CHECK YOUR UNDERSTANDING
>
> 1. When writers put parts of the main idea into different sentences, what should readers do?
>
> _____
>
> 2. When writers don't even give readers parts of topic sentences, how should readers respond?
>
> _____
>
> _____

Five Types of Paragraphs Likely to Imply the Main Idea

There's no way to say for sure when a writer will or will not imply the main idea of a paragraph. However, here are five types of paragraphs where it's quite likely that the author will suggest, rather than state, the main idea.

Just the Facts

In the following example, the author uses a series of specific details to describe the public response to a 1938 radio broadcast based on H. G. Wells's book *War of the Worlds*. The author does not offer a conclusion based on those specific details. That task is left for the reader.

> On October 30, 1938, CBS Radio broadcast a dramatized version of H. G. Wells's book *War of the Worlds*. Although announcements before and during the story identified the radio play as fictional, the broadcast took the form of a newsflash interrupting regular programming. Nationally, about six million people listened to a reporter's alarming description of an invasion by Martians, who had landed on Earth and were killing humans with heat-rays and a toxic black gas. Immediately,

thousands of hysterical people swamped radio and police stations, requesting advice about how to protect themselves. Frantic listeners began searching for household materials to use as gas masks. Some people even loaded their belongings into their cars. In New York and New Jersey, where the supposed Martian landing had occurred, fleeing residents created massive traffic jams. Thousands of others hid in their basements and cellars. Hospitals administered sedatives to people suffering from shock and hysteria. All over the country, police stations had to broadcast the message that the radio program was only a dramatization and that there was no cause for alarm.

In this case, the specific details lead the reader to infer an implied main idea like the following: "The broadcast of H. G. Wells's *War of the Worlds* caused widespread panic among thousands of radio listeners, who thought they were hearing about a real space invasion."

> **READING TIP** When a writer describes an event or experience by piling up specific details without including a topic sentence that interprets or evaluates them, you need to infer the main idea implied by the author.

Question and Answer

② ? and the rest is the answer

Writers sometimes open a paragraph with a question that immediately gets answered by the topic sentence (see Chapter 4). Frequently, however, the opening question can't be answered in a single sentence. In this case, writers leave it up to readers to infer the answer, which is also the implied main idea. Here's an example:

How did the circle containing a straight line separated into three prongs come to be the symbol or peace sign of the antinuclear movement? According to one explanation, an opponent of nuclear power in the 1950s created the peace sign by combining two symbols normally used as railroad signals. One symbol was a horseshoe-shaped curve that stood for the letter *d*. The other was a circle with a slash through it, which represented the letter *n* and the word "no." When these two signs were combined, the modern peace sign emerged to symbolize nuclear disarmament (ND). Yet another explanation says the symbol was designed by the Campaign for Nuclear Disarmament

(CND) in the 1950s. The organization's president at the time, British philosopher Bertrand Russell, said that the sign originated with the navy's flag signaling system. In this system, a signaler with two flags holds one flag straight up and one straight down to symbolize the letter *d*. Holding both flags down at a forty-five-degree angle from the body symbolizes the letter *n*. Combining these two signals creates the straight line with three prongs that symbolizes the plea for nuclear disarmament. Still another explanation claims that someone in the campaign for nuclear disarmament mixed two historic Christian symbols, with the outer circle representing Earth and the line with three prongs inside suggesting God reaching down to humans.

In this example, the author begins the paragraph with a question that has three different answers, making the implied main idea something like the following: "There are at least three different accounts of how the peace sign originated."

READING TIP When the opening question of a paragraph is *not* followed by an immediate answer, it's usually the reader's job to infer an answer that is also the implied main idea.

③ Competing Points of View

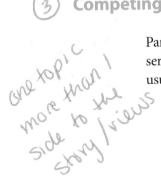

one topic / more than 1 side to the story / views

Paragraphs that offer competing points of view about the same event or series of events *without* saying which point of view is more accurate are usually implying, rather than stating, the main idea. Here's an illustration:

Wilbur and Orville Wright are usually credited with being the first to fly an airplane. On December 17, 1903, in Kitty Hawk, North Carolina, Orville flew the brothers' new invention for twelve seconds. However, some people argue that New Zealand farmer Richard Pearse, who designed his own engine-powered flying machine, was actually the first to fly when his craft rose fifty yards into the air on March 31, 1903, eight months *before* the Wrights' flight. Others argue that Gustave A. Whitehead deserves the credit for making the first powered flight. Although there is no eyewitness evidence for that claim, Whitehead supposedly flew his aircraft for the first time in Bridgeport, Connecticut, on August 14, 1901, more than two years before the Wrights' flight.

Then there are those who insist that Brazilian Alberto Santos-Dumont was the first man to achieve powered flight when he flew his invention fifty meters on October 23, 1906. Because the Wrights launched their plane into the air with a catapult* device and Santos-Dumont's plane, which had wheels, took off under its own power alone, his countrymen believe that he is actually the true Father of Aviation.

In this case, the author describes competing points of view but doesn't offer a judgment on any single one. That means it's up to you to infer an implied main idea like the following: "Controversy still exists over who first took flight in an airplane."

READING TIP When the author offers several competing points of view without evaluating them, you need to infer a main idea that expresses the variety of opinions concerning the issue, person, or event under discussion.

---

④ Comparison and Contrast

Same/different
2 or more
topics

In a comparison-and-contrast paragraph, the writer points out similarities or differences—or both—between two people, events, objects, or ideas. Sometimes the main idea is stated in a topic sentence. But, frequently the author lets the similarities and differences speak for themselves. Here's an example:

Most people know about the tragic destruction of the *Titanic,* the luxury ocean liner that sank on April 15, 1912, after hitting an iceberg. They may not know, however, about the *Lusitania,* another "floating palace" that went down a little more than three years later, on May 7, 1915. When the *Titanic* sank, 1,523 people died from injuries, drowning, and exposure to frigid temperatures. That number accounted for 68 percent of those on board. The death toll for the *Lusitania,* which was 1,198 people (or 61 percent of those aboard), was just as devastating. Those victims, too, died from injuries, drowning, and hypothermia.* The *Lusitania*'s destruction also resulted in the loss of treasures as rich

---

*catapult: launch.
*hypothermia: abnormally low body temperature.

as those lost aboard the *Titanic*. And although both disasters had significant consequences, the *Lusitania*'s sinking had an even greater international impact. The *Titanic* accident led to stricter lifeboat rules. The *Lusitania,* torpedoed by a German submarine, generated support for the entrance of the United States into World War I.

Here the author compares and contrasts the consequences of the *Titanic* disaster with those arising from the sinking of the *Lusitania*. The writer's point is that the lesser-known *Lusitania* tragedy was as significant as the far more famous sinking of the *Titanic*. The author never specifically says that, however. Instead, the main idea is implied by a series of specific statements comparing and contrasting the two disasters to suggest the following main idea: "Although the sinking of the *Titanic* is better known, the sinking of the ship called the *Lusitania* had similar and equally tragic consequences."

> **READING TIP** If a paragraph lists similarities and differences between two topics but doesn't tell you what those similarities and differences *mean* or how to evaluate them, you need to infer a main idea which makes a general point that can include all or most of them.

Results of Research

Writers frequently use research to prove a point. However, sometimes they simply cite research and assume readers will figure out what theory or idea the research supports. In the following paragraph, note how the author lets the research results lead readers to her implied main idea:

Someone is doing research

> Researchers at the Harvard University School of Public Health wanted to find out if it's healthier for men to express their anger or to keep their feelings to themselves. So they conducted a study of 23,522 men aged fifty to eighty-five. These participants completed a survey that asked them to identify how they behaved when they got angry, choosing from options such as "I argue with others" and "I do things like slam doors." Then the researchers followed the men over a two-year period. They found that men who expressed their anger in moderate ways were half as likely to suffer from a nonfatal heart attack as

men who rarely vented their anger. In addition, the study showed that the risk of stroke decreased as the levels of anger expression increased.

In this illustration, the author describes the question being researched: Is it better for men to express their anger or keep it to themselves? The author then explains how the study was conducted and offers the research results, leading the reader to infer the following main idea: "Research at Harvard suggests it may be healthier for men to express anger instead of keeping it to themselves."

READING TIP

If the author cites research but doesn't interpret the results, you need to infer what the research results suggest about the problem or issue under study.

SUMMING UP THE KEY POINTS

Five types of paragraphs are likely to imply rather than state the main idea.

1. Paragraphs that bring together a number of different facts about the topic without drawing any conclusions based on those facts rely on the reader to infer the appropriate conclusion.

2. Paragraphs that open with a question but do not provide an explicitly stated answer expect the reader to infer the answer.

3. Paragraphs that offer competing points of view about the topic without making one point of view more important than the others require readers to infer an idea that reflects a variety of opinion.

4. Paragraphs that point out similarities and differences between two topics often let the reader decide what the similarities and differences suggest about the paired topics.

5. Paragraphs that describe a study or several studies without saying directly what the study or studies show rely on readers to infer the meaning of the research results.

VOCABULARY CHECK

The following words were introduced in pages 316–40. Match the word to the definition. Review words, definitions, and original context two or three times before taking the vocabulary tests. (The page numbers in parentheses indicate where the word first appeared.)

1. quips (p. 316) _____
2. chortles (p. 317) _____
3. terrain (p. 320) _____
4. palpitations (p. 323) _____
5. gravitas (p. 330) _____
6. suffrage (p. 331) _____
7. distillation (p. 331) _____
8. dissembled (p. 332) _____
9. catapult (p. 340) _____
10. hypothermia (p. 340) _____

a. unusually fast heartbeat

b. an area of ground or land

c. abnormally low body temperature

d. quick one-liners

e. pretended

f. dignity, seriousness

g. launch

h. the process of heating a liquid until it boils and then collecting what's left after boiling; also, reducing something to its most basic elements

i. the right to vote

j. laughs, chuckles

♦ **EXERCISE 7**   Recognizing the Implied Main Idea

DIRECTIONS   Circle the appropriate letters to identify the implied main idea and the type of paragraph used to suggest it.

EXAMPLE   For the last twenty years, the Drug Abuse Resistance Education (D.A.R.E.) program has been encouraging America's schoolchildren to "just say no" to drugs. But until recently no one asked a key question: How effective has this program been in reducing drug use among young people? D.A.R.E. is based on the "gateway," or "stepping stone," theory, which suggests that experimentation with drugs like marijuana leads to the use of more dangerous and addictive drugs like cocaine and heroin. However, the National Academy of Sciences, America's leading scientific organization, says that there is no basis for this theory. And while 80 percent of school districts offer D.A.R.E. to students, close to 50 percent of high school seniors still admit to having tried marijuana, while 80 percent have drunk alcohol. What's more, a 1991 University of Connecticut study of 2,000 students found no difference in the drug use of sixth-grade D.A.R.E. graduates and nongraduates two years after the D.A.R.E. graduates completed the program. A 1998 survey of 1,798 students by the University of Illinois also showed no difference in illegal drug use among D.A.R.E. graduates and nongraduates. Similarly, a 2004 study reported in the *American Journal of Public Health* agreed with the findings of other similar studies that D.A.R.E. was "ineffective."

Paragraph Type   a.   just the facts

(b.)   question and answer

c.   competing points of view

d.   comparison and contrast

e.   results of research

Implied Main Idea (a.)   The D.A.R.E. program does not seem to reduce drug use among young people.

b.   The D.A.R.E. program is currently being reevaluated.

c.   The D.A.R.E. program has been effective despite the lack of statistical evidence.

EXPLANATION   In this case, the passage opens with a question about the drug-abuse-prevention program called D.A.R.E. However, the answer does not appear in the paragraph. You have to infer the answer, which is also the implied main idea.

1. In 1977, Dr. Alan Scott of the Smith-Kettlewell Eye Research Institute wanted a treatment for lazy eye, a condition in which the eye muscles are hyperactive and cross the eyes. So Dr. Scott became the first to prescribe botulinum toxin, or Botox, which is a poison that destroys nerve function and helps muscles relax. Ten years later, eye doctor Jean Carruthers used the same toxin to treat patients' eye twitches. She began to notice that patients receiving these treatments looked younger, which led to the discovery that Botox smoothes facial wrinkles to produce a more youthful appearance. Then doctors began to notice that patients using Botox stopped having migraine headaches. They also realized that the toxin could help ease the symptoms of cerebral palsy and Tourette's syndrome.[†] Both

---

[†]Tourette's syndrome: a disease characterized by involuntary movements and sounds.

disorders are characterized by uncontrollable muscle spasms that can be calmed with Botox injections. Now, researchers have even begun to experiment with Botox as a possible cure for obesity. When injected into patients' stomachs, the toxin makes them feel fuller faster.

Paragraph Type

a. just the facts

b. question and answer

c. competing points of view

d. comparison and contrast

e. results of research

Implied Main Idea

a. Botulinum toxin's use as an eye treatment led to discoveries of its effectiveness for a variety of cosmetic and medical uses.

b. Botox has unexpected medical properties, but most of them are related to improving appearance.

c. Medical discoveries often happen by chance, as the history of Botox makes clear.

2. In 1982, the American Cancer Society began evaluating 900,000 people who were cancer free. In this study, researchers examined each participant's body mass index, or BMI, which is calculated using height and weight. Based on BMI, participants were divided into three categories: normal weight, overweight, or obese. During the sixteen years of the study, 57,145 of the participants died of cancer. When researchers compared the mortality rates of the three different groups, they found that those with the highest BMI had death rates from all cancers combined that were 52 percent (for men) and 62 percent (for women) higher than the rates in men and women of normal weight. In both men and women, a higher BMI was also linked to higher rates of death from cancers of the esophagus, colon and rectum, liver, gallbladder, pancreas, and kidney. In addition, men with higher BMIs had higher rates of stomach and prostate cancers, and women had higher rates of cancer of the breast, uterus, cervix, and ovary. Subsequent studies done in 2007 by researchers at the University of Texas and at Boston's Mass. General Hospital in 2009 produced similar results.

Paragraph Type

a. just the facts

b. question and answer

c. competing points of view

d. comparison and contrast

e. results of research

Implied Main Idea

a. Medical research has repeatedly shown that being overweight leads to an early death.

b. Some studies suggest that having a high body mass index increases one's risk of dying of cancer.

c. The American Cancer Society study has not yet been adequately evaluated.

3. Some of today's flightless birds, such as the ostrich, have long legs and feet that are strikingly similar to those of some dinosaurs. Both birds and dinosaurs also have an expanded upper hipbone. As a matter of fact, birds and dinosaurs share more than one hundred different skeletal features. In addition, like many dinosaurs, birds have light, hollow bones and a dense system of blood vessels. Birds' feathers are similar in structure to the scales that covered dinosaurs' bodies, and many scientists believe that some dinosaurs may have had feathers that kept them warm. Furthermore, birds lay eggs, nest in colonies, and care for their young in nests, just as dinosaurs did.

Paragraph Type

a. just the facts

b. question and answer

c. competing points of view

d. comparison and contrast

e. results of research

Implied Main Idea

a. The similarities between birds and dinosaurs suggest that birds may be descendants of dinosaurs.

b. Physical similarities are no proof that dinosaurs and birds are related.

c. Like the dinosaurs they resemble, birds lay eggs and care for their young in nests.

4. Catholics, Jews, and Muslims all regularly practice "intercessory prayer," or praying for someone who is sick or hospitalized. They believe that prayer helps the people being prayed for. To find out if intercessory prayer can heal, scientists have tried to measure the

effect of prayer on patients' health. A 1999 study of 1,000 heart patients conducted by University of Missouri professor William Harris found that prayed-for patients fared better than those who were not prayed for. Harris's results seemed to confirm those of a similar 1997–1998 Duke University Medical Center study involving 150 patients who had undergone surgery to open blocked coronary arteries. Unbeknownst to anyone involved, some of these patients were prayed for by seven prayer groups, while other patients weren't prayed for at all. Those who received intercessory prayer turned out to be 25 to 30 percent less likely to experience adverse* outcomes like heart attack, heart failure, and death. Yet, when Duke University repeated the same study in 2004 by having Christian, Muslim, Jewish, and Buddhist groups pray for 371 of 700 patients, researchers found that those who received prayers were no less likely to avoid later complications. The results of this study were similar to those of a 2001 Mayo Clinic study of 799 heart patients. Half of the patients were unknowingly assigned to a prayer group, half were not. All were evaluated after twenty-six weeks. Researchers found little difference between the two groups' rates of death, cardiac arrest,† or rehospitalization.

Paragraph Type

a. just the facts

b. question and answer

c. competing points of view

d. comparison and contrast

e. results of research

Implied Main Idea

a. Research on heart patients has confirmed that intercessory prayer improves the health of those who are prayed for.

b. Despite the claims of the faithful, intercessory prayer actually has no effect on the health of those being prayed for.

c. So far, scientific studies haven't conclusively proved or disproved the effectiveness of intercessory prayer.

5. When a cute and cuddly panda cub was born at the National Zoo in Washington, D.C., in 2005, the public snapped up the 13,000 tickets offered for two-hour daily viewing sessions in just two hours. To help satisfy the public's passion for panda bears, both the National

*adverse: negative.
†cardiac arrest: the stopping of the heart.

Zoo and the San Diego Zoo offer online "panda cams" that allow observation of the animals 24 hours a day. The cameras are so popular viewers are asked to limit viewing to just 15 minutes so that everyone gets a chance to see the bears. Pandas also appear in the logos* of many organizations and businesses, such as the World Wildlife Fund, the Panda Express fast-food chain, and Panda Energy International. The panda is likewise the national symbol of China, which is why a cartoon panda named Jing Jing was one of the mascots for the 2008 Summer Olympics in Beijing. In the 1960s and 1970s, the adorable bears helped China establish diplomatic relations with other nations. In 1972, for instance, President Richard Nixon returned from China with pandas Hsing-Hsing and Ling-Ling. The gift gave birth to the term "panda diplomacy."

Paragraph Type

a. just the facts

b. question and answer

c. competing points of view

d. comparison and contrast

e. results of research

Implied Main Idea

a. Pandas have always been the most popular animals at America's zoos, and visitors seem to dote on the cuddly creatures.

b. China has long used its national symbol, the panda bear, for political purposes.

c. Around the world, the popular panda has inspired feelings of affection and good will.

♦ **EXERCISE 8**   **Inferring the Implied Main Idea**

DIRECTIONS   Read each paragraph. Then write the implied main idea in the blank.

EXAMPLE   It's distressing but true that thousands of species of cockroaches are living in all kinds of places: at busy schools, under mossy stones, in subway stations, among fallen leaves, at fancy restaurants, in stinky sewer pipes. The cockroach's flattened body makes it easy for the insect to fit into tiny cracks in walls or slip into spaces under objects.

---

*logos: symbols representing institutions or companies, e.g., Apple Computer's apple or the Hartford Insurance Company elk.

In addition, cockroaches are fast runners, with nervous systems that allow the bugs to get moving as soon as they sense danger. The cockroach's survival is also aided by the long, sensitive antennae that help the insect collect information about its surroundings. In lab experiments, cockroaches have even used those antennae to detect and avoid areas sprayed with poison. Their antennae also ensure that cockroaches can locate food and water. Eating, however, is seldom a problem. To survive, cockroaches munch on a wide variety of substances, including pet food, wallpaper glue, house insulation, and paper. If necessary, the insects can go without food and water for weeks at a time. (Adapted from Doris, *Insects*, p. 42.)

Implied Main Idea   Cockroaches are masters of survival.

EXPLANATION   The paragraph offers a series of specific facts about cockroaches. Every specific statement in the paragraph describes how well adapted they are. Thus, the implied main idea suggests their ability to survive under any conditions.

1. How do you fight the urge to underachieve? Start by reflecting on and evaluating messages you received from family and friends while growing up. Did family members or friends resent those who experienced career success or were wealthy? Did they tell you to let other children win at games or various contests, otherwise no one would like you? Once you get a sense of how a "fear of success" pattern might develop, think about how you might showcase your abilities. This might involve volunteering to work on a new project that will allow you to demonstrate your skills. Finally, learn how to sell yourself to people who make decisions about your earnings and your advancement. In other words, don't be afraid to toot your own horn. (Adapted from Reece and Brandt, *Effective Human Relations in Organizations*, p. 190.)

Implied Main Idea   *There are things you can do to avoid underachieving*

2. For some, the 2009 publication of Chris Anderson's book *Free: The Future of a Radical Price* was a major event. In their minds, Anderson's book offered an astute description of how digital technology was positively transforming the marketplace. For others, though, the

book was a ludicrous* and superficial attempt to claim that businesses can make money by giving their wares away. One of Anderson's supporters was David Weinberger, co-author of *The Cluetrain Manifesto: The End of Business as Usual*, a 1999 book that made many of the same points Anderson's book does. Weinberger considers Anderson to be an "intellectual agitator," who is "largely right." In fact, from Weinberger's perspective Anderson is performing something like a public service: "to throw a big idea at us and throw it at us in the strongest form possible." Best-selling author Malcolm Gladwell, to put it mildly, did not agree. Reviewing Anderson's book in *The New Yorker*, Gladwell could barely conceal his contempt for the author's claims that both companies and employees could thrive under a new, "free" business model: "It would be nice to know . . . how a business goes about reorganizing itself around getting people to work for 'nonmonetary' rewards. Does he [Anderson] mean that the *New York Times* should be staffed by volunteers, like Meals on Wheels?" Somewhere between celebrating and ridiculing Anderson was writer Matt Yglesias, who argued on his blog Thinkprogress.org that Anderson had a valid point but went "off the rails" by suggesting "that this 'give it away' business model is actually a *promising business model*." (Source of Weinberger quotation: www.boston.com/bostonglobe/ideas/articles/2009/06/28/the_future_of_8216free.)

Implied Main Idea _____

_____

3. While it may seem strange to some, there are people who think that pythons make wonderful pets. At least they think that when the python is a year old and costs around $70 at a reptile fair or ordered online. Pythons, though, can grow to be 20 feet in length and weigh 200 pounds. Around this point, many owners decide they made a mistake buying the once-cute little snake. Fearful of what might happen with a snake that can stretch across a room to swallow dogs as big as Dobermans, owners often dump full-grown snakes in some out-of-the-way place. When this happens in New York City, the snakes, which are tropical creatures, don't survive. However, they do quite well in places where the weather is warm year-round, which may be how so many Burmese pythons ended up in Florida's Everglades

_____
*ludicrous: absurd, laughable, ridiculous.

National Park. Hundreds of the snakes have been discovered in the park, either captured by park employees or found as road kill. Unfortunately, park biologists, who routinely cut open the stomachs of the snakes to determine what they are feeding on, have identified a depressing array of remains: mice, rabbits, squirrels, possum, even bobcat and alligator have made it into the bellies of adult pythons. Park officials have also located nests containing fertile python eggs.

Implied Main Idea *Many ppl think pythons are wonderful pets but then dump them where they don't belong, because they can't take care*

4. Who was the greatest baseball player of all time? Well, that depends. If we ask sports fans, many would probably name Babe Ruth number one. Thanks to his astonishing home-run record and colorful personality, Ruth was voted baseball's Greatest Player Ever in a 1969 poll. Thirty years later *The Sporting News* still put Ruth at the top of its list of "Baseball's 100 Greatest Players." In 1999, The Associated Press named him "Athlete of the Century." However, if we look at statistical achievements, we might have to conclude that one of Ruth's teammates, Lou Gehrig, is equally deserving of the greatest player title. Although it's been seventy years since Gehrig played, many of his accomplishments—such as his twenty-three grand slams—remain at or near the top of the record books. Then again, limiting ourselves to batting averages and home runs from what were once all-white leagues would mean leaving out a man like the black player Satchel Paige. Widely believed to be the greatest pitcher in the history of the Negro League, Paige's achievements included pitching sixty-four consecutive scoreless innings. Finally making it to the Major League in 1948 as its first black pitcher, he promptly led his team to a World Series victory that same year. From Paige's perspective, though, the legendary Joe DiMaggio was "the best and fastest pitcher I've ever faced." (Source of quotation: www.satchelpaige.com/bio2.html.)

Implied Main Idea *Who was the greatest baseball player of all time is still the argument to this day.*

5. As most parents or teachers know, boys and girls begin school with different mental and physical abilities. Boys tend to have better spatial reasoning and hand-eye coordination than girls, and they are usually more active and energetic. Girls tend to have more advanced verbal and organization skills, and they are less impulsive. Despite their

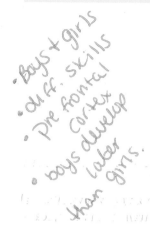

• Boys + girls
• diff. skills
• Pre frontal cortex
• boys develop later
than girls.

strengths, however, boys are twice as likely as girls to have problems with reading and writing. By eighth grade, boys are scoring an average of 11 points lower than girls on standardized reading tests and 21 points lower on writing tests. This gap has been blamed on everything from society's differing expectations to inappropriate teaching methods. However, as it turns out, the prefrontal cortex, the part of the brain responsible for organizing complex thoughts and controlling impulses, processes information differently in boys than in girls. Tests on eleven- to eighteen-year-olds show that when boys are shown pictures of fearful faces, they register activity on both sides of their prefrontal cortex. Girls, however, use only one side, just like adults. By age eighteen, of course, boys' and girls' brains are processing information with the same speed and sophistication. But brain scans have revealed that the prefrontal cortex reaches its maximum thickness in girls by age eleven. In boys, this development happens later on.

Implied Main Idea The development of the prefrontal cortex effects boys and girls different development

✔ CHECK YOUR UNDERSTANDING

1. With paragraphs that offer numerous facts about a topic, the reader's job is to

_____.

2. When a paragraph opens with a question but does not _____, it's the reader's job to _____.

3. If a paragraph offers competing points of view about a topic but doesn't say _____, then the reader has to imply the main idea.

4. In a comparison-and-contrast paragraph, the writer points out_____ _____ and leaves it up to the reader to explain their meaning.

5. Paragraphs that describe a study or studies without explaining_____ _____ rely on the reader to draw the appropriate inference.

More on Evaluating Your Inferences

Any time you infer the main idea of a paragraph, you need to make sure your inference is logical. **Logical inferences** are firmly based on statements in the paragraph. They do not contradict or undermine what the author actually says, and they keep the reader in touch with the author's intended meaning. **Illogical inferences** are based more on the reader's personal experience or common sense than on the author's words. They are likely to ignore or contradict what the author actually says. Illogical inferences often divert readers from the writer's train of thought, leading them to develop a meaning the writer never intended.

Illustrating Logical and Illogical Inferences

To see the difference between logical and illogical inferences, read the following passage about Joan of Arc. Then look carefully at the two possible implied main ideas that follow. One is a logical inference that follows from, or is based on, the paragraph. The other is not. It reflects the reader's point of view more than the author's. Your job is to decide which is which.

> Joan of Arc, the national heroine and patron saint[†] of France, was born in 1412 to a family of poor peasants. In 1425, at the age of thirteen, Joan claimed to hear voices that she believed belonged to the early Christian saints and martyrs.[*] Four years later, in 1429, those same voices told her to help the young king of France Charles VII fight the British, who were trying to take control of France in the Hundred Years War.[†] When the king believed her story and gave her troops to command, Joan put on a suit of armor and led her soldiers to victory. Yet when the British captured Joan in 1430 and tried her for heresy[*] and wearing masculine dress, Charles refused to help her, allowing her to be condemned to death. On May 30, 1431, Joan was burned at the stake, still swearing loyalty to the king of France.

[†]patron saint: the saint protecting or guarding a nation, a place, an activity, or a person.
[*]martyrs: people willing to die for their faith or to save the lives of others.
[†]Hundred Years War (1337–1453): an episodic struggle over land that varied from times of peace to periods of intense violence.
[*]heresy: challenging church law.

Now which of the following implied main ideas effectively sums up the above paragraph?

Implied Main Idea 1 Even though Joan of Arc sacrificed her life to save his throne, the king of France failed to return her loyalty.

Implied Main Idea 2 Although she died swearing her loyalty to the king of France, Joan of Arc must have hated him for his betrayal.

Did you decide that the first implied main idea was a more logical inference than the second? If you did, you are absolutely correct. The paragraph definitely implies that Joan sacrificed everything for a king who did not return her loyalty. Because we can safely say that statement 1 sums up the message of the paragraph in the same way that a topic sentence might have, we can also say that it's the implied main idea of the paragraph.

Statement 2, in contrast, is an illogical inference. It could easily lead the reader away from the writer's real point. There is simply no evidence in the paragraph to support the notion that Joan hated the king for his betrayal. True, many people might well despise someone who betrayed their loyalty as Charles VII did Joan's. Yet a reader's inferences can't be based on what many—or even most—people might feel. Logical inferences have to be grounded primarily on the author's words. Inference 2 does not fulfill this requirement. Thus it is not the implied main idea of the paragraph.

SUMMING UP THE KEY POINTS

- ➤

1. Logical inferences
   - follow from or are based on what's said in the paragraph.
   - do not favor the reader's experience or knowledge over the author's words.
   - are not contradicted by any statements appearing in the paragraph.
   - do not divert the reader from the author's intended meaning.
2. Illogical inferences
   - give more weight to the reader's feelings than they do the author's words.
   - are based on a few stray words rather than several different sentences.
   - are likely to be contradicted by one or more statements appearing in the paragraph.
   - are likely to lead readers far from the author's intended meaning.

◆ **EXERCISE 9**   **Identifying the Implied Main Idea**

DIRECTIONS   Read each paragraph. Then circle the letter of the implied main idea. *Note*: Be sure the answer you choose fits the description of a logical inference.

1. The drug called cocaine was formally identified in 1855. By the 1870s, surgeons used it as an anesthetic for minor surgery. In the 1880s, it was used to treat opium addiction and alcoholism. The drug came to the notice of the young Sigmund Freud when he read reports of how small doses could restore exhausted soldiers. Trying it out on himself, Freud was enthusiastic, calling cocaine a wonder drug and recommending it to his wife. Freud was so enthusiastic that he prescribed cocaine for a young colleague who was addicted to morphine. The drug, however, did not produce a cure. Instead, the young man began hallucinating wildly. Believing that snakes were crawling under his skin, he committed suicide, leaving Freud devastated.

Implied Main Idea

   a. Sigmund Freud never got over his guilt about driving a colleague to suicide.

   b. Sigmund Freud never got over the mistake he made when he prescribed cocaine for a colleague who then killed himself.

   c. Sigmund Freud was sadly mistaken in his early enthusiasm for cocaine.

2. Entrants in the Little Miss of America beauty contest—girls between the ages of three and six—are not asked to pay a fee. Their indulgent* parents, however, willingly pay hundreds of dollars just to have their children's photographs included in the pageant catalog. They also must pay for the singing and dancing lessons that will allow their child to participate in the talent section of the contest. But perhaps even more costly than the lessons are the extensive wardrobes of party dresses that the girls must have in order to participate in the contest and its related functions. Furthermore, traveling expenses for the children and the relatives who accompany them can easily run into thousands of dollars.

Implied Main Idea

   a. It costs a lot of money to enter the Little Miss of America beauty contest.

---

*indulgent: lenient; inclined to spoil.

    b. Little girls should not be encouraged to participate in beauty pageants.

    c. When parents enter their little girls into beauty pageants, they have no idea of the costs associated with being in the pageant.

3. On January 30, 1889, young Crown Prince Rudolf of Austria was found shot to death in his hunting lodge on the outskirts of Vienna. Lying next to him was the body of his lover, seventeen-year-old Baroness Maria Vetsera. She, too, had been shot. In the years since that tragic event, some have claimed that Rudolf ended his life because he was depressed over a terminal illness. According to this theory, when Maria found him, she decided to take her life. Others insist, however, that Rudolf was murdered by members of the court who feared his progressive* beliefs would become public policy when Rudolf reached the throne. According to another theory, Maria and Rudolf entered into a suicide pact when their parents forbade the couple to marry.

Implied Main Idea

    a. Although there are many theories about how Crown Prince Rudolf and Maria Vetsera died, the theory that they were murdered makes the most sense.

    b. No one really knows for sure how Crown Prince Rudolf and Maria Vetsera died.

    c. Love drove Crown Prince Rudolf of Austria to suicide.

4. Can babies remember sounds heard when they were in the womb? Anthony DeCasper and Melanie Spence (1986) asked pregnant women to read Dr. Seuss's *The Cat in the Hat* to their unborn infants twice a day for the last six weeks of their pregnancies. After birth, the researchers tested the newborns by using a nipple connected to a tape recorder. By sucking in one pattern of short and long sucks, a baby could hear a recording of the mother reading *The Cat in the Hat*. Another sucking pattern produced a recording of the mother reading a different rhyming story. The babies, some only hours old, chose *The Cat in the Hat* most often. (Rubin et al., *Psychology*, p. 222.)

Implied Main Idea

    a. The research of Anthony DeCasper and Melanie Spence suggests that babies do remember sounds they hear in the womb.

---

*progressive: supporting social or political change.

b. Without question, babies remember everything they experience in the womb.

c. One study proved that babies have a special fondness for the sounds of Dr. Seuss.

♦ **EXERCISE 10**   Inferring the Main Idea

DIRECTIONS   Read each paragraph. Then, in the blanks that follow, write the implied main idea of the paragraph.

EXAMPLE   The plow was invented during the Middle Ages. Thanks to its invention, farmers could dig more deeply into the soil and do it with much greater ease. That meant they could farm more land, using less labor. Another important innovation* in the Middle Ages was the collar harness. The old yoke harness had worked well with oxen, but tended to choke horses. With the collar harness, farmers could exchange oxen for horses. Horses had more stamina* and worked faster than oxen. Thus farmers could work fewer hours while still covering the same amount of ground. The Middle Ages also saw the invention of the water mill. With water-powered mills, farmers could grind more corn with less effort.

Implied Main Idea   During the Middle Ages, several important inventions made farming easier and more productive.

EXPLANATION   The paragraph describes three separate inventions that appeared in the Middle Ages. Each of those inventions helped farmers do more work with less effort. Because this inference is general enough to include all three inventions, it effectively sums up the implied main idea of the paragraph.

1. During World War II, women of childbearing age had, on average, 2.5 children. But the 1950s saw an increase in the fertility rate. It edged up to more than 3.3 children per woman in the first half of the decade and then peaked at 3.6 children in the decade's last half. Fifteen years later, the fertility rate had dropped to the point where the average woman had 1.7 children. This trend eventually reversed itself, with fertility increasing to 2.0 children per woman of childbearing

---

*innovation: introduction of something new.
*stamina: ability to stay strong over time.

age in 1989. However, this apparent baby boomlet was the result of baby-boom women having children. (Adapted from Gelles, *Contemporary Families*, p. 261.)

Implied Main Idea _____

_____

2. Anyone who orders a milk shake in Rhode Island and expects a drink made with ice cream is in for a surprise. In Rhode Island, a "milk shake" contains no ice cream. It's made of milk and flavored syrup. That's all. If you want ice cream in your drink, you'd better call it a "cabinet." The name comes from the wooden cabinet encasing the mixer that shakes up the milk. Similarly, anyone in search of a long sandwich made with layers of meat and cheese should ask for a "sub" or a "hero" in the North. But in the South, you had better request a "poor boy," or the waiter will be confused. If you want a soda in Boston, you should probably ask for a "tonic." However, if you are in Minneapolis, you'd better ask for a "pop," or else you're likely to get a glass of flavored seltzer water.

Implied Main Idea _____

_____

3. When Annie Sullivan first arrived to teach her young pupil, Helen Keller, she found a little girl who could not see or hear or speak. Cut off from the world around her, the child behaved like a little savage, biting and kicking whenever anyone approached her. In less than a month, however, Sullivan had taught the wild little girl that each thing has a name and that human beings could use those names to communicate with one another. In the years that followed, with Sullivan as a teacher and confidante,* Helen Keller learned to read Braille[†] in English, Latin, Greek, French, and German. She learned to use sign language and, above all, she learned to speak.

Implied Main Idea _____

_____

---

*confidante: friend.
[†]Braille: a system of printing for those who are visually impaired.

4. The Beatles' song "I Am the Walrus" was inspired by Lewis Carroll's classic work of children's literature, *Alice's Adventures in Wonderland*. The same book also gave rock group Jefferson Airplane the idea for its song "White Rabbit" and Steely Dan its idea for "The Mock Turtle's Song." Mary Shelley's great science fiction novel, *Frankenstein*, inspired songs performed by rock band Blue Oyster Cult and singer-songwriter Bob Dylan, who also got many of his ideas for lyrics from great works of literature like Samuel Taylor Coleridge's "The Rime of the Ancient Mariner," Dante's *The Inferno*, and the poetry of William Blake. Several of Led Zeppelin's songs are derived from J. R. R. Tolkien's *The Lord of the Rings*. The band Styx also performed a song based on that same fantasy classic. Rock group Pink Floyd's entire *Animals* album was inspired by George Orwell's classic, *Animal Farm*. Homer's *The Odyssey* has influenced songs by Steely Dan, Cream, and others. (Source of information: www.artistsforliteracy .org/famous.html.)

Implied Main Idea _____

_____

✔ CHECK YOUR UNDERSTANDING

Explain the difference between logical and illogical inferences.

_____

_____

_____

_____

VOCABULARY CHECK

The following words were introduced in pages 347–58. Match the word to the definition. Review words, definitions, and original context two or three times before taking the vocabulary tests. (The page numbers in parentheses indicate where the word first appeared.)

1. adverse (p. 347) _____

2. logos (p. 348) _____

3. ludicrous (p. 350) _____

4. martyrs (p. 353) _____

5. heresy (p. 353) _____

6. indulgent (p. 355) _____

7. progressive (p. 356) _____

8. innovation (p. 357) _____

9. stamina (p. 357) _____

10. confidante (p. 358) _____

a. people willing to die for their faith or to save the lives of others

b. lenient; inclined to spoil

c. friend

d. challenging church law

e. ability to stay strong over time

f. absurd, ridiculous

g. negative

h. introduction of something new

i. symbols representing institutions or companies

j. supporting social or political change

DIGGING DEEPER Black Baseball

Looking Ahead Page 351 introduced the name of Satchel Paige, considered by many to be one of the greatest baseball players of all time. The following reading describes the Negro League, which flourished in the years before Jackie Robinson broke the color barrier in baseball.

1 In 1947, the general manager of the Brooklyn Dodgers, Branch Rickey, decided to integrate the major leagues by hiring Georgia-born infielder Jackie Robinson. Ignoring death threats, Robinson made his debut on April 15 at Brooklyn's Ebbets Field, and major league baseball was never the same again. The color bar separating black and white players had finally been broken, and it was down for good.

2 For decades now, Robinson's story has been told and retold—and rightly so, for it illustrates how discrimination can be eradicated when people decide it has to be. Yet, as James A. Riley, the author of *The All-Time Stars of Black Baseball*, has written, great black players in the tradition of Hank Aaron, Willie Mays, and Willie Stargell didn't just spring up out of nowhere as a result of Robinson's debut. From the beginning, Jackie Robinson was standing on the shoulders of countless black players who came before him. Unfortunately, the players' names and their struggles to make a living playing the game they loved have been largely ignored.

3 As early as the 1860s, mixed crowds were watching championship games played by all-black teams like the Uniques, the Pythians, and the Excelsiors. Yet despite the obvious skill of the players and the enthusiasm shown by fans of both races, the National Association of Base Ball Players (NABBP), organized in 1868, would not accept the all-black teams for membership. Instead the association established the first official "color line" in baseball by voting unanimously to bar "any club which may be composed of one or more colored persons."

4 Fortunately for black players, the association only had amateur status. Thus, professional players weren't bound by its rules, and black ballplayers continued to appear on integrated teams (some black teams even played in integrated leagues). The noose, however, was tightening: Black players were slowly being cut off from all integrated team play. The year 1876 saw the birth of the National League, and it was clear from the start that the league was going to remain lily white. When talented black players like the brothers Moses and Wellday Walker, Frank Grant, and the near-legendary

pitcher George Stovey began flocking to the International League's integrated teams, editorials began to appear, asking questions similar to the one posed in the magazine *Sporting Life*: "How far will this mania* for engaging colored players go?"

5   After a few more such editorials, some protests by angry fans, and several on-field confrontations, integrated teams quickly became a thing of the past. To be sure, black players could found their own teams, like the Cuban Giants, organized in 1885. They could also start their own leagues, like the Negro National League established in 1920 by Rube Foster, the father of black baseball. But black players weren't going to appear on the field with white players. Talent wasn't the issue; race was what mattered.

6   Had talent been the issue, only the most die-hard racists would have argued that black players weren't the equal of white ones. It's revealing that in the era prior to Robinson's debut, many white players publicly proclaimed their admiration for their black counterparts. When the great Pittsburgh Pirates shortstop Honus Wagner heard that black shortstop John Henry Lloyd was called "the black Wagner," he called the comparison "an honor and a privilege."

7   In fact, some white players, including the celebrated Babe Ruth, were so anxious to have black players on the field, they organized their own exhibition games. Because the teams weren't paid, blacks could partici-pate, and Ruth, for one, could test his mettle against the likes of Josh Gibson, considered the most dangerous hitter in black baseball. Following Ruth's example, the famed pitcher Dizzy Dean organized numerous exhibition games, largely because they allowed him to compete against Satchel Paige, the black pitcher widely known as the "Mound Magician." In 1934, Dean got a taste of the magician's magic when Paige beat him 1–0 in an exhibition game that went down in sports history.

8   Ironically,* the Negro leagues, which had done so much to foster the talent of players like Paige and Gibson, became a thing of the past once Robinson broke the color barrier. The Negro National League, for example, folded just one year after Robinson ran onto Ebbets Field. Robinson had led his team to the World Series, and the once all-white leagues were now eager to sign young black players who showed signs of talent. The era of two separate base-ball leagues, one black and one white, was finally over. Sadly, the end of that era had been a long time coming, much longer than many people realize.

---

*mania: madness.
*ironically: contrary to what one might expect, implying the opposite of what one says. If asked how your day went, you might make a face and say "Oh, just great," meaning it was a horrible day.

Sharpening Your Skills

DIRECTIONS   Answer the following questions by filling in the blanks or circling the letters of the correct response.

1. Based on the context, what is the meaning of *mettle* in paragraph 7?

     a. dislike and anger
     b. courage and strength
     c. past and present
     d. string of awards

     According to a dictionary, what is the idiom that uses the word *mettle*? What is the meaning of the idiom?

     _____

     _____

2. What is the main idea of paragraph 2?

     a. Nobody before or after his time has ever been a match for the great Jackie Robinson.
     b. James A. Riley's book *The All-Time Stars of Black Baseball* has managed to preserve the true story of black baseball.
     c. Jackie Robinson was a creation of newspaper reporters who needed a good story; he was never as talented as the press claimed.
     d. Many great black ballplayers came before Jackie Robinson; they just never got a chance to show their ability.

3. What is the main idea of paragraph 6?

     a. With a few exceptions, no one ever doubted that black ballplayers could play as well as white ones.
     b. Honus Wagner was one of the few ballplayers to openly acknowledge the talent of black ballplayers.
     c. Black shortstop John Henry Lloyd was a great admirer of the Pittsburgh Pirates shortstop Honus Wagner.
     d. Honus Wagner was insulted at hearing that a black ballplayer was called "the black Wagner."

4. In paragraph 7, which sentence is the topic sentence?

a. In fact, some white players, including the celebrated Babe Ruth, were so anxious to have black players on the field, they organized their own exhibition games.

b. Because the teams weren't paid, blacks could participate, and Ruth, for one, could test his mettle against the likes of Josh Gibson, considered the most dangerous hitter in black baseball.

c. Following Ruth's example, the famed pitcher Dizzy Dean organized numerous exhibition games, largely because they allowed him to compete against Satchel Paige, the black pitcher widely known as the "Mound Magician."

d. In 1934, Dean got a taste of the magician's magic when Paige beat him 1–0 in an exhibition game that went down in sports history.

5. What's the implied main idea of the entire reading?

a. For almost a century, black ballplayers were forced to create their own baseball teams and leagues in order to play ball, even though they were clearly superior to the all-white teams.

b. We should not forget the many black baseball players who paved the way for Jackie Robinson's triumphant civil rights breakthrough in 1947.

c. In the early years of the game, baseball was open to any player who had talent.

d. Without the courage of Jackie Robinson and Branch Rickey, baseball would have remained a segregated sport for at least another decade.

Making Connections You've just read about how Jackie Robinson changed the face of baseball. On page 351, you also read about Babe Ruth's achievements in baseball. Can you come up with *one* general statement that sums up how each man influenced the game? Were they similar in influence or different?

_____

_____

_____

Drawing Your Own Conclusions Many baseball fans say that baseball is now "past its time" rather than what it used to be, America's favorite "pastime." What's their point?

_____

_____

Does baseball currently have any heroes equal to Ruth or Robinson?

_____

_____

▶ **TEST 1**   **Vocabulary Review**

DIRECTIONS   Fill in the blanks with one of the words listed below.

palpitations	hypothermia	quips	distillation	catapulted
dissemble	terrain	gravitas	suffrage	chortled

1. The director did not get the joke at first, but as the joke's sly meaning dawned on him, he suddenly _____ out loud.

2. The writer's last novel was a(n) _____ of everything he had learned in life.

3. After weeks of heart _____, the coach finally consulted a doctor.

4. When the explorers stepped out of the boat, they were confronted by the coldest and most barren _____ imaginable.

5. In the nineteenth century, Victoria Woodhull became notorious as a woman who dared to say out loud that _____ was a woman's right.

6. As the youngest and least experienced member of the team, the engineer tried to project a sense of _____, but she could not completely control her girlish giggle.

7. Chris Rock's _____ at the president's expense delighted the audience.

8. When he needed to, the prosecutor could _____ and hide his intentions.

9. The dog fell through the ice and almost died of_____ before he was rescued by a passerby.

10. Almost unknown before John McCain's 2008 campaign for president, Sarah Palin was _____ into the spotlight when McCain chose her as his vice-presidential running mate.

▶ **TEST 2**   **Vocabulary Review**

DIRECTIONS   In the blank, write a definition for each italicized word.

1. The comedian made a sexist joke at the journalists' dinner and knew immediately from the audience's *adverse* reaction that he'd made a huge mistake.

   Adverse means _____.

2. Companies like Nike and Apple have *logos* that are recognized around the world.

   Logos means _____.

3. When Giordano Bruno claimed that the earth revolved around the sun, as opposed to the sun moving around the earth, he was burned at the stake because his *heresy* challenged church teaching.

   Heresy means _____.

4. When Franklin Delano Roosevelt became president in the midst of a disastrous economic downturn, he surrounded himself with *progressive* thinkers who challenged all previous notions about the relationship between government and society.

   Progressive means _____.

5. The soldier did not have the *stamina*, mentally or physically, to return to duty, but he had no choice.

   Stamina means _____.

6. At one time, centuries ago, the fork was considered a real *innovation* that dramatically changed what people ate.

   Innovation means _____.

7. Makers of the diet pills have made absolutely *ludicrous* claims about the product's safety and effectiveness.

   Ludicrous means _____.

8. Hotel owner Leona Helmsley made life miserable for her employees, but she was extremely *indulgent* when it came to her dog to whom she bequeathed a fortune.

   Indulgent means _____.

9. In nineteenth-century women's fiction, women were often portrayed as *martyrs*, who willingly sacrificed their own lives for their selfish husbands; the message of the novels was that sainthood brought with it power.

   Martyrs means _____.

10. For many years, novelist Truman Capote was a *confidante* of the rich and famous; then he wrote a novel that revealed the secrets of his former friends and was forever banned from their circle.

    Confidante means _____.

▶ **TEST 3**   Recognizing the Implied Main Idea

DIRECTIONS   Read the paragraph. Then circle the letter of the implied main idea.

1. The word *natural* in advertisements clearly sells products. Juices and foods filled with "natural" goodness along with "natural" vitamins and herbs are big sellers. Consumers seem to believe that anything coming straight from nature has to be good for you. Yet if you're one of those consumers, you might want to reconsider your trust in Mother Nature. Aflatoxin, one of the most potent cancer-causing substances that exists, is a natural product of mold. Ricin, one of the deadliest poisons on earth, comes from nature's own castor beans. Take just one bite of the naturally growing mushroom *Amanita phalloides*, and you won't be around long enough to discuss its bitter aftertaste. Next time you're thinking of buying an herbal supplement because it's "natural"—and therefore has to be good for you—just remember, bee stings and poison ivy are also part of nature.

Implied Main Idea
     a. Synthetic products are better for you than natural ones are.

     b. We shouldn't just assume that "natural" products are safe.

     c. The word *natural* is a big selling point for all kinds of products.

2. After Timothy J. McVeigh was convicted of bombing a federal office building in Oklahoma City, causing the deaths of 168 people, reporters swarmed to McVeigh's hometown of Pendleton, New York.[†] The journalists sought comments on the verdict from McVeigh's friends, family, and acquaintances in the small town, which has about five thousand residents. The reporters also wanted to ask if Pendleton people thought McVeigh deserved the death penalty. But in short order, community members slammed their doors in journalists' faces. McVeigh's family pulled down the shades and refused to leave the house. When television crews approached Pendleton folks at a supermarket, the shoppers tried to slam their carts into expensive TV equipment. One woman grabbed a phone and started dialing local police. Other Pendleton residents just pressed their lips together and stared.

[†]The bombing took place on April 19, 1995; McVeigh was convicted in June 1997. He was executed on June 11, 2001.

a. People in Timothy McVeigh's hometown didn't want to talk to reporters.

b. People in Timothy McVeigh's hometown thought he was innocent.

c. People in Timothy McVeigh's hometown were ashamed to have known him.

3. In 1995 gray wolves, listed as an endangered species, were reintroduced into Yellowstone Park, where they had once roamed freely. To the surprise of biologists, the wolves multiplied faster than expected, so much so that their status is now listed as "threatened" rather than endangered. Perhaps because of the population spurt, the wolves have begun to stray outside the park's boundaries. In a few cases, they have ventured onto bordering ranch lands and killed domestic livestock. The U.S. Fish and Wildlife Service responded quickly by shooting or capturing the wolves believed to be preying on livestock. But some ranchers have taken the law into their own hands and shot the wolves themselves. The ranchers want the legal right to shoot any wolf that ventures onto their property. Many are furious that the Fish and Wildlife Service insists on fining and prosecuting any rancher caught wolf hunting.

a. The reintroduction of gray wolves was a bad idea from the beginning.

b. The reintroduction of gray wolves into Yellowstone Park proves that endangered animals can be saved by human intervention.

c. The 1995 reintroduction of gray wolves into Yellowstone Park has saved them from extinction; however, it has also caused some serious problems.

4. Currently, children in the United States receive more vaccinations than ever before. On average, they get nineteen inoculations for ten different diseases. As a result, potential killers such as polio and diphtheria are all but unknown in the United States. One would think that would be cause for gratitude among parents anxious to protect their children from illness. But some parents are not so thrilled. Instead, they want to know more about the possible adverse effects. One such parent is Barbara Loe Fisher, president of the National Vaccine Information Center, who pointedly asks if the vaccines children receive "could be doing something else which isn't so

good." Fisher charges that parents don't get enough information about the relationship between vaccines and chronic physical and mental disorders. Lisa Mayberry is another parent troubled by the numerous vaccines given to children. She watched her child develop autism† after he was inoculated against measles, mumps, and rubella (MMR). Although a study of 498 autistic children found no connection between the MMR shot and autism, the Centers for Disease Control and Prevention (CDC) is continuing to investigate. The CDC has recommended that physicians discontinue use of the oral vaccine against polio because it has been proven to induce polio in several instances. It has also called a halt to the new rotavirus vaccine designed to eliminate gastrointestinal ailments in infants. As it turns out, the vaccine causes bowel obstructions in some recipients. (Source of information: Claudia Kalb and Donna Foote, "Necessary Shots," *Newsweek*, September 13, 1999, p. 73.)

Implied Main Idea

a. Although vaccinating America's children has had obvious benefits, some parents are worried about possible adverse reactions.

b. All the vaccination programs for children should come to an immediate halt.

c. Anxious about their children's health, some parents have launched a fight against vaccinations.

---

†autism: a disorder that makes it hard for affected children to make contact with the world around them.

▶ TEST 4   Recognizing the Implied Main Idea

DIRECTIONS   Read the paragraph. Then circle the letter of the implied main idea.

1. According to the rules of their order, Carmelite nuns begin their days at the crack of dawn. Rising at 5:00 a.m., they sing hymns and eat breakfast. Breakfast, like the rest of their meals, is simple. The nuns are not allowed to eat meat. In addition, they have taken a vow of poverty, so rich food is out of the question. Once breakfast is over, the Carmelites spend their days doing chores or saying prayers. Conversation of any sort is forbidden, as are visitors. If the nuns speak at all to outsiders, it is through an iron grill that symbolizes their separation from the world. As one might expect, radio, television, and computers are not usually found among the Carmelites.

Implied Main Idea

    a. In time, the rules of the Carmelite order are bound to become less strict.

    b. Most Carmelite nuns enter the order because they have been wounded by the world.

    c. The Carmelites will never change the strict rules of their order.

    d. The rules of the Carmelite order ensure that the nuns lead a life of solitude and simplicity.

2. History books have long insisted that the Spanish explorer Hernando Cortés defeated the Aztec Empire after Montezuma, the empire's too trusting king, welcomed Cortés into Tenochtitlan (now Mexico City) and extended him his hospitality. Cortés returned the courtesy by throwing Montezuma into jail. Then with the help of a few hundred men and the arrival of European diseases like typhus and smallpox, he turned the Aztec Empire into a Spanish colony. That, in any case, is the conventional version of events. But now researchers at an archaeological dig about one hundred miles east of modern Mexico City have unearthed hundreds of skeletons, bones, and ancient objects that tell another story. The remains found are from a 1520 caravan of Spanish conquistadors, their families, and servants, all of whom were on their way to Tenochtitlan, probably to help put the finishing touches on Cortés's defeat of the Aztecs. According to Enrique Martinez, director of the dig, the newfound evidence strongly suggests that the travelers were set

upon and captured by Aztec warriors. The captors then apparently kept their victims in cages for an extended period of time, perhaps up to six months. During that time, Aztec priests made regular selections of those who were to be used as human sacrifices in religious rituals. Close examination also suggests that the caravan's captors engaged in cannibalism, eating the bodies of those who had been sacrificed. This seems to explain why Cortés named the town where it all happened "Tecuaque," which means "where people were eaten."

Implied Main Idea

a. Historians have long underestimated the courage of Montezuma's warriors.

b. Enrique Martinez has found conclusive evidence that cannibalism was part of Aztec society.

c. A new archaeological discovery disputes the notion that the Aztecs let themselves be conquered without a fight.

d. In at least one instance, Cortés's followers got exactly what they deserved for plundering the great Aztec Empire.

3. Spectacled cobras—six-foot-long brown snakes that can kill with a single bite—are everywhere in the country of Sri Lanka. It's not surprising, therefore, that thousands of people are bitten yearly. Many victims are children, and some of them die. What's surprising is that most Sri Lankans will not harm a cobra that happens to venture into a nearby woodpile or rice field. The majority of Sri Lankans are Buddhists. According to their religion, the spectacled cobra once gave shelter to Buddha by opening the hood at the back of its neck. To show that the cobra was under his protection, Buddha is said to have given the snake the spectacles-like red mark that appears on the back of its head.

Implied Main Idea

a. Given the number of people who die from snake bites, the people of Sri Lanka should stop worshipping cobras.

b. The people of Sri Lanka should do something about the threat of cobra bites to their children.

c. The people of Sri Lanka do not kill cobras because they believe the snakes are under the protection of Buddha.

d. Should the number of victims suffering from cobra bites continue to rise, the people of Sri Lanka are bound to change their attitudes toward cobras.

4. Listeria is a food-borne bacterium that has been found in hot dogs, deli meats, soft cheeses, undercooked meat, poultry, and seafood. On a yearly basis, listeria sickens about 2,500 Americans. One serious outbreak of listeria poisoning, in 1998, was traced to meat processed at a Sara Lee Corporation plant in Michigan. The company had to recall 15 million pounds of hot dogs and luncheon meats. In 2002, seven people died from eating Wampler brand turkey tainted by listeria. In the healthy, listeria is an unpleasant nuisance, causing flu-like symptoms that last several days. But if the elderly are stricken by listeria poisoning, they can die from it. If a pregnant woman ingests the bacterium, a miscarriage or a stillbirth often results, even if the mother herself experiences no symptoms. In the 1998 outbreak, at least one hundred people got sick, and fifteen of those died.

Implied Main Idea

   a. Processed meats have long been the source of food poisoning.

   b. Given the high incidence of listeria poisoning, it is amazing that meatpacking plants are not required to test for it.

   c. Outbreaks of listeria poisoning are bound to increase.

   d. Depending on who is stricken, listeria poisoning can be an unpleasant nuisance or a horrible tragedy.

▶ **TEST 5** **Recognizing the Implied Main Idea**

DIRECTIONS Read the paragraph. Then circle the letter of the implied main idea.

1. Some people claim that declawing a cat does no real harm, but for reasons of their own, they are denying the obvious. Cats remove old skin and dry hair by scratching themselves. A cat without claws can't groom itself properly. Cats also need their claws to jump. Their claws are like landing gear. They help cats maintain their balance. If deprived of claws, the animals find it hard to jump from place to place. Worst of all, if a declawed house cat escapes its home, it could quickly die of starvation. Grabbing for a mouse or bird would be an empty gesture, leaving the cat to go hungry. An even more horrible fate awaits the declawed cat who gets into a fight with another animal.

Implied Main Idea

 a. It's a mistake to declaw a cat.

 b. Cats need their claws for grooming.

 c. Too many pet owners don't consider their animals' needs.

 d. The practice of declawing cats is increasing.

2. On December 18, 1912, an amateur archaeologist named Charles Dawson and his friend Arthur Smith Woodward presented what they claimed were extraordinary findings to the Geological Society of London.[†] Woodward and Dawson presented the skeleton of a creature alleged to be half man and half ape. The two men claimed they had discovered what was believed to be the missing link between humans and apes. With relatively little investigation, Piltdown man—as the skeleton came to be called—was accepted as genuine. As time went by, however, doubts began to surface, and researchers examined and reexamined the skeleton. In 1953, close analysis of the skeleton revealed that someone had created it by fusing together the bones of a human being and an orangutan.

Implied Main Idea

 a. Dawson and Woodward were con men.

 b. The Piltdown man was a fraud.

---

†Geological Society of London: a group devoted to the study of the earth.

c. The Piltdown man hoax illustrates a basic truth in science: The experts are often the easiest to fool.

d. Dawson knew the Piltdown man was a hoax, but Woodward believed the skeleton was the real thing—the missing link.

3. In the eighteenth century, the English economist Thomas Malthus predicted that future populations would increase faster than food supplies—with disastrous results. But in the past two hundred years, scientific advances have profoundly influenced food-production methods. In heavily industrialized countries, the same amount of food can be produced in less time than it took half a century ago. Similarly, increased knowledge of agriculture has helped grow more food on less land. By the same token, land once considered unfit for food production has become fertile. With time, as we learn more about the ocean, we may be able to produce food not just from the land but from the sea as well.

Implied Main Idea

a. Malthus's prediction may yet be proven true.

b. Technology will always outwit Mother Nature.

c. The theory that population increases faster than food supplies has not proved true for industrialized countries.

d. Malthus inaccurately predicted a problem with overpopulation.

4. Vitamin A helps with vision, bone growth, and healthy skin. A deficiency in vitamin A can produce eye diseases. Dairy products, nuts, and yellow vegetables all contain vitamin A. Vitamin C helps fight colds and is essential to healthy teeth. Oranges, lemons, tomatoes, and strawberries all contain this important vitamin. Vitamin D, the sunshine vitamin, helps keep bones and teeth strong; a lack of this vitamin can contribute to arthritis. Fish and eggs are the best sources of vitamin D. The vitamin B complex—B_1, B_2, B_6, and B_{12}—is also extremely important. It keeps the skin healthy and develops muscle tone. Vitamin B may even help reduce stress and tension. Green, leafy vegetables, milk, and grains help supply this important group of vitamins.

Implied Main Idea

a. Of all the vitamins, the B complex is the most important.

b. Vitamin A is the key to good health.

c. We can get all the vitamins we need from a balanced diet; vitamin pills are unnecessary.

d. Vitamins are important for maintaining good health.

▶ TEST 6   Recognizing the Implied Main Idea

DIRECTIONS   Read each paragraph. Then write the implied main idea in the blanks that follow.

1. Left on his own at a young age, the comedian Charlie Chaplin quickly learned how to survive on London's city streets. Living in part from money earned as a mime,[†] he also charmed friends and strangers alike into giving him food and shelter. Above all, he learned how to outwit the police, who were not fond of a young boy without a home or a job. Arriving in the United States in 1910, Chaplin quickly got work in silent films. After that, it did not take him long to develop the character that made him famous—the "Little Tramp." Dressed in shabby clothes, begging for money and food wherever he could find it, the Little Tramp spent most of his twenty-five years onscreen avoiding the police, who pursued him in one hilarious scene after another.

Implied Main Idea   _____

                        _____

2. During the Civil War, the first war to be covered by newspaper journalists, some reporters considered it their duty to rally the troops. During the famous battle of Bull Run, for example, Edmund Clarence Stedmen of the *New York World* would wave the regiment flag whenever he thought the troops he was covering were losing their will to fight. Junius Brown from the *New York Tribune* went a step further. If he thought a rebel sniper was in the surrounding area, he would pick up a gun and start firing. Aware that Union[†] leader Ulysses S. Grant liked to drink, Sylvanus Cadwallader of the *Chicago Times* did his part to win the war: He locked himself and Grant in the bathroom to keep the general from hitting the bottle. Even more than his colleagues, Samuel Wilkeson of the *New York Times* participated in the war he covered. After the bloody battle of Gettysburg, Wilkeson wrote his report standing beside the grave of his oldest son.

Implied Main Idea   _____

                        _____

[†]mime: a performer who acts out situations without speaking.
[†]Union: loyal to the U.S. government during the Civil War.

3. In the stable and moist conditions of the tropical rain forests, plants and animals are more varied and diverse than anywhere else on Earth. The variety and diversity of the rain forest makes it a treasure trove for all kinds of riches, from exotic perfumes to cures for deadly diseases. Yet every year, a rain-forest region the size of Belgium is cut down to make way for agriculture. The cutting occurs despite the fact that the soil in the rain forest is not particularly suitable for either growing or grazing. The soil is sandy. Lacking nutrients from the trees, it quickly becomes too dry to be useful for farming or herding. Still, the cutting continues, although no one knows what miraculous cure for disease has been lost in the process.

Implied Main Idea _____

_____

4. Lasers, devices that produce an intense, focused beam of light, have been around since 1960, when Theodore H. Maiman put the first one together. At the time, however, no one quite knew what to do with the laser. In fact, in the 1960s and early 1970s, the laser was often described as a solution looking for a good problem. But today, no one makes that little joke any more. Laser technology is being used with increasing frequency on people who wear glasses. Many who undergo laser surgery discover that once it is over, they can see without glasses. Lasers are also now commonly used to remove cataracts and gallstones, and heart surgeons use them to remove blood clots from coronary arteries. In addition to medical uses, lasers are important tools of the military. They are central to all kinds of weaponry, including the so-called smart bombs. Moreover, traveling at the speed of light, lasers can burn a hole in missiles or their warheads and thereby render them ineffective. They are also a central part of military warning and detecting systems. In addition, lasers have found their place in industry. They play a key role in machine-tool operations, communication systems, tunnel construction, and welding.

Implied Main Idea _____

_____

5. The first successful blood transfusion was performed in the seventeenth century, but the practice was outlawed because of the dangers it posed to the patient. The practice was revived in the nineteenth century, but it was accompanied by terrible risks, like blood clots and kidney failure. Austrian-born Karl Landsteiner (1868–1943), however, had a theory. He argued that the blood of humans had inborn differences and similarities. The key, from Landsteiner's perspective, was to understand both the differences and the similarities. Once they were understood, Landsteiner thought the risks of blood transfusion might be eliminated. To that end, he analyzed numerous blood samples. By 1901, he had classified blood donors into three different categories called A, B, and O (AB was added in 1902). Following that discovery, the transfusion of blood became a relatively safe procedure.

Implied Main Idea _____

_____

Drawing Inferences from Visual Aids

IN THIS CHAPTER, YOU WILL LEARN

- when pie charts are likely to turn up in a passage.

- why line graphs are so popular with writers.

- when bar graphs are preferable to line graphs.

- how drawings and cartoons reaffirm or expand the author's message.

"Reading and understanding information is more than a matter of words."
—From the publishers of Ashgate Books

Writers use visual aids such as pie charts, graphs, and drawings to help readers understand their message. Sometimes visual aids reinforce the author's point by repeating it in visual terms. But just as frequently they offer more evidence for the author's claim. Occasionally, visual aids add details that the text can't provide because the explanation might become too long and tedious for the reader.

None of these objectives could be fulfilled, however, without help from the reader. Except for the title, label, and caption, or explanation, visual aids don't rely heavily on language. Sometimes visual aids don't even appear on the same page as the passage they illustrate. That means it's the reader's job to draw the necessary inferences that tie text and image together.

In this chapter, we'll look at some common visual aids and focus on the inferences readers need to draw to make visual aids enhance the text as the author intended.

Pie Charts

As their name implies, pie charts look like pies (Figure 7.1). In pie charts, circles are divided into segments, or shares, to show the percentage, or contribution, of each piece. Pie charts are usually used to identify all the individual components of some larger entity—for example, government spending, federal debt, criminal offenses—and they allow the reader to see immediately how each share or piece compares to the other shares making up the larger whole.

Pie charts are fairly straightforward, so authors often let them speak for themselves. In Figure 7.2, for example, the author uses the title to pose a question and lets the pie chart provide the answer for the reader willing to draw an inference.

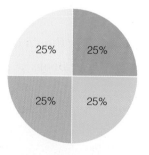

Figure 7.1 Pie Chart

Who Owns the U.S. Federal Debt?
As of January 31, 2009

Owned by U.S. private sector firms and citizens: $3,245 B (31%)

Owned by foreign governments and citizens: $3,072 B (29%)

Owned by U.S. government: $4,315 B (41%)

Chinese: $740 B

Japanese: $635 B

OPEC: $186 B

All other countries: $1,512 B

Figure 7.2

Source of data: www.optimist123.com/optimist/2009/04/pie-chart-who-owns-the-national-debt.html.

Based on the pie chart in Figure 7.2, we can infer that there are three central owners of the U.S. federal debt: (1) the U.S. government, (2) private individuals and firms in the United States, and (3) foreign governments and citizens. The chart shows quickly and clearly that among the three, the U.S. government owns the major portion of federal debt.

That's the beauty of pie charts: At a glance, you can draw conclusions from them.

Doubling Up

Writers often make comparisons by including two pie charts. In these cases, readers need to respond by inferring the connections between the two charts.

Take, for example, the following passage, which draws an interesting conclusion based on the sleep differences between adults and newborns.

If it's true, as research suggests, that rapid eye movement, or REM, sleep is a time when the brain is energetically storing, sorting, and understanding new information, then newborns clearly experience a much more active and energetic sleep than adults do. Newborns spend almost sixteen hours a day sleeping, and eight of those hours are passed in REM sleep. The rest of the time, newborns doze their way through eight hours of less mentally active, non-REM sleep or else remain awake. Adults, if they are lucky, sleep eight hours each day, and of those eight hours, only 1.6 hours consist of REM sleep with

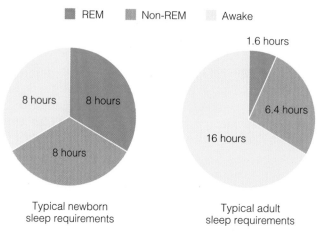

Figure 7.3 Developmental Changes in Sleep Requirements

Source of data: Seifert, Hoffnung, and Hoffnung, *Lifespan Development*, p. 113.

its wildly active brain waves. Because a growing body of research suggests that REM sleep is essential to ordering and storing information in the brain, the sleep differences between newborns and adults may well reflect the amount of new information babies are receiving daily compared to the amount adults need to process.

In this case, the pie charts illustrate one of the author's key points: Babies get a lot more REM sleep than adults do. Note, however, that the author does not explicitly say why the pie chart is there. Instead, she expects the reader to make the appropriate connections between chart and text.

Steps in Reading a Pie Chart
◆

1. If you spot a pie chart during your preview of a chapter, check to see if the title tells you what's being divided into shares or segments.

2. When you read a passage that refers to a pie chart, look at the figure either while you are reading or as soon as you finish reading the passage that refers to it.

3. Pay attention to the number of pieces in the pie and the percentage of the whole each one represents. Notice if the shares are very different in size. If they are, note which shares are largest or smallest.

4. Be sure you understand what point the author wants to reinforce by including the pie chart. For instance, is she offering it as evidence to prove that among all the union organizations in the country,

the largest is the AFL-CIO? Or is he using a pie chart to illustrate that government spending on foreign aid is minuscule?

5. If the author provides two pie charts, make sure you know what each one represents. Pay attention to similarities in the makeup of the segments. However, pay particular attention to differences. Writers don't include two pie charts unless the differences the charts reveal are important.

READING TIP

Look at pie charts both before and after reading. Look the first time to make predictions about the reading, the second to make sure you understand what the pie chart adds to the author's point.

SUMMING UP THE KEY POINTS

1. Pie charts show how the individual pieces, or shares, of some larger whole compare to one another.

2. To understand pie charts, readers need to look at the individual shares and note any large differences among them. But above all, readers need to understand what the chart contributes to the writer's overall point, or main idea.

3. Writers sometimes include two separate pie charts to encourage comparisons between two groups of individuals, institutions, or things. If you see a passage accompanied by two pie charts, make sure you recognize the differences between them and can connect those differences to the author's overall point.

◆ **EXERCISE 1**   **Understanding Pie Charts**

DIRECTIONS   Read the passage and study the accompanying pie chart. Then circle the appropriate letter to identify the purpose of the chart.

1. **State and Local Spending**

The principle of diversity in state and local finance is evident in terms of what state and local governments choose to do with their revenues. First, these governments spend a great deal of money. State and local spending has been increasing much faster than the gross national product and the level of inflation. The functional distribution of spending varies from state to state. As indicated in Figure 7.4, education consumes the largest portion of total state and local spending, followed by public welfare, which includes public assistance, medical services, and health care.

Within each of these categories lies a wide range of financial commitments. For instance, higher-education expenditures in a recent year ran from 16.6 percent of total state and local spending in Utah to only 5.4 percent in New York. South Dakota dedicated 14.9 percent to highways, whereas New York set aside just 4.4 percent for the same purpose. Such differences represent historical trends, local economic circumstances, and citizens' willingness to incur debt to pay for services.

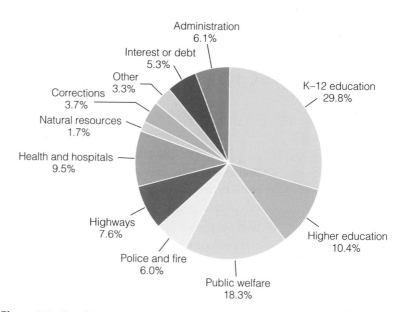

Figure 7.4 Total State and Local Government Spending, by Service Delivered

Source of data: Bowman and Kearney, *State and Local Government*, pp. 356–57.

When considered in relation to the text, the purpose of the pie chart is to

a. show how the state of Utah spends its money.

b. show how the states overall spend money.

c. show that more federal money is spent on education than people realize.

d. show how the state of New York spends its money.

2. Who Controls Health Care Reform?

Listening to the 2009 debates about reforming U.S. health care, one would think that the fate of health care in this country lay in the hands of a few influential government officials, who must determine how more people can get access to health care. But even a quick glance at Figure 7.5 indicates how naive this notion is. The biggest portion of health care spending goes to hospitals, the second biggest goes to doctors. It should be obvious, then, that reforming health care delivery cannot be decided solely through government legislation. Reforming health care requires the involvement and support of the country's physicians.

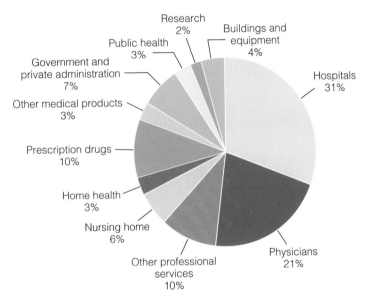

Figure 7.5 U.S. Spending in 2007 by Type of Service and Activity

Source of data: Center for Medicare and Medicaid Services (CMS).

When considered in relation to the text, the purpose of the pie chart is to

a. indicate that doctors are overpaid in the United States and that the first issue of health care reform has to address physicians' fees.

b. indicate that more than half of health care spending goes to doctors or hospitals, making them extremely influential in the decisions about health care.

c. indicate that the fate of health care reform is doomed because physicians would have to accept lower fees if we are to insure more people without increasing spending.

d. indicate that prescription drugs, so often blamed for the high costs of health care, actually play only a small role in health care spending.

CHECK YOUR UNDERSTANDING

1. What's the purpose of a pie chart?

_____

_____

_____

2. What do readers need to do when they look at a pie chart?

_____

_____

3. How do authors use pie charts to encourage the making of comparisons?

_____

_____

Line Graphs

Line graphs usually show how **variables**, or things capable of change, are affected by the passage of time.

Line graphs are very effective for tracking subtle changes and revealing trends. On the left side of a line graph, going from top to bottom, is the *y-axis*. This is where you'll see represented items that can be counted, for instance, dollars, barrels, births, and deaths. The units, or increments, of time are plotted, or tracked, along what's called a horizontal line or *x-axis*, the line running from left to right; for example, a graph tracking the divorce rate over a period of years would start off looking something like the one shown in Figure 7.6 on page 389.

However, as with pie charts, the function of a line graph in relation to the text is not always explicitly explained by either the title or caption. Instead, authors expect readers to infer the logical connection. Look, for instance, at the line graph (Figure 7.7) accompanying the text about the effects of divorce (page 389).

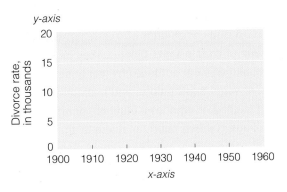

Figure 7.6   Line Graph
Line graphs use the *x*- and *y*-axis to record different kinds of information.

Effects of Divorce on Kids

Divorce is especially hard for school-age children. Having outgrown the self-centeredness of the preschool years, school-age children increasingly identify with and rely on their parents as role models to help them establish their own sense of who they are and how they should behave. At a time when children are just learning to be independent from home life, divorce threatens the safe base they have come to rely on to help make increasing independence possible. The loyalty conflicts frequently created by parents who are competing for their children's allegiance can make children fearful that they will lose one of their parents in the process.

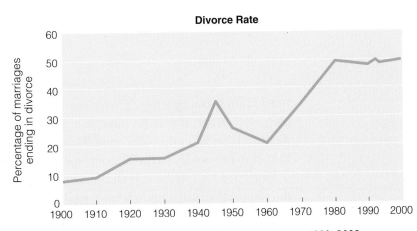

Figure 7.7   Percentage of U.S. Marriages Ending in Divorce, 1900–2000
Since the mid-1980s, approximately half of all marriages in the United States have ended in divorce.

Source of data: U.S. Bureau of the Census (2000).

Judith Wallerstein and Sandra Blakeslee (1996)[†] conducted a long-term follow-up study of children who were between six and eight years old at the time of their parents' divorce. They found that even ten years later, these children were burdened by fear of disappointment in love relationships, lowered expectations, and a sense of powerlessness. When compared to children who were older or younger at the time of the breakup, school-age children fared far worse in their emotional adjustment and overall competence, including school and social relationships. The profound unhappiness with current relationships and concerns regarding future ones that these children experienced often were masked by their overall conformity to social expectations. (Adapted from Seifert and Hoffnung, *Child and Adolescent Development*, p. 404.)

In this example, the line graph does not directly illustrate anything said in the text. Instead, the authors expect readers to draw an inference something like this: "Divorce can be hard on children, and there is every indication [based on the line graph] that divorce is becoming so prevalent, many children will have to deal with it."

Note, too, how the line graph in Figure 7.7 clearly conveys a trend. As the graph illustrates, in 1900, divorce occurred in less than 10 percent of all marriages. However, the divorce rate steadily increased and spiked between 1940 and 1950. (One would suspect that the spike is related to social changes that emerged after World War II.) It dipped again but then began to rise around 1962 and kept climbing until reaching its current 50 percent rate for first marriages. (According to divorcerate.org, the divorce rate for second marriages is higher.)

Doubling Up for Comparison

In addition to tracking trends, writers also use line graphs to make comparisons.[†] When this is the case, two lines will appear in the graph. Readers have to study both carefully and make sure they understand how each line relates to the author's words.

In Figure 7.8 (on page 391), for instance, the title of the line graph does not really match up to what is said in the text, and it's the reader's job to infer the right connection between words and image. Note that the text discusses how the sleep cycle changes during a lifetime. But the

---

[†]This study has been the subject of much criticism and its conclusions disputed due to the methods used.
[†]Bar graphs (see pp. 396–403) are also used for comparison.

caption accompanying the graph focuses solely on sleep during childhood. Thus, it is up to the reader to infer the graph's true purpose: to give readers a visual illustration of how the amount of REM sleep decreases and non-REM sleep increases over the course of a lifetime.

Sleep Deprivation: Getting By on Less

Sleep patterns change during the life cycle. Newborn infants sleep for about two-thirds of the day (see Figure 7.8). Infants spend about one-half of their time in REM sleep while adults spend about one-fifth. Children spend more time in REM sleep than adults, but as they mature, the proportion of REM sleep declines, while periods of non-REM sleep and wakefulness increase. During adulthood, amounts of REM sleep, deep sleep, and total sleep decline. By the time we reach our sixties or seventies, we may require only six hours of sleep per night. (Nevid, *Psychology: Concepts and Applications*, p. 150.)

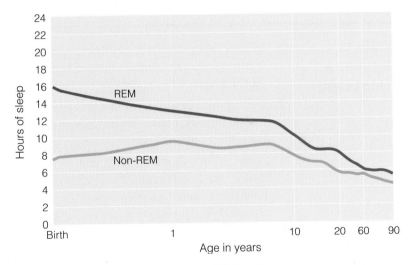

Figure 7.8 Changes in Sleep Patterns in Childhood
During early childhood, the proportion of REM sleep declines, while the proportion of non-REM sleep increases.

Source of data: Nevid, *Psychology: Concepts and Applications*, p. 150.

Based on the graph's title, it's easy to miss the connection between the graph and the text. The title emphasizes just childhood sleep patterns. But the graph itself illustrates the point of the passage: how REM sleep declines over a lifetime. The graph shows readers what the text does not specifically say, that the decline is slow but steady. By the time adults are in their seventies, they get very little REM sleep.

Reader-Supplied Inferences

Note that grasping the information in the graph relies almost totally on the reader's willingness to draw inferences. Readers have to register the meaning of both lines: The green line identifies hours of non-REM sleep, and the blue line identifies hours of REM sleep. Note, too, that the *y*-axis identifies hours of sleep and the *x*-axis indicates age in years. Thus, contrary to the title, which focuses solely on childhood, the graph actually highlights how REM sleep declines over the course of a lifetime. Infancy is the high point of our REM sleep time.

The length of REM sleep then declines steadily until almost all the sleep we get is non-REM. In truth, then, the graph tells us more than the caption or title suggests. However, readers who didn't take the time to draw the appropriate inferences would miss much of the information the graph provides.

Steps in Reading a Line Graph ♦	
	1. In your preview, look at any line graphs present in the chapter. See if you can make any predictions about the chapter's content based on the graphs.
	2. During your reading, when a line graph is referred to in the text, look at it quickly to see if you understand the connection between the author's words and the graph.
	3. After you finish the chapter section where the graph appeared, look at the graph again. Note what items, incidents, events, etc., have been plotted on the *y*-axis. If the amount of time covered on the *x*-axis is *not* plotted, make sure you understand what standard of measurement is used.
	4. Look for notable features of the graph, such as big spikes or deep valleys, and ask yourself how these relate to what you learned from the text.
	5. If there are two or more lines plotted on the graph, note their differences and similarities, and make sure you know what each one represents.
	6. Check the source or sources of the graph, noting the age of the information. Be wary of a graph used as evidence if the information is more than ten years old. If the graph illustrates a historical trend, say the rise in divorce after 1900, then the dates are less significant.

7. See if you can mentally sum up the reason for the line graph's presence in the text, e.g., "The line graph shows how cell phones are steadily replacing the use of land lines."

8. If you can't determine why the line graph is present in the text, mark the passage for a second reading.

SUMMING UP THE KEY POINTS

1. Line graphs usually show how a variable, or something capable of change, is affected by the passage of time.

2. Line graphs are especially good at revealing patterns or trends that can begin subtly and then plunge or spike dramatically.

3. The *y*-axis, which is at the left end of the graph and runs from top to bottom, shows the item being tracked, usually over the course of time. It identifies what's being analyzed, often for time-related change—for example, births, deaths, and wages.

4. The *x*-axis runs horizontally. This is where you'll usually see represented the different increments of time being used as a measure. Those time increments might consist of years, hours, or ages. The time increments plotted along the bottom line will change according to what's being measured.

5. When studying a line graph, note any marked spikes or dips in the plotted line or lines. Ask yourself if these strong increases or decreases reflect some idea mentioned in the text the graph accompanies.

◆ EXERCISE 2 Understanding Line Graphs

DIRECTIONS Read the passage and study the accompanying line graph. Then circle the letter of the correct response.

Chronic Sleep Deprivation

1 If you miss a few hours of sleep, you may feel a little groggy the next day but will probably be able to muddle through. What you may not realize is that sleep deprivation slows reaction times and impairs concentration, memory, and problem-solving ability. It also makes it more difficult to retain newly acquired information and impairs academic performance, such as

performance on math tasks (Bowman, 2000; Carpenter, 2000; Harrison & Horne, 2000; Lorenzo et al., 1995; Stickgold, LaTanya, & Hobson, 2000).

2   Not surprisingly, sleep deprivation is among the most common causes of motor vehicle accidents ("Odds Against Weary Driver," 2000). Motor vehicle accidents are most likely to occur in the early morning hours when drivers are typically at their sleepiest (Figure 7.9).

3   Chronic sleep deprivation is a major stress faced by medical residents and a cause of concern for patients treated by doctors who may be nearly asleep on their feet (Lingenfelser et al., 1994). Fortunately, temporary periods of sleep deprivation are not known to produce lasting ill effects (Anch, Browman, Mitler, & Walsh, 1988). We shouldn't become alarmed if we miss a few hours of sleep; rather, we should attempt to restore our normal sleep pattern the following night.

4   It's not just the total amount of sleep that affects our functioning but also the type of sleep. From laboratory studies in which volunteers have been deprived of REM sleep, we know that loss of REM sleep impairs learning ability and memory (T. Adler, 1993). After REM deprivation, people experience a "rebound effect"—they make up for the loss by spending more of their next sleep period in REM sleep. (Adapted from Nevid, *Psychology: Concepts and Applications*, p. 151.)

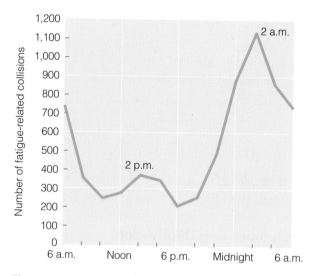

Figure 7.9   Motor Vehicle Accidents in Relation to Time of Day
The greatest risk of motor vehicle accidents occurs in the early morning hours when drivers are typically at their sleepiest.

Source of data: Adapted from AAA Foundation for Traffic Safety, 2007.

1. In this context, the line graph is included to

   a. reaffirm the idea that chronic sleep deprivation creates medical hazards when sleep-deprived residents treat patients.

   b. offer evidence that sleep deprivation leads to auto accidents.

   c. prove that sleep deprivation does not have lasting ill effects.

2. During what time of night do the most motor vehicle accidents occur?

   a. 1 a.m.

   b. 2 a.m.

   c. 5 a.m.

   Were you able to answer this question based on

   a. the text?

   b. the line graph?

✔ CHECK YOUR UNDERSTANDING

1. What do line graphs usually show?

   _____

   _____

2. Define the terms *x-axis* and *y-axis*.

   _____

   _____

   _____

3. What should you pay particular attention to when studying a line graph?

   _____

   _____

   _____

Bar Graphs

Like line graphs, bar graphs can show changes over time. But when bar graphs track changes over time, the increases and decreases are usually large. When the changes are subtle, line graphs are more appropriate. Bar graphs also frequently accompany comparisons of specific prices, fees, products, or incidents. They are less effective at revealing subtle changes or early trends.

By looking at the varying heights or lengths of the bars in a bar graph, readers can quickly visualize any differences or similarities mentioned by the author. Bar graphs, for example, are likely to accompany statements like the following: "The number of female CEOs[†] running Fortune 500[†] companies is much smaller than the number of males." A bar graph accompanying a statement like this one would immediately reveal how many more male Fortune 500 CEOs there are than female ones.

Bar graphs can present information with either horizontal or vertical bars. The important point to note about bar graphs is the height or length of the bars—the greater the height or length of the bars, the bigger the number or amount they represent.

Vertical Bar Graphs

Vertical bar graphs, where the bars run from top to bottom, are the most likely choice when only one or two variables are being tracked over time. See, for example, the bar graph in Figure 7.10.

From the graph in Figure 7.10, you can see that the number of police officers employed between 1994 and 1996 decreased, but started increasing again in 1997. The graph also makes it easy to compare or contrast the number of police officers for any combination of years.

Horizontal Bar Graphs

Horizontal bar graphs, such as the one shown in Figure 7.11, are more likely to be used when several items are being measured, each with a different label, and some of the labels are too long to fit along the x-axis.

[†]CEOs: chief executive officers.
[†]The list of Fortune 500 companies is compiled by *Fortune 500* magazine, which lists the country's largest companies.

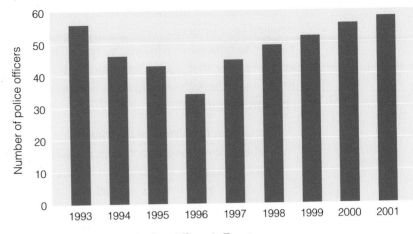

Figure 7.10 Number of Police Officers in Tarrytown

Source of data: www.statcan.ca/english/edu/power/ch9/bargraph/bar.htm.[†]

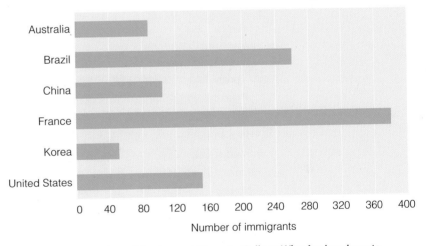

Figure 7.11 Number of Students at Diversity College Who Are Immigrants

Source of data: www.statcan.ca/english/edu/power/ch9/bargraph/bar.htm.

Expanding the Main Idea

Bar graphs often act as a visual reinforcement of the author's main idea. But bar graphs can also add to the main idea, providing information not mentioned in the text.

[†]The bar graphs shown in Figures 7.10 and 7.11 are both based on imaginary locations and were created purely to illustrate principles of reading bar graphs. The website from which these data were drawn is worth a look.

This additional information should not be ignored, because the more detailed your understanding of the author's thinking is, the more likely you are to remember what you've read. For an illustration of how a bar graph—or, for that matter, any visual aid—can add to the writer's main point, read the following excerpt on taxes in the United States. Then check out Figure 7.12.

Throughout the history of the United States, a fair tax law has generally been viewed as one that keeps the overall tax burden low, requires everyone to pay something, and requires the better-off to pay at a higher rate than the less-well-off. The law, in short, was viewed as good if it imposed modest burdens, prevented cheating, and was mildly progressive. On the first count at least, Americans appear to have succeeded. The tax burden in the United States is lower than it is in most other democratic nations. (Adapted from Wilson and Dilulio, *American Government*, p. 505.)

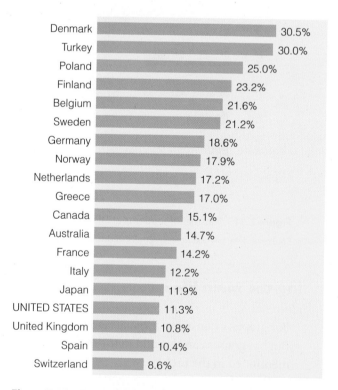

Figure 7.12 Tax Burdens in Democratic Nations (Taxes as a Percentage of Income of a Family with Two Children)

Source of data: Wilson and Dilulio, *American Government*, p. 507.

In the previous example, the bar graph provides only a title. There's no caption to explain its meaning. However, because the passage accompanying the bar graph talks about Americans' success at keeping the tax rate low, readers can correctly infer that the graph supplies evidence for the authors' claim.

But readers who truly want to understand and remember the authors' point would also draw one or two other inferences based on the data shown in the graph. For instance, by looking at the length of the bars, readers can rightly infer that Americans who complain about the country's current tax rate should consider themselves lucky. When the bar showing American tax rates is compared to the two bars representing tax rates for Denmark and Turkey, it's clear that the tax rates for these two countries are almost triple those of the United States.

Although this supporting detail implied by the graph does not appear in the accompanying passage, it still reinforces the authors' main idea. It also makes more specific the authors' claim that American taxes are much lower than those of other countries. Implied supporting details like this one help readers store both main idea and support in long-term memory.

Double-Bar Graphs

In some instances, a writer may want you to compare how two related variables, for instance, the wages of male and female managers, changed over the course of thirty years. When this is the case, the bars in the graph may be paired for ease of comparison.

For an illustration, read the text that follows. Then look at Figure 7.13, a double-bar graph following the excerpt. The bar graph illustrates a point made in the paragraph: Support for civil rights legislation increased dramatically in the 1980s and 1990s, even among southern Democrats[†] who once routinely opposed it. However, the graph also adds to that point by showing readers, by means of the twin bars, that the two branches of Congress, the Senate and the House of Representatives, have differed over the years in their support of civil rights legislation.

Since the 1960s, congressional support for civil rights legislation has grown—so much so, indeed, that labeling a bill a civil rights measure, once the kiss of death, now almost guarantees its passage. In 1984,

---

[†]Between 1952 and 1964, the South was heavily Democratic.

the Supreme Court decided that the federal ban on discrimination in education applied only to the "program or activity" receiving federal aid and not to the entire school or university. Four years later, Congress passed a bill making it clear that antidiscrimination rules applied to the entire educational institution and not just to that part receiving federal money. When President Reagan vetoed the bill, Congress overrode the veto. In the override vote, every southern Democrat in the Senate and almost 90 percent of those in the House voted for the bill. This was a dramatic change from 1964, when over 80 percent of the southern Democrats in Congress voted against the Civil Rights Act. (Wilson and Dilulio, *American Government*, p. 139.)

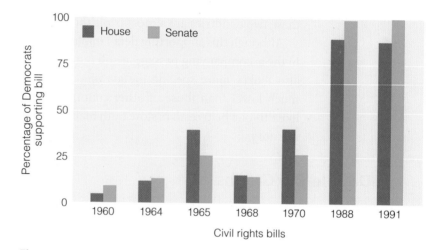

Figure 7.13 Growing Support Among Southern Democrats in Congress for Civil Rights Bills

Source of data: Congressional Quarterly, *Congress and the Nation*, vols. 1, 2, 3, 7, 8.

In the above bar graph, the height of the paired bars indicates a dramatic change over the course of time: Since 1964, southern Democrats have increased their support of civil rights bills by a large percentage. Note as well that the double bars add to readers' understanding of the text. The double bars indicate that the Congress and the Senate have not always been in agreement in their support of civil rights legislation.

An additional inference that can be drawn from the bar graph is that progress on civil rights legislation came slowly between 1957 and 1970. However, progress accelerated, or sped up, in the 1980s and 1990s.

Steps in Reading a Bar Graph
◆

1. Pre-read any bar graphs in the chapter. If possible, make predictions based on their contents.

2. When the bar graph is referred to in the text, look at it quickly to see if you can understand how it relates to the author's words. Does it repeat the main idea or offer support for the author's claim?

3. When you finish reading the text that refers to the bar graph, look for any extremes in the length or width of the bars. Ask yourself how this visual information fits the author's verbal explanation.

4. If the graph measures changes over time, try to sum up some of those changes. Was there a particular time period when a dramatic change occurred? Ask yourself how that fits the author's description or claims.

5. See if you can mentally sum up the reason for the bar graph's presence in the text—e.g., "the bar graph illustrates how cigarette consumption dropped dramatically after the connection between cigarettes and cancer was made public."

6. If you can't determine the relationship between the text and the accompanying visual aid, mark the passage for a second reading.

SUMMING UP THE KEY POINTS

- - - - - - - - - - - - - - - - - - - ▶

1. Bar graphs, like line graphs, sometimes track changes over time, but they are usually used when the changes are extreme rather than subtle.

2. Bar graphs can also give readers a quick visual picture of how much of something exists in comparison to something else, for instance, how much corn is grown in Ukraine versus Iowa. Unlike line graphs, bar graphs aren't used to reveal general trends. They are more likely to provide specific information concerning differences in amount or frequency.

3. The bars in a graph are usually arranged horizontally when there are several different groups, all of which require labels.

4. Pay attention to the length and width of the bars, and make sure you understand how they develop the point of the text.

♦ EXERCISE 3   Understanding Bar Graphs

DIRECTIONS   Read the text and study the accompanying bar graph. Then circle the letter of the correct response.

Death Rates and Accidents Among Schoolchildren

The sign of good health in schoolchildren is their very low **mortality**, or the proportion of children who die at a given age. However, for both children and adolescents, deaths by accidents outnumber deaths by life-threatening illness.

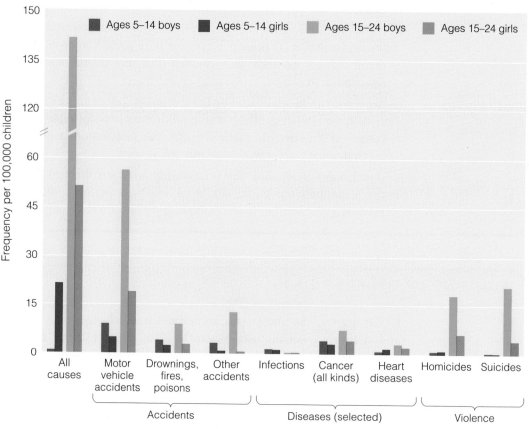

Figure 7.14   Causes of Death Among Children and Young Adults

Source of data: Seifert and Hoffnung, *Child and Adolescent Development*, p. 345.

1. Look closely at the bar graph in Figure 7.14. Note the heights of the bars for all the possible causes of death. Which inference can you draw from the graph?

a. Girls between the ages of five and fourteen are more likely to die in motor vehicle accidents than boys are.

b. Girls between the ages of five and fourteen are more likely to be homicide victims than boys are.

c. Between the ages of five and fourteen, girls have a higher mortality, or death, rate than boys do, but boys overtake and surpass girls dramatically between the ages of fifteen and twenty-four.

2. Which of the following inferences can you draw from the graph?

a. Between the ages of fifteen and twenty-four, girls and boys are about equal when it comes to dying from activities involving personal risk-taking.

b. Between the ages of fifteen and twenty-four, boys are much more likely to die from activities that involve personal risk-taking than girls are.

c. Between the ages of fifteen and twenty-four, suicide is likely to claim more girls than boys.

✔ CHECK YOUR UNDERSTANDING

1. What are two of the most common uses for bar graphs?

_____

_____

2. When reading a bar graph, what should you pay close attention to?

_____

_____

3. What should you do if the bar graph tells you even more than the text it accompanies?

_____

_____

Interpreting Drawings and Cartoons

For the most part, drawings generally restate the point of a passage, often by implicitly comparing the situation described in words to a different set of circumstances that has similar characteristics. Read, for example, the following paragraph, which claims that knowledge about current events offers an advantage. Then study the accompanying drawing:

> In the late 1960s, Professors Phillip Tichenor, George Donahue, and Clarice Olen of the University of Minnesota came upon a sobering survey finding that relates to the difference in the amount of current events information that different people learn from the media. They found that people who are information-rich to begin with tend to get richer faster than people who are information-poor. If the difference in the amount of knowledge between the two types of people grows wider, so does the difference in financial success. (Source of information: Turow, *Media Today*, p. 150.)

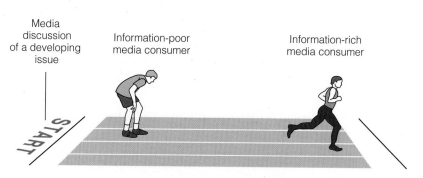

Figure 7.15   Research Shows Information Is an Advantage

In this case, Figure 7.15 supplies a visual image that mirrors the main idea of the text: Like fast runners competing against slower ones, well-informed people can charge ahead of the less well-informed in the race for success. Still, without inferring an answer to the question, "What does a foot race have to do with the author's point about access to information?" the drawing would be meaningless. Readers need to infer the connection between people supplied with (or lacking) necessary information and faster (or slower) runners in a race.

Drawing a Chain of Inferences

Although the race image is a familiar metaphor, or comparison, not all drawings or cartoons will be quite so straightforward. For an illustration, read the following passage about the public's early anxiety over monopolies. Then look at the nineteenth-century political cartoon that accompanies it.

> Much of the antitrust legislation passed in this country, including the Sherman Anti-Trust Act (1890), parts of the Federal Trade Commission Act (1914), and the Clayton Anti-Trust Act (1914), has been the result of public protest. Toward the end of the nineteenth century, there arose a broadly based criticism of business monopolies (called "trusts" at the time). The Grange, an organization of farmers, was especially outspoken in its criticism, and popular opinion generally—insofar as we can know it in an era without pollsters—seems to have been indignant about trusts and in favor of "trustbusting." Newspaper editorials and magazine articles frequently dwelt on the problem. (Adapted from Wilson and Dilulio, *American Government*, p. 480.)

The Grange sought to warn the public about the dangers of a railroad monopoly.

From Culver Pictures.

In this example, the cartoon reinforces a supporting detail used to develop the main idea—that public protest produced anti-monopoly legislation. To drive that idea home in the passage, the writers mention "the Grange," a farmers' organization, which spoke out against monopolies. The cartoon then makes a similar point in its caption, "The Grange sought to warn the public about the dangers of a railroad monopoly." But a reader who doesn't make inferences about the cartoon, despite its caption, will miss much of its meaning.

Note how the cartoon shows a crowd of people lying peacefully (one man is even reading the newspaper) under railroad tracks. The creator of the cartoon has put them there for a reason. They symbolize what the railroad monopoly will do to people's lives: crush them. Yet the people lying under the tracks seem peacefully ignorant of the oncoming danger. Only the farmer, who symbolizes the Grange movement, seems aware of the threat. His pointing finger is a warning to his fellow citizens that they are in danger of being crushed by the railroad industry.

Unlike the drawing of the race, which employs a familiar metaphor, or implied comparison, this cartoon requires more work from the reader. We have to ask ourselves why people have been placed underneath the railroad tracks, where they would normally never be. We also have to connect the cartoon to the passage about monopolies. Since the text itself doesn't mention railroads, the caption of the cartoon links the two, monopolies and railroads, so that we can infer the connection between the image and the authors' claims.

Steps in Understanding Drawings and Cartoons ♦	1. During your preview, look at the drawing or cartoon and determine what's being depicted. If there's a caption, read it. Try to make a prediction about the chapter's content.
	2. Ask yourself during your reading if the drawing or cartoon realistically depicts a point made in the passage or if it's meant to function as a metaphor and calls up a situation similar to, but not the same as, the one you are reading about.
	3. Make sure you understand the point of the cartoon or drawing first. Then ask yourself how it relates to what you have read.
	4. Determine whether the visual aid repeats or adds something to the textbook passage it illustrates. Even if the drawing or cartoon makes an additional point, be sure you understand what that point is.

SUMMING UP THE KEY POINTS

1. Drawings and cartoons often restate the point of the reading. They function, that is, as a visual image that mirrors the author's words. Sometimes, though, the drawing or cartoon depicts a situation that is like the one described in the text. However, the point illustrated by the situation will be the same. This was true, for example, of the foot race image used on page 404 to emphasize how being information-rich is a big advantage.

2. In interpreting the function of the drawing, be ready to draw a chain of inferences that relates the drawing, which may be about something entirely different from the topic of the text (as the drawing on page 405 illustrates). There has to be a connection between the two, but it's almost always the reader's job to infer it.

3. If drawings or cartoons are used to emphasize the author's point, make sure you understand the point of the image and can tie it to what the author explicitly says.

◆ **EXERCISE 4**   **Understanding Cartoons and Drawings**

DIRECTIONS   Read the following passage and study the accompanying cartoons and drawings. Then circle the appropriate letters to identify (1) the inference readers need to make about the visual aid and (2) the main idea of the reading.

1. **Just How Lame Is a "Lame Duck" President?**

Although the phrase "lame duck" was initially used to describe people who couldn't pay off their debts, it eventually acquired a different meaning. The phrase "lame duck" now is usually applied to political officeholders who have lost an election or who are ineligible to serve another term. Thus, they finish out their term but allegedly have no real power.

While a politician's lame duck status is beloved by cartoonists fond of sketching a wounded duck napping in office, lame duck officials have been known to get their licks in before riding off into the sunset. This is particularly true of presidents.

As Senator Patrick Leahy (D–Vt.) expressed it, "No president is ever a lame duck. He is still a president." Ronald Reagan was a lame duck president when he met with Soviet premier Mikhail Gorbachev to hammer out the details for an era of peaceful coexistence between Russia and the

United States. Bill Clinton was a lame duck president when he outraged many by pardoning one of his most controversial fund-raisers, fugitive financier Mark Rich. As a lame duck president, Jimmy Carter tried desperately to get freedom for the American hostages held in Iran, and he almost did it. But time ran out, and the hostages were freed just as Ronald Reagan took office. (Source of Leahy quotation: http://history.howstuffworks.com/american-history/lame-duck-president2.htm.)

© Ulrich Flemming

Figure 7.16   Just How Lame Is a Lame Duck?

1. The main idea of the reading is that

   a. lame duck officials are usually involved in activities they don't want to make public.

   b. the stereotype of the lame duck official doing nothing in office is not really accurate.

   c. presidents in particular use their lame duck status to pay off supporters and make plans for the future.

2. The cartoon of the duck with the bandaged foot makes which point?

   a. The lame duck political official is generally assumed to be doing absolutely nothing in office.

b. The lame duck political official actually has more power than some might think.

c. When they are lame ducks, political officials have more power than they ever had in office.

2. Famous Filibusters

The *filibuster*, the use of prolonged speechmaking to delay legislative action, has a long history. South Carolina's J. Strom Thurmond filibustered for 24 hours and 18 minutes in an attempt to delay a vote on the Civil Rights Act of 1957. But even before Thurmond, there was the tireless senator from Louisiana, Huey P. Long, who repeatedly used the filibuster to hold up bills he thought favored the rich. In the thirties, Long once held the Senate floor for fifteen hours. He infuriated his opponents but generally delighted spectators. Most filibusters are famous for their mind-numbing tedium, but Long used up his time by reciting Shakespeare and giving out recipes for Southern snacks. Strom Thurmond, in his record-breaking filibuster, also included a few recipes, but Thurmond didn't have Long's punchy delivery or range of reference, and he left both critics and supporters stupefied with boredom.

© Ulrich Flemming

Figure 7.17 Filibusters Use *Prolonged* Speechmaking to Delay Legislative Action

3. The main idea of the reading is that

   a. Huey Long was better at filibustering than Strom Thurmond, who generally put his listeners to sleep.

   b. Huey Long may have been a scoundrel but he was a charming one.

   c. Politicians have a long history of using the filibuster to delay legislation.

4. The cartoon reinforces the point that

   a. some filibusters, like the ones favored by Huey Long, were enjoyed by listeners.

   b. filibusters were widely used to discourage civil rights legislation.

   c. filibusters might have a political purpose but they are usually stupefyingly tedious.

DIGGING Voting Goes High-Tech
DEEPER

Looking Ahead The following reading uses a pie chart to make a point about voting.

1   It wasn't that long ago when voters cast their ballots by going to the local polling place, marking an X on a paper ballot to indicate which candidate they preferred, and depositing the ballot in a box. When the polls closed, official poll workers would count the ballots and report the results. Obviously, vote counting was time consuming and had the potential for human error and misconduct.

2   The next improvement came with lever voting machines—massive metal structures, complete with wrap-around privacy curtains, in which a voter pulled a lever next to the name of the candidate she preferred. The tally of the votes was mechanical, and at the end of the day, poll workers could read the vote totals from the automatic counter in each machine. The machines themselves were costly to purchase, to store, and to maintain; furthermore, they required complicated logistics to haul them to and from polling places during the election period.

3   Fast forward to contemporary times: Less than 12 percent of the electorate uses lever voting machines; less than 1 percent votes with paper ballots. (See Figure 7.18.) Punch card voting, introduced in the 1970s, had been promoted as the solution to paper ballots and lever machines. A county could set up several punch card booths to replace a lever machine, thereby allowing a speedier voting process; tallying the vote required nothing more than running the cards through a card reader. But as the 2000 presidential election showed, punch card voting carried its own set of problems. (Remember the "hanging chads"?[†]) By 2006, only an estimated 5 percent of the electorate was still using a punch card voting system. However, the optical scan ballot, a process akin to marking answers on a machine-graded exam, has proven a much more popular alternative: 41 percent of the electorate uses this method.

4   So what is the latest and newest in voting machine technology? The federal government passed the Help America Vote Act of 2002 (HAVA), which provided funds so that states could upgrade their election equipment. Many election administrators considered paperless electronic voting

---

[†]hanging chad: A chad is a small piece of paper that is supposed to be removed when a hole is punched. But in Florida during the 2000 presidential election, the chads in many voter cards were not completely removed. They were left hanging, making it difficult to say whom the voter had actually chosen.

machines (similar to the touch screens in automatic teller machines) as the best alternative, but concerns about their accuracy and security have slowed implementation. However, as of 2006, approximately 38 percent of the electorate was voting with these electronic machines.

5   Still, opponents of paperless voting have pushed for a paper trail, that is, a way to verify the actual vote cast. Now 25 states have VVPATs (voter-verified paper audit trails) to supplement the record of the count stored in the electronic machine's memory. And although Internet voting holds great promise, concerns about security, unequal access, and the civic consequences of moving elections out of polling places have kept it from being anything more than an experiment at this point. (Bowman and Kearney, *State and Local Government*, pp. 86–87.)

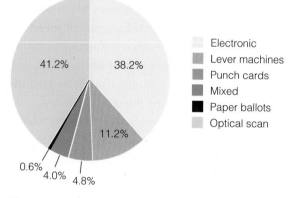

Figure 7.18   Voting Equipment Used: 2006

Source of data: Bowman and Kearney, *State and Local Government*, p. 87.

Sharpening Your Skills

DIRECTIONS   Answer the following questions by filling in the blanks or circling the letter of the correct response.

1. The topic of the reading is methods of voting or voting machines. (Just count the number of times that word or phrase appears.) However, as with paragraphs, you still need to figure out what point the author wants to make about the topic. Of the following statements, which best expresses the main idea?

   a. In 2006, voting had to go "high tech" because there were so many problems with counting the paper ballots.

   b. It's hard to make the voting process truly democratic.

    c. Electronic voting machines are increasingly in use at the polls, but, like past methods, they, too, have their problems and their critics.

    d. Electronic voting machines may provide the most accurate method of counting votes, but they are so expensive, many states cannot afford them.

2. What transitions do the authors use to link paragraphs 2 and 3?

_____

3. Why do the authors bring up "hanging chads"? What inference do they expect readers to draw?

_____

_____

4. The pie chart that accompanies the reading is there to

    a. add additional information about voting methods not mentioned in the chapter.

    b. identify the current voting methods in use and the percentage of 2006 voters using each method.

    c. indicate the need for improved voting machines because fewer and fewer registered voters are using older methods.

Making Connections Like avoiding jury duty, many people do not vote. Two readings in Chapter 6 identified some of the reasons people try to get out of jury duty. Why do you think so many people in the United States do not vote in elections?

_____

_____

Drawing Your Own Conclusions What method of voting do you favor? Please explain.

_____

_____

▶ **TEST 1**   **Reviewing Visual Aids**

DIRECTIONS   Fill in the blanks with the correct response.

1. In pie charts, each piece, or slice, represents _____
_____ .

2. Pie charts allow the reader to see immediately _____
_____ .

3. Line graphs usually show how some _____ is _____
_____ .

4. Line graphs are an excellent tool for _____
_____ .

5. In line graphs, the horizontal line running from left to right across the bottom is called _____ .

6. The vertical line running from top to bottom is called _____ .

7. In line graphs, the line going from top to bottom usually indicates _____ . The line going from left to right shows
_____ .

8. Bar graphs are often used when the writer wants readers to compare large increases or decreases in _____ .

9. With bar graphs, readers need to pay close attention to _____
_____ of the bars.

10. Drawings and cartoons sometimes realistically depict what's said in the text, but sometimes they _____
_____ .

▶ **TEST 2**   **Reading Charts and Graphs**

DIRECTIONS   Read each passage. Then look carefully at the figure that accompanies it. Answer the questions that follow by filling in the blanks.

1. Every year the Gallup polling organization tries to get a sense of how Americans identify their political leanings. The annual figures are based on multiple national surveys, which can encompass as many as 40,000 interviews. In 2009, given the election of President Barack Obama, who was considered by many to be one of the country's more liberal presidents, the expectation was that the number of Americans who described themselves as liberal would dramatically increase in comparison to figures for the year 2000, when the more conservative George W. Bush was elected. As shown in Figures 7.19 and 7.20, the Gallup poll figures for 2009 did not bear out this expectation.

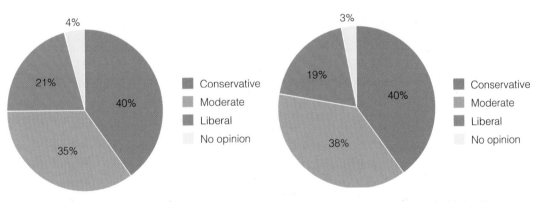

Figure 7.19   Political Views in the United States, 2009

Source of data: www.gallup.com/poll/120857.

Figure 7.20   Political Views in the United States, 2000

Source of data: www.gallup.com/poll/120857.

At the end of the above reading, the author says that the "Gallup poll figures for 2009 did not bear out this expectation." But the author doesn't offer any further explanation. Instead, she lets the two pie charts speak for her. What inference are readers expected to draw after comparing the two charts?

_____

_____

_____

2. As influential as parents and family are in the lives of preschoolers, television has become a potent force in teaching them about the wider world. An exploration of preschoolers' TV viewing patterns shows the extent to which TV has become a part of daily life. (Seifert and Hoffnung, *Childhood and Adolescent Development*, p. 323.)

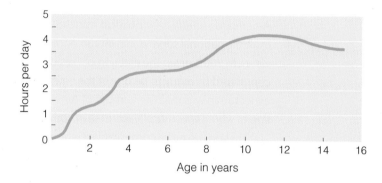

Figure 7.21 Changes in the Amount of Television Viewing, Based on Age[†]

Source of data: Seifert and Hoffnung, *Childhood and Adolescent Development*, p. 323.

(1) According to the line graph shown in Figure 7.21, how many hours of television is a three-year-old likely to watch per day?

_____

(2) According to the line graph, when does television watching peak among preschoolers?

_____

(3) What is the purpose of the line graph that accompanies this text?

_____

_____

_____

[†]Research that looks more closely at how much time kids spend watching television programming along with other kinds of games and videos on a computer would probably show that visual media have increased their influence.

3. According to the bar graph shown in Figure 7.22, is it correct to say that most people in the group see no difference between store and manufacturer brands for beverages but big differences between brands for most other products? Please explain your answer, using evidence from the bar graph.

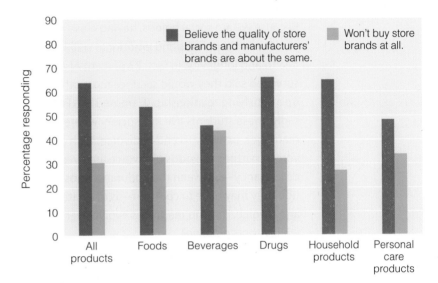

Figure 7.22   The Effect of Brands on Consumers

Source of data: Pride and Ferrell, *Marketing*, p. 303.

_____

_____

▶ **TEST 3**   Understanding Visual Aids

DIRECTIONS   Read the passage and study the accompanying line graph. Answer the questions that follow.

1. Is There a Pattern to Marriage?

1   Because we are social beings, having close relationships is important to us all—for our happiness and emotional well-being and even for our physical health and longevity. In fact, 73 percent of American college students surveyed said they would sacrifice most other life goals rather than give up a satisfying relationship (Hammersla & Frease-McMahan, 1990). Yet sadly, these students live in a society where 40 to 50 percent of first marriages are likely to end in divorce. With at least one previously divorced partner, the odds of divorce are even greater (Gottman, 1998). This discrepancy—between the endurance most people want and the disruption they may have to confront—is dramatic. Couples break up, separate, and divorce. How do marriages evolve over time, and why do some last while others dissolve?

2   Ellen Berscheid and Harry Reis (1998) say that for social psychologists who study intimate relationships, this is the most frequently asked and vexing question. Is there a typical developmental pattern? No and yes. No, it's clear that all marriages are different and cannot be squeezed into a single mold. But yes, certain patterns do emerge when survey results are combined from large numbers of married couples that are studied over long periods of time. Recently, Lawrence Kurdek (1999) reported on a longitudinal study of married couples in which he measured each spouse's satisfaction every year for ten years (out of 522 couples he started with, 93 completed the study). Look at Figure 7.23, and you'll see that there is an overall pattern of decline in ratings of marital quality—and that the ratings given by husbands and wives were very similar. Look more closely and you'll also see that there are two particularly sharp periods of decline. The first occurs during the first year of marriage, apparently while newlyweds tend to idealize each other and to enjoy an initial state of marital bliss (Murray et al., 1996). This "honeymoon" is soon followed by a decline in satisfaction (Bradbury, 1998). A second decline is then observed at about the eighth year of marriage—a finding that is consistent with the popular belief in a "seven-year itch" (Kovacs, 1983). (Adapted from Brehm, Kassin, and Fein, *Social Psychology*, pp. 344–45.)

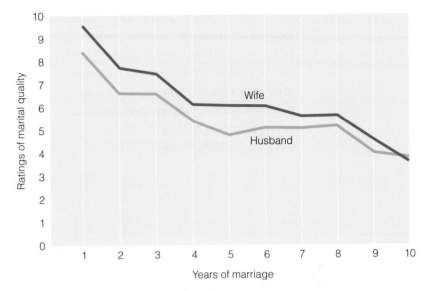

Figure 7.23   Marital Satisfaction Over Time

In a longitudinal study that spanned ten years, married couples rated the quality of their marriage. On average, these ratings were high at the beginning, with ten being the highest rating, but tended to decline over time.

Source of data: Brehm, Kassin, and Fein, *Social Psychology*, p. 344.

Which one of the following points from the reading does the line graph reinforce?

a.   We are social beings who value close relationships and will sacrifice a lot to maintain them.

b.   Almost half of all marriages end in divorce.

c.   The marriages described in the study by Kurdek did not get better over time; they got worse.

2. Are Stock Market Decisions Logical?

If stock market decisions are not made on strictly economic grounds, then on what are they based? As described in *Beyond Greed and Fear*, Hersh Shefrin's (2000) book on the psychology of investing, predictions of the future on Wall Street are heavily influenced by social psychological factors. In October 1987, for example, the U.S. stock market crashed, resulting in an estimated loss of $500 billion. Shortly afterward, economist Robert Shiller sent questionnaires to a group of active traders to try to determine what caused the crisis. For the one thousand or so investors who responded, the key event was news concerning the market itself—including a sharp decline that occurred on the morning of the crash. In other words, price movements in the stock market were triggered not by objective economic information but by other price movements in the market. Does this phenomenon ring a bell? Studies on the process of social comparison and conformity have shown that when people feel they cannot clearly and concretely measure their own opinion, they turn to others for guidance. Perhaps that is why investors are more influenced by news and stock market tips during periods of rising or falling prices than during periods of relative stability (Schachter et al., 1985). (Brehm, Kassin, and Fein, *Social Psychology*, p. 505.)

"I don't buy stocks simply because others are buying them. I buy them because many, many others are buying them."

Which one of the following points in the reading does the cartoon reinforce?

a. In 1987, the U.S. stock market crashed with a resulting loss of $500 billion to investors.

b. When people feel they have no way to evaluate their opinions, they often turn to others for guidance.

c. In an effort to determine what caused the crash, Robert Shiller circulated a questionnaire to traders.

3. Low Birth Weight

As infant and childhood diseases have come under greater control in recent decades, the treatment and prevention of low-birth-weight infants (those weighing less than twenty-five hundred grams, or five-and-a-half pounds) has gained increased attention. Mortality rate rapidly declines as birth weight increases to near normal levels. The United States has a higher proportion of infants born with low birth weight than many other developed countries, a major reason that its infant mortality rate is also higher than in many other industrialized countries (see Figure 7.24). (Bukatko and Daehler, *Child Development*, p. 138.)

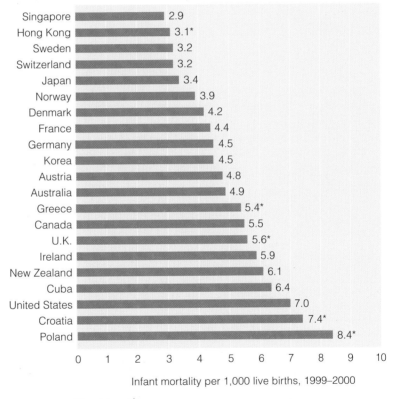

Infant mortality per 1,000 live births, 1999–2000

*Provisional.[†]

Figure 7.24   Infant Mortality in Selected Developed Countries
The infant mortality rate (deaths before one year of age per thousand live births) is a measure that provides an indication of the overall health of a nation. A number of countries have a lower infant mortality rate than the United States.

Source: Data from United Nations, *Population and Vital Statistics Report*, 2001.

[†]provisional: temporary, subject to change.

a. According to the bar graph, _____ had the lowest infant mortality rate in 2000, while _____ had the highest.

b. Taken together, the text, the caption for the graph, and the graph itself indicate what about the overall health of the United States?

_____

_____

_____

Beyond the Paragraph: Reading Longer Selections

IN THIS CHAPTER, YOU WILL LEARN

- how to adapt what you know about reading paragraphs to longer, multi-paragraphed selections.
- how to monitor your comprehension with informal outlines.
- how to take notes on longer readings.

"God may very well be in the details, but don't we still need to look at the bigger picture to make sense of what's going on?"

—Frances Marciano, author of the novel *The End of Manners*

Chapter 8 shows you how to adapt everything you have learned about paragraphs to longer readings. It also tells you more about two methods for note-taking introduced in Chapter 1: outlining and diagramming. Finally, Chapter 8 introduces a crucial element of writing we have not discussed in relation to paragraphs—the writer's purpose.

Moving Beyond the Paragraph

Reading longer, multi-paragraph selections takes more time than reading single paragraphs. However, the extra time needed should not suggest to you that reading essays, articles, or chapter sections requires a brand-new set of skills totally different from the ones you use to read paragraphs. What you need to do, instead, is adapt the skills you practiced on paragraphs to make them suitable for longer, multi-paragraph selections. That means you need to understand exactly how the structure and content of multi-paragraph readings differ from single paragraphs, so that's where we'll start.

Titles and Headings Are Tip-offs

Single paragraphs don't usually have headings or titles. Longer readings do. Longer readings are likely to have titles, headings, even subheadings. Fortunately for readers, these titles and headings usually say a good deal about the reading's topic. For instance, if you are asked to read a chapter section titled "Brand Loyalty," you could correctly predict that the topic of the chapter section is "consumer attachment to a particular brand." Similarly, many textbooks use questions as titles—for example, "Is Romance Essential to Marriage?" The answer to the question is almost always the main idea of the reading.

One Main Idea Controls and Unifies the Others

Like paragraphs, longer readings are unified by one general main idea. In composition classes, this main idea is often called a *thesis*, and it usually appears in the first two or three paragraphs (if the reading is longer, the introduction of the main idea can also be delayed). The paragraphs that follow state or imply a new series of main ideas. However, these demonstrates his or her power over the situation. Unconsciously, teenagers who diet to the point of starvation may be attempting to teach their parents the same lesson: Control is not in the hands of the parents.

6   According to another theory, anorexia may indicate a young girl's deep-rooted fear of growing up. From this perspective, starving the body can be viewed as a way of maintaining its childish contours and rejecting adult femininity. Yet another hypothesis views the disease as a form of self-punishment. The victims may have extraordinarily high standards of perfection and punish themselves for failing to meet their goals.

Paragraph 1: Thesis Statement
However, for some teenagers, dieting is no laughing matter. For them, dieting is not a momentary whim to be pursued and forgotten; instead, it is the symptom of a serious emotional disorder called *anorexia nervosa*, a disease that can have terrible, even fatal, consequences.

Major Supporting Paragraph

Paragraph 2
The disease usually strikes adolescent and preadolescent girls who have no reason to diet. . . .

Major Supporting Paragraph

Paragraph 3
Some teenagers who are obsessed with the need to diet seek treatment. . . . A few victims manage to keep it a secret. . . .

Major Supporting Paragraph

Paragraph 5
To date, the actual cause of the starvation disease has not been determined. According to one theory . . .

Major Supporting Paragraph

Paragraph 6
According to another theory, anorexia may indicate a young girl's deep-rooted fear of growing up. . . .

Minor Supporting Paragraph

Paragraph 4
Unfortunately, members of this group are in the most serious danger . . .

As the diagram shows, the first paragraph of this reading introduces the thesis statement. Keep in mind, however, that longer readings sometimes open with one or more introductory paragraphs that pave the way for the thesis statement.

The reading on pages 428–29 also contains four major supporting paragraphs. They answer the questions "Which teenagers get this disease?" and "What are its symptoms and causes?" One minor supporting paragraph fleshes out, or further explains, a point made in a major supporting paragraph: Some victims keep their illness a secret, which can be deadly.

As the selection and the diagram illustrate, reading multi-paragraph selections does not require a new set of reading strategies. Longer readings require you to refine the reading skills you already have.

SUMMING UP THE KEY POINTS

1. With longer, multi-paragraph readings, titles and headings often identify the author's subject matter along with the point he or she wants to convey.

2. Figuratively speaking, when reading longer selections, you need double vision. You still need to identify main ideas in paragraphs. However, you also need to identify the main or controlling idea of the entire reading. That's the general idea that determines and unifies the content of all the paragraphs.

3. Topic sentences govern paragraphs, but it's thesis statements that govern multi-paragraph readings.

4. The main differences between topic sentences and thesis statements are length and level of generality. Thesis statements can consist of several sentences and express broader and more general ideas than topic sentences normally do. "Florida has been hit hard by the housing crisis" could be the controlling idea of an article. However, "Families in Fort Myers, Florida, have been hit hard by the housing crisis" could be developed in a paragraph.

5. Once you think you know the overall, or controlling, idea of a reading, start asking yourself what each paragraph contributes to that thought. To relate supporting details to the overall main idea, ask questions like these: (1) What kind of specific information does the author supply through supporting details? Are the supporting details examples, statistics, studies? (2) What questions about the main idea does that information answer for readers?

6. It varies with the length of the reading, but for chapter sections in textbooks, if you haven't spotted a thesis statement by the third or fourth paragraph, consider inferring one. To draw your inference, use the various points made in the other paragraphs as the basis for a larger implied generalization.

♦ **EXERCISE 1**   Recognizing Main Ideas in Longer Readings

DIRECTIONS   Read each selection. Then circle the letter of the sentence that best expresses the main idea of the passage.

EXAMPLE

On the Trail of Typhoid Mary

1 On November 11, 1938, a woman called Mary Mallon died of a stroke. She was seventy years old at the time. During her seventy years on earth, death and disease had followed in her wake.* By the time Mary Mallon died, at least three deaths and fifty-three cases of typhoid had been attributed to her, and the press had dubbed* her "Typhoid Mary."

2   In 1906, while working as a cook for New York City banker William Henry Warren, Mallon prepared a sumptuous* dinner—cold cucumber soup, lobster, wild rice, and strawberry ice cream with peaches. Warren and his guests ate heartily. But less than ten days later, several guests ended up in the hospital. All of them were eventually diagnosed with typhoid fever.

3   Careful research and some clever detective work by Dr. George Soper, a sanitary engineer employed by the New York Department of Health, traced the disease to Mary Mallon. Unfortunately, by the time Soper had identified Mallon as the source of infection, she was gone, on to yet another job as a cook or housekeeper. Hot on Mallon's trail, Dr. Soper discovered that the woman changed jobs frequently; wherever she worked, someone developed typhoid fever.

4   When Soper finally caught up with Mallon in 1907, she was hardly apologetic. On the contrary, she chased him away with a carving knife. Mallon only submitted to testing when Soper returned with three policemen. Tests done over her objections showed Mallon carried the bacteria that caused typhoid, but for some reason she herself showed no symptoms of the disease. Told to have her gall bladder removed—the gall bladder was believed to be the site of the infection—Mallon refused and began a lengthy court battle to gain her freedom from hospital isolation.

5   In 1910, Mary Mallon was released. However, she had to promise never to work as a cook again. She also had to report to the New York Department of Health every ninety days so that officials could keep her under close scrutiny.* But by now, the newspapers all knew who Mallon was. Hounded

---

* wake: the course or track left behind by someone or something that has passed.
* dubbed: named.
* sumptuous: delicious, rich, fancy.
* scrutiny: careful study or observation.

by reporters, Mallon disappeared again only to resurface in 1915 when an outbreak of typhoid was reported at the Sloane Hospital for Women.

6   As George Soper had suspected, Mary Mallon had been working in the hospital kitchen shortly before the outbreak. This time, when police caught up with Mallon, they arrested her. By order of the courts, she was confined to Riverside Hospital in New York, where she spent the rest of her life.

Main Idea   a.   In the United States, typhoid fever was once a dangerous disease that took many lives.

b.   Mary Mallon, also known as "Typhoid Mary," fought a lengthy court battle to win her freedom.

ⓒ   By the time she died, Mary Mallon had truly earned her nickname "Typhoid Mary."

EXPLANATION   Statement *c* is correct because it's the answer that best states the main idea of the selection. Statement *a* is incorrect because the selection does not discuss typhoid in general but focuses on how Mary Mallon spread the disease. Statement *b* is inappropriate because the reading has only one sentence about Mary's court battle.

1. Is Romance Essential to Marriage?

1   The majority of Americans and Europeans believe that couples should first fall in love and then get married. Yet in many other countries, including India and China, the reverse is much more common. First, an individual marries someone chosen by family members; *then* the couple find love. Anthropologists say that the arranged marriage is actually common throughout history, with even colonial[†] Americans approaching matrimony in this way. Today, in fact, as many as 60 percent of the world's marriages are still arranged. There appear to be two main reasons why arranged marriages have never gone out of fashion.

2   First of all, in many cultures marriage is viewed as the union of two families, rather than just two people. Because marriage is a valuable tool for creating alliances that benefit both parties, the selection of a mate is considered too important to be left up to the young and inexperienced. Often with the help of professional matchmakers, parents search for someone who possesses the specific temperament, interests, and background that will suit both their child *and* their family.

---

†colonial: relating to the period of time in which America was a colony under British control.

3   Unlike western relationships, which usually begin from chance encounters between two people who may or may not have much in common, the arranged marriage involves a focused search that ends by matching up two very compatible people. Thus, children are raised with the expectation that their parents will help them find the best possible husband or wife so that the blending of the two families will be permanent.

4   The other reason why the tradition of arranged marriage remains strong is the belief that romantic love can hinder the establishment of a lasting partnership. Proponents of arranged marriage believe that in a union based on romance, serious problems can arise when the excitement of courtship begins to fade and the partners' flaws and differences become more apparent. Because arranged marriages are not based on love to begin with, they are not usually dissolved, as many western marriages are, once passion dies. Thus, while about half of romantic marriages end in divorce, only about 5 percent of arranged marriages fail.

5   Still, arranged marriages are not necessarily loveless. On the contrary, in societies that arrange marriages, couples often become loving life partners. Because the spouses were matched based on compatible characteristics, they usually possess the necessary foundation for building mutual respect, affection, and even love. In western marriages, passionate love is often damaged by the intrusion of everyday life. In arranged marriages, however, couples begin their courtship *after* the wedding as they blend gradually blossoming affection with the realities of day-to-day existence.

6   Today, more and more Americans, disillusioned with the dating scene and failed relationships, are beginning to explore some of the methods used in arranged marriages. It's no coincidence that participants of one television reality show called *Married By America* agreed to give viewers the power to decide whom they would marry, based on assessments of the contestants' compatibility. Online dating and matchmaker services, especially those that allow participants to search for someone with very specific qualities, have also grown in popularity. While most Americans are unlikely to change their belief that marriage requires love, they are less scornful of the idea that a successful, happy marriage can be arranged by family, friends, or an interested third party.

Main Idea a. Unlike Americans, people in other countries do not believe that romance is essential to marriage.

        b. Americans and Europeans both believe that romantic love is essential to a good marriage.

        c. Generally speaking, two essential advantages account for the long-standing popularity of arranged marriages.

2. Blind Tom: A Forgotten Prodigy*

1 Born blind and the son of slaves, Thomas Greene Wiggins (1849–1908) was unusually musical. Even as an infant, he could mimic whatever tune he heard. By the age of five, he was composing music. Surprisingly, the boy's owner, a lawyer named James Neil Bethune, fostered Wiggins's obvious talent. As might be expected, however, Bethune, an avid supporter of slavery, had a less than altruistic* motive in mind. Bethune hoped to exhibit the boy around the country as a musical oddity and earn money from the boy's special ability. As it turned out, Bethune was right about the promise of financial gain. Over the years his investment in Thomas Wiggins paid off handsomely: Bethune earned a fortune exploiting Wiggins's natural talent.

2 It wasn't very long before Wiggins, whose stage name was "Blind Tom," was earning Bethune around $100,000 annually, a munificent* sum for the nineteenth century. Needless to say, Wiggins never collected a penny of the money he earned. It all went directly into the pockets of Bethune and Perry Oliver, the white planter who managed Wiggins's career.

3 Although Wiggins could play serious classical music, and his early compositions show real musical merit, both owner and manager insisted on portraying him as a musical oddity. While on stage, Wiggins would sing one song while playing a different one with his right hand. With his left hand, he played still a third. He also performed classical favorites with his hands crossed, imitated famous political speakers, and did on-the-spot imitations of musical instruments, animals, or objects. Labeled by Bethune and Oliver as a freak of nature with a flair for imitation, Wiggins was actually a gifted musician, who could play serious music and needed no weird noises to please the audience.

4 He could play the music of Bach, Beethoven, and Liszt. Even the Europeans, notably critical of American artists, were enthralled by Blind Tom. Respected musicians like Charles Halle and Ignaz Moscheles glowingly praised both the African-American's wit and his technique. Still, no amount of money or praise seemed capable of winning Wiggins the thing he prized most—his freedom.

5 When the end of the Civil War brought freedom within Wiggins's grasp, Bethune found a way to maintain his income at the musician's expense. He persuaded the young man's parents to sign an agreement that bound him over to Bethune for a period of five years. The Bethune family then regularly renewed those contracts until, by 1887, Blind Tom had been in service to his

---

*prodigy: a person of unusual gifts.
*altruistic: unselfish.
*munificent: generous.

former owners for thirty-eight years. He only managed to escape their clutches by retiring from the stage and refusing to perform. Although he did return to the stage occasionally to lay to rest rumors about his death or to challenge the performance of impersonators, he made almost no money from any of those infrequent appearances. Those profits went to Eliza Bethune, James's daughter-in-law. When he died in 1908 of a stroke, Thomas Greene Wiggins was still under the legal guardianship of Eliza.

6   If there is a bright side at all to Wiggins's sad story, it is this: Almost one hundred years after his death, he has finally found a champion. The acclaimed pianist John Davis has released a CD called "John Davis Plays Blind Tom." It contains fourteen pieces of Wiggins's original music, and all of them attest to his skill and originality. In addition, Mr. Davis has created a one-man show devoted to Wiggins's performing life. It is titled "Will the Real Thomas Wiggins Please Stand Up." (Source of information: Thomas L. Riis, "The Legacy of a Prodigy Lost in Mystery," *New York Times,* March 5, 2000, pp. 35–36.)

Main Idea   a.   The life of Thomas Greene Wiggins—also known as "Blind Tom"—is a superb illustration of how spirit can battle circumstance.

b.   Unfortunately, the talents of Thomas Greene Wiggins were exploited by others for most of his life.

c.   In his heart, James Bethune thought he was being generous to allow a slave to play the piano; he never realized what a terrible thing he had done to Thomas Greene Wiggins, the man who made Bethune rich.

◆ **EXERCISE 2**   Recognizing Main Ideas in Longer Readings

DIRECTIONS   Read each selection. Then circle the letter of the sentence that best expresses the main idea of the passage.

1. **No Diet Books on the Fiji Islands**

1 On the Fiji Islands of the South Pacific, diet books would never be the big sellers they are in the United States. Although Fiji Islanders have definite ideas about how a person should look, they don't much care about being overweight. On the contrary, Fijians like sturdy muscles and a generally well-fed look in both men and women. To a large degree, the preference for plumpness among Fijians stems from their culture's emphasis on community rather than appearance.

2   Unlike Americans, who prize individualism, the Fijians care more about the good of the community than they do about themselves as individuals. For them, standing out in a crowd is never as important as showing a nurturing and caring attitude toward friends. And what is the primary vehicle for showing your friends you care for them? It's serving them food, of course. For the Fijians, offering food to friends and family is a way of showing you're concerned about their physical and emotional well-being. At dinnertime, Fijians routinely open their windows and doors so that the aroma of the meal will waft outside and attract passersby. Extra food is always prepared so that anyone attracted by the smell of dinner can stop by for a snack. It is, in fact, a social disgrace not to have enough food for drop-in guests.

3   Because of their perspective on food and its cultural significance, Fijians consider dieting socially unacceptable. Dieting prevents the person invited to dine from accepting the invitation. In addition, what dieter would willingly prepare huge, tempting meals for friends and family? Thus, parents watch their children carefully for signs that they might be losing weight. They do so not because they want their children to achieve and maintain a certain weight but because they want to make sure their children are fully participating in the community through the sharing of food.

4   As a result of the Fijians' attitude toward food, children in particular are spared the painful experience so common to Americans of all ages—the failed diet. They aren't obsessed by their personal appearance and they don't constantly compare themselves to those a bit trimmer or thinner. If anything, they pity others for failing to be appropriately plump. However, the Fijian emphasis on food and the celebration of body fat does have one drawback. Children who need to limit their intake of calories for reasons of health—say, a child with diabetes—can become anxious or depressed because they are unable to fully participate in the community's common feasting. (Source of information: Seifert, Hoffnung, and Hoffnung, *Lifespan Development*, pp. 264–65.)

Main Idea a. Thanks to Fijians' attitudes toward dieting, children don't feel that their personal appearance is all that counts in life.

b. The Fijians don't care about being overweight because for them the sense of community created by the sharing of food is more important than one's personal appearance.

c. Americans are extremely individualistic; as a result, they tend to place too much emphasis on personal appearance and are overly obsessed with being thin.

d. On the whole, Fijian children are happier and more confident than American children.

2. The Ebbinghaus Experiments

1 At the end of the nineteenth century, a German psychologist named Hermann Ebbinghaus became interested in the carefully controlled laboratory experiments being used to do research in the fields of physiology* and physics. He was so impressed with the experiments' results that he decided to introduce similar methods into the study of human memory.

2 Using only himself as a subject, Ebbinghaus devoted six years of research to his experiments. In one of his experiments, he memorized lists of nonsense syllables, put them aside for specified amounts of time, and then relearned them. By comparing the time taken to learn the lists with the time taken to relearn them, Ebbinghaus was able to reach several important conclusions about the role of memory in learning. After more than a century of research, these conclusions have been repeatedly confirmed.

Rates of Forgetting

3 As a result of his research, Ebbinghaus maintained that the rate of forgetting becomes progressively slower over time. A list of nonsense syllables that he had memorized and put aside for an hour required more than half the original study time to relearn. But a list that had been put aside for nine hours was not, as one would expect, totally forgotten. The rate of forgetting had slowed down, and only two-thirds of the original study time was required to relearn the nonsense syllables.

4 Since 1885, when Ebbinghaus first published his work, investigators have studied the rate of forgetting. They have used not only nonsense syllables but also passages of prose, lists of facts, and excerpts from poetry. Like Ebbinghaus, they have discovered that the rate of forgetting slows down over time. It is rapid at first but becomes slower as the amount of time between learning and relearning increases.

Overlearning

5 Another of Ebbinghaus's conclusions confirmed by modern research is that overlearning during the initial learning period makes relearning at a later time easier. Based on his experiments, Ebbinghaus maintained that the more repetitions involved in the original learning, the fewer repetitions needed for relearning. Later investigators have come to a similar conclusion. However, they have also concluded that each repetition will not produce an equal return in time saved during the relearning period. After a

---

*physiology: the study of how the body functions.

point, the repetition of material already memorized does not produce a sufficient reward.

Distributed Learning

6 Research that followed Ebbinghaus's experiments by more than half a century also confirmed his belief that learning sessions devoted to memorizing are more effective if they are distributed over time. In 1940, an American psychologist, A. P. Bumstead, decided to do a series of experiments to determine whether it was better to have several short learning sessions spaced out over a period of time or one long, unbroken learning session. Using only himself as a subject, Bumstead memorized several different poetry selections, spacing his learning sessions at intervals that varied from one hour to eight days. After finishing the experiment, Bumstead concluded that increasing the time between learning sessions actually decreased the amount of time needed to memorize the material.

Main Idea a. Thanks to Ebbinghaus, we know how to do controlled laboratory experiments that test the power of human memory.

b. More research is needed to confirm Ebbinghaus's early conclusions about the nature of memory.

c. Research has shown that Ebbinghaus's claims about learning and memory are correct.

d. Research has proven that Ebbinghaus was right when he claimed that the rate of forgetting slows down with the passage of time.

CHECK YOUR UNDERSTANDING

1. What extra clues to the topic and main idea do longer readings provide?

_____

_____

2. With longer readings, what should you do in addition to identifying the main idea of individual paragraphs?

_____

_____

3. What are the two main differences between topic sentences and thesis statements?

_____

_____

4. What questions should you ask once you think you understand the point of the reading?

_____

_____

_____

5. If you haven't spotted the thesis statement of a chapter section by the third or fourth paragraph, what should you do?

_____

Implied Main Ideas in Longer Readings

In longer readings, the controlling main idea is usually expressed in a thesis statement. Much of the time, that statement appears somewhere in the first three or four paragraphs, right after the title, heading, or introduction.

However, authors do sometimes expect readers to infer the implied main idea that unifies the entire reading. Here's an example:

The Gorilla's Two Faces

1 Even die-hard wrestling fans don't remember his name anymore, but in the mid-sixties, the wrestler Gorilla Monsoon was a major star. At 6 feet and 6 inches, Monsoon was a towering figure. He weighed more than four hundred pounds and fought some eight thousand bouts. When announcers said his name, their voices tended to quaver a little, for Gorilla was wrestling's first real "bad guy." He was the wrestler audiences loved to hate because he was tougher and meaner than anyone else around.

2 Wearing a body suit with one strap draped over his massive shoulder, Gorilla would enter the ring looking as if he could, in a hungry moment, chew rusty nails and easily digest them. After toying with his opponent for a while, he liked to end the bout with the wrestling hold that helped make him famous. Knocking his opponent to the floor, he would wrap the man's

feet around his enormous waist. Seemingly without effort, he would then lift and twirl his opponent round and round, keeping the man just about at waist level for at least thirty seconds. To further embroider his image of pure evil, Gorilla would cackle with laughter the entire time. Staged or not, it was a terrifying display, and the audience couldn't get enough of it.

3   Out of the ring, however, Gorilla Monsoon was Robert Morella. Quiet and soft-spoken, he had a college education. Prior to becoming a wrestler, he had been a high school teacher. But the money was bad, and wrestling was more lucrative. Mr. Morella, as he liked to be called, also had a way with words. When asked why anyone would ever pay to see grown men throw one another around in a ring, he paused for a moment and then paraphrased St. Augustine:[†] "For those who believe in our sport, no explanation is necessary."

4   He was equally articulate when interviewed, long past his heyday, about the current state of wrestling. Asked about the new and more profitable face of wrestling, he didn't have to think twice before shrugging it off as little more than people from the pages of "comic books." From his perspective, wrestling in the old days was a more serious sport, and "people really thought I was the Devil incarnate."[*] (Source of information: David Hadju, "When Wrestling Was Noir," *New York Times Magazine*, January 2, 2000, p. 43.)

© Bettmann/Corbis

Out of the ring, Robert Morella, a.k.a. Gorilla Monsoon, was quiet and gentle, but in the ring he was a loud and terrifying presence.

Generally speaking, this reading breaks into two sections. In the first section, we learn about Gorilla Monsoon's professional image as the wrestler everyone loved to hate. But in the second, a new image emerges along with Gorilla's real name, Robert Morella. Out of the ring, Morella was anything but the hulking bully he portrayed in it. Yet if we look for a thesis statement that sums up both sides of Gorilla's personality, we won't find it. Almost all the sentences in the reading are equally specific, and there is no general statement summarizing them. On the contrary, we have to infer one like the following: "Sixties wrestler Gorilla Monsoon may have looked like the

---

[†]St. Augustine (354–430): Catholic saint who, when questioned about his faith, responded, "For those who believe, no explanation is necessary."
[*]incarnate: in the flesh; representing a perfect example of something.

Devil incarnate in the ring, but out of it, he was a thoughtful man who took his profession seriously."

Much of the time, longer, multi-paragraph readings will contain a thesis statement. But just like paragraphs, they won't always. If you read an article, an essay, or a chapter section and don't find any general statements that combine and summarize the meaning of the more specific ones, you need to infer a main idea that sums up the reading.

◆ **EXERCISE 3**   Recognizing Implied Main Ideas

DIRECTIONS   Read each selection. Then circle the letter of the sentence that best expresses the implied main idea.

EXAMPLE

Death, Past and Present

1 In the early nineteenth century, when the country was still largely rural, families cared for their dying relatives and friends. They prepared the corpses for burial and dug the graves by hand. They laid out the bodies of the dead in the parlors of their homes and commemorated the lives of the departed. Then they buried the deceased in family or community cemeteries.

2   The beginning of the nineteenth century was a time when epidemics and famines wiped out huge numbers of people, so there were constant reminders that death was a reality. Communities were small and closely knit, and death was taken personally by most members. Mourning rituals were community-wide events. Because adult life expectancy was short, and infant mortality high, death seemed a natural, if distressing, part of daily life.

3   Now, however, medical advances have added years to the average life span. As a result, more people die in hospitals or nursing homes, to which they have gone because they are too ill or too frail to live at home by themselves or in the homes of relatives. Living in facilities separated from their family members, many of those who die are no longer widely known to all of their kin. Burial of the dead has also been handed over to funeral parlors and takes place far away from the home of the deceased. Relatives participate in but do not organize the commemorative ceremonies. That job is handled by funeral directors who prepare the body for viewing and determine the hours of public mourning.

4   In contrast to times past, workplaces have now established rules governing the time employees can take off from work following the death of a
close family member. Such institutional constraints on behavior have
imposed social uniformity and a more formal aura* on what were once
individual and diverse patterns of grief and bereavement. In short, death
has become institutionalized, with, for instance, funeral homes deciding on
the manner of grieving and mode of burial. In some cases, it is also the
funeral home that shapes the expression of mourning by providing grief
counseling programs for the relatives of those who have died. (Adapted
from James, *Crisis Intervention Strategies*, p. 364.)

Implied Main Idea a. Modern medicine has destroyed the American family.

b. Family ties have become so weakened by the stresses of modern life
that adult children no longer care when their elderly parents die.

ⓒ Death is handled very differently now than it was in the early nineteenth century.

d. Although the way people handle the death of relatives has changed,
one thing has stayed the same: People have always feared dying and
pretended it would not happen to them.

EXPLANATION   This is an example of an extended reading that contrasts death in the early nineteenth century with death in modern life.
The author, however, does not explicitly state the point of the contrasts.
Readers are meant to infer the idea that we treat death today in a way
very different from the way we did in times past.

1. What Makes a True Believer?

1 If astrology and handwriting analysis have no scientific basis, why do they
remain so popular? One explanation is the "Barnum effect"—the tendency
for people to accept vague, ambiguous,* and general statements as
accurate descriptions of their personalities (French, Fowler, and McCarthy,
1991). The Barnum effect is named after the famous circus owner
P. T. Barnum, who declared, "There's a sucker born every minute."

2   Handwriting analysis and astrological readings often sound something
like this (based on Forer, 1949):

> You have a great need for other people to like you and admire you. You
> have a tendency to be critical of yourself. You have a great deal of unused

---

*aura: feeling, atmosphere.
*ambiguous: open to interpretation.

capacity, which you have not used to your advantage. At times, you are extroverted,* affable, and sociable. At times, you are shy, wary, and reserved. Some of your aspirations* tend to be pretty unrealistic. Security is one of your major goals in life.

3   People are often amazed by how "accurate" such reports are. As a result, they may conclude that there must be something to horoscopes or handwriting analysis (French, Fowler, and McCarthy, 1991; McKelvie, 1990). The trick is that such a general statement is likely to sound accurate to just about *anyone*. In P. T. Barnum's words, it has "a little something for everyone."

4   The Barnum effect goes hand in hand with another aspect of human reasoning that encourages illogical beliefs. We tend to give the most credence* to information that confirms our expectations and to discount information that doesn't confirm our expectations (Nisbett and Ross, 1980). So we are likely to remember the few times that our horoscope precisely matched our experience and forget the many other times it didn't. Or we focus on the two or three accurate statements in our handwriting analysis and ignore the seven or eight inaccurate ones. The mass media reinforce these biases. If an astrologer correctly predicts the date a world leader is assassinated, for example, the prediction will be picked up as "news," but the thousands of times such predictions are false do not make the headlines. (Rubin et al., *Psychology*, p. 35.)

Implied Main Idea   a.   There are two different reasons why people believe in pseudosciences like astrology and handwriting analysis.

b.   The public's belief in astrology continues to grow despite the fact that there is no scientific basis for astrological forecasts.

c.   The term "Barnum effect" refers to the readiness of people to believe what they wish to believe, avoiding all evidence to the contrary.

d.   Particularly in times of social unrest, people are far too ready to believe in shaky science that is not backed by sound evidence.

2. The Future of Genetic Testing

1   In August 2000, a test-tube baby named Adam Nash was born in Denver, Colorado. After cutting Adam's umbilical cord, doctors collected some cells from that cord. A month later, they infused those same cells into the circulatory system of Adam's six-year-old sister, Molly. The procedure was necessary to save Molly's life.

---

*extroverted: outgoing.
*aspirations: hopes, desires.
*credence: belief.

2   Afflicted with a rare bone marrow disease called Fanconi anemia, Molly's only hope was a cell transplant from a sibling. Because both parents carried the Fanconi gene, which gave them a 25 percent chance of giving birth to a child carrying the same disease as Molly, doctors needed to select an embryo not affected by the disease-carrying gene. That selection process could only be carried out in an in vitro–produced pregnancy followed by sophisticated gene testing. Doctors would test embryo cells to discover which of them did not carry the diseased gene and then impregnate the mother with only those cells that tested normal.

3   In part at least, the Nash case resembles a similar one from 1989, which involved sixteen-year-old Anissa Ayala, a young girl diagnosed with a lethal form of leukemia. In an effort to save her life, the girl's father, Abe Ayala, had his vasectomy reversed so that he and his wife, Mary, could have a third child who would be a bone marrow donor for Anissa. Although the Ayalas had a one-in-four chance of having a child with the right cells to be a donor, luck was on their side. Genetic testing showed that Anissa's newborn sister, Marissa, had inherited all the right genes, and she did, in fact, prove to be an ideal donor. Thanks to Marissa, Anissa got a new lease on life.

4   In situations like these, genetic testing does indeed seem a godsend. Certainly, this perspective is promoted by Charles Strom, director of the Illinois Masonic Medical Center, which was heavily involved in both cases. Thanks to genetic testing, lives can be saved and tragedy avoided. As long as the children born to be donors are loved, says Strom, that's all that matters; and in both cases, the children born to save their siblings are very much cherished.

5   Yet both cases raise a serious question: Are the increasing sophistication and use of genetic testing always a cause for jubilation?* If you ask Jeffrey Kahn, director of the University of Minnesota's Center for Bioethics,† the answer is no. Mr. Kahn takes issue not with the subject of children who come into the world to be donors but with the use of genetic testing to search out or avoid specific traits. He fears a future in which reproductive technology allows some parents—primarily those who can afford it—to choose their children's physical and mental makeup. Kahn, who is as pessimistic as Strom is optimistic, claims that having a child "is quickly becoming like buying a car." Parents can choose the options they do or do not want. He believes that as genetic tests become more available to the

---

*jubilation: joy, celebration.
†bioethics: the study of moral and ethical implications caused by new scientific discoveries.

public, there will be more and more parents asking for "embryos without a predisposition* to homosexuality or for kids who will grow to more than six feet tall."

6   Although Kahn's argument smacks of slippery slope† logic, it does seem plausible that some parents, intent on shaping their children's future, would insist on genetic testing in order to select or reject certain traits. The question is, Will those researchers and doctors currently involved in creating even more sophisticated forms of genetic testing allow parents easy access to the tests, or will they restrict access to cases of dire emergency? Because there's no guarantee that genetic tests won't become available for a price, it's hard not to share Kahn's concerns that the tests will be used not solely to save lives, but also to create "designer babies" tailored to suit their parents' specifications.* (Sources of information: Rick Weiss, "Test-Tube Baby Born to Save Ill Sister," *Washington Post*, October 3, 2000; Abigail Trafford, "Miracle Babies Draw Us into an Ethical Swamp," *Washington Post*, November 14, 2000, p. 28.)

Implied Main Idea a. The negative consequences of genetic testing far outweigh its positive uses.

b. Genetic testing can be positive or negative, depending on the uses to which it's put.

c. Thanks to genetic testing, children like Molly Nash now have a chance to lead a normal life.

d. Genetic testing has rightly become the center of a serious ethical controversy.

3. Side Effects of Using Physical Punishment on Children

1 Concerned about how to safely and effectively discipline their children, most parents, even the highly authoritarian* ones, want to know if there is a drawback to using a physical punishment like spanking. The answer to that question is not simple. Certainly, one problem with physical punishment has to do with the pain and discomfort it causes. As a result, both the parents who punish and the situation that brings punishment about

---

*predisposition: leaning.
† slippery slope: an error in logic in which it's assumed that one event will lead to similar, and even more serious, events no matter what the context.
*specifications: requirements, desires.
Note: As of 2006, Adam and Molly were both doing well.
*authoritarian: demanding strict obedience.

become associated with fear, resentment, and dislike, sometimes all three. This negative response to physical punishment makes it especially ineffective to use when toilet training children or teaching them table manners.

2   **Learning Avoidance Techniques**   A second problem is that aversive stimuli[†] encourage escape or avoidance learning. With *escape learning*, the child responds to the threat of punishment by misbehaving and then disappearing. With *avoidance learning*, the child finds a way to postpone or prevent the pain of punishment. Children who run away from punishing parents (escape learning) may start to lie about their behavior or spend long stretches away from home (avoidance learning).

3   **Encouraging Aggression**   A third problem with physical punishment is that it often increases *aggression* in the same way that animals react to pain by attacking whoever or whatever else is around (Azrin et al., 1965). Likewise, humans who are in pain have a tendency to lash out at others.

4   We also know that aggression is one of the most common responses to frustration. Generally speaking, punishment is painful, frustrating, or both. Punishment, therefore, sets up a powerful environment for learning aggression. Children who are spanked often feel angry, frustrated, and hostile. Then they engage in aggressive acts like slapping other children in order to release feelings of anger and frustration. In this vicious cycle, aggression gets rewarded and will tend to occur again in similar situations. (Source of information: Coon, *Essentials of Psychology*, pp. 258–59.)

Implied Main Idea   a. The problem with physical punishment is that it greatly increases aggressive behavior in children.

     b. Punishment, particularly physical punishment, encourages children to lie.

     c. Parents who physically punish their children are likely to become objects of fear.

     d. Using physical punishment to control behavior has several major drawbacks.

4. The Presidency of John F. Kennedy

1 President John F. Kennedy was, as novelist Norman Mailer wrote, "our leading man." Young and handsome, the new chief executive was the first president born in the twentieth century. Considered an intellectual by the

---

[†]aversive stimuli: things that provoke avoidance or escape behavior.

public, he had a genuinely inquiring mind, and, as a patron of the arts, he brought wit and sophistication to the White House.

2   In contrast to the Eisenhower administration, the new president surrounded himself with young men who had fresh ideas for invigorating* the nation. (Kennedy appointed only one woman to a significant position.) Secretary of Defense Robert McNamara, age forty-four, had been an assistant professor at Harvard at twenty-four and later the whiz-kid president of the Ford Motor Company. Kennedy's special assistant for national security affairs, McGeorge Bundy, age forty-one, had become a Harvard dean at thirty-four with a bachelor's degree. Kennedy was only forty-three, and his brother Robert, the attorney general, was thirty-five.

3   Still, Kennedy's ambitious program, known as the "New Frontier," promised more than the president could deliver: an end to racial discrimination, federal aid to education, medical care for the elderly, and government action to halt the economic decline the country was suffering. Only eight months into his first year, it was evident that Kennedy lacked the ability to move Congress, which was dominated by a conservative group of Republicans and southern Democrats. In that year, Kennedy saw the defeat of bills providing for federal aid to education and a boost in the minimum wage.

4   Struggling to please conservative members of Congress, the new president did not pursue civil rights with vigor. Kennedy did establish the President's Committee on Equal Employment Opportunity to eliminate racial discrimination in government hiring. But he waited until late 1962 before honoring a 1960 campaign pledge to issue an executive order† forbidding segregation in federally funded housing. The struggle for racial equality was the most important social issue of the time, and Kennedy's performance disappointed civil rights supporters. (Adapted from Norton et al., *A People and a Nation*, p. 620.)

Implied Main Idea   a. During his short term as president, John F. Kennedy introduced far-reaching social legislation that still affects our lives today.

         b. There has never been another president as handsome and cultured as John F. Kennedy.

         c. Despite his glamorous image and brilliant administration, John F. Kennedy never fulfilled his plans for the New Frontier.

         d. Over time, John F. Kennedy's image has been tarnished.

---

*invigorating: energizing.
†executive order: an order issued by the president and having the force of law.

5. **The Pros and Cons of Tort Reform**

1   In Houston, a woman who scalded herself with hot coffee sued McDonald's and won $2.9 million (later reduced to a "mere" $480,000). In Maine, a woman golfer hit a shot that bounced off an obstacle and struck her in the face. She sued the country club and won $40,000. In Connecticut, a twelve-year-old Little League baseball player uncorked a wild throw that conked a woman in the stands. The woman promptly sued the player and the local government. In New York City, several prison inmates somehow shot themselves in the feet and then sued the city for negligence.

2   Such stories seem to be increasingly common, as 800,000 lawyers in the United States seek to justify their existence and citizens look for an easy dollar instead of for a sense of personal responsibility. The results are a reduction in the gross national product of an estimated $2.5 million per attorney, personal and corporate financial tragedies, and local governments that must hike taxes to cover legal fees and liability settlements.

3   The biggest problem is that of *torts,* damage suits over product liability, personal injury, medical malpractice, and related claims. Throughout the twentieth century, state courts gradually eliminated restrictions on tort liability and substituted legal doctrines favoring plaintiffs* over defendants. For example, nearly all states have a strict liability rule for product safety. This means that manufacturers of defective products (or even very hot coffee) may be held fully liable for damages caused by their product, regardless of whether the manufacturer was negligent.

4   Today, state legislatures are actively engaged in tort reform that shifts the advantage more toward defendants. Punitive damage awards have been capped in Alabama, New Jersey, Illinois, Texas, and other states. Laws protecting local governments and their employees from exorbitant* liability awards have been adopted in several states. There has been a surge of business interest in judicial* elections in California and other states, as judges known for generous tort decisions have come under electoral* attack and, in some cases, gone down to defeat.

5   Aligned against tort reform are powerful trial lawyers; litigation,* product liability, and personal injury suits are their bread and butter. Also against tort reform are certain consumer groups, who see unlimited tort liability as a fundamental right for injured citizens and a means to hold individuals

---

*plaintiffs: people who bring the suit to court wanting damages.
*exorbitant: excessive, especially in the sense of price or demands.
*judicial: related to the courts and judges.
*electoral: related to voting.
*litigation: lawsuits.

and firms accountable for shoddy and dangerous practices and merchandise. These opponents of tort reform are fighting against insurance companies, manufacturers, and others in courtrooms and in state capitols. Recently, the supreme courts of several states (e.g., Indiana, Ohio, and Oregon) have overturned tort reforms. (Adapted from Bowman and Kearney, *State and Local Government*, p. 268.)

Implied Main Idea
a. Tort reform has been a long time coming, but the public, fed up with lawsuits, has decided to take the plunge and reduce the rewards of litigation.

b. While many states are actively engaged in tort reform, both lawyers and consumers fear that the reforms will go too far.

c. Lawsuits over product liability are a menace to the economy and to citizens' sense of personal liability; they are fueled more by the lure of easy money than by any real harm done by a product.

d. Although state legislators are working hard to protect companies from lawsuits over product liability, consumers are worried that injured citizens will lose their right to sue those who caused the damages.

READING TIP Look at the beginning of paragraphs for the answer to two questions that should *always* be on a reader's mind: Why does this paragraph follow the previous one? What connects them to one another?

♦ **EXERCISE 4** Inferring the Main Idea

DIRECTIONS Read each selection. Then infer the implied main idea and write it in the blank lines that follow.

EXAMPLE

Are You Sure You Want to Be a Leader?

1 The word *leader* has positive connotations for most people. Thus, most of us, if asked whether we would like to be in a position of leadership, will say yes. To be sure, being a leader has its satisfactions. Leadership brings with it power and prestige. Often it brings status, respect, and opportunities for professional advancement and financial gain. Yet those of us intent on pursuing leadership roles in our professional lives don't always take

into account the fact that leaders are usually expected to work longer hours than other employees are. Actually, people in organizational leadership positions typically spend about fifty-five hours per week working. During periods of peak demand, this figure can rise to eighty hours per week.

2   Being a leader is also a good way to discover the validity of Murphy's law: "If anything can go wrong, it will." A leader is constantly required to solve numerous problems involving both people and things. Because of those problems and the difficulties attendant on solving them, many people find leadership positions enormously stressful. As a result, many managers experience burnout and abandon their positions.

3   In addition, people in managerial positions complain repeatedly that they are held responsible for things over which they have little control. As a leader, for example, you might be expected to work with an ill-performing team member, yet you might not have the power to fire him or her. You might also be called on to produce a high-quality service or product but not be given the staff or the funds to get the job done effectively.

4   In a sense, the higher you rise as a leader, the more lonely you are likely to be. After all, leadership limits the number of people in whom you can confide. It is awkward, not to mention unprofessional, to complain about one of your employees to another employee. Then, too, you need to be wary about voicing complaints against your superiors to the people who work for you. Such complaints are bad for morale. Even worse, they can threaten your job security. Not surprisingly, people in leadership positions complain that they miss being "one of the gang."

5   People at all levels of an organization, from the office assistant to the chairperson of the board, must be aware of political factors. Yet you can avoid politics more easily as an individual contributor than you can as a leader. As a leader you have to engage in political byplay from three directions: below, sideways, and upward. Political tactics such as forming alliances and coalitions are a necessary part of a leader's role. (Adapted from Dubrin, *Leadership,* pp. 16–17.)

Implied Main Idea   Although being a leader has some very positive consequences, it also has some negative ones that need to be carefully considered.

EXPLANATION   Although the first paragraph opens by describing the positive consequences of being a leader, most of the paragraphs describe the negative effects of assuming a leadership role. But if you look for a general statement that sums up both the positive and the negative consequences of leadership, you won't find it. What this means is that the reader has to draw an inference like the one shown above.

1. The Reality of Prison Life

1 Many Americans firmly believe that prison inmates spend their days lifting weights, watching television, or playing basketball while hard-working taxpayers pay for prisoners' food, clothing, shelter, education, and health care. However, in a minimum-security prison, the day typically begins with a wake-up call at 6:00 a.m. Prisoners then head for the community bathrooms. Because hundreds of men often share a bathroom, they usually wait in line to use the facilities. Inmates are also expected to make their beds and clean their cells.

2 Prisons are noisy. Arguments, fistfights, and robberies among convicts are common. Many prisons, even those in sweltering southern states, are not air-conditioned. In spite of regular cleaning, they often smell of urine and body odor because fresh air cannot enter the sealed buildings.

3 At many institutions, prisoners might attend psychological counseling or educational programs for part of the day, the goal of which is to provide some therapeutic* benefit. But everyone who is able usually works between four and eight hours daily. At some of this country's penal institutions, inmates labor in prison factories where they are paid somewhere between $0.25 and $1.35 per hour. Others are assigned to food service, laundry, maintenance, or janitorial service. A typical workday lasts from 7:30 a.m. to 3:30 p.m., with a break for lunch. Yet the majority of prisoners earn less than $25 a month, out of which they must buy their snacks, sodas, aspirins, and toiletries.

4 At 4:00 p.m. every day, prisoners must be in their cells and on their feet while guards count heads and make sure everyone is present. From 4:30 p.m. until the evening meal and then again until about 9:30 p.m., prisoners read mail, watch one of three available television channels, exercise, play cards and board games, or receive visitors. After these visits, prisoners are strip-searched before going back to their cell blocks, where they can watch television, wait in long lines to use the telephone, or visit with other inmates until lights out at 11:30.

Implied Main Idea _Although many Americans think prisoners spend their day having fun, they actually have many responsibilities_

*therapeutic: related to healing.

[handwritten margin note: Many americans think prison life is easy, when it actually isn't]

2. **Is Local News Really News?**

1 News is frequently defined as the telling of factual stories meant to inform the public about significant events. Thus, when you turn on your local television newscast every evening, you probably expect to hear about recent events in your community. You might even consider yourself an informed citizen because you're in the habit of watching your local news program. However, while watching your local news, it's unlikely that you will see or hear many reports about significant events concerning politics, culture, business, and government. Instead, you're probably learning about violent crimes, major accidents, deadly disasters, and celebrity breakups.

2 In a half-hour local news broadcast, only about fifteen minutes are left once the time for commercials, weather, sports, traffic, and bantering by news anchors is subtracted. This is not much time to relate all of the news of the day. Therefore, each individual news story is necessarily quite short. In fact, studies have shown that 70 percent of all news stories are no more than a minute long. Forty-three percent are less than thirty seconds long. Only about 16 percent of stories are longer than two minutes; in the television news industry, any story more than a minute and a half long is billed as an "in-depth" report.

3 Typically, the television news anchors who introduce or read these stories are not experts in any of the fields—such as education, the environment, business, government, and health—that are covered. Most are hired not for their understanding of the news but for their ability to read a story well while conveying the specific emotion (anger, fear, sympathy, admiration, disgust, etc.) appropriate to that story. The reporters who gather the stories are not experts either. They are hired primarily for their ability to communicate well on camera, as well as for their writing skill and general common sense. Plus, reporters are under tremendous pressure to produce a story. They are usually assigned a particular story about midmorning; then they have but a few hours to gather the facts and write the story so that it can be edited with video and ready for a 5:00 or 6:00 p.m. broadcast. As a result, reporters have little time for research, and their sources tend to be thin: Only 25 percent of TV news stories have more than one source. Not surprisingly, news directors avoid assigning hundreds of important stories that would require some real research.

4 The truth is that television news broadcasts feature stories that readily lend themselves to videotape footage and pictures. This is why there's so little coverage of events that are important but difficult to illustrate, such as political speeches, school board meetings, or city council sessions. One

survey revealed that only about 7 percent of news stories cover economic issues. Another study of 6,000 news stories showed that only 9 percent of them concerned poverty or welfare. Instead, TV news focuses on events that are relatively trivial but also very visual, and it tends to sensationalize those events by making them look even more dramatic than they actually were.

5   In addition to avoiding nonvisual news stories, TV newscasts seldom include negative stories about their advertisers or about police officers and firefighters. According to one survey, more than half of news directors interviewed said that they had been pressured by advertisers to either kill critical stories or promote favorable ones. The largest number of consumer complaints concern new car dealerships, but because car dealers buy a lot of commercial airtime, they are rarely subjected to a news station's scrutiny.

6   Neither will viewers see many critical stories about grocery and clothing stores, shopping malls, banks, insurance and health care providers, soda manufacturers, or fast-food restaurants, all of which buy a significant amount of commercial airtime. Police and firefighters are also rarely cast in a negative light on local TV news stations because reporters need the cooperation of law enforcement and public safety officials to get the crime stories that are their lifeblood. That's why viewers see few, if any, stories about issues like radar traps, brutality, and/or police or firefighter mistakes. (Sources of statistics: Amy Mitchell, "The Big Picture," *Columbia Journalism Review*, January/February 1999, www.archives.cjr.org/year/99/1/pej/picture .asp; Greg Byron, "TV News: What Local Stations Don't Want You to Know," www.tfs.net/~gbyron/tvnews1.html.)

Implied Main Idea _____

The local news is often decieving to the viewers.

of local news

The local news

VOCABULARY CHECK

The following words were introduced in pages 431–51. Match the word to the definition. Review words, definitions, and original context two or three times before taking the vocabulary test. (The page numbers in parentheses indicate where the word first appeared.)

1. wake (p. 431) _____
2. dubbed (p. 431) _____
3. sumptuous (p. 431) _____
4. scrutiny (p. 431) _____
5. prodigy (p. 434) _____
6. altruistic (p. 434) _____
7. munificent (p. 434) _____
8. physiology (p. 437) _____
9. incarnate (p. 440) _____
10. aura (p. 442) _____
11. ambiguous (p. 442) _____
12. extroverted (p. 443) _____
13. aspirations (p. 443) _____
14. credence (p. 443) _____
15. jubilation (p. 444) _____
16. predisposition (p. 445) _____
17. specifications (p. 445) _____
18. authoritarian (p. 445) _____
19. invigorating (p. 447) _____
20. plaintiffs (p. 448) _____
21. exorbitant (p. 448) _____
22. judicial (p. 448) _____
23. electoral (p. 448) _____
24. litigation (p. 448) _____
25. therapeutic (p. 451) _____

a. generous
b. the study of how the body functions
c. open to interpretation
d. the course or track left behind by someone or something that has passed
e. belief
f. hopes, desires
g. people who bring a suit to court wanting damages
h. excessive, particularly in relation to prices or demands
i. lawsuits
j. demanding strict obedience
k. unselfish
l. close study or observation
m. a person of unusual gifts
n. delicious, rich, fancy
o. related to healing
p. celebration, joy
q. named
r. leaning
s. outgoing
t. requirements, desires
u. atmosphere, feeling
v. in the flesh, representing a perfect example of something
w. related to the courts and judges
x. energizing
y. related to voting

Taking Notes with Informal Outlines

Even when you don't create a skeletal outline to test your comprehension, think about using informal outlining for note-taking. Informal outlines are an excellent device for readings with lots of details that are more abstract* than concrete.*

Making an Informal Outline

As you know from Chapter 1, informal outlines have no fixed format. You can mix phrases with sentences and leave an *a* without a *b*. The only test of an informal outline is how well it works for you. If your outline (1) records the main idea of the entire reading, (2) identifies the details essential to understanding that idea, and (3) shows the relationship between them, it's perfect. Here's an informal outline based on the reading on pages 446–47 about John F. Kennedy's New Frontier.

Main Idea Kennedy's New Frontier made promises it couldn't keep.

Supporting Details 1. Failed Promises: ① end to racial discrimination, ② more federal aid to education, ③ medical care for elderly, ④ government intervention in economy

    a. lacked ability to move Congress

    b. 1961: defeat of federal aid to education and increase in minimum wage

2. K. didn't pursue civil rights agenda.

    a. waited until '62 before issuing an executive order stopping segregation in federally funded housing

    b. did establish Commission on Equal Employment Opportunity

To a large degree, how you organize an informal outline is up to you. Still, there are some definite guidelines to follow if you want to take notes that are brief, complete, and well organized.

---

*abstract: describes ideas that cannot be understood or felt by the physical senses, e.g., justice, honesty.
*concrete: describes ideas that can be comprehended by one or more physical senses.

Guidelines for Informal Outlining
◆

1. **Indent to show relationships.** Even with a quick glance, your outline should clearly identify the main idea of the entire reading. Always start off by writing the main idea close to the left-hand margin. Underneath and indented, list the supporting details used to explain it.

2. **Condense and abbreviate.** Whenever you can, use phrases instead of sentences. If possible, make up your own shorthand for common words and use it consistently. If a name appears several times, spell it out once, then use initials. For example, in the sample notes, Kennedy becomes K.

3. **Paraphrase the author's words.** If you just copy the author's words into your outline, you can't be sure you've understood them. An outline of ideas you haven't completely grasped is not going to do you much good when finals roll around.

4. **Leave plenty of space.** Think of your outline as a work in progress. As you gather additional information from lectures or outside reading, you may want to add to it, so leave plenty of space in your initial outline in the margins and between sentences.

5. **Reorder the material if it helps you remember it.** There's no law saying you have to re-create the author's original pattern of presentation. If you think combining facts or ideas that actually appear in separate paragraphs will help you remember them more easily, then, by all means, do it.

◆ **EXERCISE 5** **Note-Taking with Informal Outlines**

DIRECTIONS Read and outline each selection.

EXAMPLE

Harriet Tubman and the Underground Railroad[†]

1 Even though the famed abolitionist* Harriet Tubman (1820?–1913) gave several interviews about her early life, the facts are hard to verify.* There are, for example, no exact records of her birth, although most history books cite 1820 as the year she was born. However, one item in Harriet Tubman's

---

[†] Underground Railroad: an organization that helped slaves escape to freedom.
*abolitionist: a person who wanted to end slavery.
*verify: prove true.

biography needs no verification: Because of her efforts, hundreds of slaves found their way to freedom.

2   According to Tubman's own account, she decided on her life's work when she was only thirteen years old. Badly beaten and wounded in the head by her owner, she prayed that guilt would make him repent and see the light. But when he came to visit her, intent only on seeing if she was well enough to sell, the girl realized that prayers were not enough. From that moment on, she knew that she had no choice but to escape to the North and wage a battle against slavery.

3   Although Tubman married in 1844, she did not forget her vow to fight. Quiet as she seemed to those around her, she was only biding her time until she could escape with her two brothers, and, in 1849, the three set out together. Although her brothers eventually gave up, Tubman did not. Hunger and exhaustion could not deter her. From her point of view, death was a better alternative than slavery. Spending long nights alone in the woods, Tubman traveled hundreds of miles until she arrived in Philadelphia, a free woman. The year was 1850, and Tubman was just thirty years old.

4   Before long, Tubman made contact with members of the Underground Railroad, learning the names of people and places that could guarantee safety for fleeing slaves. With her knowledge of the underground network, Tubman returned to the South for her sister and her sister's children. One year later, in 1851, she returned again for her brothers. That same year, she returned for her husband, only to find that he had a new family and was content to stay where he was.

5   During the next ten years, Tubman traveled back and forth between the free and slave states, making about twenty secret journeys in all. Ultimately, she was personally responsible for the escape of more than three hundred men, women, and children.

6   Because some of the escapes were extraordinary and because she was subject to strange seizures, some people thought Harriet Tubman had magical powers. But those who traveled with her knew otherwise. To them, Tubman's success was not mysterious. It was the result of brains, daring, and ingenuity.* Magic had nothing to do with it.

7   Tubman planned her rescues with enormous attention to detail and flatly refused to take any chances that might endanger her charges. If, for example, wanted notices were posted describing the number and appearance of her group, she would change the group's makeup. If the description

---

*ingenuity: imagination, originality.

said one man and two women, she would dress one of the women in men's clothes to outwit her pursuers. If any member of her party aroused her suspicions, she would refuse to take that person. It was this attention to minute detail that made her rescue attempts so successful and earned her the nickname "Moses."

8   Yet another black American to escape slavery and become an influential abolitionist was Frederick Douglass, whose contributions are outlined in the section that follows.

Main Idea Harriet Tubman enabled hundreds of slaves to gain freedom.

Supporting Details 1. After being badly beaten, she decided to escape slavery and take

   action against it.

2. 1844; got married but did not forget her vow to fight.

   a. 1849; escaped.

   b. 1850; arrived in Philadelphia a free woman at the age of thirty.

3. Made contact with the Underground Railroad to learn who could

   guarantee safety.

   a. Made twenty secret journeys.

   b. She was so successful, people thought she had magical powers.

4. Planned her rescues with great attention to detail.

   a. If wanted notices described her party, she would change the

      group's appearance.

   b. If she had doubts about a person, she wouldn't take that person.

   c. Earned the nickname "Moses."

EXPLANATION   Because most of the reading deals with Tubman's efforts to free other enslaved people, the last sentence in paragraph 1 is the thesis statement. It effectively sums up the reading. Although there are eight paragraphs, only four of them contain major details that are essential to explaining the main idea. Note, too, the transitional sentence that ends the reading. This kind of transition could help you focus your reading of the next section, but it need not appear in your notes.

1. Journalist and Activist: Ida B. Wells

1 Ida B. Wells is not as well known as early black civil rights advocates Frederick Douglass,[†] W. E. B. Du Bois, or Booker T. Washington.[†] However, she is gaining recognition today for being a trailblazing black female, noteworthy for her accomplishments as a journalist but above all for her passionate commitment to civil rights.

2 Born a slave during the Civil War, Wells grew up in an era when few women pursued careers outside of the home. However, she discovered a love of journalism while working as a schoolteacher and launched her writing career with a series of articles about an 1883 experience in which she refused—seventy-two years before Rosa Parks's civil disobedience aboard a Montgomery, Alabama, bus—to sit in a train car designated for black passengers. When the conductor insisted that she move to the other car, she bit him. It took three men to forcibly remove her from the train as white onlookers applauded. The next year, she sued the railroad and won, although her victory was later overturned. Her articles about the case led Wells to begin writing a column for African-American newspapers, and she eventually bought part ownership in the *Free Speech*, a black Memphis newspaper, becoming its coeditor. When she was thirty-two years old, she bought a Chicago newspaper called *The Conservator*.

3 In addition to her work in journalism, Wells was also a tireless social activist. She established the Negro Fellowship League, which assisted southern blacks who moved to Chicago. In 1909, she became one of the founders of the National Association for the Advancement of Colored People (NAACP). In 1913, Wells organized what was probably the first black female suffrage group in America, inspiring black women all over the country to organize and form the National Association of Colored Women. In 1930, at age sixty-seven, she became the first black woman to run for public office in the United States when she tried but failed to win a seat in the Illinois state senate.

4 However, Wells is also remembered today for risking her own life in a crusade to end the practice of lynching by vigilante mobs. Between 1830 and 1930, about 3,220 black Americans were murdered in this way. One of the victims, grocery-store owner Thomas Moss, was a close friend of Wells. When Moss was lynched in 1892, an angry and grief-stricken Wells launched a campaign to eliminate this atrocity. She plunged into a wide-ranging

---

[†]Frederick Douglass (1817–1895): Douglass escaped slavery and went on to become a famous writer and abolitionist.
[†]Booker T. Washington (1856–1915): Washington was a former slave who went on to become a famous educator.

investigation of lynching practices, interviewing witnesses and researching newspaper accounts. She published the results of her study in a pamphlet titled *Lynching in All Its Phases* that she later expanded into a book. Wells even toured Great Britain in 1893 and 1894, delivering lectures that caused British citizens to threaten a boycott of U.S. goods if lynching did not end.

5   Wells's militant tactics were effective, and lynching did decline as the result of her campaign. However, she often outraged her fellow Americans with her frank and forceful response to the injustices suffered by her race. She was both black and female, so she was expected to be silent. Instead, Wells wrote candidly* about the horrors of lynching. Her scathing editorials were met with hatred and death threats. Yet decades before the civil rights movement of the 1950s and 1960s gathered momentum* and produced lasting change, Wells was a powerful leader in the fight for equality, compassion, and justice. (Source of information: Clarissa Myrick-Harris, "Against All Odds," *Smithsonian*, July 2002, pp. 70–78.)

Main Idea _____

_____

Supporting Details _____

_____

_____

_____

_____

_____

_____

_____

_____

_____

_____

_____

_____

_____

*candidly: openly, directly.
*momentum: force or speed of movement.

_____

_____

_____

_____

_____

2. Athletes and Injuries

1 When an athlete has been restricted, removed from play, or been advised of a permanent disability, he or she may have a mental battle to overcome as well as a physical one. If competitive activity is restricted for only a short time, the athlete's confidence or motivation to resume activity is not likely to change significantly. However, when an athlete is out of competition for an extended time, psychological mechanisms often emerge in response to the change in lifestyle. In fact, the athlete may experience something similar to the five stages defined by Elisabeth Kübler-Ross in her timeless book, *On Death and Dying*.

2 When an athlete sustains a severe injury, the *denial stage* usually occurs first. More than likely the athlete will experience denial when told of the severity of the injury. He or she will insist that the situation is not all that serious, that the physician is wrong or overreacting. Although the physician provides the athlete with a diagnosis and prognosis,* other vital information about the injury may be left to the trainer to impart. At this point, the athlete may start to face the reality of the injury or may still insist it's not that serious. If the latter is true, it's the trainer's responsibility to insist that the injury is serious while at the same time reassuring the athlete that he or she will survive the setback.

3 During the next stage, the *anger stage*, the athlete is mad at the world. He or she is also mad at the trainer as the bearer of unwelcome news. In some cases, the athlete's anger stimulates an increased desire to play despite injury. The athlete may also need to be reminded not to jeopardize relationships with teammates by showing misdirected anger at them because they can still participate in the sport. This is the time for the trainer to be realistic with encouragement and to use supportive statements such as "I can see how this is difficult for you, but you'll get through it."

_____

*prognosis: indication of how the injury or disease will respond to treatment.

4   Injured athletes who see that anger does not work may try *bargaining*. They will insist that they will take some time off to recover if only they can play in a specific game or series of games. They will also play one person against the other using half-truths in order to return to their sport. They may also go from doctor to doctor looking for one who will say what the athlete wants to hear. Frequently when bargaining fails, the athlete may return to the anger stage.

5   Because rehabilitation* after an injury can often be long, tedious, and painful, *depression* often adds to the athlete's misery. All kinds of symptoms can emerge during this period, including weight gain, loss of self-esteem, apathy,* or trouble at home and in school. At this point, it's important for the trainer to try to minimize the negative ideas that accompany a depressed state.

6   *Acceptance* is the stage in which athletes are able to fully understand and appropriately deal with the extent of their injuries, as well as their responsibilities in the recovery process. This understanding includes coming to grips with the time frame involved in recovery or even acknowledging that return may not be possible. If the athlete is going to return to the sport, then it's the trainer's job to emphasize the role confidence and determination can play in recovery.

7   Some athletes whose injuries require an extended recovery do not experience any of the stages described above; others may experience only some of them. Still others may experience each stage but not necessarily in the order listed. Even some athletes with only short-term injuries experience some of the five stages. In any case, the trainer must be proactive, anticipating and preventing as many obstacles to recovery as possible. Knowing about the five stages an injured athlete may go through is one way for the trainer to be prepared and responsive. (Source of sequence: Clover, *Sports Medicine Essentials*, pp. 569–70.)

Main Idea ~~~~~~ Injured athelets encounter 5 stages
_____

Denial stage

Supporting Details   1) Realising the Depth of the Injury

@ Set-back Idenial   b) reality /overcoming

---

*rehabilitation: being restored to good health.
*apathy: lack of feeling or energy.
Note: In reading on privately run prisons, the context required a different definition.

2) Anger Stage
   ⓐ More denial/motivation ⓑ Control emotions
3) Barganing
   ⓐ doctor who says right ⓑ only use half-truths
4) Depression occurs
   ⓐ rehabilitation time   ⓑ minimize neg.
5) Acceptence
   ⓐ aknowledge injury ⓑ recover/break
   ⓒ Not everyone experinces the
   same stages in the same order

More on Diagramming

As you learned in Chapter 1, not everyone uses the same method to take notes. This point also applies to longer readings, where outlines might be the perfect method of note-taking for some but not for others. Many people, for instance, prefer to use diagrams or drawings, also known as **graphic organizers** or **concept maps**, to record the key points of a chapter section.

For that matter, even those who generally prefer informal outlines are inclined to switch to a diagram whenever a reading assignment focuses on steps in a sequence or a physical description. That's because the diagram more readily reflects the underlying structure or form of the content. Remember, for instance, the diagram from Chapter 1, which provided a visual image of the Earth's layers.

Diagrams, however, are not restricted to paragraphs, as the following reading and accompanying diagram illustrate.

Information-Processing Model of Memory

1 Historically, the most influential and comprehensive theories about memory have been based on a general **information-processing model** (Roediger, 1990). The information-processing model originally suggested

that in order for information to become firmly embedded in memory, it must pass through three stages of mental processing: sensory memory, short-term memory, and long-term memory (Atkinson & Shiffrin, 1968).

2   Information from the senses—sights or sounds, for example—is held in *sensory memory* for a very brief period of time, often for less than a second. To be remembered, information in the sensory memory must be attended to, analyzed, and encoded as a meaningful pattern. This is the process of *perception*. If the information in sensory memory is consciously perceived,* it enters short-term memory. If new information is not made the focus of attention, it will disappear in less than twenty seconds. If information in short-term memory is then processed further, it enters long-term memory, where it may remain indefinitely.

3   The act of reading illustrates all three stages of memory processing. As you read any sentence in this book, light energy reflected from the page reaches your eyes, where it is converted to neural* activity and registered in sensory memory. If you pay attention to these visual stimuli, your perception of the patterns of light can be held in short-term memory. This stage of memory holds the early parts of the sentence so that they can be integrated* and understood as you read the rest of the sentence. As you read, you are constantly recognizing words by matching your perceptions of them with the patterns and meanings you have stored in long-term memory. In short, all three stages of memory are necessary for you to understand a sentence.

4   Today's versions of the information-processing model emphasize these constant interactions among sensory, short-term, and long-term memory (Massaro & Cowan, 1993; Wagner, 1999). For example, sensory memory can be thought of as that part of your knowledge base (or long-term memory) that is momentarily activated by information sent to the brain via the sensory nerves. And short-term memory can be thought of as that part of your knowledge base that is the focus of attention at any given moment. Like perception, memory is an active process, and what is already in long-term memory influences how new information is encoded (Cowan, 1988). (Bernstein et al., *Psychology*, pp. 241–42.)

---

* perceived: recognized and understood.
* neural: related to the nerves.
* integrated: connected to or made part of something else.

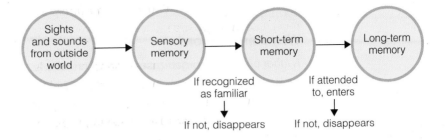

In this particular diagram, a **flow chart** represents the steps or stages in a process by showing each one in a circle or a box. The circles or boxes are accompanied by arrows identifying the sequence of steps.

Whenever you use boxes or symbols to represent the steps in a process, the symbols should be arranged in a way that highlights the order in which each stage occurs. This flow chart does just that, which is what makes it an effective learning tool. You can look at it and easily identify each individual stage information goes through as it makes its way into long-term memory.

READING TIP Any time you read descriptions of physical characteristics or chains of events, try to visualize the characteristics, the events, or both while you read.

INTERNET RESOURCE For some really good ideas on how to match your diagram to the material, go to www.writedesignonline .com/organizers. You can find this link at the student companion website for this text: www.cengage.com/devenglish/flemming/rfr11e.

◆ **EXERCISE 6**   **Diagramming a Chapter Section**

DIRECTIONS   Read the selection and answer the questions. Then take notes using a diagram.

EXAMPLE

Why Join a Union?

1 A *labor union* is an organization of workers who act together to negotiate their wages and working conditions with employers. Some workers, especially those with dull or repetitive jobs, decide to start or join a union because they feel they are merely parts of a machine. Therefore, they band together with others to avoid losing their sense of identity as individuals while they are on the job. Another reason for joining a union is to increase job security. Unions cannot completely guarantee their members' jobs, but they can enforce rules that protect workers from being fired for no good reason. Finally, workers start or join unions to improve unsatisfactory aspects of their jobs. For example, they may believe that a union will get them better pay, benefits, or working conditions.

2 The first step in forming a union is to conduct an organizing campaign. The goal of this campaign is to stimulate employee interest in having a union. The campaign may begin when a national union sends organizers to a particular firm to talk to employees. Or, the employees of a firm might contact a national union to get help with organizing. During the organizing campaign, the organizers ask employees to sign authorization cards. These cards indicate, in writing, the employees' support for the union.

3 If at least 30 percent of eligible employees sign authorization cards, the National Labor Relations Board (NLRB) holds an election. The NLRB distributes secret ballots to the employees at the workplace during normal working hours and then counts the votes. The vote of the majority determines the outcome of the election.

4 If the majority of eligible employees vote *against* having a union, a year must pass before another election can occur. If the majority of employees vote *for* having a union, the union becomes the official bargaining agent for its new members. In the final step of the process, the NLRB certifies* the results of the election. Then, the union begins the process of negotiating a labor contract with the employer. (Source of information: Pride, Hughes, and Kapoor, *Business*, pp. 335–37.)

1. What's the main idea of the reading?

   There are a number of reasons why people form a union.

2. Take notes in the form of a diagram.

---

*certifies: formally confirms as accurate.

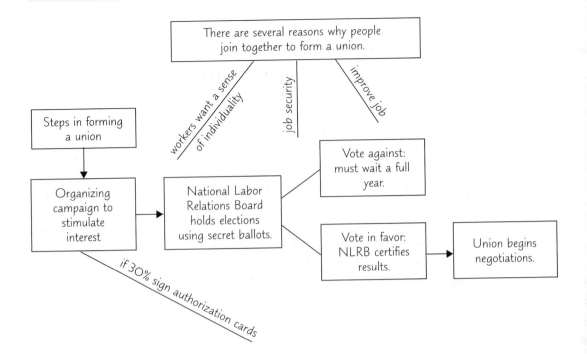

EXPLANATION   Your diagram of this reading might not look exactly like the one shown here. But if it identifies the reasons why people form a union along with the steps involved in creating one, it effectively fulfills its function. Exactly how you "picture" the material and its underlying organization is up to you.

1. The Jury Deliberation Process

1   During a courtroom trial, the jury listens as both the defense and the prosecution present their witnesses and their evidence. Both sides finish presenting their cases by making closing arguments to the jury. Then, the judge sends the jury to the jury room to decide on a verdict of "guilty" or "not guilty." To reach this verdict, the jurors must deliberate, discussing the information presented in the courtroom. Their decision-making process usually goes through three stages.

2   The first stage is a relaxed period of *orientation*. The jury begins its deliberation process by selecting a group leader (the foreperson), setting an agenda, and discussing the judge's instructions. Next, jurors begin to explore what they heard in the courtroom. They talk about the facts and the evidence the lawyers presented. They raise questions. This initial discussion ends with a vote, and each jury member reveals his or her opinion about the verdict.

3   If the necessary consensus* is not reached, the jury shifts into a period of *open conflict*. During this phase, the discussion becomes more argumentative. The two opposing groups go over the evidence and try to construct stories to explain it. The majority group tries to convince the members who disagree to change their minds by presenting information to support its argument. The majority group may also try to pressure the minority group to conform to the majority's opinion.

4   When a consensus is finally reached, the group enters a *reconciliation* phase. During this period, group members smooth over the conflicts between them. They express their satisfaction with their decision. On some juries, however, the majority is not able to persuade the holdouts to change their minds. In that case, the jury is "hung." A hung jury causes a mistrial, and the case must be retried with a new jury. (Source of information: Brehm et al., *Social Psychology*, p. 460.)

1. What's the main idea of the reading?

_____

2. Take notes in the form of a diagram.

_____

*consensus: form of group agreement.

VOCABULARY CHECK

The following words were introduced in pages 455–67. Match the word with the definition. Review words, definitions, and original context two or three times before taking the vocabulary tests. (The page numbers in parentheses indicate where the word first appeared.)

1. abstract (p. 455)   _____

2. concrete (p. 455)   _____

3. abolitionist (p. 456)   _____

4. verify (p. 456)   _____

5. ingenuity (p. 457)   _____

6. candidly (p. 460)   _____

7. momentum (p. 460)   _____

8. prognosis (p. 461)   _____

9. rehabilitation (p. 462)   _____

10. apathy (p. 462)   _____

11. perceived (p. 464)   _____

12. neural (p. 464)   _____

13. integrated (p. 464)   _____

14. certifies (p. 466)   _____

15. consensus (p. 467)   _____

a. force or speed of movement

b. lack of feeling or energy

c. formally confirms as accurate

d. being restored to good health

e. describes ideas that cannot be understood or felt by the physical senses, e.g., justice, honesty

f. form of group agreement

g. prove true

h. describes ideas that can be comprehended by one or more physical senses

i. indication of how the injury or disease will respond to treatment

j. connected to or made part of something else

k. a person who wanted to end slavery

l. openly, directly

m. imagination, originality

n. recognized and understood

o. related to the nerves

DIGGING Legal Rights for Animals
DEEPER

Looking Ahead The reading on tort reform suggested that there might be too many law-yers at work in the U.S. This reading suggests that their number might well increase due to a growing number of cases involving the legal rights of animals.

1 A little more than two decades ago, something called "animal law" started gaining public notice. There were several pet custody and wrongful death cases mentioned in the press that immediately became fodder for late-night comedians. Except for those involved, almost everyone seemed to think that talking about the legal rights of animals was a huge joke. In addition to the comic monologues, there were numerous cartoons showing a dog or cat sitting in the witness chair of a courtroom with paw raised in preparation for taking an oath. These were often accompanied by editorials with titles like "It Really Is a Kangaroo Court."[†]

No Joke Anymore

2 But make no mistake; these days, no one is laughing. Animal law, once unheard of both in and out of law school, is now being taught at more than a dozen law schools. Among them are some of the most prestigious: Georgetown, Harvard, and the University of California at Los Angeles. According to Stephen Wise, a Boston lawyer who teaches animal law at Harvard, the number of animal law classes is "sky-rocketing," and the first animal law casebook[†] is now in publication. Wise himself, the former president of the Animal Legal Defense Fund, has also written a book on animal law. It's called *Rattling the Cage: Toward Legal Rights for Animals*. The New York City Bar Association has even scheduled a conference on the legal rights of animals, and additional conferences are expected around the country.

3   In August 1999, for the first time ever, an appellate[†] court in New York reversed a trial court decision and awarded custody of Lovey, a ten-year-old cat, on the basis of the cat's "best interests." This is in direct contrast to what used to be the basis for awarding pet ownership: the animal would

---

[†] kangaroo court: a court that's dishonest or illegal.
[†] casebook: a collection of source materials, often used in teaching or research.
[†] appellate: having the power to hear appeals and review decisions.

go to whoever came up with the bill of sale or certificate of adoption. In other words, the animal was a piece of property. The New York decision, however, challenges the long-held assumption that, like jewelry or furniture, animals are property, devoid of interests or rights.

4   In 2000, Tennessee became the first state in the nation to approve emotional-distress damages for a pet's loss, and according to Michigan state's Animal Legal and Historical Center, other states are following Tennessee's lead. Attorneys specializing in animal law are intent on making the legal system recognize and respond to the human suffering caused by the loss of a beloved pet.

5   The noticeable toughening of anticruelty laws is further evidence that animal law is no longer a laughing matter. In 1994, all but six states considered cruelty to animals a misdemeanor and punished it with small fines or short jail sentences. At the present time, "aggravated cruelty" to animals has been elevated from a misdemeanor to a felony in forty-six states. In short, if someone intentionally kills or causes serious physical injury to a pet or other animal, that person can end up paying a large fine and spending time in prison. Such tough sentencing is a far cry from the days when hurting or killing an animal was punished with a fifty-dollar fine. It is also a further indication of the justice system's changing attitude toward animals.

6   The much-publicized 2007 case of Atlanta Falcon quarterback Michael Vick is a perfect illustration of how much the law has revised its stance on cruelty to animals. Indicted by a grand jury in July 2007, Vick was sentenced to twenty-three months in prison. Although many people thought the sentence too short given the deadly abuse Vick and his co-conspirators had meted out to the dogs they had used as fighters or, even worse, as bait, there was a time when imprisonment would not have been part of the penalty. After all, Vick's dogfighting ring had harmed only animals, not people, and it was once generally assumed that laws were designed to protect only the latter, not the former.

7   In a country of devoted pet owners, though, that assumption has been reexamined and found wanting. Witness the fact that there now exists an entire textbook devoted to animal law. There are also websites focusing on the same subject and many of the sites link to a "Bibliography of Animal Law Resources." There are also student chapters of the Animal Legal Defense Fund across the country, and law schools routinely host discussions and debates dedicated to the subject of animal law.

8   Although some of the groups involved in monitoring and changing the laws governing relationships between humans and animals sport amusing names like "Pawtropolis" and "Kitty Crusaders," their intent is serious—to

make the general public aware that animals can no longer be neglected, hurt, or, in the worst cases, killed with impunity. If the toughening stance vis-à-vis animal cruelty wasn't evidence enough, the number of lawyers registered with the Animal Legal Defense Fund continues to rise, and no one thinks that number has anywhere to go but up. (Source for the discussion of "Lovey" the cat: www.animallaw.com/adoptionandcustody cases.htm.)

Sharpening Your Skills

DIRECTIONS   Answer the questions by circling the letter of the correct response.

1. Which statement best expresses the main idea of the entire reading?

   a. Animal law is better known than it once was, but it is still not being taken seriously by legal scholars.
   b. The penalties for the abuse of animals need to be harsher.
   c. If animal law gains serious recognition, all experiments involving animals will result in lawsuits.
   d. Animal law is no longer the subject of jokes; it is taken seriously by both the legal system and the general public.

2. The main idea is

   a. stated.
   b. implied.

3. What does the pronoun "this" refer to in sentence 2 of paragraph 3?

   a. an appellate court in New York
   b. Lovey's custody being awarded on the basis of her "best interests"
   c. August 1999
   d. conflict over a cat in a divorce case

4. What does the phrase "in other words" (paragraph 3) signal about the sentence that follows?

   a. The author is going to reverse the previous point.
   b. The author is going to introduce a new point.
   c. The author is going to restate the previous point.

5. Which sentence best sums up the main idea of paragraph 3?

   a. The 1999 appellate court decision awarded Lovey to the person who had the cat's best interests at heart.

   b. The 1999 appellate court decision undermines the notion that pets are property.

   c. In the past, pets involved in divorce cases were treated as property.

   d. Thanks to the 1999 appellate court decision involving Lovey the cat, animals involved in divorce cases will never again be treated like property.

6. Which statement best paraphrases the topic sentence of paragraph 5?

   a. Although a few states have made cruelty to animals a felony, the majority have not followed suit.

   b. Anyone who purposely injures an animal deserves to serve time in prison.

   c. The growing tendency to make animal cruelty a serious crime is another indication that animals are winning legal rights.

   d. There was a time when people who purposely injured animals would be punished with a small fine and nothing more.

7. To make sense of paragraph 5, readers have to add what inference?

   a. No one laughs at anticruelty laws these days.

   b. Harsh punishment for a crime indicates that society takes the crime seriously.

   c. Many people still think animal cruelty is a joke, despite fines and jail sentences.

8. Look up the word *fodder*, used in sentence 2 of paragraph 1: "There were several pet custody and wrongful death cases mentioned in the press that immediately became *fodder* for late-night comedians." In this case, the word is being used

   a. literally.

   b. figuratively.

9. Based on the context in which the words *misdemeanor* and *felony* appear in paragraph 5, "At the present time, 'aggravated cruelty' to

animals has been elevated from a *misdemeanor* to a *felony* in forty-six states," which makes more sense to you?

a. A misdemeanor is the more serious crime.

b. A felony is the more serious crime.

10. Based on the context in which *vis-à-vis* is used in paragraph 8, "If the toughening stance *vis-à-vis* animal cruelty wasn't evidence enough, the number of lawyers registered with the Animal Legal Defense Fund continues to rise, and no one thinks that number has anywhere to go but up," which definition makes the most sense?

a. in contrast to

b. in relation to

c. up against

d. as a way out of

Look up *vis-à-vis* in a dictionary. The first *s* sounds like

a. the *z* in *buzz*.

b. the *s* in *hiss*.

The second *s* is

a. silent.

b. pronounced like the *z* in *buzz*.

c. pronounced like the *s* in *hiss*.

Making Connections Do you think the author of the article on tort reform on pages 448–49 and the author of the reading on animal law would agree that there are too many lawyers? Please explain your answer.

_____

_____

Drawing Your Own Conclusions Do you think Michael Vick's sentence was appropriate to the crime? Why or why not?

_____

_____

▶ TEST 1   **Vocabulary Review**

DIRECTIONS   Fill in the blanks with one of the words listed below.

ambiguous	prodigy	wake	extroverted	sumptuous
dubbed	incarnate	physiology	munificent	altruism

1. Because he was always such a quick thinker, his classmates _____ him the brain.

2. The little girl was a(n) _____ when it came to mathematics, but when it came to social interactions she was much less advanced.

3. For Americans, Osama bin Laden is evil _____.

4. To be a physical therapist, one has to understand the body's _____.

5. In 2009, many people were infuriated by the _____ bonuses given to stock traders, whose companies had gone broke and been bailed out by the government.

6. The language of the contract was a little too _____ when it came to explaining who owned the rights to the material on the website, and contributors were worried about how their personal information was going to be used.

7. The character of Prince Hal in Shakespeare's *Henry V* is the most _____ of men, delighting in the company of others, but as king, Hal is more withdrawn and not so delighted by the company of old friends.

8. In the _____ of September 11, 2001, many people who lived far away from the scene of the tragedy felt anxious and fearful of the future.

9. Dressed in a(n) _____ ball gown, bestowed on her by a fairy godmother, Cinderella went unrecognized even by her nasty stepsisters, who thought she was a princess rather than their servant.

10. Mother Teresa, who lived to care for the poor and the sick, personified _____.

▶ TEST 2   ## Vocabulary Review

DIRECTIONS   Fill in the blanks with one of the words listed below.

plaintiff	judicial	litigation	authoritarian	credence
invigorating	aspirations	specifications	predisposition	electoral

1. Like many high-ranking military men, General George Patton had a(n) _____ personality: He demanded strict obedience from those he commanded.

2. Those who disliked Supreme Court Justice Earl Warren were convinced that his court's rulings were destroying the _____ system and allowing criminals to go free.

3. The mountain air was supposed to be _____, but instead of making the climbers feel energetic, the high altitudes were making them feel tired and light-headed.

4. When the judge ruled in favor of the _____, the courtroom erupted with shouts of joy.

5. Our _____ system is not an example of direct democracy, where every single vote carries the same weight.

6. There are people who seem to be in love with _____: If anything goes wrong in their lives, they look for someone to sue.

7. Because his mother and father both had diabetes, he knew that he had a(n) _____ to develop the disease.

8. The consultant was trying to create a software program that would meet the client's _____, but she was having a hard time writing the program within the time allotted.

9. There had been rumors for years that the investment company was engaging in fraudulent practices, but investors had given the rumors no _____, until, that is, the owner of the company admitted the rumors were true.

10. In mid-life, F. Scott Fitzgerald's wife Zelda decided to fulfill her long-held _____ of becoming a ballerina.

   c. A variety of industries benefited from the invention of air conditioning.

   d. The food industry reaped huge profits from the invention of air conditioning.

4. Which sentence best expresses the main idea of paragraph 6?

   a. Air conditioning had a dramatic effect on architecture.

   b. Air conditioning changed American architecture, and those architectural changes produced social ones.

   c. Porches became a thing of the past once families could buy air conditioners.

5. The primary purpose of this reading is

   a. to describe the effect of air conditioning's arrival on industry and society.

   b. to persuade readers that the invention of air conditioning was the most important invention of the twentieth century.

Recognizing Patterns of
Organization in Paragraphs

9

IN THIS CHAPTER, YOU WILL LEARN

- how to identify six patterns commonly used to organize paragraphs: definition, time order, simple listing, comparison and contrast, cause and effect, and classification.

- how to recognize topic sentences and transitions that signal these patterns.

- how to make your notes match the patterns.

- how to determine the *primary* pattern of organization.

"To understand is to perceive patterns."
—Isaiah Berlin, historian

"What we call chaos is just patterns we haven't recognized."
—Chuck Palahniuk, novelist

Chapter 9 introduces six patterns of organization that authors commonly use to explain ideas. Recognizing these organizational patterns will serve you by helping you (1) make predictions to guide your reading, (2) identify key points, (3) decide how best to take notes, and (4) develop a framework for remembering details.

Pattern 1: Definition

As you already know from Chapter 2, the **definition pattern** includes a key term—usually highlighted in boldface, color type, or italics—followed by a detailed definition that can consist of several sentences. It also frequently includes examples or illustrations to make the meaning clearer.

Because textbook authors need to identify the specialized vocabulary of their subject, paragraphs like the following appear in almost every college textbook:

> **Epithelial tissue**, or *epithelium* (ep-ih-THE-le-um), forms a protective covering for the body and all the organs. It is the main tissue of the outer layer of the skin. Epithelial tissue forms the lining of the intestinal tract, as well as that of the respiratory and urinary passages. It also lines the blood vessels, the uterus, and other body cavities. (Adapted from Memmler et al., *The Human Body in Health and Disease,* p. 40.)

Typically for the definition pattern, the authors have highlighted the term they are defining, **epithelial tissue**. Then that highlighted term is followed by a definition. The authors also provide examples of where the tissue can be found in the body.

Typical Topic Sentences

Sentences like the ones that follow are a strong indication that the definition pattern plays an important role in the paragraph.

> 1. Nineteenth-century America was guided by the concept of **Manifest Destiny**, the belief that the United States was on a mission from God to occupy North America from coast to coast.

2. The *greenhouse effect* is the name for what happens when excessive carbon dioxide and other gases build up in Earth's atmosphere.

3. Ozone is the name for a specific form of oxygen containing three atoms instead of the two found in regular oxygen.

4. A "browser" is software that allows you to travel on the Internet and find out what is available.

Taking Notes on Definition Paragraphs

Notes on the definition pattern should include three elements:

1. the term being defined
2. a complete definition
3. any other details that might help clarify the definition—e.g., examples, contrasting words, origins

To illustrate, here are notes on the definition paragraph from the previous page:

Main Idea *Epithelial tissue* is the main tissue covering the skin and organs; it protects the body and its organs.

Supporting Details
1. Lines the intestinal tract along with respiratory and urinary passages.

2. Lines the blood vessels, uterus, and other body cavities.

Sometimes authors include background material about how a word came into being, or they define a key term by telling you what it is *not*. This information is not always essential, so look at it carefully and decide if it needs to be included in your notes.

NOTE-TAKING TIP When taking notes in your textbook, it's a good idea to make the word or words being defined stand out by circling, boxing, underlining, or highlighting them. This way, during review, you'll be sure to study important key terms.

If you are a fan of diagramming, you'll be happy to learn that definition passages readily lend themselves to that format, for instance:

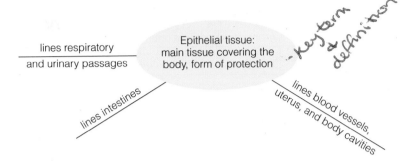

lines respiratory and urinary passages

Epithelial tissue: main tissue covering the body, form of protection

Key term & definition

lines intestines

lines blood vessels, uterus, and body cavities

SUMMING UP THE KEY POINTS

1. Paragraphs devoted to the definition pattern always open with the term being defined, and that term is usually highlighted in some way, through either boldface, italics, colored ink, or marginal notation.

2. The sentence introducing the term is usually the topic sentence. However, it's possible to introduce the term and then define it in the next sentence, which is the topic sentence.

3. Topic sentences in the definition pattern often use phrases such as "refers to," "is the name for," "is said to be," and "is defined as."

4. Notes on the definition pattern should include (1) the term defined, (2) a clearly stated definition, and (3) examples or explanations of origins that clarify the word's meaning.

◆ **EXERCISE 1** **Understanding Definition Patterns**

DIRECTIONS Read and take notes on each paragraph, making sure to paraphrase and abbreviate in your notes.

EXAMPLE The psychiatric term **psychodrama** refers to a particular kind of group therapy created and developed by therapist Jacob Moreno in the early 1950s. In a psychodrama, individuals act out disturbing incidents from their lives, often playing multiple roles. The purpose of a psychodrama is to help patients better understand the troubling situations that may have contributed to their psychological problems. Moreno believed that the insights gained during a psychodrama could then be transferred to real life. For example, a teenager jealous of and in conflict with a twin might better understand both his own feelings and the feelings of his brother by acting out one of their quarrels.

Main Idea In the 1950s, Jacob Moreno developed a special kind of group

therapy called psychodrama.

Supporting Details 1. During psychodrama, individuals act out disturbing real-life situations.

2. Objective is to better understand situations that may contribute

to psychological disturbance.

3. Moreno thought insights gained during a psychodrama could be applied

to real life.

a. A teenager in conflict with his twin might gain understanding

by acting out a typical quarrel.

EXPLANATION   Here, the key term is *psychodrama* and our notes clearly
define it. They also include some essential background about the word—
the name of Jacob Moreno and the approximate time when the term
came into being. Note, too, that an example clarifying the key term has
also been included.

1. A **self-concept** is a person's perception, or view, of his or her personality and character traits. It consists of all your ideas and feelings
about how you define yourself. To discover your self-concept, you
might ask yourself, "What kind of person am I? Am I compassionate?* Selfish? Stubborn?" Self-concepts are built out of daily experiences and our reactions to those experiences. For example, let's say
that you consistently do well in sports but find it hard to be part of a
team. You might then begin to describe your self-concept in the following terms: "I'm a good athlete, but I'm not much of a team player."
Self-concepts, however, can—and sometimes should—be revised,
particularly if they are overly negative.

Main Idea Self-concept: a persons view
of his/her personality

Supporting Details 1) revealed when asked "what kind
of person am I".

*compassionate: caring of others.

2) built out of our daily experiences
and our reactions to them.
• Good athlete but bad team player
3) Self concepts should be revised
over time

2. During the nineteenth century, the absence of effective government in many of the newly settled parts of the West created a vacuum that was often filled by **vigilante groups**—private citizens taking the law into their own hands at almost any provocation.* Vigilante groups, which typically consisted of a few hundred people led by the town elite, would track down criminals or people creating disorder in the settlement and administer "justice" to them. At some "trials" the captured outlaws were given a chance to present a defense. Determination of guilt most often resulted in the execution of the "defendant," usually by hanging. Vigilante groups were generally well organized along military lines and had written manifestos or constitutions to which the members would subscribe. (Adapted from Adler et al., *Criminal Justice*, p. 136.)

Main Idea _____

_____

Supporting Details _____

_____

_____

_____

3. By definition, **blood pressure** is the force exerted against the walls of the arteries as the heart contracts and relaxes. The force is measured in millimeters of mercury (mm Hg), and a "typical" blood pressure is 120/80

*provocation: stimulus to anger or punishment.

(read 120 over 80). The "120" refers to the force exerted by the blood just as the heart contracts and is called the **systolic** pressure. The "80" refers to the force exerted when the heart muscle is relaxed and is called the **diastolic** pressure. (Mullen et al., *Connections for Health*, p. 349.)

Main Idea   _____

_____

Supporting Details   _____

_____

_____

_____

_____

_____

4. The word *Spanglish* is said to be the creation of the Puerto Rican linguist Salvador Tió. Tió coined the word to describe the mix of English and Spanish spoken by Spanish-speaking people who live among or have heavy contact with native English-speakers. Spanglish is common along the U.S.-Mexico border and in places with large bilingual communities like Texas and Florida. Spanglish is also spoken in Panama, where America's control of the Panama Canal brought Panamanians into close contact with English. Spanglish can also be found wherever American or British movies and music have become popular. Although the characteristics of Spanglish can vary according to where it is spoken and who is describing it, the main feature is the combining of English and Spanish grammar and vocabulary in the same sentence or conversation. For instance, a speaker of Spanglish might say "Ya me voy a get up" instead of "Ya me voy a levanter" ("I'm just getting up"). (Source of information: wikipedia.org/wiki/Spanglish.)

Main Idea   _____

_____

Supporting Details _____

_____

_____

_____

✔ CHECK YOUR UNDERSTANDING

1. How do paragraphs based on the definition pattern usually begin?

_____

_____

2. Topic sentences signaling the definition pattern often include what phrases?

_____

3. Notes on the definition pattern should include what?

_____

_____

Pattern 2: Time Order

Two different types of paragraphs rely heavily on the **time-order pattern**. The first paragraph type lists a sequence of dates and events according to when they happen (or happened) in real time. The other type explains a process, telling readers how something works or develops.

Sequence of Dates and Events

Textbook authors in all fields frequently use a **sequence of dates and events** to (1) describe how a smaller series of events led up to a larger and more major event; (2) chart the career of an important figure; or (3) explain how some theory, invention, or activity came to be part of culture or history. Here, for example, is a time-order paragraph that traces a sequence of dates and events according to the order in which they occurred.

> What we now call the Internet began in 1969 when the U.S. Defense Department linked up computers at four universities to create ARPANET (Advanced Research Projects Agency Network). By 1972, thirty-seven universities were connected over ARPANET. In 1983, ARPANET inter-linked with other computer networks to create the Internet. Between 1983 and 1990, the Internet was used mainly to transmit messages known as electronic mail, or *e-mail*, among researchers. In 1991, a group of European physicists devised a system for transmitting a wide range of materials, including graphics* and photographs, over the Internet. By 1994, households all over the United States were "surfing the net." (Adapted from Janda et al., *The Challenge of Democracy*, p. 181.)

The topic of this paragraph is the growth of the Internet. The implied main idea suggests that the Internet as we know it did not happen over-night. Rather, it took more than twenty years to develop. Notice how the dates and events in the paragraph all contribute to this implied main idea.

Transitional Signals

Many of the sentences in the previous paragraph open with transitions that help readers follow the order of events. Phrases like "by 1972," "in 1983," and "between 1983 and 1990" tell readers to pay attention because the next significant event is coming up. They are the author's way of saying, "I've finished describing the previous event and I'm ready to tell you about the one that followed it." Because they usually introduce major details, time-order transitions are worthy of your attention. Here's a list of transitions likely to appear in a paragraph tracing a sequence of dates and events.

Transitions Commonly Used to Organize Dates and Events ◆	After that
	At that time or point
	Before
	Between _____ and _____
	By the end of the year
	By the year _____ †

---

*graphics: visual images.
†Blanks indicate dates.

During _____
During that time, period
Finally
From _____ to _____
In January (etc.) _____
In the days (weeks, months, years, century) following
In the spring (summer, fall, winter) of
In the following year
In the next year
In the years since
In the year _____
On the day (afternoon, evening) of _____
Until
When
While
_____ years later

Typical Topic Sentences

Transitions like those shown above are clues to the time-order pattern. So, too, are the topic sentences like the following. Note how they all identify a particular period of time.

1. The life of Mexican painter Frida Kahlo is a lesson in how art can be an antidote to pain.
2. The years leading up to the Great Depression were filled with a sense of optimism that was destroyed almost overnight.
3. Between 1939 and 1944, most of Europe descended into a nightmare world of terror, violence, and death.
4. In their youth, the inventors of the airplane, Wilbur and Orville Wright, seemed destined for failure.

Any time a topic sentence mentions a specific period of time or evaluates a life or career, there's a good chance the organization is a sequence of dates and events.

Telltale Visual Aids

Timelines like the following indicate that the sequence of dates will likely play a heavy role in the material you are reading.

Chronology of Events ◆	1860	Lincoln elected president
		Secession begins
	1861	Fort Sumter attacked
		Lincoln institutes martial law in the border states
		First Battle of Bull Run
		Trent Affair
	1862	Peninsular campaign
		Battle of Shiloh
		Union navy seizes Memphis and New Orleans
		Battle of Antietam
		Battle of Fredericksburg
		Confederate Conscription Act
		Homestead Act
		Morrill Land Grant Act
	1863	Emancipation Proclamation
		Union army enrolls black enlistees
		Federal Conscription Act
		New York City draft riot
		Battle of Chancellorsville
		Battle of Gettysburg
		Vicksburg falls

(Adapted from Gillon and Matson, *The American Experiment*, p. 571.)

Taking Notes on Dates and Events Patterns

When you take notes on paragraphs devoted to dates and events, include the following information:

1. the main idea
2. the dates and events used to develop the main idea
3. any other supporting details that lack dates but still seem essential to developing the main idea

Here, to illustrate, are notes on the paragraph about the Internet.

Main Idea The Internet was developed over an extended period of time.

Supporting Details 1. 1969: The first step toward developing the Internet came when the Defense Department linked computers at four universities to form ARPANET (Advanced Research Projects Agency Network).

2. 1972: Thirty-seven universities were connected over ARPANET.

3. 1983–1990: ARPANET interlinks with other computers to create Internet, used primarily for e-mail among researchers.

4. 1991: European physicists created a standardized system for encoding and transmitting graphics.

5. Early 90s: Ordinary citizens start exploring the Net.

NOTE-TAKING TIP The supporting details in the sample notes above all start off with the dates mentioned in the paragraph. This is a good format to use when taking notes on several dates and events. It will help keep the sequence of dates and events clear in your mind.

SUMMING UP THE KEY POINTS

1. In the sequence of dates and events pattern, the *order* of events as they happened in real time plays an essential role.

2. Paragraphs using this pattern often describe how a series of smaller events preceded some larger one. The pattern is also used to chart the career of famous people or explain how some institution, activity, or invention became part of the culture.

3. Transitional phrases like "in 1999," "before 2001," and "after the election of 2008" are clues to this pattern. So, too, are topic sentences

that emphasize a particular span of time; for instance, "During the 1950s, America underwent some startling changes in lifestyle."

4. Readings accompanied by timelines are likely to include paragraphs tracing a sequence of dates and events.

5. Notes on this pattern should include the dates and events used to explain the main idea, along with any other undated details that seem relevant to the main idea.

◆ **EXERCISE 2** **Understanding Dates and Events Patterns**

DIRECTIONS Read and take notes on each paragraph. Circle the time-order transitions.

EXAMPLE The son of a Spanish immigrant, Cuban leader Fidel Castro quickly rose to power. Castro was educated at a Roman Catholic school in Santiago, and (from 1945 to 1950) he attended the University of Havana. (In 1947) he participated in an unofficial raid on the Dominican Republic, and (in July 1953) he organized an attack on the army barracks in Santiago. The attack was unsuccessful, and Castro was sentenced to fifteen years in prison. (In 1955,) Castro was released from prison, and (the following year) he went to Mexico to build a Cuban revolutionary movement. (In December 1959,) he returned to Cuba, and (in January 1960) he led a successful attempt to overthrow dictator Fulgencio Batista. Since that time, Castro has ruled Cuba with an iron hand although (in 2006) he was rumored to be close to death.

Main Idea   It did not take many years for Fidel Castro to rise to power in Cuba.

Supporting Details 1. 1945–1950: Attended University of Havana

2. 1947: Took part in unofficial raid on Dominican Republic

3. July 1953: Organized attack on army barracks in Santiago

4. 1955: Released from prison

5. 1956: Went to Mexico to organize Cuban revolution

6. December 1959: Returned to Cuba

7. January 1960: Overthrew Batista

8. Since 1960: Rules with iron hand, although rumors of death

began in 2006

EXPLANATION   To prove the claim made in the topic sentence—that Castro's rise to power was rapid—the paragraph provides a sequence of dates and events. Using the "date-first" format, the sample notes briefly record all the significant events in Castro's rise to power. *Note*: The year 1956 is not mentioned in the paragraph, but you can figure out when Castro went to Mexico because of the phrase "the following year." Sometimes, authors don't include specific dates but instead expect you to figure them out.

1. It took some time before American colonists learned how to grow their own tea. The first tea shrub was planted in the early nineteenth century, sometime between 1810 and 1820. In 1848, more extensive* experiments with tea production were carried out; ten years later, plans were made to distribute tea seed throughout the South. These experiments, however, were cut short by the Civil War (1861–1865), and it was not until 1880 that the United States Department of Agriculture resumed tea production. In 1890, Charles U. Shepard of Summerville, South Carolina, devoted his private fortune to growing tea. By 1900, he had planted sixty acres and harvested five thousand pounds of tea. However, despite the efforts of Shepard and others who came after him, tea has never successfully competed with coffee as America's favorite drink.

Main Idea   _____

_____

_____

Supporting Details   _____

_____

_____

_____

_____

_____

_____

*extensive: large, wide-ranging.

2. Born in 1912, future German rocket scientist Wernher von Braun demonstrated his interests early on. As a boy, he tried to make his wagon fly by attaching rockets to its sides. By 1932, von Braun—a fresh-faced youth of twenty—had earned an engineering degree and was heading a newly created rocket program in Kummersdorf, Germany. By 1934, von Braun had received a doctorate in physics and was being funded by the new German leader, Adolf Hitler, who was enthusiastic about the potential of rocket science. It was only four years later that von Braun's team had developed the deadly V-2 missile, which could carry explosives almost two hundred miles. The V-2, in fact, was instrumental in Germany's deadly bombing raids on London. However, by 1945, the Nazi regime was collapsing. Von Braun, who was always careful to advance his own interests, decided to get on the winning side and surrendered to American troops. At first skeptical of von Braun, who had helped Hitler wage his bloody and horrific war, the Americans quickly realized how valuable he was to their own rocket program and decided to overlook his dubious* past. After all, the Cold War was heating up, and von Braun was a gold mine of information. By 1960, von Braun was the head of NASA's George C. Marshall Flight Center. Von Braun was jubilant when his agency landed a man on the moon in 1969, and the country celebrated with him. In 1975, he was awarded the National Medal of Science. Wernher von Braun's story is worth remembering the next time anyone tells you with great certainty that "what goes around, comes around."

Main Idea
_____

_____

Supporting Details
_____

_____

_____

_____

*dubious: questionable, suspicious.

_____

_____

_____

_____

_____

_____

The Panama Canal officially opened in 1914, creating a water passage between the Atlantic and Pacific oceans.

© John Barrett Collection, Library of Congress

3. Although the idea of constructing a canal across Panama dates back to the sixteenth century, the canal did not become a reality until the twentieth century. As early as 1534, Holy Roman Emperor Charles V suggested that building a waterway across the narrowest part of Central America would allow ships to travel more easily to Peru and Ecuador. His idea was revived now and then as the years went by, but construction was not actually attempted until 1880, when the French broke ground on January 1. Thirteen years later, in 1893, they abandoned the project as too difficult. In 1903, the United States, under President Theodore Roosevelt, gained control of the unfinished Panama Canal, and in 1904 construction resumed. Over the next ten years, workers built the canal's foundation and system of locks. On August 15, 1914, the canal formally opened when the cargo ship *Ancon* became the first to use it. After World War II, controversy swirled around the canal over who the rightful owners were, the Americans or the Panamanians. In 1977, U.S. President Jimmy Carter signed a treaty returning control of the canal zone to Panama.

Main Idea

_____

_____

Supporting Details

_____

_____

_____

_____

_____

_____

4. The civil rights, student, and antiwar movements of the 1950s and 1960s produced large numbers of young women activists.* Like the women in the earlier abolitionist movement, these activists called attention to their own inequality in America. Thus, the 1960s saw significant advances in the rights of women. Responding to increased lobbying by women, President John F. Kennedy, in 1961, created a Commission on the Status of Women. The commission's report openly criticized the fact that women continued to be second-class citizens in America, and it led to the establishment of similar state commissions. In 1966, Betty Friedan, author of the bestseller *The Feminine Mystique*, led a movement to form the first important national feminist organization in America since Susan B. Anthony's† National Women's Suffrage Association. The new organization was called the National Organization for Women (NOW). Even today, it continues to be a vocal and visible force in America on such issues as equal employment opportunity for women. In 1967, pressured by NOW, Lyndon Johnson formally prohibited sex discrimination in federal employment. Although the decades that followed the sixties have seen progress in women's rights, none quite equals the 1960s. (Adapted from Harris, *American Democracy*, pp. 170–71.)

Main Idea 1950's - 1960's were important in terms of womens rights.

Supporting Details 1) 1961: JFK created commission on Status of Women
   a) criticized how women were considered second class citizens.
2) 1966: Friedan started new organization

---

*activists: people devoted to fighting for a cause.
†Susan B. Anthony (1820–1906): a nineteenth-century leader in women's fight for the right to vote.

a feminist organization called (NOW)

3) 1967 : Johnson prohibited sex discriminat

✔ CHECK YOUR UNDERSTANDING

1. In the sequence of dates and events pattern, what plays an essential role?

_____

2. Paragraphs using a sequence of dates and events are likely to fulfill what three purposes?

_____

_____

_____

3. What kinds of transitional phrases can you expect to find in this pattern? Please give examples.

_____

_____

4. Give an example of a topic sentence that would signal the presence of the sequence of dates and events pattern.

_____

_____

5. What kind of visual aid is likely to turn up next to the sequence of dates and events pattern?

_____

6. Are only details with dates important to this pattern? Please explain.

_____

_____

Process

Writers use the **process pattern** of development to tell their readers how something works, happens, or develops. Thus the process pattern is particularly common in science and business textbooks. For an illustration of the process pattern, see the following paragraph, where the author describes the three stages of growth in identical twins.

> There are three basic stages involved in the development of identical twins. Their growth begins when the father's sperm pierces the egg of the mother. The fertilized egg then splits and divides into equal halves, each half receiving exactly the same number of chromosomes* and genes.* The halves of the egg then develop into two babies who are of the same sex and who are identical in all hereditary traits, such as hair and eye color.

The topic of this paragraph is "the development of identical twins." The topic sentence tells us there are three specific stages. The supporting details then describe each of the three stages.

Transitions

Whenever an author explains how something develops over time, look for transitions that help readers keep track of the individual steps or stages. The transitions listed below are some of the most common.

Transitions That Describe a Process ◆			
	After	In	Once
	At the onset	In the beginning	Over time
	At this point	In the early stages	Right after
	Before	In the end	Shortly after
	By	Last	Soon
	During	Later	Then
	Eventually	Meanwhile	Today
	Finally	Next	When
	First, second, third	Now	Within hours
	Following	On	(or days)

---

*chromosomes: bodies within a cell that consist of hundreds of clear, jellylike particles strung together like beads. They carry the genes.
*genes: the elements responsible for hereditary characteristics, such as hair and eye color.

Typical Topic Sentences

Any time a topic sentence uses words and phrases like *process, sequence of steps,* or *series of stages,* you are probably dealing with a paragraph that employs the time-order pattern.

1. Children go through several different stages before arriving at a sense of gender.
2. The process of photosynthesis is essential to plant life.
3. Storing information in long-term memory involves several distinct steps.
4. The red-headed owl follows an intricate courting ritual.

Telltale Visual Aids

Flow charts like the ones described in Chapter 8 are a dead giveaway to the process pattern. If you see a paragraph or chapter section accompanied by a flow chart, it's more than likely that the process pattern organizes the selection.

Taking Notes on Process Patterns

Notes on paragraphs describing a process should include the following:

1. the larger process being described
2. the specific steps in the process
3. the order in which they are presented
4. any specialized vocabulary used to describe the steps or stages

As you can see, the following sample notes identify all four essential elements of this pattern.

Main Idea There are three stages in the development of identical twins.

Supporting Details
1. Father's sperm pierces mother's egg.
2. Fertilized egg splits and divides into equal halves; each half receives same number of chromosomes and genes.
3. Halves of egg develop into two babies of same sex, identical in all hereditary traits, such as hair and eye color.

> **NOTE-TAKING TIP** You might also try using a flow chart to take notes on a process. Just make sure to include arrows and brief but complete explanations of each step with one box or circle per step.

SUMMING UP THE KEY POINTS

1. The goal of the process pattern is to explain how something works, functions, or develops by outlining the crucial steps in real-time order. The process pattern is particularly common in science and business texts.

2. In the process pattern, transitions that introduce each new step in the larger sequence are especially important. The presence of words and phrases such as "in the first step," "then," "next," and "finally" are all signals to the underlying process pattern.

3. Flow charts frequently accompany the process pattern. Writers use them to make the individual steps clear to readers.

4. Notes on the process pattern need to clearly identify the overall process being described. They also need to list and describe, in the correct order, the individual steps that make up the larger whole.

5. When specialized vocabulary is included in the pattern, it should appear in your notes.

6. Flow charts are a good note-taking strategy for recording information organized by the process pattern.

◆ **EXERCISE 3**   **Understanding Process Patterns**

DIRECTIONS   Read and take notes on each paragraph. Circle the time-order transitions.

EXAMPLE   (In spring,) the stickleback, a small fish found in both fresh and salt water, goes through a strange courtship ritual. (With the coming of) the spring months, the male stickleback begins to look for a place where he can build his nest. (Once he has found it,) he grows aggressive and fights off all invaders. (After) finishing the nest, he searches for a female. (When he finds one, he leads her to the nest, and she enters it. The male then hits the tail of the female, forcing her to deposit her eggs. Once she lays the eggs, the female swims off, and the male enters the nest.

Main Idea   In spring, the stickleback goes through an odd courtship ritual.

Supporting Details   1. Male stickleback looks for place to build nest.

2. Finding one, he grows aggressive.

3. After finishing nest, he looks for female.

4. Leads her to nest, which she enters.

5. Male hits female's tail, forcing her to deposit eggs.

6. Once eggs are laid, she swims off and male enters nest.

EXPLANATION   Because the notes contain the main idea and all the steps described in the paragraph, we have everything of importance.

1. The first act of a newly hatched queen bee is to seek a mate. Three to five days after hatching, she attempts her first flight, flying far from the hive to avoid inbreeding.* When she is far enough, the queen produces a scent that attracts drones from distant hives. Once a drone arrives, mating takes place at an altitude of about fifty feet. Following the mating, the queen flies home to lay her eggs. A queen who does not mate by the time she is two weeks old will never mate and will remain barren.

Main Idea   _____

_____

Supporting Details   _____

_____

_____

_____

*inbreeding: reproducing by mating with a closely related individual.

2. The psychological disorder known as paranoia develops in four basic stages. At the illness's onset, victims begin to distrust the motives of others. The paranoid are constantly alert for ulterior, or secret, motives in the actions of others. If suspicion marks the first stage, self-protection is central to the second. At this point, any personal failure is seen as the fault of others, and victims no longer take responsibility for their actions. In the third stage, paranoia sufferers become hostile; they are openly angry at their supposed ill treatment at the hands of others. This period of anger usually leads to a moment of paranoid illumination.* In this final stage, everything falls into place, and the truly paranoid wholeheartedly believe that a plot or conspiracy is being directed against them. Seeing enemies everywhere, they are now convinced that someone, often a whole group, is trying to do them bodily harm and perhaps even kill them.

Main Idea _____

Supporting Details _____

3. A volcanic eruption begins when lava, or liquified rock, in a volcano becomes charged with steam and gas. The lava then shoots upward

*illumination: understanding.

and falls back to earth in fragments of stone. In the next stage, the lava in the volcano's center builds up and flows over the rim. At this point, the volcano's eruption is at its crisis, or critical, point. After a final massive explosion of lava, the volcano begins to cool. During the cooling stage, the volcano emits gases and vapors. This phase is often followed by the appearance of hot springs or geysers, like the ones that can be seen in Yellowstone National Park. Eventually the last traces of volcanic heat disappear, and cold springs may appear around the volcano.

Main Idea   _____

_____

Supporting Details   _____

_____

_____

_____

_____

_____

_____

_____

_____

4. The eggs of the king salmon hatch in freshwater streams; within a year after hatching, however, the young salmon head out to sea. During their journey, many are killed by bears, ducks, raccoons, and industrial waste. Only a small portion of the salmon actually reaches the sea. Those that do, stay anywhere from four to six years. Then they begin their journey back to the river in which they hatched. When they reach that river, they lay thousands of eggs that will hatch and go through the exact same life cycle. Once the adult king salmon have laid their eggs, life is over for them. They change color and turn slimy. Slowly, they float downstream with their tails forward. Within days, they are dead.

Main Idea
_____

_____

_____

Supporting Details
_____

_____

_____

_____

_____

_____

_____

_____

_____

Pattern 3: Simple Listing

In time-order patterns, the order of the supporting details is extremely important. The dates and events or the steps in a process have to be presented according to how they occur (or occurred) in real time. The same is not true, however, of the simple listing pattern. With this method of organization, the order of the details can vary with the writer. That's because the content does not rely on any specific order. Look, for example, at the following paragraph:

> If you ask several American citizens who the country's greatest presidents were, don't expect a consensus of opinion. For each person, greatness in a president depends on an individual's sense of what presidents should accomplish for the country. Those who believe it's the government's job to create social equality are likely to name Abraham Lincoln, Franklin Delano Roosevelt, maybe even Lyndon Johnson, all of whom proudly announced their determination to use the power of government for the creation of social justice. For those convinced, though, that the best president is one who governs least, Ronald Reagan is likely to be named the greatest president of all time. It was Reagan who repeatedly proclaimed that each individual was

responsible for his or her own destiny. The government could not and would not step in to help those who had failed to adequately advance on society's economic ladder. For those who argue, however, that the Constitution is what makes the country both strong and special, the greatest presidents will be men like Thomas Jefferson, James Madison, and John Adams, all of whom helped frame the Constitution that guides our lives to this very day.

According to the above paragraph, Americans decide who is the best president based on their personal ideas of how government should function. The writer then expands on that general point by giving examples. Those examples, however, do not have to be presented in any particular order. In fact, after a little fiddling with the transitional links, the details could reappear with a totally different order:

> If you ask several American citizens who the country's greatest presidents were, don't expect a consensus of opinion. For each person, greatness in a president depends on the individual's sense of what presidents should accomplish for the country. Those who believe that what makes our country great is its Constitution would be likely to choose presidents like Thomas Jefferson, John Adams, and James Madison, men who played central roles in framing the Constitution. However, for those convinced that the best president is the one who governs least, Ronald Reagan is likely to be named the greatest president of them all. It was Reagan who repeatedly proclaimed that each individual was responsible for his or her own destiny. The government could not and would not step in to help those who had failed to adequately advance on society's economic ladder. But for those citizens passionately convinced that it's the government's job to help create social equality, the greatest presidents would be men like Abraham Lincoln, Franklin Delano Roosevelt, maybe even Lyndon Johnson, all of whom proudly announced their determination to use the power of government for the creation of social justice.

As you can see, the simple listing pattern does not rely on the order of events or steps to make a point.

Typical Topic Sentence

Topic sentences that signal the listing pattern usually contain some general word or phrase that needs to be illustrated to be meaningful—for example, "African honeybees have a number of *characteristics* that make them especially dangerous." Often, the general word or phrase is an explicit or implied plural form. For instance, in the example on the previous page, the phrase "for each person" suggests many people with conflicting ideas about what the president should be doing in office. That phrase paves the way for the writer to provide some specific examples.

The following are all topic sentences that suggest a listing pattern.

1. Unlike the previous generation who relied on letters and phone calls to keep in touch, people today have many different ways to stay connected to friends and family.
2. Crime shows are a staple of television programming.
3. Abused children tend to exhibit similar behavior.
4. Across cultures, certain moments in life count as unforgettable.
5. There are a number of reasons why memorizing poetry has practical benefits.

READING TIP In the listing pattern, it's unlikely that the topic sentence would be in the middle of the paragraph. In this pattern, the topic sentence appears at the very beginning or the very end.

Transitional Signals

Transitions like *for instance* and *for example* are likely to appear in this pattern. So, too, are transitions such as *first*, *second*, and *third*.

Taking Notes on the Simple Listing Pattern

Notes on the simple listing pattern should include the following:

1. the main idea
2. any supporting details necessary to itemize and explain the plural word or phrase included in the topic sentence—for example, different reasons, crime shows, characteristics

Because order does not play a significant role in this pattern, you might consider using a diagram to take notes.

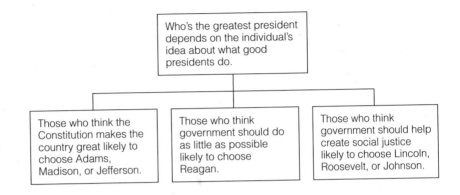

SUMMING UP THE KEY POINTS

1. In the simple listing pattern, the order of the supporting details can vary dramatically, depending on how the writer chooses to arrange the details. Because the order of information is not a significant factor in this pattern, your notes can present the details in any way that makes them easy to remember.

2. Topic sentences in this pattern will appear at the very beginning or at the very end.

3. Topic sentences in the simple listing pattern are also likely to include some general word that needs to be more specific to be meaningful. That word or term is likely to be plural in form, for instance, "indications" and "strategies."

4. Typical transitions are "for instance" and "for example," along with transitions like "first," "second," and "third." These transitions help readers identify the individual items being listed.

◆ **EXERCISE 4**   **Understanding Simple Listing**

DIRECTIONS   Read each passage. Then take notes using the space provided to create an outline or a diagram.

EXAMPLE   There are many common signs and symptoms of respiratory disease. One typical symptom is difficulty breathing in a prone position. This symptom is especially significant if breathing becomes easier when the person sits or stands up straight. Coughing is another common symptom, and it's caused by irritation of the airways or a buildup of fluid in the lung tissue. Coughing up blood is called *hemoptysis* and can be a sign of serious respiratory disease. Nasal discharge is another symptom of respiratory problems and is present in both inflammation and allergic respiratory reactions. Most frequently, nasal discharge is a symptom of the common cold, but it can also be a symptom of other more serious respiratory disorders. Surprisingly, hiccups, at least if they are persistent, can be a sign of respiratory disease. A barrel-chested appearance and enlarged fingertips can also be signs that a respiratory disease is present.

A number of different symptoms can be signs of respiratory disease.

- difficulty breathing in a prone position
- gets better standing
- coughing
- caused by irritation to lungs or fluid buildup
- coughing up blood serious
- barrel-chested appearance
- enlargement of fingertips
- persistent hiccups
- nasal discharge

EXPLANATION As is typical of this pattern, the topic sentence appears at the beginning and includes a phrase "signs and symptoms" that needs to be narrowed if it is to convey any information to the reader. The symptoms are then listed in a way the writer finds effective. However, another writer might just as easily choose to start with the most severe symptoms followed by those that are less severe. Yet another writer might decide to start with symptoms related to physical appearance and then progress to symptoms that are more overtly a sign of illness, such as difficulty breathing.

1. Everyone feels unhappy or sad in response to disappointment, failure, or personal loss. This is a perfectly normal reaction to painful experiences. However, persistent and prolonged feelings of sadness lacking any particular cause are often a sign of clinical depression, and they require treatment, particularly if the following symptoms are also present. People who are clinically depressed often feel hopeless and worthless. Try as they might, they find it difficult to control their negative thoughts. Another sign that a serious depression may

be brewing is loss of appetite, and the seriously depressed take no pleasure in food. Insomnia or the tendency to sleep too much is yet another symptom of depression. Finding previously easy-to-handle tasks difficult is an additional indication that a person is clinically depressed. So, too, is the inability to concentrate or stay focused on a task. Probably the most important warning sign, though, is the feeling that life is not worth living. Often this feeling is accompanied by the persistent idea that suicide might be the only way out. When this happens, the person experiencing these thoughts should seek help immediately.

2. Until the 1930s, memorizing poems was considered an essential part of a child's education, but at some point, memorization got a bad name, and students stopped learning how to commit poems to memory. But as novelist and poet Carol Muske-Dukes points out in her essay "A Lost Eloquence," to memorize a poem is to "own" it with both the body and the brain, making the benefits of memorizing poetry more numerous than many realize. In his article "In Defense of Memorization," essayist and teacher Michael Knox Beran insists that memorizing poems is a significant vocabulary booster. When students memorize a poem, they learn new words plus a context to go with them. Because the context stays with the student in the form of a memorized poem, so do the meanings of the words. By memorizing poetry, students also automatically learn which words typically make sense together and which ones don't. In addition, the reading and re-reading that memorization requires encourage students to read phrase by phrase, while pausing to make connections between each line of poetry. This close reading helps students recognize subtle word meanings that might well go unnoticed if the student were not re-reading in order to memorize.

3. There are three essential learning strategies students should use to make sure they understand and remember new information. One strategy is *rehearsal*, or repetition, of what's just been read or heard. Thus, students who repeat the main idea of a paragraph right after they finish reading it are more likely to understand and remember the paragraph's point. *Synthesizing** is another key learning strategy. For instance, students reading a chapter that compares the press's role during the first and second Gulf War will have a better understanding of the material if they can link the chapter sections with a synthesis statement. A synthesis statement makes connections between different chapter sections (or even different readings), for example: "During the first Gulf War, the government and the military, worried about a possibly adversarial* press, imposed blanket censorhip. But in the second, they used embedding† to keep the press informed and cooperative." The third strategy, *elaboration*, requires the learner to relate new information to prior knowledge by, for instance, comparing the author's point of view to another writer who disagrees or shares the same opinion, for example: "Robert Caro despises Johnson as a man and president, but Robert Dallek is a more sympathetic critic on both counts."

---

*synthesizing: the combining of separate thoughts to create a new idea.
*adversarial: challenging; ready to criticize.
†embedding: journalists were assigned to military units engaged in armed conflicts.

4. Fans of the iPhone claim that it has applications, or apps, for just about every waking minute. In addition to its more basic functions as a cell phone, the iPhone app store can provide, for a price and for free, any number of services. Looking in the refrigerator and wondering what you can whip up for dinner with the four ingredients sitting in there, try the *Betty Crocker Mobile Cookbook* app. It suggests recipes based on ingredients on hand. Insecure about what to wear, then consider tapping *Stylish Girl*. It stores images of your clothes and can mix and match them to create outfits. And if you need to know how to dress for the day, always check *The Weather Channel* to see if a heavy coat is really necessary. If you walk to school or work and want to know how many steps you take, turn to *Step Trak Lite* to start the count. And if you think you need a cup of coffee to keep you going, the application *My Yelp* will tell you where you can find one. By the time you get home and finish studying, you're probably ready to kick back and watch a little television. As it turns out, there's an app for that, too. *What's On* is just a tap away on the iPhone.

✔ CHECK YOUR UNDERSTANDING

1. How does the simple listing pattern differ from a process pattern?

_____

_____

_____

2. In the simple listing pattern, where is the topic sentence most likely to occur?

_____

_____

3. What kind of word is likely to appear in a topic sentence that introduces the simple listing pattern?

_____

_____

4. What are some transitions that are likely to accompany this pattern?

_____

_____

Pattern 4: Comparison and Contrast

Paragraphs based on comparison and contrast mention the similarities, and/or differences between two people, events, animals, or objects. Take, for example, the following paragraph:

> Much attention, perhaps too much, has been paid to the differences between Japanese and American workers. *But* perhaps we should examine more carefully the differences between Japanese and American management at the highest levels of decision making. In Japan, the heads of companies are discouraged from earning more than fourteen times the salary of their highest-paid workers. In America, *in contrast,* the company's chief officer can be expected to earn as much as fifty times more than the highest-salaried worker. In Japan, if someone in top management makes a serious blunder, he is in disgrace and will publicly acknowledge it. *However,* if the same thing happens in America, the company may suffer bankruptcy, but the person who erred is unlikely to publicly take responsibility.

While the introductory sentence suggests a paragraph that will focus on the differences between Japanese and American workers, the transition *but* reverses the opening train of thought and paves the way for the topic sentence—"But perhaps we should examine more carefully the differences between Japanese and American management at the highest levels of decision making." That topic sentence makes it clear that the paragraph will concentrate on differences between Japanese and American management. The major supporting details then cite specific differences.

In some cases, paragraphs do both: They compare *and* contrast two topics. Here's an example:

> The African or so-called killer bees have entered the United States, and their arrival has, for good reason, aroused intense fear. *Although* in some ways the African bees are similar to harmless honeybees, they are different in a significant and dangerous way. *In terms of similarities*, the African bee's venom is no more poisonous than the honeybee's, and individually the African bee is not much more aggressive than the honeybee. What distinguishes the African bee from the American honeybee is its determined defense of territory. If African bees are disturbed in their nest, they mount a furious attack and pursue intruders for miles, *whereas* honeybees quickly give up the chase.

In this paragraph, the topic sentence tells readers to expect a discussion of both similarities and differences: "Although in some ways the African bees are similar to harmless honeybees, they are different in a significant and dangerous way." The supporting details fulfill the promise of that sentence, specifically identifying two similarities and one dangerous difference.

Transitions

Notice, too, the italicized transitions that signal both comparison and contrast. Such transitions are useful clues to the comparison and contrast pattern. They can also help you distinguish between major and minor supporting details. Transitions signaling comparison or contrast almost always introduce major rather than minor details.

Transitions That Signal Similarity ♦	Along the same lines	In like fashion (manner)	Just as
	Also	In much the same way (manner)	Just like
	By the same token		Like
	Comparatively	In terms of similarities	Likewise
	In comparison	In the same vein	Similarly

Transitions That Signal Difference ♦	Actually	In reality	Opposing that position
	Although	Instead	Rather
	And yet	Ironically	Still
	But	Just the opposite	Though
	Conversely	Nevertheless	Unfortunately
	Despite that fact	Nonetheless	Unlike
	Even though	On the contrary	Whereas
	However	On the one hand	While
	In contrast	On the other hand	Yet
	In opposition		

Typical Topic Sentences

Transitions like those listed above are good clues to the comparison and contrast pattern. So, too, are topic sentences like the following:

[handwritten: Contrast]

1. Scientists Edward Teller and J. Robert Oppenheimer had very different feelings about the success of the Manhattan Project.[†]

[handwritten: Contrast]

2. Unlike African Americans, Mexican Americans were not forced into segregated military units during World War II.

[handwritten: Both]

3. France and Germany were both against the 2003 war with Iraq, but they showed their disagreement in very different ways.

[handwritten: Compare ✗]

4. Roy Cohn and Joseph McCarthy showed the same approach to the truth: If it stood in their way, they just ignored it.

Topic sentences that identify two topics and review the similarities and the differences, or both, are a dead giveaway to the comparison and contrast pattern. However, it's also true that authors frequently identify similarities and differences, letting the details imply the overall point.

[†]Manhattan Project: the name given to the research group that focused on building the atom bomb. Teller was enthusiastic about the successful detonation of the bomb. Oppenheimer was appalled.

Taking Notes on Comparison and Contrast Patterns

Notes on a paragraph using a comparison and contrast pattern should clearly identify three essential elements:

> **1.** the two topics being compared and/or contrasted
> **2.** the similarities and/or differences between the two
> **3.** the main idea they explain or support

Here, to illustrate, are notes on the paragraph on page 525.

Main Idea Although there are some similarities between American honeybees and African bees, there is an important and dangerous difference.

Supporting Details **1.** African bees' venom no more poisonous than honeybees'.

2. The two bees about equally aggressive.

3. What makes African bees different and dangerous is determined defense of territory.

    a. Attack in a group and pursue for miles.

    b. Honeybees quickly give up the chase.

When taking notes on the comparison and contrast pattern, consider making a diagram that looks something like this:

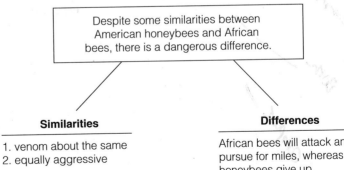

Despite some similarities between American honeybees and African bees, there is a dangerous difference.

Similarities
1. venom about the same
2. equally aggressive

Differences
African bees will attack and pursue for miles, whereas honeybees give up.

> **READING TIP** Make sure you know what main idea is developed by the description of differences and similarities.

SUMMING UP THE KEY POINTS

1. Paragraphs based on the comparison and contrast pattern of organization always present the reader with two different topics. Based on the needs of the main idea, the supporting details then highlight similarities and differences between the two. Some paragraphs using this pattern describe both similarities and differences.

2. Transitions such as *likewise*, *similarly*, *but*, and *however* are clues to this pattern. However, the real clues are the presence of the two topics and the references to similarities and/or differences.

3. Topic sentences that explain how two things, people, ideas, or events do or do not resemble one another are also a clue to this pattern. It's also true that in the comparison and contrast pattern, the main idea is frequently implied rather than stated. In this case, the author lets the similarities and differences speak for themselves.

4. Notes on the comparison and contrast pattern need to include the two topics being compared and/or contrasted. They also need to include the central similarities and differences between the two, along with the implied or stated main idea that the details develop.

5. Crucial to notes on the comparison and contrast pattern is the presence of the main idea. Sometimes readers get caught up in the similarities and differences and forget to indicate why they are present in the paragraph.

◆ EXERCISE 5 Understanding Comparison and Contrast Patterns

DIRECTIONS When you finish reading each paragraph, circle the appropriate letter to indicate whether the author has (1) compared two topics, (2) contrasted two topics, or (3) compared *and* contrasted two topics. Circle all comparison and contrast transitions, and use the blank lines to take notes on the paragraph.

EXAMPLE Between 1890 and 1900, millions of people from southern and eastern Europe left their homes in search of the American dream. The new immigrants hoped to find a comfortable place where they could settle and live out their lives. (But) the cities to which they came were not prepared for the new arrivals, and many immigrant families ended up in ugly apartments that were poorly supplied with light, heat, and water. The new arrivals had dreamed of finding work that could make them independent, even rich. (Instead) they found that jobs were scarce. Immigrants often had to take jobs for which they were unsuited, and the work left them exhausted and depressed. (Moreover,) many found that they were treated as outsiders, and their accents were subject to insults or ridicule.

In this paragraph, the author
    a. compares two topics.
    (b.) contrasts two topics.
    c. compares and contrasts two topics.

Main Idea Immigrants who came in search of the American dream between

1890 and 1900 were terribly disappointed.

Supporting Details 1. Instead of comfortable place to live, had to settle for ugly apartments

with little light, heat, or water.

2. Instead of suitable jobs, found unemployment or exhausting,

depressing work.

3. Instead of warm welcome, treated as outsiders with odd customs and odd

way of speaking.

EXPLANATION   The paragraph contrasts what immigrants hoped to find in their new country with what they actually found. Each difference reinforces the implied main idea: "Immigrants who came in search of the American dream between 1890 and 1900 were terribly disappointed."

1. The ancient Greek philosophers Plato and Aristotle differed widely in their worldviews. Plato, the mystic, was a believer in intuition rather than reason. For him, nature was only a dark reflection of a higher, more spiritual world revealed in occasional flashes of insight. Aristotle, however, was a firm believer in logic and hard evidence. Unlike Plato, he believed that truth could be found through the observation of nature. Yet despite their basic differences, the two had a similarly negative effect on scientific progress during the Middle

Ages and early Renaissance.[†] Thanks to their teaching, the scientific understanding of astronomy and physics slowed to a standstill. Insisting that all motion was in perfect circles completed at a uniform speed, both Plato and Aristotle delayed the recognition of what the astronomer Johannes Kepler proved in the seventeenth century: Kepler demonstrated that the planets moved in oval rather than circular orbits. Kepler's discoveries laid the groundwork for the laws of motion later discovered by Isaac Newton. Both Kepler's description of the planets and Newton's laws of motion might have come a good deal sooner had the ideas of Plato and Aristotle not been influential for so many centuries.

In this paragraph, the author

a. compares two topics.

b. contrasts two topics.

c. compares and contrasts two topics.

Main Idea _____

_____

Supporting Details _____

_____

_____

_____

_____

_____

_____

[†]Renaissance: A cultural movement that was marked by a renewed interest in classical literature, advances in art, and political change. The movement occurred across Europe and happened in different times in different countries. The dates of the Renaissance, which means "rebirth," are roughly between the fourteenth and seventeenth centuries.

2. Gerald Ford, the thirty-eighth president of the United States, was fond of alluding* to one of his predecessors, Harry S. Truman. Ford used the allusions to emphasize what he believed were similarities between himself and Truman. A less than charismatic president, Ford seemed to think that likening himself to Truman would increase his hold on the public's imagination. Like Ford, Truman had been a vice president who became president only by chance. Truman took over when Franklin Roosevelt died in office, a circumstance that resembled Ford's own ascent* to the presidency when Richard Nixon resigned from office. Neither Truman nor Ford was an intellectual, and both men tended to exaggerate their lack of learning, insisting that they were just simple men with simple tastes. Ford also liked to emphasize that both he and Truman came to office at a difficult time. Truman led the nation during the final months of World War II, and Ford entered office in the wake of the Watergate scandal that destroyed Nixon's career.

In this paragraph, the author
a. compares two topics.
b. contrasts two topics.
c. compares and contrasts two topics.

Main Idea _____

_____

Supporting Details _____

_____

_____

_____

_____

_____

_____

*alluding: referring, mentioning.
*ascent: climb.

3. Laws and ethics are not quite the same. In general, laws are society's attempt to formalize—reduce to written rules—the general public's ideas about what is considered right and wrong conduct in various spheres of life. However, it is rarely possible for written laws to capture all of the subtle shadings that people include in the codes of ethics they use to govern their lives. Ethical concepts, or moral principles—like the people who believe in them—are more complex than written rules of law. Ethical concepts are ideas about right or moral conduct, and they cannot always be expressed in the formal language of law or in rules. (Adapted from Frederick et al., *Business and Society*, p. 68.)

In this paragraph, the author

a. compares two topics.

b. contrasts two topics.

c. compares and contrasts two topics.

Main Idea _____

_____

Supporting Details _____

_____

_____

_____

_____

4. To some degree, all societies are altered by time. But for Nigerian society, the changes between life in early-nineteenth-century Nigeria and now are especially striking. Most notable is the shift in economic and political power, which was originally in the hands of local leaders who governed Nigeria's twenty-three individual states. Currently, power is concentrated in the hands of a small group of business and military leaders. While local leaders in the early nineteenth

century often waged war in pursuit of expanding their territory or province,* modern tribal leaders exert influence through behind-the-scenes political wheeling and dealing rather than military conquest. Although the power and influence of local leaders has been dramatically curtailed by the arrival of democratic traditions, one thing has not altered. Community leaders are still regarded as the custodians of past tradition and as the final word on questions about what it means to be a Nigerian in moral or ethical terms. Another area where dramatic change has occurred is in the conduct of courtship. In the past, there was no such thing as dating. If a couple was seen together in public, they were expected to marry. City couples, at least, are now free to date without expectations of marriage. In the countryside, however, courtship rules are somewhat stricter, and dating as we know it is not encouraged.

In this paragraph, the author

a. compares two topics.

b. contrasts two topics.

c. compares and contrasts two topics.

Main Idea _____

_____

Supporting Details _____

_____

_____

_____

_____

_____

_____

*province: area governed as a unit of a country or an empire; area of knowledge or interest.

> ✔
> # CHECK YOUR UNDERSTANDING
>
> 1. What are the essential characteristics of the comparison and contrast pattern?
>
> _____
>
> _____
>
> 2. Name four transitions that are typical of this pattern.
>
> _____
>
> _____
>
> 3. What kind of topic sentence is likely to appear in this pattern?
>
> _____
>
> _____
>
> 4. What should notes on this pattern include?
>
> _____
>
> _____
>
> 5. What mistake do readers sometimes make when taking notes on this pattern?
>
> _____
>
> _____

Pattern 5: Cause and Effect

"Life is a perpetual instruction in cause and effect."

— Ralph Waldo Emerson, American writer and philosopher

Whatever type of reading you do, you are bound to run across passages that explain how one event—the **cause**—leads to or produces another event—the **effect**. Look, for example, at the following paragraph:

Fear has a profound effect on the human body. When you become frightened, you breathe more deeply, thereby sending your muscles more oxygen and energy. *Consequently*, your heart beats faster, making your blood circulate more quickly and thereby rushing oxygen to all parts of your body. *In response* to fear, your stomach and intestines stop contracting and all digestive activity ceases. Your saliva also stops flowing, causing your mouth to become dry. Fear also causes the body's blood vessels to shrink, making your face lose its natural color.

In this paragraph, the topic sentence identifies the cause and effect relationship under discussion: Fear has a profound effect on the human body. The supporting details then describe those effects more specifically. Note, too, that some details also describe *cycles of causes and effects* in which one effect turns into the cause of another. Fear, for example, causes your blood vessels to shrink, which, in turn, produces another effect—your face loses color. If diagrammed, the relationships among these statements would look like this:

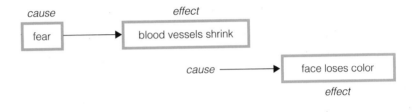

Transitions

As the italicized transitions in the paragraph above suggest, transitions are often clues to the cause and effect pattern. Should you see any of the following in a paragraph, there's a good chance that the cause and effect pattern is at work.

Cause and Effect Transitions ◆	As a result	For this reason	In response to
	As a side effect	Hence	Thanks to
	Consequently	In the aftermath of	Therefore
	Due to	In consequence	Thus

Cause and Effect Verbs

In addition to the above transitions, watch for the following verbs. They, too, are clues to the cause and effect pattern. Like the transitions, they can also help you sort out the individual causes and effects mentioned in a paragraph.

Verbs Frequently Used to Link Cause and Effect ◆	Affect	End	Result
	Begin	Foster	Revolutionize
	Bring about	Generate	Set in motion
	Cause	Halt	Set off
	Change	Increase	Spur
	Contribute	Induce	Start
	Create	Introduce	Stimulate
	Decrease	Lead to	Stop
	Encourage	Produce	Trigger

Typical Topic Sentences

Topic sentences like those listed below all suggest a cause and effect pattern.

1. General Alfredo Stroessner took control of Paraguay in 1954 and turned the country into a haven for international outlaws.
2. Artist Andy Warhol's paintings of ordinary objects like the Campbell's soup can revolutionized modern art.
3. In the 1980s and 1990s, rock star Madonna profoundly influenced the image of women in pop music.
4. The fabulous success of Daddy Yankee's album *Barrio Fino* brought the music known as Reggaeton international interest and acclaim.
5. Three factors contributed to the decline in union membership between 1950 and 1990.

If you encounter a topic sentence that says one event led to or caused another, you are undoubtedly dealing with a cause and effect pattern.

Taking Notes on Cause and Effect Patterns

As you might expect, cycles of causes and effects such as the one already illustrated should be included in your notes along with the following:

1. The general cause and effect relationship described by the topic sentence.
2. The specific causes and/or effects mentioned in the paragraph.

For an illustration, look at the following sample notes for the paragraph on fear:

Main Idea Fear has a powerful effect on the human body.

Supporting Details 1. Breathe more deeply, sending muscles more oxygen and energy.

2. Heart beats faster, making blood circulate more rapidly.

    a. Blood rushes oxygen to all parts of body.

3. Stomach and intestines stop contractions so that all digestion ceases.

4. Saliva stops flowing and mouth gets dry.

5. Blood vessels shrink.

    a. Causes face to lose color.

NOTE-TAKING TIP When taking notes on a cause and effect passage, consider using a diagram like the one shown on page 535.

SUMMING UP THE KEY POINTS

1. Paragraphs organized to show cause and effect always explain how one event produced or created another or other events.
2. Although they do not always appear, transitions such as *thus, therefore, consequently*, and *as a result* suggest that the cause and effect pattern is present. So, too, does the presence of verbs such as *triggers, causes*, and *stimulates*.
3. Topic sentences in the cause and effect pattern are likely to explain how some event or series of events led to specific effects or had powerful consequences—for example, "The study indicates that letting small children watch television throughout the day increases their risk of having concentration problems later on in school."

4. When a paragraph describes a cycle of causes and effects, it shows how one effect can then become the cause of yet another effect, producing what amounts to a chain of cause and effect relationships.

5. Notes on this pattern should include the overall cause and effect relationship outlined in the topic sentence, along with any specific causes and effects identified in the paragraph.

◆ **EXERCISE 6**   **Understanding Cause and Effect Patterns**

DIRECTIONS   Read each paragraph. Circle the cause and effect transitions. Then take notes on each pattern.

EXAMPLE   No one would deny that several events led to America's Revolutionary War. But one of the most important was the introduction of the Coercive* or Intolerable Acts. The Coercive Acts, which were designed to punish Americans for the Boston Tea Party,[†] treated Bostonians with great severity. The Port of Boston was closed until the tea that had been destroyed was paid for. In addition, any English officials accused of committing murder in the course of suppressing a riot or enforcing the law could no longer be tried in the colony where the incident had taken place. Moreover, Massachusetts officials would no longer be locally elected; instead, they had to be appointed by the king. Perhaps most offensive to the Americans was the new Quartering Act. It specified that British troops could be housed in all inns or homes even without the owners' permission. (As a result) of the Coercive Acts, many Americans who had been undecided about rebellion became committed to the idea of throwing off British rule.

Main Idea The Coercive Acts played a key role in America's decision to rebel against

the British.

Supporting Details 1. Port of Boston closed until tea was paid for.

2. English officials who committed murder while putting down a riot or

enforcing the law tried outside of the colony where murder had occurred.

---

*coercive: forcing someone to do something against his or her will.
[†]Boston Tea Party: In 1773, Bostonians angry over British taxes on tea hurled 342 chests of English tea into the ocean.

3. Massachusetts officials had to be appointed by king rather than locally elected.

4. Most offensive was the Quartering Act, which said that British troops could be housed in inns and homes without owners' permission.

EXPLANATION   This paragraph tells readers that Americans fought the Revolutionary War, in part at least, because of the hated Coercive Acts. The major details describe the acts so that readers understand the source of the hatred.

1. In his book *The Bounty of the Sea*, Jacques Cousteau, the underwater explorer, writer, and filmmaker, painted a terrifying portrait of what will happen if, in his words, we let the ocean "sicken and die" from pollution. From Cousteau's point of view, the death of the ocean, or extinction of sea life, will have terrifying consequences for all of humanity. Without sea life, the ocean would become a rotting grave. Billions of decaying bodies would create a stench* that would make its way into coastal regions. Consequently, people would have to abandon their homes to escape the smell. In addition, the death-filled seas would no longer be able to maintain a balance between the gases that make life possible. The carbon dioxide in the atmosphere would increase, trapping the heat that normally radiates outward from Earth into space. As a result, temperatures at sea level would dramatically increase. Yet another consequence would be visible on the ocean's surface. It would be covered with a thick film of decayed matter. Thus, the ocean would no longer give water to the skies through evaporation. Rain would be a rarity. Drought would range* over the land, and multitudes would starve.

Main Idea _____

_____

Supporting Details _____

_____

_____

*stench: smell, stink.
*range: move about, travel.

_____

_____

_____

_____

_____

_____

_____

2. There are at least two different, though occasionally overlapping, reasons why people decide to join groups. In some cases, the group's activities offer a chance to fulfill civic* or religious obligations we consider valuable. Thus, a person concerned about the plight of the homeless might decide to become part of a community soup kitchen to fulfill her sense of social responsibility. Then, too, we frequently join groups because we care more about the group's members than we do about the group's goals. For example, a person might decide to join a bowling group even if he's not all that fond of bowling. The appeal here is a chance to get together with friends—not the dream of winning a bowling tournament.

Main Idea _____

_____

Supporting Details _____

_____

_____

_____

_____

_____

_____

*civic: relating to the city or citizenship.

3. By the 1830s and 1840s, the growth of cities and the increase in literacy* had dramatically changed the face of American newspapers. Initially, newspapers had been written primarily for the well-to-do who wanted news about the arts, social events, and commerce.* But thanks to the growing urban landscape and the increase in the reading public, papers like the New York *Sun* started a trend toward cheap, mass-produced newspapers. The new "penny press," as it was called, broadened the range of topics covered in newspapers, telling of everyday events, sensational crimes, gossip, sports, and human-interest stories. By the 1890s, some penny papers had more than a million readers.

Main Idea

_____

_____

Supporting Details

_____

_____

_____

_____

_____

_____

_____

4. The causes for the dinosaurs' extinction remain one of science's great mysteries. Although there are several theories as to why the dinosaurs disappeared, only one seems truly sound. According to this theory, dinosaurs became extinct because a comet or an asteroid crashed into Earth, producing huge quantities of dust. As a result, clouds of dust blocked out sunlight for many months, and plants dependent on photosynthesis† for survival died out. Thus, the dinosaurs, who lived mainly on vegetation, were left without much food. The absence of

_____

*literacy: ability to read and write.
*commerce: trade.
†photosynthesis: process conducted by plants during which they use the sun's energy to convert carbon dioxide and water into food.

sunlight would have also caused temperatures to drop sharply, subjecting the dinosaur to twin forces of destruction—freezing and starvation.

Main Idea   _____

_____

Supporting Details   _____

_____

_____

_____

_____

_____

Pattern 6: Classification

"When we name something, then, we are classifying. The individual object or event we are naming, of course, has no name and belongs to no class until we put it in one."

—S. I. Hayakawa, American teacher, writer, Republican senator

In the classification pattern, the order of the supporting details is, once again, not important. However, there is a critical difference between simple listing and classification. Paragraphs relying on the classification pattern always make the same point: They tell the reader how some larger group can be broken down into smaller subgroups, or classes, each with its own defining set of characteristics. For example, in the following paragraph, the authors classify voting methods in the House of Representatives.

> Members of the House of Representatives may vote in four different ways. The most common method is the *voice vote*. Members in favor of a bill say "yea," while those opposed say "nay." The Speaker of the House then judges which side has the most voice votes and announces the result. If any member feels that the Speaker is mistaken, the Speaker can be forced to call for a *standing vote* in which the members stand to be counted for or against. A third method is the *teller vote*. If one-fifth of the members present demand, all the members of the House pass between "tellers" and are counted as they do so, first those in favor and then those opposed. The *roll call* is the procedure used for important measures. The Clerk of the House calls the

roll, and each of the members responds by answering "yea" or "nay." Roll-call voting takes about forty-five minutes. (Adapted from Shick and Pfister, *American Government: Continuity and Change*, p. 29.)

As is typical of the classification pattern, the authors open by telling their readers two things: (1) the larger group to be subdivided, Voting in the House of Representatives, and (2) the number of categories produced by classification, four. They then proceed to describe each category in more specific detail.

Typical Topic Sentences

Topic sentences like those listed here practically guarantee that a classification pattern organizes the paragraph.

1. There are primarily four different types of computer crime.
2. Most of the major speech defects are found within five main categories.
3. Researchers in interpersonal communication have come up with four kinds of conversations.
4. The Indian caste system once assigned human beings to four different groups, with Brahmans at the top of the heap and the untouchables at the bottom.

If a topic sentence announces that some larger group can be divided into separate categories or groups, you should prepare to take notes on the classification pattern.

Frequently Used Words in Classification Topic Sentences ◆		
	Categories	Elements
	Components	Features
	Fields	Problems
	Ranks	Types
	Groups	Kinds
	Parts	Classes
	Factors	

Telltale Visual Aids

Tables like the following frequently signal the presence of the classification pattern. Keep in mind, though, that you can also use them to review (just cover the right-hand side and see what you can remember about each classification category) or as a model for note-taking.

Table: The Four Basic Components of a Strategy

Scope	• Identifies the markets or industries in which firm will compete
Resource Deployment	• Indicates how company will allocate or use resources
Competitive Advantage	• Specifies what advantages a firm has relative to competitors
Synergy	• Reflects extent to which businesses inside the firm can draw upon one another

Source of information: Van Fleet and Peterson, *Contemporary Management*, pp. 73–74.

Taking Notes on the Classification Pattern

To be complete, notes on the classification pattern require the following information:

1. The name of the larger group being broken down into subgroups
2. The names of the categories if they are supplied
3. A brief description of each category

Here to illustrate are notes on the paragraph on pages 542–43.

Main Idea Members of the House have four different ways to vote.

Supporting Details 1. "Voice vote." Members voting in favor say "yea," those opposed say "nay," and the Speaker judges who has the stronger voice.

2. "Standing vote." If someone thinks the Speaker is mistaken, then members must stand to be counted.

3. "Teller vote." If 1/5 of all present members demand, members must be counted as they walk between tellers.

4. "Roll call." Used for really important measures; the House clerk calls the roll and each member responds "yea" or "nay."

NOTE-TAKING TIP If names of categories do appear in the classification paragraph, put those names first in your notes. This note-taking format nicely highlights the individual categories. However, you should also be aware that the subgroups in this pattern are not always named.

SUMMING UP THE KEY POINTS

1. Like simple listing, the classification pattern does not require that supporting details be presented in a particular order. However, the classification pattern, unlike simple listing, always makes the same point: It explains how some larger group can be broken down into smaller subgroups. Then the supporting details describe each subgroup in detail.

2. The topic sentence of the classification pattern usually names the number of subgroups that make up the larger whole—for example, "Currently, there are three different kinds of medication that deal with anxiety."

3. Categories in the classification pattern are not always identified by name. However, if they are identified by name, the names should be included in your notes. Include as well the characteristics that describe each subgroup.

◆ **EXERCISE 7** **Understanding Classification Patterns**

DIRECTIONS Read and take notes on each paragraph.

EXAMPLE Psychological problems are generally classified into two categories: externalizing disorders and internalizing disorders. The **externalizing disorders** are characterized by aggression diverted outward, such as striking out at other people or the environment. People suffering from these kinds of disorders exhibit behaviors such as lying, stealing, disobedience, and delinquency. Other common symptoms of externalizing disorders include fighting, cruelty to animals, property destruction, temper tantrums, hostility toward authority figures, and violating the rights of others. The **internalizing disorders** are directed inward. These affect the individual rather than other people or the environment. These disorders include anxiety, depression, worrying, withdrawal, phobias, and panic attacks. (Source of information: Kaplan, *Adolescence*, pp. 463–64.)

Main Idea Psychological problems are generally divided into two groups:

externalizing disorders and internalizing disorders.

Supporting Details 1. Externalizing disorders are directed toward others or the environment.

   a. Include lying, stealing, disobedience, and delinquency.

   b. Also include violence, fighting, animal cruelty, property damage,

      temper tantrums, hostility, and violation of others' rights.

2. Internalizing disorders are directed inward, toward self.

   a. Include anxiety, depression, worrying, withdrawal, phobias, and panic attacks.

EXPLANATION   As you can see, the notes contain the essential elements of the classification pattern. The larger group is divided into two smaller categories, and the names and characteristics of each group are listed.

1. In the human body, blood circulates through elastic, tubelike canals called *blood vessels*. Consisting of three different types, blood vessels are well adapted to their functions. The vessels called *arteries* carry blood away from the heart to all parts of the body. The largest artery in the human body is the *aorta*. Arterial blood appears bright red because it is filled with oxygen. In contrast, blood in the *veins*, another type of blood vessel, appears purplish because it is no longer carrying a supply of oxygen. Veins, which carry blood back to the heart, contain small valves that prevent the blood from flowing backward. This is important in the lower parts of the body where the blood has to move against the pull of gravity. The third type of blood vessel is the *capillary*. Capillaries are tiny vessels connecting arteries and veins. Capillary walls are extremely thin. They have to be thin so that digested food can pass through them to the cells of the body.

Main Idea _____

   _____

Supporting Details _____

   _____

   _____

_____

_____

_____

_____

_____

_____

_____

_____

2. Studies indicate that learning can be divided into two categories: *incidental learning* and *intentional learning*. Incidental learning takes place by chance; there is no clearly defined intention to learn. For example, a student wanting to check if he knows the first sixteen presidents of the United States may ask a friend to listen while they are named. During the recitation, the friend may, by chance, also learn the names of the first sixteen presidents. Intentional learning occurs when a clearly defined purpose exists from the very beginning. For example, a student may sit down with a list of the fifty states and their capitals because she needs to learn them for a test. Current research suggests that intentional learning is more effective because it stays with us over time.

Main Idea _____

_____

Supporting Details _____

_____

_____

_____

_____

_____

_____

3. In management, the phrase "downward communication" refers to messages from superiors to subordinates. According to D. Katz and R. Kahn, authors of the text *The Social Psychology of Organizations*, there are five different types of downward communication in organizations. (1) **Job instructions** are messages that specify how tasks should be conducted: "Always submit budget requests two months in advance." (2) **Job rationale** messages explain why tasks must be performed and how they relate to other activities of the organization: "We require advance notice so that we can plan ahead." (3) **Procedures and practices** messages inform members about organizational responsibilities, obligations, and privileges: "According to the procedures manual, we follow affirmative action[†] guidelines to the letter." (4) **Feedback** messages inform employees of their performance in the organization: "I am happy to note that your last project was a real success." (5) **Instruction about goals** messages teach employees the mission, goals, and objectives of the organization: "As you can see from our shared-values list, we feel that customer service is our number-one job." Downward communication may seem simple and clear-cut on the surface, but it is a complicated process that doesn't always go smoothly. (Adapted from O'Hair, Friedrich, and Shaver, *Strategic Communication*, p. 58.)

Main Idea _____

_____

Supporting Details _____

_____

_____

_____

_____

_____

_____

———————————

[†]affirmative action: term for a variety of efforts to ensure employment opportunities for women and minorities.

4. The sociologist Max Weber (1864–1920) classified authority into three major types. **Traditional authority** is authority based on custom and accepted practice. In England, for example, the authority to be the head of government is traditionally a birthright. The person who becomes the king or queen does so because a parent or some other ancestor reigned before. **Charismatic authority** stems from the personality or personal appeal of the individual. Salvador Allende,[†] Martin Luther King Jr., and Princess Diana are examples of people whose power stemmed partly or wholly from their *charisma*. **Legal-rational authority** comes from rules or laws created to make institutions function effectively. Elected government officials hold this type of authority. Neatly divided as Weber's categories are, however, it should be pointed out here that all three types of authority are present in most societies, and they do occasionally overlap. (Adapted from Poponoe, *Sociology*, pp. 436–37.)

Main Idea _____

_____

Supporting Details _____

_____

_____

_____

_____

_____

_____

_____

_____

_____

[†]Salvador Allende (1908–1973): The first democratically elected Marxist head of government, he ruled Chile between 1970 and 1973.

✔ **CHECK YOUR UNDERSTANDING**

1. What's the major difference between the simple listing and the classification pattern?

   _____

   _____

2. What does the topic sentence in the classification pattern usually do?

   _____

   _____

3. When taking notes on the classification pattern, what should you include in your notes?

   _____

   _____

Identifying the Primary Pattern

Until now, you've been working with one organizational pattern at a time. But from now on you'll be asked to select one particular pattern among several possibilities. You need to be aware that, at this point, you are being asked to identify the *primary* pattern. The primary pattern organizes all or *most* of the details. If, for instance, a paragraph describes a cause and effect relationship for six of seven sentences and sentence seven makes a comparison, the primary pattern—and the correct answer—is cause and effect, not comparison and contrast.

◆ **EXERCISE 8**   **Recognizing Primary Patterns of Organization**

DIRECTIONS   Identify the primary organizational pattern for each paragraph by circling the appropriate letter.

EXAMPLE   With the arrival of twentieth-century technology, medical professionals were able to think seriously about creating artificial replacements for damaged human hearts that no longer functioned effectively. In 1957, Dr. Willem Kolff created the first artificial heart and implanted it in a dog, who promptly died from the experiment. Still, animal research continued, and, in 1969, Dr. Denton Cooley implanted the first artificial heart into the body of a human. The device, made largely of plastic, only had to function for a brief period of time, while the patient awaited a transplanted human heart. In 1979, Dr. Robert Jarvik patented the first artificial heart. Three years later, the Jarvik heart, as it came to be called, was implanted in the body of Barney Clark, a retired dentist dying of heart disease. Clark lived for 112 days after the surgery, and his survival raised hopes for the future success of artificial hearts. But by 1985 it was clear that artificial-heart patients were prone to fatal strokes and infections. Still, to this day, researchers—among them Robert Jarvik—are convinced that artificial heart transplants will one day be successful.

a. definition
b. time order: dates and events
c. time order: process
d. comparison and contrast

EXPLANATION   Because the paragraph is heavily laced with dates marking major events, time order: dates and events is the primary pattern.

1. A **generic product** (sometimes called a **generic brand**) is a product with no brand name at all. Its plain package carries only the name of the product—applesauce, peanut butter, potato chips, or whatever—in black type. Generic products, available in supermarkets since 1977, usually are made by the major producers that manufacture name brands. They appeal mainly to consumers who are willing to sacrifice consistency in size or quality for a lower price. However, generic products are not necessarily lower in quality. Even though generic brands may have accounted for as much as 10 percent of all grocery sales several years ago, they currently represent less than 1 percent. (Pride, Hughes, and Kapoor, *Business*, p. 403.)

a. definition
b. comparison and contrast
c. cause and effect
d. classification

2. The painting known as the *Mona Lisa* has fascinated art lovers for centuries. But it wasn't until the twentieth century that one man fell so in love with the *Mona Lisa* that he decided to steal her from the Louvre.[†] In 1909, Italian-born Vincenzo Peruggia was employed by the Louvre to do some painting; it was at this point that Peruggia first got a look at the masterpiece that was to get him into so much trouble. On August 21, 1911, Peruggia returned to the Louvre as a visitor and headed straight for the *Mona Lisa.* Twenty minutes later, he left the museum with the painting tucked inside his jacket. For more than two years, investigators hunted unsuccessfully for the painting. Then, on November 29, 1913, a wealthy Italian art dealer received a letter saying the *Mona Lisa* would be returned for a price. On December 10, 1913, the art dealer arranged to meet with the painting's new owner. After Peruggia produced the painting, police took him into custody. At his trial in 1914, Peruggia explained that he had stolen the *Mona Lisa* because he couldn't forget her smile. The unsympathetic judge sentenced the would-be art collector to three years in jail.

a. time order: dates and events
b. comparison and contrast
c. cause and effect
d. simple listing

3. Child psychologists are inclined to label aggressive behavior as *overt* or *relational.* Overt aggression harms others through actual physical damage or the threat of physical harm. Children who engage in overt aggression are likely to push, hit, or kick a peer. At the very least, those who are overtly aggressive will make explicit threats to do some kind of physical harm in the future. Relational aggression is more psychological than physical and it revolves around threats to or criticism of peer relations. Children who use relational aggression, for example, may taunt a peer by saying that he or she is unlikable and has no friends. At one time, parents and educators focused on strategies to avoid overt aggression among children, because this kind of aggression seemed the more harmful of the two. But research

---

[†]Louvre: a famous museum in Paris.

has shown that children also suffer from being the target of relational aggression.

a. time order: process
b. simple listing
c. cause and effect
d. comparison and contrast

4. The term **alluvial deposits** refers to layers of broken rocky matter formed from material that has been carried by the waves of a river or stream and dropped when the current's speed lessened. River plains and deltas consist of alluvial deposits. The elements that make up alluvial deposits can range widely in size, from chunks of boulders, to small pebbles, to grains of sand. A large portion of the world's richest farmland is located on top of alluvial deposits, which can also be the source of minerals such as gold or tin. These mineral deposits are called "placer deposits." (Source of information: *Scientific American Desk Reference*, 1999, p. 289.)

a. time order: process
b. comparison and contrast
c. definition
d. classification

5. Certain attitudes, or ways of thinking, help us move smoothly through our daily life. However, if those same attitudes are strictly maintained and never deviate, no matter what the situation, they sometimes prove a hindrance.* The behavior of a problem-solver, someone who immediately tries to find solutions to difficult situations, perfectly illustrates how a useful attitude can turn negative. There are, after all, problems that have no solutions. They are simply facts of life. Why is it, for example, that the pets we love always have a much shorter lifespan than we do? Unfortunately, people who focus on coming up with the right solution are inclined to get frustrated whenever the problem or question at hand has no neat solution. When pushed to extremes, over-reliance on logic is another attitude

*hindrance: obstacle.

that can prove harmful. There are situations in life where understanding human emotion is extremely important, and in these cases sympathy and empathy are more crucial than logic. Yet another attitude that can have a down side is fear of failure. If we try hard to succeed because we fear failure, that's a good thing. But if we are overly terrified of failing, we are unlikely to engage in original thought because, by definition, it has no proven history of success. Yet original thought, and the success it can bring, has no track record. It requires us to face and accept the possibility of failure.

a. comparison and contrast
b. simple listing
c. classification
d. time order: process

6. The human brain has two hemispheres—the right and the left. Although the hemispheres cooperate for many functions, research suggests that they control highly different activities. Thanks to the left side of our brain, we are able to master and manipulate language, using it to communicate our thoughts. The left side of our brain helps us make sense by giving order and logic to our utterances.* The right hemisphere is less crucial to language production and appears to be more concerned with the creation of images. Research suggests that the right brain dominates during infancy. Babies make sense of the world by visualizing, rather than naming, and visualization is controlled by the right side of the brain.

a. time order: dates and events
b. comparison and contrast
c. cause and effect
d. simple listing

7. Adolescent rape victims seem to have more subsequent behavior problems than do other crime victims. This is probably because the adolescent experiences the attack at the time when she is trying to develop a sense of self. Immediate reactions to rape can include loss

---

*utterances: verbal statements.

of self-trust, turning away from friends, retreating to the protection of the family, and avoiding social activities. Long-term reactions include anxiety, sleep disturbances, and abnormal fears. (Adapted from Greenberg et al., *Sexuality*, p. 513.)

a. time order: process

b. comparison and contrast

c. cause and effect

d. classification

8. An attacker has put you in a wristlock to force you to submit. He has grabbed your wrist, pressing hard on the bones and nerves to cause you pain. If you try to pull away, you cause yourself more pain, and you could actually break your own wrist in an attempt to escape. However, if you remember a simple self-defense technique, you can free yourself. First, fight your instinct to tighten the muscles in your hands and arms. Doing so will actually cause you more pain because the tension will exert more pressure. If you are in pain, you cannot strike out to free yourself from your opponent. Second, let your hand and wrist relax and go limp. This will lessen the pain you're experiencing long enough for you to punch, kick, or bite your attacker to force him to let you go. Relaxing your hand may also surprise him, causing him to loosen his grip for a moment. Third, the thumb is the weakest link in a person's grip, so rotate your arm and pull your hand toward your attacker's thumb for the best chance of breaking free.

a. definition

b. time order: process

c. comparison and contrast

d. classification

9. There are four common types of vegetarians, each of whom follows a different set of rules. Lacto-ovo vegetarians don't eat meat, but they do eat eggs and dairy products. Lacto vegetarians consume dairy products but won't touch eggs, whereas ovo vegetarians eat eggs but avoid dairy products. For members of the fourth category, vegans, eggs and dairy products are completely off the menu. So, too, are all animal by-products. Some vegans won't even touch honey. The

restriction on animal by-products can extend to other aspects of life: Some vegans refuse to wear leather, silk, or wool.

a. comparison and contrast

b. classification

c. cause and effect

d. time order: process

10. Samuel Gompers was born in London in 1850. After only four years of elementary school, he was apprenticed to a cigar maker and learned the trade that he followed for more than a quarter of a century. But it was as a labor leader rather than a cigar maker that Samuel Gompers made his mark on history. Gompers moved to America with his family in 1863. The next year, he became a member of the Cigar Makers' International Union. Young as he was, he took an immediate interest in the union's progress and began speaking at local meetings. The hard times of the 1870s only strengthened Gompers' belief in the importance of unions, and he became even more active. Elected president of the local union in 1874, he was ousted* from that position by the socialist* opposition in 1880. But this defeat left him free to take a prominent role in founding the Federation of Organized Trades and Labor Unions, established in 1881 to influence legislation on behalf of labor. When the American Federation of Labor (AFL) was created in 1886, Gompers was elected president. Until his death in 1924, Gompers was repeatedly reelected as president of the AFL.

a. definition

b. time order: dates and events

c. comparison and contrast

d. simple listing

---

*ousted: removed.

*socialist: a person who believes that the means of production in a society should be owned by a large group rather than an individual.

VOCABULARY CHECK

The following words were introduced in the chapter. Match the word with the definition. Review words, definitions, and original context two or three times before taking the vocabulary tests. (The page numbers in parentheses indicate where the word first appeared.)

1. compassionate (p. 496) _____
2. provocation (p. 497) _____
3. graphics (p. 500) _____
4. extensive (p. 505) _____
5. dubious (p. 506) _____
6. activists (p. 508) _____
7. chromosomes (p. 510) _____
8. genes (p. 510) _____
9. inbreeding (p. 513) _____
10. illumination (p. 514) _____
11. synthesizing (p. 522) _____
12. adversarial (p. 522) _____
13. alluding (p. 531) _____
14. ascent (p. 531) _____
15. province (p. 533) _____
16. coercive (p. 538) _____
17. stench (p. 539) _____
18. range (p. 539) _____
19. civic (p. 540) _____
20. literacy (p. 541) _____
21. commerce (p. 541) _____
22. hindrance (p. 553) _____
23. utterances (p. 554) _____
24. ousted (p. 556) _____
25. socialist (p. 556) _____

a. referring, mentioning
b. challenging; ready to criticize
c. a person who believes that the means of production in a society should be owned by a large group rather than an individual
d. caring of others
e. forcing someone to do something against his or her will
f. trade
g. the elements responsible for hereditary characteristics, such as hair and eye color
h. stimulus to anger or punishment
i. visual images
j. large, wide-ranging
k. verbal statements
l. removed
m. move about; travel; extend
n. questionable, suspicious
o. bodies within a cell that consist of hundreds of clear, jellylike particles strung together like beads. They carry the genes.
p. people devoted to fighting for a cause
q. reproducing by mating with a closely related individual
r. the combining of separate thoughts to create a new idea
s. smell, stink

t. understanding

u. relating to the city or citizenship

v. obstacle

w. ability to read and write

x. climb

y. area governed as a unit of a country or an empire; area of knowledge or interest

DIGGING Types of Love
DEEPER

Looking Ahead   You probably know that the way a person loves a dog or cat is quite different from the way he or she loves a parent or spouse. But did it ever occur to you that there might actually be six different kinds of love?

1   Although there are many theories about love, one in particular has captured the attention of researchers in interpersonal communication. According to this theory, there are actually six different kinds of love.

Eros: Beauty and Sexuality

2   Like Narcissus, who fell in love with the beauty of his own image, the erotic lover focuses on beauty and physical attractiveness, sometimes to the exclusion of qualities you might consider more important and more lasting. Also like Narcissus, the erotic lover has an idealized image of beauty that is unattainable in reality. Consequently, the erotic lover often feels unfulfilled. Not surprisingly, erotic lovers are particularly sensitive to physical imperfections in the ones they love.

Ludus: Entertainment and Excitement

3   Ludus love is experienced as a game, as fun. The better he or she can play the game, the greater the enjoyment. Love is not to be taken too seriously; emotions are to be held in check lest they get out of hand and make trouble; passions never rise to the point where they get out of control. A ludic lover is self-controlled, always aware of the need to manage love rather than allow it to be in control. Perhaps because of this need to control love, some researchers have proposed that ludic love tendencies may reveal tendencies to sexual aggression (Sarwer, Kalichman, Johnson, Early et al. 1993). Not surprisingly, the ludic lover retains a partner only as long as the partner is interesting and amusing. When interest fades, it's time to change partners. Perhaps because love is a game, sexual fidelity is of little importance. In fact, recent research shows that people who score high on ludic love are more likely to engage in "extradyadic" dating and sex than those who score lower (Wiederman and Hurd 1999).

Storge: Peaceful and Slow

4   Storge love lacks passion and intensity. Storgic lovers don't set out to find lovers but to establish a companionable relationship with someone they

know and with whom they can share interests and activities. Storgic love is a gradual process of unfolding thoughts and feelings; the changes seem to come so slowly and so gradually that it's often difficult to define exactly where the relationship is at any point in time. Sex in storgic relationships comes late, and when it comes, it assumes no great importance.

Pragma: Practical and Traditional

5 The pragma lover is practical and seeks a relationship that will work. Pragma lovers want compatibility and a relationship in which their important needs and desires will be satisfied. They're concerned with the social qualifications of a potential mate even more than with personal qualities; family and background are extremely important to the pragma lover, who relies not so much on feelings as on logic. The pragma lover views love as a useful relationship, one that makes the rest of life easier. So the pragma lover asks such questions of a potential mate as "Will this person earn a good living?" "Can this person cook?" "Will this person help me advance in my career?" Pragma lovers' relationships rarely deteriorate. This is partly because pragma lovers choose their mates carefully and emphasize similarities. Another reason is that they have realistic romantic expectations.

Mania: Elation and Depression

6 Mania is characterized by extreme highs and extreme lows. The manic lover loves intensely and at the same time intensely worries about the loss of the love. This fear often prevents the manic lover from deriving as much pleasure as possible from the relationship. With little provocation, the manic lover may experience extreme jealousy. Manic love is obsessive; the manic lover has to possess the beloved completely. In return, the manic lover wishes to be possessed, to be loved intensely. The manic lover's poor self-image seems capable of being improved only by love; self-worth comes from being loved rather than from any sense of inner satisfaction. Because love is so important, danger signs in a relationship are often ignored; the manic lover believes that if there is love, then nothing else matters.

Agape: Compassionate and Selfless

7 Agape is a compassionate, egoless, self-giving love. The agapic lover loves even people with whom he or she has no close ties. This lover loves the stranger on the road even though they will probably never meet again.

Agape is a spiritual love, offered without concern for personal reward or gain. This lover loves without expecting that the love will be reciprocated. Jesus, Buddha, and Gandhi practiced and preached this unqualified love (Lee 1976). In one sense, agape is more a philosophical kind of love than most people have the strength to achieve. (Adapted from DeVito, *The Interpersonal Communication Book*, pp. 343–45.)

Sharpening Your Skills

DIRECTIONS   Answer the questions by filling in the blanks or circling the letter of the correct response.

1. Which statement best expresses the main idea of the entire reading?
   a. Unlike erotic love, storge love is gradual and not particularly intense.
   b. Most people do not realize that there are six different kinds of love.
   c. Experts in interpersonal communication generally embrace the notion that there are six different kinds of love.
   d. Although there are six different kinds of love, only erotic love gets much attention from researchers involved in interpersonal communication.

2. What's the primary pattern of this reading?

   _____

3. What's the main idea of paragraph 4?
   a. Storge love is based on companionship.
   b. Storge love does not involve sex.
   c. Storge love is not as lasting as erotic love.
   d. Storge lovers are usually middle aged.

4. What's the main idea of paragraph 6?
   a. The manic lover is never happy even when loved in return.
   b. Manic lovers make the lives of those they love utterly miserable.
   c. Manic lovers are psychologically unbalanced.
   d. Manic lovers love with great passion and are always anxious about losing those they love.

5. In the last sentence of paragraph 5, the author says, "Another reason is that they have realistic romantic expectations." To make sense of that statement, readers need to infer that *they* refers to

_____ and the expectations are about

_____.

Making Connections

Re-read the selection about arranged marriage on pages 432–33. Based on that description, arranged marriages would fall into which of the six categories described by Professor DeVito? Please explain.

_____

_____

_____

Drawing Your Own Conclusions

Think of people you know or have heard about who illustrate each kind of love. Can you offer examples of behavior that show why these people personify the various kinds of love described in the essay?

_____

_____

_____

▶ TEST 1

Vocabulary Review

DIRECTIONS Fill in the blanks with one of the words listed below.

utterance	stench	literacy	ousted	synthesize
alluding	provocation	coercive	province	illumination

1. All of the articles about the Southern senator Henry Clay were either wildly positive or furiously negative, and the researcher was having a hard time finding a way to _____ the competing viewpoints into a broader, more complete picture of the man and his career.

2. In prison, no one had time to figure out the best way to get prisoners to follow the rules, so the tendency was to rely solely on _____ measures.

3. Anyone who lives near a factory farm that raises pigs or cows is painfully aware of the _____ this kind of animal crowding produces.

4. In a moment of sudden _____, the scientist finally understood what the cellular evidence was telling him.

5. Both mother and father were eagerly awaiting their child's first _____.

6. After the revolutionary movement _____ Fulgencio Batista, Fidel Castro and the communists took over the Cuban government.

7. _____ to past rumors of his infidelity, the presidential candidate made it clear that they were just that, rumors, nothing more.

8. Almost everyone readily admits that verbal _____ is important, but for some reason, many of those same people are far less concerned about "innumeracy," or the inability to understand numbers.

9. Although art is not my _____, I can't help thinking that some of Jackson Pollock's fame was due to his rugged good looks and wild cowboy ways.

10. Without _____, the male snake suddenly turned and bit the female snake lying in the sun alongside him.

▶ **TEST 2**   **Vocabulary Review**

DIRECTIONS   Fill in the blanks with one of the words listed below.

activists	hindrance	inbreeding	graphics	genetic
ranged	civic	compassionate	ascent	commerce
dubious	extensive	chromosomes	adversarial	socialist

1. The journalists were openly skeptical of the candidate's _____ claim that he had been an unsung war hero, whose bravery under fire had gone unnoticed.

2. In 1920, America's most famous _____, Eugene V. Debs, ran for president while he was in prison; Debs won more than nine hundred thousand write-in votes.

3. Their relationship had grown so _____, the two law-yers decided they had to break up their office and go their separate ways.

4. The _____ of pedigreed dogs has caused many breeds to develop serious health problems.

5. When _____ at the meeting began shouting out accu-sations, the moderator stopped the discussion and pleaded for quiet.

6. People in that part of the state regularly attend town council meet-ings; they consider attendance to be an important part of their _____ duty.

7. In humans, sex is determined by two _____, *x* for a female and *y* for a male.

8. The website's use of _____ was especially pleasing to the eye.

9. As a young man, he had started at the bottom in the newspaper business and gotten _____ experience in just about every aspect of the newspaper profession.

10. There was a time when people believed that criminality had a _____ basis and could be passed on from generation to generation.

11. The surgeon was a rare creature: She had extraordinary surgical skills and a _____ heart.

12. Amateurs should not attempt the _____ of Mount Everest; the climb is a punishing one that requires much skill and experience if one is to survive it.

13. With the coming of the railroad, _____ between East and West increased dramatically.

14. Instead of being a help on the campaign trail, the vice president was proving a _____ because he tended to speak without thinking.

15. The physicist had a number of interests that _____ widely from playing baseball to writing poetry.

▶ **TEST 3**   **Recognizing Primary Patterns**

DIRECTIONS   Identify the primary pattern of organization by circling the appropriate letter.

1. The meaning of silence can vary with one's culture. Americans, for example, often view silence as negative. At business meetings, participants frequently force themselves to speak; they fear that being silent will make it appear as if they had nothing to say. On a personal level, silence is often interpreted as a sign that things are not going well. In a group, for example, members frequently mistrust the person who remains silent. It's assumed that he or she is bored or disinterested in the group's activities. In Japan, however, silence is viewed in an altogether different light. Silence, in a personal or a professional context, is often interpreted as positive. People who are silent at meetings are thought to reflect more deeply on the issues under discussion. During personal conversations, remaining silent so that the other person has a chance to speak is considered the height of politeness and courtesy. The Japanese, in general, prefer silence to speech.

   a. definition
   b. time order: dates and events
   c. time order: process
   d. comparison and contrast

2. New York City's size and layout changed greatly between 1728 and 1890. A flourishing center of trade, New York grew in the early and mid-1700s without a definite plan. Farmers sold land for buildings plot by plot, as need demanded, and this stop-and-start development is reflected in lower Manhattan's irregular streets. After the Revolutionary War, the 1782 Act of Confiscation took land away from anyone who had sided with the British, leaving many areas of New York available for organization and urban planning. A commission was set up in 1807 to create a street layout that would keep New York orderly, no matter how much trade or industry boomed. In 1811, the commission revealed its plan: a simple pattern of horizontal and vertical lines that didn't follow the natural landscape. A piece of wasteland purchased in 1853 was eventually turned into the 843-acre Central Park. Otherwise, little open land remained

for games or sports. By 1890, the island of Manhattan had grown into a thriving checkerboard of streets and buildings.

a. definition

b. time order: dates and events

c. simple listing

d. comparison and contrast

3. During the Middle Ages (600–1500) in Europe, most ordinary people could not read. They had to rely on village gossip and on tales relayed by bands of storytellers. During this period, four main types of storytellers developed, each specializing in particular themes and characters. In northern Europe, *bards* recited poems about heavenly gods and earthly heroes. The poem *Beowulf*, for example, was probably first recited by an English bard. In France and Spain, *minstrels* related the great deeds performed by King Charlemagne's knights in stories like the *Song of Roland*. In France and Italy, *troubadours* spun tales of courtly romance that placed women on a pedestal with men at their command. In Germany, *minnesingers* told stories of passion and romance.

a. time order: process

b. comparison and contrast

c. cause and effect

d. classification

4. In Northern India, a wasp known as *Rogas indiscretus* kills the gypsy moths that harm trees in the foothills of the Himalayas.[†] Scientists say the wasp's methods are simple yet quite efficient. The female wasp stings a gypsy moth caterpillar and deposits an egg inside it. After hatching, the wormlike baby wasp eats the moth's insides. The infant wasp then spins a cocoon inside the moth's dead body; the cocoon is protected by the mummified husk. A few weeks later, the infant wasp grows into an adult—which, if female, is ready to lay at least two hundred eggs in other gypsy moth caterpillars. (Adapted from *U.S. News & World Report*, April 7, 1997, pp. 70–71.)

[†]Himalayas: mountains in south central Asia.

a. simple listing
b. time order: process
c. comparison and contrast
d. classification

5. Jon Krakauer's best-selling book *Into the Wild* tells the story of Chris McCandless, an idealistic young man who traveled to a remote region in Alaska to live off the land. McCandless cut himself off from the world and vowed to make his way with no money or map. In August 1992, four months after he walked into the Alaskan wilderness, McCandless's body was discovered by hunters who were hiking by an abandoned bus. At the time, no one knew how or why McCandless had died until Krakauer, investigating McCandless's case for a national magazine, uncovered the cause: poisoning from the seed pods of wild potato plants. As was his habit, McCandless had used a field guide to identify edible plants, and the book said nothing about any ill effects from eating potato seeds. But, as Krakauer found after taking some seeds for laboratory tests, the seeds contain a poisonous substance that causes weakness, depression, muscle fatigue, and nervousness. The poison also makes it hard to eat and drink and prevents the body from turning food into usable energy. McCandless was already very thin because his wilderness diet consisted of berries he had gathered, and the potato-seed poison hit him hard. Unable to leave his remote campground or call for help, he slowly starved to death.

a. simple listing
b. comparison and contrast
c. cause and effect
d. classification

▶ **TEST 4**   **Recognizing Primary Patterns**

DIRECTIONS   Identify the primary pattern of organization by circling the appropriate letter.

1. Industrial psychologists who have studied work teams have come up with five different categories. First, *production teams* consist of the employees who actually produce a product or service. These are the employees who make the ball bearings, computer chips, or automobile parts. Second, *management teams* coordinate workers who report to them while the product is being made, developed, or refined. Unlike members of the production team, the members of the management team are not on the front line. Instead, they are responsible for the planning, staffing, budgeting, and sequencing of work projects. *Service teams* consist of employees who work together to serve the needs of customers. An example of a service team is the technical support group that addresses a software problem customers call or e-mail about. Fourth, *project teams* carry out specific projects and are dissolved upon project completion. For example, book publishers might assign the publication of a book to a specific team that no longer exists once the book is in stores. Finally, there are *advisory teams*. These teams offer advice about a specific problem—for example, the presence of low morale in the workplace. (Adapted from Levy, *Industrial/Organizational Psychology*, pp. 368–69.)

     a. time order: dates and events

     b. time order: process

     c. comparison and contrast

     d. cause and effect

     e. classification

2. The body's response to flesh wounds is remarkably quick and efficient. The first stage in the body's response occurs when the blood begins to clot. Next, tiny bodies in the bloodstream called **platelets** rush to the wound site and disintegrate, or dissolve. Fibrous proteins begin to form, and the blood that has already escaped hardens into a scab. Once the bleeding stops, the body releases chemicals called **pyrogens**. These chemicals cause the area surrounding the wound

to grow warm. In turn, blood vessels grow wider, allowing nutrients, oxygen, and white blood cells to flood the wounded area and start the formation of new tissue.

a. definition

b. time order: dates and events

c. time order: process

d. simple listing

e. comparison and contrast

3. Few events are more bizarre or unbelievable than sudden death said to be caused by "voodoo" or "magic." Nevertheless, death caused by voodoo does, indeed, seem to occur. Here is one account of what happened in a tribe when a man discovered that he had been cursed. "His body begins to tremble and the muscles twitch involuntarily. He sways backwards and falls to the ground. . . . From this time onwards he sickens and frets, refusing to eat and keeping aloof from the daily affairs of the tribe. Unless help is forthcoming in the shape of a countercharm, death is only a matter of a comparatively short time (Basedow, 1925; cited in Cannon, 1942)."[†] It has been argued that voodoo deaths seem to require belief in the power of magic. But all they really require is belief in the power of emotion. Walter Cannon, a well-known medical researcher, studied many voodoo deaths and concluded that they are explained by the bodily changes that accompany strong emotion. More specifically, Cannon argued that intense fear and its effects on the body are what causes someone to die from a curse.

a. time order: dates and events

b. time order: process

c. simple listing

d. comparison and contrast

e. cause and effect

4. **Syndicates** provide important materials for newspapers. A syndicate is a company that sells editorial matter that is not hard news to newspapers. Hundreds of syndicates supply a variety of content for

---

[†]Dennis Coon, *Introduction to Psychology* (St. Paul: West Publishing, 1989), p. 308.

different departments and different audiences. The Washington Post Writers Group, the syndication arm of the *Washington Post*, circulates the work of columnists such as Ellen Goodman, George Will, and David Broder. Copley News Services sells editorial cartoons. Universal Press Syndicate offers a wide range of choices from "Dear Abby" and Jeane Dixon's "Your Horoscope" to Marshall Loeb's "Your Money" column to the "Doonesbury" strip. As you might imagine, syndicates supply some of the most popular parts of a paper. (Adapted from Turow, *Media Today*, pp. 132–33.)

a. definition

b. time order: dates and events

c. time order: process

d. comparison and contrast

e. classification

5. First ladies Eleanor Roosevelt and Hillary Rodham Clinton shared many similarities. While their husbands served as U.S. presidents, both women actively assisted and advised their spouses. Mrs. Roosevelt frequently made fact-finding trips to gather information for her husband, and Mrs. Clinton helped her husband by advising him during his political campaigns. Both women engaged in humanitarian work. Mrs. Roosevelt advocated equal rights for minority groups and worked with children and the poor. Mrs. Clinton served as national chairperson for the Children's Defense Fund, an organization dedicated to helping neglected children. Finally, both first ladies became role models for women in politics and public affairs by pursuing distinguished careers of their own. After death cut short her husband's fourth term in office, Mrs. Roosevelt went on to serve as a delegate to the United Nations General Assembly, where she chaired the Human Rights Commission. Mrs. Clinton was elected a U.S. senator for New York State and went on to become U.S. Secretary of State.

a. simple listing

b. time order: process

c. comparison and contrast

d. cause and effect

e. classification

◗ **TEST 5**   **Recognizing Primary Patterns**

DIRECTIONS   Identify the primary pattern of organization by circling the appropriate letter.

1. Though the U.S. president, unlike a prime minister, cannot command an automatic majority in the legislature, he does have some impressive powers. Simply by virtue of the office, the president is the official commander-in-chief of the armed forces. He[†] can also grant reprieves and pardons for federal offenses, call Congress into special sessions, receive visiting dignitaries, and commission officers of the armed forces. Along with the Senate, the president has the power to make treaties with foreign countries, appoint judges to the Supreme Court, and place other high officials, like the Secretary of State, in office. The president also has the right to veto legislation and the power to ensure that legislation, once passed, is properly enforced. (Adapted from Wilson and DiIulio, *American Government*, p. 370.)

   a. time order: process

   b. simple listing

   c. comparison and contrast

   d. cause and effect

   e. classification

2. No one really knows for sure when table tennis, more commonly known as *Ping-Pong*, actually came into being. But some authorities on the game believe that it originated in 1890, when British Army officers began playing it in India. By 1900, table tennis was popular throughout the world. Although table tennis was called a variety of names, among them *Whiff Whaff* and *Gossimar*, by 1902 most amateur players referred to it as Ping-Pong (the name was taken from the patented trademark of a company that produced table tennis equipment). By 1910, table tennis—under any name—had become a popular pastime. In fact, in the United States, it was practically a craze. But like so many fads, its popularity quickly faded. In 1921, however, a movement started in several parts of the world, the goal of which was to make table tennis a serious sport. In 1926, seven nations came together in Berlin, Germany, for a meeting that resulted in the formation of a group called the International Table Tennis

---

[†]It would be nice to one day write *he or she* in this context.

Federation. By 1933, the United States had its own governing group called the U.S. Table Tennis Association. To this day, the group governs all tournament competition in the United States.

a. definition

b. time order: dates and events

c. time order: process

d. comparison and contrast

e. cause and effect

3. Traditionally, musical instruments are grouped into five categories, based on the way sound is produced. When the sound results from the vibration of air through a tube or mouthpiece, the instrument is known as an *aerophone*. Clarinets, flutes, and trumpets belong to this musical family. A second type, *idiophones*, make sound when they are stamped, shaken, scraped, or rubbed. Members of this group include rattles and washboards. A third classification, *membranophones*, produce sound through the movement of a stretched membrane, or skin. All drums are membranophones. Another category is the *chordophones*. These instruments create sound through the movement of strings. Harps, violins, and cellos are good examples of chordophones. *Electrical instruments* comprise the fifth group, which includes electric organs and guitars, keyboards, and chimes.

a. time order: dates and events

b. time order: process

c. comparison and contrast

d. cause and effect

e. classification

4. There's no denying that high heels glamorize the leg, which may be one reason why so many women wear them despite the fact that heels are rarely comfortable for walking. High heels are also popular with teenagers, and that may be why doctors say foot problems are showing up in relatively young women, who, twenty years ago, would never have seen the inside of a podiatrist's[†] office. The sad truth is that high heels may do wonders for the look of the legs, but they have horrific consequences for the feet. Bunions, a bony swelling at the base joint of the big toe, are one

---

[†]podiatrists: doctors who specialize in foot problems.

common long-term problem caused by wearing heels on a regular basis. But bunions are only one potential problem. Wearing high heels can also cause Morton's neuroma, a condition in which the nerves thicken and cause a lump on the underside of the foot. Morton's neuroma is painful and can cause numbness in the toes. High heels also raise the heel and push the body's center of gravity forward. This causes the back to bend and puts pressure on the nerves in the back, which can lead to sciatica, a painful nerve inflammation that shoots waves of pain down the leg. Tendons in the heel can also shorten and tighten from being pushed upward. When this happens, the feet have a hard time adapting to a flat surface and need to be permanently raised to feel comfortable. Women and girls can avoid these problems by not wearing heels higher than 1.5 inches, but given our culture's emphasis on physical appearance, no one expects that to happen any time soon.

a. time order: process

b. simple listing

c. comparison and contrast

d. cause and effect

e. classification

5. Edgar Schein's model for looking at organizational change and growth is evolutionary in nature; that is, it describes distinct stages of change. Schein created a model that identified three separate stages. In the first stage, the organization's founders are the source of inspiration. Their ideas guide the organization and hold it together. The second stage is often defined by an identity crisis. At this point, members sometimes doubt their commitment to the group, and the organization's goals frequently come under fire. In stage two, the organization needs to redefine its underlying rules and objectives; otherwise, it may simply disappear. Organizations that survive stage two and enter stage three often disavow some of the early ideas that motivated or guided the group's behavior. New rules and goals that reflect a changing world take the place of the old.

a. time order: process

b. simple listing

c. comparison and contrast

d. cause and effect

e. classification

▶ **TEST 6**   **Recognizing Primary Patterns**

DIRECTIONS   Identify the primary pattern of organization by circling the appropriate letter. *Note:* Time order in this exercise includes both process and sequence of dates and events.

1. If you are thinking about leaving your job either by choice or at the request of your employer, here are some things you should and should *not* do when you leave. Don't tell off either your co-workers or your superiors, even if you feel that you have been badly treated. You never know when you might meet them again in a professional setting. Unless you have been fired for some truly horrible offense in which you have been caught red-handed, do ask for a reference. In looking for your next job, you will have to indicate where you have worked before, and even if it's bad, you want to know what your previous employer will say if asked for a recommendation. Plus, many employers who might have written a bad evaluation if they thought you weren't going to see it, might well write a more neutral one if they know you are going to be reading what they've written. If a replacement has already been hired, don't tell him or her anything bad about the company. Your problems may have been a matter of personal chemistry, and your replacement might not share your difficulties. By the same token, when you interview for a new job, don't criticize your previous employer. Your criticism may be justified, but your potential new employer doesn't know you and is likely to assume you are a complainer or a troublemaker. Do speak about your former employer and co-workers with respect. You don't have to praise them, but you do need to show that you aren't someone who gossips or spreads rumors. Not surprisingly, employers don't look kindly on people who do.

   a. definition

   b. time order

   c. simple listing

   d. comparison and contrast

   e. cause and effect

   f. classification

2. It is easy enough to confuse cheetahs with leopards. Even in Africa, where people are used to seeing these animals, they are often called by

the same Swahili name, *ngari*. The confusion is understandable. On a superficial level, the two have much in common. Both have light tan fur and dark spots. Both have about the same body weight, approximately 110 to 130 pounds. However, on closer inspection, there are clearly more differences than similarities between the two. The cheetah has longer legs and a much smaller head. An agile climber, the leopard climbs trees to hunt monkeys; the cheetah, one of the fastest animals on Earth, takes its prey on the ground, running it down at full speed. The leopard consumes a varied diet. Even when game is scarce, it can subsist on mice and fruits. The cheetah, by contrast, relies primarily on antelope for food.

a. definition

b. time order

c. simple listing

d. comparison and contrast

e. cause and effect

f. classification

3. The process of human digestion begins at the very moment that food enters our mouth. At this point, both teeth and saliva begin preparing the food for safe entry into the intestine. Once the chewed and liquefied food is swallowed, it moves downward through the esophagus by means of muscle contractions. When it reaches the stomach, the food is mixed with enzymes and acid that ready the partially digested food for entry into the small intestine. There, more enzymes will be added, and digestion will essentially be completed. After all the food nutrients have been absorbed by the body, the indigestible parts will move on to the large intestine in preparation for being excreted from the body.

a. definition

b. time order

c. simple listing

d. comparison and contrast

e. cause and effect

f. classification

4. In the next decade, hundreds of thousands of convicted felons who were locked up as a result of tough anticrime policies in the 1980s and 1990s will be released from America's prisons. Their release in such large numbers is bound to cause problems, placing a too heavy burden on government and community reentry programs created to help former inmates adjust to life outside of prison. Most of these programs are already underfunded and understaffed. As a result, it will be even harder to arrange adequate social services for all those who need them. Yet if former inmates do not receive psychological counseling, job training, and some help finding employment, they are bound to drain community welfare programs and food banks. Ex-prisoners left to sink or swim on their own will probably see no alternative except returning to the criminal behavior that got them into trouble in the first place. Although some increased funding for reentry programs is already in the works at both the state and federal level, much more is desperately needed.

a. definition

b. time order

c. simple listing

d. comparison and contrast

e. cause and effect

f. classification

Combining Patterns in Paragraphs and Longer Readings

10

Jokerpro/Shutterstock

IN THIS CHAPTER, YOU WILL LEARN

- how to recognize two or more patterns in a paragraph.

- how to recognize patterns in longer readings.

- how to decide what's important in readings that combine two, three, or even four patterns.

"Usually, if I see a pattern, I can remember the point."
—Joe Kelly, writing teacher and friend

Until now, you've worked with paragraphs based primarily on one organizational pattern. But if their ideas require it, writers often use more than one pattern. Particularly in longer readings, authors frequently combine two, three, or even four patterns, instead of relying solely on one. Thus, it's important for you to learn how to (1) identify the different patterns used in a reading and (2) figure out which pattern or patterns are primary, or central, to developing the main idea.

Combining Patterns in Paragraphs

The following paragraph combines two different patterns. Read it through. Then, on the blank line below it, identify the two patterns you think are at work in the paragraph.

> [1]Increased spells of warm weather and decreased use of a pesticide called Mirex have resulted in a plague of what laypeople call fire ants. [2]Indeed, pleasant weather and an absence of pesticides have encouraged whole armies of ants to make their homes in farmers' fields, where they can leisurely munch on potato and okra crops. [3]Should a tractor overturn one of their nests, the furious ants swarm over the machine and attack the driver. [4]Using their jaws to hold the victim's skin, they thrust their stingers into the flesh, holding the same position for up to twenty-five seconds. [5]The sting produces a sharp burning sensation and frequently produces painful infections that can last weeks and even months. [6]Some victims who were especially allergic to the ants' poison have not survived a fire-ant attack.

The first clue to a pattern in the paragraph is the verb *resulted* in the first sentence. That verb suggests a cause and effect pattern. And, in fact, that is exactly the pattern that first appears in the paragraph. In the opening sentence, the author explains how two causes—more warm weather and decreased pesticide use—have produced an effect—a plague of fire ants.

But look what happens in sentence 3. At this point, the author starts to describe a process—an attack by angry fire ants. Step by step in the remaining sentences, the paragraph outlines what happens when fire ants attack. Thus, we can rightly say that the paragraph is organized according to two different patterns, cause and effect *and* time order (process).

Because the paragraph describes a cause and effect relationship and outlines the steps in a process, you need to first identify the key elements in each pattern. Then you need to decide if all of those elements are essential to the main idea.

Because cause and effect is central to the main idea—more warm weather and decreased use of the pesticide Mirex have made fire ants a serious threat—we definitely need to identify and link both cause and effect in our notes. However, to further illustrate the threat posed by the ants, we also need to include the steps in their attack. Complete notes would look something like this:

Main Idea More warm weather and decreased use of the pesticide Mirex have produced a plague of fire ants.

Supporting Details 1. Whole armies of ants have moved into farmers' fields and are eating potatoes and okra.

2. If tractor overturns nest, ants swarm over machine and attack driver.

3. They thrust stingers into flesh, holding the same position for up to 25 seconds.

4. Sting produces painful burning sensation and can cause infections.

5. Some especially allergic victims have died following fire-ant attacks.

Not All Patterns Are Equal

When taking notes on a paragraph with two or more organizational patterns, don't assume all patterns are equal. Instead decide which pattern or patterns are most important based on two questions: (1) which pattern is most central to explaining the main idea? and (2) which one organizes the most sentences? The answers to those two questions will tell you which patterns are essential to explaining the main idea. The key elements of those patterns should appear in your notes.

SUMMING UP THE KEY POINTS

1. The pattern or patterns of organization used in a paragraph are dictated by the main idea they develop. Some thoughts lend themselves perfectly to one pattern of organization, e.g., "Panda bears were once thought to be relatives of raccoons, but the differences between the two creatures eventually convinced researchers that they were not related." Other ideas, however, clearly require more than one organizational pattern in order to be fully explained: "According to researchers Raymond Cattell and John Horn, there are two types of intelligence, fluid and crystallized, and each displays a unique developmental course."

2. Because an author combines patterns in a paragraph, it doesn't mean that all the patterns present are equally important. Only those essential to developing the main idea are really significant. The key elements of these patterns are the ones that should go into your notes.

◆ **EXERCISE 1**   **Recognizing Combined Patterns**

DIRECTIONS   Circle the appropriate letters to identify the patterns used in each paragraph. *Note*: In this exercise and those that follow, "time order" refers to "sequence of dates and events" *and* process patterns.

EXAMPLE   In the early part of the nineteenth century, tennis was a leisurely diversion* favored by the wealthy, but between 1913 and 1915, the game underwent some dramatic changes, becoming more like the game we know today. The year 1913 saw the rise of tennis champion Maurice E. McLoughlin, a player with an aggressive and competitive style that left his opponents stunned and panting for air. Known as the "California Comet," McLoughlin had the game's most powerful serve. In doubles, McLoughlin was so aggressive that the *New York Times* claimed he appeared to be playing by himself. The players who challenged McLoughlin and ultimately followed in his footsteps played as hard as he did, and they too helped transform the game. In 1915, the national tennis championship was moved from the privileged environment of Newport, Rhode Island, to the far less sophisticated and

---

*diversion: pleasant activity.

posh* West Side Tennis Club at Forest Hills, New York. At long last, tennis was ready to break free of its image as the sport of the privileged and ready to welcome, in the years to come, players like Pancho Gonzales, Jimmy Connors, John McEnroe, and the incomparable* Williams sisters, athletes and competitors who went on the court charged up and ready to win.

a. definition
(b.) time order
c. simple listing
(d.) comparison and contrast
(e.) cause and effect
f. classification

EXPLANATION The paragraph's use of dates suggests that time order is in play. However, when you examine McLoughlin's effect on the game, it's also true that cause and effect is involved. Perhaps you circled simple listing as well. However, because the changes occurred over a fixed period of time, it's all but impossible to order them any way other than earliest event to latest, so simple listing is incorrect.

1. Anyone who has ever cheered on his or her favorite athlete knows that yelling can produce hoarseness. When a person yells or screams, the vocal cords—two thick, muscular strings—close tightly and create a huge amount of air pressure. As they open to let out a sound, the sudden release of air causes the cords to slam together. When the cords collide, especially over a long period of time, they can bruise and swell. If this happens, they will not fit together properly. Air then leaks between the cords, and the voice sounds hoarse. Hoarseness is a sign that the vocal cords need rest. Trying to talk as a way of getting rid of the hoarseness only makes matters worse, for the cords may begin bleeding. Many vocalists, especially rock singers who shout a lot, suffer from bleeding and irritated cords.

   a. definition
   b. time order
   c. simple listing

---

*posh: fancy.
*incomparable: having no equal.

d. comparison and contrast

e. cause and effect

f. classification

2. Hurricanes and tornadoes both pack a wallop. But of the two, tornadoes produce the more deadly effects. On average, tornadoes kill at least 100 people a year. In the worst tornado on record, the Tri-State tornado of 1925, a mile-wide killer tornado hurtled through Missouri, Illinois, and Indiana, destroying over 15,000 homes, killing 695 people, and injuring 2,207. Like tornadoes, hurricanes can sweep through several states, but today's improved weather tracking systems have made it easier to prepare for and avoid death and destruction from hurricanes, usually by evacuating those in danger. In 1928, however, such tracking systems did not exist. When a hurricane struck Lake Okeechobee in Florida, it killed 1,836 people. Still even with modern tracking systems, 1999's Hurricane Floyd caused 56 deaths. And those locations lacking sophisticated weather monitoring systems are still in serious danger when a hurricane hits. In 1991, a typhoon (as hurricanes are called in the western Pacific and Indian oceans) tore through Bangladesh and left in its wake 140,000 deaths.

[handwritten margin note: dates are out of order / = Simple listing]

a. definition

b. time order

c. simple listing

d. comparison and contrast

e. cause and effect

f. classification

3. The venom of a bee resembles the venom of a snake, and the sting of a bee can, in some instances, prove dangerous. Yet while most people react quickly to a snake bite, they tend to ignore a bee sting. That failure to act, however, can be a mistake. Bee stings can actually have deadly consequences if a person is allergic to bee venom. Thus it is better not to take any chances with bee stings. Anyone who gets stung by a bee should react quickly, just as he or she would in reaction to a snake bite. First, remove the stinger by brushing it away; don't try to pull it out. Then apply one of the several professional bee-sting remedies to the whitish swelling that appears almost

immediately following the sting. If the swelling continues through-out the day or if breathing becomes difficult, call a doctor.

a. definition
b. time order
c. simple listing
d. comparison and contrast
e. cause and effect
f. classification

4. The Hollywood propaganda* films created during World War II fall into three general categories: (1) films that praise American traditions, (2) films that introduce World War II allies, and (3) films that criticize the enemy. Around 1938, Hollywood began producing a series of bio-graphical* films that glorified the American democratic tradition. John Ford's *Young Mr. Lincoln* (1939) and John Cromwell's *Abe Lincoln in Illinois* (1940) were Hollywood tributes to an America that gave every-one an equal chance at success. In the early 1940s, Hollywood began to introduce America's British allies. Films such as *Mrs. Miniver* (1942) and *Journey for Margaret* (1942) presented a sympathetic picture of the British people. During the mid-1940s, Hollywood concentrated on in-troducing American audiences to the enemy, and movies like *Hitler's Children* (1943) and *Behind the Rising Sun* (1943) portrayed German and Japanese brutality. Many of these later films have since been criti-cized because of their distorted and simplistic themes that presented the German and Japanese people as half-mad beasts. It has been argued that vicious stereotypes are not appropriate, even during wartime when propaganda supposedly serves a useful, if not a positive, function.

a. definition
b. time order
c. simple listing
d. comparison and contrast
e. cause and effect
f. classification

---

*propaganda: a method of persuasion that relies on emotional appeal and discourages logical thinking.
*biographical: related to a person's life.

5. The Workplace Bullying Institute (WBI) is an advocacy group determined to eliminate bullying in the workplace. To accomplish that goal, the group is trying to make the public aware of how big a problem workplace bullying really is. As WBI defines it, bullying is driven by the need to feel powerful through controlling the behavior of someone else and has several distinct characteristics. These include verbal abuse; constant criticism; and threatening, humiliating, or intimidating actions. According to a survey that WBI conducted with the polling group Zogby in 2007, over one-third of all employees claim that they have been bullied, and the person doing the bullying is usually the boss. Although the majority of those targeted for bullying are women, the survey also showed that in 40 percent of the reported cases, both the person doing the bullying and the individual targeted for abuse were women. Oddly enough, while the male bullies in the study tended to attack males and females equally, the female bullies focused mainly on their own sex. According to its website, WBI claims that being bullied at work is much like being a battered spouse. Like the domestic abuser, the workplace bully wants to keep the target off balance and, therefore, purposely doesn't use any predictable pattern of attack. Eruptions can happen anytime and anywhere. That way, the person being bullied never knows when he or she will be the focus of unwanted and painful attention. According to WBI, 45 percent of those bullied suffer stress-related health problems, but only 3 percent ever file lawsuits in an effort to make the misery stop. (Source of statistics: www.workplacebullying.org/research.html.)

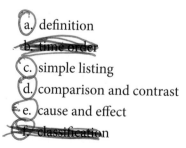

a. definition

b. time order

c. simple listing

d. comparison and contrast

e. cause and effect

f. classification

✔ CHECK YOUR UNDERSTANDING

1. What decides the pattern of organization a writer uses?

2. Should you assume that every pattern present in a paragraph is equally important? Please explain your answer.

_____

_____

_____

Seeing Patterns in Longer Readings

Longer, multi-paragraph readings do occasionally rely on a single pattern of organization. Look, for example, at the following selection, which relies almost exclusively on the cause and effect pattern of development. As you read, note the italicized transitions that are clues to the cause and effect pattern.

Hunger and the Ik

1 The Ik are a small tribe located in East Africa. Formerly a society of hunters, the Ik were forced to become farmers when their government confiscated most of their land for a national park. Deprived of their right to hunt and unable to support themselves through farming, the Ik have learned to live with constant hunger and the threat of starvation. As the anthropologist Colin Turnbull has shown in his book *The Mountain People*, starvation brought profound changes to Ik society.

2 Painfully aware of every extra mouth to feed, the Ik do not regard children as a blessing. They know that children expect to be fed, and that is exactly what Ik parents cannot do. *Therefore*, children are forced from home around the age of three. Left to fend for themselves, the children run in packs, constantly searching for food. They fight among one another, squabbling over scraps.

3 Understandably, children treated in this fashion harbor no great love for their parents or grandparents. *Thus* Turnbull's book contains numerous examples of starving parents being turned away when they sought their grown-up children's help. From the children's point of view, they have enough trouble feeding themselves and cannot possibly feed their aging parents. The parents, apparently remembering their own attitude toward

their children, do not consider such behavior unusual. They simply accept it and go away.

4   *Another consequence of starvation* is that married love seems to have disappeared from Ik lives. Men care little or nothing for their wives, valuing the women only if they are able to provide food. The women share this practical attitude. They will quickly abandon a husband who does not provide food or money and will search for a mate who can. To the Ik, the idea of caring for an aging or ailing spouse is ridiculous. Unable to take care of themselves, they find it hard to care for others.

5   *Like love*, sex doesn't interest the Ik. Sex is viewed primarily as a way of getting food or gifts from neighboring tribesmen who are better off than the Ik. It's important only when it puts food on the table. Otherwise, sex requires far too much energy, energy that could be better spent in search of something to eat.

In this reading, the thesis statement tells us that the Ik, at least according to Colin Turnbull, have been profoundly affected by the starvation that haunts their society. Each major supporting paragraph then describes a different tragic effect. Basically, the whole reading follows a cause and effect pattern of development.

Now, what about the following reading? Would you say that it, too, relies on only one pattern?

Ancient Beliefs About Mental Illness

1 Some half a million years ago, ancient societies apparently did not recognize any difference between mental and physical disorders. Abnormal behaviors, from simple headaches to convulsions,* were believed to be caused by evil spirits that lived in the victim's body. According to this system of belief—called *demonology*—those suffering from disease were considered responsible for their misfortune.

2   For this reason, some Stone Age cave dwellers appear to have treated behavior disorders by a surgical method called *trephining*. During this procedure, part of the skull was chipped away to make an opening. Once the skull was opened, the evil spirits could escape. It was believed that when the evil spirit left, the person would return to his or her normal state. Surprisingly, several trephined skulls that healed over have been found. This indicates that some patients survived what had to be an extremely crude operation. (Adapted from Sue et al., *Understanding Abnormal Behavior*, p. 16.)

---

*convulsions: uncontrolled fits in which the muscles contract wildly.

In this example, the authors' thesis statement identifies a cause and effect relationship: In early societies, illness was considered to be a result of demonic possession. The second paragraph then defines and describes a primitive surgical procedure—*trephining*—that our ancestors may have used to free the body from evil spirits. All together, the authors use three different organizational patterns: (1) cause and effect, (2) definition, and (3) process.

Generally, most of the longer readings you encounter in textbooks, magazines, and newspapers are going to resemble the second sample selection rather than the first. They will rely, that is, on two, three, and, occasionally, even four patterns of organization. True, one pattern may be primary, or be more important, than the rest. But that doesn't mean you should ignore the others. Instead, search out and evaluate the elements of each pattern.

Taking Notes on Mixed Patterns

To take complete notes on a reading that combines two or more patterns, you need to (1) identify the essential elements of each pattern, (2) select the elements that are essential to explaining the overall main idea, and (3) record those elements in your notes.

To illustrate, here are some sample notes on the previous reading:

Main Idea   According to prehistoric beliefs, disease was a result of possession by demons, and the victims were responsible for their illness.

Supporting Details   1. Because they believed demons caused illness, Stone Age cave dwellers treated illness with a procedure called "trephining."

     2. Part of the skull was chipped away to make an opening for evil spirits to escape.

       a. Surprisingly, some patients appear to have survived.

As you can see, complete notes on the reading clearly describe the cause and effect relationship central to the reading. They also define and describe the process of trephining.

◆ **EXERCISE 2**   **Identifying Patterns in Longer Readings**

DIRECTIONS   Circle the letters of the pattern or patterns you recognize in the readings.

EXAMPLE

Scott Joplin: The King of Ragtime

1 Born in 1868 in Texarkana on the Texas-Arkansas border, musician and composer Scott Joplin began his career playing piano in the saloons of St. Louis, Missouri, at the age of seventeen. During the next ten years, he perfected the style of jazz that came to be known as ragtime. Then, from 1896 to 1900, Joplin studied at George R. Smith College in Sedalia, Missouri, so that he could write down the music he played so naturally.

2 In 1899, Joplin published his first piece of music, "Maple Leaf Rag." Less than a year later, ragtime—a unique American blend of African and European musical forms—took the country by storm. Suddenly, everyone wanted to hear "Maple Leaf Rag," and Scott Joplin became the first composer in the world to sell more than one million copies of a single tune.

3 But the King of Ragtime didn't want to devote his life to writing popular music. A serious artist, he was hurt by white Americans' tendency to dismiss his music because it had black origins. To prove the value and beauty of ragtime, Joplin decided to compose an opera. By doing so, he was demanding direct comparison with the greatest European composers.

4 Joplin's opera, *Treemonisha*, is the story of a black orphan girl educated by whites. The opera combines elements of ragtime with black work songs and rousing gospel music. When Joplin published it at his own expense in 1911, it was called "an entirely new form of operatic art."

5 But the timing was wrong. Joplin had invested his hopes in a work based solely on black music just as ragtime was declining in popularity. The one disastrous performance in New York City in 1915 humiliated him, and two years later he was dead.

6 Had he lived to see it, Joplin would have been overjoyed to read the review of *Treemonisha* that appeared in 1972 in the *New York Times*. According to the reviewer, "the audience went out of its mind," applauding what Joplin believed was his greatest failure.

a. definition
(b.) time order
c. simple listing
d. comparison and contrast
(e.) cause and effect
f. classification

EXPLANATION   In this reading the author has two goals: (1) to trace Scott Joplin's career and (2) to explain why writing a successful opera was so important to him. To fulfill those goals, she uses two patterns: a time-order pattern to trace the composer's career, and a cause and effect pattern to explain why *Treemonisha* meant so much to him.

1. The Chernobyl Catastrophe

1 In April 1986, technicians at a Swedish nuclear power plant were puzzled by the abnormally high levels of radiation in the air. They were even more puzzled when an inspection turned up no evidence of a leak. Then reports began to come in from Denmark, Finland, and Norway that they too were experiencing unusually high levels of radiation. Horrified, the technicians now realized that somewhere—they had no idea where—a full-scale nuclear meltdown was taking place. Then, on the night of April 16, the Russian government announced that an accident had taken place at Chernobyl, a nuclear power plant in Ukraine.

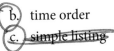

2 Actually the disaster had started days earlier when an explosion ripped through one of Chernobyl's four reactors† and sent 100 million curies† of radiation into the air. For some reason, once the explosion occurred, the plant's cooling system did not work well enough to put out the resulting fire, and the plant had been burning for two weeks. According to the government, thirty-one people died during that period from radiation sickness, but the figure may well have been a good deal higher. As a result of the explosion, 135,000 people were evacuated from a three-hundred-square-mile area. In addition, the land and water within twenty miles of the reactor were now contaminated.

3 Later investigations of the disaster revealed that plant managers had been lax* about safety controls and that human error, along with poor design, had played a key role in the explosion. Consequently, officials in charge of the plant were put on trial in 1987, and several of those responsible were sentenced to long prison terms. But the real result of Chernobyl was the lurking fear that it could happen again someplace else, with even more horrifying consequences.

a. definition
b. time order
c. simple listing

---

†reactors: devices using heat to generate power.
†curies: units of radioactivity.
*lax: careless.

    d. comparison and contrast

    e. cause and effect

    f. classification

2. The Donner Party

1 In 1846, two brothers named George and Jacob Donner, along with a prosperous businessman named James Reed, organized a party to travel to California. They, like many others of the time, hoped to buy land and make a better life for themselves. Their group grew to include a number of families and individuals, reaching a total of eighty-seven people, thirty-nine of them children, all of whom set out from Illinois in May of the same year. However, the Donner Party, as the group came to be known, would meet with disaster and become infamous in American history.

2 During the first leg of their journey, the group experienced the expected hardships that accompanied wagon-train travel. It was difficult to transport all of their belongings, which included furniture, clothing, food, and cattle. River and creek crossings were especially hazardous. Wagons often became stuck and had to be pulled free of obstacles like mud and rocks. Yet despite these complications, the Donner Party was still on schedule when it reached Wyoming in June.

3 Unfortunately, however, the party's leaders then made an ill-fated decision. They decided to take a little-used shortcut to save time. Ignoring an experienced wilderness explorer named James Clyman, who advised James Reed not to travel the shortcut, the Donner Party decided to try the more direct route. In August, the pioneers faced their first serious obstacle, eighty miles of desert near the Great Salt Lake. Although they were able to successfully cross the barren land, they suffered terribly, enduring sweltering daytime heat and freezing nighttime cold. In addition, many of the livestock suffocated during sandstorms.

4 By October, the group had managed to reach the Sierra Nevada outside California. Tensions, however, were running high. After killing another man in a fight, James Reed had been banished. Exhausted, frustrated by the many delays they had encountered, and increasingly concerned about the approaching winter, the travelers pressed on into the mountains. Although the food supply was getting low, members of the group assured the rest of the party that the route through the Sierras would be passable for another month. The travelers decided to rest their livestock for a few days before continuing. It was their second bad decision.

5   They were just below the summit of the Sierra Nevadas and only 150 miles from Fort Sutter in California when a blizzard struck on October 31. By the next day, the party could not locate the road under several feet of snow, let alone move the wagons. The group quickly erected makeshift cabins and shacks, and butchered the few remaining cattle for food. But the weather continued to worsen, and the situation quickly grew desperate. The first death from starvation occurred on December 15.

6   Seventeen of the group's members decided to make one last-ditch effort to walk the trail to California. But they got lost in heavy snow, and after three of the men died of starvation in one night, the desperate survivors resorted to cannibalism to stay alive. When their grisly provisions ran out, the starving band turned on their Native American guides, killed them, and ate them, too.

7   Meanwhile, back at the Sierra Nevada camp, twelve people had starved to death by February, and others had gone mad from hunger. When rescuers finally reached the camp on February 19, they found a ragged group of emaciated survivors who had also been desperate enough to resort to cannibalism.

8   Four different relief parties journeyed to the Donner camp over the next several weeks. The first two rescue groups were each able to take only about twenty survivors with them due to limited supplies. The second group was beset by another blizzard, which killed four more people, and that group, too, was forced to cannibalize the dead before the third relief party arrived. By the time the third group of rescuers arrived at the camp, fewer than ten people were still alive. A few refused to leave those who were sick or were too ill themselves to travel, so they stayed behind. By the time a fourth rescue team arrived, after a month's delay, only one survivor remained.

9   Following their ordeal, the survivors told their stories to the newspapers, horrifying the entire nation and even briefly putting a stop to westward migration. Those who lived through the experience disagreed about who was to blame for their disastrous trip. However, it seems clear that this group of Midwestern flatlanders seriously underestimated the dangers of mountain travel. They probably also underestimated the lengths they would go to in order to stay alive. (Source of information: McGill, "Donner Party," *American History & Politics, 1850–1914*, pp. 5–8.)

a. definition
b. time order

be reliable, yielding consistent results over time, but invalid as a measure of intelligence.

5   There are several types of validity. One type is *predictive validity*, the degree to which test scores accurately predict future behavior or performance. IQ tests are good predictors of academic achievement and performance on general aptitude, or ability, tests, such as the Scholastic Aptitude Test (SAT) and the Graduate Record Examination (GRE) (Neisser et al., 1996; Wadsworth et al., 1995). However, though intelligence tests do predict future academic performance, they are far from perfect predictors, and they should not be used as the only basis for evaluating children's ability. (Adapted from Nevid, *Psychology: Concepts and Applications*, pp. 283–84.)

a. definition

b. time order

c. simple listing

d. comparison and contrast

e. cause and effect

f. classification

READING TIP   In a reading that combines several patterns, one pattern might well dominate, or be primary, but you still need to find and evaluate the key elements in the less important patterns. Then you can decide which of those elements are important enough to appear in your notes.

◆ **EXERCISE 3**   **Identifying the Primary Patterns**

DIRECTIONS   Identify the main idea of each reading along with the pattern or patterns used to develop it.

EXAMPLE

The Dual Nature of Curare

1 *Curare* is a blackish, powderlike substance made from the roots and bark of a woody vine that grows in South America. Although many people know that curare is a deadly poison, they do not know that it can save life as well as take it. Once known only as the "flying death," curare has become one of medicine's most trusted weapons in the fight against disease.

2   Rumors of curare's deadly powers began to circulate as early as the sixteenth century, when explorers came back from journeys to the

Amazon. Upon their return, they described Indian hunters who could bring down prey with a single blow from a dart gun. According to eyewitness accounts, hunters boiled the roots and bark of a woody vine into a heavy syrup. Then they dipped darts into the thick liquid. Expert hunters, capable of finding a target more than a hundred yards away, would blow the darts through hollow reeds, killing their prey almost instantly. Birds died in less than five seconds, and human beings in less than five minutes.

3   Because the jungles were all but unreachable to everyone but the Indians, no one really understood how curare worked until the mid-nineteenth century, when experimenters began to uncover its secrets. It was found that curare, if swallowed, is fairly harmless. But if it penetrates the skin, curare is lethal. Because it relaxes all the muscles in the body—including those that control breathing—the victim quickly suffocates and dies.

4   Once researchers knew how curare worked, they were in a better position to figure out how it might be used to more beneficial ends. However, researchers were reluctant to experiment with curare imported from South America. Its strength varied, and one could never be sure how strong a dosage to use.

5   During World War II, Daniel Bovet, an Italian pharmacologist, developed the first synthetic* form of curare, and the stage was set to discover curare's benefits to humans. In 1942, Dr. Harold Griffith successfully used it as an anesthetic during surgery. From that time on, a synthetic and diluted* form of curare was used in many operations because its ability to relax the patient's muscles made the surgeon's work easier. Eventually, it was also used to treat rabies and tetanus, diseases that produce severe muscle cramps.

1. What is the overall main idea of the reading?
   a. Curare is an incredibly dangerous poison that can kill in seconds.
   b. A deadly poison, curare can also save lives.
   c. Curare has a long and ancient history.
   d. The jungle kept curare a secret for centuries.

2. Which pattern or patterns does the author use to develop that main idea?
   a. definition
   b. time order

---

*synthetic: artificial, made by people rather than nature.
*diluted: weakened.

ⓒ simple listing

d. comparison and contrast

ⓔ cause and effect

f. classification

3. If more than one pattern organizes the reading, identify the most important.

cause and effect; definition; sequence of dates and events
_____

Please explain.

Without definition and the cause and effect pattern, the writer couldn't

explain how curare kills and cures. Without the sequence of dates and

events, the writer couldn't explain how scientists unraveled the poison's

secrets with the passage of time.
_____

EXPLANATION   Everything in the reading, including the title, points to answer *b* as the overall main idea: Curare has a double nature: It can kill *and* it can heal. To explain that main idea, the author needs the definition pattern to tell readers what curare is. The cause and effect organizational pattern is central to explaining curare's dual nature as killer and healer. The sequence of dates and events pattern plays a key role in organizing the description of how curare's other, more beneficial, uses came to light. Process, probably the least important pattern, helps explain how hunters turned curare into a poison so that they could dip their arrows into it.

1. Schizophrenia, the Mind in Two

1 The term *schizophrenia* was coined in 1911 by the Swiss psychiatrist Eugene Bleuler. Literally, the word means "split mind." Bleuler thought the term effectively expressed one of the disease's central symptoms—a split between the patient's internal world and the external world of social reality.

2   Since Bleuler's time, researchers still have not figured out what causes this mysterious and devastating disease. However, they have been able to identify and name three distinct types.

3   *Disorganized schizrenia* expresses itself through bizarre and childlike behavior. Victims pay little attention to personal grooming. Sometimes they remain unwashed for days. Behaving like children, they are prone to making faces and given to bouts of giddiness.*

_____

*giddiness: silliness.

4 Those suffering from a second form of the disease, called *catatonic schizophrenia*, can remain immobile for hours. Mentally withdrawing from their environment, patients adopt rigid postures and fall silent for days, even months. Sometimes, without reason, sufferers will suddenly grow violent and attack anyone who comes near.

5 In *paranoid schizophrenia*, the most marked symptom is the presence of delusions or fantasies that bear no relation to reality. Patients suffering from this form fear that a person or group is trying to harm them. They often think they are surrounded by enemies and may, in response, become violent.

6 As research continues, it's becoming more and more likely that schizophrenia is not a single disease but a family of diseases that may arise from a variety of causes. By learning more about each type of schizophrenia, researchers hope to find more effective treatments.

1. What is the overall main idea of the reading?

    a. The term *schizophrenia* means "split mind," and was coined by Eugene Bleuler.

    b. Schizophrenia may well be a family of diseases.

    c. Although no one knows the cause of schizophrenia, researchers have identified three distinct types.

    d. Paranoid schizophrenia is perhaps the worst and most debilitating form of the disease.

2. Which pattern or patterns does the author use to develop that main idea?

    a. definition

    b. time order

    c. simple listing

    d. comparison and contrast

    e. cause and effect

    f. classification

3. If more than one pattern organizes the reading, identify the most important.

_____

Please explain.

_____

_____

_____

_____

2. The Johari Window

1   The Johari Window, named after its inventors, Joseph Luft and Harry Ingham, is a useful model for describing the complex process of human interaction. The window, or box, is divided into four panes, or areas, with each area labeled to indicate the kind of information that can be revealed or concealed when we communicate or interact with others: (1) open, (2) blind, (3) hidden, and (4) unknown. Because each person's window reflects his or her psychological makeup, the size of each pane varies with the individual.

2   The **open area** of the Johari Window represents your "public" or "awareness" area. This section symbolizes the information about yourself that both you and others recognize. It includes the information that you are willing to admit or make public. For example, you and everyone you know may be aware that you are a competitive person who doesn't like losing an argument or that your temper is easy to trigger.

3   The **blind area** in the Johari Window represents the information about yourself that others may know, or think they know, but that you are not aware of. For instance, you may think that you have a tendency to be shy and a bit withdrawn, whereas others may see you as open, relaxed, and friendly. Over time, information in the blind area can shift to the open area if other people are willing to mention their view of your behavior.

4   The **hidden area** in the Johari Window shows information that you know but that others do not. This area reflects the private thoughts and feelings you prefer to keep to yourself. For example, you may not want people to know that you are terrified of public speaking despite the fact that you do it frequently. Unlike the open and blind areas, the hidden area may not change over time. In other words, you may always choose to keep certain things about your life a secret.

5   The **unknown area** of the Johari Window is made up of things unknown both to you and to others. This area is reserved for those feelings, talents, and motives that are below the surface of awareness and have never been acknowledged or displayed. For example, you may have a talent for verbal expression, but if you are shy and avoid speaking a lot, you may never know that you have the ability. To offer another example, you may know that you grow angry when conversing with authority figures but have no idea that

Known to self   Not known to self

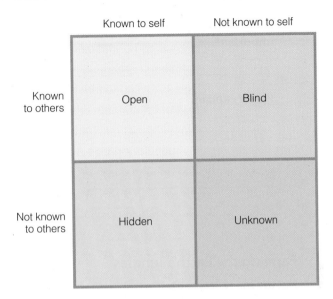

	Known to self	Not known to self
Known to others	Open	Blind
Not known to others	Hidden	Unknown

Figure 10.2 The Johari Window
The Johari Window is used primarily with groups on the assumption that self-disclosure and feedback improve communication among group members.

your anger stems from an unhappy relationship with your older brother. Obviously, if you don't recognize the cause and effect relationship between your childhood and your adult behavior, no one else is likely to either.

1. What is the overall main idea of the reading?
   a. The Johari Window is the creation of Joseph Luft.
   b. The Johari Window consists of four separate panes, or sections.
   c. The Johari Window offers an effective way to describe the human psyche.
   d. The size of the panes in the Johari Window varies with the individual.

2. Which pattern or patterns does the author use to develop that main idea?
   a. definition
   b. time order
   c. simple listing
   d. comparison and contrast
   e. cause and effect
   f. classification

3. If more than one pattern organizes the reading, identify the most important.

_____

Please explain.

_____

_____

_____

_____

3. Farming the Earth's Jungles

1 Not too many years ago, it was thought that food shortages could readily be solved by farming the world's jungles. Because the lush region of the Amazon Basin of Brazil seemed the perfect site, an agricultural colony was formed and farming was begun. To the surprise of many, the project failed—and failed badly. Yet, in retrospect, several major problems can be readily identified.

2 The first and most fundamental problem is the tropical soil. Although rain forests are lush and rich in foliage, the soil itself is poor. When foliage falls to the ground, very little is absorbed by the soil because of heavy rains. When the rains come—and they come often—most of the decaying foliage is washed away before it can enrich the earth. As a result, the soil in the tropical jungles never has enough time to absorb nutrients from fallen leaves, making it less appropriate for cultivation than one might assume.

3 Then, too, there is the problem of how quickly the jungle grows. Workers on the project would spend a day clearing a space for planting, only to return a day or two later and find it partially overgrown. The jungle is simply too powerful for humans' puny efforts to make any lasting imprint. One can fly over the area for hours and see no sign of human settlement.

4 Finally, there is the effect of sunlight on jungle soil. In many areas, when the soil is exposed to sunlight, it first hardens, then it turns into _laterite_, a red, rocklike substance containing high concentrations of aluminum and iron. While laterite is so beautiful it has been used to build temples in places such as Cambodia and Vietnam, it is all but impossible to use for agricultural purposes.

1. What is the main idea of the reading?

   a. There is still hope that the world's food shortages can be eliminated by farming the earth's jungles.

   b. People who dream of using the Amazon jungle for farming forget how quickly the jungle overruns everything in its path.

   c. The rain forests cannot be farmed without causing considerable damage to the environment.

   d. There are several reasons why attempts at farming the Amazon Basin of Brazil failed.

2. Which pattern or patterns does the author use to develop that main idea?

   a. definition

   b. time order

   c. simple listing

   d. comparison and contrast

   e. cause and effect

   f. classification

3. If more than one pattern organizes the reading, identify the most important.

   _____

   Please explain.

   _____

   _____

   _____

   _____

   _____

4. **Congratulations, Dad! Are You Nuts, Mom?**

1   Usually when a woman announces she is ready to give birth, most people, be they friends, relatives, or complete strangers, clap for joy. Impending motherhood is a miracle, after all, worthy of celebration. But that's hardly the response that British mother-to-be Elizabeth Adeney received when it was discovered in May 2009 that she was about to give birth.

2   Elizabeth Adeney, you see, was sixty-six years old and pregnant thanks to modern fertility treatments, which allow women long past childbearing age to bear children. As it was with sixty-six-year-old Adriana Iliescu, a Romanian woman who gave birth to a child in 2006, the public's view of Elizabeth Adeney was hotly critical. Her decision evoked numerous public attacks.

3   Among the nicer reactions was one from a blogger who said that much could be forgiven if Adeney, like some other older moms, had had a younger partner. Then the partner could presumably care for the child if anything happened to Adeney. But Adeney was divorced with no partner. She also didn't have brothers and sisters to step in if something happened to her.

4   Few took the position of one writer, who insisted that the whole affair was no one's business except the mother's. That mind-your-own-business take on the subject was, in fact, very much in line with what Adeney herself had said: that her pregnancy was no one's business except her own. As newspapers, blogs, and tweets around the world confirmed, very few agreed. Adeney's situation was fodder for the tabloids, and everyone seemed ready and willing to take potshots at Adeney's decision to become an elderly mom.

5   Far fewer people asked the question posed by journalist Gail Parker of the *Belfast Telegraph*, who wondered in print why old moms, but not old dads, are the subject of scorn and abuse. As Parker wrote, "If Adeney had been a 66-year-old man, it would have been cigars all around and to hell with the actuary tables."[†] And she's right, no one batted an eyelash when Warren Beatty became a dad at fifty-five, and even the most stodgy art critics can't restrain a smile at the mention of Pablo Picasso's fathering a child at sixty-eight.

6   Although there are probably legitimate reasons for thinking that having a child after the age of fifty is not the best idea in the world, it's clear that those reasons aren't applied equally. We seem to think old dads are kind of cute whereas old moms should have their heads examined. (Source of quotations: www.anorak.co.uk/media/210798.html; www.belfasttelegraph.co.uk/opinion/columnists/gail-walker/why-are-the-old-mums-so-disliked-but-not-old-dads-14306592.html.)

1. What is the main idea of the reading?

   a. Women who decide to give birth to children when they are way past childbearing age are making a terrible mistake, but men who father children in their sixties are even worse.

[†]actuary tables: tables indicating the average length of life given specific circumstances.

b. For some reason, people are appalled when women in their fifties and sixties use fertility technology in order to give birth, but men never experience the same amount of outrage if they decide to become fathers late in life.

c. The public's willingness to attack and demean women who choose to have children in their fifties and sixties is just another sign of how sexist the world remains.

d. The 2009 example of the British woman who decided to give birth in her sixties is another example of how badly the feminist movement failed women by encouraging them to put off having children in favor of a career.

2. Which pattern or patterns does the author use to develop that main idea?

a. definition

b. time order

c. simple listing

d. comparison and contrast

e. cause and effect

f. classification

3. If more than one pattern organizes the reading, identify the most important.

_____

Please explain.

_____

_____

_____

_____

VOCABULARY CHECK

The following words were introduced in the chapter. Match the word with the definition. Review words, definitions, and original context two or three times before taking the vocabulary tests. (The page numbers in parentheses indicate where the word first appeared.)

1. diversion (p. 582) _____

2. posh (p. 583) _____

3. incomparable (p. 583) _____

4. propaganda (p. 585) _____

5. biographical (p. 585) _____

6. convulsions (p. 588) _____

7. lax (p. 591) _____

8. synthetic (p. 597) _____

9. diluted (p. 597) _____

10. giddiness (p. 598) _____

a. careless

b. artificial, made by people rather than nature

c. silliness

d. weakened

e. fancy

f. related to a person's life

g. without equal

h. pleasant activity

i. uncontrolled fits in which the muscles contract wildly

j. a method of persuasion that relies on emotional appeal and discourages logical thinking

DIGGING DEEPER The Development of Self in Childhood

Looking Ahead Ever say "I'm not myself today" or "I know myself; I don't do well in high-stress situations"? Most of us talk about our "self" without ever really asking the question that underlies this reading, "How do we become who we are?"

1   How do we acquire a sense of identity, or self? Well, it doesn't happen overnight. In Europe and the United States, at least, identity formation is a process that involves several different steps, each occurring at a different age. By the second year of life, for example, most children can correctly label their gender, a key component in identity formation. Around two, children start to make statements like "I am a boy" or "I am a girl." Labels like these then pave the way for a later, more complete and more sophisticated sense of identity.

2   Initially, however, such labels lack permanence. Between the ages of two and three, a boy may claim he can become a girl under certain circumstances—"when I grow up" or "if I grow my hair long." Similarly, a girl might imagine she can change her gender by changing her name—"I'm going to call myself Bob and become a boy." At this early stage in identity formation, children are also prone to thinking they can throw off human identity and become an animal: "Bow-wow, I'm a dog."

3   After the age of five or six, however, children begin to develop a sense of **self-constancy** (the belief that identity remains permanently fixed). At this point, children start to believe that they will stay the same person indefinitely on into the future. They now believe that they will remain human forever and maintain the same gender under all circumstances. Permanent beliefs like these are the most basic and earliest core of a personal identity.

4   Around the age of eight, children begin to include psychological characteristics in their description of self. They say, for example, "I am brave" or "I am happy." What's missing from this early description of self is any sense of context. The child does not realize that he or she is brave in certain situations and fearful in others. Nor does the child recognize that he or she can be brave and fearful at the same time. Rather, the tendency is to focus on one particular feeling or trait and disregard all others. At this point, ambiguous, or conflicting, feelings seem too threatening to be expressed or even acknowledged, perhaps because the child's internal sense of identity still feels weak and fragile.

5   By the end of middle childhood, both boys and girls are clearly able to think of themselves in more complicated ways. They can, for example, describe themselves as relaxed and skillful when in the classroom but ill-at-ease or uncomfortable in social settings. They are now much less likely to define themselves in simplistic terms—for instance, "I am always angry." Instead, they are more likely to describe themselves in relation to particular situations: "I get angry when I think people are not listening to what I have to say." But generally speaking, it isn't until adulthood that children develop a more flexible sense of self and are able to integrate, or combine, conflicting traits: "I am a friendly person and like to be around people, but I also need some time alone on a regular basis."

6   It's worth pointing out, however, that the process of creating and maintaining a sense of identity does not appear to be the same in all cultures. In Asian countries like India, Japan, and Nepal, for example, three distinct senses of self appear to develop in childhood and persist on into adulthood—the familial, the spiritual, and the individual. The familial self relates only to how one appears or behaves within the context of the family: "I am very obedient to my parents' wishes." In contrast, the spiritual self is defined and organized strictly in terms of religious beliefs: "My relationship to my god is central to my life." As one might expect, the individual self is closest to the European sense of identity described in the preceding paragraphs: "I am a generally happy person." (Source of information: Seifert, Hoffnung, and Hoffnung, *Lifespan Development*, pp. 301–2.)

Sharpening Your Skills

DIRECTIONS   Answer the questions by filling in the blanks or circling the letters of the correct response.

1. How would you paraphrase the main idea of the entire reading?

_____

_____

2. Overall, what is the primary pattern in this reading?
   a. definition
   b. time order
   c. simple listing
   d. comparison and contrast
   e. cause and effect
   f. classification

3. To connect paragraph 5 to paragraph 4, readers have to draw what inference?

  a. By the end of middle childhood, children are better able to express their feelings.

  b. By the end of middle childhood, children's intelligence has increased.

  c. By the end of middle childhood, children have a sense of context when describing themselves.

4. What two patterns of organization are at work in the last paragraph?

  a. definition

  b. time order

  c. simple listing

  d. comparison and contrast

  e. cause and effect

  f. classification

5. Which statement better describes the purpose of this reading?

  a. The author wants to describe the stages we go through to develop a sense of personal identity.

  b. The author wants to persuade readers that our society overemphasizes the sense of personal individuality.

Making Connections In paragraph 5, the author gives an illustration of how children's sense of themselves develops over time, using as an example the sentence, "I am a friendly person and like to be around people, but I also need some time alone on a regular basis." Look back to the Johari Window (Figure 10.2). In which box does this statement belong?

_____

Drawing Your Own Conclusions Based on the reading, how do you think children between the ages of two and three would answer if someone said to them, "That's impossible. A person can't be in two places at the same time."

_____

_____

_____

▶ **TEST 1**   **Vocabulary Review**

DIRECTIONS   Use one of the following words to fill in the blanks.

incomparable	synthetic	posh	propaganda	convulsions
lax	biographical	diluted	diversion	giddiness

1. After the dog went into _____, they knew his condition was serious.

2. Because the company was _____ about security, spies were able to steal the new designs.

3. The restaurant's canopy was made of some _____ material that could not tear no matter what was done to it.

4. If they _____ the medicine with a glass of water, the child would drink it without crying.

5. The girl's _____ suggested the Coke bottle had more than Coke in it.

6. Right before he died in 2007, David Halberstam, considered by his peers to be a(n) _____ journalist, issued some strong criticisms about his chosen profession.

7. There was a little _____ note next to the author's picture, but it failed to mention that he had spent time in prison.

8. Whenever the scholar had to attend a social function in really _____ surroundings, he would dress very stylishly and hope that no one would notice how ill at ease he felt.

9. The elderly man had once been a race-car driver, but at eighty-four, golf was his only _____; he had become as passion-ate about playing golf as he had once been about driving fast cars.

10. The government used _____ to drum up support for an unpopular war.

▶ **TEST 2**   Identifying Main Ideas and Patterns of Organization

DIRECTIONS   Circle the appropriate letter to identify the main idea along with the patterns used to organize the reading.

1. Rattlesnakes

1   The rattlesnake's tail is ringed with several rattles that make a whirring sound when the snake is disturbed and about to attack. Each time the snake molts and loses its skin, a new ring is added to the rattle. However, after several years, the end rattle becomes worn and falls off. Therefore, it is a myth that the age of the snake can be determined by the number of its rattles.

2   What's not a myth, however, is that rattlesnakes can be dangerous. In general they prefer to hide from humans, but they will attack if threatened, and their venom can be deadly.

3   The venom of the rattler contains two different poisons. One stops the action of both heart and lungs. The other destroys tissue. The rattler's venom is contained in two glands, one in each cheek. Long ducts connect the glands to two hollow fangs in the upper jaw. The fangs protrude, or stick out, if the rattler is ready to strike, but they fold back into the mouth when the snake is at rest.

4   Unlike other poisonous snakes—copperheads, water moccasins, and coral snakes—rattlers have never been known to attack human beings without reason. They will attack only if they are disturbed by some sudden intrusion. They also always warn in advance that they are about to strike. Although a rattler's venom is indeed deadly, no one need die of a rattlesnake bite if medical attention is available. There are several antidotes for the snake's poison, all of which render it harmless. The main thing is for the victim to receive the antidote as soon as possible.

1. What is the main idea of the entire reading?
    a. It's not true that the age of a rattler can be determined by counting the number of rings.
    b. Rattler attacks are dangerous and can be deadly.
    c. There are many myths surrounding rattlesnakes.
    d. Rattlers are famous for attacking without reason.

2. Which patterns does the author use to develop that main idea?

    a. definition

    b. time order

    c. simple listing

    d. comparison and contrast

    e. cause and effect

    f. classification

2. Open Versus Closed Questions

1   The questions we ask can be open or closed (Goodman and Esterly, 1988). *Closed questions* are ones that people can answer with a "yes" or a "no" or some other equally short answer. If we meet other people for the first time and ask them, "How long have you lived here?" we are asking a closed question. *Open questions*, in contrast, are designed to obtain more information than closed questions. Open questions are asked in such a way so that people cannot give a one-word answer. Asking someone "What kinds of experiences have you had since you moved here?" is an open question that would produce more information than a closed question such as "Do you like your new school?"

2   If we really want a direct answer, we should ask a closed question. To illustrate, if we want to know if our spouse or partner wants to go to a movie tonight, we shouldn't ask, "When's the last time we went to the movies?" The answer to this question may or may not lead the other person to suggest that we go to the movies. But if we really want to go to the movies that night, a closed question such as "Would you like to go to a movie tonight?" would prove more effective.

3   Keep in mind, too, that asking several closed questions instead of one good open question can make a small problem seem like a big one (Goodman and Esterly, 1988). To illustrate, suppose you are in conflict with your roommate, and you have just explained your position. Now you want to know how your roommate feels about what you have just said. Unfortunately, if you ask a number of closed questions, your roommate is likely to feel like she or he is being interrogated.[†] To get more information, you could ask an open question such as "How do you feel about what I just said?" (Gudykunst et al., *Building Bridges*, p. 281.)

[†]interrogated: required to answer questions as if in a police station.

1. What is the main idea of the entire reading?

    a. There are two types of questions: open and closed.

    b. Closed questions are always better than open ones.

    c. Open questions almost never produce the necessary information.

    d. To get honest answers, we need to ask closed questions.

2. Which patterns does the author use to develop that main idea?

    a. definition

    b. time order

    c. simple listing

    d. comparison and contrast

    e. cause and effect

    f. classification

▶ **TEST 3**   ## Identifying Main Ideas and Patterns of Organization

DIRECTIONS   Circle the appropriate letter to identify the main idea along with the patterns used to organize the reading.

1. ### Radio Rescues

1   The invention of radio had a profound effect on the safety of ships at sea. When ships got into trouble, it became possible to summon aid by radio. One of the first such cases occurred in 1898, when radio signals were used to help a sinking vessel.

2   A truly dramatic rescue at sea took place in 1909. When the SS *Republic* began to sink off New York, the wireless[†] operator immediately sent out a distress signal. Other ships detected it and came to the position indicated. Luckily, all the passengers were rescued. The rescue made newspaper headlines, and the public was thrilled.

3   Unfortunately, a historic rescue effort in 1912 was less successful. When the "unsinkable" *Titanic* struck an iceberg in the North Atlantic, the wireless operator tried to alert nearby ships. Unfortunately, their radio crews had gone to bed for the night. However, he was able to make contact with a station on shore (in Wanamaker's department store in New York City), whose stronger signal could reach more distant points. The young operator, David Sarnoff, stayed at his post for many hours, making contact with other vessels. Unfortunately, by the time the ships he had contacted arrived the next morning, the great passenger liner had sunk to the bottom of the ocean. Some 1,500 people drowned, including the *Titanic*'s heroic wireless operator, who tried all night to summon aid until he went down with the ship. (Adapted from DeFleur and Dennis, *Understanding Mass Communication*, pp. 190–91.)

1. What is the main idea of the entire reading?
   a. When the *Titanic* sank, the wireless operator went down with the ship.
   b. The dramatic rescue of the SS *Republic* dramatically illustrated the effect of radio on ship safety.
   c. Even radio communication could not help the *Titanic*.
   d. Although the invention of radio profoundly improved ship safety, even radio communication could not help the *Titanic*.

[†]wireless: a radio telegraph.

2. What patterns does the author use to develop that main idea?

a. definition

b. time order

c. simple listing

d. comparison and contrast

e. cause and effect

f. classification

2. What Differences Actually Exist?

1 In the light of stereotypes about "femaleness" and "maleness," it is logical to ask whether researchers have documented actual differences in the characteristics or behaviors of females and males. For many human traits, the data show that average differences *between* the sexes are smaller than the variability in performance *within* each sex. Nonetheless, in some areas the characteristics of females and males have been found to differ.

2 **Physical Attributes** Females and males physically differ in a number of ways, including the makeup of their chromosomes, their genitalia, and levels of certain hormones. Females are physically more mature at birth, whereas males show a special physical vulnerability during infancy. Compared with females, males are more likely to be miscarried, die in infancy, or develop hereditary diseases (Jacklin, 1989). Later in infancy and childhood, females walk, talk, and reach other developmental milestones earlier than males. Males, on the other hand, are more physically active and are more likely to engage in vigorous rough-and-tumble play (Eaton & Ennis, 1986; Pellegrini & Smith, 1998). By later childhood and adolescence, females reach puberty earlier and males develop greater height, weight, and muscle mass than females (Maccoby & Jacklin, 1974).

3 **Cognition** One aspect of cognition for which males and females have been thought to differ is in verbal abilities. The popular belief has been that girls are more skilled than boys at verbal tasks, a belief that was modestly supported by an early review of the relevant research (Maccoby & Jacklin, 1974). A close analysis of cognitive sex differences, however, indicates only small sex differences in verbal skills favoring females (Feingold, 1988; Hyde & Linn, 1988). Females have a slight advantage on tests that measure reading comprehension, spelling, word meaning, or grammar (Feingold, 1993; Halpern, 1997), but most researchers agree that the differences are not large enough to warrant much notice.

4 **Social Behaviors**   One of the most consistent findings in the research on sex differences is that, beginning in the preschool years, males are more aggressive than females. They engage in more rough-and-tumble play, display more physical aggression, try to dominate peers, and subsequently display more antisocial behaviors than girls (Block, 1983; Huston, 1985; Loeber & Hay, 1997). Analyses substantiate that sex differences in aggression are greatest among preschoolers and decrease through the college years (Eagly & Steffen, 1986; Hyde, 1984, 1986).

5   Even though males generally are more aggressive than females, however, the magnitude of the sex difference varies as a function of where the aggression occurs and the type of aggression being measured. The largest sex differences are found in natural settings, such as playgrounds, and when physical aggression is being measured. Conclusions about sex differences in aggression must be tempered by how this term is defined, however. When aggression is described as an attempt to harm another person through manipulation, gossip, or excluding peers from a social group (called *indirect* or *relational aggression*), girls are found to be more aggressive than boys starting in the preschool years (Bjorkqvist, 1994; Crick, Casas, & Mosher, 1997; Crick & Grotpeter, 1995). (Adapted from Bukatko and Daehler, *Child Development*, pp. 468–70.)

1. What is the main idea of the entire reading?
    a. Sex differences between males and females are largely a result of the stereotypes that govern our thinking.
    b. Although the differences between males and females are not that large, they do exist in certain areas.
    c. Although it may not be politically correct to say so, there are major differences between males and females, almost from the moment of birth.
    d. Researchers consistently show that boys are more aggressive than girls in almost every possible setting or situation.

2. What patterns does the author use to develop that main idea?
    a. definition
    b. time order
    c. simple listing
    d. comparison and contrast
    e. cause and effect
    f. classification

More on Purpose, Tone, and Bias

IN THIS CHAPTER, YOU WILL LEARN

- how to evaluate an author's writing in relation to purpose.

- how to distinguish between fact and opinion.

- how to recognize and respond to a writer's tone.

- how to tell when an author's bias has become excessive.

- how to recognize opinions based on faulty logic.

"Question everything."
—Maria Mitchell, first female professor of astronomy

Chapter 8 briefly discussed purpose in writing. This chapter examines the writer's purpose more closely so readers can determine when an informative purpose has crossed the line into persuasion. Chapter 11 also identifies the clues that reveal when writers intent on persuasion have forgotten the ethical responsibility of persuasive writing—to present opposing points of view with fairness and respect.

Why Think About Purpose?

We tend to assume that certain written materials—textbooks, news reports, reference works, and manuals—have a purely informative purpose. They are there to provide information without expressing judgment or opinion. Thus, we often read such materials as if we were absorbing purely factual information, agreed upon and undisputed by all sane people.

Yet even authors whose primary intention is to inform can occasionally let personal bias creep in. If you start to see signs of persuasive writing in an essentially informative text, take note. The material you are reading may not be untouched by bias. There may very well be other ways to think about the topic or issue, different from the one the author presents.

For that matter, knowing from the very beginning that a writer's purpose is persuasive is equally important. Writers intent on persuasion are biased in favor of the idea or action they support. There is nothing wrong with that. The danger lies in their letting personal bias overwhelm their judgment. To really evaluate an author's position, you need to be alert to logic or language suggesting that the author's bias might have clouded his or her ability to think clearly or treat opposing points of view fairly.

The Signs of Informative Writing

Writers whose primary purpose is to inform want to make readers knowledgeable about a particular person, idea, or issue. They aren't interested in promoting any one perspective, or point of view. On the contrary, they are likely to present opposing points of view so readers can compare and contrast different positions and come to their own conclusions.

Informative writing tends to lean heavily on **factual evidence**. This is the kind of agreed-upon evidence that can be verified or checked against outside sources, for example, "As a result of the explosion, nine miners died" or "Seventy-five percent of the students who took a study-skills course improved their grades." Both of these statements are factual and can be checked for accuracy.

Writers intent on informing do include opinions, but they are the opinions of others. They are not, at least not explicitly, the writer's. In addition, the tone, or voice, called up by informative writing is likely to be coolly neutral, or impersonal, and lacking in emotion. Here is an example of writing meant primarily to inform.

The Controversy Surrounding Forrest Carter

1 *The Education of Little Tree* is the story of an orphaned boy named Forrest who learns about life from his Cherokee grandparents. Written by Forrest Carter, the book, which has remained in print since its publication in 1976, has been an extraordinary literary success. The book's author, however, has not had the same unqualified success; he has, in fact, been the subject of enormous controversy.

2 As the author of *Little Tree*, Carter was revered as a man dedicated to preserving the richness and wisdom of Native American culture. He was, as an old friend maintained, "somebody who wanted to see right done to Indians." Yet Forrest Carter was also Asa Carter, a devout, even zealous,* Ku Klux Klan member and a speechwriter for the segregationist* Alabama governor George Wallace. Although Carter tried to keep his Klan past a secret, it was uncovered when he went on television to promote one of his books that was being made into a movie. The newspapers picked up the story, and Forrest Carter's other life came to light. Yet few seemed to care, least of all the book's publisher, the University of New Mexico Press. Happy with the book's sales, the publisher generally ignored Carter's past. The twenty-fifth anniversary edition, for instance, appeared in 2001 without any reference to Carter's other self.

Note here how the author describes some very unpleasant parts of Carter's past without passing judgment. That lack of a personal opinion or point of view is essential to informative writing.

---

*zealous: excessively enthusiastic.
*segregationist: someone who believes in strict separation of races.

Note, too, the tone the author assumes. Is she a fan or a critic of Carter's? You can't tell. And that's as it should be if an author's purpose is to inform.

Ten Signs of Informative Writing ♦	1. Opens with a neutral title that does not judge or evaluate: "Latino Rock Pioneers of the 50s"; "World War II Propaganda."
	2. Describes a subject, an event, or an issue without offering a personal opinion or making a value judgment: "In 2005, surgeons successfully performed a face transplant for the first time in medical history."
	3. Relies mainly on a denotative language, which makes the author sound cool and personally uninvolved: "On the first day of the riots, one hundred people died."
	4. Leans heavily on factual evidence that can be verified, or checked, in other sources: "In May of 1968, approximately nine million workers went on strike in France."
	5. Describes the opinions of others without revealing if the author agrees or disagrees: "In a recent *New York Times* editorial, William Baude argued that states might 'use custody laws to curtail the movements of pregnant women.'"
	6. Avoids using the first-person singular (*I*) or plural (*we*): "It has been argued by some" as opposed to "I would argue here."
	7. Often gives both sides of an issue: "Judge William Rehnquist, who died in 2005 at the age of eighty, was considered by many to be an arch-conservative who helped divide the country. Others, however, saw him as a consensus builder."
	8. Expresses only value judgments that are attributed to others: "Some hold the opinion that both Republicans and Democrats failed to adequately help victims of Hurricane Katrina. Critics cite failures among Democrats at the local level and Republicans at the federal level."
	9. Emphasizes the role of research that illustrates or supports the main idea: "The leading medical researcher at Harvard Medical School disputes the notion that eight glasses of water a day are essential. His claim is supported by a number of studies done on athletes."
	10. Commonly appears in reference works, textbooks, manuals, newspapers, and institutional reports.

◆ **Persuasive Writing**

Although writers intent on persuasion may present opposing opinions, they usually make it clear that one opinion—theirs—is more informed or better supported than anyone else's. In other words, they openly express a bias for or against a particular position.

Writers hoping to convince may well supply readers with facts that can be verified. However, those facts have usually been chosen because they support the opinion being promoted. Writers intent on persuasion often don't supply facts equally. They are more likely to tip the scale in favor of their position because they want the reader to share their viewpoint, not the opposition's.

In contrast to the neutral tone of informative writing, persuasive writing often conveys an emotionally charged tone that underscores the author's personal involvement in the subject matter. See the following box for the various tones an author can assume.

Some Words That Describe Tone ◆		
admiring	disbelieving	outraged
amazed	disgusted	passionate
angry	doubtful	patriotic
anxious	enthusiastic	proud
appalled	friendly	puzzled
arrogant	horrified	regretful
breezy	insulting	respectful
cautious	ironic (saying the opposite of what is intended)[†]	rude
comical		sarcastic
confident		shocked
contemptuous	mistrustful	skeptical
critical	neutral	solemn
cynical	nostalgic (longing for a past time)	sympathetic
determined	objective	worried
disapproving		

[†]We use irony all the time in daily conversation. If traffic was bad, upon arriving at our destination, we might say to the host, "The traffic was a real pleasure," meaning, of course, the opposite.

Here's another reading about writer Forrest Carter. Only this time the purpose is persuasive. Note how the title already suggests a point of view, and the very first sentence introduces a mistrustful tone that turns outright critical, even disgusted.

The Dark Side of Forrest Carter

1   Although Forrest Carter originally claimed that *The Education of Little Tree* was autobiographical, there is amazingly little evidence to prove his claim. Carter was not orphaned at five years of age, nor was he raised by his grandparents. There is even some disagreement about the accuracy of Carter's portrayal of Cherokee life. Geary Hobson, an active member of the Cherokee tribe, is dubious concerning Carter's knowledge of Cherokee culture, while writer Daniel Heath Justice claims that some of the customs described in the book are authentic.

2   What is not subject to disagreement is the fact that Forrest Carter was born Asa Carter and grew up to be a bitter, hard-drinking, die-hard racist. In his Alabama hometown, Carter was a high-ranking Ku Klux Klan member and a speechwriter for the state's fiery segregationist governor, George Wallace. Although some literary critics, like the esteemed Henry Louis Gates Jr., claim that Carter's racist background does not influence the value of his most famous work, that point of view seems naïve. As an open and unashamed bigot, Carter could not help but portray his characters in demeaning terms. When closely examined, *The Education of Little Tree* displays typical stereotypes about Native Americans: The Cherokees in *The Education of Little Tree* are innocent children of nature who desperately need the benevolent protection of white people.

The writer of this selection doesn't just describe Asa Carter and his work. She also makes a value judgment: Bigotry mars Carter's work.

Notice as well the use of phrases like "racist background" and "open and unashamed bigot." The heated language, heavy with negative connotations, creates a disapproving tone that encourages readers to share the author's contempt.

Ten Signs of Persuasive Writing ◆	**1.** Opens with a title that suggests a point of view: "Voting Matters"; "Turkey Haunted by the Nightmare of Armenia."†

---

†Although many of his fellow citizens disagree with Turkish writer Orhan Pamuk, many others share his opinion. Pamuk insists his country carried out genocide, or planned mass slaughter designed to wipe out a specific group, against the Armenians in 1915.

2. Expresses a personal opinion about a subject, an event, or an issue: "From my perspective, the best thing about the Winter Olympics is that they are over."

3. Frequently uses language that reveals strong feelings: "How many stories about desperate, terrified, and homeless people do we need to hear before we really commit to rebuilding New Orleans?"

4. Mentions an opposing point of view mainly to contradict it: "The notion that alcoholics can learn to drink moderately is wishful thinking."

5. Uses more facts that favor the writer's point of view. For instance, a writer who does not want readers to support the use of animals in research might include statistics about the number of mice killed in pursuit of a cancer treatment, while leaving out any statistic about the number of people living longer now that the drug is available.

6. Gives reasons why the author's opinion should be held by others: "There are several reasons why censorship during wartime is absolutely necessary."

7. Often uses the first-person pronoun (*I*) or addresses the audience: "I know that you too must cringe when politicians claim to speak for America."

8. Refers to the audience as if agreement had already been established between the writer and the audience: "We all know that elections are not won by merit; they are won by money."

9. Uses rhetorical questions that neither expect nor want an answer: "Except to undermine parental authority, what other reason could there be for telling a small child to question authority?"

10. Commonly appears in essays, editorials, biographies, and books written to make readers aware of an issue or revise a long-held opinion.

Belong to a group

On the Meaning of "Primary Purpose"

The more you consider writing in relation to purpose, the more you will be aware that where persuasive writing is concerned, the two purposes are bound to blend. For instance, even the passage on page 623, which describes Asa Carter's views with outright contempt, has some informative moments: Forrest Carter was born Asa Carter, and he did write speeches for George Wallace. As a thoughtful reader, you have to weigh the amount of persuasion versus the amount of pure information in a reading and make a decision about which purpose is primary. In the case of the passage on page 623, it's clear that the primary purpose is persuasion. The informative statements are only there as part of the writer's attempt to convince readers of two things—Carter was a wholesale bigot and a fraud.

SUMMING UP THE KEY POINTS

1. When reading reference books, textbooks, or newspaper articles, most people assume the goal of the writer is to inform, or lay out the facts and perspectives associated with a particular idea or issue. Thus, they are inclined to read uncritically, simply trying to absorb the information they are being given. But even writers who try hard to be completely objective can't always do so, especially if they have strong opinions on the subject. Because writers intent on dispensing information do slip into persuasion, often without even realizing it, readers need to be aware when bias has crept into a supposedly informative piece of writing.

2. Informative writing is marked by a heavy emphasis on facts that can be verified, or checked for accuracy.

3. In informative writing, the opinions included are never ascribed, or linked, to the author personally. They belong to outside sources, and they are present so that the author can give readers some perspective on the topic under discussion.

4. Writers whose sole purpose is to inform use a cool, unemotional tone that does not reveal a personal point of view.

5. Persuasive writing is supposed to present an opinion, and there's nothing wrong with that unless the author is so committed to a particular position, he or she can't treat opposing points of view fairly.

6. Writers intending to persuade may also include facts, but those facts will usually support those writers' opinions. Facts supporting an opposing point of view are usually in short supply.

7. When the goal of writing is persuasion, writers may well present opposing points of view, but when they do, they usually point out what's wrong with those points of view.

8. Tone plays a key role in persuasive writing. Writers use a range of tones from humorous to outraged as a way to encourage readers' agreement. They generally choose the tone they consider most likely to persuade their particular audience.

9. Authors may intentionally or unintentionally combine purposes, starting off informative and veering into persuasion. It's the reader's job to determine which purpose is primary because one usually is.

◆ EXERCISE 1   Identifying the Main Idea and Primary Purpose

DIRECTIONS   Circle the correct letters to identify the main idea and primary purpose.

EXAMPLE

Study Focuses on High School Dropout Rate

1 For a while now, studies of the U.S. education system have shown that about one-third of all high school students drop out before they receive their diploma. While the United States used to rank first when it came to adults 25–34 who had finished high school, it has dropped to 11th. Many in both government and education view this situation with concern, and the results of a new study seem to support their worries. "Education at a Glance" was released by the Paris-based Organization for Economic Cooperation and Development (OECD) on September 12, 2006. The study's goal was to compare the educational performances of students around the world and help world leaders see how well or poorly their countries are doing in comparison to their international neighbors. According to the results, only Denmark equals the United States when it comes to high school dropouts.

2   The study did reveal, though, that high school dropouts all over the world face a stiff penalty for not graduating: They earn significantly less money than those who do get a degree. This is especially true in the United States. Forty-four percent of adults who don't graduate high school make half or less of the country's median income.[†] It also seems that students who drop out of high school can't make up for their missing degree. One reason for this, according to Barbara Ischinger, director of education for the OECD, is

---

[†]median income: the middle point of all income possibilities, with everyone else above or below that point. In 2002, the U.S. median income was $42,409, down $500 from 2001.

that adult education and job-training programs don't seem to be closing the gap between those with degrees and those without: "Those with poor initial qualifications remain disadvantaged throughout their life because they have fewer opportunities to catch up later on."

3   In discussing the study, Ischinger also pointed out that the importance of a high school degree on economic achievement varies according to the country. Dutch and Swiss governments, for instance, have federal regulations in place that help support those who have weak educational backgrounds or who lack highly marketable skills. The United States with its strong emphasis on a free market economy does not, making the penalties for dropping out greater.

4   According to OECD's study, college graduation rates in the United States were also below average when compared to other nations. Still, the study did show that for those who complete their college training, the rewards in the United States are great: An adult with a degree earns 72 percent more than someone who only has a high school degree. The United States also remains the most popular place for foreign students to study, although that number, too, showed a decline. Overall, the study did say that the United States has a high proportion of educated adults and a greater degree of gender equality among the educated than many other countries. It also points out that the United States, despite the high dropout rate, remains economically competitive and strong. (Source of statistics: http://news.yahoo.com/s/ap20060912/ap_on_go_ot/education-compared.)

1. Which statement best expresses the main idea?

   a. A new study indicates that the United States is no longer economically competitive.

   b. The study called "Education at a Glance" proves that the United States does not spend enough money on education, and that failure to commit financially to education has important consequences for the country's workforce.

   ⓒ A recent study by the Organization for Economic Cooperation and Development points out that the high school dropout rate in the United States is higher than in many other countries and has significant financial consequences.

   d. The 2006 "Education at a Glance" study done by the Organization for Economic Cooperation and Development shows how money can affect education, with wealthier students going to better schools and consequently making more money.

2. The author's primary purpose is to

    (a.) inform readers about the results of the study by the Organization for Economic Cooperation and Development.

    b. persuade readers that the results of the study by the Organization for Economic Cooperation and Development prove how ineffective the U.S. education system is.

EXPLANATION   For the main-idea question, answer *a* is wrong because it contradicts the reading, which explicitly says that the country remains competitive. Answers *b* and *d* cannot be correct because the amount of money spent on education is never discussed. Answer *c*, however, does correctly identify the main idea. The reading reports on the results of the study done by OECD, and it focuses on the financial consequences of dropping out before earning a diploma.

Despite the fact that this reading could be used to persuade readers that American education needs an overhaul, its purpose is informative. Note the neutral title and the equally neutral tone. The language is very denotative. It's never used to charm, excite, or inflame readers. The author is also careful to report what the study says rather than what she thinks about American education and the problem of high school dropouts.

1. Fingerprints on Trial

1 Fingerprints have long been considered an essential part of crime solving. If a trained expert said in a courtroom that fingerprints found at the scene of a crime matched those of the accused, the expert's testimony usually decided the case. The defendant was found guilty, case closed. But fingerprint evidence may no longer be considered unassailable proof of guilt. While fingerprints might not lie, the experts who analyze them can and do make mistakes. Sometimes poorly trained, they are not always subject to regular review by outside experts. Consequently, the use of fingerprint evidence is currently on trial, and the jury is still out as to whether fingerprint analysis makes for reliable evidence.

2   Fingerprint evidence was first admitted into a U.S. courtroom in 1911 and went unchallenged for so long, in part, because no one really knew what standards should be applied to what was considered scientific evidence. However, all that changed with a 1993 case called *Daubert v. Merrell Dow Pharmaceuticals*. The case involved a child whose mother had taken a drug made by Merrell Dow Pharmaceuticals. The child suffered from serious birth

defects, and lawyers representing the child's family argued that the drug had caused the defects. The pharmaceutical company insisted that there was no valid proof that the drug was at fault and raised the issue of what constituted scientific proof. The judge ruled in favor of the pharmaceutical company and laid down a set of standards for what could qualify as proof. Chief among them was the criterion that an evidence-gathering technique with a high error rate could no longer be accepted as solid evidence. As a consequence of the *Daubert* ruling, judges were now required to take a more active role evaluating and deciding the "quality of evidence." It was at this point that the sacred cows of forensic* science came under attack. Handwriting evidence was no longer considered scientific, use of lie detector results as evidence was severely limited, and even ballistic tests claiming to match bullets to specific guns came into question.

3   Suddenly, questions were being asked that had rarely been posed in pre-1993 courtrooms: Has fingerprint identification been adequately tested? What's the error rate? What are the standards and controls for evaluating fingerprint experts? People like lawyer Robert Epstein, who has repeatedly challenged the validity of fingerprint evidence, would say that none of these questions has been adequately answered. And even when they have been answered, the result does not bode well for the survival of fingerprint analysis. Epstein is not alone in his opinion. Professor David Faigman of the University of California, Hastings College of Law, predicts "that . . . some judge somewhere in the country will write an opinion excluding fingerprinting. It's inevitable. The research is just too thin to let it in." (Source of statistics: Malcolm Ritter, "Fingerprint Evidence Faces Hurdles," April 7, 2001, www.scafo.org/Library/PDF/FP%20Evidence%20 Faces%Hurdlespdt.)

1. Which statement best expresses the main idea?
   a. Fingerprint evidence has been totally discredited as a result of the *Daubert* standards; it is no longer used in courtrooms.
   b. The FBI still defends fingerprint evidence, but no one else seems to believe in it any longer.
   c. It's not certain whether fingerprint evidence will continue to appear in our nation's courtrooms.

---

*forensic: related to courts of law and criminal investigations.

    d. Thanks to attorney Robert Epstein, who had the courage to singlehandedly challenge fingerprint evidence, fingerprints as evidence have been completely discredited.

  2. The author's primary purpose is

    a. to inform readers about the controversy over fingerprint evidence.

    b. to persuade readers that fingerprint evidence may not survive the current challenge to its credibility.

2. Should a Drug-Abusing Expectant Woman Be Charged with Child Abuse?

1   Consider the circumstances surrounding the prosecution of Cornelia Whitner of South Carolina. Her son was born with cocaine in his system. In 1992 Cornelia pled guilty to a charge of child neglect after admitting to the use of cocaine in her third trimester of pregnancy. She was sentenced to eight years in prison.

What Is the Controversy?

2   Although the conviction of Cornelia Whitner has since been overturned, the issues surrounding this and similar cases deeply divide law enforcement, medical, and social service agencies in the United States, Canada, and many Western European countries (Capron, 1998; Peak & Del Papa, 1993). Since the mid-1980s, more than two hundred American women in thirty states have been prosecuted on charges of child abuse and neglect, delivery of drugs to a minor, or assault with a deadly weapon for allegedly harming their offspring through prenatal exposure to cocaine or other illegal drugs (Paltrow et al., 2000). Court cases with policy implications for whether a woman can or should be arrested if she exposes a fetus to illegal drugs are continuing to be debated at the highest judicial levels, including the Supreme Court in the United States (Greenhouse, 2000; Paltrow et al., 2000). Is this an effective way to reduce the likelihood of drug use and any of its accompanying risks for the fetus?

What Are the Opposing Arguments?

3   Some say a concerned society should impose criminal or other charges on a pregnant woman who uses a drug that may be dangerous to the fetus. A number of jurisdictions in the United States and provinces in

Canada have implemented laws permitting a newborn to be removed from a parent on the grounds of child abuse or neglect because of drug exposure during pregnancy. In some cases, the woman has been ordered to be confined to a drug-treatment facility during pregnancy. After all, anyone found to provide such illegal substances to a child would certainly expect to face criminal or other charges. Are the circumstances that much different in the case of a pregnant woman and her fetus?

4   Others believe the situation is vastly different and further claim that criminal charges, imprisonment, or mandatory treatment are counterproductive (Beckett, 1995; Farr, 1995). Legislation specifically targeted to pregnant drug users might actually drive prospective mothers, out of fear of being prosecuted, away from the care and treatment needed for both themselves and their fetuses. Moreover, the tendency to rely on criminal procedures could limit the resources available for the implementation of innovative, well-funded public health efforts for treating addiction and its consequences for the fetus (Chavkin, 2001).

What Answers Exist? What Questions Remain?

5 At the present time no research has been carried out on whether threats of criminal procedures or other forms of punishment dissuade a woman from using drugs during her pregnancy. If studies with this or other populations demonstrate that these kinds of actions are effective in reducing drug use, perhaps greater justification would exist for the extension of this approach to expectant women. But given the recent findings that the negative consequences for the fetus often stem less from the illegal drugs themselves than from the myriad of other factors that are associated with drug use, would such actions be helpful? In other words, are poor nutrition and a host of other social and economic factors, as well as the chaotic lifestyle that often accompanies drug use and over which a woman may not always have control, the primary culprits in impaired fetal development? If so, then intervention must take place at the public health level. (Adapted from Bukatko and Daehler, *Child Development*, pp. 123–24.)

1. Which statement best expresses the main idea?
    a. The conviction of Cornelia Whitner deserved to be overturned. The notion that convicting a pregnant woman who takes drugs of child abuse is misguided at best.

b. A society that cares about its children should impose criminal charges on a pregnant woman who takes drugs.

c. The idea of imposing criminal charges on a pregnant woman who takes drugs is highly controversial.

d. Most Americans believe that legislation targeting pregnant women who take drugs for criminal prosecution will do more harm than good.

2. The author's primary purpose is

a. to inform readers about the controversy over legislation targeting pregnant women who take drugs.

b. to persuade readers that imposing criminal charges on a pregnant woman who takes drugs is a huge mistake that will do nothing to help unborn children.

✓ CHECK YOUR UNDERSTANDING

1. Why should readers check for bias even in written materials that were specifically created with an informative purpose in mind?

_____

_____

2. Informative writing shows heavy emphasis on what kind of statements?

_____

3. What kind of tone do authors use when their purpose is informative?

_____

4. When should persuasive writing be treated with skepticism?

_____

_____

5. How does a writer intent on persuasion treat facts?

_____

6. How do writers intending to persuade handle an opposing point of view?

_____

7. What kind of tone do writers with a persuasive purpose use?

_____

Separating Fact and Opinion

Although the ultimate goal in this section is to identify opinions that have been mixed in with what seem to be pure textbook fact, let's start with a quick review of how fact and opinion differ.

Facts

Statements of fact describe people, places, and events without benefit of interpretation, inference, or value judgment. "The sun is red," for example, is a statement of fact. "The red sun is beautiful" is a statement of opinion that offers a value judgment.

Checking the Facts

Unlike opinions, facts can be checked for accuracy through observation or reference to written records. In contrast to opinions, which cannot be verified, facts can be labeled "true" or "false," "accurate" or "inaccurate." They don't vary from person to person or from place to place.

Look up the dates of the American Civil War anywhere in the world, and they will be the same: 1861 to 1865. Similarly, you can check the date Nancy Pelosi was first elected Speaker of the U.S. House of Representatives, and it will always be January 4, 2007, whether you look the date up today or ten years from now.

> The following are all statements of fact:
>
> 1. The union leader and civil rights activist César Chávez was born in 1927 in Yuma, Arizona.
> 2. Rapper Snoop Dogg's real name is Calvin Broadus.
> 3. Most human cells contain forty-six chromosomes arranged in twenty-three matching pairs.

Facts and Tone

As you can see from the three boxed statements above, a writer dealing in facts is likely to keep the language unemotional and minimize colorful imagery. Factual statements are, more often than not, expressed in a cool, objective tone. Note, for example, how the writer avoids conveying any emotion about the war described in this brief passage:

> The shortest war on record was between the United Kingdom and Zanzibar. It took place on August 27, 1896. It lasted from 9:02 a.m. to 9:40 a.m.

As is typical for factual statements, the writer reveals nothing about his personal point of view toward the war he describes.

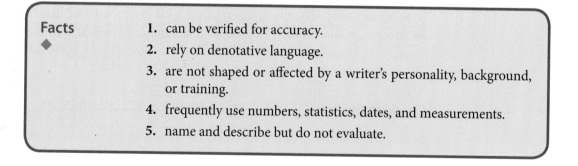

Facts
◆

1. can be verified for accuracy.
2. rely on denotative language.
3. are not shaped or affected by a writer's personality, background, or training.
4. frequently use numbers, statistics, dates, and measurements.
5. name and describe but do not evaluate.

Opinions

In contrast to facts, statements of opinion cannot be verified. Opinions are shaped by a person's background, temperament, and training. They cannot be proven true or false. There is no way, for example, to prove to cat lovers that dogs make better pets. Which pet a person favors is a matter of personal opinion.

Informed, Valid, or Sound Opinions

Opinions can be labeled "valid" or "invalid," "sound" or "unsound," "informed" or "uninformed." Such labels indicate whether the writer or speaker has supplied adequate evidence for the opinion expressed. Although everybody has a right to his or her own opinion, everyone's opinion does not deserve the same degree of attention or consideration. If a writer doesn't argue an opinion by telling you how he or she arrived at it, then be skeptical and do more research before agreeing.

Opinions and Tone

In contrast to facts, opinions can be expressed in a wide variety of tones. Here are three different opinions on the same subject—an affirmative action decision. Note the differences in tone, which range from critical to enthusiastic.

> It's probably the worst affirmative action decision ever issued by the Supreme Court. (Linda Chavez, former staff director of the United States Commission on Civil Rights)

> The opinion is very important because it emphasizes the fact that in most job situations, the differences between candidates are rather insignificant. (Drew S. Days, professor, Yale Law School)

> It's a wonderful decision. (Joyce D. Miller, vice president of the Amalgamated Clothing and Textile Workers Union)[†]

Depending on the speaker, the decision was "wonderful," "important," or "the worst." As is typical, the opinion changes from person to person, and so does the tone.

Opinions ◆	1. cannot be verified for accuracy.
	2. can only be labeled *valid* or *invalid*, *sound* or *unsound*, *informed* or *uninformed*, depending on the amount and type of support offered.
	3. rely on connotative language.

[†]"This Week in Review," *New York Times*, March 29, 1987, p. 1.

4. are affected by a writer's personality, background, and training.

5. frequently express comparisons using words such as *more, better, most,* and *least.*

6. often make value judgments suggesting that some action or event has a positive or negative effect.

7. are often introduced by verbs and adverbs that suggest doubt or possibility, such as *appears, seems, apparently, probably, potentially,* and *possibly.*

◆ **EXERCISE 2**   **Labeling Facts and Opinions**

DIRECTIONS   Label each statement *F* (for fact) or *O* (for opinion).

EXAMPLE   On the night of July 13, 1977, New York City experienced a blackout.

_____F_____

EXPLANATION   This statement is a clear-cut fact. You can check it in any number of reference sources.

1. Harvard student Mark Zuckerberg first launched a version of Facebook in 2003.

F

2. Physicists are <u>notoriously scornful</u> of scientists from other fields.

O

3. Moenia is the <u>best alternative rock group</u> ever to come out of Mexico.

O

4. Politicians <u>too often</u> base their positions on polls rather than on the public good.

O

5. In 2005, comedian George Lopez received a kidney transplant; the kidney was donated by his wife, Ann.

   F

6. The 1973 U.S. Supreme Court case *Miller v. California* resulted in a method for testing obscenity.

   F

7. The singer Beyoncé first became famous as a member of the girl group Destiny's Child.

   F

8. Campaign contributions <u>should not be</u> considered a form of free speech.

   O

9. The movie *Frida* <u>does a poor job</u> of illuminating the life of artist Frida Kahlo.

   O

10. The 1950s were not as <u>boring</u> as <u>most</u> people seem to think.

    O

Combining Opinions with Facts

Writers intent on informing their readers often, without realizing it, include a word or phrase that expresses their personal point of view. For an illustration, read the following sentence in search of a word that evaluates Sigmund Freud's discussion of dreams: "Sigmund Freud's *Interpretation of Dreams* was published in 1900, and its revolutionary impact is still being felt today" (Rubin et al., *Psychology*, p. 52).

Did you decide that the word *revolutionary* expressed an evaluation? If you did, good for you. That's precisely the word that pushes an otherwise factual statement into the realm of opinion. The statement is, to be sure, *primarily* factual. But it definitely puts a personal opinion into the mix. In this context, *revolutionary* carries with it positive associations that suggest Freud's theories were original and groundbreaking. They were so *revolutionary* they transformed the study of dreams and remain relevant today.

But consider now *this* sentence: "Sigmund Freud's *Interpretation of Dreams* was published in 1900, and the theories of dreaming it introduced are still used by some therapists despite the fact that Freud's theories have not been supported by scientific research on dreams and sleep." Well now, there's another way to look at Freud's theories, which is not to say that this less positive view is the correct one.

What the second sentence does suggest is that you need to remain skeptical. Before you assume *Interpretation of Dreams* was so groundbreaking its influence is still powerful over a century later, you might want to know a bit more about the current research on dreaming. Remember, an author's word choice counts a great deal when it comes to separating fact and opinion. A single word or phrase with strong connotations can inject a personal opinion into a statement that, at first glance, seems like hard fact.

SUMMING UP THE KEY POINTS

1. Statements of fact offer descriptions of topics or issues. They do not evaluate them.

2. Factual statements can be verified, or checked, against outside sources. They don't vary from place to place or person to person.

3. Factual statements employ a cool, neutral tone, using words that don't carry strong emotional associations.

4. Unlike facts, opinions can't be verified. They can't be proven right or wrong, true or false. That doesn't mean, however, that opinions can't be evaluated. They can. Opinions backed by sound evidence and reasoning are termed *sound, informed,* or *valid.* Those that have no such backing because the writer or speaker can't explain his or her position are labeled *unsound, uninformed,* or *invalid.* Yes, everyone has a right to an opinion, but not every opinion deserves equal respect.

5. Writers can assume any number of tones when expressing an opinion. The tone they choose reflects their feelings about the subject and their attitude toward their audience.

6. Without realizing it, writers sometimes add a word or phrase with positive or negative associations. That word or phrase then mixes an opinion in with facts.

> **READING TIP** Sometimes what writers leave out of an explanation is as important as what they put in.

◆ **EXERCISE 3** **Recognizing Opinions in Factual Statements**

DIRECTIONS Label each statement *F* (for fact), *O* (for opinion), or *M* (for a mix of both).

EXAMPLE In 1963, the Supreme Court prohibited the Lord's Prayer and Bible reading in schools. This misguided decision should be reversed.

_M_

EXPLANATION The first sentence is indeed a fact, one that can be easily verified. The second sentence, however, is an opinion that makes a value judgment.

1. Measles has an incubation period of seven to fourteen days.

   F

2. Within twenty years, online colleges will replace brick-and-mortar ones.

   O

3. From full moon to full moon, the lunar cycle is about 29.5 days.

   F

4. In 1985, Tommy "Muskrat" Green ate six pounds of oysters in one minute and thirty-three seconds. That's sick.

   M

5. The tragic battle of the Alamo, where frontier hero Davy Crockett died, began on February 23, 1836.

   M

6. The Jamaican iguana[†] is on the list of endangered species.

F

7. Fortunately, support for euthanasia appears to have decreased among cancer specialists.

Ⓞ M

8. *It's a Wonderful Life*, probably the corniest movie ever made, first appeared in 1946, and it wasn't a particularly popular film until it turned up on television.

M

9. Ann Richards, the former governor of Texas who died in 2006 at age 73, broke through the gender barriers that had kept Texas women out of high political office.

 M

10. Maine, Vermont, and New York were the first states to finally enact laws allowing judges to include pets in the orders of protection that keep abusers away from their victims.

M

◆ **EXERCISE 4**   **Drawing Conclusions About the Author**

DIRECTIONS   After reading each textbook excerpt, label it *V* if you think the author is simply reporting facts and opinions of others, both of which can be *verified*. Label the excerpt *M* if you think the author has *mixed* some personal opinion in with factual statements. Then circle the letter of the conclusion you think readers can draw about the author's point of view.

EXAMPLE   A ruthless land grab, the Cherokee removal exposed the prejudiced and greedy side of Jacksonian democracy. (Divine et al., *America Past and Present*, vol. 1, p. 285.)

M

_____

[†]iguana: a type of lizard.

Based on the excerpt, which conclusion can you draw about the authors?

a. The authors are probably great admirers of Andrew Jackson, the seventh president of the United States.

(b.) The authors probably believe that Andrew Jackson, the seventh president of the United States, presided over a government that acted dishonestly.

c. The authors probably believe that writers of American history books should describe events in a way that puts the country in a positive light.

d. It's impossible to draw any conclusions about the authors' opinions.

EXPLANATION Although it is a fact that the removal of the Cherokee from their lands took place under President Andrew Jackson, words like *ruthless* and *greedy* have very negative connotations. Thus, the authors are also interpreting that event and making it clear that the government under Andrew Jackson behaved improperly. Based on their words, answer *a* cannot be correct. It's unlikely that the authors could be admirers of Jackson's, for who else but Andrew Jackson could have presided over the removal of the Cherokee? Thus, he is responsible for the behavior the authors describe as *ruthless* and *greedy*. Answer *c* is off the mark because the authors do not describe this event in a positive light. The only valid conclusion is answer *b* because there is evidence that the authors considered Jackson's behavior disreputable. It would be impossible to choose *d*, given the negatively charged language of the excerpt.

1. Despite its mixed economic record, the [Cuban] revolution's achievements in the areas of employment, equitable* distribution of income, public health, and education are remarkable. (Keen and Haynes, *A History of Latin America*, p. 457.)

———

Based on the excerpt, which conclusion can you draw about the authors?

a. The authors are likely to agree with those who believe that the revolution has brought nothing but ruin to Cuba.

b. The authors believe that the United States should have done everything possible to undermine Cuba's revolutionary government.

———

*equitable: fair, balanced.

c. The authors are likely to believe that some Cubans are better off now than they would have been under the pre-revolutionary government.

d. It's impossible to draw any conclusions about the authors' personal opinions.

2. **Rehearsal** is a convenient means by which information can be stored in short- and then long-term memory. Also chunking—the grouping of bits of information into meaningful and manageable clusters—aids the retention and retrieval of information. (Matsumoto, *People: Psychology from a Cultural Perspective*, p. 55.)

Based on the excerpt, which conclusion can you draw about the author?

a. The author believes that having a good memory is an inherited trait, and people are born with memories that are either good or bad.

b. The author believes that people can do things to improve their ability to store information in long-term memory.

c. The author believes that most people don't make an effort to remember, and that's why they forget.

d. It's impossible to draw any conclusions about the author's personal opinions.

3. One of the first challenges to the idea that the higher the self-esteem the better was based on the observation that aggressive adolescents appear confident, and even arrogant, to the outside world because they are so accepting of themselves and their behaviors (Baumeister, 1997). Aggressive children and adolescents often have inflated ratings of their own competence. After reviewing the literature, Baumeister and colleagues (1996) suggested that violence may result when overly positive views of the self are threatened by others. (Kaplan, *Adolescence*, p. 311.)

Based on the excerpt, which conclusion can you draw about the author?

a. The author is convinced that high self-esteem is a greater danger than low self-esteem.

b. The author does not agree with Baumeister's findings.

c. The author agrees with Baumeister that high self-esteem can lead to aggressive behavior.

d. It's impossible to draw any conclusions about the author's personal opinions.

4. In his March 12, 1947, speech to Congress, Truman requested $400,000 in aid to Greece and Turkey. He had a selling job to do. The Republican 80th Congress wanted less, not more, spending. Senator Arthur Vandenberg of Michigan, a bipartisan leader who backed Truman's request, bluntly told the president that he would have to "scare the hell out of the American people" to gain congressional approval. With that advice in mind, the president delivered a speech laced with alarmist* language intended to stake out the American role in the postwar world. In it, he claimed that "communism . . . imperiled* the world." (Adapted from Norton et al., *A People and a Nation*, p. 775.)

Based on the excerpt, which conclusion can you draw about the authors?

a. The authors believe that Truman was right to sound the alarm about the threat of communism.

b. The authors believe that Truman exaggerated the threat of the Communist peril.

c. The authors believe that Truman would never have given his speech about the Communist threat if Senator Vandenberg had not made his comment about the American people.

d. It's impossible to draw any conclusions about the authors' personal opinions.

5. If you dislike campaign oratory,* put yourself in the candidate's shoes for a moment. Every word you say will be scrutinized, especially for slips of the tongue. Interest group leaders and party activists will react sharply to any phrase that departs from their

---

*alarmist: given to exaggerating real or potential danger.
*imperiled: emdangered.
*oratory: speech making.

preferred policies. Your opponent stands ready to pounce on any error of fact or judgment. You must give countless speeches every day. The rational reaction to this state of affairs is to avoid controversy, stick to prepared texts and tested phrases, and shun anything that sounds original (and hence untested). . . . Voters may *say* that they admire a blunt, outspoken person, but in a tough political campaign, they would probably find such bluntness a little unnerving. (Wilson and DiIulio, *American Government*, p. 243.)

———

Based on the excerpt, which conclusion can you draw about the authors?

a. The authors probably believed that a presidential candidate who speaks his or her mind without worrying about polls is precisely what the public wants.

b. The authors probably believe that a presidential candidate who speaks his or her mind, without reservation or censorship, is making a big mistake.

c. The authors believe that many Americans are waiting for a presidential candidate who is willing to speak his or her mind, but the candidates are too worried about polls to recognize what the public wants.

d. It's impossible to draw any conclusions about the authors' personal opinions.

CHECK YOUR UNDERSTANDING

1. What do statements of fact do for readers?

_____

_____

2. How can statements of fact be evaluated?

_____

3. What kind of tone do writers use when stating facts?

_____

4. Are all opinions equally deserving of respect? Please explain your answer.

_____

_____

5. What kind of tone do writers use when expressing an opinion?

_____

_____

6. Can one word or phrase turn a statement of fact into an opinion? Please explain your answer.

_____

_____

Evaluating Bias in Persuasive Writing

"We are all tolerant enough of those who do not agree with us, provided only they are sufficiently miserable."

—Ray Stannard Baker, journalist

By definition, persuasive writing has a bias. Bias only becomes a drawback in persuasive writing when (1) the author's belief in a particular point of view has turned him or her into a verbal bully, someone who won't let readers even consider an opposing point of view, or (2) the author consciously misrepresents opposing opinions.

When Bias Goes Overboard

In the following reading, the author has a stake in the long-running controversy over who actually got to the North Pole first, Robert E. Peary or Frederick A. Cook. The author's on Peary's side, and he's not about to let his readers so much as wonder if there might be another perspective.

Who Got There First Is Not in Question

1 On September 6, 1909, Robert E. Peary announced to the world that he had just returned from the Arctic, where he had been the first person to reach the North Pole. He claimed that he had arrived at the Pole on April 6, 1909, and had then spent the next five months traveling back to civilization. To his astonishment, however, Peary learned that just five days before, Frederick A. Cook had made the exact same announcement, claiming that he had been the first human being to discover the North Pole. Cook insisted that he had reached the Pole on April 21, 1908, a full year before Robert Peary did. According to Cook, he had been unable to communicate the news for more than a year because he had been lost in the Arctic wilderness, where he had spent the winter in a cave.

2 Which man was telling the truth? That question has generated controversy to this day. Yet the controversy is somewhat inexplicable, given that Peary was backed by the scientific community and Cook was not. Even the rather staid National Geographic Society deemed Peary more believable than Cook. And while it's true that Cook's description of the Pole's geography and physical conditions was accurate, his rather shady past doesn't exactly lend him credibility. The man was, after all, imprisoned for mail fraud.

3 Ask some current scholars what they think of the controversy, and they might argue that both Cook and Peary were lying. That's certainly the point of Robert Bryce's book *Cook and Peary: The Polar Controversy*. But Bryce, who is even-handed when it comes to Cook, seems to have an ax to grind when he discusses Peary's achievements. He fails to take into account evidence that supports Peary's claim, evidence that is overwhelming to all but the most biased fan of that milkman-turned-doctor, Frederick Cook.

In this reading, the author does not initially acknowledge that he is taking sides. Particularly in the first paragraph, he appears to be intent on telling readers something about the controversy surrounding the claims of both Peary and Cook. But as the reading develops, it's clear that he is excessively biased in favor of Peary. More to the point, the author's bias has made him an unreliable source of information because he doesn't adequately address opposing points of view.

After mentioning that Cook did in fact give accurate descriptions of the North Pole, the author insists that this is not meaningful proof because Cook had been imprisoned for mail fraud. This response is an example of faulty logic in which the author substitutes a **personal attack** for evidence. Writers sometimes launch an attack on a person's character or beliefs when they have no convincing reasons or evidence to prove their point or challenge an opposing position. Some writers even stoop to insults in place of solid reasons or hard evidence for their claims. However, if they were able to supply those, they wouldn't need to engage in personal attacks.

Note, too, how the author concludes by telling readers that only biased Cook fans could ignore the "overwhelming" proof that Peary made it to the North Pole first. If the evidence were so overwhelming, we should have seen a lot more of it in this reading.

An Example of Acceptable Bias

In the reading that follows, the writer has a definite bias. But this time the bias isn't excessive. The author doesn't use a personal attack to undercut the opposition. Instead, the author uses evidence to convince readers that Peary was telling the truth.

Charisma or Not, Peary's the One

1 On September 6, 1909, Robert E. Peary jubilantly announced to the world that he had done what no man before had accomplished. He had reached the North Pole. According to Peary's account, he had reached the North Pole on April 6 and had spent the next five months making his way back to civilization. To his annoyance and astonishment, however, Peary learned that, just five days earlier, Frederick A. Cook had made the same claim. Cook insisted that he had reached the Pole on April 21, 1908, a full year before Peary. According to Cook, he had been unable to communicate the great news because he had been lost in the cold Arctic wilderness and had survived by taking shelter in a cave.

2 The question these competing claims raised was obvious: Who was telling the truth? Established experts like the National Geographic Society took Peary's part, insisting that his photographs and journals proved his claim. The *New York Times* put Peary on the front page while the various naturalist societies of the day pinned medals on him.

3 Yet somehow, the general public wouldn't, or couldn't, give up its faith in Cook. Even the *New York Herald* took his side. In part at least, Cook had his champions because no one liked Peary very much. Selfish, vain, and greedy for glory, Peary was too desperate to be famous and too unwilling to give any credit to others. From his very first expedition, he had been accompanied by an African American named Matthew Henson. A skilled dog and sled handler, Henson was also fluent in the

Inuit[†] language, which Peary hadn't bothered to learn. Henson's help, in other words, was invaluable, particularly after Peary had lost most of his toes to frostbite. But Peary was forever trying to pretend that Henson played a completely subordinate role in the quest to reach the Pole. In Peary's accounts, he was more servant than fellow-explorer.[†]

4   Despite his stint in jail, Cook by many accounts was charming, courageous, and charismatic. So much so that Robert M. Bryce, the author of *Cook & Peary: The Polar Controversy Solved*, started writing the story of both Cook and Peary in order to prove that Cook had been the first one at the Pole. Yet whatever his aspirations, Bryce ended up believing that neither man told the truth. According to Bryce, Peary couldn't have made it in the time he claimed—thirty-seven days—because later explorers with better equipment and technology hadn't been able to match or beat that record. Unfortunately, when Bryce got a look at a heretofore undiscovered diary written by Cook, along with some of Cook's private papers, he was forced to admit that his hero occasionally doctored the evidence to prove his claims.

5   Critically heralded and widely read, Bryce's book seemed to have resolved the controversy over who got to the North Pole first. The key word here, though, is *seemed* because, like it or not, the vain, overbearing, glory-hound Peary apparently was the one who made it to the Pole first. Conclusive proof for that claim came from a team of five explorers who arrived at the North Pole in April 2005, using the same equipment Peary had used, huskies and wooden sleds. The four men and one woman arrived there in a little under the thirty-seven days Peary had claimed for his journey. They made the trip because they were long-time Peary fans, who wanted to give their man his due. As leader Tom Avery expressed it, "We hope we have restored Peary's name to its rightful place and put the controversy to rest once and for all." While diehard Cook fans may not like the idea, it was indeed Robert E. Peary who made it to the North Pole ahead of everyone else. (Sources of quotations: members.tripod.com/PolarFlight/controversy1.htm; http://news.bbc .co.uk/1/hi/england/southern_counties/4505333.stm.)

In this reading, readers can infer from the title that the author is going to take Peary's side. But taking sides in persuasive writing is expected. The question is how strong is the writer's bias? Is it so strong that this author, like the previous one, can't be considered a reliable source of information?

[†]The people living in the Arctic regions prefer *Inuit* to *Eskimo*.
[†]According to Robert M. Bryce, in one of history's typical ironies Henson's account of the journey is much read. Peary's isn't.

The answer is no. Look at the way the reading challenges the opposing position of Robert Bryce. Instead of ridiculing Bryce's opinion, the writer contradicts it with factual evidence. Writing before the 2005 expedition, Bryce argued that Peary wasn't telling the truth because no one had matched his record in getting to the Pole. In response to Bryce, the author points to an expedition that disproves his argument. In April 2005, five people, traveling exactly like Peary did, made it to the North Pole in almost the same time the earlier explorer had claimed it took him.

That's not to say that Cook's supporters won't still claim that Cook should also be believed. But that's not the issue here. The point is that this reading reveals a bias but doesn't go overboard defending it. The author refuses to insult the opposition or launch personal attacks. Instead, she treats the opposing point of view with respect and counters it by giving readers a solid, factually based reason for thinking Peary should be believed. That's what a persuasive piece of writing should do. It shouldn't browbeat the reader or disparage the opposition. Instead, it should offer readers the kind of logic and evidence that rightfully sways opinions.

READING TIP   Any time a writer decides to do your thinking for you by saying that a particular point of view is "undeniable" or evidence is "overwhelming," it probably means that the person writing hasn't built a convincing case.

SUMMING UP THE KEY POINTS

1. Bias in persuasive writing is to be expected. However, it can become a drawback under two conditions: (1) the writer assumes a bullying tone and refuses to even acknowledge opposing points of view, and (2) the writer acknowledges opposing points of view but misrepresents them in order to bolster his or her argument.

2. Some writers are so desperate to discredit the opposition, they don't even address the other side's argument. Instead, they use an "attack the person" approach. They criticize the person's character, beliefs, or past experience and avoid addressing the argument put forth.

3. In persuasive writing, it's perfectly acceptable to point out flaws in the opposition's logic. What's not acceptable is insulting opposing points of view or suggesting that anyone who doesn't agree with the writer's position is a fool or worse.

c. by leaving out the drawbacks of bypass surgery, the media has been irresponsible.

The tone is
a. accusing.
b. friendly but firm.
c. puzzled.

For a persuasive piece of writing, the author's bias is
a. acceptable.
b. excessive.

2. When architectural student Maya Lin won the contest to design the Vietnam Veterans Memorial in 1981, many people—especially veterans—were shocked and angry. Her design, a long black wall inscribed with the names of those who died, was described as a "black gash of shame," and the resulting opposition and controversy came close to preventing Lin's design from ever being built. However, when people now visit Lin's completed monument, they see a black granite wall that, although it makes no political statement about the war, cuts into the earth like the shiny scar of a deep wound. The wall lists the names of all of the men and women who lost their lives in the conflict. It is long and low, and every name is within reach. In its effect, the memorial invites the living to reach out and touch the names of the dead. When visitors look at the wall, its polished mirrored surface reflects the ghosts of their own faces behind the names of fallen friends and loved ones. As a result, many visitors openly grieve, demonstrating the monument's ability to evoke powerful emotional responses that can help assuage grief. Even the memorial's opponents have changed their initial opinion about the monument's design. They now agree that the wall is a moving tribute that encourages visitors to reflect on the price of war while still honoring those who served. The pity is that it took so long for Lin's critics to recognize her achievement.

The author wants to persuade readers that
a. Maya Lin produced exactly the right design for the Vietnam Veterans Memorial, and the recognition of her accomplishment took much too long.

  b. Maya Lin's design for the Vietnam Veterans Memorial was meant to elicit powerful emotions.

  c. if Maya Lin had not been a woman, people would have recognized her accomplishment sooner.

The tone is

a. impressed.

b. ironic.

c. disbelieving.

For a persuasive piece of writing, the author's bias is

a. acceptable.

b. excessive.

3. ## Columbus Revisited

When Columbus set sail in 1492, King Ferdinand and Queen Isabella of Spain wanted him to spread Christianity while fulfilling his promise of finding a route to Asia. Columbus, as it turned out, did neither. When Columbus first made land, he thought he was somewhere in the East Indies, but he was actually stepping on shore of what is now Barbados. Claiming everything in sight as the property of Spain, Columbus demanded that the indigenous* population pay tribute, preferably in gold. If they refused outright or seemed to be making insufficient efforts to pay, their hands were to be chopped off per order of the admiral—Christopher Columbus.

In 1493, as the governor of Hispaniola, now Haiti, Columbus gifted the New World population with imported European diseases, malnutrition, overwork, and harsh punishments. Eventually, Columbus's rule and its aftermath took a terrible toll, reducing the population to 22,000 people.

With time even the Spanish missionaries, sent to help Columbus spread God's word, were alarmed by his behavior. One missionary reported that Columbus was guilty of "robbing and destroying the land." Columbus apparently thought nothing of cutting down a whole forest in order to have enough wood for building and heat. By 1500, even his Spanish sponsors knew their man was a failure. Stripped of his authority, Columbus was returned to Spain in chains at the command of the new governor.

*indigenous: native to the region.

In the light of these facts, we have to wonder about those people who claim that Columbus's voyage began a new era of exploration and that his great achievement is worthy of a federal holiday. Who will we honor next, the serial killer Charles Manson?

The author wants to persuade readers that

a. Columbus was a terrible leader.

b. Columbus was generally incompetent.

c. Columbus is not deserving of a federal holiday.

The tone is

a. outraged.

b. discontented.

c. soothing.

For a persuasive piece of writing, the author's bias is

a. acceptable.

b. excessive.

CHECK YOUR UNDERSTANDING

1. When does bias in persuasive writing become a drawback?

_____

_____

_____

2. When a writer uses an "attack on the person" approach to the opposition, what does he or she do?

_____

_____

_____

3. If pointing out flaws of an opponent's argument is acceptable, when does the writer go too far?

_____

Sound Opinions Need Solid Reasoning

"To every complex question, there is a simple answer and it is wrong."
—H. L. Mencken, journalist

To be persuasive, writers need to put forth a sound argument. They need to clearly identify the opinion they would like you to share or consider and provide reasons and evidence for their position. Look, for example, at the following passage:

> For decades, we Americans have shunned the $2 bill and the $1 coin. Although both are still legal tender, they are rarely used. Most of us prefer to throw them in our drawers at home rather than spend them. There are, however, some very good reasons to start using these two forms of currency more. The best reason is that both the $2 bill and the $1 coin save taxpayer dollars. Because the government can print half the number of $2 bills than $1 bills to put the same amount of money in circulation, production costs are lower. The same is true of the $1 coin. Although it costs three times as much as a paper dollar to make, it lasts twenty times as long. In the long run, then, fewer new coins must be produced, and the government again saves money. Another reason to spend our $2 bills and $1 coins is their lack of value as collectors' items. Apparently, many of us assume that because these forms of currency are unusual, they must be keepsakes that could one day be worth more than their face value. This idea causes many people to hoard them for the future. However, expert collectors like the editor of *Money Talks* say that this belief is a mistake. Thus, saving $2 bills and $1 coins makes no sense. (Sources of information: "Money for Sale," editorial, *USA Today*, June 13, 2003, 15A, www.usatoday.com/usaonline/20030613/5240970s/html; Associated Press, "Government May Revive $2 Bill," *The Atlanta Journal-Constitution*, May 12, 2003, www.ajc.com/news/content/news/0603/12twodollar.html.)

The author of this paragraph believes that people should stop hoarding the $2 bill and the $1 coin. But notice that she doesn't just state her opinion and expect you to accept it without reasons or evidence. Respecting her readers' right to an argument—instead of an unsupported assertion, or claim—she carefully supplies reasons for her belief.

Shaky Arguments

Now that you've seen an example of a solidly argued opinion, you'll probably be less impressed by the shaky, or poorly supported, arguments that follow.

Hasty Generalizations

One example or, for that matter, a few instances are never enough to prove a broad generalization about huge numbers of people. Yet, writers who want to persuade are sometimes guilty of offering readers precisely this kind of **hasty generalization**. Here's an example:

Generalization   Without a doubt, the 1.5 to 2 million American children who are being home-schooled are learning more and learning it faster than children who are attending public or private schools. According to a study conducted in 2004 by the Home School Advocates organization, which examined the progress of 102 home-schooled children in 50 families, students who are taught at home by their parents consistently score in the 80th percentile or above on standardized achievement tests. This same study also revealed that 75 percent of these 102 home-schooled children are enrolled in one or more grades higher than their public- and private-school counterparts of the same

Generalization   age. Clearly, a home-school education is far superior to that of an education in any institutional setting.

Don't be fooled by the presence of a study supporting the idea that children who are home-schooled do better than children who are not. One small study seldom proves anything. And in this case, readers are being asked to accept a generalization about more than a million children based on a single study of 102 kids. Where broad generalizations are concerned, writers need to give readers lots of examples. *The broader the generalization the more examples required.* Look, for instance, at the following paragraph to see an illustration of a generalization that is not hasty.

Generalization   What has come to be known as the Forer effect may well explain why people, despite all evidence showing that astrologers don't know anymore than the rest of us, continue to read the astrology columns of their local newspapers: They do so because they, like most people, are ready to believe any statement that is positive and vague enough to apply to just about anyone. In 1948, psychology instructor Bertram R. Forer gave his students a personality test, ignored their answers, and gave them all the same evaluation. The evaluation read as follows:[†] "You have a need for other people to like and admire you, and yet you tend to be critical of yourself. While you have some personality weaknesses you are generally able to compensate for them. You have

---

[†]The evaluation is too long to quote in its entirety here.

considerable unused capacity that you have not turned to your advantage. Disciplined and self-controlled on the outside, you tend to be worrisome and insecure on the inside. . . ." Almost everyone in the class agreed with their "personality assessment," despite the fact that everyone received the same one. The first such experiment was done in 1948 but has been repeated hundreds of times since. On every occasion at least 80 percent of the people tested have rated the descriptions of themselves as accurate. (Source of information: http://skepdic .com/forer.html.)

The generalization in this paragraph is based on numerous studies conducted over a long period of time. It is well supported rather than hasty.

Irrelevant Evidence

When you analyze a piece of persuasive writing, always be on the lookout for **irrelevant**, or **unrelated, evidence**. Authors in the grip of excessive bias will sometimes supply you with a fact or reason that fills up space but has no particular bearing on the subject at hand. Look, for example, at the following paragraph, where the writer argues that John F. Kennedy does not deserve his high ranking on surveys of best presidents. Can you find a piece of irrelevant evidence?

When surveyed for its opinion about America's best presidents, the public consistently and mistakenly ranks John F. Kennedy either first or second. In reality, Kennedy was not a particularly effective president. No doubt, much of his appeal rests upon his image. He was seen as a dynamic leader reigning over a new "Camelot."[†] Kennedy's quick wit, excellent speaking skills, and good looks helped make him the media's darling, and his charm and charisma played well on television. Yet while the press portrayed him as a devoted family man, Kennedy actually was a womanizer who had a number of extramarital affairs, including one with a nineteen-year-old White House intern. He suffered from chronic health problems and took many drugs, including painkillers, to relieve colitis, back pain, and Addison's disease. His precarious physical state made him ill-suited to the nation's highest office, yet he irresponsibly duped the American people into believing that he was capable and fit. In truth, Kennedy was living on borrowed

---

[†]Camelot: According to legend, King Arthur's royal court.

time; had he lived to be reelected to a second term, his failings eventually would have been exposed, and his house of cards would have come tumbling down.

The author of this passage argues that John F. Kennedy was not a particularly good president. To support that opinion, she offers two reasons: Kennedy was a womanizer, and he had serious health problems that he kept hidden.

John F. Kennedy may well have been a womanizer, but unless the author can explain how that interfered with Kennedy's performance of his duties as president, the author has not supplied you with evidence relevant to her claim. To make Kennedy's immoral behavior matter in this context, the author would have to describe how Kennedy's affairs with women kept him from the business of the presidency.

More relevant to the author's point are Kennedy's hidden health problems and the medications he was forced to take. Painkillers are notorious for clouding a person's ability to think clearly, so they may well have interfered with Kennedy's performance. But even this piece of supporting evidence needs to be made relevant in order to be truly convincing. The author needs to cite some instance in which President Kennedy's presidential decisions were affected by the drugs he took.

Circular Reasoning

It's easy to determine the opinion expressed in the following paragraph: The U.S. government should regulate night-shift hours. What's not so clear is why the author takes this position. Much of the paragraph simply repeats the opening opinion. That's why it's an example of **circular reasoning**: The opinion and the reason for holding it are one and the same.

> The government of the United States should regulate the number of hours a worker can put in on a night shift. It is a disgrace that this has not been done already. The United States is one of only six industrialized countries that do not regulate night-shift hours. This lack of regulation is a dangerous and costly oversight that will one day prove disastrous.

But imagine now that the author had recognized his failure to provide an argument and revised the above paragraph to make it more persuasive.

> The government of the United States should regulate the number of hours a worker can put in on a night shift. According to studies com-

pleted by the National Commission on Sleep Disorders, the loss of sleep, whether voluntary or involuntary, is a dangerous and deadly threat. The commission concluded that literally millions of accidents are caused every year by drivers and workers trying to function normally on too little sleep. Yet another study by the Congressional Office of Technology pointed to the importance that changes in the sleep cycle play in human errors within the workplace. Additional studies suggest that people are more likely to make errors of all kinds if they have not slept seven to eight hours within the last twenty-four hours. These studies strongly suggest that limits be placed on disturbances in the human sleep cycle. Although the government cannot determine how many hours employees sleep, it can and should place limits on the number of hours they spend on night shifts.

In this paragraph, the author now anticipates and answers the question he rightly assumes his readers might pose: "Why should I accept this opinion?" To argue his claim and make it persuasive, he tells his readers about some studies that helped him to form his opinion. Although critical readers might not immediately embrace the author's opinion as their own, they would certainly give it serious consideration.

Offering False Alternatives

Authors determined to persuade may insist that there are only two possible alternatives or answers to a problem or question when, in fact, there are several. Here's an example:

> Moviemakers intent on creating a realistic atmosphere are forced to engage in *product placement*—the use of brand names in exchange for a fee. Were an actor in a scene to open a can simply labeled tuna, the audience's attention would be distracted by the label, and the effect of the scene would be destroyed. People are used to seeing brand names such as Chicken of the Sea and Bumble Bee. Filmmakers who want realism in their films aren't doing anything wrong when they engage in product placement.

According to this author's reasoning, either moviemakers must accept fees for using brand names or they will be forced to use general names that distract the audience. Left out of this reading are two other alternatives: (1) arrange the scene so that audiences don't see labels or

(2) invent brand names and labels that resemble the real ones. Faced with the above either-or thinking, critical readers would start looking for other alternatives.

Making Careless Comparisons

Comparisons used to illustrate a point are a useful tool for writers. Look how Gail Sheehy uses a comparison between humans and lobsters in order to illustrate the stages we go through in life.

> We are not unlike a particularly hardy crustacean.* The lobster grows by developing and shedding a series of hard, protective shells. Each time it expands from within, the confining shell must be sloughed off. It is left exposed and vulnerable until, in time, a new covering grows to replace the old shell.
>
> With each passage from one stage of human growth to the next, we, too, must shed a protective structure. We are left exposed and vulnerable. (Sheehy, *Passages*, p. 24.)

Be wary, though, of authors who use comparisons not to illustrate a point but to prove it. Often the differences between the two things compared are more crucial than the similarities. Here, for example, the author compares producers who get paid for product placement with athletes who get paid to wear their sponsor's clothing:

> Filmmakers who accept fees for using brand names in their films are just like athletes who are paid to wear name brands in public.

Although that reasoning might sound convincing at first, the differences between the two practices may, in fact, be more important than the similarities. Certainly that is what the writer of the following passage believes:

> Product placement and celebrity endorsements are not the same at all. Highly publicized celebrity contracts have made the public fully aware that athletes are paid large sums of money to sport a sponsor's clothing or footwear. In contrast, the average moviegoer is not so knowledgeable about the fees paid to filmmakers using brand names. Thus, the effects of product placement in films work on a far more subconscious level. Audience members have no idea they are seeing paid advertising.

*crustacean: shellfish.

As the author of this passage points out, there are some crucial differences between athletes who wear name-brand clothing and filmmakers who use brand names in their movies. Those differences considerably weaken the first author's argument for product placement.

SUMMING UP THE KEY POINTS

1. To be taken seriously, opinions need to be backed by relevant reasons and evidence. They need to be part of a solid argument that offers readers a basis for sharing the opinion put forth in the reading.

2. Hasty generalizations cover large numbers of people, experiences, and ideas, while offering only one or two examples as proof—for instance, "Getting a college degree is worthless. My aunt dropped out of high school, and she owns her own company."

3. Irrelevant evidence is related in some way to the topic at hand but has nothing to do with backing up the opinion being put forth—for instance, "Despite swindling numerous people out of their pensions, the broker should not pay for his crimes with a prison term. After all, he founded several organizations that take care of abandoned animals."

4. Circular arguments restate the opinion being proposed in different language, and the restatement is supposed to function as evidence—for example, "Ten years from now, there will no longer be print books; everything will be digitalized. It's bound to happen because books composed of paper are going to disappear and e-books are going to take their place."

5. Writers using false alternatives insist that a problem with several solutions actually has only two—for example, "The only choice we have where swine flu is concerned is to either slaughter every single pig in countries where the disease emerges or face the death of millions around the world."

6. Careless comparisons use the similarities between two groups, experiences, or ideas to prove a point. Although comparisons are a useful method of clarification, they are often shaky as evidence because the differences usually outweigh the similarities. For example, "Why is there always so much talk about the corruption of politics through campaign contributions? Campaign donations are just like speech. They are another form of self-expression."

◆ **EXERCISE 6**   **Recognizing Faulty Logic**

DIRECTIONS   The following passages all present you with arguments in favor of an opinion. But each one reveals flawed logic. Circle the appropriate letter to identify the error.

EXAMPLE   In far too many American cities, homelessness has become a major problem. In some cities, whole families live on the street. In a country this rich, homelessness is a national disgrace. In response to this social problem, Americans must dig more deeply into their pockets to support the work of local charities, or the number of homeless people will continue to grow.

a.   irrelevant evidence
b.   false alternatives
c.   careless comparison
d.   hasty generalization
e.   personal attack

EXPLANATION   The author insists that we have only two choices about how to treat the homeless: give to local charities or allow the problem of homelessness to increase. It doesn't take a sociologist to realize that there are other alternatives, as well.

1. Stephen King is an underrated artist who is every bit as gifted as Shakespeare. Evidence of King's greatness can be found by examining the similarities in the work of both authors. Shakespeare often wrote about love and relationships. An excellent example of this is his play *Romeo and Juliet*. Stephen King also writes about relationships. *The Stand* and *It* both focus on the importance of love and the power of friendship. Both authors examine issues of morality and are interested in the power of evil. If Shakespeare were alive today, I think he and Stephen King might even work on writing a book or screenplay together. That's just how talented Stephen King is.

a. irrelevant evidence
b. false alternatives
c. careless comparison

d. hasty generalization

e. personal attack

2. As a writer, Ernest Hemingway is overrated. His novels and short stories are of little general interest. He wrote about experiences that appeal only to a certain kind of man: the hypermasculine male who loves hunting, fishing, and safaris. Hemingway's range as a writer was very narrow. But that should come as no surprise to people familiar with Hemingway's personal life. Hemingway was a womanizer and a heavy drinker. He was the worst kind of "man's man." It's no wonder that his writing is limited and shallow: Hemingway was a limited and shallow man.

a. irrelevant evidence

b. false alternatives

c. careless comparison

d. circular reasoning

e. personal attack

3. On July 13, 1977, the lights went out in New York City, and almost as soon as it happened, the fighting and looting began. But the city would never have been the scene of such confusion had the police done their job. It was the police's incompetence that caused the epidemic of theft, violence, and arson. Had the police been more in control, there never would have been so much chaos.

a. irrelevant evidence

b. false alternatives

c. careless comparison

d. circular reasoning

e. personal attack

4. Sociologists have long claimed that a lack of daily or weekly contact with a parent has few negative effects on the children of divorce; however, new research shows that a lack of regular contact with one of the parents is actually destructive. In one study, fifty college freshmen with divorced parents completed a questionnaire about their experiences and feelings. A number of the students who were

geographically separated from one of their parents following a divorce admitted to having a more difficult time adjusting. In comparison to those whose parents continued to live near each other after divorcing, this group also claimed to feel more hostility. (Source of information: Mackenzie Carpenter, "Experts Disagree on Best Interests of Children of Divorce," *Pittsburgh Post-Gazette*, http://singleparents.about.com/cs/divorce/a/childofdiv81503.htm.)

a. irrelevant evidence

b. false alternatives

c. hasty generalization

d. careless comparison

e. circular reasoning

5. Currently, many health maintenance organizations (HMOs) in the United States do not adequately meet the medical needs of their participants. Part of the problem stems from the amount of money HMOs are forced to spend not on medical care but on the bureaucratic* apparatus they need to function. HMOs rely heavily on disease management and review boards that advise insurers about which treatments and drugs should be allowed. The boards cost money, not just to pay the salaries of board members but also to finance the paperwork they generate. In addition to the management and review boards, HMOs require legal services to defend against the possibilities of lawsuits that might be filed when specific treatments are disallowed. In addition to their billing agencies, HMOs rely heavily on marketing consultants to help them attract business. All of these services require substantial amounts of cash, and even in the most efficient HMOs, overhead consumes 14 percent of insurance premiums compared to only 3 percent in Canada, where there is a national health insurance and 97 percent of the premium payment goes to doctors, hospitals, and clinics.[1] No wonder states like Illinois are demanding the right to fill their prescriptions in Canada.

a. irrelevant evidence

b. false alternatives

---

*bureaucratic: typical of institutions with many departments and numerous regulations.
[1]James Weinstein, *The Long Detour* (Boulder, Colo.: Westview Press, 2003), pp. 240–41.

c. careless comparison

d. circular reasoning

e. hasty generalization

◆ **EXERCISE 7**   **Recognizing Faulty Logic**

DIRECTIONS   Read each passage. Identify the error in reasoning by circling the appropriate letter. *Note:* Read the passages slowly. You may even need to read them twice.

EXAMPLE   The media often call attention to teachers' poor working conditions and low pay. However, the teaching profession has improved in many ways during the last forty years. For one thing, today's teachers are responsible for fewer students. A National Education Association survey of the 2000–2001 school year revealed that elementary school teachers have about 21 students per class. In contrast, teachers in 1961 had an average of 29 students. Teachers in secondary schools have seen a slight increase— from 27 to 28 students in a class—since 1961; however, they teach fewer students overall. High school teachers in 1966 taught 132 students a day; by 2001, that total was down to 89. In addition, the NEA survey showed that today's teachers have more preparation time than their 1960s counterparts had. Teachers now hold more advanced degrees, too. Fifty percent of today's teachers have earned a master's degree; this percentage has more than doubled since 1961. What's more, a teacher's average salary has steadily increased since the 1960s, when teachers made the equivalent of $32,598 in today's dollars. In 2001, the average teacher's salary was $43,262. Plus, some researchers say that when salaries are computed on an hourly basis, teachers usually earn an hourly wage exceeding that of registered nurses, accountants, engineers, and other middle-class professions. (Sources of statistics: Fredreka Schouten, "Public School Teachers' Hourly Pay Tops Many Professions, Study Finds," *USA Today*, June 3, 2003, p. 9D; Greg Toppo, "Teachers Have Smaller Classes But Spend More Time There," *USA Today*, August 28, 2003, p. 9D.)

(a.) irrelevant evidence

b. circular reasoning

c. false alternatives

d. careless comparison

e. hasty generalization

"A Farewell to Traditional Valedictorians," *Washington Post*, June 26, 1997, p. J01, www.washingtonpost.com/wp-srv/local/longterm/library/valedict/novdict.htm.)

The tone of this passage is

a. neutral.

b. friendly.

c. angry.

d. puzzled.

For a persuasive reading, the author's bias is

a. acceptable.

b. excessive.

◆ **TEST 5**   **Locating Errors in Logic**

DIRECTIONS   Circle the appropriate letter or letters to identify the error in logic.

1. Fast-food restaurants such as McDonald's, Burger King, and Taco Bell should be required to display warning notices about the fat content of the foods they sell. Animal studies have suggested that eating fatty foods seems to provoke addictive behavior. For example, rats fed a diet high in sugar exhibit signs of anxiety when the sugar is removed. Other research suggests that high-fat foods may stimulate the brain's pleasure centers, producing an effect similar to that of drugs such as nicotine and heroin. As a result, consumers have the right to be informed that eating fast food is just like getting hooked on drugs. The government requires cigarette manufacturers to print warning labels on every pack to inform consumers that smoking is an addictive habit that causes cancer and death. It stands to reason, then, that every fast-food wrapper and carton should be similarly labeled to make it clear that their addictive contents will lead to obesity and death. (Sources of studies: Bruce Horovitz, "Fast-Food Restaurants Told to Warn of Addiction," *USA Today*, June 17, 2003, www .usatoday.com/money/industries/food/2003-06-17warning_x.htm; "Fast Food 'as Addictive as Heroin,'" *BBC News*, January 30, 2003, http://news.bbc.co.uk/2/hi/health/2707143.stm.)

   a. irrelevant evidence

   b. careless comparison

   c. false alternatives

   d. personal attack

   e. hasty generalization

   f. circular reasoning

2. Kids today are being assigned far too much homework, so schools should require teachers to limit their after-school assignments to a maximum of one hour's worth of work. For one thing, when children are forced to spend school nights doing hours and hours of homework, they quickly form a dislike of both school and learning. Kids burn out quickly if their free time is filled up with assignments and projects. Children need their evenings free to play and

to relax. Plus, now more than ever, children should be spending quality time with their families in the evenings. If kids are always doing homework instead of bonding with their loved ones, how can they possibly grow up with any sense of family values? Either we limit homework now, or kids will grow up believing that academic achievement is more important than cultivating family relationships.

a. irrelevant evidence

b. careless comparison

c. false alternatives

d. personal attack

e. hasty generalization

f. circular reasoning

3. George Balanchine, the Russian-born choreographer and dance teacher, founded the School of American Ballet in 1934. Best known as the prime mover at the New York City Ballet from 1948 to 1983, Balanchine has been called one of the finest creators of ballets the world has ever known. But if we examine his career without the blinders of hero worship, it's obvious that Balanchine possessed neither enormous talent nor great artistic vision. Without a doubt, Balanchine was a cruel tyrant who worked his dancers to exhaustion and gave them little praise. His criticism during rehearsals was often so sharp it reduced young dancers to tears. Out of the studio, Balanchine ignored dancers he had trained for years, pretending not to recognize members of his troupe when he bumped into them in restaurants or stores. Even Balanchine's fellow choreographers had to endure rude treatment: He was so self-centered he could scarcely remember their names. All in all, George Balanchine was not a very nice person.

a. irrelevant evidence

b. careless comparison

c. false alternatives

d. personal attack

e. hasty generalization

f. circular reasoning

4. According to a 2001 American Management Association report, 78 percent of U.S. firms monitor their employees' communications in some way, and 47 percent read their workers' e-mail messages. Why are we Americans not more alarmed by these blatant invasions of our privacy? Companies may argue that they monitor their workers only to guard company secrets or to protect themselves from potential lawsuits over harassment and other violations. But the fact remains that employers are spying on Americans whose privacy is protected by the U.S. Constitution, and workers are giving up their rights if they allow employers to read employees' messages, record their telephone conversations, and videotape them with surveillance cameras. Employees cannot just give up the fight and submit to this kind of snooping. They should be outraged by their employers' attempts to monitor their every move and should speak out against attempts to infringe upon their privacy. What's more, companies themselves should realize that stooping to snoop on their workers communicates a lack of trust that ultimately translates into low employee morale, diminished motivation, and reduced productivity. Given how many firms keep their employees under surveillance, it's no wonder that four out of five workers surveyed by the Johnson Foundation report dissatisfaction with their chances for professional advancement.

   a. irrelevant evidence
   b. careless comparison
   c. false alternatives
   d. personal attack
   e. hasty generalization
   f. circular reasoning

5. Today's zookeepers claim to have learned the lessons of the past and are creating habitats for animals that take into account the animals' needs. Unfortunately, though, no matter how many plants, trees, rocks, and waterfalls are added to create more naturalistic settings, the creatures confined in zoo exhibits are still suffering from mistreatment. They may not be cruelly locked up in cramped cages as in the past, but they are still neglected and even beaten. When an elephant handler at the Oregon Zoo inflicted 176 gashes and cuts

upon one of the beasts in his care, the truth became clear. The pretty, naturalistic settings of modern zoos do nothing more than camouflage the animal abuse occurring there.

a. irrelevant evidence

b. careless comparison

c. false alternatives

d. personal attack

e. hasty generalization

f. circular reasoning

Putting It All Together

The following readings give you a chance to practice everything you have learned about comprehension and critical reading. As you read, think about where you stand on the various events and experiences described. Ultimately reading is not just about understanding and remembering what other people say about the world. It's also about discovering your own point of view.

◆ **READING 1**   Beyond Time Management

Dave Ellis

Looking Ahead   One of the biggest problems students have when they first enter school is how to manage their time. This reading will help you figure out not just where the time goes every day but also what you can do to get the most out of the hours in the day.

Word Watch   Some of the more difficult words in the reading are defined below. The number in parentheses indicates the paragraph in which the word appears. An asterisk marks its first appearance in the reading. Preview the definitions before you begin reading and watch for the words while you read.

> **finite (5):** limited
>
> **procrastinating (11):** postponing
>
> **nurturing (14):** developing, supporting, caring for
>
> **synchronize (17):** to match different activities in time
>
> **harmonize (18):** make compatible

Flexible Reading Tip   This reading is divided up by numerous headings. Pose a question based on each heading. Then read for the answer. For instance, "What does the author mean when he says, 'Discover Your Style'?"

1   Sometimes people who pride themselves on efficiency are merely keeping busy. In their rush to check items off a to-do list, they might be fussing over activities that create little value in the first place.

2   A better strategy is to think beyond time management to the larger concept of *planning*. The point of planning is not to load your schedule with obligations. Instead, planning is about getting the important things done and still having time to be human. An effective planner is productive and relaxed at the same time.

Discover Your Style

3   Many time-management techniques appeal to "left-brained" people—those who thrive on making lists, scheduling events, and handling details. These suggestions might not work for people who like to see wholes and think visually. Remember that there are many styles of

planning. Some people prefer a written action plan that carefully details each step leading to a long-range goal. Others just keep a list of current projects and periodically assess their progress. Both approaches can work.

4   Do give time-management strategies a fair chance. Some might be suitable, with a few modifications. Instead of writing a conventional to-do list, for instance, you can plot your day on a mind map.[†] . . . Or write to-do's, one per 3 × 5 card, in any order in which tasks occur to you. Later you can edit, sort, and rank the cards, choosing which items to do.

Focus on Values

5 View your activities from the perspective of an entire lifetime. Given the finite* space between birth and death, determine what matters most to you. As a way to define your values, write your own obituary. Describe the ways you want to be remembered. List the contributions you intend to make during your lifetime and the kind of person you wish to become. . . . Or simply write your life purpose—a sentence or short paragraph that describes what's most important to you. . . .

Focus on Outcomes

6 You might feel guilty when you occasionally stray from your schedule and spend two hours napping or watching soap operas. But if you're regularly meeting your goals, there's probably no harm done. Managing time and getting organized are not ends in themselves. It's possible to be efficient, organized, and miserable. Larger outcomes such as personal satisfaction and effectiveness count more than the means used to achieve them.

7   Visualizing a desired outcome can be as important as having a detailed action plan. Here's an experiment: Write a list of goals you plan to accomplish over the next six months. Then create a vivid mental picture of yourself attaining them and enjoying the resulting benefits. Visualize this image several times in the next few weeks. File the list away, making a note on your calendar to review it in six months. When six months have passed, look over the list and note how many of your goals you have actually accomplished.

Do Less

8 Planning is as much about dropping worthless activities as about adding new ones. See if you can reduce or eliminate activities that contribute little

---

[†]mind map: a diagram of what you want to accomplish.

to your values. When you add a new item to your calendar or to-do list, consider dropping a current one.

Buy Less

9 Before you purchase an item, estimate how much time it will take to locate, assemble, use, repair, and maintain it. You might be able to free up hours by doing without. If the product comes with a 400-page manual or 20 hours of training, beware. Before rushing to the store to add another possession to your life, see if you can reuse or adapt something you already own.

Slow Down

10 Sometimes it's useful to hurry, such as when you're late for a meeting or about to miss a plane. At other times, haste is a choice that serves no real purpose. If you're speeding through the day like a launched missile, consider what would happen if you got to your next destination a few minutes later than planned. Rushing might not be worth the added strain.

Handle It Now

11 A long to-do list can result from postponing decisions and procrastinating.* An alternative is to handle the task or decision immediately. Answer that letter now. Make that phone call as soon as it occurs to you. Then you don't have to add the task to your calendar or to-do list.

12   The same idea applies when someone asks you to volunteer for a project and you realize immediately that you don't want to do it. Save time by graciously telling the truth up front. Saying "I'll think about it and get back to you" just postpones the conversation until later, when it might take more time.

Remember People

13 Few people on their deathbed ever say, "I wish I'd spent more time at the office." They're more likely to say, "I wish I'd spent more time with my family and friends." The pace of daily life can lead us to neglect the people we cherish.

14   Efficiency is a concept that applies to things—not people. When it comes to maintaining and nurturing* relationships, we can often benefit from loosening up our schedules. We can allow extra time for conflict management, spontaneous visits, and free-ranging conversations.

Forget About Time

15 Take time away from time. Schedule "downtime"—a space in your day where you ignore to-do lists, appointments, and accomplishments. This is a period when you're accountable to no one else and have nothing to accomplish. Even a few minutes spent in this way can yield a sense of renewal. One way to manage time is periodically to forget about it.

16 Experiment with decreasing your overall awareness of time. Leave your watch off for a few hours each day. Spend time in an area that's free of clocks. Notice how often you glance at your watch, and make a conscious effort to do so less often.

17 If you still want some sense of time, then use alternatives to the almighty, unforgiving clock. Measure certain activities with a sundial, hourglass, or egg timer. Or synchronize* your activities with the rhythms of nature, for example, by rising at dawn.

18 You can also plan activities to harmonize* with the rhythms of your body. Schedule your most demanding tasks for times when you're normally most alert. Eat when you're hungry, not according to the clock. Toss out schedules when it's appropriate. Sometimes the best-laid plans are best laid to rest.

19 Strictly speaking, time cannot be managed. The minutes, hours, days, and years simply march ahead. What we can do is manage *ourselves* with respect to time. A few basic principles can help us do that as well as a truckload of cold-blooded techniques.

Using a Long-Term Planner

20 Long-term planning allows you to avoid scheduling conflicts—the kind that obligate you to be in two places at the same time three weeks from now. You can also anticipate busy periods, such as finals week, and start preparing for them now. Good-bye, all-night cram sessions. Hello, serenity.

Monitoring Your Comprehension For each heading, try to come up with a specific example of how to apply the advice given in the chapter section.

Comprehension and Critical Reading Questions Answer the following questions by filling in the blanks or circling the letter of the correct response.

Overall Main Idea 1. Which statement best expresses the main idea of the entire reading?

    a. Time-management techniques don't work. They are designed for left-brained people, and most of us are more right-brained than left-brained.

    b. Instead of focusing on specific time-management techniques that require, for instance, to-do lists, it might be better to think about the more general concept of planning as a way of getting important things done and ignoring or postponing the unimportant.

    c. Time management only works when people are willing to do the specific things that help us monitor how we are using time, i.e., We have to be ready to make numerous lists that identify what we intend to accomplish and when we plan to complete those tasks.

    d. Time-management strategies are only effective if we have clearly identified what we want to achieve by getting an education. Once we know where we are going, we can figure out the specific steps we need to take to get there.

Patterns of 2. The second sentence in paragraph 4, "Some might be suitable, with
Organization   a few modifications," suggests which pattern of organization?

    a. definition

    b. simple listing

    c. comparison and contrast

    d. classification

Paraphrase Practice 3. Explain in your own words why the author suggests it's a good idea to "write your own obituary" (paragraph 5).

_____

_____

Inferences 4. In paragraph 7, what does the author imply about the practice of visualization and the achievement of goals?

_____

_____

Supporting Details **5.** According to the author, what is the purpose of scheduling "downtime," a suggestion he offers in paragraph 15?

_____

Patterns of Organization **6.** In paragraph 19, the author says, "What we can do is manage *ourselves* with respect to time. A few basic principles can help us do that as well as a truckload of cold-blooded techniques." Based on these two sentences, what pattern of organization is likely to follow?

a. comparison and contrast

b. simple listing

c. definition

d. time order

Paraphrase Practice **7.** In your own words, what do you think the author means when he says, "Strictly speaking, time cannot be managed. . . . What we can do is manage *ourselves* with respect to time" (paragraph 19)?

_____

_____

Inferences **8.** Circle the letter or letters of the inferences the author expects readers to draw to connect these three statements: "You can also anticipate busy periods, such as finals week, and start preparing for them now. Good-bye, all-night cram sessions. Hello, serenity" (paragraph 20).

a. If you anticipate and plan for busy periods, you won't have to resort to cram sessions.

b. Studying in cram sessions is directly related to poor grades in college.

c. Cram sessions make students anxious.

d. When students are prepared, they feel more relaxed.

e. Cram sessions are not a bad way to study as long as you prepare for them early in the semester.

Purpose **9.** How would you describe the author's primary purpose?

a. The author wants to tell readers about the many different methods of time management available.

b. The author wants to make students realize that there is more to managing time than using specific strategies and techniques.

Tone **10.** How would you describe the author's tone?

    a. cool and formal

    b. friendly and approachable

    c. solemn

    d. bossy and overbearing

Drawing Your Own Conclusions Imagine a student complained to the author of "Beyond Time Management" that she regularly makes to-do lists but never completes more than one or two of the items listed. Based on the reading, how might the author respond?

_____

_____

_____

_____

_____

Making It Personal Do you think you have a problem managing time? If so, do you think this reading might be of help? Please explain. If you don't have a problem, then what's your secret?

Writing Suggestion Try out the author's suggestion of writing your own obituary to determine what it is you think you want to achieve in life.

◆ **READING 2**   ## Arriving at a Crossroads†

Tracy Gordon Fox

Looking Ahead   In this selection, reporter Tracy Gordon Fox describes how, after twenty-three years as a reporter, she decided to become a nurse.

Word Watch   Some of the more difficult words in the reading are defined below. The number in parentheses indicates the paragraph in which the word appears. An asterisk marks its first appearance in the reading. Preview the definitions before you begin reading and watch for the words while you read.

> **epiphany (4):** sudden flash of understanding
>
> **diversity (4):** variety
>
> **inflammation (6):** a reaction of tissue to some sort of injury or infection, characterized by pain, redness, and swelling
>
> **oncology (6):** study and treatment of tumors
>
> **travesties (7):** mishaps, mistakes
>
> **random (7):** lacking in order or plan
>
> **copious (12):** numerous, many

Flexible Reading Tip   This reading is a narrative with a storyline, so previewing it is unnecessary. However, to thoroughly understand the author's point, you do need to closely follow the chain of events and understand how each one affected her final decision. As with most narrative writing, be prepared to draw numerous inferences.

1   "If I couldn't be a reporter, then who was I? What would I do?" I had read these words of Michael Weisskopf, senior correspondent for *Time* magazine, in an excerpt from his book *Blood Brothers*, published in the magazine in September 2006. The excerpt begins on Dec. 10, 2003, the day Mr. Weisskopf's writing hand was blown off by a grenade in Iraq.

2   As a police reporter for *The Hartford Courant*, I had roamed drug-infested areas, gone 140 miles per hour in a police cruiser, even been bitten by a police dog. But covering a war zone? I couldn't begin to imagine the pain that Mr. Weisskopf went through. And yet I understood exactly how he felt.

---

†To arrive, be, or come to a crossroads literally is to come to a place where one has to choose which road to take. Figuratively, it means a person has to make a crucial decision.

I had wanted to do nothing other than be a reporter since I was 9. His words had brought me to tears. Two years later, they brought me to a crossroads.

3   In the spring of 2008, as buyout packages were being strewn about the newsroom where I had worked for 23 years, and more and more of my colleagues either took the buyout or were laid off, I asked myself, with far greater urgency than ever before: What would I do if I weren't a reporter? The answer came in bits and pieces, held together by a string of bad news. Somewhere between my teenage daughter's hospitalization, my breast surgery and my mother's cancer, I decided to become a nurse.

4   This was a decision made by fate as much as by the economy. The idea came not so much as an epiphany,* but as a seed planted one night in November 2007 at Connecticut Children's Medical Center, where my oldest daughter, Sarah, was suffering a painful bout of pancreatitis. As Sarah began to feel better, she talked to the nurses about their jobs. All of them seemed to love the flexibility and diversity,* and the feeling at the end of the day that they had helped someone. "Mommy," she said, turning over in bed to look at me, "you should be a nurse."

5   That night, as I slept in a cot beside her, I watched out the window as a Life Star helicopter landed across the street on the roof of Hartford Hospital. I had witnessed the Life Star crew work countless times at the scenes of accidents, once a triple fatality a mile from my house. I had tuned my ear to listen for the "Code 100" on the police scanner, which means an emergency call for a critically injured person. Now I wondered what it would be like to be on the lifesaving end of a tragedy rather than on the observer's side. I may have discarded the idea had nothing else gone wrong in 2007 and 2008.

6   Just three weeks after Sarah recovered, an inflammation* and infection in my breast that I had had the year before came back with a vengeance. Fearing I had breast cancer, I went to a comprehensive breast center at St. Francis Hospital and Medical Center in Hartford. By chance and, as I later realized, luck, Dr. James L. Frank, director of surgical oncology,* was assigned my case. He told me he would have to operate to take out the offending tissue and rule out breast cancer. He and his nurses were kind and reassuring, and helped ease my fears. The biopsy was negative. I had dodged a bullet, but another one was headed straight for my mother.

7   After years of writing about people's travesties* and tragedies, I had come to believe life was random chaos, not a predetermined path. Of that I am no longer certain. That breast infection, which had no apparent cause, had one major effect: I had met a top oncology surgeon and knew whom to contact when my mom learned she had uterine cancer three months

later. In a 10-hour surgery in April 2008, Dr. Frank and Dr. Alan Mayer removed the cancer and benign pancreatic tumor. Sitting in my mother's hospital room during her recovery, I watched how the nurses cared for her and kept her comfortable. And when she returned home and needed her bandages changed twice a day, I put on blue surgical gloves and gently applied gauze pads and tape, just as I had seen the nurses do.

8   I liked the feeling of helping her, of being needed, of nursing her back to health. But how could I, a divorced mother of three in my mid-40s, reinvent myself? All I ever knew was writing and reporting, having completely avoided math and science in college. What would I do if I weren't a reporter? The push I needed to walk away from a 23-year career came last June in a strange, fateful way, less than 12 hours before I had to decide whether to take the newspaper's buyout offer.

9   I had to pick Sarah up from work at 10:30 p.m. and stopped to get gas at a small, deserted convenience store in my hometown. A car pulled in front of mine as I was pumping gas, and out stepped a man dressed in bright blue scrubs and Crocs. I stared at him as if he were some kind of mirage, and asked, "Are you a nurse?"

10   Yes, he was. And he was headed for his shift at St. Francis Hospital, where he worked on one of the floors where my mother had been taken after surgery. I told him that I was thinking about becoming a nurse, but that I wasn't sure I could get through the program at Three Rivers Community College, where I had already enrolled in a summer math class.

11   He told me he had just graduated from Three Rivers's two-year registered nursing program. He said he had been in the military, had never gotten a four-year college degree and had gotten through it. He told me that I could do it, that I should do it. What were the odds of a chance meeting with a nurse who had gone to my college, at a place 30 miles from the hospital where both my mother and I had been treated, on the night before I had to make a decision about the buyout?

12   The next day I signed my buyout papers and enrolled in full-time classes at Three Rivers. Since then, after getting B's in two math classes and an A in biology, I've come to realize that the work habits I had developed as reporter—taking copious* notes, staying focused, finishing what I started—had translated into good study habits. And my experience in dealing with people as an observer has been very helpful in my current role, as a hands-on volunteer in the emergency department at St. Francis.

13   Sometimes, when the list of classes I still have to take to become a nurse seems overwhelming, I think of William J. Dopirak Jr., who was my biology professor at Three Rivers Community College last semester.

Mr. Dopirak was 19 when he suffered traumatic brain injury in a horrific car wreck, and he had to relearn to walk, talk and think. Now, in his 40s, with the use of only his left side, he teaches science. He tells his students they can do anything they put their minds to. And I think, yes, I will be a nurse.

Monitoring Your Comprehension   The author describes a number of profound changes in her life. See if you can describe how each one brought her one step closer to a crossroads in life.

Comprehension and Critical Reading Questions   Answer the following questions by filling in the blanks or circling the letter of the correct response.

Overall Main Idea   1. Which statement best expresses the main idea of the entire reading?

    a. People are never too old to change their careers, even if it requires learning a whole new set of skills.

    b. Cancer teaches us hard lessons about life's tragedy.

    c. For those willing to pay attention, life's hard knocks sometimes show us the road we need to take.

    d. Women find it harder than men to make a radical change in how they earn their living.

Inferences   2. What is the implied main idea of paragraph 3?

_____

_____

Literal and Figurative Language   3. In paragraph 4, the author says a "seed" was planted. Does she mean that literally or figuratively? _____

Please explain.   _____

_____

_____

Patterns of Organization and Transitions   4. Paragraphs 5, 6, and 7 open with transitions that suggest which underlying pattern of organization?

    a. definition

    b. comparison and contrast

c. time order

d. classification

5. Identify the transitions that gave you the answer to the previous question.

_____

Literal and 6. Is the author speaking figuratively or literally in paragraph 6, when
Figurative Language she says, "I had dodged a bullet, but another one was headed straight for my mother."_____

Please explain. _____

_____

_____

Inferences 7. What does the author imply by means of the question in paragraph 11?

_____

8. In paragraph 13, the author expects readers to draw what inference from her description of William Dopirak?

_____

_____

Tone 9. How would you describe the author's tone?

a. angry

b. frustrated

c. inspirational

d. sad

Purpose 10. What do you think is the author's primary purpose?

a. The author wants to describe how her life has changed.

b. The author wants to describe how her life has changed and encourage others to reconsider the influence of fate.

Drawing Your If someone said to the author of this reading, "Life has no rhyme or rea-
Own Conclusions son; it just happens," how do you think she would respond?

_____

_____

_____

_____

Making It Personal Can you describe a time in your life when you felt yourself to be at a crossroads? Does everything in life happen for a reason, or is life a series of random, unrelated events that just happen with no rhyme or reason behind them?

Writing Suggestion Write a paper in which you describe how you or someone you know (or have just read about) faced the need to make a life-changing decision.

◆ **READING 3** Marla Ruzicka: Activist Angel

Ann Marie Radaskiewicz

Looking Ahead Would you risk your life to correct some injustice? Throughout history, many brave people have persisted in trying to right a wrong even when doing so was extremely dangerous. Many of these heroes have lost their lives as they attempted to make the world a better place. Marla Ruzicka was one of them.

Word Watch Some of the more difficult words in the reading are defined below. The number in parentheses indicates the paragraph in which the word appears. An asterisk marks its first appearance in the reading. Preview the definitions before you begin reading, and watch for the words while you read.

> **humanitarians (1):** people who care about the welfare of other people
>
> **activist (1):** person who works to change something
>
> **undeterred (2):** not stopped
>
> **routed (3):** defeated; drove from power
>
> **fundamentalist (3):** adhering rigidly to religious principles
>
> **lobbied (4):** tried to influence or persuade
>
> **compensation (5):** payment for damage or injury
>
> **jittery (6):** nervous
>
> **quantify (6):** determine an amount
>
> **noncombatant (6):** related to civilians during wartime
>
> **casualties (6):** injuries and deaths
>
> **detonated (8):** caused to explode

Flexible Reading Tips 1. The title suggests that the author considers Marla's life angelic or saintly. As you read, keep asking yourself what in the reading justifies that title. Every time you see a sentence that makes the title more meaningful and lends support to the idea that Marla's actions were above those of ordinary humans, mark that sentence with a star or an exclamation point.

2. The reading includes a number of dates. Pay particular attention to the event or events those dates identify.

1 Some humanitarians* crusade to change laws or raise money for charities. Others leave comfort and security behind, go to people in need, roll up their sleeves, and pitch in, often endangering their lives in the process. American activist* Marla Ruzicka did both. Before her life exploded in a car bomb, this passionate and courageous woman did whatever was necessary to help innocent civilian victims of the wars in Afghanistan and Iraq.

2 Early in life, at an age when her peers cared for little more than fashion and football games, Marla dedicated herself to saving the world. "Since the adults won't talk," she proclaimed, "the youth will lead the way." Fiercely anti-war at only fifteen, she led a protest against the first Gulf War that got her suspended from high school. Undeterred* by such punishments, Ruzicka took her protests to a wider stage. In high school, and later while enrolled in Long Island University's Friends World Program, she traveled to tense places like Cuba, Palestine, Guatemala, South Africa, and Israel.

3 Upon graduating from college in 1999, she took a job at Global Exchange, a human rights organization. With no intention of sitting behind a desk and playing it safe, she flew to the war zone in Afghanistan in 2001, just after the U.S. military routed* the Taliban, the fundamentalist* Islamic government. As stray bombs demolished buildings and sometimes whole neighborhoods, Marla went door to door and into hospitals, collecting first-person accounts of citizens who had been killed, injured, abused, or left homeless as a result. It was a heart-wrenching job, but Marla was determined to do it.

4 In early 2002, armed with thousands of stories of shattered lives, twenty-five-year-old Marla arrived in Washington, D.C. Smiling and talking to anyone who would listen, she insisted that the U.S. government had a responsibility to the innocent people injured by its weapons, especially the children. She lobbied* lawmakers relentlessly for financial aid to rebuild Afghan homes, schools, and businesses. In the end, her one-woman crusade for compassion and fairness achieved what had never before been done: the U.S. Congress agreed to pay $2.5 million to Afghan victims. Despite this amazing victory, Marla wasn't finished. Creating the Campaign for Innocent Victims in Conflict (CIVIC) soon after American forces invaded Iraq in 2003, she began raising millions of dollars in private donations for civilians in both Afghanistan and Iraq.

5 Not content to simply collect money for aid, Marla continued to return to the world's worst danger zones. From 2003 to 2005, she traveled repeatedly to Afghanistan and Iraq. Clad in the traditional black robe

of Iraqi women to better blend in, she helped locate dead and injured citizens, documented their suffering, and worked to obtain compensation* for them and their families. She kept in touch with the people she assisted, updating them when she received new information. Through her case-work, she personally verified about 2,000 casualties.

6   Because of her efforts, Marla made it much harder for the U.S. military and the American public to ignore the human costs of war. Exposing the war's "collateral damage" through her large network of journalist friends, Marla told the stories of American rocket attacks that had mistakenly blown up cars or homes containing entire families, of children whose arms and legs had been ripped off in mine explosions, of nonthreatening civilians accidentally shot by jittery* soldiers. She wanted them all to be counted. As she wrote in an essay for Human Rights Watch, "A number is important not only to quantify* the cost of the war, but to me each number is also a story of someone whose hopes, dreams, and potential will never be realized, and who left behind a family." Believing that the United States should be accountable for these losses, she wanted the government to do what *she* was doing. It should take responsibility for errors, heal wounds already inflicted, and do more to prevent them from happening in the future. Marla dreamed, for example, of creating a government office responsible for maintaining records of noncombatant* casualties.*

7   Her work became increasingly dangerous. Iraqi terrorists were kidnapping and beheading Americans and other foreign citizens, and it was a rare day that did not feature at least one deadly bomb explosion. Nevertheless, Marla refused to abandon her mission. According to her closest friends, her activism was not only her calling and her obsession but also a form of self-therapy. Often battling anxiety and depression, Marla threw herself into her work, hoping to save herself by saving others.

8   But in the end, she couldn't save herself. Marla was in Iraq in April 2005 when an Iraqi suicide bomber detonated* his explosives beside her car, taking her life. She was just twenty-eight years old. All over the world reports of her death overflowed with praise for her courage, energy, persistence, and her ferocious desire to help the suffering. She was hailed as a "humanitarian angel," "a mix of Mother Teresa and Buffy the Vampire Slayer," and "the best of America." (Sources of information: Ellen Knickmeyer, "Victims' Champion Is Killed in Iraq," *The Washington Post*, April 18, 2005, p. A13; Glen Kessler, "U.S. Activist Mends Lives Torn by War," *The Washington Post*, August 23, 2004.)

Monitoring Your Comprehension In the opening paragraph, the author explains two ways that humanitarians choose to help others. If you can explain how Marla's actions illustrated both of these two methods, your comprehension was excellent.

Comprehension and Critical Reading Questions Answer the following questions by filling in the blanks or circling the letter of the correct response.

Overall Main Idea 1. Which statement best expresses the main idea of the entire reading?

    a. The U.S. government does not do enough to help the innocent victims of war.

    b. Marla Ruzicka sacrificed her life to help innocent victims of war.

    c. Marla Ruzicka's fundraising was her most important contribution to Afghan and Iraqi victims of war.

    d. In human terms, the first war in Iraq was much more costly than the war in Afghanistan.

Context 2. Based on the context, *collateral damage* in paragraph 6 means

    a. the use of military might against civilians.

    b. the damage to buildings done by bombs.

    c. unintentional injury or damage occurring as a result of a military operation.

Main Idea 3. Which statement best expresses the main idea of paragraph 3?

    a. Marla left behind the comfort and security of her life in America to do a very difficult job in a war zone.

    b. The war in Afghanistan took a terrible toll on innocent civilians.

    c. Global Exchange is one of the best human rights organizations in existence today.

    d. Marla went door to door to determine the number of civilian war victims.

Inference 4. What is the implied main idea of paragraph 4?

    a. Marla had a talent for persuading politicians to do the right thing.

    b. An activist can raise more money through private donations than by lobbying elected officials.

    c. Marla's CIVIC organization was amazingly successful.

    d. To help the victims of war, Marla raised money from public and private sources.

Supporting Details 5. In paragraph 2, why does the author mention Marla's protests and travels?

    a. They illustrate the idea that she became an activist at a young age.

    b. They show that she was fiercely opposed to war.

    c. They illustrate her thirst for adventure.

    d. They provide examples of her talent for persuading politicians to change their minds.

Inferences and 6. What inference must the readers draw to completely understand the
Conclusions following sentence from paragraph 2? "Fiercely anti-war at only fifteen, she led a protest against the first Gulf War that got her suspended from high school."

    a. School officials did not approve of student protests.

    b. The protest Marla led became destructive.

    c. Anti-war sentiment in Marla's home town was not strong.

7. The author expects readers to infer the reason for civilians being shot by "jittery" soldiers in paragraph 6. What inference does the author expect readers to draw?

_____

_____

Patterns of 8. What two patterns organize the entire reading?
Organization

    a. dates and events; comparison and contrast

    b. definition; cause and effect

    c. dates and events; cause and effect

    d. cause and effect; comparison and contrast

Purpose 9. What do you think is the author's primary purpose?

    a. The author wants to inform readers about the events that led up to Marla Ruzicka's death.

    b. The author wants to persuade readers that Marla Ruzicka was a very special and very heroic young woman.

Tone 10. The author's tone is _____.

Drawing Your Own Conclusions The anthropologist Margaret Mead said, "Never doubt that a small group of thoughtful, committed citizens can change the world. . . ." How do you think Marla Ruzicka would have felt about those words?

_____

_____

_____

Making It Personal Can you imagine yourself doing what Marla Ruzicka did? Why or why not?

Writing Suggestion Write a paper in which you explain why you admire or disapprove of Marla Ruzicka's actions.

◆ **READING 4**   The Altruistic Personality

Sharon S. Brehm, Saul M. Kassin, and Steven Fein

Looking Ahead What qualities make an individual more likely to help others? In this selection from a social psychology textbook, the authors explore the characteristics of people who are there when we need them.

Word Watch Some of the more difficult words in the reading are defined below. The number in parentheses indicates the paragraph in which the word appears. An asterisk marks its first appearance in the reading. Preview the definitions before you begin reading and watch for the words while you read.

---

altruistic (2): exhibiting unselfish concern for the welfare of others

genetically (2): related to biological inheritance

longitudinal (4): long-term

empathy (5): understanding of another person's situation or feelings

fraternal twins (5): developed from two separate eggs (identical twins develop from one egg)

heritable (5): capable of being passed by birth from one generation to the next

variables (9): characteristics, events, or things that can change with time or context

prosocial (9): beneficial to society

collectivist (10): valuing the group's well being over all else

individualist (10): valuing the individual person's well being over all else

extroversion (10): interest in other people, interest in the world outside one's own mind

---

Flexible Reading Tip Note that the headings in this reading are questions. After reading each section, see if you can answer the question posed in the heading. If you can't, mark that section for re-reading.

1   When we think about extreme acts of helping, or of failing to help, or when we think about long-term, well-planned acts of helping such as volunteering at a clinic or shelter or serving as a Big Brother or Big Sister, we tend to wonder about the nature of the people involved.

2   Researchers have even tried to identify an *altruistic* personality*, one that distinguishes people who help from those who don't. Some research

has focused on whether certain people tend to be more helpful across situations than others. Other research has asked whether and to what extent unselfishness and a willingness to give to others might be genetically* based. Several studies have sought to identify what general personality characteristics and traits comprise the altruistic personality.

Are Some People More Helpful Than Others?

3   When Daniel Santos's friends and co-workers learned of his heroics in jumping 150 feet off the Tappan Zee Bridge to save a stranger, they were not surprised. "That's just how he is," said a fellow volunteer firefighter. "If he sees something, he's going to go and try to help out that person." A receptionist at the company where he worked as a mechanic added, "He will help anyone at any place and any time." His sister noted that he leaped into the water even though he's not a strong swimmer. "He has a good heart," she said (Fitz-Gibbon & Siemaszko, 1996, p. 7).

"The purpose of human life is to serve and to show compassion and the will to help others."

—Albert Schweitzer

4   Are there many people who are generally helpful across all situations? Are there others who are generally unhelpful? Although the specific situation clearly can overwhelm individual differences in influencing helping behaviors (Latané & Darley, 1970), researchers have provided some evidence for individual differences in helping tendencies. These tendencies seem to endure in a variety of settings. People who are more helpful than others in one situation are likely to be more helpful in other situations as well (Hampson, 1984; Rushton, 1981b). In addition, a longitudinal* study by Nancy Eisenberg and others (1999) suggests that this individual difference may be relatively stable over time. Specifically, they found that the degree to which preschool children exhibited spontaneous helping behavior predicted how helpful they would be in later childhood and early adulthood.

5   According to J. Philippe Rushton and his colleagues (1984), this individual difference in helpfulness is, in part, genetically based. Studies of twins offer some support for Rushton's argument. Genetically identical twins are more similar to each other in their helpful behavioral tendencies and their helping-related emotions and reactions, such as empathy,* than are fraternal twins* who share only a portion of their genetic make-up (Davis et al., 1994; Rushton et al., 1986; Zahn-Wexler et al., 1992). These findings suggest that there may be a heritable* component to helpfulness.

What Is the Altruistic Personality?

6   Even if we identify some people who help others a lot and other people who don't, we have not addressed the question of what distinguishes

people who help from those who don't—other than their helpfulness, of course. What are the various components of the altruistic personality? Can we predict who is likely to be altruistic by looking at people's overall personalities?

7   Consider some examples of people who have acted very altruistically. Do they seem to have very similar personality traits and characteristics? Think, for example, about Oskar Schindler[†] and how he cheated in business and in his marriage. Could anyone have predicted his altruistic actions from his overall personality? It is doubtful.

8   What about more contemporary models of altruism? In 1997, Ted Turner, founder of numerous cable stations and owner of professional sports teams, pledged a personal donation of one billion dollars to the United Nations. Not to be outdone, by July 2000 Microsoft Chairman Bill Gates had pledged 22 billion dollars to charity. Actor Paul Newman donated all of the millions of dollars in profits that were generated by his brands of salad dressing, spaghetti sauce, popcorn, and the like to charities, such as his camp for children living with a fatal disease. And until her death in 1997, Mother Teresa devoted her life to the poor in India. These four well-known figures seem quite different from each other in overall personality—except for their concern with helping others.

9   The quest to discover the altruistic personality has not been an easy one. Much of the research conducted over the years has failed to find consistent, reliable personality characteristics that predict helping behavior across situations. Situational variables* have predicted people's helping behaviors much better than personality variables (Latané & Darley, 1970; Piliavin et al., 1981).

10   Some researchers have changed the nature of the quest, however, focusing on personality variables that predict helping in some specific situations rather than across all situations; and their studies have been more successful in identifying traits that predict such behavior (Carlo et al., 1991; Penner et al., 1995). George Knight and his colleagues (1994) have suggested that an interacting group of personality traits influences prosocial* behavior and responses differ depending on the situation. For example, in dangerous emergencies, people who are high in self-confidence and independence are more likely to help than other people,

---

[†]German businessman famous for helping Jews to escape from Nazi Germany and the subject of the hit film *Schindler's List*.

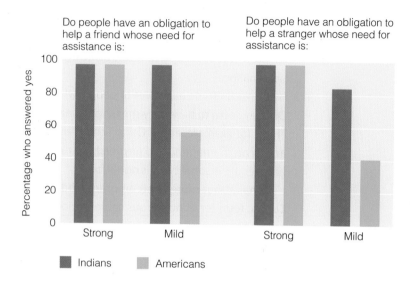

Figure 1 The Sense of Social Responsibility in India Compared to the United States

These results compare the proportion of children and adults in India with the proportion of children and adults in the United States who said that people have an obligation to help others, both friends and strangers.

Source of data: J. G. Miller et al., 1990.

but they are no more likely to help in response to a request to donate money to a charity (Wilson, 1976).

11　　Personality variables, or traits, that have been associated with greater helpfulness in some contexts include the following: empathy toward others; a tendency to attribute the causes of events to individual control rather than external circumstances; a collectivist* rather than an individual-ist* orientation; and extroversion,* openness to experience, and agreeable-ness (Bierhoff et al., 1991; Kosek, 1995; Moorman & Blakely, 1995). And whether or not people have the traits associated with prosocial behavior, if they can be convinced or motivated to believe that they are altruistic, their behavior may follow. For example, labeling someone as a helpful person seems to increase that individual's helpful behavior (Kraut, 1973; Strenta & DeJong, 1981).

12　　In sum, research provides some insight into the traits and characteris-tics that may be associated with helpful behavioral tendencies. However, more research is needed before a conclusion can be reached about the make-up of the altruistic personality. The research thus far does point to two qualities that seem essential for such a personality: empathy and advanced moral reasoning.

Monitoring Your Comprehension Make a list of the questions posed by the headings in the reading. Write out answers to each question. The question you have the most difficulty answering will identify the sections you've understood along with those you need to review.

Comprehension and Critical Reading Questions Answer the following questions by filling in the blanks or circling the letter of the correct response.

Overall Main Idea **1.** Which statement best expresses the main idea of the entire reading?

    a. Research has proven that altruistic behavior has no genetic basis.

    b. Research on the elements of the altruistic personality continues, but evidence suggests that certain factors do seem to predispose, or encourage, an individual to helping others.

    c. So far, researchers have been unable to construct any reliable studies for identifying the characteristics that make up an altruistic personality.

    d. People who readily help others all have very similar personalities: They are affectionate by nature and enjoy helping others.

Supporting Details **2.** Why do the authors mention Oskar Schindler, Ted Turner, Bill Gates, Paul Newman, and Mother Teresa?

    a. They illustrate the idea that donating large sums of money is a common behavior of people with altruistic personalities.

    b. They are all examples of people who were altruistic from childhood on.

    c. They illustrate the idea that people who behave in altruistic ways can have very different personalities.

    d. They support the authors' point that extremely altruistic people always become famous.

Topic Sentence **3.** In paragraph 4, which sentence is the topic sentence?

    a. sentence 1

    b. sentence 2

    c. sentence 3

    d. sentence 6

Inferences and **4.** What do the authors imply with the description of Daniel Santos in
Conclusions paragraph 3?

    a. People with altruistic personalities do not care about risking their own lives or the lives of others.

    b. Altruistic people have certain personality traits in common.

    c. People who have altruistic personalities are liked and admired by others.

    d. People with altruistic personalities are just naturally willing to help others even in dangerous situations.

5. The authors open the reading with the question, "Who is likely to help?" What is their implied answer?

_____

_____

Patterns of **6.** The heading for paragraph 6, "What Is the Altruistic Personality?"
Organization suggests which pattern of organization?

    a. definition

    b. simple listing

    c. classification

    d. comparison and contrast

Paraphrasing **7.** How would you paraphrase this statement from paragraph 9? "Situational variables have predicted people's helping behaviors much better than personality variables."

_____

_____

Understanding **8.** Based on the bar graph on page 712, what is the difference between
Visual Aids Indians and Americans when it comes to helping others?

_____

_____

Purpose **9.** What do you think is the authors' primary purpose?

    a. The authors want to describe current research suggesting that altruism may be inborn.

    b. The authors want to encourage their readers to be more altruistic.

Tone 10. How would you describe the authors' tone?

      a. confident

      b. casual

      c. skeptical

      d. neutral

Drawing Your Own Conclusions Based on the information in this reading, what do you think the authors would say about some preschools' attempts to develop altruism in young children? Would they say that these efforts are useful or that they might not be effective? What statements in the reading led you to your conclusion?

_____

_____

_____

Making It Personal On a scale of 1 to 10—10 being the highest degree of altruism—how would you rate yourself, and why would you give yourself that rating?

Writing Suggestion Write a paper in which you define and illustrate the altruistic personality. Think of people you know who might illustrate your definition. What personality traits do they have in common?

◆ **READING 5** Where Does Free Speech End?

Ann Marie Radaskiewicz and Laraine Flemming

Looking Ahead Should there ever be limitations upon citizens' right to express themselves freely? In this selection, the authors explore the case of David Irving, who was sentenced to prison for denying that the Holocaust ever happened.

Word Watch Some of the more difficult words in the reading are defined below. The number in parentheses indicates the paragraph in which the word appears. An asterisk marks its first appearance in the reading. Preview the definitions before you begin reading and watch for the words while you read.

---

unicorns (1): mythical creatures pictured as horses with a single horn growing from their head

leprechauns (1): elves in Irish folklore

appalled (2): alarmed, horrified

railed against (2): criticized or condemned

affront (2): insult

crackpot (2): foolish, crazy

fascism (3): dictatorship form of government; powered by force

dictum (3): saying

Flexible Reading Tip As you come to each argument for or against David Irving's jail sentence, underline it and write "pro" or "con" in the margins.

1 In February 2006, an Austrian court sentenced British history writer David Irving to three years in prison. His crime? In the past, he has said that scholars writing about the Holocaust—Nazi Germany's systematic execution of six million European Jews—might as well be novelists writing about unicorns* and leprechauns.* Horrified by these views, government officials in Austria, Germany, Canada, Australia, New Zealand, and South Africa informed Irving that he was no longer welcome in their countries. Austria went so far as to issue a warrant for his arrest in 1989 after he denied the Holocaust's existence in two of his speeches. When Irving boldly defied banishment and visited Austria in 2005, he was promptly arrested for violating a law that explicitly prohibits Holocaust denial. His subsequent conviction and sentence to three years' imprisonment sparked strong controversy.

2   Appalled* and outraged, civil rights advocates railed against* this affront* to Irving's freedom of speech. Protecting the right to freedom of expression, they argued, demands that all citizens be allowed to speak their mind, without exception. Misguided opinions, crackpot* ideas, and outright lies should be allowed expression, for censorship in any form must not be tolerated. Even historian Deborah Lipstadt, whom Irving had sued a decade before for libel,† opposed his sentence, saying, "I am not happy when censorship wins, and I don't believe in winning battles via censorship. . . . The way of fighting Holocaust deniers is with history and truth." In the opinion of Lipstadt and many others, imprisoning Irving was also a tactical mistake. It made him into a freedom-of-speech martyr, garnering him and his theories attention they did not deserve.

3   Those in favor of Irving's jail term took a different position. They were less concerned about free speech and more concerned about a return of fascism.* From their standpoint, the original purpose of Austria's law against denying the Holocaust had to be taken into account. The law had been formulated because the Austrians took seriously the old dictum* that those who fail to remember history are condemned to repeat it. Many feared that speech or writing that diminished the horror of the Holocaust could also drive it from public memory and pave the way for a renewal of a society rife with prejudice and hatred, in other words, a world much like Austria just prior to World War II. Considered from this perspective, Irving's persistent denial of the Holocaust minimized the tragedy that had taken place and opened the doors to its happening again. The German historian Hans-Ulrich Wehler lent support to Irving's imprisonment by arguing that "the denial of such an unimaginable murder of millions, one-third of whom were children under the age of 14, cannot simply be accepted as something protected by freedom of speech."

4   After Irving appealed his sentence, the Austrian Supreme Court took into account the time he had already served in prison and replaced the rest of his jail term with probation. The author was then expelled from the country. Upon his arrival in England, Irving repaid the court's consideration by announcing that he no longer felt the need to "show remorse" for his views, an emotion he had claimed to experience when threatened by a prison sentence. At that point, Irving was banned from ever again setting foot on Austrian soil.

5   In 2008, Irving was again at the center of a controversy when he was invited to the Norwegian Festival of Literature, which was to take

---

†libel: making a false claim in writing that hurts a person's reputation.

place in May 2009. Several of Norway's most respected authors protested the invitation, and it was withdrawn. The withdrawal led writer Stig Sæterbakken, who had invited Irving to the festival, to resign his position as director of program content. Once again at issue was the right to freedom of speech, even if the speech in question is vile, inaccurate, and repellent. As the head of the festival, Randi Skeie complained, "Everything is fine as long as everyone agrees, but things get more difficult when one doesn't like the views being put forward." As the case of David Irving illustrates, "difficult" is an understatement. (Source of quotations: http://en.wikipedia.org/wiki/DavidIrving.)

Monitoring Your Comprehension If you can summarize the arguments for and against David Irving's imprisonment for denying the Holocaust, you have successfully understood this reading.

Comprehension and Critical Reading Questions Answer the following questions by filling in the blanks or circling the letter of the correct response.

Overall Main Idea 1. Which statement best expresses the main idea of the entire reading?

   a. David Irving committed no crime and should not have been punished.

   b. The Austrian court of law that convicted David Irving was justified because Holocaust deniers increase the chances of the same thing happening again in other parts of the world.

   c. As the case of David Irving illustrates, defending freedom of speech raises complicated questions.

   d. In all the controversy over David Irving's jail sentence, no one ever mentioned a key fact: Irving was delusional.

Supporting Details and Paraphrasing 2. According to the authors, why do countries like Austria prohibit Holocaust denial?

   _____

   _____

   3. Paraphrase the viewpoints of those who oppose David Irving's jail sentence.

_____

_____

_____

4. Paraphrase the viewpoint of those who supported Irving's sentence.

_____

_____

Inferences and Conclusions
5. In paragraph 2, when historian Deborah Lipstadt says, "I don't believe in winning battles via censorship. . . . The way of fighting Holocaust deniers is with history and truth," she means that

   a. historically, censorship has never been successful at stopping the spread of dangerous ideas.

   b. censorship always makes a bad situation even worse.

   c. dangerous ideas can be defeated by bringing to light evidence that shows how inaccurate and false they are.

   d. she herself has suffered for openly expressing an unpopular opinion, and she doesn't want to do that to someone else.

6. In saying that scholars writing about the Holocaust "might as well be novelists writing about unicorns and leprechauns" (paragraph 1), Irving was trying to make what point?

_____

Purpose
7. The title suggests that the reading is primarily

   a. persuasive.

   b. informative.

Fact and Opinion
8. Which of the following best describes this sentence? "Appalled and outraged, civil rights advocates railed against this affront to Irving's freedom of speech" (paragraph 2).

   a. This is a statement of fact.

   b. This is an opinion.

   c. The statement mixes opinion with fact.

Tone 9. How would you describe the authors' tone?

    a. angry

    b. neutral

    c. ironic

    d. anxious

Is that tone maintained throughout the reading? Please explain.

_____

_____

Bias 10. Which statement describes the authors' position on David Irving's views?

    a. The authors reveal a bias in favor of David Irving's viewpoint.

    b. The authors reveal a bias against David Irving's viewpoint.

    c. The authors are neutral or impartial on the subject of David Irving's viewpoint.

Drawing Your Own Conclusions The French philosopher Voltaire is credited[†] with the famous saying, "I disapprove of what you say, but I will defend to the death your right to say it." What does the saying mean, and whose side do you think Voltaire would be on in the controversy over imprisoning David Irving?

_____

_____

_____

Making It Personal In your opinion, should David Irving have been convicted and imprisoned for what he said or not? Please give reasons for your opinion.

Writing Suggestion The philosopher and Harvard University professor George Santayana said many things, but among his most famous statements is the following: "Those who cannot remember the past are condemned to repeat it." Write three or four paragraphs in which you do the following: (1) open with the quotation; (2) explain what it means; (3) show how it supports or undermines the idea that Holocaust deniers like Irving are a serious threat.

_____

[†]It's not clear that Voltaire actually said anything so succinct and direct. Instead he appears to have expressed these sentiments, while the actual quote that has become so famous appeared in a book about Voltaire, called *Friends of Voltaire*.

◆ **READING 6**   Is Facebook Growing Up Too Fast?

Brad Stone

Looking Ahead   The author of the following reading looks at the astonishing success of the social-networking site Facebook.com and wonders if the site can maintain its stunning momentum.

Word Watch   Some of the more difficult words in the reading are defined below. The number in parentheses indicates the paragraph in which the word appears. An asterisk marks its first appearance in the reading. Preview the definitions before you begin reading and watch for the words while you read.

> **mojo (1):** magic charm; spell
>
> **peripatetic (1):** on the move or in motion
>
> **surnames (2):** last names
>
> **dispersed (2):** spread out
>
> **genealogy (2):** the study of family history
>
> **arbitrary (3):** based on chance rather than reason or necessity
>
> **disheveled (4):** careless, sloppy
>
> **metrics (4):** measures
>
> **caustic (5):** harsh, sharp
>
> **dissenters (6):** people who disagree, critics
>
> **quandary (6):** difficulty, dilemma, problem
>
> **vested (6):** invested
>
> **disseminate (8):** publish, give out, spread
>
> **jarring (9):** unpleasant, disagreeable
>
> **realms (9):** areas, fields
>
> **modicum (9):** small amount
>
> **disparate (9):** different, varied
>
> **discreetly (11):** cautiously

Flexible Reading Tip   The author poses a question in the title. Look for passages that suggest an answer.

1   By any measure, Facebook's growth is a great accomplishment. The crew of Mark Zuckerberg, the company's 24-year-old co-founder and chief executive, is signing up nearly a million new members a day, and now more than 70 percent of the service's members live overseas, in countries like Italy, the Czech Republic and Indonesia. Facebook's ranks in those countries swelled ... after the company offered its site in their languages. All of this mojo* puts

Facebook on a par with other groundbreaking—and wildly popular—Internet services like free e-mail, Google, the online calling network Skype and e-commerce sites like eBay. But Facebook promises to change how we communicate even more fundamentally, in part by digitally mapping and linking peripatetic* people across space and time, allowing them to publicly share myriad and often very personal elements of their lives.

2   Unlike search engines, which ably track prominent Internet presences, Facebook reconnects regular folks with old friends and strengthens their bonds with new pals—even if the glue is nothing more than embarrassing old pictures or memories of their second-grade teacher. Facebook can also help rebuild families. Karen Haber, a mother of two living outside Tel Aviv, logs onto Facebook each night after she puts the children to bed. She searches for her family's various surnames,* looking for relatives from the once-vast Bachenheimer clan of northern Germany, which fractured during the Holocaust and then dispersed* around the globe. Among the three dozen or so connections she has made on Facebook over the last year are a fifth cousin who is a clinical social worker in Woodstock, N.Y.; a fourth cousin running an eyeglasses store in Zurich; and another fifth cousin, living in Hong Kong selling diamonds. Now she shares memories, photographs and updates with them. "I was never into genealogy* and now suddenly I have this tool that helps me find the descendants of people that my grandparents knew, people who share the same truth I do," Ms. Haber says. "I'm using Facebook and trying to unite this family."

3   Facebook has also become a vehicle for broad-based activism—like the people who organized on the site last year and mobilized 12 million people to march in protests around the globe against practices of the FARC† rebels in Colombia. Discussing Facebook's connective tissue, Mr. Zuckerberg recalls the story of Claus Drachmann, a schoolteacher in northern Denmark who became a Facebook friend of Anders Fogh Rasmussen, Denmark's prime minister. Mr. Drachmann subsequently invited Mr. Rasmussen to speak to his class of special-needs children; the prime minister obliged last fall. Mr. Zuckerberg says the story illustrates Facebook's power to cut through arbitrary* social barriers. "This represents a generational shift in technology," he says. "To me, what is interesting was that it was possible for a regular person to reach the prime minister and that that interaction happened."

4   As Facebook has matured, so has Mr. Zuckerberg. He has recently traded his disheveled,* unassuming image for an ever-present tie and

---

†FARC: Fuerzas Armadas Revolucionarias de Colombia, Revolutionary Armed Forces of Colombia.

making visits to media outfits like *The Oprah Winfrey Show*. And he says Facebook's most important metrics* are not its membership but the percentage of the wired world that uses the site and the amount of information—photographs, news articles and status updates—zipping across its servers. Facebook's mission, he says, is to be used by everyone in the world to share information seamlessly. "Two hundred million in a world of six billion is tiny," he says. "It's a cool milestone. It's great that we reached that, especially in such a short amount of time. But there is so much more to do."

5   As Facebook stampedes along, it still has to get out of its own way to soothe the injured feelings of users like Liz Rabban. Ms. Rabban, 40, a real estate agent and the mother of two from Livingston, N.J., joined the site in November 2007, quickly amassing 250 friends and spending hours on the site each day. But these days, she spends less time on the site and posts caustic* comments about Facebook's new design, which turns a majority of every user's home page into a long "stream" of recent, often trivial, Twitter-like updates from friends. "The changes just feel very juvenile," Ms. Rabban says. "It's just not addressing the needs of my generation and my peers. In my circle, everyone is pretty devastated about it."

6   Ms. Rabban is not alone. More than two and a half million dissenters* have joined a group on Facebook's own site called "Millions Against Facebook's New Layout and Terms of Service." Others are lambasting the changes in their own status updates, which are now, ironically, distributed much more visibly to all of their Facebook friends. The changes, Facebook executives say, are intended to make the act of sharing—not just information about themselves but what people are doing now—easier, faster and more urgent. Chris Cox, 26, Facebook's director of products and a confidant of Mr. Zuckerberg, envisions users announcing where they are going to lunch as they leave their computers so friends can see the updates and join them. "That is the kind of thing that is not meaningful when it is announced 40 minutes later," he says. The simmering conflict over the design change speaks to the challenges of pleasing 200 million users, many of whom feel pride of ownership because they helped to build the site with free labor and very personal contributions. "They have a strange problem," says S. Shyam Sundar, co-director of the Media Effects Research Laboratory at Pennsylvania State University, of Facebook's quandary.* "This is a technology that has inherently generated community, and it has gotten to the point where members of that community feel not only vested* but empowered to challenge the company."

7   Those tensions boiled up previously, when Facebook announced the intrusive Beacon advertising system† in 2007, and again when Facebook introduced new service terms earlier this year, which appeared to give the company broad commercial control over the content people uploaded to the site. Facebook responded to protests over the second move by promising users a vote in how the site would be governed.

8   But while Facebook is willing to give users a voice, it doesn't necessarily want to listen. Users are widely opposed to terms that grant Facebook the right to license, copy and disseminate* members' content worldwide. But Facebook says it has to ignore those objections to protect itself against lawsuits from users who might blame the company if they later regret having shared some piece of information with their friends. (Other Web sites have similar stipulations.) While Facebook addressed the feedback on its unpopular design changes last week—partly by saying it would give users more control over the stream of updates that appear on their pages—it also said members' pages would soon become even busier and more dynamic, updating automatically instead of requiring users to refresh their browsers to see new posts.

9   That's a change that may irk users like Ms. Rabban, who don't like how busy their pages have become. Facebook executives counter that it will help users share more information, and that they will eventually come to appreciate it, just as they have with previous changes that were initially jarring.* "It's not a democracy," Mr. Cox says of his company's relationship with users. "We are here to build an Internet medium for communicating and we think we have enough perspective to do that and be caretakers of that vision." People, of course, sometimes like to keep secrets and maintain separate social realms*—or at least a modicum* of their privacy. But Facebook at almost 200 million members is a force that reinvents and tears at such boundaries. Teachers are yoked together with students, parents with their children, employers with their employees. Uniting disparate groups on a single Internet service runs counter to 50 years of research by sociologists into what is known as "homophily"—the tendency of individuals to associate only with like-minded people of similar age and ethnicity.

10   Facebook's huge growth is creating inevitable collisions as the whole notion of "friend" takes on a highly elastic meaning. When the Philadelphia Eagles allowed the star safety Brian Dawkins to leave for the Denver

---

†Beacon is part of Facebook's advertising system. Members were outraged to discover that their activities on other websites were being tracked and recorded.

Broncos earlier this month, Dan Leone, a gate chief at Lincoln Financial Field, the Eagles' stadium, expressed his disappointment by referring to the situation with an obscenity on his Facebook status update. Mr. Leone's boss, who was his Facebook friend, forwarded the update to an Eagles guest services manager, who fired him. The team has since refused to reconsider the matter, despite Mr. Leone's deep remorse and his star turn on countless radio talk shows across the country to discuss the situation. "If you know your boss is online, or anyone close to your boss is online, don't be making comments that can be detrimental to your employment," Mr. Leone advises.

11   Facebook is trying to teach members to use privacy settings to manage their network so they can speak discreetly* only to certain friends, like co-workers or family members, as opposed to other "friends" like bosses or professional colleagues. But most Facebook users haven't taken advantage of the privacy settings; the company estimates that only 20 percent of its members use them.

12   Other problems are trickier, especially among true friends and family members. How, for example, can Facebook remain a place for teenagers to share what they did on Saturday night when it is also the place where their parents are swapping investment tips with old friends? In the six weeks since Rich Hall, a 52-year-old theater manager in Mount Carroll, Ill., joined Facebook, he has reconnected with more than 400 friends and acquaintances, including former high school friends, his auto mechanic and former buddies from his days as a stock car driver. In the course of his new half-hour-a-day Facebook habit, Mr. Hall also "friended" the 60 high school students he is directing in a school play, so he could coordinate rehearsal times. That led some of them to deny his request because, as he says they told him, their parents "found it creepy." Along the way, Mr. Hall also found photographs of his 19-year-old son on the site, drinking beer at a Friday night bonfire. "He denied it and said he wasn't there," Mr. Hall says. "I said, 'Let's go to this page together and look at these photos.' Of course he did it. There are no secrets anymore."

Monitoring Your Comprehension   See if you can paraphrase how the author answers the question posed in the title.

Comprehension and Critical Reading Questions   Answer the following questions by filling in the blanks or circling the letter of the correct response.

Overall Main Idea   **1.** Which statement best expresses the main idea of the entire reading?

    a. Facebook has become the hottest social-networking site on the Internet, and the signs are that it will leave all of its competitors in the dust.

    b. Although Facebook has increased its membership at an astonishing rate, not all of its members are happy with the site's new rules and features.

    c. Facebook has lost much of its popularity as a result of how it has handled privacy concerns.

    d. Facebook members are learning the hard way that postings on the site can lead to serious problems on the job.

Supporting Details   **2.** In paragraph 2, Karen Haber appears in the reading in order to

    a. illustrate the clever methods Facebook has used to attract new members.

    b. give an example of how Facebook can help connect family members.

    c. show the negative reaction many members have had to the site's new format and features.

    d. prove that Facebook is fast overtaking all competitors.

  3. In paragraph 3, Claus Drachmann is mentioned in order to

    a. illustrate how Facebook can be a vehicle for social activism.

    b. offer an example of Facebook's stunning growth in membership.

    c. explain why many Facebook members are currently so angry.

Sentence Sense   **4.** In paragraph 5, these two phrases, "As Facebook stampedes along" and "But these days," are

    a. words with strong connotations.

    b. transitions.

    c. introductions.

    d. topics.

  5. In paragraph 6, the sentence "Ms. Rabban is not alone" is

    a. an introductory sentence.

    b. a transitional sentence.

    c. a topic sentence.

Supporting Detail 6. Liz Rabban is used to illustrate what point about Facebook?

_____

Inferences 7. What does the author imply when he says, "But while Facebook is willing to give its users a voice, it doesn't necessarily want to listen" (paragraph 8)?

_____

_____

_____

Paraphrase Practice 8. In your own words, how would you paraphrase the definition for *homophily* mentioned in paragraph 9?

_____

_____

Supporting Details According to the article, is *homophily* something that speaks for or against the goals of Facebook's founders? Please explain your answer.

_____

_____

_____

_____

Purpose 9. What do you think is the author's primary purpose?

    a. The author wants to describe what has made Facebook a success and indicate what elements might lead to its failure.

    b. The author wants to tell readers why Facebook's stunning success is not going to last much longer.

Bias 10. Which statement best describes the author's attitude toward his topic?

    a. The author appears to be a big Facebook fan.

    b. The author seems to be a Facebook critic.

    c. It's impossible to identify the author's personal feelings.

Drawing Your Own Conclusions Based on the reading, how do you think Facebook's Chris Cox would respond to a statement like this one: "The creators of Facebook need to run proposed changes in the site by users before implementing those changes"?

_____

_____

_____

_____

Making It Personal Facebook was once limited to college students. However, now it's for everyone, and kids are being "friended" by their parents, while employees like Dan Leone (paragraph 10) make their bosses (or ex-bosses) their Facebook friends. Do you consider this change an improvement, a disaster, or something in between?

Writing Suggestion For a while now, Facebook has been in the midst of a raging controversy over allowing Holocaust deniers on its social-networking site. Although Facebook administrators have removed some of the groups from the site, they have refused to institute an outright ban—a lack of action that has infuriated many, some of whom have formed protest groups like the one created by the Jewish Internet Defense Force. Write a paper in which you argue for or against the presence of Holocaust denial groups on Facebook.

To understand some of the arguments made by both sides, you may want to type "Holocaust denial on Facebook" into your search engine box and study some of the different responses.

◆ **READING 7**   Memory, Perception, and Eyewitness Testimony

Douglas A. Bernstein, Louis A. Penner, Alison Clarke-Stewart, and Edward J. Roy

Looking Ahead   The U.S. justice system depends heavily on eyewitnesses who testify during trials. In many cases, defendants are convicted based on what those witnesses say they saw. However, in this selection from a psychology textbook, the authors point out the dangers of relying on the testimony of eyewitnesses.

Word Watch   Some of the more difficult words in the reading are defined below. The number in parentheses indicates the paragraph in which the word appears. An asterisk marks its first appearance in the reading. Preview the definitions before you begin reading and watch for the words while you read.

---

constructive (1): related to assembling or combining parts

DNA evidence (1): proof based on the body's DNA molecules, which are like a blueprint for everything in an individual's body. This means that, except in the case of identical twins, DNA evidence is unique to the person from whom it was derived.

perceive (2): recognize; absorb into consciousness

stimulus (2): something that causes a response

assumption (3): belief or conviction considered to be a given

prosecution (4): related to the lawyers who make a case against a defendant during legal proceedings

inherent (6): inborn; naturally a part of

amplified (6): made more powerful

miscarriages (8): failures

arrays (8): arrangements

Flexible Reading Tip   In this selection, the authors are inclined to follow general statements with specific examples. Try paraphrasing the general statements in the margins. Then use arrows to point out the examples. To take your understanding a step deeper, write your own examples in the margins across from the authors' examples.

1   There are few situations in which accurate retrieval of memories is more important—and constructive* memory is more dangerous—than when an

eyewitness testifies in court about a crime. Eyewitnesses provide the most compelling evidence in many trials, but they can sometimes be mistaken (Loftus & Ketcham, 1991; Wells, Olson, & Charman, 2002). In 1984, for example, a North Carolina college student, Jennifer Thompson, confidently identified Ronald Cotton as the man who had raped her at knifepoint. Mainly on the basis of Thompson's testimony, Cotton was convicted of rape and sentenced to life in prison. After eleven years behind bars, DNA evidence* revealed that he was innocent (and it identified another man as the rapist). The eyewitness-victim's certainty had convinced a jury, but her memory had been faulty (O'Neill, 2000). Let's consider the accuracy of eyewitness memory and how it can be distorted.

2   Like the rest of us, eyewitnesses can remember only what they perceive,* and they can perceive only what they attend to (Backman & Nilsson, 1991). Perception is influenced by a combination of the stimulus* features we find "out there" in the world and what we already know, expect, or want.

3   Witnesses are asked to report exactly what they saw or heard; but no matter how hard they try to be accurate, there are limits to how faithful their reports can be (Kassin, Rigby, & Castillo, 1991). For one thing, during the time that information is encoded and stored in long-term memory, certain details can be lost (Fahsing, Ask, & Granhag, 2004). Further, the appearance of new information, including information contained in questions posed by police or lawyers, can alter a witness's memory (Belli & Loftus, 1996). In one study, when witnesses were asked, "How fast were the cars going when they *smashed into* each other?" they were likely to recall a higher speed than when they were asked, "How fast were the cars going when they *hit* each other?" (Loftus & Palmer, 1974; see Figure 2). There is also evidence that an object mentioned during questioning about an incident is often mistakenly remembered as having been there during the incident (Dodson & Reisberg, 1991). So if a lawyer says that a screwdriver was lying on the ground (when it was not), witnesses often recall with great certainty having seen it (Ryan & Geiselman, 1991). This *misinformation effect* can occur in several ways (Loftus & Hoffman, 1989). In some cases, hearing new information can make it harder to retrieve the original memory (Tversky & Tuchin, 1989). In others, the new information may be integrated into the old memory, making it impossible to distinguish the new information from what was originally seen (Loftus, 1992). In still others, an eyewitness report might be influenced by the person's assumption* that if a lawyer or police officer says an object was there or that something happened, it must be true.

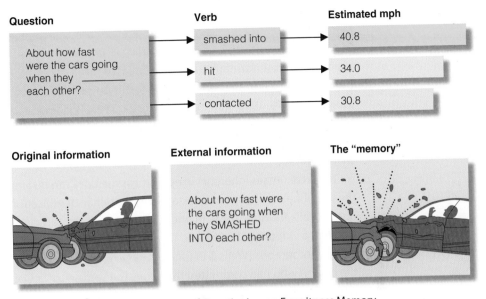

Figure 2   The Impact of Questioning on Eyewitness Memory

After seeing a filmed traffic accident, people were asked, "About how fast were the cars going when they (smashed into, hit, or contacted) each other?" As shown here, the witnesses' responses were influenced by the verb used in the question; "smashed" was associated with the highest average speed estimates. A week later, people who heard the "smashed" question remembered the accident as being more violent than did people in the other two groups (Loftus & Palmer, 1974).

4   A jury's belief in a witness's testimony often depends as much (or even more) on *how* the witness presents evidence as on the content or relevance of that evidence (Leippe, Manion, & Romanczyk, 1992). Many jurors are impressed, for example, by witnesses who give lots of details about what they saw or heard. Extremely detailed testimony from prosecution* witnesses is especially likely to lead to guilty verdicts, even when the details reported are irrelevant (Bell & Loftus, 1989). When a witness gives highly detailed testimony, such as the exact time of the crime or the color of the criminal's shoes, jurors apparently assume that the witness paid especially close attention or has a particularly accurate memory. At first glance, these assumptions seem reasonable. However, the ability to divide attention is limited. As a result, witnesses might be able to focus attention on the crime and the criminal, or on the surrounding details, but probably not on both—particularly if they were emotionally aroused and the crime happened quickly. So witnesses who accurately remember unimportant details of a crime scene may not accurately recall more important ones, such as the criminal's facial features (Backman & Nilsson, 1991).

5   Juries also tend to believe witnesses who are confident (Leippe, Manion, & Romanczyk, 1992). Unfortunately, witnesses' confidence in their testimony often exceeds its accuracy (Shaw, 1996). Repeated exposure to misinformation and the repeated recall of misinformation can increase a witness's confidence in testimony, whether or not it is accurate (Lamb, 1998; Mitchell & Zaragoza, 1996; Roediger, Jacoby, & McDermott, 1996). In other words, as in the Jennifer Thompson case, even witnesses who are confident about their testimony are not always correct.

6   The weaknesses inherent* in eyewitness memory can be amplified* by the use of police lineups and certain other criminal identification procedures (Wells & Olson, 2003). In one study, for example, participants watched a videotaped crime and then tried to identify the criminal from a set of photographs (Wells & Bradfield, 1999). None of the photos showed the person who had committed the crime, but some participants nevertheless identified one of them as the criminal they saw on tape. When these mistaken participants were led to believe that they had correctly identified the criminal, they became even more confident in the accuracy of their false identification (Semmler, Brewer, & Wells, 2004; Wells, Olson, & Charman, 2003). These incorrect, but confident, witnesses became more likely than other participants to claim that it had been easy for them to identify the criminal from the photos because they had had a good view of him and had paid careful attention to him.

7   Since 1973, at least 115 people, including Ronald Cotton, have been released from U.S. prisons in twenty-five states after DNA tests or other evidence revealed that they had been falsely convicted—mostly on the basis of faulty eyewitness testimony (Death Penalty Information Center, 2004; Scheck, Neufeld, & Dwyer, 2000; Wells, Malpass, et al., 2000). DNA evidence freed Charles Fain, who had been convicted of murder and spent almost eighteen years on death row in Idaho (Bonner, 2001). Maryland officials approved $900,000 in compensation for Bernard Webster, who served 20 years in prison for rape before DNA revealed that he was innocent (Associated Press, 2003).

8   Frank Lee Smith, too, would have been set free after the sole eyewitness at his murder trial retracted her testimony, but he had already died of cancer while awaiting execution in a Florida prison. Research on memory and perception helps explain how these miscarriages* of justice can occur, and it is also guiding efforts to prevent such errors in the future. The U.S. Department of Justice has acknowledged the potential for errors in eyewitness evidence, as well as the dangers of asking

witnesses to identify suspects from lineups and photo arrays.* The result is *Eyewitness Evidence: A Guide for Law Enforcement* (U.S. Department of Justice, 1999), the first-ever guide for police and prosecutors who work with eyewitnesses. The guide warns these officials that asking leading questions about what witnesses saw can distort their memories. It also suggests that witnesses should examine photos of possible suspects one at a time and points out that false identifications are less likely if witnesses viewing suspects in a lineup are told that the real criminal might not be included (Wells & Olson, 2003; Wells, Malpass, et al., 2000).

Monitoring Your Comprehension Look at the drawing (Figure 2) accompanying the reading. What does it illustrate, and how does it contribute to the authors' point? If you can answer those two questions, you've understood the gist of the reading.

Comprehension and Critical Reading Questions Answer the following questions by filling in the blanks or circling the letter of the correct response.

Overall Main Idea 1. Which statement best expresses the main idea of the entire reading?

    a. The wording of questions can distort the memories of crime victims and eyewitnesses.

    b. Because eyewitnesses can and do make mistakes, innocent people have been wrongly convicted of crimes.

    c. People's memories are, in general, not very reliable, but eyewitnesses are particularly inclined to distort reality.

    d. Many innocent people have been convicted of crimes they did not commit; fortunately, DNA evidence has been used to exonerate them and set them free.

Main Idea 2. What is the main idea of paragraph 6?

    a. People's memories aren't always very reliable.

    b. Having crime victims look at photographs is an ineffective criminal identification technique.

    c. Procedures that police use to help victims or eyewitnesses identify criminals can encourage distorted memories of events.

    d. So many studies have revealed the flaws of both eyewitness memory and the criminal justice system that we need to consider the legality of the death penalty.

Supporting Details 3. Why do the authors mention victim Jennifer Thompson and/or accused rapist Ronald Cotton three times throughout the reading?

    a. They illustrate the authors' point that the wording of questions often distorts eyewitnesses' memories.

    b. Their example supports the idea that, in spite of its flaws, eyewitness testimony is usually accurate.

    c. They illustrate the idea that bystander-eyewitnesses tend to recall details more accurately than victim-eyewitnesses do.

    d. Their stories support the idea that an individual can be falsely convicted on the basis of eyewitness testimony.

4. Which statement best describes paragraphs 4 and 5?

    a. Paragraphs 4 and 5 introduce two different major details that support the overall main idea of the reading.

    b. Paragraph 4 introduces a major detail further explained by paragraph 5.

    c. Paragraphs 4 and 5 both further explain the main idea of paragraph 3.

Inferences and Supporting Details 5. What inference do readers need to supply in order to understand the following supporting detail from paragraph 3? "In one study, when witnesses were asked, 'How fast were the cars going when they *smashed into* each other?' they were likely to recall a higher speed than when they were asked, 'How fast were the cars going when they *hit* each other?'"

    a. They recalled a higher speed because they were being questioned.

    b. The change in verbs from *smashed* to *hit* affected what witnesses remembered.

    c. Being asked a question by an authority figure affected the witnesses' memory of what happened.

Inferences and Conclusions 6. The authors use the phrase "constructive memory" in the opening sentence of the reading. That phrase is meant to imply what about how we remember?

    a. Human memory functions like a camera. The brain takes "snapshots" of the past and stores them away.

    b. Human memory is a process that pieces together or combines fragments of experience and stores away a version of what happened in the past.

c. Human memory is a completely unreliable witness to events, subject to forgetting and distortion; it's a wonder that people can ever agree on anything.

Understanding Visual Aids 7. The accompanying visual aid

    a. adds new information to the reading.

    b. further emphasizes an idea mentioned in the reading.

Purpose 8. What do you think is the authors' primary purpose?

    a. The authors want to identify the various ways eyewitness testimony can be inaccurate.

    b. The authors want to persuade readers that eyewitness testimony cannot be completely trusted.

Tone 9. The authors' tone is _____.

Bias 10. Which of the following sentences reveals the authors' personal point of view?

    a. "Witnesses are asked to report exactly what they saw or heard; but no matter how hard they try to be accurate, there are limits to how faithful their reports can be" (paragraph 3).

    b. "Extremely detailed testimony from prosecution witnesses is especially likely to lead to guilty verdicts, even when the details reported are irrelevant" (paragraph 4).

    c. "Since 1973, at least 115 people, including Ronald Cotton, have been released from U.S. prisons in twenty-five states after DNA tests or other evidence revealed that they had been falsely convicted—mostly on the basis of faulty eyewitness testimony" (paragraph 7).

Drawing Your Own Conclusions Based on what the authors say in the reading, do you think they are or are not likely to support the death penalty? Please explain.

_____

_____

_____

Making It Personal You are a juror in a murder trial. The prosecutor's case is weak. The only compelling evidence comes from an eyewitness account. When you enter the jury room, you realize that all the jurors are leaning toward conviction. What will you do, agree to convict or discuss the problem of eyewitness testimony with other jury members? Please explain your reasoning.

Writing Suggestion Write two or three paragraphs summarizing why eyewitness testimony can be inaccurate.

◆ **READING 8**   Is a Monster Pandemic Around the Corner?

Laraine Flemming

Looking Ahead   In 1918, millions died from a mysterious flu that traveled around the world at breakneck speed. Oddly enough in the aftermath of the flu's lethal destruction, not much was written about it. But currently the 1918 influenza epidemic is much on the mind of the general public and members of the scientific community. The worry is, will a similar flu return and have the same catastrophic effects?

Word Watch   Some of the more difficult words in the reading are defined below. The number in parentheses indicates the paragraph in which the word appears. An asterisk marks its first appearance in the reading. Preview the definitions before you begin reading and watch for the words while you read.

> **virologists (5):** people who study viruses
>
> **virulence (6):** strength
>
> **incidence (6):** frequency
>
> **genetic (7):** related to biological inheritance
>
> **respirator (8):** machine that simulates breathing
>
> **swabbings (9):** pieces of cotton used to wipe the patient's throat
>
> **orifices (11):** openings, holes
>
> **mutate (13):** change
>
> **prototype (16):** original or first example

Flexible Reading Tip   When you finish reading, see if you can answer the question posed in the title and explain why members of the scientific community have answered with a *yes* and a *no*.

1   Between 1916 and 1917, at a British encampment at Étaples, France, perfectly healthy young British soldiers began coming down with what was first diagnosed as an ordinary influenza, or flu. Then something strange happened. Stricken one day, some victims died the next, their faces purple from lack of air, their lungs filled with fluid. Then in 1918, another respiratory ailment, again with what started out as common flu-like symptoms, hit a small Spanish resort town called San Sebastián. Shockingly, the same thing happened as in France. The faces of some victims turned blue. After coughing until their ribs cracked, they choked to death.

to humans, could work its way relentlessly through an unprotected population. Because the avian virus had never before turned up in humans, none of its victims would have antibodies built up from previous influenza strains circulating in the population. Bird flu could, in short, go on an unimpeded killing spree.

11   This scenario seemed increasingly possible as eighteen people in Hong Kong were infected and six people died. All were suffering from avian flu. Meanwhile, more and more chickens on sale in Hong Kong's outdoor markets were also showing signs of a vicious flu that left them bleeding from all orifices* before they expired. It was at this point that the then Secretary of Economic Services in Hong Kong, Stephen Ip, made an announcement. His department would oversee the destruction of "all the chickens on Hong Kong Island, Kowloon Island, and the New Territories." In the end, more than 1.2 million chickens were slaughtered, disinfected, and buried. As a result, what might have been a deadly pandemic was stopped dead in its tracks.

12   The hope was that slaughtering the poultry flocks had bought virologists some time to get ready for another pandemic in the years to come. That future pandemic, however, seems set to arrive sooner than anyone anticipated because, as of 2006, three different strains of avian flu had infected about 120 people in Southeast Asia. The most deadly of the three has been H5N1, with an alarming 50 percent mortality rate. At the same time, there was also a violent outbreak of influenza among poultry flocks in the countries of Vietnam, Indonesia, Thailand, and India. The outbreak killed millions of birds. In addition, millions were slaughtered in efforts to limit contamination. By 2006, bird flu had also been found in Europe's wild bird population.

13   As if that reality weren't frightening enough, there is another even more terrifying possibility. To this point, the avian flu virus seems to have spread only to humans who had direct contact with birds. Thus it is no coincidence that the little boy in Hong Kong had been exposed to sickly looking pet birds in his classroom before he got sick. The birds were probably what led to his death. However, the avian flu virus is a shape-shifter. It has the ability to mutate* to suit the circumstances, which is one of the reasons there are already three different strains. If cases of humans infected with avian flu increase, the virus will have more chances to exchange genetic material with its human host and the worst fears of virologists could be realized: Avian flu could be transmitted from person to person.

14   Many of those who have written about or researched the flu are deeply concerned about the possibility of avian flu being transmitted from person

to person. Mike Davis, the author of *The Monster at Our Door: The Global Threat of Avian Flu*, paints a bleak picture of governments unprepared to handle a global pandemic as well as a public primed for contagion: "Our terrifying vulnerability to this [avian flu] has been shaped by concentrated urban poverty, the neglect of vaccine development by a pharmaceutical industry that finds infectious disease 'unprofitable' and the deterioration, even collapse, of public-health infrastructures in some rich as well as poor countries."

15   Yet surprisingly, Dr. Edwin Kilbourne, a world-renowned expert on influenza, whose earlier work Davis cites as cause for alarm, is now more cautious about his own previous predictions that a devastating pandemic is imminent. Like other researchers, Kilbourne cites Influenza A's astonishing ability to mutate. However, he offers another possibility—that the virus, in its adaptation to the human body, might actually grow less rather than more lethal.

16   Still, Kilbourne, like every authority writing about the disease today, is far from sanguine. Like Davis, he insists that a vaccine based on the existing strains of avian flu need to be developed now even if it proves not to be the perfect match for the virus that actually launches an epidemic. If a pandemic does strike, the first batch of vaccine might provide some protection while a more refined and improved vaccine is in production. In other words, the first vaccine would probably be a stopgap measure until the right vaccine could be produced and distributed.

17   Fortunately, Kilbourne's and Davis's warnings are being heeded. In February 2007, the Food and Drug Administration endorsed an experimental vaccine made by the French firm Sanofi Pasteur. Based on an avian virus that was circulating in Vietnam three years ago, there is evidence that the vaccine will provide some protection against avian flu. At least sixteen other companies are also developing a prototype* vaccine to be used at the first sign of a pandemic, and even the World Health Organization, which, in 2005, had warned that the world was insufficiently prepared for a global pandemic, has noted the increase in available vaccines. There is also no doubt that the swine flu of 2009, caused by a virus that mixed human, pig, and bird strains, was an added stimulus to the development of an effective vaccine against avian flu.

18   This time around, if a monster pandemic hits, one like the killer of 1918, the world will not react with puzzlement and surprise. It will be ready for an opponent, which, history tells us, should not be underestimated.

Monitoring Your Comprehension See how many key dates and events you can remember from the reading. Make a timeline showing what new information about bird flu emerged during each year mentioned in the reading.

Comprehension and Critical Reading Questions Answer the following questions by filling in the blanks or circling the letter of the correct response.

Overall Main Idea 1. Which statement best expresses the main idea of the entire reading?

   a. There is no doubt that a flu virus like the one that killed millions in 1918 will return very soon, and when it does, the world will not be prepared with the appropriate vaccines.

   b. Avian flu might well become a pandemic, and if the pharmaceutical companies do not act quickly, the world will suffer for their delay in producing a vaccine against the disease.

   c. It seems likely that the avian flu might become capable of human-to-human transmission and, when it does, it could threaten the world with a pandemic; however, the world is much better prepared for such an event than it was in 1918.

   d. It is unlikely that the avian flu virus will become capable of human-to-human transmission, and, if it does, there is enough vaccine to protect the global population; so, currently at least, there is no real cause for alarm.

2. According to the reading, what defines a "pandemic"?

   _____

Supporting Details 3. Which statement best expresses the main idea of paragraph 4?

   a. In 1957, another killer influenza arrived and signaled that pandemics were not a thing of the past.

   b. When a deadly influenza arrived in 1957, researchers knew it was caused by a virus.

   c. By 1957, doctors could treat the flu with antibiotics.

   d. When another killer influenza arrived in 1957, the disease did not take the same death toll because doctors were better prepared.

Paraphrase Practice 4. In your own words, what does it mean to say that the pandemic flu has a "one-two punch"?

_____

Inferences 5. In your own words, what was it that stopped the potentially deadly 1997 avian influenza from spreading all over the world?

_____

_____

Supporting Details 6. In the reading, why is the avian flu virus called "a shape-shifter" (paragraph 13)?

_____

Analyzing Opinions 7. Which statement best describes the difference between writer Mike Davis and researcher Edwin Kilbourne?

a. While the writer Mike Davis believes that the development of an avian flu that can be transmitted from human to human will be a catastrophe, Kilbourne believes that the virus, when it gets transmitted by humans, might become less deadly.

b. Unlike the researcher Edwin Kilbourne, writer Mike Davis believes that should avian flu develop the ability to be transmitted from human to human, it will, in fact, become weaker and not pose the same threat it once did.

c. The researcher Edwin Kilbourne was one of the first to warn the world about the deadly dangers posed by avian flu. Writer Mike Davis, drawing on the work of Kilbourne, expresses similar fears.

Purpose 8. How would you describe the author's primary purpose?

a. The writer wants to tell readers why many people believe that the avian flu could become the world's next pandemic, but without the same consequences as the pandemic of 1918.

b. The writer wants to warn readers that the avian flu could become the world's next pandemic and not enough is being done to prevent that from happening.

Tone **9.** How would you describe the author's tone?

   a. concerned

   b. disgusted

   c. neutral

   d. terrified

Bias **10.** Which statement do you think is accurate?

   a. The writer believes that Mike Davis is accurate in his assessment of the threat posed by avian flu.

   b. The writer believes that Mike Davis is not correct in his assessment of the threat posed by avian flu.

   c. It's impossible to determine the writer's personal bias.

Drawing Your Own Conclusions What effect do you think the swine flu attack of 2009 will have on the search for a vaccine that offers protection against avian flu?

_____

_____

Making It Personal In countries where avian flu has already taken a toll, in Indonesia, for instance, some farmers who raise chickens have refused to report signs of illness among their flocks. Can you come up with an explanation for this behavior?

_____

_____

_____

_____

Writing Suggestion Go to Bartleby.com and read Edgar Allan Poe's *The Masque of the Red Death*. Write a few paragraphs explaining how Poe's story illustrates one response to the threat of a pandemic.

◆ **READING 9**   Whaddya Have to Do to Get a Kidney
Around Here?

Frances Kissling

Looking Ahead   The author of the following reading suffers from kidney disease so severe she needs a kidney transplant. In her search to find a donor, she
learned a good deal about the generosity of friends and even more about
the complexity of the transplant process.

Word Watch   Some of the more difficult words in the reading are defined below. The
number in parentheses indicates the paragraph in which the word appears.
An asterisk marks its first appearance in the reading. Preview the definitions before you begin reading and watch for the words while you read.

> **ineluctably (1):** inescapably
>
> **euphemistically (1):** expressed
> in a positive way
>
> **discreet (1):** careful, tactful
>
> **infirmity (2):** illness
>
> **circumspect (4):** cautious,
> careful
>
> **provisional (4):** serving only
> for the time being
>
> **dementia (4):** deterioration
> of memory, concentration,
> and judgment, which results
> from disease or disorder of
> the brain
>
> **viable (5):** capable of living
> or developing
>
> **renal (6):** related to the
> kidneys
>
> **procurement (6):** acquiring,
> acquisition
>
> **incentives (9):** things that
> encourage people to act
>
> **autonomous (10):** independent
>
> **ethicists (12):** people con-
> cerned with the study of moral
> or ethical behavior
>
> **provision (14):** written rule,
> agreement, or qualification

Flexible   The preview of the reading says that the author learned about the "com-
Reading Tip   plexity of the transplant process." Mark the passages that offer specifics
about that complexity, and when you finish, see if you can summarize
the author's explanation of that point.

1   It was almost a year ago that I found out my kidneys were slowly but
ineluctably* failing. I'd been diagnosed with kidney disease a few years
earlier but the beans had been stable at 50 percent. Then a consult at Mass

General concluded with the news that it could be as early as a year before I would need what was euphemistically* called "renal replacement therapy." Doctors are often discreet* in the way they describe things, but the message was clear. I would face three choices: death, dialysis, or transplant.

2   I am an odd duck, but I was energized by what was now to be a great adventure. I was going to have the opportunity to face my own mortality. At 65, I had a wonderful life, a public voice, and made a modest contribution to a better world. . . . I loved my life and would enjoy more if it were available, but death was OK. I would take it as the last wonderful journey. I'd also do what needed to be done to continue to live a long and fruitful life, free of infirmity.* That meant finding a person who would donate his or her spare kidney to me before mine failed. It was not, the doctors said, too soon to begin the search.

3   I think I instinctively knew what I had to do. I'd spent a lot of my time raising money, and I had that Bible verse "ask and you shall receive" burned into my consciousness. I decided to compose an e-mail about my need. In it, I shared my sense of the adventure before me and asked if anyone would like to give me one of their kidneys. I noted: "To be dependent on the generosity of others is a new experience for me and I am thinking a lot about what it means to share one's body with another person. Also trying to figure out how I ask for a gift that I really want without expectation or making friends and colleagues uncomfortable."

4   I sent this off in batches to about 150 friends and colleagues whom I thought would want to know and might fit the criteria for donating. Within three days I had five offers. Within a month, 24 people, some I did not even know, came forward to donate. I was in the midst of a new phase in my life's journey. I have always seen myself as an open person, but I have also been pretty circumspect* about sharing my life. I never married, and I have no children. Now, not only was I planning on being part of the remarkable biotechnological revolution in which a part of someone else's body would become mine, but I was also engaged with others in reflecting on the meaning of friendship. I was bowled over by how people responded. One friend wrote: "I want you to know I am willing to consider being a donor. I am facing a different kind of provisional* diagnosis of a rare inherited form of dementia,* one that would take my life in the next two decades. Since I probably won't need a kidney to last more than another 15–20 years, I am happy to share one of mine. I planned to donate my useable organs anyway, and it would be a blessing and a joy to see one of them help you." . . .

5   But most people are not so lucky. They have no viable* offers. My nephrologist told me the story of a senior surgeon at the hospital who had recently had a transplant. His kidney came not from a family member, friend, or colleague—but from a Web site.

6   Some basics: According to the National Kidney Foundation, there are 485,000 Americans with end-stage renal* disease. More than 341,000 are on dialysis,† 140,000 have functioning transplants. About 87,000 people die each year from end-stage renal disease, some on the waiting list, others who could benefit from a transplant but never get on the list. Each year, through death or transplantation, more new people go on the list than get off the list. For example, in 2007 there were only 16,629 kidney transplants; 10,588 were from organs donated by 7,241 deceased people and 6,041 from living donors. In spite of all the heart-rending stories about the lady from Dunkin' Donuts who gave her kidney to a customer and the millions of dollars the federal government has given to nonprofits charged with organ procurement* to educate the public about the social good and medical ease of donating organs, the number of kidneys donated has risen only modestly over the last decade. In 2007 the number donated was the lowest since 2000.

7   Having had such a positive reaction to my own need, I was left wondering: What the hell is going on? Why are so few people donating kidneys to people they know? And is anyone doing anything about it? Answers to the first question are hard to come by. As I talked to people and read more about the issue, there were clues. People wanted to save their kidneys for their kids or their spouses. Some friends reported that other family members discouraged them from giving. Transplants are still a little creepy, and the idea of sharing your body with someone else is still science fiction. It's scary. It's not a simple procedure. And people who need kidneys stay quiet about it. A recent study of people considering transplant showed that 54 percent of them had not asked anybody to donate.

8   Publicity about improvements in dialysis has probably made people think it's not so bad. We imagine people go sit in a nice chair for four hours three times a week, read a book, and then go about their daily lives. In fact, as nephrologist Benjamin Hippen notes in the scientific journal *New Atlantis*, "Life on dialysis is a fragile, vulnerable existence." Far too often, things do not go well, and people on dialysis are unable to work, experience multiple complications, and die quickly. The average span of life once one goes on dialysis is eight years for a person 40–44 years old and 4.5 years for someone 60–64.

---

†dialysis: a process for maintaining kidney function with the help of a machine.

9   The "is anyone doing anything about it" question is easier to answer. Some leaders in the field—transplant surgeons, nephrologists, and policy analysts—have suggested that it's time to provide donors with incentives,* from health insurance to tax credits and pension contributions to promote donations. My friend Sally Satel has been in the forefront of promoting this idea, and she has been a thorn in the side of the kidney establishment, which has been moving around the deck chairs on the *Titanic* rather than face the core ethical questions in the debate: Do potential donors own their bodies and have a right to decide? Do we treat potential donors fairly? These questions take on special urgency when you realize that 23 percent of Medicare expenditures go to treating kidney disease and the number of people with end-stage renal disease in the U.S. is projected to reach 712,000 by 2015.

10   Even without incentives, no group of do-gooders is treated with more suspicion by the medical community than living organ donors. Even a free glass of orange juice or an unnecessary lollipop given to a donor is interpreted by some leaders in the field as a "bribe" or a crime. Appropriate concern for the international organ trafficking problem (WHO[†] estimates that the annual total of internationally trafficked kidneys is about 6,000) has so distorted the concept of altruism and eroded the principle of mutual respect that potential kidney donors are denied the basic safety net that a just and giving society should provide people who offer to risk their own lives to save the lives of others. And let's be clear. The best way to stop first-world people with money from exploiting poor people by bargain basement organ trafficking is to procure more organs from well-informed, healthy, and autonomous* people in the first world.

11   This insanity is so widespread that a new and creative transplant practice, known as daisy chains, needed federal legislation to assure hospitals and donors that they would not be arrested for performing them. In a daisy chain, two or more people who need kidneys but have potential donors who are not a match, trade donors. Those concerned worry that the 1984 National Organ Transplant Act (NOTA), which prohibits the sale or transfer of human organs for "valuable consideration," would be invoked. Would my trade of my donor's kidney for another be a form of "valuable consideration"? Legislation to clarify this was introduced and failed in three successive sessions of Congress. It was not till 2007 when Rep. Charles Norwood died and the bill was named after him that Congress could get this bill passed.

[†]WHO: World Health Organization.

12   But more disturbing is the attempt by some transplant professionals and ethicists* to so constrain government benefits to potential donors that the large number of low-income and minority candidates for transplant are almost automatically precluded from receiving kidneys while they are healthy enough to benefit from them. Almost half of those on the kidney waiting list are African-American or other ethnic minorities. . . .

13   The donor costs of the kidney transplant are covered by the recipient's medical insurance (most often Medicare) and the recipient can reimburse the donor for medical costs, travel, and lost wages. Low-income recipients may not have the money to do that. Charitable funds for this purpose are woefully inadequate to meet the need and when they apply for funds donors wait months to find out if these costs will be paid.

14   More important, we financially abandon the donor almost immediately after we take their kidney. There is no provision* for comprehensive long-term health insurance for donors, or for life and disability insurance. Opponents of any form of compensation or benefit to donors beyond costs directly attributable to the transplant itself fight efforts to provide these benefits. One example of such stinginess is the current "End the Wait" campaign of the National Kidney Foundation. In a grudging concession, the NKF supports post-transplant health insurance, but insists that it only cover medical expenses directly related to complications from the transplant. How mean can you be?

15   No matter. This over-scrupulosity has to stop. It's time to rescue the debate about organ transplant policy from the deck chair rearranging and simply treat potential donors with the same generous spirit with which they have offered their kidneys. No donor should spend a single dollar in the process of giving an organ. And donors should have the safety net they need to stay healthy, to support their family if they cannot work and life insurance should they die. We can and should do even more; but health, life, and disability are bottom lines. One member of Congress who gets it is Arlen Specter, who is circulating the Organ Trafficking Prohibition Act of 2009. The bill increases the penalties for really buying and selling organs, but makes clear that state and federal government can provide the kind of benefits donors deserve without going to jail. Anyone disagree?

16   My own story? I'm still waiting to hit the magic number when the transplant will be needed. Two potential donors were found to have kidneys not quite strong enough to share and are very sad. A third, my buddy Rita Nakashima Brock, is in the final stages of the rigorous testing, and it is looking good. I have no idea whether taking better care of donors will result in more kidneys available for transplantation, but I am very certain it is the right thing to do. . . .

Monitoring Your
Comprehension

In paragraph 7, the author poses a question: "Why are so few people donating kidneys to people they know?" See how well you can paraphrase her answer to that question.

Comprehension
and Critical
Reading Questions

Answer the following questions by filling in the blanks or circling the letter of the correct response.

Main Idea 1. Which statement best expresses the main idea of the entire reading?
   a. When the author, Frances Kissling, found out she needed a kidney transplant, she asked her friends if one of them would donate a kidney; the response of her friends proves that altruism is more widespread than is commonly assumed.
   b. In trying to find a kidney donor, the author discovered that attitudes and procedures related to organ donors were serious obstacles to increasing the number of kidneys available for donation.
   c. In trying to locate someone who would donate a kidney to save her life, the author realized that people with a strong religious faith were more likely to become organ donors.
   d. In her search for a kidney transplant, the author discovered that women are more likely to be organ donors than men are, indicating that women are more compassionate and altruistic than men are.

Inference and
Paraphrase Practice

2. In paragraph 3, the author suggests that she had learned what from the Bible? Please paraphrase rather than quote.

_____

Sentence Function 3. In paragraph 5, the first sentence is
   a. an introductory sentence.
   b. a topic sentence.
   c. a transitional sentence.

Inference 4. What is the point of the "basics" introduced in paragraph 6?
   a. Kidney dialysis is not the easy solution to renal disease that many people imagine it to be.
   b. Offers for organ donations have begun to rise thanks to the efforts of nonprofit organizations dedicated to increasing the number of organ donors.

      c. Most people who get on the list of those in need of an organ do-
        nation leave it because they die before they can get a transplant.

      d. Renal disease in the United States is a serious problem, but, so far
        at least, organ donations have not increased enough to come any-
        where close to solving that problem.

Paraphrasing   **5.** The author offers four answers to the question she poses in paragraph 7: Why are so few people donating to people they know? Para-
phrase those four answers.

_____

_____

_____

_____

_____

_____

Supporting Details   **6.** In paragraph 9, the author calls her friend "a thorn in the side of the
and Inferences   kidney establishment." Based on the rest of the reading, who is the
kidney establishment?

_____

_____

Literal and   **7.** What does the author imply by calling her friend "a thorn in the side
Figurative Language   of the kidney establishment"?

_____

_____

    8. In paragraph 9, the author also says that the kidney establishment
has been "moving around the deck chairs on the *Titanic* rather than
face the core ethical questions in the debate." In this statement, she is
speaking

      a. literally.

      b. figuratively.

Tone 9. How would you describe the author's tone?

    a. grateful then outraged

    b. angry then resigned

    c. sad then furious

    d. worried then enthusiastic

Purpose 10. How would you describe the author's purpose?

    a. The author wants to explain to readers the process that people in need of a kidney must go through in order to find a donor.

    b. The author wants to convince readers that agencies involved in organ donation must re-evaluate and radically change their procedures for handling kidney donors.

Drawing Your Own Conclusions In the last decade, a number of organ donors have given a kidney to people they never met. These donors, known as "altruistic donors," simply decided that they had a kidney to spare and would be willing to give it up to help someone in need of a transplant. This decision, however, has not always been treated as an act of great compassion. In fact, many of these donors report that they were treated as if they were crazy by both members of their family and members of the medical community. How do you think the author of the reading would react? Please explain your answer.

_____

_____

_____

Making It Personal Explain why you think you would or would not donate a kidney for a friend suffering from renal disease. Or, as an alternative, explain why you think you would (or would not) do what the author did—ask a friend to help save your life by donating a kidney for transplant.

Writing Suggestion Write a few paragraphs in which you give your thoughts on people who donate a kidney to complete strangers. Do you think they are being altruistic and doing something positive and good? Or are their actions completely beyond your understanding and, therefore, suspect?

◆ **READING 10**   Debating Parental Notification Laws

Paul S. Kaplan

Looking Ahead Taken from a textbook on adolescence, the following reading discusses a question that arouses passionate opinions: "Do parents have the right to know that their daughter is seeking an abortion?"

Word Watch Some of the more difficult words in the reading are defined below. The number in parentheses indicates the paragraph in which the word appears. An asterisk marks its first appearance in the reading. Preview the definitions before you begin reading and watch for the words while you read.

---

sibling (3): brother or sister

waive (3): ignore or negate

judicial (4): related to the courts

onerous (4): very burdensome and unpleasant

mandatory (7): forced, officially demanded

erratic (11): not consistent, unreliable

exemptions (11): freedom from certain obligations

rationale (14): reason or basis

Flexible Reading Tip As the preview of this reading suggests, people don't always agree that parents should be notified if their daughter is going to have an abortion. As you read, be especially alert to two kinds of passages: (1) those that describe legislation related to parental notification, and (2) those that explain why some people are for it and some people opposed.

1 Nancy is a 16-year-old girl who discovers she is pregnant. She has been having sex with her 17-year-old boyfriend for about 6 months. They thought they had taken sufficient contraceptive precaution, but obviously they were mistaken. After talking it over with her boyfriend, Nancy decides to seek an abortion. Should she be forced by law to inform her parents that she is contemplating an abortion?

2   In a landmark 1992 case, *Planned Parenthood v. Casey*, the Supreme Court of the United States held that states may require minors seeking abortions to obtain parental consent as long as a procedure allowing a

minor to bypass parental notification laws in certain cases is in place (Bach, 1999). Most states have laws requiring parental notification for abortion (Planned Parenthood, 2001).

3   Some state laws require only parental notification, whereas others require parental consent (Tomal, 2000). Some states require notification of one parent, and others require notification of both parents. Some states allow notification of grandparents as an alternative to parents, or even notification of a sibling* who is at least 25 years old. Some states allow a physician to waive* notification if the doctor thinks it is not in the best interest of the minor (perhaps because of evidence that notification could lead to abuse or the doctor's belief that the teenager is mature enough to make her own decision) (Planned Parenthood, 2001).

4   State laws are routinely tested for their constitutionality. For example, the New Jersey Supreme Court struck down a parental notification bill in 2000 even though it included a judicial* bypass procedure (Lovell, 2000). The court's majority argued that the practical difficulties involved in going to court, getting a lawyer, obtaining transportation, taking time off from school, and maintaining anonymity were onerous* and only delayed the abortion, making it more dangerous. The majority argued that the law violated the rights of the minor. The justices who voted to sustain the law argued that it protected the interests of both minors and parents, as well as fostered family integrity. They also argued that the judicial bypass procedure was not an undue burden. When these justices measured the law against the right of parents to be informed of the significant health issues in their children's lives, they saw it as sustainable.

5   Parental notification laws do not really affect the majority of pregnant teenagers, for most girls voluntarily inform their parents when they seek an abortion. A study of unmarried minors having abortions in states without parental notification and consent laws found that 61 percent reported that at least one of their parents knew about their abortions (Henshaw & Kost, 1992). About a third of the teens who did not tell their parents had histories of violence in their families, feared violence, or were afraid of being thrown out of their homes.

6   Advocates of parental notification and consent legislation, often called *parental involvement legislation*, use a number of arguments to bolster their view. They state, for example, that parents are responsible for their children and have a right to know when their minor children are going to make an important medical decision. Advocates also argue that parental notification allows parents to provide their children with emotional support (Harris, 1997). Adolescents do not have much experience in making

important decisions, and parents can help their teenagers consider their alternatives. Finally, advocates note that parents have a right to decide what medical services their minor children receive and that any routine overriding of parental authority threatens the parents' right to raise their children in the way they think best. One medical provider noted that he could not remove a splinter from the finger of a minor without a parent's consent, but that without parental notification laws a minor could receive an abortion without the family's knowing.

7   Opponents of laws regarding mandatory* parental involvement argue that we do not live in an ideal world, and many adolescents do not feel they can tell their parents about an abortion (Planned Parenthood, 1999). Teens who do not wish to notify their parents often have a very good reason. In addition, being forced to notify parents or to receive their consent often causes a delay in seeking medical care; and because earlier abortions are safer, delaying an abortion increases the physical and emotional risk to the teenager (Raab, 1998).

8   Individuals opposed to parental notification also argue that states have routinely allowed minor adolescents to consent to their own medical care in critical areas, such as treatment for STIs[†] and drug or alcohol addiction, when confidential care is deemed a public health necessity (Donovan, 1998b). Many states allow minors to consent to contraceptive services, and a majority of states allow pregnant minors to obtain prenatal care and delivery services without parental consent.

9   Two pieces of legislation have been introduced into Congress to further limit access to abortions. One, the Child Custody Protection Act, makes it a federal crime for a nonparent to take a pregnant minor across state lines to obtain an abortion for the purpose of avoiding laws requiring parental involvement in their home states. Another, the Putting Parents First Act (PPFA), would require minors to get parental consent for abortion referrals or contraceptives obtained at any facility receiving federal funds, and it would reverse many years of public policy (Katz, 1999).

10   People who passionately believe in a woman's right to choose whether to have an abortion argue against almost any limitation on abortion rights. People who passionately believe that abortion is wrong and should be illegal argue for just about anything that limits abortion rights. However, many people in between consider bypass procedures to be a feature that would protect the pregnant teen who has reason to believe she would

---

[†]STIs: sexually transmitted infections.

suffer negative consequences from parental notification. However, what seems reasonable in theory may not work in practice.

11   Bypass procedures have proved to be both erratic* and problematic. Some states deny very few petitions. For example, in Massachusetts only 13 of 15,000 waivers were denied, and of the denied petitions, 11 were reversed on appeal, meaning that only 2 minors were denied their request for an abortion without parental notification (Lovell, 2000). In other states the situation is very different, and teens have more trouble obtaining exemptions.* Even within states, courts function very differently. Some counties almost routinely grant abortion petitions, whereas other counties routinely reject them (Bach, 1999). Another problem is the requirement in some states that both parents must be notified. Many teens do not live with both parents, and they may have little or no contact with their noncustodial parent or fear involving that parent.

12   On the other side is the question of whether an occasional horrific story about a teenage girl beaten by her father because he was notified of her impending abortion is sufficient to certify that parents generally should not be informed. There will always be some parents who act improperly, but that fact does not mean that the vast majority of parents who can and will provide emotional support and guidance should not be involved.

13   The issue of parental notification seems to pit parental rights against the minor's right of self-determination. Parents are told that they are responsible for their children, the argument goes, but without legislation they may not participate in an important decision made by their minor daughter. However, it can be argued that a teenage girl faced with an unwanted pregnancy who does not want to tell her parents should not be forced to do so. It is unfortunate that judicial bypass seems so erratic and problematic that it does not solve the problem in a practical way.

14   We are faced with the same questions that have been raised over and over. Should adolescents have the same rights as adults? If not, what rationale* should be used to determine which rights minors should have and which rights they should not have? Both questions are difficult to answer, and balancing parental rights and responsibilities with adolescent rights and responsibilities remains difficult.

Monitoring Your Comprehension   Can you paraphrase some of the reasons why parents favor parental notification? What are the reasons expressed by those opposed?

Comprehension and Critical Reading Questions   Answer the following questions by filling in the blanks or circling the letter of the correct response.

Main Idea 1. Which statement best expresses the main idea of the entire reading?

    a. Parental notification laws exist all over the country, but they are routinely ignored.

    b. Parental notification laws treat teenagers as if they had no right to decide their own future.

    c. Both critics and supporters of parental notification laws have some good arguments, and there seems to be no simple answer to the question: Should parents be notified if their daughter is having an abortion?

    d. Critics of parental notification don't realize that they are depriving young people of the emotional support only a parent can provide during times of intense emotional distress.

Inference 2. What is the implied main idea of paragraph 3?

    a. Parental notification means different things in different states.

    b. The number of states that require parental notification proves that it should be the law of the land.

    c. Parental notification laws should be made more consistent from state to state.

Supporting Details and Paraphrasing 3. Paragraph 4 opens with this statement: "State laws are routinely tested for their constitutionality." In your own words, what happens when a law is tested for "constitutionality"?

_____

_____

4. The topic sentence in paragraph 6 suggests which pattern?

    a. cause and effect

    b. comparison and contrast

    c. simple listing

    d. classification

Patterns of Organization 5. The topic sentence in paragraph 9 suggests which patterns?

_____

Transitions 6. What two transitions are used in paragraph 9?

_____

Analyzing Arguments

7. List and paraphrase the reasons given in paragraph 6 in favor of parental notification.

_____

_____

_____

_____

_____

_____

_____

Transitions

What transition or transitions does the author use to separate some or all of those reasons?

_____

Analyzing Arguments

8. List and paraphrase the arguments against parental notification (paragraphs 7 and 8).

_____

_____

_____

_____

_____

_____

Transitions

What transition or transitions does the author use to separate some or all of those arguments?

_____

Purpose

9. How would you describe the author's purpose?

a. The author wants to sum up the arguments for and against parental notification, in order to inform readers about the controversy surrounding it.

b. The author wants to persuade readers that parental notification should be standardized and applied in every state.

c. The author wants to persuade readers that parental notification does more harm than good.

Bias 10. Which statement most accurately describes the author's point of view?

a. The author supports parental notification.

b. The author thinks parental notification laws have serious draw-backs.

c. It's impossible to determine the author's personal point of view.

Drawing Your Own Conclusions How do you think members of the National Right to Life organization, which is committed to making abortion illegal, would feel about parental notification legislation?

_____

_____

_____

How do you think members of NARAL (National Abortion and Reproductive Rights Action League) would feel about parental notification legislation?

_____

_____

_____

_____

Making It Personal Imagine that you are the parent of an eighteen-year-old who is pregnant and seeking to have an abortion. How would you feel if you were not notified of her desires?

Writing Suggestion Write four or five paragraphs in which you first explain the general goal of parental notification legislation (refer to paragraphs 2 and 3 to summarize the general goal and perhaps one or two variations on how that goal is implemented in different states). Then state your opinion on the legislation and give at least two reasons why you hold that opinion.

Acknowledgments

Douglas A. Bernstein, Louis A. Penner, Alison Clarke-Stewart, and Edward J. Roy: From *Psychology, 7/e.* © 2006 Wadsworth, a part of Cengage Learning, Inc. Reproduced by permission. www.cengage.com/permissions.

Ann O'M. Bowman and Richard Kearney: From *State and Local Government, 7/e.* © 2008 Wadsworth, a part of Cengage Learning, Inc. Reproduced by permission.www.cengage.com/permissions.

Sharon S. Brehm, Saul Kassin, and Steven Fein: From *Social Psychology, 5/e.* © 2002 Wadsworth, a part of Cengage Learning, Inc. Reproduced by permission. www.cengage.com/permissions.

Danuta Bukatko and Marvin Daehler: From *Child Development, 5/e.* © 2004 Wadsworth, a part of Cengage Learning, Inc. Reprinted by permission. www.cengage.com/permissions.

Richard W. Bulliet: From *The Earth and Its Peoples, 3/e.* © 2006 Wadsworth, a part of Cengage Learning, Inc. Reproduced by permission. www.cengage.com/permissions.

Dennis Coon: From *Essentials of Psychology, 9/e.* © 2003 Wadsworth, a part of Cengage Learning Inc. Reproduced by permission. www.cengage.com/permissions.

Joseph A. DeVito: *The Interpersonal Communication Book, 9/e* © 2001. Published by Allyn and Bacon, Boston, MA. Copyright © 2001 by Pearson Education. Reprinted by permission of the publisher.

Dictionary definitions: Copyright © 2006 by Houghton Mifflin Harcourt Publishing Company. Reproduced by permission from *The American Heritage College Dictionary, 4/e.*

Dave Ellis: From *Becoming a Master Student, 12/e.* © 2009 Wadsworth, a part of Cengage Learning, Inc. Reproduced by permission. www.cengage.com/permissions.

Tracy Gordon Fox: "A Series of Troubling Events, a Change of Career" by Tracy Gordon Fox from the *New York Times*, May 17, 2009, p. NJ8. Copyright © 2009 The New York Times Co. Reprinted by permission.

Steven M. Gillon and Cathy D. Matson: From *The American Experiment, 2/e.* © 2006 Wadsworth, a part of Cengage Learning, Inc. Reproduced by permission. www.cengage.com/permissions.

Google: Google screen shots. Courtesy of Google, Inc.

Paul Kaplan: From *Adolescence.* © 2004. Cengage Learning, Inc. Reproduced by permission. www.cengage.com/permissions.

Frances Kissling: "Whaddya Have to Do to Get a Kidney Around Here?" by Frances Kissling from Salon.com, March 27, 2009. Reprinted by permission of the author.

Robert Kreitner: From *Management, 10/e.* © 2007. Cengage Learning, Inc. Reproduced by permission. www.cengage.com/permissions.

Marianne Neighbors and Ruth Tannehill-Jones: From *Human Diseases, 2/e.* © 2006 Delmar Learning, a part of Cengage Learning, Inc. Reproduced by permission. www.cengage.com/permissions.

Jeffrey S. Nevid: From *Psychology, 1/e.* © 2003 Wadsworth, a part of Cengage Learning, Inc. Reproduced by permission. www.cengage.com/permissions.

Howard L. Nixon and James H. Frey: From *Sociology of Sport*, p. 175. Wadsworth, 1996. Reprinted by permission of the author.

Optimist123.com: Reprinted by permission of Optimist123.com.

William M. Pride and O. C. Ferrell: From *Marketing 2000, 11/e.* © 2000 South-Western, a part of Cengage Learning, Inc. Reproduced by permission. www.cengage.com/permissions.

Sagehistory.net: "The Cold War: The Balance of Terror." Reprinted by permission.

Michael G. Schneider and Judith L. Gerstin: From *Invitation to Computer Science.* © 2007. Cengage Learning, Inc. Reproduced by permission. www.cengage.com/permissions.

Kelvin L. Seifert and Robert J. Hoffnung: From *Child and Adolescent Development, 5/e,* pp. 345, 404. Copyright © 2000. Reprinted by permission of Kelvin L. Seifert.

David Shaffer: From *Social and Personality Development, 6/e.* © 2009 Wadsworth, a part of Cengage Learning, Inc. Reproduced by permission. www.cengage.com/permissions.

Ethel Sloane: From *Biology of Women, 4/e.* © 2002 Delmar Learning, a part of Cengage Learning, Inc. Reproduced by permission. www.cengage.com/permissions.

Brad Stone: "Is Facebook Growing Up Too Fast?" by Brad Stone from the *New York Times*, March 29, 2009. Copyright © 2009 The New York Times Co. Reprinted by permission.

Jonathan Turk and Amos Turk: From *Physical Science with Environmental and Other Practical Applications.* © 1987 Brooks/Cole, a part of Cengage Learning, Inc. Reproduced by permission. www.cengage.com/permissions.

R. E. Ulrich, T. J. Stachnik, and N. R. Stainton: Adapted and reproduced with permission from authors and publisher from "Student acceptance of generalized personality interpretations" by R. E. Ulrich, T. J. Stachnik, and N. R. Stainton from *Psychological Reports*, 1963, 13, pp. 831–834.

David D. Van Fleet: From *Contemporary Management, 3/e.* © South-Western, a part of Cengage Learning, Inc. Reproduced by permission. www.cengage.com/permissions.

Claire Waughfield: From *Mental Health Concepts, 5/e.* © 2002 Delmar Learning, a part of Cengage Learning, Inc. Reproduced by permission. www.cengage.com/permissions.

James Q. Wilson and John J. DiIulio: From *American Government, 10/e.* © 2006 Wadsworth, a part of Cengage Learning, Inc. Reproduced by permission. www.cengage.com/permissions.

Index

Irony Writers who use irony say the opposite of what they mean.

Main idea The main idea is the central point or message of a passage or reading. It controls and unifies all the other sentences in the reading.

Major supporting details These details are essential to explaining the topic sentence and making it convincing.

Metaphor Metaphors make comparisons that reveal a hidden similarity between two very different things.

Minor supporting details These details are the most specific sentences in the paragraph. They further explain major details, repeat key points, or add colorful facts. They can be essential or nonessential to the paragraph, depending on their context.

Opinions Statements of opinion reflect a person's point of view. Unlike statements of fact, they are shaped by personal experience, training, and background. They cannot be checked for accuracy, but they can be labeled informed or uninformed, justified or unjustified.

Paraphrase A paraphrase translates an author's ideas into someone else's words without altering or changing the original meaning. An *inaccurate paraphrase* alters an author's meaning along with the words.

Persuasive writing Persuasive writing expresses an opinion that the writer wants readers to share or at least to consider.

Purpose The term *purpose* refers to the author's goal or reason for writing. Most writing falls into one of two categories, informative or persuasive.

Relevant reasons Relevant reasons are clearly related to the opinion being discussed.

Similes Comparisons using the words *like* or *as*. Similes, like metaphors, make a point by revealing hidden similarities between things that are outwardly quite different.

Simple listing An organizational pattern that orders supporting details according to the writer's preference rather than any inherent order in the material.

Slippery slope thinking Writers who use this logic say that if one event happens, a host of similar and much worse events are bound to follow.

Specific sentences Unlike general sentences, specific sentences focus on individual events, dates, and experiences. They help clarify or explain general ones.

SQ3R SQ3R is a study technique for reading and understanding textbooks. The letters stand for survey, question, read, recall, review.

Supporting details Supporting details are the examples, reasons, studies, statistics, and so on, that develop, explain, or prove an author's point.

Synthesizing In the process of synthesizing, readers find a way to link different sources that discuss the same topic.

Thesis statement Thesis statements sum up main ideas in longer readings. Like topic sentences, thesis statements give written form to the main idea of an extended reading.

Time order Readings that rely on this pattern of organization present events according to their order in real time.

Tone Like tone of voice in speaking, tone in writing is the author's way of expressing his or her attitude toward a particular subject. Depending on audience and subject matter, a writer's tone can range from angry and sarcastic in one context to humorous or light-hearted in another.

Topic The topic of a paragraph is the subject the author chooses to discuss or explore. It's the person, place, or event most frequently mentioned or referred to in a passage or selection.

Topic sentence The topic sentence uses the author's words to express the main idea.

Transitions Transitions are verbal bridges that help readers move smoothly from one sentence to another. *Moreover*, *therefore*, and *however* are all examples of transitions.

Web search engines Search engines are used to scan the World Wide Web and locate information based on the search term provided by the user. The more precise the search term is, the more useful will be the information located by the search engine.